# Language, Culture, and Society

SEVENTH EDITION

# Language, Culture, and Society

## *An Introduction to Linguistic Anthropology*

JAMES STANLAW
NOBUKO ADACHI
ZDENEK SALZMANN

WESTVIEW
PRESS

Westview Press
Hachette Book Group
1290 Avenue of the Americas, New York, NY 10104
westviewpress.com

Printed in the United States of America

Seventh Edition: July 2017

Published by Westview Press, an imprint of Perseus Books, LLC, a subsidiary of Hachette Book Group, Inc.
The Hachette Speakers Bureau provides a wide range of authors for speaking events. To find out more, go to www.hachettespeakersbureau.com or call (866) 376-6591.
The publisher is not responsible for websites (or their content) that are not owned by the publisher.

Print book interior design by Timm Bryson

Library of Congress Cataloging-in-Publication Data has been applied for.

ISBNs: 978-0-8133-5060-8 (paperback), 978-0-8133-5073-8 (e-book)

LSC-W

10 9 8 7 6 5 4 3 2 1

# CONTENTS

# PREFACE TO THE SEVENTH EDITION

Once again it gives us great pleasure to offer another edition of *Language, Culture, and Society*. As we explained in the last edition, our intent has been to maintain our original "Americanist" vision of linguistic anthropology—as established by the discipline's forerunners such as Franz Boas and Edward Sapir—while addressing some of the newer pressing and exciting challenges of the twenty-first century, among them issues of language and power, language ideology, and contemporary digital and computer-mediated communication. In this vein, we have substantially reworked our materials on language variation based on race and ethnicity (Chapter 14), linguistic anthropology in the global digitized world (Chapter 15), and how meaning emerges from conversation (Chapter 12). About 20 percent of the text is new, and unfortunately about 20 percent of the text has been reduced or eliminated. However, we have now added dozens of photographs and numerous new figures, problems, sidebars, and boxes. We have also added a newly revised and up-to-date glossary.

And speaking of problems and activities, as we mentioned last time, linguistic anthropology is a lot like swimming: you can study hydraulics, kinesiology, or the theory of the backstroke all you want, but it is a lot more fun—and ultimately more rewarding—to actually get wet. So we encourage everyone to step into the linguistics pool (we have tried to make sure the water is not too deep). To encourage this—knowing the current generation of students is not only Internet friendly but Web addicted—we have given at least three or four multimedia links in each chapter through which teachers and students can explore in more detail some of the issues brought up in the text. Sometimes these include things that are purely for fun—who can resist Sacha Baron Cohen in character as Ali G "interviewing" one of the world's foremost linguists and intellectuals, Noam Chomsky!—to current political affairs, such as the language of the 2016 presidential debates. So these problems and "projects" and Internet activities should not be considered extraneous. They are a vital part of the learning experience.

Now, as we said last time, we *do* understand that some students are a bit intimidated by such words as *grammar* and all those strange symbols found in a phonetic alphabet. To this we have two responses. First, we have tried to be more clear in this edition about why we introduce these things, and we offer motivations for needing some formalism—and how it reveals things that cannot be shown in any other way. We also want to remind students that this is *not* an algebra class, and that many of these problems are closer to crossword puzzles than math equations. So enjoy! Second, in this edition we continue to offer a transcription system that we feel is much easier for beginning students to master than the International

Phonetic Alphabet (IPA): the so-called American System, popular among anthropologists, especially before World War II, when exotic fonts were not so easy to typeset. We feel the problem with the IPA for beginners is the conflation of pure vowels and diphthongs, and excessive use of diacritics, in its orthography. In comparison, the American System is much more transparent and less confusing.

Throughout the text, statistics have been updated and the references expanded, with the addition of about one hundred and fifty new sources.

Once more we are indebted to many people for all their help. We are extremely grateful to all the students and instructors—and referees—who have continued to give us many valuable suggestions and comments, some of which we have been able to incorporate in this edition. Linguistics graduate student Su Yin Khor created a new glossary for us and also contributed several sidebars. She also helped with editing and reading chapters, and she prevented us from making naïve mistakes especially in the arenas of emoji usage, Twitter, and text messaging. We are once again indebted to the fine staff at Westview Press for all their editing and production. In particular, we'd like to thank previous editors Leanne Silverman, Evan Carter, Sandra Beris, Karl Yambert (who initially suggested our collaboration), and Catherine Craddock, and acquisitions director Grace Fujimoto. Our current sociology and anthropology editor, James Sherman, has been a voice of clarity and reason in the sometimes complicated revision process. Their support and encouragement has been enormous.

We hope the readers of this new edition will gain as much from using this book as we did from writing it.

*Jim Stanlaw*
*Nobuko Adachi*
*Zdenek Salzmann*

# 1

# Introducing Linguistic Anthropology

## LEARNING OBJECTIVES

- Explain some of the "myths" people have about language, and why; be able to refute them
- Give a brief overview of the history of anthropology and identify its four subfields
- List some of the assumptions underlying "Americanist" linguistic anthropology
- Identify Franz Boas and Edward Sapir and explain their importance to linguistic anthropology
- Describe some ways languages can differ in terms of grammar and vocabulary

The first thing that someone reads in any introductory textbook is the authors' capsule definition of the subject matter at hand. In this book we have two disciplines that, at first glance, might appear to be very different. Stereotypically, people think of anthropologists in pith helmets out in a jungle someplace uncovering bizarre tribal customs. Likewise, they imagine a linguist as someone who can speak a dozen languages fluently, or else as a scholar poring over ancient texts deciphering secret hieroglyphic messages. In reality these two fields are hardly like that, but that does not make them any less exciting. This book is about how those people who call themselves linguistic anthropologists study the universal phenomenon of human language. But before we go into the specifics of how they do that, we should ask ourselves an even more basic question.

## WHY SHOULD WE STUDY LANGUAGE? LANGUAGE IN DAILY LIFE

"Why should I study language?" is hardly a rhetorical question. Most people never formally study language, and they seem to get along fine. But do they? For example, have you ever arranged to meet someone "next Tuesday," only to find that your friend was planning to show up a week later than you had anticipated? Or why do we need lawyers to translate a contract for us when the document is written in a language that all parties share? David Crystal (1971:15) points out that communication between patients and physicians can be extremely difficult, given the differences in training and perspective of the persons involved. The doctor often has to take a general phrase, such as "a dull ache in my side," and formulate a diagnosis and treatment based solely on this description. And when responding to what the patient has said, the doctor must choose her words carefully. What a doctor calls a "benign growth" might be heard as "cancer" by the patient.

At school we are confronted with language problems the minute we walk in the door. Some are obvious: "I can't understand Shakespeare. I thought he spoke English. Why is he so difficult?" Other problems are not so obvious: "What is the difference between who and whom? Doesn't one make me sound British?" "Why do I have to say 'you and I' instead of 'me and you'?" Some problems, such as the subtle sexism found in some textbooks, may be beyond our everyday psychological threshold. Problems of ethnicity and community-identity can be seen in such controversial issues as bilingual education or the teaching of **Ebonics**.

Language is involved in a wide variety of human situations, perhaps *every* situation. If something permeates every aspect of human life and is so complex that we cannot fathom its influence, we should study it. The scientific study of language is one of the keys to understanding much of human behavior.

The study of language will not in itself solve all the world's problems. It is useful enough to make people aware that these problems of language exist and that they are widespread and complex. Besides being of intellectual interest, then, the study of language offers a special vantage point of "linguistic sensitization" (Crystal 1971:35) to problems that are of concern to everyone, regardless of discipline and background.

Some of the questions we will address in this book, then, are broad but fundamental—for example:

1. How can language and culture be adequately described?
2. Do other animals, such as chimpanzees using American sign language, show linguistic capacities?
3. How did language originate? How did it contribute to human evolution and the development of culture?
4. How are languages acquired?
5. How can languages be classified to show the relationships among them?
6. What is the relationship between language and thought?
7. What is meaning? How is it bestowed? How is it learned?
8. What does it mean to be human?

## MODERN MYTHS CONCERNING LANGUAGES

This may be a good place to provide information about languages in general to set some basic matters straight. Every human being speaks a language, but what people think about languages—particularly those about which they know little or nothing—is quite another matter. Consider the following statements. Which ones do you think are true?

- Almost everywhere in the world, everyone is monolingual or monodialectal, just as in America.
- Spelling in English is basically phonetic and governed by clear rules.
- Most writing systems in the world are based on some kind of alphabet.
- If you really want to learn Spanish, don't take a class in school. It is better to just go, say, to Mexico for a month or two.
- Some languages are naturally harder to learn than others.
- Some languages are naturally more "primitive" than others.
- Language itself is not ambiguous; it is people's misinterpreting things that causes problems.
- Some dialects are, well . . . stupid, demonstrating that a person is uneducated.
- The use of language somehow reflects one's intelligence.
- People who are fluent in another language may not have complete mastery of their native language.
- The ability to learn a foreign language is a special kind of skill that some of us have, and others don't.
- As our grade school teachers taught us, if you want to get it right, go to the dictionary!
- People who use double negatives ("I don't need no anthropology classes") are really not thinking logically.
- It is easier to learn Chinese if you come from a Chinese family background than from a European family.
- Languages seem to have special characteristics or personalities: for example, French is romantic; German is scientific; Russian is soulful; Spanish is hot-blooded; Italian is emotional; Chinese is simple and straightforward; Japanese is mysterious, spiritual, and Zen-like; English is logical; Greek is philosophical, and so on.
- All Native Americans generally speak the same language; that's why they could communicate with each other using sign language (like in the movies).
- The more words you know, the better you know your language.

Most anthropologists and linguists would say that all of these statements are suspect, if not outright wrong. Let us briefly consider a few of these misconceptions concerning languages in more detail because they appear to be widespread, even among those who are otherwise well educated and knowledgeable. These misconceptions we can refer to as myths, in the sense of being unfounded, fictitious, and false beliefs or ideas.

### *Primitive Languages . . . Or Not?*

The most common misconception is the belief that unwritten languages are "primitive," whatever that may mean. Those who think that "primitive" languages still exist invariably associate them with societies that laypeople refer to as "primitive"—especially the very few remaining bands of hunter-gatherers. There are of course differences in cultural complexity between hunting-and-collecting bands and small tribal societies, on the one hand, and modern industrial societies, on the other, but no human beings today are "primitive" in the sense of being less biologically evolved than others. One would be justified in talking about a primitive language only if referring to the language of, for example, the extinct forerunner of *Homo sapiens* of a half million years ago. Even though we do not know on direct evidence the nature of the system of oral communication of *Homo erectus*, it is safe to assume that it must have been much simpler than languages of the past several thousand years and therefore primitive in that it was rudimentary, or represented an earlier stage of development.

Why are certain languages mistakenly thought to be primitive? There are several reasons. Some people consider other languages ugly or "primitive sounding" if those languages make use of sounds or sound combinations they find indistinct or "inarticulate" because the sounds are greatly different from those of the languages they themselves speak. Such a view is based on the ethnocentric attitude that the characteristics of one's own language are obviously superior. But words that seem unpronounceable to speakers of one language—and are therefore considered obscure, indistinct, or even grotesque—are easily acquired by even the youngest native speakers of the language in which they occur. To a native speaker of English, the Czech word *scvrnkls* "you flicked off (something) with your finger" looks quite strange, and its pronunciation may sound odd and even impossible because there is no vowel among the eight consonants; for native speakers of Czech, of course, *scvrnkls* is just another word. Which speech sounds are used and how they are combined to form words and utterances vary from one language to the next, and speakers of no language can claim that their language has done the selecting and combining better than another.

### *The Grammar of Non-Western Languages*

Another myth has to do with grammar. Some think that languages of peoples whose societies are not urbanized and industrialized have "little grammar," meaning that such languages have few, if any, of the sort of grammar rules students learn in school. According to this misconception, members of simple societies use language in rather random fashion, without definite pattern. To put it differently, grammar in the sense of rules governing the proper use of cases, tenses, moods, aspects, and other grammatical categories is erroneously thought to be characteristic of "civilized" languages only. Once again, nothing could be further from the truth. Some languages have less "grammar" than others, but the degree of grammatical complexity is not a measure of how effective a particular language is.

What sorts of grammars, then, characterize languages spoken by members of tribal societies? Some of these languages have a fairly large and complicated grammatical apparatus, whereas others are less grammatically complex—a diversity similar to that found in Indo-European languages. Edward Sapir's description of the morphology of Takelma, based on material collected in 1906, takes up 238 pages (Sapir 1922). In Takelma, the now extinct language spoken at one time in southwestern Oregon, verbs were particularly highly inflected, making use of prefixes, suffixes, infixes, vowel changes, consonant changes, and reduplication (functional repetition of a part of a word). Every verb had forms for six tense-modes, including potential ("I can . . . " or "I could . . . "), inferential ("it seems that . . . " or "I presume that . . . "), and present and future imperatives (the future imperative expressing a command to be carried out at some stated or implied time in the future). Among the other grammatical categories and forms marked in verbs were person, number, voice (active or passive), conditional, locative, instrumental, aspect (denoting repeated, continuing, and other types of temporal activity), and active and passive participles. Sapir's description of verb morphology fills more than 147 pages—yet is not to be taken as exhaustive. Although the brief characterization here is far from representative of Takelma verb morphology, it clearly indicates that Takelma grammar was anything but simple. A similar and more detailed demonstration of morphological complexity could easily be provided for hundreds of other so-called primitive languages.

### *Vocabulary Deficiencies?*

When it comes to the vocabulary of languages, is it true, as some suppose, that the vocabularies of so-called primitive languages are too small and inadequate to account for the nuances of the physical and social universes of their speakers? Here the answer is somewhat more complicated. Because the vocabulary of a language serves only the members of the society who speak it, the question to be asked should be: Is a particular vocabulary sufficient to serve the sociocultural needs of those who use the language? When put like this, it follows that the language associated with a relatively simple culture would have a smaller vocabulary than the language of a complex society. Why, for example, should the Inuit people (often known by the more pejorative term "Eskimo") have words for chlorofluoromethane, dune buggy, lambda particle, or tae kwon do when these substances, objects, concepts, and activities play no part in their culture? By the same token, however, the language of a tribal society would have elaborate lexical domains for prominent aspects of the culture even though these do not exist in complex societies. The Agta of the Philippines, for example, are reported to have no fewer than thirty-one verbs referring to types of fishing (Harris 1989:72).

For Aguaruna, the language serving a manioc-cultivating people of northwestern Peru, Brent Berlin (1976) isolated some 566 names referring to the genera of plants in the tropical rain forest area in which they live. Many of these genera are further subdivided to distinguish among species and varieties—for example, the generic term *ipák* "achiote or annatto tree (*Bixa orellana*)" encompasses *baéŋ ipák*, *čamíŋ ipák*, *hémpe ipák*, and *šíŋ ipák*, referring respectively to "kidney-achiote," "yellow achiote," "hummingbird achiote," and "genuine achiote." Very few Americans, unless they are botanists, farmers, or nature lovers, know the names of more than about forty plants.

Lexical specialization in nonscientific domains is of course to be found in complex societies as well. The Germans who live in Munich are known to enjoy their beer; accordingly, the terminology for the local varieties of beer is quite extensive. Per Hage (1972) defined ten "core" terms for Munich beers according to strength, color, fizziness, and aging. But when local connoisseurs also wish to account for the degree of clarity (clear as against cloudy) and the Munich brewery that produced a particular beer, the full list now exceeds seventy terms. Such a discriminating classification of local beers is likely to impress even the most experienced and enthusiastic American beer drinker.

### *So, Are All Languages the Same?*

However, even though no languages spoken today may be labeled primitive, this does not mean that all languages are the same, do all things in the same way, or are equally influential in the modern transnational world. The linguistic anthropologist Dell Hymes claims that languages are not functionally equivalent because the role of speech varies from one society to the next. One of his examples is the language of the Mezquital Otomi, who live in poverty in one of the arid areas of Mexico. At the time of Hymes's writing, most of these people were monolingual, speaking only Otomi, their native language. Even though they accepted the outside judgment of their language as inferior to Spanish, they maintained Otomi and consequently were able to preserve their culture, but at a price. Lack of proficiency in Spanish, or knowledge of Otomi only, isolated the people from the national society and kept them from improving their lot. According to Hymes, no known languages are primitive, and all "have achieved the middle status [of full languages but not] the advanced status [of] world languages and some others. . . . [But though] all languages are potentially equal . . . and hence capable of adaptation to the needs of a complex industrial civilization," only certain languages have actually done so (Hymes 1961:77). These languages are more successful than others not because they are structurally more advanced, but because they happen to be associated with societies in which language is the basis of literature, education, science, and commerce.

The Otomi example is not an isolated case in Mexico. An important factor that contributes to the success of a language is the literacy of its speakers. In countries where many languages are spoken, the language or languages that people learn to read and write are associated with knowledge and therefore also with political and economic power. In Mexico, whose official language is Spanish, more than 250 indigenous languages or regional dialects are spoken (Lewis 2009). These include Nahuatl (several dialects of a Uto-Aztecan language) and Yucatec (a Mayan language), each spoken by more than a million speakers, and about fourteen others that are used by more than 100,000 speakers each. During the last seventy years, however, the percentage of monolingual and bilingual Mexican Indians has been steadily declining in favor of Spanish (from 16 percent in 1930 to about 7 percent in 2005). Although speakers of Indian languages use them in family life, in the fields, at traditional ritual gatherings and curing ceremonies, and in village markets and other local settings, an increasing number use Spanish in schools, agricultural or other training, hospitals and clinics, and political and administrative meetings organized by representatives of the state or federal government. Speaking knowledge and literacy in Spanish have come to be viewed as a mark of "cultural advancement" and self-confidence; the use of only an indigenous language is viewed as a sign of ignorance, backwardness, and a passive attitude. (Although the absence of writing in no way implies inferiority of a language, it is particularly ironic that in pre-Columbian times a number of Mesoamerican peoples did have writing systems.) Today, "Spanish is . . . exerting a tremendous pressure, particularly among the young, and the rejection of the Indian language has been a first step toward assuming a mestizo [mixed European and American Indian ancestry] identity, 'passing over' from one ethnic group to another" (King 1994:170). But can one talk about unsuccessful languages when their subordinate status is being assigned to them by outsiders and accepted by their own speakers?

To say, however, that some languages may be considered more successful than others must not be taken as justifying linguistic profiling—that is, judging the worth of persons on the basis of their speech. This may happen (and is happening) whenever one of two (or several) languages spoken in a particular area of the world is thought to have more prestige than another. Such valuation may easily lead to language prejudice and result in an irrational attitude of superiority toward an individual, a group, or a population using that language. And strange as it may seem, language prejudice can exist even in situations in which two (or more) languages in question have equally long histories and distinguished literary traditions. A case in point may be the attitude in the eastern United States of some white Americans toward Puerto Ricans. The use of "good" English (whatever "good" may mean in this context) is associated by these white Americans with political and economic prestige, but Spanish (or English, the second language of the Puerto Ricans, if spoken with a decided accent and grammatical mistakes) is equated with poverty, a lower-class status, lower intelligence, and the like. In other words, languages, dialects, choice of words, and accents become the means by which people are classified and then treated accordingly. Linguistic prejudice and racial prejudice are close relatives.

## A BRIEF HISTORY OF ANTHROPOLOGY

This book is a text on linguistic anthropology, so let us now discuss what these two disciplines—anthropology and linguistics—entail. We begin with anthropology. A very simple definition of anthropology is "the holistic study of humankind," but this may not be especially enlightening. More insightful might be these propositions, which summarize the overall scope of anthropology (Pi-Sunyer and Salzmann 1978:3):

1. Because members of the species *Homo sapiens* are biological organisms, the study of human beings must try to understand their origin and nature in the appropriate context.
2. As hominids (that is, recent humans and their extinct ancestors) strove to adapt to a great variety of natural and self-made conditions, they engaged in a long series of innovations referred to by the term *culture*.
3. In the course of their cultural evolution during the past million years, humans have been immeasurably aided by the development of an effective means of communication, the most remarkable and crucial component of which is human language.

Many other fields, of course, are also concerned with aspects of the human condition. Among these fields are anatomy, physiology, history, political science, economics, art history, literature, and sociology. With all these specialized areas focusing on the human experience, why would there be a need for such a broad discipline as anthropology?

When Herodotus, a Greek historian of the fifth century BCE, wrote briefly about the ethnic origin of the Carians and Caunians of southwestern Asia Minor and took into consideration the dialects they spoke, he engaged in (stretching the point a bit) what could be called linguistic anthropology. During the Age of Discovery, European scholars became intrigued by the many different peoples of the American continents and the languages they spoke. Nevertheless, linguistic anthropology in the modern sense is a relatively recent field of study that developed in the United States and has been practiced predominantly by North American academics.

The stimulation for the earliest phases of what was to become linguistic anthropology came from the exposure of European immigrants to Native Americans. The cultures and languages of these peoples were studied by educated Americans of varying professions—physicians, naturalists, lawyers, clerics, and political leaders. Among these amateur linguists, for example, was Thomas Jefferson (1743–1826), who collected the vocabularies of Native American languages. In his *Notes on the State of Virginia* (1787) Jefferson wrote,

**Photo 1.1 Franz Boas. Courtesy of the Library of Congress, LC-USZ62-36743.**

"Great question has arisen from whence came those aboriginals of America" and then offered the following suggestion: "Were vocabularies formed of all the languages spoken in North and South America . . . and deposited in all the public libraries, it would furnish opportunities to those skilled in the languages of the old world to compare them with these, now, or at any future time, and hence to construct the best evidence of the derivation of this part of the human race" (Jefferson 1944:225–226). In this passage, Jefferson referred to more than just the comparative study of languages; he must have had in mind using linguistic evidence to address questions concerning the cultural prehistory of humankind.

By the middle of the nineteenth century the world was basically a well-known place, both geographically and culturally. The details certainly remained to be filled in, but no one expected to find a new hemisphere or uncover an unknown civilization. What puzzled scholars, however, was why there was so much human variety. Peoples looked vastly different; they spoke different languages; and their religions, marriage practices, and other customs also seemed very different. One of the main intellectual and scientific tasks of the day was to try to explain this diversity of race, language, and culture, past and present.

Modern anthropology began as the study of subjects that were not already claimed by scholars in other fields. But to say that anthropology just gathered these intellectual leftovers is not quite accurate. It was thought that the study of human biological and cultural development would shed light on the pressing "race, language, and culture" question. Because at that time "primitives" were thought to be the remnants of an evolutionary ancestral past, the study of preindustrial societies naturally became anthropology's main domain. Early anthropologists, then, focused especially on the nonliterate tribal peoples others considered "primitive" or "savage." These humble beginnings are still reflected in the popular conception of anthropologists as people who supply museums with exotic specimens from societies in remote parts of the world or who dig up the remains of past human life and cultures. Many modern anthropologists, however, study their own cultures as well, and some of their findings and comments on them are illuminating.

During the nineteenth century, the study of Native Americans and their languages occupied both distinguished Americans and a number of European explorers who traveled in the western part of the United States. Some of them collected and published valuable data on Native Americans and their languages that would otherwise have been lost. Serious and purposeful study of Native American languages and cultures, however, did not begin until after the establishment of the Bureau of (American) Ethnology of the Smithsonian Institution in 1879. John Wesley Powell (1834–1902), perhaps better known as the first person to run the Colorado River throughout the entire length of the Grand Canyon, became its first director. In 1891, Powell published a still-respected classification of American Indian languages north of Mexico.

**Photo 1.2 Edward Sapir. Portrait of Edward Sapir, Canadian Museum of History, 85901 LS.**

Because the early anthropologists were interested in peoples other specialists neglected, they concerned themselves with all aspects of a society. The German-born Franz Boas (1858–1942) was a dominant figure in the early days of American anthropology and held the first academic position in anthropology in the United States (at Clark University in Worcester, Massachusetts, from 1888 to 1892). He authored, coauthored, or edited more than seven hundred publications, ranging from articles on Native American music, art, folklore, and languages to studies in culture theory, human biology, and archaeology. As early as 1911, Boas edited the first volume of *Handbook of American Indian Languages*, followed by two other volumes (1922 and 1933–1938) and part of a fourth (1941). Even though he emphasized the writing of grammars, the compiling of dictionaries, and the collecting of texts, research concerning the place of languages in Native American societies and the relation of languages to cultures began to be undertaken with increasing frequency. Because of Boas's advocacy, the study of the relationship among language, culture, and society became fully recognized as important enough to be considered one of the four subfields of anthropology. Boas's direct influence was felt until his death at the age of eighty-four, and the course of American anthropology after him was shaped to a great extent by his students at Columbia University.

Probably the most important founder of today's linguistic anthropology was Edward Sapir (1884–1939), whom we met previously in our discussion of Takelma grammar. Sapir was undoubtedly the most accomplished linguist and anthropologist of the first half of the twentieth century. His seminal *Language* (1921), was one of the first linguistics books written for a popular audience, and it is still in print today. Sapir was perhaps the most prolific anthropologist, ever—his works have been collected in a (so-far) nine-volume collection of some 7,000 pages (with fourteen volumes in the series being projected). He was mainly a specialist in Native American languages, doing work on Yana, Wishram, Chinook, Navajo, Nootka, and Paiute, among others. But he was also one of the most influential general scholars of his day, impacting the fields of anthropology, linguistics, and psychology.

By World War II, anthropology was well established as an academic field and was taught at major US universities. The four main subfields then recognized—in large part a legacy of Boas—were **biological** (or physical) **anthropology, cultural anthropology, archaeology**, and **linguistic anthropology**. More specialized areas of concern and research have developed within the subfields, among them political, economic, urban, feminist, medical, legal, nutritional, visual, and psychological anthropology, and the anthropology of area studies such as Latin America, Asia, Africa, and Europe, to mention a few.

The one commitment that anthropologists profess regardless of their specialization is to the holistic approach. The term **holistic** refers to concern with a system as a whole rather than with only some of its parts. Because studying an entire culture in full detail could easily become a lifetime project, anthropologists focusing on only certain of its aspects invariably study and discuss them in full cultural context. In the study of humanity, applying the holistic approach means emphasizing the connections among the many different facets of the human condition so that humankind can be understood in its full complexity: cultural, social, and biological.

One characteristic that sets anthropology apart from the other social sciences is a strong fieldwork component, sometimes augmented (especially in archaeology and biological anthropology) by work in the laboratory. Archaeologists survey land for sites and excavate and analyze the remains of past cultures. Biological anthropologists study such topics as the relationship between culture and disease, the behavior of nonhuman primates (such as chimpanzees and gorillas), gene pool frequencies, and nutritional patterns. They also search in particular locations of the world for skeletal remains relating to human evolution. For some time now, cultural anthropologists have not limited themselves to the study of tribal societies, peasant villages, or bands of hunter-gatherers in remote parts of the world. Many today work in postindustrial modern societies such as Japan and the United States or those found in Europe. This is certainly as it should be: if anthropology is truly the study of humankind, then it must concern itself with all of humankind.

## ANTHROPOLOGY, LINGUISTICS, AND LINGUISTIC ANTHROPOLOGY

Another discipline that also focuses on uniquely human attributes is linguistics, the scientific study of language. **Linguistics** does not refer to the study of a particular language for the purpose of learning to speak it; rather, it refers to the analytical study of language, any language, to reveal its structure—the different kinds of language units (its sounds, smallest meaningful parts of words, and so on)—and the rules according to which these units are put together to produce stretches of speech. There is a division of labor, then, between linguists and linguistic anthropologists. The interest of the linguist is primarily in language structure, whereas the interest of the linguistic anthropologist is in speech use and the relations that exist between language, on the one hand, and society and culture, on the other. As for the prerequisite training, the linguist does not need to study anthropology to become fully proficient in linguistics; a linguistic anthropologist, in contrast, must have some linguistic sophistication and acquire the basic skills of linguistic analysis to be able to do significant research in linguistic anthropology.

A terminological note is appropriate here. Although **anthropological linguistics** has frequently been employed to refer to the subfield of anthropology otherwise known as linguistic anthropology, and a respected journal exists under that name (*Anthropological Linguistics*), the term **linguistic anthropology** is to be preferred, as Karl V. Teeter argued some years ago (1964). Briefly, if anthropology is the study of humanity, and language is one of the most characteristic features of humankind, then the study of language is an obvious and necessary aspect of anthropology as a whole. To modify the noun *linguistics* by the adjective *anthropological* is clearly redundant, because even though members of all animal species communicate, so far as is known no other species uses anything comparable to human language. Only if, say, members of the cat family (Felidae) or of the class of birds (Aves) had something like human speech (not just some system of communication, no matter how intricate) would it make sense to speak of anthropological linguistics to distinguish it from some such field of study as felid or avian linguistics (that is, the study of the language of cats or birds). As we have already seen, there are several subfields of anthropology; just as the subfield concerned with culture is referred to as *cultural anthropology*, the one concerned with language is aptly referred to as *linguistic anthropology*. This is the term used throughout this book: it states exactly what the subfield is about—the study of language (or speech) within the framework of anthropology.

Others, however, have been quite adamant about these apparently picayune differences in terminology, which to the uninitiated would seem to matter little. Dell Hymes (2012), for example, argued that there were political and academic consequences to these choices of words. Hymes said it was important to be clear that the work discussed here was not just a kind of linguistics that anthropologists decided to do, but rather an integral part of the anthropological paradigm. But in the 1960s, the formalist study of grammar and language, as advocated by Noam Chomsky and his followers, came to dominate much of all intellectual thought (as we will see in Chapter 4). Chomsky and others stressed the notion of linguistic **competence**—the underlying knowledge and ability a person has for a language, regardless of his or her actual manifestation—or **performance** of that language in a social context at any given time. But to Hymes and others it was exactly this communicative ability of language to produce results in social life that held the most interesting problems and prompted the most important questions. Communicative competence and the social life of language, then, was what anthropologists should be studying, and the way to best describe this activity was to use the cover term *linguistic anthropology*.

### *The Americanist Tradition*

Hymes (2012:160) also asks another pertinent question: "What happened to our foundations in Native American languages?" By this he is referring to the long-standing historical connection between anthropology in general—and linguistic anthropology in particular—with "the tradition and kind of work that first brought linguistics and ethnographic research together in the United States, that is, work with American Indian people and American Indian languages." Although he laments that less stress is placed on Indian languages now than before, and that the analysis of Indian myth, verse, and poetry has been largely supplanted by more formal studies, he makes the important point that anthropology, linguistics, and Native Americans were inexorably linked in the first half of the twentieth century.

Because of this close connection, some (e.g., Darnell 1999, 2001; Valentine and Darnell 1999) have called this the "Americanist" tradition in anthropology. By this they mean not just a subject matter—American Indian languages and cultures—but also a set of premises that underlie much of the discipline. Some of these are listed in Box 1.1. Often these assumptions are not explicitly stated, but Darnell and others argue that they permeate anthropology as practiced and taught in North America. Many go back directly to Franz

Boas. Although anthropological theory has changed greatly over the course of a century of often hard-fought and groundbreaking debate, the continuity from Franz Boas to the present can be seen through the works of Alfred Kroeber, Ruth Benedict, Edward Sapir, Elsie Clews Parsons, Benjamin Lee Whorf, A. Irving Hallowell, Claude Lévi-Strauss, and others.

## SUMMARY AND CONCLUSIONS

In its modern form, linguistic anthropology was the last subfield of anthropology to be developed and recognized and was practiced primarily by North American anthropologists.

### BOX 1.1 SOME ASSUMPTIONS OF THE "AMERICANIST" TRADITION

1. Language, thought, and reality are presumed to be inseparable; that is, cultural worlds are constructed from linguistic categories; this, then, posits or implies the following:
   a. linguistic determinism (a relationship between language and thought): language determines the way people perceive and organize the world;
   b. linguistic relativitism: the distinctions encoded in one language are not found in any other language;
   c. linguistic equality: anything can be said or thought in any language; no language is more complex or simpler or easier than any other; no language is innately harder or easier to learn than any other; and
   d. linguistic indeterminacy: the distinctions a language makes are arbitrary; there is no a priori way to predict ahead of time what distinctions a language might or might not make.

2. For each linguistic assumption given above there is a corresponding cultural counterpart:

   linguistic determinism => cultural determinism
   linguistic relativitism => cultural uniqueness
   linguistic equality => cultural relativism
   linguistic indeterminacy => cultural indeterminacy

3. Culture is defined in terms of a system of symbols—in turn, these symbols reify and legitimate the culture; in other words, culture is a set of symbols in people's heads, not just the behaviors that arise from them.
4. Discourse and "texts" of various kinds are the primary basis for both linguistic and ethnographic study.
5. An intimate, intensive, and long-term working relationship with a number of key informants, using the native language, is an absolute necessity.

*continues*

Its beginnings go back to the interest of nineteenth-century scholars in the great variety of Native American societies and the languages they spoke. Linguistic anthropologists view language in its cultural framework and are concerned with the rules for its social use; the analysis of its structure is therefore only a means to an end. By contrast, linguists in their study of languages emphasize linguistic structure and the historical development of languages.

Just as in the rest of anthropology, the data for linguistic anthropology are for the most part obtained in the field. Over several decades fieldworkers have developed techniques and methods to the point that anthropology departments with a sizable program in linguistic anthropology now offer courses in linguistic field methods.

*continued*

6. It is assumed that there is a link between linguistics and what anthropologists sometimes call "culture and personality" studies (i.e., culture and the individual are inseparable).
7. It is assumed that culture is mutable and historic—that is, traditional cultures are not static; native peoples—like Euro-Americans—also have a history; "traditional" cultures change and adapt to new circumstances.
8. There is an emphasis on long-term fieldwork (often two or three decades spent in the same community).
9. There is a strong commitment to preserving knowledge encoded in the oral tradition.
10. Native peoples are not objects to be studied; there is a dialogic relationship between the researched and those doing the researching.
11. There is also a strong link among the informant, the researcher, and the researcher's work; some native peoples are linguists and anthropologists themselves, and many are at least readers of and commentators on the research product.
12. There is often a rather strong emphasis on "native" categories; they are at least as important as the researcher's categories.
13. There often is a de-emphasis on theory over data (at least in the pre–World War II era).
14. The strict separation of race, language, and culture is something never to be forgotten; indeed, when this is forgotten, dire social consequences can result.
15. Although relativism is assumed, this by no means implies that linguistic and cultural universals are to be dismissed or ignored.

Jim Stanlaw (based on Darnell, *Theorizing American Anthropology* [1999], 45–48, and *Invisible Genealogies* [2001], 11–20; Stanlaw, *Review of Invisible Genealogies* [2002])

## RESOURCE MANUAL AND STUDY GUIDE

Following are some questions related to the text you have just read. This format is followed in all subsequent chapters. For the true-false questions, circle T or F, as applicable, to the left of each statement. For each multiple-choice question, select the most easily defensible complement or choice and indicate your answer by entering the appropriate capital letter in the space to the left of the question number. For the completions, complete each statement using the most suitable word(s). The number of words is indicated in parentheses. In some chapters, there are problems asking you to apply the methods of analysis just presented to actual linguistic data. Solutions to the problems and answers to all objective questions are given in the answer key. For each chapter, there are questions for discussion and sometimes projects. Because these are open-ended questions, we have not provided answers for them. Finally, please note that definitions for all the key terms bolded throughout the text can be found in the glossary at the back of the book.

### *Questions for Discussion*

1. Imagine people growing up without language. Can they still "think" the same as someone *with* language? That is, can we think without language? What about visual artists or musicians? Do they think in language? What personal experiences might you have had yourself to use as evidence for your answers?
2. One of the authors of this book has just been made king of America, and his first decree is that everyone must study a foreign language in school for at least six years, starting in the first grade. Will this edict start a revolution? Would you be one of the rebels? Is this un-American? What do you think the king has in mind with this decree, and does it make any sense? What if we told you that this actually has happened in numerous countries?
3. Enrollments nationwide for Arabic language classes in institutions of higher education have risen well over 100 percent in recent years, and the number of colleges offering Arabic instruction has nearly doubled. Why do you think that is?

### *Project*

In this project we will consider notions some people might have about language. Take all or some of the items on the list on page 2 and show them to a friend, roommate, or family member. Ask that person what she or he thinks, and why. The answers may actually surprise you. (As mentioned previously, each of these statements would be considered wrong or exaggerated by most anthropologists and linguists.)

### *Objective Study Questions*

**TRUE-FALSE TEST**

T F 1. For the most part, the terms *linguistic anthropology* and *anthropological linguistics* mean exactly the same thing, and neither is to be preferred over the other.

T F 2. Natural language itself is not ambiguous; it is people's misinterpreting things that causes problems.

T F 3. According to Boas, there is no intrinsic connection among race, language, and culture.

T F 4. Almost everywhere in the world, everyone is monolingual or monodialectal, just as in America.

T F 5. No language is really more complex or simpler or easier than any other; no language is harder or easier to learn than any other.

T F 6. Whereas *linguists* are primarily interested in the structure of languages, *linguistic anthropologists* study the relationship between language, on the one hand, and culture and society, on the other.

**MULTIPLE-CHOICE QUESTIONS**

____ 1. The person who is said to be the "founding father" of American anthropology is (A) Edward Sapir. (B) Dell Hymes. (C) Franz Boas. (D) Karl V. Teeter.

____ 2. Anthropology as a recognized science began in the (A) seventeenth century. (B) eighteenth century. (C) nineteenth century. (D) twentieth century. (E) twenty-first century.

____ 3. According to Edward Sapir, it is the (A) syntax, (B) vocabulary, (C) grammar that more or less faithfully reflects the culture whose purposes it serves.

____ 4. During the last seventy years, the percentage of monolingual and bilingual Mexican Indians has been steadily declining in favor of Spanish by about what percent? (A) From 16 percent in 1930 to about 7 percent in 2005. (B) From 10 percent in 1930 to 1 percent in 2005. (C) There actually has been not much change. (D) Spanish has for the most part replaced almost all indigenous languages.

____ 5. Lexical specialization—that is, a large inventory of words pertaining to a particular domain—is found in which of the following instances? (A) The Agta of the Philippines have more than thirty verbs referring to types of fishing. (B) The natives of the German city of Munich are said to have more than seventy terms referring to the local varieties of beer. (C) Americans have a hundred or so names for makes and types of automobiles. (D) Only two of the preceding three choices are true. (E) All three choices, A–C, are true.

**COMPLETIONS**

1. In the nineteenth century, one of the main intellectual and scientific tasks was to try to explain the great diversity of __________, __________, and __________, past and present (three words).
2. Sapir's description of the morphology of the __________ language demonstrated that non-Western languages can be as complex as any found in Europe (one word).
3. A very brief and simple definition of anthropology might be "the __________ study of humankind" (one word).

**ANSWER KEY**

True-false test: 1-F, 2-F, 3-T, 4-F, 5-T, 6-T
Multiple-choice questions: 1-C, 2-C, 3-B, 4-A, 5-E
Completions: 1. race, language, culture (any order), 2. Takelma, 3. holistic

## *Notes and Suggestions for Further Reading*

Those who wish to explore even more language myths than those discussed here should see the lively Bauer and Trudgill (1999). There are a number of books on linguistic anthropology for beginning students, including Ahearn (2012), Ottenheimer (2013a, 2013b), and Bonvillain (2010). Duranti (1997), and Hanks (1995) are more advanced; Agha (2007) even more so, but is excellent. Duranti (2001a) is a convenient encyclopedic dictionary of key terms for studying language and culture, and Duranti (2006) is an edited overview of articles on topics covering the whole field of linguistic anthropology. Another encyclopedic approach of a different kind—but also very useful for beginning students—is Crystal (2010). Enfield, Kockelman, and Sidnell (2014) is a fantastic resource, but a bit advanced for beginners. Bauer (2007) is a different kind of handbook, but it provides much interesting information on languages and linguistics in one convenient place. For general-reader introductions to the field of linguistics, see Burton et al. (2012)—it is not really for dummies!—or Rowe and Levine (2015), who are actually anthropologists. For interesting overviews of the languages of the world for beginning students, see Andresen and Carter (2016) or Austin (2008).

Edward Sapir's *Language* has been in print in various editions since it first appeared in 1921, for good reason. The greatest expert in Native American languages before World War II, Sapir could also write in an entertaining manner. Darnell (2010) gives him a sensitive biography. The most accessible of Franz Boas's linguistic works is his "Introduction" to the *Handbook of American Indian Languages* (1911). His grandson Norman Boas (2004) has written his definitive biography. The "Americanist" tradition in linguistic anthropology is covered by Darnell (2001), Valentine and Darnell (1999), and the review by Stanlaw (2002). A very useful collection of readings on topics germane to linguistic anthropology can be found in Blum (2013).

# 2

# Methods of Linguistic Anthropology

### LEARNING OBJECTIVES

- Define—and compare and contrast—autonomous linguistics and linguistic anthropology
- List and define the two major paradigms of autonomous linguistics
- List and define the three major paradigms of linguistic anthropology
- Explain the importance of language in doing anthropological fieldwork
- Discuss the role of informants in doing fieldwork
- Explain some of the techniques of fieldwork methodology

What linguistic anthropology is concerned with are the consequences of the process that led to language. Because linguistic anthropologists try to view language from the very broad base of anthropology, their research interests are correspondingly comprehensive: from communication among the primates to language origins to structural characteristics of language to nonverbal types of communication to language in social context, and so on—too many to fully enumerate here. If the study of language is the main concern of linguistic anthropologists, then how does linguistic anthropology differ from linguistics?

## CONTRASTING LINGUISTICS WITH LINGUISTIC ANTHROPOLOGY

Linguistics is the scientific study of language. The term does not refer to the study of a particular language or languages for the purpose of learning to speak them; rather, it refers to the analytical study of language, any language, to reveal its structure—the different kinds of language units (its sounds, smallest meaningful parts of words, and so on)—and the rules according to which these units are put together to produce stretches of speech.

The subject matter of linguistic anthropology, which can be briefly defined as the study of language in its biological and sociocultural contexts, is best illustrated by the table of contents of this book. Perhaps only the term **sociocultural** needs a comment. The term **society** is frequently used almost interchangeably with the term **culture**, and the compound "sociocultural" points out their interconnection. There is a fine distinction, though, between society and culture, and linguistic anthropologists deal with aspects of both concepts: when they study and describe the communicative links between individual members of a group and between groups within a society, and when they study and describe traditional learned behavior (culture) and how it relates to the values of the members of a group, their linkages with language are sociocultural.

To give concrete examples of the difference between linguistics and linguistic anthropology, consider the following four statements: The first two illustrate statements made by a linguist, the last two statements by a linguistic anthropologist.

The two linguistic statements:

1. In English, the nasal consonant *n* as in *sin* and ŋ (written as *ng*) as in *sing* are in contrast because they differentiate the meanings of two English words.
2. The Modern English word *woman* developed over the centuries from the Old English *wīfman*.

One will notice that there is no reference in these statements about the speakers or the circumstances under which the words have been used.

Statements from linguistic anthropology:

1. In Javanese, the choice of words is determined by such characteristics of the speaker and the addressee as their age, gender, wealth, education, and occupation; the more refined the level of speech, the slower, softer, and more even the presentation will be.
2. The remarkable cave-wall paintings and carvings of the **Upper Paleolithic** Cro-Magnons serve as an indirect proof that these prehistoric people had a full-fledged language.

To sum up, then, a division of labor exists between linguistics and linguistic anthropologists. The interest of the linguist is primarily in language structure and less often in language changes over time; the interest of the linguistic anthropologist is in speech use and the relations that exist between language, on the one hand, and its users, on the other.

## THREE STRAINS OF LINGUISTIC ANTHROPOLOGY, AND MORE: THEORETICAL AND HISTORICAL PERSPECTIVES

To sum up the last section, we could say that formal linguistics and linguistic anthropology in some ways address complementary issues. Autonomous linguistics tends to deal with formal structures—the code of language—whereas linguistic anthropology focuses more on social structures, speakers, and language use. Of course these are not necessarily exclusive, but things like "use," "speech communities," and "characteristic of the speaker" cover a lot of ground. Thus, before we begin a discussion of methodology, we will make some remarks on the current state of the discipline of linguistic anthropology and offer some advice on mastering its tenets.

Many names and theories are discussed in this book. A simple presentation of facts, findings, and results of experiments will not suffice to fully understand the phenomena of human language and all its facets. A theoretical lens is needed to help us make sense of applicable data (or even recognize them when we see them). Theory helps us to interpret the world around us or even to know the important questions to ask. Practitioners and researchers always keep these things in mind as they do their work, even if they do not always make them clear when reporting results.

To help make some sense of all the material to come later in the book, it might be helpful for students to be exposed to a few of the major theories or approaches that will be encountered. These are given in summary form in Tables 2.1 and 2.2. It is recommended that students come back to these tables often as they read the book. Not every name or term given in the tables is explained in detail right now, but all will be encountered later in some other chapter. In each table, the paradigm is named ("trend"), its years of origin given, and a few names associated with it are listed. The goals of the theory, its views of language, its units of analysis, outstanding issues, and method of obtaining data are provided in thumbnail sketches in subsequent columns.

To keep things manageable, these theories, approaches, or paradigms are presented chronologically. Two major themes are discussed for (non-anthropological) linguistics: (1) structuralism and (2) Chomsky's generative grammar. These are shown in Table 2.1.

For linguistic anthropology, Alessandro Duranti (2003) sees the discipline as having gone through three paradigms since the turn of the twentieth century. These are listed in Table 2.2: (1) the "first paradigm" of *anthropological* linguistics, (2) the "second paradigm" of *linguistic* anthropology or sociolinguistics, and (3) the "third paradigm" of social constructivism. In addition, we also present what we believe will be a fourth possible paradigm: cognitive linguistic anthropology.

These paradigms are briefly discussed below—two for autonomous linguistics in Table 2.1, and four for linguistic anthropology in Table 2.2—but students should be aware that these themes reappear numerous times in the course of this book. Thus some of the information in the tables may become clearer then. We suggest using these tables as signposts and coming back to them periodically as more material is learned. We hope that with these tables as guides, these theoretical "big questions" will not be so daunting.

**TABLE 2.1** TWO MAJOR PARADIGMS AND TRENDS IN MODERN LINGUISTICS

| | *Trend* | *Years* | *Proponents* | *Goals* | *View of Language* | *Preferred Units of Analysis* | *Theoretical Issues* | *Preferred Method of Data Collection* |
|---|---|---|---|---|---|---|---|---|
| 1. | Classic structural linguistics | WWI–c. 1950s | Leonard Bloomfield, Ferdinand de Suassure, Eugene Nida, Charles Hockett | To scientifically describe the world's languages, and to trace their typologies and connections | Language is an agreed-upon set of arbitrary signs people use unconsciously | Typically analysis of sounds (phonology), word components (morphology), and grammatical rules (syntax) are emphasized | How do arbitrary signs obtain and convey meaning; tied to psychological behaviorism? | One-on-one work with an informant, especially in a field setting for an extended period of time |
| 2. | Modern formal linguistics; generative grammar | 1960–present | Noam Chomsky and his students | To discover the innate properties of language and what they all have in common; how innate deep structures become manifested in speech | Language reflects innate conditions of the human mind; universal grammar | Sentences, phonological patterns, and the competence of the ideal speaker-listener | Mentalism; internalized "I-language" is taken to be the object of the study; language as a kind of "mental organ"; Plato's problem | The ideal speaker-listener acceptability judgments; oneself can also be an informant |

**TABLE 2.2** SOME PARADIGMS AND TRENDS IN LINGUISTIC ANTHROPOLOGY*

| *Trend* | *Years* | *Proponents* | *Goals* | *View of Language* | *Preferred units of Analysis* | *Theoretical Issues* | *Preferred Method of Data Collection* |
|---|---|---|---|---|---|---|---|
| "first paradigm": anthropological linguistics | 1900–1960 | Franz Boas, Edward Sapir, and their students | "[D]ocumentation, description and classification of indigenous languages, especially North American"; "salvage anthropology" | Language "as lexicon and grammar, that is, rule-governed structures, which represent arbitrary relations between language as an arbitrary symbolic system and reality" | "[S]entence, word, morpheme, and from the 1920s, phoneme; also texts (e.g., myths, traditional tales)" | "[A]ppropriate units of analysis for comparative studies (e.g., to document genetic linguistic relativity)" | "[E]licitation of word list grammatical patterns, and traditional texts from native speakers" |
| "second paradigm": *linguistic* anthropology or sociolinguistics | 1960s–1980s | Dell Hymes, John Gumperz | "[T]he study of language use across speakers and activities" | Language "as a culturally organized and culturally organizing domain" | "[S]peech community, communicative competence, repertoire, language variety, style, speech event, speech act, genre" | "[L]anguage variation, relationship between language and context" | "[P]articipant observation, informal interviews, audio recording of spontaneous language use" |
| "third paradigm": social constructivism | 1990s–present | Alessandro Duranti, Mary Bucholtz, Susan Gal, Kira Hall, William Hanks | "[T]he use of linguistic practices to document and analyze the reproduction and transformation of persons, institutions, and communities across space and time" | Language "as an interactional achievement filled with indexical values (including ideological ones)" | "[L]anguage practice, participation framework, self/person/identity" | "[M]icro-macro links, heteroglossia, integration of different semiotic resources, entextualization embodiment, formation, and negotiation of identity/self/narrativity/language ideology" | "[S]ocio-historical analysis; audiovisual documentation of temporarily unfolding human encounters, with special attention to the inherently fluid and moment-by-moment negotiated nature of identities, institutions, and communities" |
| A fourth paradigm?: cognitive linguistic anthropology | 1990s–present | John Lucy, Charles Briggs, George Lakoff, Ronald Langacker | To account for and to explain the various patterns of shared cultural knowledge | Language is not innate but is embodied and situated in specific cultural and physical environments | Concepts, cultural categories, lexical semantics (what words mean, and how and why), metaphors | Explaining culture/behavior/grammar in terms of conceptualization | Participant observation, audiovisual recordings, experiments and formal protocols, computer simulations and modeling |

***Quoted material based on Duranti (2003:326, 329–330, 333).**

## *Two Paradigms of Autonomous Linguistics*

### 1. Structural Linguistics

The classic **structuralist paradigm** (Table 2.1, row 1) dominated linguistics for the first half of the twentieth century until the 1960s, when Noam Chomsky's generative grammar largely replaced it. The pre–World War II structural linguists had an easy relationship with the Americanist anthropologists, and many important figures like Edward Sapir comfortably wore both hats. They saw language as consisting of largely arbitrary **signs** (things that stand for, or represent, something else). There is nothing natural about calling Secretariat a "*horse*," a "*kuda*," an "*uma*," a "*cheval*," a "*caballo*," or a "*Pferd*"—the word used would only depend on whether you lived in the United States, Indonesia, Japan, France, Mexico, or Germany, respectively. The important thing is that signs between and within languages contrast with one another, and that we all agree on these contrasts. But another important point that Sapir made—one the consequences of which would be explored more fully by Chomsky and others—was that these signs and the "unconscious patterning" that underlie them were largely used by speakers without their being aware of them.

Structural linguists, then, were interested in scientifically and objectively analyzing and describing the world's languages, as well as tracing their historical relationships and typologies. They developed extensive methodologies and tools to find the rules and patterns that governed a language's sound system (**phonology**), word structure (**morphology**), grammar (**syntax**), and vocabulary (**lexicon**); they also tried to develop ways to find the structure of **meaning** (**semantics**). They borrowed certain ideas from American behaviorist psychology (e.g., stimulus-response learning theory) to explain language acquisition.

### 2. Chomsky's Transformational-Generative Grammar

In the 1950s, Noam Chomsky (Table 2.1, row 2) revolutionized the field of linguistics with his theory of **generative grammar**. (This theory has gone through a series of name changes over the past fifty years—that is, "transformational grammar," "government and binding," "minimalism," and "move α," to mention only a few you may encounter—as it has been refined and refocused, but for our purposes we just call it "generative grammar." In Chapters 3 and 4 we will have more to say about these things.) Chomsky basically said linguists were not asking the right questions and were not setting their bar high enough. Instead of describing the various structures a language had, we needed to ask what the tacit rules were that allowed speakers to create and use languages in the first place. If viewed from afar, Chomsky showed the remarkable similarities shared by all languages (which he sometimes called **universal grammar**), even though French might appear to be very different from English on the surface, especially if a student has a French quiz on Friday. Thus, each native speaker possessed in his or her head *competence* in all the aspects of how that language operates. Later called **I-language**—the *I* vaguely standing for all the *internalized* and *intensional* knowledge an *individual* possesses—this part of language contrasts with **E-language**, the speech actually produced by speakers under specific *external* conditions (the material that often holds the most interest for linguistic anthropologists). While admitting that people's manifestations of language can be quite disparate, Chomsky and his followers believe it is by examining this underlying formal code that the most important things about language will be revealed. This often is done by giving informants test sentences (looking for hypothetical underlying rules) and asking them for their judgments on their acceptability.

Chomsky revisited a philosophic question he called **Plato's problem**: the fact that we seem to know more things than we are explicitly taught. For example, we seem to possess all kinds of geometric knowledge already—like how lines and squares and triangles operate—even if we are high school dropouts. No one has actually ever seen a "perfect triangle"; no matter how good a drawing in a geometry book, there will always be some inaccuracies or imperfections. Real perfect triangles exist only in our heads. Likewise, Chomsky argues that a basic knowledge of language is also largely unobtainable by mere exposure to the environment, so it too must exist only in our heads. Thus, language in general as a human property must be largely innate, biologically based, and the same for everyone. Methodologically, this means that we do not need a plethora of informants because no one's knowledge of some language is any better than any other (assuming they are normal native speakers). Sometimes one can even use oneself as an informant.

**Photo 2.1 Noam Chomsky. deepspace/Shutterstock.com**

## *Three Trends in Linguistic Anthropology . . . and More*

### 1. Americanist Anthropological Linguistics

As for linguistic anthropology, the "first" Americanist paradigm (Table 2.2, row 1) was initially proposed by Franz Boas as he developed his vision of anthropology in the United States. Boas saw linguistics as a tool for cultural and historical analysis, and, indeed, a necessary component of the kind of "salvage linguistics" and "salvage anthropology" he felt was also a mission of the new fledgling field. Thus, a high level of technical linguistic ability was expected of practitioners so all the data could be gathered correctly (in some cases, for the last time). Much of the early work by both structural linguists and "anthropological linguists" (the preferred term of the day) was on Native American languages. This emphasis on description implied that, in a sense, language is culture, and "therefore one can be assumed to be doing something anthropological by studying grammar" (Duranti 2003:325). Indeed, the categories of descriptive linguistics often determined the units of analysis for the anthropological linguists of this period. One important theoretical issue that arose in this climate was the **Sapir-Whorf hypothesis**: the idea that "languages provide their native speakers with a set of hard-to-question dispositions (e.g., to hear only certain sound distinctions, to favor certain classifications, to make certain metaphorical extensions) that have an impact on their interpretation of reality, and consequently, on their behavior" (Duranti 2003:326).

### 2. Linguistic Anthropology and Sociolinguistics

This first paradigm lasted from about 1900 to 1960, when the "second," sociolinguistic or linguistic anthropology "paradigm" (Table 2.2, row 2) was developed. This approach was largely due to the scholarship of two important linguistic anthropologists working in the

1960s and 1970s, Dell Hymes and John Gumperz. Their approach—sometimes called the ethnography of communication or the ethnography of speaking—was seen as a major alternative to Chomsky's generative grammar, which largely dismissed language-in-use. At this time Hymes strongly advocated the use of the term *linguistic anthropology* to stress that the work he and others were doing was not just a kind of linguistics that happened to be done by anthropologists, but rather a legitimate research project within anthropology itself.

Hymes and Gumperz said that language should be studied in ways very different from those of the Boasians and Chomskyans. Language must be studied within a social context or situation and go beyond the study of grammar. Ethnographers need to examine and describe the patterns of the spoken "**speech activity**" in the "**speech community**." The unit of interest, then, is not the ideal speaker-listener informant, but the speech community and its speech events. Language performance is to take precedence over knowledge of a language. Language became not so much a way to get at cognition (which both Boas and Chomsky believed), but a way to express social phenomena and social relationships. Language register and language variation—as a means of seeing how speech practices organize culture and society—came to take precedence over grammar as a way of seeing how people organize the world.

### 3. Social Constructivism

The "third" paradigm (Table 2.2, row 3) began in the late 1980s and early 1990s and is the one that guides most of the current research in linguistic anthropology. Duranti calls this trend "**social constructivism**" because this work focuses on the role language plays in constituting social encounters. Although speech events and speech communities are not dismissed, many people working in this tradition are acutely aware of the interactionism and improvisational aspects of language use. There has been a shift away from looking at language forms to looking at the way language is involved in symbolic domination, identity construction, power relations, and other issues of ideology. Some of the areas of interest are language and gender; performativity; race and racism; language and space; temporality; and language use in gay, lesbian, and transgendered communities. As Duranti says (2003:332), "The interest in capturing the elusive connection between larger institutional structures and processes and the 'textual' details of everyday encounters (the so-called **micro-macro connection**)" has produced a whole range of projects; whereas earlier generations of students who were interested in "linguistic forms and languages (in the first paradigm) or from their use in concrete and culturally significant social encounters (in the second), students today typically ask questions such as 'What can the study of language contribute to the understanding of this particular social/cultural phenomena (e.g., identity formation, globalization, nationalism)?'" This means, then, that linguistic anthropologists today are "using language as a tool for studying what is already being studied by scholars in other fields" and the rest of anthropology (2003:333).

### 4. A Cognitive Linguistic Anthropology?

We suggest that a cognitively informed linguistic anthropology may be considered an upcoming fourth paradigm (Table 2.2, row 4). In this "**cognitive linguistic anthropology**" we see that some of the insights from the new discipline of cognitive science are influencing research by those working in the linguistic anthropology tradition. This is not so much a radical departure because, as we saw in our earlier discussions, an interest in the relationships among language, thought, culture, and mind goes back to the earliest work of Boas in the early part of the twentieth century, through Sapir and Whorf at the time of World War II. A cognitive linguistic anthropology could be seen as a way of trying to connect the mentalism of current Chomskyan autonomous linguistics; the earlier work in cognitive anthropology of the 1970s; the conceptualizing of speech events of the "second paradigm"; and the interest in social life, social justice, and social constructivism found in the "third paradigm."

A cognitive linguistic anthropology attempts to find patterns of shared cultural knowledge within and across societies: what people from different groups know and how this knowledge is conceived, organized, and transmitted linguistically. Both language (and its formal properties like grammar) and society (and it manifestations like social structure) are understood as conceptualizations and mental representations. Cognitive linguistic anthropology interprets language use in terms of concepts—sometimes universal, sometimes culturally specific. In short, cognitive linguistic anthropology uses language as the doorway to enter the study of cognition and the study of language-in-use: how people perceive the real physical world, the constructed social world, and the imagined conceptual world.

## THE FIELDWORK COMPONENT, AND THE COMPONENTS OF FIELDWORK

### *Participant Observation*

Research concerning the cultures and languages of contemporary societies is for the most part conducted in the field. Exposure of anthropologists to the societies or communities they wish to study is usually not only prolonged (lasting at least several months, and frequently a full year) but also repeated (once accepted by a group, anthropologists tend to return for follow-up research). The immersion of anthropological fieldworkers for an extended period in the day-to-day activities of the people whom they study is referred to as **participant observation**. To be able to communicate in their own language with the people under study is very helpful to the anthropologist. Lacking such skills, the anthropologist must rely on interpreters who, no matter how eager they are to help, may unwittingly simplify or distort what is being said by those who supply cultural or linguistic data. Because members of a society who are fluent in two languages are sometimes culturally marginal people, they should be selected with care: individuals who have adapted to or borrowed many traits from another culture could have lost a substantial number of traits from their own. To be sure, studies of how and to what extent individuals or whole groups may have modified their culture by prolonged or vigorous contact with another society are of great importance and interest, but these studies cannot be carried out satisfactorily unless the traditional base of the culture undergoing change is well understood.

The availability of someone who can communicate with the anthropologist does not excuse the researcher from needing to become acquainted with the language of the group. The knowledge of a language serves the anthropologist as an invaluable tool for gaining an informed understanding of the many aspects of a culture—for example, enabling the researcher to judge the relative standing of members of a community on the basis of how they address one another. As early as 1911, Boas emphasized this point in his introduction

**Photo 2.2 Bronislaw Malinowski. Courtesy of the London School of Economics, Malinowski/3/18/8.**

to the first volume of *Handbook of American Indian Languages* when he insisted that "a command of the language is an indispensable means of obtaining accurate and thorough knowledge [of the culture that is being studied], because much information can be gained by listening to conversations of the natives and by taking part in their daily life, which, to the observer who has no command of the language, will remain entirely inaccessible" (Boas 1911:60).

### *Malinowski: Language in Daily Life*

What Boas insisted on was underscored by Bronislaw Malinowski (1884–1942), the Polish-born anthropologist who pioneered participant observation during his **fieldwork** in Melanesia and New Guinea between 1914 and 1920. In discussing the advantage of being able to speak one of the local languages, he wrote: "Over and over again, I was led on to the track of some extremely important item in native sociology or folklore by listening to the conversation of . . . Igua [his young helper] with his . . . friends, who used to come from the village to see him" (Malinowski 1915:501). And seven years later, in his introduction to *Argonauts of the Western Pacific*, Malinowski offered additional reasons why the command of the native language is useful: "In working in the Kiriwinian language [spoken on the island of Kiriwina in the Trobriand Islands], I found still some difficulty in writing down . . . [a] statement directly in translation . . . [which] often robbed the text of all its significant characteristics—rubbed off all its points—so that gradually I was led to note down certain important phrases just as they were spoken, in the native tongue" (Malinowski 1922:23). Decades later, Malinowski was still being cited for his emphasis on participant observation (see Box 2.1).

For linguistic anthropologists, reasonably good speaking knowledge of the language of the society being studied is indeed indispensable. ("Reasonably good" speakers are those who can express themselves comfortably on nontechnical subjects; fluency, if it refers to nativelike command of a language, is very difficult to attain even after an extended period of fieldwork.) It is also necessary for linguistic anthropologists to learn a great deal about the culture of a foreign society, for much of what they study concerns the sociocultural functions of linguistic behavior. In short, both a knowledge of the language and a fair acquaintance with the culture are called for if inquiries made in the field are to be relevant and statements about the relationship between language and culture or society are to be accurate and valid (see Box 2.2).

### BOX 2.1 PARTICIPANT OBSERVATION

During [Malinowski's] trip to do his first fieldwork, World War I broke out. When he landed in Australia, he learned that he was now the enemy, and the Australians informed him that he was stuck for the duration. But he convinced them that they should let him go and wander the territories, do a little ethno-exploring. He spent two extensive periods of time on a little string of atolls called the Trobriand Islands.

Malinowski became the patron saint of ethnography. He dived right in, lived with the "natives," and learned their language as they spoke it while they went about their everyday business. He talked about the goal of it all in romantic tones—"to grasp the native's point of view, his relation to life, to realize *his* vision of *his* world," or, as he sometimes put it, "to get inside the native's skin."

The name of this approach to fieldwork, a name that is now enshrined in the jargon, is participant observation. You don't just stand around and *watch* like a parody of a lab technician; you jump in and *do* everyday life with people to get a firsthand feel for how things go. At the same time, you keep a third eye at an altitude of several feet above the action and watch what's going on in a more distant way.

Never mind that this is difficult, to passionately commit to the flow of experience and keep your distance at the same time. The concept expresses the right contradiction. Besides, participant observation hides Malinowski's secret about culture. Like Boas and Whorf, he wrote about culture as what "those people" have. But participant observation carries with it a commitment to connect, to put your body and mind on the line, to engage what "those people" are doing and figure out why, at first, you didn't understand. Participant observation signals that culture *has* to get personal.

Given the gregarious nature in general and his devotion to participant observation in particular, it's no surprise that Malinowski['s . . . ] first love was the real situations that made up the daily life of the Trobriand Islanders. Language wasn't an isolated object that consisted of words and the rules for stringing them together into sentences. Language was the way that people came together in those situations and got things done.

### *Informants, Consultants, Collaborators*

The native speaker from whom the researcher collects linguistic (or cultural) information is referred to as an *informant*. In recent years, the term *consultant* has been used with increasing frequency, in part because some members of the public confuse *informant* with the uncomplimentary term *informer*. More important, though, is that the term *consultant* gives recognition to the intellectual contribution made to linguistic and anthropological studies by those native speakers who work with anthropologists or linguists. The collaboration between members of a society and outsiders who study various aspects of that society is reflected in the growing number of coauthored articles. Another way of using to advantage the native speakers' insights into their own language is to enable interested individuals to receive training in linguistics and anthropology and then encourage them to use the acquired skills and knowledge, not only for the benefit of linguistic anthropology in general, but for the benefit of their own societies as well. Perhaps the most prominent among those who have urged that language informants be brought fully into collaboration was Kenneth L. Hale (1934–2001). He pioneered this approach for more than a quarter of a century. As early as 1969, Hale made the points that "for some linguistic problems [it is doubtful] whether the traditional arrangement, in which the linguistic problem is formulated in one mind and the crucial linguistic intuitions reside in another, can work at all—or, where it appears to work, whether it can be said that the native speaker is not, in fact, functioning as a linguist," and, a little further, that

> **BOX 2.2 COMMENTS ON METHODOLOGY I**
>
> In the last few decades of the twentieth century, there was considerable improvement in the tools used in documenting language use. Whereas descriptions of verbal activities such as greetings, proverbs, insults, and speechmaking used to be based on participant observation or on work with native speakers, today researchers are expected to have recordings of exchanges in which the phenomena they describe are occurring spontaneously. As the technology for visual documentation improves and becomes more accessible, we are able to notice phenomena (e.g., synchronization between talk and gestures) which used to be missed in past analysis of verbal communication. At the same time, audiovisual documentation has also increased the level of intrusion into people's lives. This means that researchers must be ever more aware of the social and ethical dimensions of fieldwork. The relationship between researchers and their subjects is as delicate and as important as any other human relationship and as such requires care, mutual respect, and honesty. If the goal of our study is a better understanding of the role played by language in the human condition, we must be guided in our efforts by the desire to improve our communication across social and cultural boundaries. This must also apply to our fieldwork situation and our relationship with the speech communities we want to study.
>
> Reprinted from Alessandro Duranti, *International Encyclopedia of the Social and Behavioral Sciences* (2001b), 8904-8905, with permission from Elsevier.

> the distribution of linguistic talent and interest which is to be found [for example] in an American Indian community does not necessarily correspond in any way to the distribution of formal education in the Western sense. If this talent is to flourish and be brought to bear in helping determine the particular relevance of the study of language to the communities in which it is located, then ways must be found to enable individuals who fit such descriptions . . . to receive training and accreditation which will enable them to devote their energies to the study of their own languages. (Hale 1974:387, 393)

Data for the analysis of a language or of language use can of course be collected away from the area where the language is spoken if an informant lives within reach of the linguistic anthropologist. Linguistic data obtained in such a manner can be quite useful if the informant's native language skills have remained good and the goal of the research is to make a preliminary analysis of the language. Determining how a language functions in a society, though, cannot be accomplished with the help of only one native speaker removed from those with whom he or she would normally communicate. (Special circumstances may merit exceptions. The description of the grammar of Tunica, a Native American language formerly spoken in northern Louisiana, was based on the speech of the only individual who could still speak the language "with any degree of fluency." The author of the grammar, Mary R. Haas [1910–1996], who did most of her fieldwork in 1933, noted that her informant "has had no occasion to converse in Tunica since the death of his mother in 1915" [Haas 1941:9]. In this case, the only available informant was clearly preferable to none at all.)

In the early twenty-first century, there are likely to remain only a few languages in the world about which nothing is known. However, there are still hundreds of languages about which linguists and anthropologists know relatively little. For the most part these languages are in Irian Jaya (West Irian) and Papua New Guinea (the western, Indonesian, and eastern, independent, halves of New Guinea, respectively) and the basin of the Amazon. According to recent estimates, some 850 languages are reported for Papua New Guinea, some 670 for Indonesia, and about 210 for Brazil—a total of nearly three-tenths of the world's languages (Krauss 1992:6). As a result of the great amount of fieldwork done the world over following World War II, it is now increasingly common for anthropologists to study communities or societies whose languages have already been described at least to some extent (and for which a system of writing may even have been devised, although speakers of such languages may have little, if any, need for writing). Such scholars are fortunate to be able to prepare in advance for their fieldwork by reading the relevant publications or unpublished manuscripts, listening to tape recordings made in the field by others, or even studying the language from native speakers if they are readily available. But occasions still arise in which the linguistic anthropologist must, or does, start from scratch. The description in Box 2.3, then, has two functions: first, to indicate very briefly how potential fieldworkers who lack any knowledge of the field language should proceed and, second, to indicate how linguists and anthropologists have coped with unknown languages in the past.

Besides being fluent in their native language, informants should be active participants in their culture. In most instances, ideal informants are older men and women not significantly affected by other languages and outside cultural influences. Such people almost always know their language better than the younger members of the society, who are likely to

### BOX 2.3 COMMENTS ON METHODOLOGY II

Fieldworkers' participation in the social life of the community must be recorded as systematically as possible. This is done by writing field notes and by transcribing recordings of social encounters, activities, and events. Field notes are important because they provide researchers with a chance to document important information (which is soon forgotten if not written down) and reflect on what they have just experienced. Transcription is equally important because it allows researchers to fix on paper (or on a computer screen) salient aspects of interactions that can then be interpreted, translated, collected, and compared. Transcription is thus a particular type of what Ricoeur called "inscription," that is an abstraction and a fixing of something that by nature is or was moving across time and space. Linguistic anthropologists strive to produce rich transcripts by relying on native speakers who have the necessary cultural background to provide the information necessary to make sense of what is being said. There are many different ways of transcribing speech and nonverbal communication, and it is important for researchers to become familiar and experiment with more than one way before choosing the one that better fits their research goals and needs. For example, those who are interested in grammatical analysis must provide word-by-word glosses; for those who are interested in the relation between speech and the spatial organization of the event, visual representations of the settings become crucial; a transcript that utilizes phonetic symbols is appropriate when writing for linguists, but would be too hard to decipher for anyone else. Similarly, a transcript that tries to cover most of the information available to the participants at the time of speaking would be too cumbersome and equally hard to interpret. More generally, a transcript is always work in progress. It constitutes a first analysis of the data collected. It forces us to make important decisions about what is salient in an interaction and, at the same time, while being produced or once completed, it can reveal phenomena that we might otherwise have missed.

Reprinted from Alessandro Duranti, *International Encyclopedia of the Social and Behavioral Sciences* (2001b), 8904-8905, with permission from Elsevier.

also use the language of whatever dominant culture may surround them. The situation of course varies from one part of the world to another. In many Native American societies in the United States, for example, young parents are no longer able to speak to their children in the language that was native to their own parents or grandparents. Not only do older members of a society tend to remember traditional narratives, which invariably preserve grammatical forms, words, and phrases that do not occur in everyday conversation, but they also are knowledgeable about the traditional aspects of their culture—ceremonies, rules of kinship, artifacts, foods, and the like—and therefore have a good command of the corresponding vocabulary.

Informants should be able to enunciate clearly. The speech of men and women missing most or all of their front teeth may be distorted to the point that a description of the sounds of their speech would not be representative of the typical pronunciation of the society's members. Most commonly, male anthropologists use male informants in the initial stages of their fieldwork and female anthropologists use women, simply because individuals of the same gender usually work more comfortably with each other, especially in traditional societies. At some point during the field research, however, it is essential to obtain data from informants of the opposite gender as well, because in some societies the language of women contains certain sounds or words that differ from those heard in men's speech. All such differences should be accounted for and described. It is also important to include younger members of a society among the informants in order to find out whether and how linguistic variation is related to age and to what extent speakers may be influenced by other languages or dialects used in the area or by the official language of the country in which the group is located. For example, even though typical American teenagers and their grandparents speak the same language, their dialects differ somewhat, especially as far as vocabulary is concerned; older speakers are not likely to be acquainted with teenager slang and, even if they are, may not want to use it. Speakers of Badaga (a Dravidian language of southern India) who learned to speak the language prior to the 1930s make use of twenty distinctive vowel sounds, whereas the younger Badaga use only thirteen (Samarin 1967:61). The result of this simplification of the Badaga vowel system is an increased number of homonyms, words pronounced alike but different in meaning (like the English words spelled *meet* and *meat*, *rode* and *rowed*, and *soul* and *sole*). In general, variations in speech may be influenced by differences in age, gender, socioeconomic class, caste, religion, and various other factors.

### *Eliciting Data*

In eliciting data—that is, in obtaining from informants words, utterances, texts, and judgments concerning their language—the fieldworker should strive to collect material that is dialectally uniform and spoken in a natural tone of voice and at a normal rate of speed. Unnaturally slow speech used by an informant to enable the linguist to transcribe utterances more easily tends to distort sounds, stress, and the length of vowels; when sentences are spoken too rapidly, there is a tendency to leave out sounds or even to change them (consider the English *Gotcha!* "I got you!" and *Betcha!* "I bet you!"). Because dialects of a language may have somewhat different repertories of sounds and words, using informants who speak different dialects could prove confusing for the fieldworker in the initial stages of research. Eventually, of course, dialectal variation is worth noting, as are the sound modifications that words undergo when they are pronounced rapidly.

During the initial stages of fieldwork, eliciting is accomplished by asking the informant relatively simple questions such as "How do you say 'I am hungry' in your language?" "What does ___ mean in your language?" "Am I repeating correctly the word you have just said?" and the like. Once the linguistic anthropologist has become accustomed to hearing the language and working with it, more spontaneous and richer data can be obtained. Informants are then asked to talk, unprompted, about topics of personal interest to them—for example, "Please tell me how your father taught you to hunt when you were young" or "When you were a child, what was your favorite way of helping your mother?"—or to give an eyewitness account of some memorable experience, narrate a traditional tale, or engage in a conversation with another native speaker. Utterances longer than just a few sentences are best recorded on tape. The recordings can later be replayed as many times as needed to ensure accurate transcription. When first used, the tape recorder may inhibit informants somewhat, but if it is used often enough, informants become accustomed to it, and their speech should not be appreciably affected.

If fieldworkers wish to include in their studies so-called body language (eye movements, gestures, and shrugs), which may be a very important component of communicative behavior, videocassette recorders are useful. They record not only the sounds of speech and the body motions of the individuals speaking, but also the reactions of the audience and the overall setting, making it possible for the linguistic anthropologist to arrive at an accurate and comprehensive description of the communicative behavior characteristic of ceremonies, conversations, and encounters of other kinds.

What should be the size of a corpus, the collection of language data available to the linguist? A corpus is adequate for studying the sounds and grammar of a language once several days of recording and analysis have passed with no new sounds or grammatical forms noted. As for vocabulary, it would be impractical or impossible to collect every word that members of a society know or use. Quite commonly, words heard in everyday conversation among the members of a group do not include words heard in such traditional contexts as the telling of myths, praying, conducting ceremonies, and the like. A comprehensive description of a language (its sound system, grammar, and sentence formation) should therefore be based on data drawn from both casual and noncasual speech; that is, speech of different styles—everyday conversations, speech of young and old and women and men, speech of traditional storytelling, language used in formal affairs, and so on.

## *The Fieldworker*

Linguistic anthropologists are of course interested in much more than just the sounds, grammar, and vocabulary of a language, as the following chapters of this book show. However, practical speaking skills and knowledge of a language's structure are prerequisites for the full understanding of the relations between a language, on the one hand, and the society and its culture, on the other.

From what has just been said, it would appear that doing anthropological fieldwork is a challenging but interesting undertaking: The anthropologist makes many friends in an environment that is usually—at least in the initial stages—exciting, even mysterious, and becomes caught up in a discovery procedure that builds from the first day until the project is completed. The overwhelming majority of anthropologists engage in fieldwork repeatedly because they enjoy being away from the paperwork and routine of teaching and being among those whom they are eager to learn about and from.

Many demands that require adjusting to, however, are placed upon fieldworkers. The common response to exposure to unfamiliar cultural surroundings and people who speak a different language is culture shock. It manifests itself, at least initially, in disorientation and some degree of anxiety on the part of the fieldworker, particularly if he or she is the only outsider in an otherwise close-knit community, and a conspicuous outsider at that. There are many things to adjust or conform to: different foods, almost invariably the absence of personal privacy, poor hygiene, and the lack of physical comfort. There can also be a variety of threats to a fieldworker's well-being: excessive heat, humidity, or cold; ever-present insects (some alarming in size or number); larger animals to beware of (snakes, for example); and bacteria and viruses to which the visitor is not immune, with no physician to consult if the need arises. Then, too, it can be frustrating to have no one with whom to discuss the puzzling issues that frequently develop in the course of research. But even if the picture is somewhat mixed, most anthropologists—students and colleagues alike—usually consider their times in the field to be among the most memorable experiences of their lives.

## SUMMARY AND CONCLUSIONS

Linguistic anthropologists view language in its cultural framework and are concerned with the rules for its social use; the analysis of its structure is therefore only a means to an end. By contrast, linguists in their study of languages emphasize linguistic structure and the historical development of languages.

Just as in the rest of anthropology, the data for linguistic anthropology are for the most part obtained in the field. Over the decades, fieldworkers have developed techniques and methods to the point that some anthropology departments with a sizable program in linguistic anthropology now offer courses in linguistic field methods.

## RESOURCE MANUAL AND STUDY GUIDE

### *Questions for Discussion*

1. People who are not well informed sometimes have strange ideas about the languages spoken by members of small tribal societies. Analyze the following statement critically point by point: unwritten languages, such as those spoken by American Indians, lack well-defined sounds, orderly grammars, and extensive vocabularies. Not having been subjected to the unrelenting demands of complex industrial civilizations, these languages are inherently incapable of assuming the functions of well-established languages.
2. Suppose you were to engage in your first fieldwork experience in linguistic anthropology. How would you select your informant(s), and why would you choose certain types of individuals over others?
3. Suppose a fieldworker discovered and then was making a study of a language spoken by the members of a village society in the jungle of the Amazon basin. What would be the benefits of having studied cultural anthropology?

### *Objective Study Questions*

**TRUE-FALSE TEST**

T F 1. The reason all anthropologists enjoy fieldwork is that living in the field places no demands on them that they must adjust to.

T F 2. The native speaker from whom the researcher collects linguistic (or cultural) data is referred to as an informer.

T F 3. One characteristic that sets anthropology apart from other social sciences is a strong fieldwork component.

T F 4. In the initial phases of fieldwork, the anthropologist prefers to use people who have had extended experience in the anthropologist's own society.

T F 5. In the initial phases of linguistic fieldwork, anthropologists endeavor to use informants who speak different dialects of the language studied.

T F 6. Unwritten languages of small tribal societies are primitive because these languages have little or no grammar.

T F 7. Vocabularies of the languages of some small tribal societies may not be as extensive as the vocabulary of, say, English, but are sufficient to serve the needs of the groups using them.

**MULTIPLE-CHOICE QUESTIONS**

____ 1. There are still hundreds of languages about which linguists and anthropologists know relatively little or nothing at all. For the most part such languages are found in (A) Irian Jaya. (B) Papua New Guinea. (C) the Amazon basin in South America. (D) only two of the areas mentioned. (E) all three of the areas mentioned.

____ 2. For initial fieldwork in linguistic anthropology concerning, for example, Native American languages, experienced anthropologists tend to choose a native informant (consultant) who (A) is of the opposite sex. (B) has had good exposure to the larger society surrounding the tribal society being studied. (C) is young and easily approachable. (D) None of the preceding three choices is fully satisfactory.

____ 3. The immersion of anthropological fieldworkers for an extended period of time in the day-to-day life of the people whom they study is referred to as (A) going native. (B) participant observation. (C) giving up one's ethnic identity.

____ 4. Which of the following statements having to do with obtaining data for a little-known language is *least* acceptable? (A) The informant should be an older person who is an active participant in his or her culture. (B) Recording a spontaneous conversation between two native speakers yields good material during the initial stages of fieldwork. (C) Tape recordings of linguistic data (with the permission of the informant) are extremely helpful. (D) In the advanced stages of fieldwork, using informants of several age groups and both genders is highly advisable.

**COMPLETIONS**

1. A collection of language data used as a basis for an analysis or description is referred to as a ____________________ (one word).
2. ____________________ (one word) is the drawing out of information or response from informants.
3. To emphasize the interconnection between culture and society, anthropologists use the compound adjective ____________________ (one word).
4. Alessandro Duranti argues that there have been three "paradigms" in linguistic anthropology. These are ____________________, ____________________, and ________________________________________ (three sets of two words each).

## *Answer Key*

True-false test: 1-F, 2-F, 3-T, 4-F, 5-F, 6-F, 7-T
Multiple-choice questions: 1-E, 2-D, 3-B, 4-B
Completions: 1. corpus, 2. elicitation, 3. sociocultural, 4. anthropological linguistics, linguistic anthropology, social constructivism

## *Notes and Suggestions for Further Reading*

For a book-sized guide to linguistic fieldwork, see Samarin (1967). However, Sakel and Everett (2012) provide much new information, as does the collection in Thieberger (2014). Bowen (2008) is also of interest and gives a fair bit of space to ethical issues. Quite possibly the earliest article discussing the training of linguistic anthropologists is Voegelin and Harris (1952). Useful although somewhat dated comments on obtaining a linguistic sample and a guide for transcribing unwritten languages may be found in Voegelin and Voegelin (1954 and 1959). Eliciting and recording techniques are discussed in Hayes (1954) and Yegerlehner (1955). For a practical guide to how to learn a field language, consult Burling (1984).

For contributions to the history of linguistic anthropology, see Hymes (1963, somewhat revised in Hymes 1983); Hallowell (1960); and Darnell (1992, 1999, and 2001). Readers on language in culture and society and on language in the social context are Hymes (1964) and Giglioli (1972). The history of linguistic anthropology is given in Duranti (2003). For a detailed account of Puerto Rican experiences with language, race, and class in the United States, see Urciuoli (1996). Duranti (2001a) (largely based on Volume 9 of the *Journal of Linguistic Anthropology*) contains seventy-five essays of two to four pages by specialists on "language matters in anthropology." The topics range from acquisition of language to writing. Any reader will find something of interest as well as short bibliographies of the most salient works on each topic. For a reader in linguistic anthropology, see Duranti (2009); the twenty-one contributions to this work include articles on speech community and communicative competence, utterances as acts, language socialization and literacy practices, and the power of language. For information on a possible cognitive strain in linguistic anthropology see Geeraerts and Cuyckens (2007); D'Andrade (1995); Lakoff (1987); Langacker (1987, 1991); Talmy (2000a, 2000b); and Shaul and Furbee (1998). For a concise "everything Chomsky" book, see McGilvray (2005).

# 3

# The "Nuts and Bolts" of Linguistic Anthropology I: Language Is Sound

## LEARNING OBJECTIVES

- Understand the articulatory phonetics approach to studying the sounds of language
- Become familiar with, and develop some utility in, phonetic transcription
- Understand the concept of the phoneme
- Develop some knowledge of the phonemes of English
- Be able to recognize prosodic features, and understand their role in speech

Even if we are not sociologists, most of us are aware that there are differences in our society based on economic class, social status, education, and other variables. This is probably true for any society in the world. These differences are encoded in numerous ways, and we perceive and demonstrate them to each other all the time. However, much of this is done unconsciously. William Labov suspected that one way social class is expressed and reified is through how people talk and listen to each other. In a classic experiment (which we will study in more detail in Chapter 14), he examined speech patterns in three New York City department stores. He found that salespeople and customers differed substantially in how, for example, they used r-sounds: whether they "dropped" them—as in the stereotypical Bronx accent, "I'm gonna pahk the cah ovah there in that big lot"—or "hyper-corrected" them, making sure they were pronounced clearly, as in "I'm going to park the car over there in that big lot." This so-called r-dropping depended on social class, though this variable was not something most people could readily identify in isolation. But people were, indeed, aware of these connections between speech and class. For example, in an attempt to sound more sophisticated, middle-class people often tried to emulate the speech and patterns of pronunciation of the upper class.

To detect such things, however, requires subtlety, and most people do not critically examine or notice their everyday surroundings. Linguistic anthropologists and sociolinguists such as Labov can help us do so. But to do so we need some special tools. In this chapter and the next, we are going to focus on (1) several formal properties of language and (2) the techniques anthropologists and linguists use to study them. These "nuts and bolts" are necessary for any further examination of how language, culture, and society are related, even though at first some of the technical details and formalism might seem a bit daunting. They are not; they are just the fundamentals required to examine problems analytically rather than just anecdotally. In this chapter we look at the sound structure of language and its analysis (phonology). In the next we look at how sounds are put together to make words (morphology) and sentences (syntax). Also, the nature of ethnographic fieldwork makes it essential for anthropologists to acquire a working knowledge of the language of those whom they study; to learn something about its structure; and to be able to write it down to record words, utterances, or traditional narratives.

## ANTHROPOLOGISTS NOTICE LANGUAGE

Traditionally, American anthropologists have long been concerned with language, in large part because of the great number and variety of Native American languages spoken in their own linguistic backyard. Each language represents a particular variety of the general language code—in other words, no two languages are alike; although some are structurally similar, others are quite different. Understanding the workings of a foreign language rather than simply learning to speak it requires some acquaintance with the plan according to which a particular language code is constructed. Such acquaintance cannot be gained by using the traditional grammar of English, or some other language taught in schools, as a framework. There are at least two important reasons for a more systematic and specialized approach: sounds and syntax.

### *Sounds and Symbols*

The first major reason has to do with converting to written form a language that previously has only been spoken. To accomplish this task, one must learn the principles of **phonetic transcription** and learn to write things in a **phonetic alphabet**. The use of the conventional spelling system of the anthropologist's own language is invariably out of the question: Not only should one expect the sounds of one language to differ from those of another, but the sounds and the orthographic conventions that represent them in the written language are not likely to correspond to each other on a one-to-one basis. English spelling is notorious for its lack of correlation with spoken English. For example, the sound *sh* in *shy* is written in English in twelve additional ways, as in *chef*, *conscience*, *fuchsia*, *issue*, *mansion*, *nauseous*, *ocean*, *potion*, *pshaw*, *schist*, *sugar*, and *suspicion*. The two sentences "The sun's rays meet" and "The sons raise meat" sound exactly alike despite their different meanings and orthographic representations, and in "Where do these lead pipes lead?" the two words written as *lead* are pronounced differently depending on their meaning. It should be obvious that the writing systems of languages with a literary tradition, English in particular, are not suitable for careful linguistic work. Therefore, some other more consistent way of writing things down must be used.

Here is another reason that learning a phonetic alphabet is a worthwhile endeavor—even though for some people, at least initially, it seems intimidating. If you put away your instinctive fear of new symbols—"It looks like mathematics!" one of our students once said to us, accusingly—we think you will see it is not so bad and can actually be pretty useful. For example, let's say you were interested in the various regional dialects of American English and wanted to find out, record, and tell others about the different pronunciations you have discovered. For instance, the word *pecan* is pronounced in at least five ways in the United States: *pee-KAHN, PEE-kahn, PEE-kan, pee-KAN*, and *pih-KAHN*. We have improvised a way to indicate these different pronunciations, in which "*pee*" sounds like the name of the "pea" vegetable; "*pih*" sounds like the first sound of the word *piddle*; "*kan*" sounds like the container that holds trash, "can"; and "*kahn*" sounds like the verb to cheat someone, "con"; stress is indicated by capital letters. Josh Katz tells us (2016:80–81) that the actual percentage distribution of these forms is:

| | |
|---|---|
| pih-KAHN | 39% |
| pee-KAHN | 16% |
| PEE-kahn | 9% |
| PEE-kan | 12% |
| pee-KAN | 9% |

But wasn't it cumbersome to do things this way, having to give an explanation for the intended pronunciation for every word? And wouldn't it be likely that someone else would come up with some other ad hoc system? A phonetic alphabet, with consistent and unambiguous symbols for each individual sound that could be used by everyone, every time, is the intent of a phonetic alphabet. We will a present a—relatively!—easy phonetic alphabet later on in this chapter.

### *Syntax and Structures*

The second major reason for a specialized approach has to do with grammatical structure—often called syntax in fancy linguistics parlance. Each language has a structure of its own that cannot be analyzed or grasped in terms of the investigator's own language. Many languages, for example, do not possess the definite and indefinite articles corresponding to the English *the* and *a(n)*. And those that do, often use them in ways slightly, or vastly, different than in English. For example, Box 3.1 shows that although Swedish does possess definite and indefinite articles, not only does it often place them in different locations, it also distinguishes plurality (i.e., uses different *the*-s or *a(n)*-s if the noun being referred to is singular or plural).

And English does not distinguish in the first person exclusive and inclusive plural forms that are common in other languages, for example, the Algonquian languages of Native North Americans. In English, when one would simply say *we*, *us*, or *our*, speakers of these languages must specify whether both the addressee (hearer) and perhaps others are included (as when a boy talks to his sister about "our mother"), or whether others are included but the addressee (hearer) is excluded (as when a mother talks to a visitor about "our children," referring to those belonging to her and her husband).

In sum, each language has its own distinctive structural characteristics, and these are likely to be overlooked if its structure is accounted for through the grammatical categories of the investigator's mother tongue or some other language serving as a model. Many grammars of American Indian languages compiled in earlier centuries by well-meaning missionaries strongly resembled Latin or Greek, even though the Native American languages could not have been more different; the descriptions betrayed their authors' thorough grounding in the classical languages and the resulting dependence on their structures.

There are many benefits to understanding the structure of a system, not only with respect to becoming acquainted with a foreign language but also in regard to other learning situations. One practical benefit is that if we are able to understand how the parts of a system function and what kinds of relationships exist among them, we are then spared having to memorize, or at least pay undue attention to, details that may well be trivial. To illustrate this point, let us use a simple example.

Bontok is a language spoken by a people in the mountains of northern Luzon in the Philippines. Among the many words corresponding to English nouns and adjectives are the following four stems: *fikas* "strong," *kilad* "red," *bato* "stone," and *fusul* "enemy." To

BOX 3.1 ARTICLE SYSTEMS: COMPARING SWEDISH AND ENGLISH

English has indefinite articles *a/an* and a definite article *the*, and these are placed before the word that they modify. The basic ESL rule is this: if the noun is an example of just one of many available, it takes *a* or *an* (e.g., "pick out *an* apple from the barrel"); if there is only one of the noun available, or there is only one kind like it in existence, the article is *the* ("Let's meet in *the* ballroom"; "*the* sun is hot today"); if it is a proper name, the noun takes nothing ("Ø Jane"). However, some other languages have a different system. Consider this table of Swedish articles:

| English gloss | Singular, indefinite | Singular, definite | Plural, indefinite | Plural, definite |
|---|---|---|---|---|
| jacket/coat | *en jacka*<br>"a jacket" | *jack**an***<br>"the jacket" | *jack**or***<br>"jackets" | *jack**orna***<br>"the jackets" |
| boy | *en pojke*<br>"a boy" | *pojk**en***<br>"the boy" | *pojk**ar***<br>"boys" | *pojk**arna***<br>"the boys" |
| phone | *en telefon*<br>"a phone" | *telefon**en***<br>"the phone" | *telefon**er***<br>"phones" | *telefon**erna***<br>"the phones" |
| stamp | *ett frimärke*<br>"a stamp" | *frimärk**et***<br>"the stamp" | *frimärk**en***<br>"stamps" | *frimärken**a***<br>"the stamps" |
| year | *ett år*<br>"a year" | år***et***<br>"the year" | år<br>"years" | år***en***<br>"the years" |

What do we notice looking at this table? First, we see that while there are only two articles in English (*a/an* and *the*), Swedish also makes a distinction between definite and indefinite nouns that can be singular or plural. An example of this can be seen in boy/*pojke* above:

*continues*

express the idea that someone is becoming what the noun or adjective refers to, the Bontok would use the following words derived from the four stems above: *fumikas* "he is becoming strong," *kumilad* "he is becoming red," *bumato* "he is becoming stone" (as in a myth), and *fumusul* "he is becoming an enemy." Those not trained in linguistics may find these forms a bit confusing, perhaps expecting, as a result of being native speakers of English, that in each example several words would be needed to indicate that an individual is undergoing some sort of change—becoming strong, red, stone, or an enemy. An examination of the Bontok data reveals a simple rule that accounts for the meaning "he is becoming—_______" (in stating the rule, we are avoiding terminology that might be unfamiliar to readers): insert the sounds (written here as *um*) after the initial consonant of the stem. This rule produces *f-um-ikas* from *fikas*, and so on. Now that we know this particular piece of Bontok structure, we can guess at the word that would most likely mean "he is becoming white" if we are

[singular]

| | |
|---|---|
| *en pojke* | e.g., a boy (say, from the group) stepped forward [indefinite] |
| *pojken* | e.g., the boy (with the red hair) stepped forward [definite] |

[plural]

| | |
|---|---|
| *pojkar* | e.g., boys (not necessarily all of them) stepped forward [indefinite] |
| *pojkarna* | e.g., the boys (say, vs. the girls) stepped forward [definite] |

In English, plurality is only marked in the noun: *boy* vs. *boys,* while in Swedish, this particular grammatical information is encoded in both the noun and the article, as seen, for example, in *en pojke* vs. *pojkarna* in the table (*a* boy vs. *the* boys). Technically, the *-ar*-infix marks the plural form of *boy,* while the *-na* suffix is the article that marks number and definiteness. In other words, there must be an agreement between the article and the number. Thus, we should note that the words listed in the "Plural Indefinite" column are like simple plurals in English.

Second, we see that there seem to be five classes or groups of nouns, each of which takes an article suffix in a slightly different way (for example, scan down the extreme right-hand column in the table. The suffixes to be added are *-orna, -arna, -erna, -a,* or *-en*). Third, compared to English the articles in Swedish are quite different in terms of form (how they appear) but not necessarily in their function (what they do). Just like English, Swedish articles mark definiteness vs. indefiniteness, like *a boy* vs. *the boy*. But the major difference is that Swedish articles also mark number.

Su Yin Khor

given *pukaw* "white"—namely, *pumukaw*; conversely, we can guess what the stem meaning "dark" would be from the word ŋumitad "he is becoming dark"—namely, ŋitad.

Focusing on recurring patterns of behavior of members of a society—in other words, trying to discover the structure of a cultural system—helps us become familiar with how the system operates. This is particularly true of the thousands of communicative systems we call languages. Let's begin with the study of **phonology**, the structures of sound in language.

## THE ANATOMY AND PHYSIOLOGY OF SPEECH

The capacity for speaking and speech itself are taken so much for granted that few individuals ever stop to wonder how sounds are produced and why they vary as much as they do. Although it is true that speakers use their mother tongue automatically, without concentrating, it is equally true that the production of a dozen to a score of speech sounds per second requires extremely well-coordinated and precise movements and positionings of various parts of the speech apparatus located between the diaphragm and the lips (see Figure 3.1).

The extent of these elaborate gymnastics is all the more remarkable when we remind ourselves that the primary functions of the various parts of the speech apparatus are not those associated with producing sounds. For example, the tongue, rich in tactile sensory nerve endings, is the seat of the sense of taste and helps in swallowing food, and the main purpose of teeth is to bite off food (incisors) and then chew it (molars). In short, speech is a secondary function for what we refer to as the vocal tract, or vocal organs.

The production of speech sounds, which is a complex process involving about one hundred muscles as well as other tissues, requires precise coordination. When one speaks, air is taken into the lungs more rapidly than in the normal course of inbreathing and then exhaled in a slow and steady stream. It is forced from the lungs through the trachea (windpipe) and undergoes important modifications in the larynx, located at the upper end of the trachea. The larynx, the position of which is marked externally by the Adam's apple, houses two bands of muscular tissue known as the vocal cords, or vocal folds. The vocal folds stretch from front to back and regulate the size of the elongated opening between them, the glottis. During swallowing, in addition to being protected by the folded epiglottis from above, the vocal cords are drawn together, with the glottis closed, to prevent liquids or food particles from entering the lungs. For the production of **voiced sounds**, such as those making up the word *buzz*, the cords are drawn together and made to vibrate as the airstream forces its way between them; in whispering, they are brought close together, with the glottis narrowed. For the production of **voiceless sounds**, such as those heard at the beginning and end of the word *ship*, they are spread apart but tensed. During normal breathing, they are relaxed and spread apart. The tension of the vocal cords determines the frequency of their vibration and therefore the pitch, whereas the force of the outgoing air regulates the loudness of sounds.

Having passed through the larynx, the air proceeds out through the pharynx toward the oral and nasal cavities. When the soft palate (velum) in the rear upper part of the mouth, just above the uvula, is lowered and the lips are closed, the air is released through the nose, producing nasal sounds, such as the three different ones in the Spanish word *mañana*

**FIGURE 3.1.** THE SPEECH APPARATUS. (A) A CROSS-SECTION OF THE HUMAN HEAD SHOWING THE PRINCIPAL PARTS OF THE VOCAL TRACT. THE LUNGS AND THE DIAPHRAGM BELOW THEM ARE NOT SHOWN.

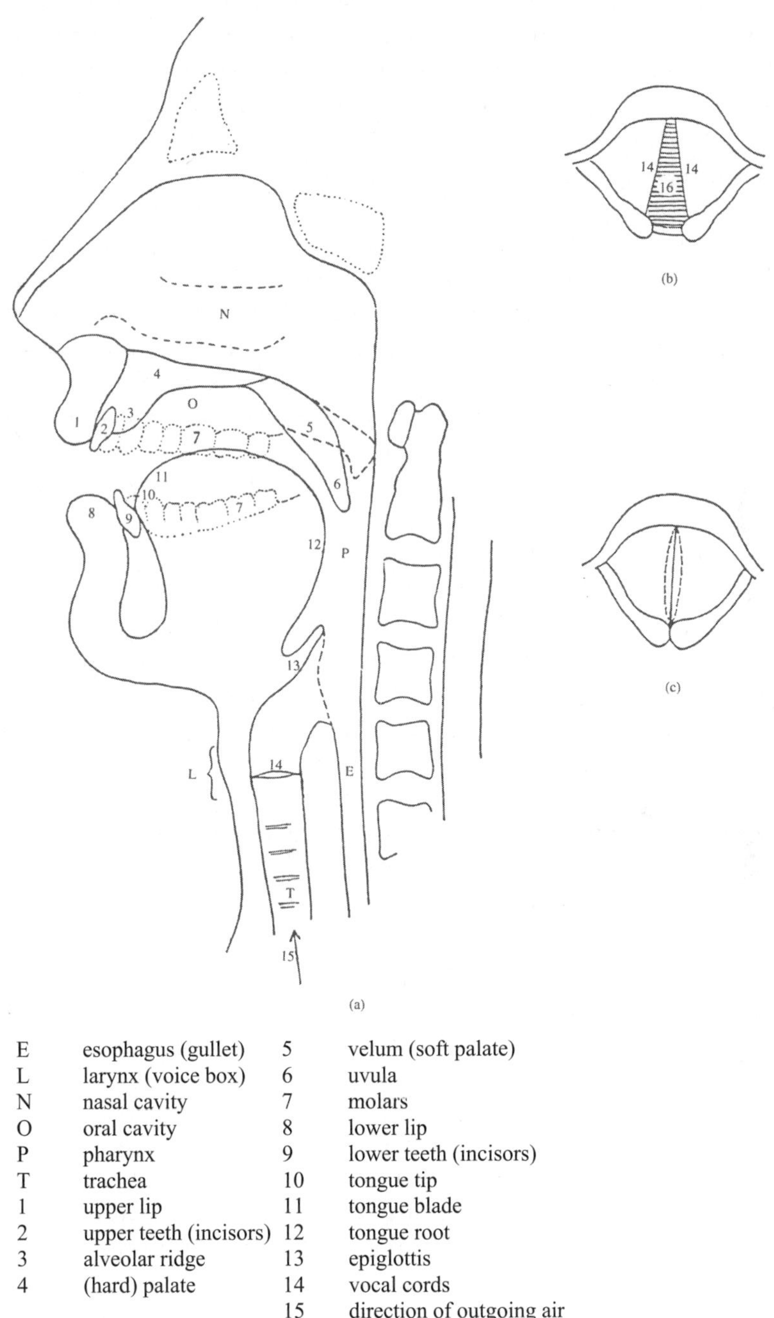


| | | | |
|---|---|---|---|
| E | esophagus (gullet) | 5 | velum (soft palate) |
| L | larynx (voice box) | 6 | uvula |
| N | nasal cavity | 7 | molars |
| O | oral cavity | 8 | lower lip |
| P | pharynx | 9 | lower teeth (incisors) |
| T | trachea | 10 | tongue tip |
| 1 | upper lip | 11 | tongue blade |
| 2 | upper teeth (incisors) | 12 | tongue root |
| 3 | alveolar ridge | 13 | epiglottis |
| 4 | (hard) palate | 14 | vocal cords |
| | | 15 | direction of outgoing air |

(b) A view of the glottis (16), with a vocal cord on each side, during normal breathing. (c) The same view, but with vocal cords vibrating during speech. Adapted from Bohuslav Hála: *Uvedení do fonetikcy češtiny*, Prague, 1962, p. 63.

"tomorrow" or the final one in the English word *king.* If the soft palate is lowered but the air is allowed to escape simultaneously through both the nose and the mouth, nasalized sounds are the result, as in the French *bon* "good." The majority of sounds in the languages of the world are oral, with the air escaping only through the mouth because the soft palate is fully raised, making contact with the back wall of the pharynx and shutting off the entrance to the nasal cavity.

As the air passes through the upper part of the speech tract, numerous modifications of the **vocal channel**, involving such articulators as the soft palate, tongue, and lips, make possible the tremendous variety of sounds heard in the world's several thousand languages. These sounds are customarily classified according to (1) the **manner of articulation** and (2) **place of articulation** and are typically transcribed by means of **phonetic symbols**, which are enclosed in square brackets [ ]. Phonetic symbols are not exactly the same thing as the symbols in the regular English alphabet. The idea is to have one symbol consistently correspond to one and only one sound. This is not the case in normal spelling, in which, for example, (a) some letters can stand for two sounds (like "c" standing for both "s" as in *certainly* and "k" as in *catch*), (b) one sound like "ch" is represented by two letters, and (c) some letters such as "q" or "x" do not really stand for unique sounds at all (representing "ku-" or "eks" respectively).

## ARTICULATION OF SPEECH SOUNDS

If you are an American, you have likely heard since elementary school there are six vowels in English; "A, E, I, O, U, and sometimes Y." But what does this mean? Is this just another example of folk beliefs regarding language we talked about in Chapter 1? The short answer is yes.

### *What Is a Vowel?*

Phonologists like to talk about main classes of speech sounds: vowels and consonants. In the production of vowels, the air that escapes through the mouth (for oral vowels) as well as through the nose (for nasalized vowels) is relatively unimpeded. **Vowels** are classified according to the part of the tongue that is raised, the configuration of the lips, and the extent to which the tongue approaches the palate above it (see Table 3.1). Another variable is the degree of muscular effort and movement that goes into the production of vowel sounds. If the tension in the tongue muscles is prominent, vowels are said to be *tense,* as in *beat* or *boot*; if it is lacking or scarcely noticeable, they are said to be *lax,* as in *bit* or *book.*

Even though an utterance may be viewed as a succession of individual sounds, most speakers tend to subdivide utterances naturally into somewhat larger units: syllables. To be fully serviceable, the term *syllable* needs to be defined separately for each language, but in general one may say that a syllable consists of a nucleus—usually but not always a vowel (V), with or without a consonant (C) or consonants before or after it. The following English words—*a, on, me, pin, spin, drift,* and *strengths*—all consist of one syllable and may be represented as V, VC, CV, CVC, CCVC, CCVCC, and CCCVC(C)CC, respectively. In the word *button,* the nucleus of the second syllable is the nasal [n], because the orthographic vowel *o* is not pronounced. A consonant functioning as the center of a syllable is said to be *syllabic.*

**TABLE 3.1** TYPES OF VOWELS ACCORDING TO THE PLACE AND MANNER OF ARTICULATION, WITH EXAMPLES

MANNER OF ARTICULATION:
If the air escapes through the mouth with no obstructions (as in the case of consonants), the sound is a normal or *oral* vowel.
If the air escapes also through the nose, it is a *nasal* or nasalized vowel.
If the lips are used in a round circular manner when pronouncing a sound, the vowel is *rounded*; if the lips are relatively flat, the vowel is *unrounded*.

POINTS OF ARTICULATION:
This refers to the position of the tongue in the mouth, in two dimensions (front, middle, or back of the mouth; and height from top to bottom: high, lower high, middle, lower middle, or low)

*According to the part of the tongue that is raised:*

*According to position of the lips:*

*According to the position of the highest point of the tongue in the mouth (according to the closeness of the tongue to the roof of the mouth):*

| | *Front* | | *Central* | | *Back* |
|---|---|---|---|---|---|
| | unrounded (spread) | rounded | unrounded | unrounded | rounded |
| high (close) | **i *beat*** | **ü German *kühl* "cool"** | **ɨ Russian быть "to be"** | **ï occurs in Turkish** | **u *boot*** |
| lower high | **ɪ *bit*** | | **ɪ̶ as in *just* (*you wait*)** | | **U *book*** |
| mid | **e *bait*; German *See* "sea"** | **ö German *schön* "lovely"** | **ə the second vowel of *sofa*** | | **o *boat*; French *beau* "beautiful"** |
| lower mid | **ɛ *bet*** | **ɔ̈ French *peur* "fear"** | | **ʌ *butt*** | **ɔ *bought*** |
| low (open) | **æ *bat*** | | **a *body*** | | **ɒ *pot*; in London English, *not*** |

**1. It is not easy to illustrate various vowel types by examples from English because of wide dialect variation. For example, people native to eastern New England, the central Atlantic seaboard, and the coastal South pronounce the words Mary, marry, and merry differently, whereas in the rest of the United States, these three words are usually pronounced alike.**

**2. The vowels here are written in the International Phonetic Alphabet (IPA). We will actually be using the American System (see Fig. 3.2 and Fig. 3.3) for many of the problems and discussions in this book, as that is an easier and more consistent method of transcription (though perhaps slightly less precise at times).**

**TABLE 3.2** TYPES OF CONSONANTS ACCORDING TO PLACE OF ARTICULATION

| *Place of Articulation* | *General Description* | *Consonant Type* | *Example(s)* |
|---|---|---|---|
| Glottis | Vocal folds are positioned so as to cause a closure or friction. | Glottal | glottal stop that in some dialects of English replaces the *t* sound (-*tt*-) in such words as *bottle* |
| Pharynx | Back wall of the pharynx articulates with the root of the tongue. | Pharyngeal | common in Arabic |
| Uvula | Back of the tongue articulates with the uvula. | Uvular | the *r* sound frequently heard in German (voiced variety) or French (voiceless) |
| Velum, or soft palate | Back of the tongue articulates with the soft palate. | Velar | initial sound of *calf* |
| (Hard) palate | Front of the tongue articulates with the hard palate. | Palatal | the final sound of the German *ich* 'I' |
| Area where the palate and the alveolar ridge meet | Blade of the tongue (and sometimes the tip) articulates with the palato-alveolar area. | Palato-alveolar | initial sound of *ship* |
| | Tip of the tongue, curled back, articulates with the palato-alveolar area. | Retroflex | typically, *t* and *d* sounds in English as spoken by East Indians |
| Alveolar ridge | Front of the tongue articulates with the alveolar ridge. | Alveolar | the initial sound of *sit* |
| Teeth | Tongue tip articulates with the upper teeth. | Dental | *t* and *d* sounds of Irish English |
| | Tongue tip is positioned between the upper and lower teeth. | Interdental | the initial sounds of *thin* and *this* |
| Lower lip and upper teeth | Lower lip articulates with the upper teeth. | Labiodental | the initial sounds of *fan* and *van* |
| Lips | Both lower and upper lips articulate. | Bilabial | the initial and final sound of *bob* |

The vowels of American English dialects occur for the most part singly, as in the words *linguistic anthropology* [-ɪ ɪ ɪ-æ-ə-ɒ-ə-i]. (See Table 3.1 for an explanation of these symbols.) However, sometimes there is a change in vowel quality within a syllable, as in the words *bite*, *bout*, and *boy*. What occurs in each of these three words and others like them is a movement from the first, more prominent vocalic part to the second, which is shorter and less distinct. A change in vowel quality within the same syllable is referred to as a **diphthong**. As a heuristic device, you might think of a diphthong as a sound in which you go from one vowel to another in close succession.

### *What Is a Consonant?*

In the production of **consonants**, the sound is altered or modified greatly as it passes through the mouth and throat. Compared to consonants, vowels are almost basically unmodified breaths of air. Typically, consonants are described by **place of articulation** and **manner of articulation**. The places of articulation range all the way from the glottis to the lips, the last place in the vocal tract where the outgoing air can be modified (described in Table 3.2).

In a sense, the places of articulation mentioned in Table 3.2 are just the top part of the cutaway face shown in Figure 3.1, where we see the lips and teeth in the front of the mouth, then the palate of the roof of the mouth, and then the back of the mouth with the glottis. The manner of articulation refers to the several kinds of constriction that may be set up at some point along the speech tract by the articulators. There are several ways of describing the manner of articulation, and some are given in Table 3.3.

The vowel and consonant types surveyed here include only the basic ones. Just as sounds can undergo lengthening or nasalization, they can be modified by secondary articulations. These give rise to labialized, palatalized, velarized, pharyngealized, and otherwise modified sounds. Some consonants may also be followed by aspiration, that is, accompanied by an audible breath. Relatively rare are clicks, sharp suction sounds made by the lips or the tongue, and ingressive sounds, those produced on the inbreath rather than the outbreath. The most common speech sounds and their modifications are represented by the phonetic symbols and diacritics of the International Phonetic Alphabet (IPA). Its various symbols and diacritics can be used to represent a great many (but by no means all) sounds occurring in the world's languages (see Chart 3.1)

Because the special characters and diacritical marks used by the IPA are not always readily available, for the sake of economy and convenience many anthropologists (and some linguists) use some symbols that do not correspond to those of the IPA. This is the so-called **American System**, which was popular among many anthropologists before World War II. One should remember, however, that phonetic symbols are arbitrary, and in principle one phonetic alphabet used for transcription is just as acceptable as another so long as each sound is represented consistently and each symbol carefully defined. As the American System is a bit easier, we will usually use it in this book.

### *The American Transcription System*

Tables 3.4 and 3.5 and Figures 3.2 and 3.3 depict the ideas we have been talking about in using the American System. Table 3.4 is a chart of the most important consonants found in the world's languages. The "manners of articulation" are given along the vertical axis,

**TABLE 3.3** TYPES OF CONSONANTS ACCORDING TO MANNER OF ARTICULATION

| *Type of Constriction* | *Subtype of Constriction* | *General Description* | *Consonant Type* | *Examples with Description* |
|---|---|---|---|---|
| CLOSURE | Total | complete closure at some point in the vocal tract, with soft palate raised; sudden release of air pressure | Plosive, or stop | the initial sound of *pick*; closure at the lips |
| | Total | complete closure at some point in the mouth, with soft palate lowered and air escaping through the nose | Nasal | the initial and final sound of *mom*; closure at the lips |
| | Total | complete closure at some point in the mouth, with soft palate raised; gradual release of air pressure | Affricate | the initial and final sound of *judge*; the tongue blade forms closure with the front of the hard palate |
| | Intermittent | an articulator flapping loose or one articulator tapping against another | Trill | the *r* sound in Scottish pronunciation or in the Spanish *perro* 'dog'; the tongue vibrates against the alveolar ridge |
| | Intermittent | a single tap by one articulator against the roof of the mouth | Flap | the *r* sound in British English pronunciation of *very* or in the Spanish *pero* 'but'; the tongue taps the alveolar ridge |
| | Partial | partial closure in the mouth allowing the air to escape around one or both sides of the closure | Lateral | the initial sound of *law*; the middle part of the tongue touches the top of the mouth |
| NARROWING | | at some point in the vocal tract the opening is narrowed so as to produce audible friction | Fricative | the initial and final sounds of *fuss*; air is forced between the lower lip and upper teeth, and between the front of the tongue and the alveolar ridge, respectively |

## CHART 3.1 THE INTERNATIONAL PHONETIC ALPHABET

CONSONANTS (PULMONIC)



| | Bilabial | Labiodental | Dental | Alveolar | Postalveolar | Retroflex | Palatal | Velar | Uvular | Pharyngeal | Glottal |
|---|---|---|---|---|---|---|---|---|---|---|---|
| Plosive | p b | | | t d | | ʈ ɖ | c ɟ | k ɡ | q ɢ | | ʔ |
| Nasal | m | ɱ | | n | | ɳ | ɲ | ŋ | ɴ | | |
| Trill | ʙ | | | r | | | | | ʀ | | |
| Tap or Flap | | ⱱ | | ɾ | | ɽ | | | | | |
| Fricative | ɸ β | f v | θ ð | s z | ʃ ʒ | ʂ ʐ | ç ʝ | x ɣ | χ ʁ | ħ ʕ | h ɦ |
| Lateral fricative | | | | ɬ ɮ | | | | | | | |
| Approximant | | ʋ | | ɹ | | ɻ | j | ɰ | | | |
| Lateral approximant | | | | l | | ɭ | ʎ | ʟ | | | |

Symbols to the right in a cell are voiced, to the left are voiceless. Shaded areas denote articulations judged impossible.

CONSONANTS (NON-PULMONIC)

| Clicks | Voiced implosives | Ejectives |
|---|---|---|
| ʘ Bilabial | ɓ Bilabial | ʼ Examples: |
| ǀ Dental | ɗ Dental/alveolar | pʼ Bilabial |
| ǃ (Post)alveolar | ʄ Palatal | tʼ Dental/alveolar |
| ǂ Palatoalveolar | ɠ Velar | kʼ Velar |
| ǁ Alveolar lateral | ʛ Uvular | sʼ Alveolar fricative |

VOWELS

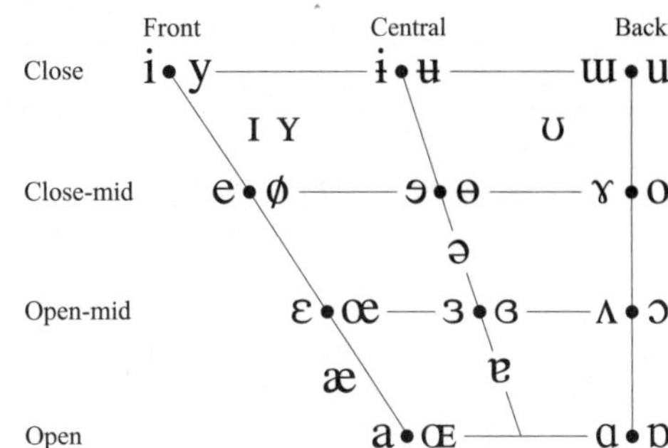


Where symbols appear in pairs, the one to the right represents a rounded vowel.

OTHER SYMBOLS

ʍ Voiceless labial-velar fricative

w Voiced labial-velar approximant

ɥ Voiced labial-palatal approximant

ʜ Voiceless epiglottal fricative

ʢ Voiced epiglottal fricative

ʡ Epiglottal plosive

ɕ ʑ Alveolo-palatal fricatives

ɺ Voiced alveolar lateral flap

ɧ Simultaneous ʃ and x

Affricates and double articulations can be represented by two symbols joined by a tie bar if necessary. t͜s k͡p

SUPRASEGMENTALS

ˈ Primary stress

ˌ Secondary stress

ˌfoʊnəˈtɪʃən

ː Long eː

ˑ Half-long eˑ

˘ Extra-short ĕ

| Minor (foot) group

‖ Major (intonation) group

. Syllable break ɹi.ækt

‿ Linking (absence of a break)

DIACRITICS Some diacritics may be placed above a symbol with a descender, e.g. ŋ̊

| | | | | | | | | |
|---|---|---|---|---|---|---|---|---|
| ̥ | Voiceless | n̥ d̥ | ̤ | Breathy voiced | b̤ a̤ | ̪ | Dental | t̪ d̪ |
| ̬ | Voiced | s̬ t̬ | ̰ | Creaky voiced | b̰ a̰ | ̺ | Apical | t̺ d̺ |
| ʰ | Aspirated | tʰ dʰ | ̼ | Linguolabial | t̼ d̼ | ̻ | Laminal | t̻ d̻ |
| ̹ | More rounded | ɔ̹ | ʷ | Labialized | tʷ dʷ | ̃ | Nasalized | ẽ |
| ̜ | Less rounded | ɔ̜ | ʲ | Palatalized | tʲ dʲ | ⁿ | Nasal release | dⁿ |
| ̟ | Advanced | u̟ | ˠ | Velarized | tˠ dˠ | ˡ | Lateral release | dˡ |
| ̠ | Retracted | e̠ | ˤ | Pharyngealized | tˤ dˤ | ̚ | No audible release | d̚ |
| ̈ | Centralized | ë | ̴ | Velarized or pharyngealized | ɫ | | | |
| ̽ | Mid-centralized | e̽ | ̝ | Raised | e̝ (ɹ̝ = voiced alveolar fricative) | | | |
| ̩ | Syllabic | n̩ | ̞ | Lowered | e̞ (β̞ = voiced bilabial approximant) | | | |
| ̯ | Non-syllabic | e̯ | ̘ | Advanced Tongue Root | e̘ | | | |
| ˞ | Rhoticity | ɚ a˞ | ̙ | Retracted Tongue Root | e̙ | | | |

TONES AND WORD ACCENTS

| LEVEL | | | CONTOUR | | |
|---|---|---|---|---|---|
| e̋ or | ˥ | Extra high | ě or | ˩˥ | Rising |
| é | ˦ | High | ê | ˥˩ | Falling |
| ē | ˧ | Mid | e᷄ | ˦˥ | High rising |
| è | ˨ | Low | e᷅ | ˩˨ | Low rising |
| ȅ | ˩ | Extra low | e᷈ | ˧˦˧ | Rising-falling |
| ꜜ | Downstep | | ↗ | Global rise | |
| ꜛ | Upstep | | ↘ | Global fall | |

and "points of articulation" are given on the horizontal axis. The white cells are important phoneme sounds used in English (we will define *phoneme* momentarily), the dark-gray cells are sounds that are commonly used in English but not phonemic, and the light-gray cells are consonants found in other languages but not used in English. Table 3.5 provides examples of these sounds that are used in English (for each symbol, examples are given for that sound as it appears at the beginning, the middle, or the end of a word).

Figure 3.2 is a chart of English vowels using the American System (as opposed to the many possible vowels found in the world's languages as described in Table 3.1, and using the International Phonetic Alphabet). Basically, you may visualize this diagram as the interior "mouth" part of the cutaway face in Figure 3.1 (the "oral cavity," O, in the picture). Each cell represents a rough place the tongue can go when it makes a vowel. For example, if air is pushed out when the tongue is toward the front of the mouth and relatively high, the i-sound is made. A bit lower, the e-sound is made, and so on. Diphthongs in English are shown in the American System in Figure 3.3.

Diphthongs are handled more elegantly in the American System than in the IPA. As noted, a diphthong is a change in vowel quality within the same syllable. Basically, in the American System, if a syllable proceeds higher and toward the front of the mouth, this is indicated by adding the symbol [-y] to the vowel. For instance, if a high front vowel [i]—as in *bit*—moves higher and more forward—as in *beat*—this is depicted as [-iy]. If a syllable proceeds higher and toward the back of the mouth, this is indicated by adding the symbol [-w] to the vowel. For instance, if a central back vowel [o]—as in *home*—moves higher—as in *hoi polloi*—this is depicted as [-oy].

### *Other Approaches to Phonology*

There are generally three ways to approach phonology. **Articulatory phonetics**—which we have just been discussing—is the study of the production of speech sounds by the vocal organs. But is not the only way to examine the raw material of language. It is also possible to examine speech sounds for their physical properties, that is, from the perspective of **acoustic phonetics**. This approach requires the sound spectrograph, a device that visually represents acoustic features of speech sounds in the form of spectrograms, or voiceprints. Spectrograms show three dimensions of sounds: Duration (time) is displayed horizontally, frequency vertically, and intensity by the degree of darkness. For example, each vowel is characterized by several resonance bands, referred to as formants, which represent the overtone structure of a vowel produced by the shape of the vocal tract. Because the position of the tongue changes with the production of different vowels, the formants vary correspondingly. Finally, **auditory phonetics** is the study of how speech sounds are perceived and interpreted by the various organs of the human body (ear, auditory nerves, and brain). We will focus on articulatory phonetics here, leaving the other two areas to physicists, neurologists, speech therapists, and other specialists.

## FROM PHONES TO PHONEMES

### *Phones: The Smallest Unit of Sound*

The smallest perceptible discrete segment of speech is a **phone**, a speech sound considered a physical event. A succession of phones in a particular language makes up a stretch of

**TABLE 3.4** CHART OF THE MOST IMPORTANT MANNERS OF ARTICULATION (VERTICAL AXIS) AND POINTS OF ARTICULATION (HORIZONTAL AXIS) OF SELECTED CONSONANTS

| | | *Bilabial* | *Labio-dental* | *Dental* | *Alveolar* | *Alveo-palatal* | *Velar* | *Uvular* | *Glottal* |
|---|---|---|---|---|---|---|---|---|---|
| STOPS | voiced | b | | d | | | g | | |
| | unvoiced | p | | t | | | k | q | ʔ |
| AFFRICATES (groove) | voiced | | | | ʒ | ǰ | | | |
| | unvoiced | | | | c | č | | | |
| AFFRICATES (lateral) | voiced | | | | λ | | | | |
| | unvoiced | | | | ƛ | | | | |
| FRICATIVES | voiced | β | v | ð | z | ž | g | | |
| | unvoiced | f | f | θ | s | š | x | | h |
| NASALS | voiced | m | | | n | ñ | ŋ | | |
| | unvoiced | | | | | | | | |
| LATERALS | voiced | | | | | l | r | | |
| | unvoiced | | | | | ł | | | |
| SEMI-VOWELS | voiced | w | | | | (r) | y | | (w) |

***Note:*** **white cells = phonemes used in English; dark gray cells = sounds common in English but not phonemic; light gray cells = not in English**

**TABLE 3.5** THE CONSONANT PHONEMES IN AMERICAN ENGLISH

| *Symbol* | *Examples* | | |
|---|---|---|---|
| | *Initial* | *Medial* | *Final* |
| /p/ | *p*it | su*pp*er | ri*p* |
| /b/ | *b*it | fi*b*er | ri*b* |
| /t/ | *t*ip | mea*t*y | ki*t* |
| /d/ | *d*ip | o*d*or | ki*d* |
| /k/ | *c*ap | loc*k*er | pic*k* |
| /g/ | *g*ap | so*gg*y | pi*g* |
| /č/ | *ch*in | it*ch*y | ri*ch* |
| /ǰ/ | *g*in | pu*dg*y | ri*dg*e |
| /f/ | *f*at | go*ph*er | belie*f* |
| /v/ | *v*at | i*v*y | belie*v*e |
| /θ/ | *th*in | e*th*er | brea*th* |
| /ð/ | *th*en | ei*th*er | brea*th*e |
| /s/ | *s*eal | i*c*y | his*s* |
| /z/ | *z*eal | co*z*y | hi*s* |
| /š/ | *sh*ow | po*ti*on | ru*sh* |
| /ž/ | — | lei*s*ure | rou*g*e |
| /h/ | *h*asp | a*h*oy | — |
| /m/ | *m*oon | si*mm*er | loo*m* |
| /n/ | *n*oon | si*nn*er | loo*n* |
| /ŋ/ | — | si*ng*er | ki*ng* |
| /l/ | *l*imb | mi*ll*er | ree*l* |
| /r/ | *r*im | mi*rr*or | rea*r* |
| /w/ | *w*et | lo*w*er | — |
| /y/ | *y*et | la*y*er | — |
| /c/ | *Ts*ar | pre*tz*el | i*ts* |
| /ʒ/ | — | — | i*ds*, arachni*ds* |

*Note:* Some other sounds that are common in English, but not phonemic:

| | | | |
|---|---|---|---|
| [q] | *c*ar | in*c*arnate | — |
| [ñ] | *ny*uck! *ny*uck! | se*ñ*or | — |
| [ʔ] | — | Oh*ʼ*oh! | — |

speech, or an utterance. Each utterance is unique, occurring if not under different circumstances at least at a different time. Yet people do not respond to each instance of speech as though it were different from all others. Such utterances as "Where have you been?" or "I have no time just now" are treated as if they were much the same every time they are said, regardless of whether the voice belongs to a woman, man, or child, or happens to be clear or hoarse. Because there is so much likeness in what is objectively different, it is possible to represent speech sounds—phones—through the written symbols of a suitable phonetic alphabet. Linguistic anthropologists make phonetic transcriptions of words or utterances whenever they wish to obtain a sample of speech for subsequent analysis.

Let us now consider the English words written as *papaya, pepper, pin, spin, up,* and *upon.* The *p* sound of *pin* is followed by a distinct puff of air, which is completely absent in *spin.* The difference between the two *p* sounds can be easily demonstrated if one holds a sheet of paper vertically between thumb and finger about two inches from one's lips and says the two words. The puff of air, or aspiration, following the *p* sound of *pin* sends a ripple through the sheet, whereas the word *spin* leaves the sheet motionless. We find that the same difference obtains between the *p*'s of *pair, peck, peer,* and *pike,* on the one hand, and those of *spare, speck, spear,* and *spike,* on the other.

In the word *upon,* the *p* sound is about as distinctly aspirated as in *pin.* In *papaya,* however, it is only the second *p* that is strongly aspirated, the first one aspirated only slightly, if at all; in *pepper,* it is the other way around. In the word *up,* especially if it stands at the end of a sentence, as in "Let's go up!" the *p* sound may remain unreleased; that is, the lips simply stay closed in anticipation of the silence that follows.

**FIGURE 3.2.** AN ENGLISH VOWEL CHART BASED ON THE AMERICAN SYSTEM

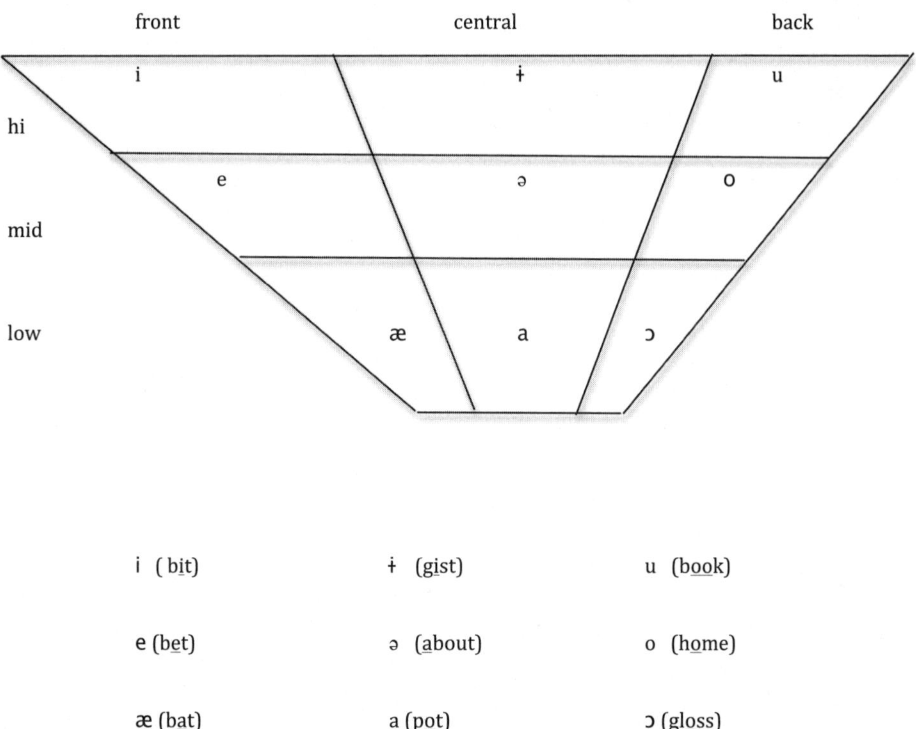

**FIGURE 3.3.** A CHART OF COMMON DIPHTHONGS (AMERICAN SYSTEM)

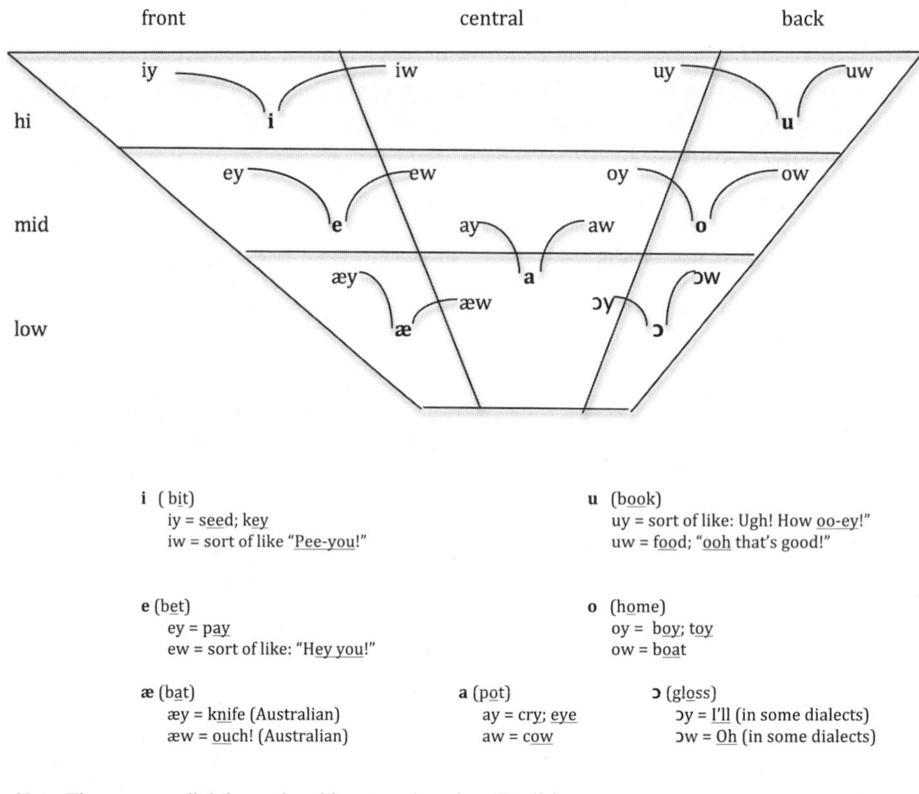


*Note*: The common diphthongs in midwestern American English are:

| | |
|---|---|
| iy | (*seed*) |
| ey | (*paid*) |
| ay | (*eye*) |
| aw | (cow) |
| uw | (food) |
| ow | (boat) |
| oy | (boy) |

To generalize about the occurrence of these phonetically similar segments, we may say that in English there are at least four varieties of the *p* sound: (1) an aspirated p (which we will write as [pʰ]) before a stressed vowel unless preceded by an *s* (such as the second *p* in *papaya*, the first in *pepper*, and in *pin* and *upon*); (2) a very slightly aspirated [p] before a weakly stressed vowel (the first in *papaya*, the second in *pepper*); (3) an unaspirated p (which we will write as [P]) with a relatively small degree of muscular effort and breath force, after an *s* of the same syllable and before a vowel (*spin*); and (4) an unreleased p (which we will write as[p˺]) in the sentence-final position, where [pʰ] or [p] may also occur. (To illustrate a principle rather than account for numerous other details, the description of the varieties of the English *p* sound and their occurrence has been simplified.)

Let us next consider the words *pin, spin,* and *bin,* which we may transcribe phonetically as [pʰin], [sPin], and [bin]. The difference between the *p* of *pin* and *b* of *bin* is clearly of another kind than that between [pʰ] and [p] or [pʰ] and [P]. By choosing either *b* or *p* for the initial sound, the speaker is distinguishing between two meaningful items of the English vocabulary, *bin* and *pin*. Even if one were to interchange the pronunciation of the *p* sounds in *pin* and *spin* and say [Pin] and [sp$^{h}$in] instead, one would no doubt be understood, though the listener would probably suspect that either English is not the speaker's native language or the speaker is trying to imitate a foreign accent. As a matter of fact, native speakers of English never have to choose consciously between [P] and [p$^{h}$]. They employ automatically the former before a vowel whenever the sound *s* precedes within the same syllable, and the latter if it occurs before a strongly stressed vowel.

### *Phonemes: The Smallest Group of Sounds That Have Psychological Reality*

With specific reference to English—because all languages must be examined and analyzed only on their own terms—linguists establish the *b* sound of *bin* and the *p* sound of *pin* as two contrastive sound units, or **phonemes**. That is, b-sounds versus p-sounds are "differences that make a difference," as the words *bin* and *pin* with different meanings demonstrate. However, if I use any of the variety of p-sounds in a certain word, it might not be a difference that makes a difference. For example, I may say the word *Stop!* while agitated—and not expelling a puff of air at the end, sucking in the sound in my excitement (i.e., using [p˺]). At other times I may say the word *stop* while disgusted ("Oh, just stop") *with* a puff of air being expelled (i.e., [p$^{h}$]). Chances are that only I, and no one else, will even notice that I have technically pronounced *stop* in two different ways.

The several varieties of the p sound—[p$^{h}$], [P], [p], and [p˺]—are called **allophones**—or variants—of the phoneme /p/. (Note the use of slant lines around the symbol to indicate its phonemic status.) To put it differently, when *p* is used to represent the English phoneme /p/, it serves as a cover symbol for a group or class of phonetically similar sounds that are in complementary distribution or free variation. Phones are in complementary distribution if they never occur in the same phonetic environment—for example, simplified, [P] is found always after *s*, where [p$^{h}$] never occurs. Phones are in free variation if substituting one for another does not cause a change in meaning. But if two phones contrast, as does [b] in *bin* with [p$^{h}$] in *pin*—that is, if substituting one for another causes a change in meaning—they are assignable to two different phonemes (or, phrased differently, they are allophones of two different phonemes).

The simplest way to establish phonemic contrasts in a language is by means of minimal sets, in which each word has a different meaning but varies from the rest in one sound only. From the foursome of words *bit*, *bet*, *bat*, and *butt*, we establish phonemic contrast among all four vowels. As for consonants, all the initial sounds (not letters!) of the following set of words contrast with one another and are therefore assignable to different English phonemes: *by*, *die*, *fie*, *guy*, *high*, *lie*, *my*, *nigh*, *pie*, *rye*, *shy*, *sigh*, *thigh*, *thy*, *tie*, *vie*, and *why*, yielding /b, d, f, g, h, l, m, n, p, r, s, š, θ, ð, t, v, w/.

To demonstrate the fundamental principles underlying phonemic analysis, we have, for obvious reasons, used English. But linguistic anthropologists typically face a different situation when they study peoples whose languages have never before been written. A thorough phonemic analysis of a language involves more than just compiling minimal sets; it takes weeks of painstaking listening for contrasting sounds, repeating words and utterances and recording them on tape, and phonetically transcribing a good deal in the initial stages of work. The following need to be established: the distinctive sounds, or phonemes, of a language; the prosodic features that characterize its utterances; the main allophones of each phoneme and the phonetic environment in which they occur; the pattern of phonemes—vowels, consonants, and their subclasses; and the rules for their combinations among each other and in higher-level units. Next, the practical task for the linguistic anthropologist is to devise an appropriate alphabet so that the language can be transcribed phonemically, without the many phonetic details of the initial transcription that have now become easily retrievable: when we write /p/ in English, we know under what circumstances this phoneme is physically realized as one of its four allophones, [pʰ], [p], [P], and [p˺].

It is important to remember that the same phonemes do not necessarily characterize every speaker of English. It is common knowledge that British, Australian, and other forms of English differ from American English, and that each of these exists in several dialectal varieties, particularly as far as vowels are concerned. In general, though, each language contains its own particular overall system of distinctive sounds. In Spanish, for example, a certain vowel sound approximates that heard in the English word *beat*, but there is no Spanish parallel to the English vowel sound of *bit*. This and similar differences are the source of the "natural" mispronunciations of native speakers of Spanish learning English, such as when they pronounce the word *mill* as though it were *meal*. Their Spanish speech habits carry over into a language they are learning or are not familiar with.

The study of the sound systems of languages—and of the sound changes that take place over time in a language or in several related languages—is called **phonology**, and the study of determining the phonemes of languages is called **phonemics**. Both are complex subdisciplines in their own right, each with its own set of books, techniques, and specialists. We will not get too detailed about these things here, but every linguistic anthropology student should understand the concept of phonemes and how to start finding and analyzing them (at least in theory, in general terms). A brief summary of how one might begin to do a phonemic analysis is given in the Resource Manual and Study Guide at the end of this chapter. This should help get students started when trying to do the problems found there. As we will see later in this chapter, this notion of "differences that make a difference versus differences that do not make a difference"—the key notion behind the phoneme—is an important aspect of cultural knowledge and categorization.

And one more remark about writing—this time about developing a writing system for languages that are spoken but not written, which means primarily for languages of small tribal societies. Today most members of such societies inevitably also speak the language of the larger society that surrounds them, and many are no longer sufficiently proficient in their native language to speak it. One may ask, Why give a written form to a language that is destined to become extinct in a generation or two? One reason would be to enable the linguistic anthropologist (or linguist) to record the society's tales, prayers, ritual speeches, and everyday language in the original form while it is still possible. But then, too, the availability of a written form helps to bolster the viability of a threatened language by giving it prestige in the outside world. It may be possible, for example, to include lessons in the native language in the elementary school system serving the group. One of the authors of this text (Salzmann), for example, compiled in 1983 a *Dictionary of Contemporary Arapaho Usage* to help Arapaho teachers remember and use the language of their grandparents. But then a problem arose—namely, how to represent some of the sounds of the language, which in linguistic literature would be done by means of phonetic symbols. (To use English spelling would be very confusing, for reasons explained elsewhere in this book.) Here the advice of informants could be very valuable. An example: one of Salzmann's informants suggested that the sound usually represented by the Greek letter *theta*, that is by θ, could be represented by a graphic symbol found on the keyboard of American typewriters, thereby enabling a teacher to type Arapaho lessons for students. This same informant suggested using the numeric symbol *3* because the English word *three* begins with this particular sound (written in English as *th*). Salzmann accepted this practical and ingenious suggestion, and so the Arapaho word for *dog* in the dictionary is written as *he3* rather than phonetically (phonemically) as *hɛθ*.

### *Phonemes of English*

The list of consonant phonemes in American English is shown in Table 3.5 (whenever possible, the occurrence of each phoneme is exemplified for the word-initial, word-medial, and word-final positions). The dialects of English vary somewhat with respect to vowels, even within the United States. The repertory of typical vowel phonemes is shown in Figure 3.2 (nine "plain vowels) and Figure 3.3 (fourteen diphthongs). These charts are representative of a great many speakers of American English, though not all.

How does the phonemic system of English compare with the systems of other languages? In the number of segments, it belongs to the middle range, along with the large majority of the world's languages. According to a survey based on the phonemic inventories of a sample of 317 languages (Maddieson 1984), some languages contain no more than a dozen segmental phonemes (for the most part they are members of the Indo-Pacific and Austronesian language families), whereas a few languages are reported to have in excess of one hundred (members of the Khoisan family in southern Africa). The mean number of consonants per phonemic inventory is in the low twenties (22.8), that of vowels close to nine (8.7). In most languages, the total number of consonants is more than twice as large as the number of vowels. The most common consonantal subsystem includes from five to eleven plosives (stops), including affricates; one to four fricatives; two to four nasals; and four consonants of other types. The most common vowels are those classified as high front unrounded, high back rounded, mid front unrounded, mid back rounded, and low central unrounded. The inventory of segmental phonemes in English appears to be much like the systems characteristic of the bulk of the world's languages. This is not to say, however, that English is a typical language. Although all natural languages are indeed distinct variations on a common theme—human language—each has its own peculiar features of structure that make it unique.

## PROSODIC FEATURES

Vowels and consonants that combine into words and sentences may be thought of as segments, or segmental units, that is, as discrete units that can be identified in the stream of speech and separated from other such units (as in *part* = *p-a-r-t* and *slept* = *s-l-e-p-t*). But there is more to speech than just ordering these segments according to the rules of a particular language. Additional features are essential for an utterance to sound natural and to be fully meaningful, especially stress and pitch, these two sometimes lumped together under the term **accent**. These other features are called **prosodic features**. It is important to note that prosodic features can be distinctive in some languages.

**Stress** refers to the degree of force, or prominence, associated with a syllable. In the word *under*, the prominent stress is on the first syllable, whereas in *below*, it is on the second. In the sentence "Will you permit me to use your permit?" the word *permit* functioning as a verb is stressed differently from *permit* used as a noun. Some linguists claim that to describe English adequately, as many as four degrees of stress are needed, ranging from primary (1) to weak (4), as in *dictionary* (1-4–3-4) and *elevator operator* (1-4–3-4 2-4–3-4). In English the placing of stress is not completely predictable, as it is in Czech, in which as a rule the main stress falls on the first syllable, or in Polish, in which it falls on the penultimate, or next-to-the-last, syllable.

A distinctive **pitch** level associated with a syllable is referred to as tone. Among the several dialect groups in China, Mandarin Chinese provides a good example of a tone system. Simpler than the systems of other Chinese tone languages or dialects, Mandarin employs four relative pitch contours, or tones, to distinguish among normally stressed syllables that are otherwise identical (see Table 3.6; the same *ma* syllable is also discussed in Table 5.1).

By contrast, the use of pitch in English is not associated with individual syllables, but rather with utterances in a variety of intonation patterns. The intonation that accompanies the question "Who ran off, Mother?" addressed to the speaker's mother, may elicit an answer such as, "Your sister." With the appropriately different intonation, the question "Who ran off—Mother?" addressed to some other member of the family may elicit an answer such as, "Yes, without even leaving a note."

The physical duration of a sound is referred to as its quantity, or **length**. In English, the difference between the short vowel in *bit* and the longer one in *beat* is not strictly or primarily a difference in length because the two vowels vary in other respects. Yet the consonant written as *tt-* in *cattail* is somewhat longer than that written as *-tt-* in *cattle.* In Czech, though, length is contrastive; such word pairs as *lak* "varnish" and *lák* "pickle (brine)" or *dal* "he gave" and *dál* "farther" are alike except for the considerable lengthening of the vowel in the second word of each pair (marked in conventional Czech spelling by the diacritic ´ over the vowel).

Some linguists also distinguish phonetic features that mark the joining of one grammatical unit to another: so-called *junctures*. English examples include the audible difference between the members of such pairs as *nitrate* and *night rate*, *I scream* and *ice cream*, and *an aim* and *a name*.

## SUMMARY AND CONCLUSIONS

For ethnographic research to be conducted as participant observation, anthropologists should have a working knowledge of the language spoken by the people they study. For a linguistic anthropologist, acquaintance with the methods of linguistic analysis and appreciation of structural differences among languages are essential.

Speech sounds are produced by various modifications of the vocal channel as the outgoing airstream passes between the vocal cords and the lips. The two main classes of speech sounds are vowels and consonants, each consisting of various types according to the place and manner of articulation. Vowels are usually associated with accent, which may take

**TABLE 3.6** THE FOUR DISTINCTIVE TONES OF MODERN MANDARIN CHINESE

| *Tone Number* | *Syllable* | *Description* | *Notation: Pinyin* | *Notation: Wade-Giles* | *Chinese Tone Name* | *Pitch Contour* | *Tone "Letter"* | *English Gloss* | *Character* |
|---|---|---|---|---|---|---|---|---|---|
| 1 | mā | high level | *mā* | *ma*$^{1}$ | *yīnpíng* | 5-5 | ˥˥ | mother | 媽 |
| 2 | má | rising | *má* | *ma*$^{2}$ | *yángpíng* | 3-5 | ˧˥ | flax fiber, hemp | 麻 |
| 3 | mǎ | dipping then rising | *mǎ* | *ma*$^{3}$ | *shǎng* | 2-1-4, 2-1 | ˨˩˦, ˨˩, | horse | 馬 |
| 4 | mà | falling | *mà* | *ma*$^{4}$ | *qù* | 5-1 | ˥˩ | to scold | 罵 |
| | ma | neutral tone | *ma* | *ma*$^{0}$ | | | | (question-tag maker) | 嗎 |

*Note:* This table gives the four Mandarin tones for one example syllable, "ma." As can be seen by the glosses and characters at the right, a difference in tone makes a difference in meaning. The table also shows how the tones are notated using the *pinyin* system, common in the People's Republic of China, and the older Wade-Giles transcription. The four tones in modern Mandarin Chinese are (1) high level, (2) rising, (3) dipping then rising, and (4) falling—though they are called various other names. Chinese also use "tone letters," which give a graphic representation of each syllable's tone. They view all speech as being spoken at one of five pitches or levels, from 5 down to 1 (with 5 being the highest), which they write as ˥ ,˦ ,˧ ,˨ , and ˩ respectively. So for the first "high level" tone as applied to the syllable ma, it is pronounced continuously for two beats at the highest 5 pitch (depicted, then, as 5-5 or ˥˥ ). The second "rising" tone starts in midrange and rises to the highest pitch (3 to 5, or ˧˥ ). The third "dipping then rising" tone starts low at 2 and drops to the lowest point 1, then rises high to the fourth level: 2-1-4, or ˨˩˦ . In the last case, the voice starts at the highest pitch (5) and drops to the lowest pitch (1): 5-1, or ˥˩ . (The unmarked syllable is a "neutral" tone, a special case that depends on the neighboring sounds.)

the form of stress, pitch, or a combination of both. Languages that make use of distinctive pitch levels are referred to as tone languages, some of those spoken in China being the best-known examples.

Analysis of the sounds of a language involves determining which phonetic differences are contrastive (distinctive, significant), that is, phonemic (for example, [b] and [pʰ] in English, differentiating between *bull* and *pull*), and which are predictable, or allophonic (for example, [P] and [pʰ] of *span* and *pan*). Each language has a characteristic phonemic system: sounds that are assignable to two or more distinct phonemes in one language may be allophones of a single phoneme in another. Although phonemes have been defined traditionally as the minimal units in the sound system of a language, they can be further analyzed into distinctive features, of which each phoneme is a bundle. The number of segmental phonemes per language varies from a mere dozen to as many as one hundred or more, but the inventories of the great majority of languages (70 percent) range between twenty and thirty-seven segments.

The phonetic and phonemic analytical approaches have been extended from the study of language to nonlinguistic aspects of culture under the terms **etic** and **emic**. Although the techniques of etics and emics have been employed for several decades, not all scholars agree on their status and mutual relationship.

## RESOURCE MANUAL AND STUDY GUIDE

### *Questions for Discussion*

1. Compare the phonetic transcription system given in the IPA in Chart 3.1 with the American System used in the text (Table 3.4, Table 3.5, Figure 3.2, Figure 3.3). How are they different? How are they similar? Why do you think differences exist? You might want to check Multimedia Link 1 in answering this question.
2. Morris Halle wrote that "the sounds . . . we emit when speaking are produced by complex gymnastics." Considering that people speak effortlessly and sometimes too fast, why did Halle make that statement?
3. Consider ten or so sounds of English and attempt to describe (at least roughly) where in the vocal tract, that is, between the lips and the larynx (marked in the neck by the so-called Adam's apple), each sound is produced and by what means.

### *Objective Study Questions*

**TRUE-FALSE TEST**

T F 1. American English has more vowel phonemes than consonant phonemes.

T F 2. English spelling and spoken English are well correlated; the writing system of English is therefore particularly suitable for careful linguistic work with unwritten languages.

T F 3. In the production of vowels, the air that escapes through the mouth (and the nose in the case of nasalized vowels) is relatively unimpeded.

T F 4. Pitch in a variety of intonational patterns is used in English—for example, in questions.

T F 5. The syllable written as *ma* has four different meanings in Mandarin Chinese, depending on the type of pitch contour the speaker employs.

T F 6. The English words *guy* and *thigh* represent a minimal pair; that is, they vary from each other in one sound only.

T F 7. Acoustic phonetics refers to the study of the production of speech sounds by the vocal organs.

T F 8. English as spoken in Great Britain, the United States, and Canada differs somewhat from one dialect to the next with regard to vowel pronunciation.

T F 9. Articulation of all the sounds in the languages of the world takes place between the glottis (the elongated space between the vocal cords) and the lips.

T F 10. In an analysis of an unwritten language, phonemic transcription precedes phonetic transcription.

**MULTIPLE-CHOICE QUESTIONS**

____ 1. When the vocal cords are drawn together and made to vibrate, they produce (A) voiced sounds. (B) voiceless sounds. (C) the glottal stop [ʔ].

____ 2. The p-sounds in the English words peak and speak are (A) two allophones of one phoneme. (B) two different phonemes. (C) in complementary distribution. (D) Of the three choices above only two are acceptable.

____ 3. Prosodic features can include all the following except (A) pitch. (B) vowel length. (C) voicing. (D) stress.

____ 4. The sound written as [b] is (A) uvular. (B) dental. (C) bilabial. (D) None of these three choices applies.

____ 5. Which among the following statements is indefensible? (A) Each language has a characteristic phonemic system. (B) The grammars of unwritten languages of small tribal societies are invariably simpler than grammars of languages of large established societies. (C) The production of speech sounds is an exceedingly complex process involving some one hundred muscles as well as other tissues. (D) Native speakers of a language use it efficiently even though they may know nothing about its structure.

**COMPLETIONS**

1. Languages that make use of distinctive pitch levels (Mandarin Chinese, for example) are referred to as ______________ languages (one word).
2. The smallest perceptible discrete segment of speech is a ______________ (one word); the contrastive sound units of a language are ______________ (plural of one word); and the varieties of a contrastive sound are its ______________ (plural of one word).

## *Problems*

### SOME TECHNIQUES FOR SOLVING PHONEMICS PROBLEMS

I. Keep in mind that there is really no ultimately "right" answer; there is only an explanation that accounts for all the data you are given, and new data may make us change our hypotheses. So remember that what you are actually doing is hypothesis testing (almost like a word game such as a crossword puzzle or on *Wheel of Fortune*) and trying to figure out what is going on.

II. First stop and look for **minimal pairs**.

 II a. If you have minimal pairs WITH the same meaning, you have ONE phoneme by the principle of **free variation**. Stop here.

 II b. If you have minimal pairs WITH NOT the same meaning, you have TWO phonemes by the principle of **contrasting distribution**.

III. If you do not have minimal pairs, try looking at similar phonetic environments (for "complementary distribution" or "overlapping distribution").

 III a. Your first try here would probably be to look at the initial/medial/final distributions. Try making a chart of the forms in question. Put a hash mark or check mark for each case you see if they look something like the following table:

| | initial | medial | final |
|---|---|---|---|
| [x] | ✓✓✓✓ | | |
| [y] | | | ✓✓✓ |

The two for ms do not seem to be occurring in the same environments. Thus, you are probably dealing with two allophones (variants) of one single phoneme (by the principle of **complementary distribution**—that is, where you find one, you do not find the other). You probably can stop your analysis here.

III b. If your distribution looks something like this table,

| | initial | medial | final |
|---|---|---|---|
| [x] | ✓✓✓ | ✓✓ | ✓ |
| [y] | ✓✓ | ✓✓✓ | ✓✓✓ |

we see that [x] and [y] DO seem to occur in similar environments. That is, they seem to overlap, or be in **overlapping distribution**. We MIGHT have two different phonemes, then, and we might be able to stop here if all else looks fine. However, we should check to be sure, as there may be some other kinds of distributions we have not noticed yet.

III b i. Some examples of distributions to check include looking at the following questions:

1. Does one form occur only initially or finally?
2. Does one form occur only before/after/between/ vowels or certain vowels?
3. Does one form occur only before/after/between/consonants or certain consonants?

III b ii. Some specific things to do:

1. Try writing the forms in isolation from the rest of the word to more easily see what is going on; for example,

| | | | |
|---|---|---|---|
| aWo | tXd | #Yo | eZ# |
| aWa | kXn | #Ya | rZ# |
| eWo | kXr | #Yr | oZ# |

In these hypothetical examples, we see that [W] seems to occur between vowels, [X] between consonants, [Y] at the beginning of words, and [Z] at the ends.

2. Check the consonant and vowel charts in Table 3.4 and Figures 3.2 and 3.3. Go across the rows and columns and see what properties the forms have in common with the sounds around them; this may be a clue to your hypothesis. For example, look at the Japanese problem given below. In this data set, what do we find? In the data, we see [m] coming before [b], [p], and [m]; [n] comes before [s], [g], [r], [k], [n], [t], and [š], and at the ends of words. What is going on here? There doesn't seem to be much in common among the sounds in this last group, BUT all three in the first group are bilabials (and in the same column in Table 3.4). Thus, our initial hypothesis might

be that there is only one phoneme distributed like this (if you wanted to write formally what we just said above, in words):

/N/ = { [m] / _b, _p, _m (i.e., bilabials); [n] / elsewhere }

WThat is, we posit one phoneme, which we will call /N/, which consists of two forms, or allophones: it appears as [m] if it comes before [b], [p], and [m] sounds; it appears as [n] when it comes before anything else (more data could actually make us change this hypothesis later).

3. Look at voicing, labial-ness, stop-ness, nasality, vowel height, and vowel distance (front or back); these are some of the most common properties that contribute to the analysis of phonemics problems.

IV. Rewrite your given phonetic data now in phonemic terms, using the phoneme(s) you have hypothesized. This is just simple substitution of your chosen phoneme symbols for the forms in the original data corpus. For example, if you think [t] and [d] are allophones of /T/, rewrite the words [ta] and [da] now as /Ta/.

**Sample problem (Japanese):** Practice checking overlapping distribution. Consider the data below. What is the status of the [m] sounds and [n] sounds? Do you think they are two phonemes or one? Either way, what are the distributions?

| | | | |
|---|---|---|---|
| šimpi | mystery | šimpuku | sincerity |
| šinsan | hardships | šinsecu | new theory |
| šimbō | patience | šinčoku | progress, advance |
| šingō | traffic signal | šimpan | referee, judge |
| šinri | mind, heart | šimpu | bride |
| šimbun | newspaper | šimmise | new store |
| šimpai | worry | šingi | deliberation |
| šinkon | newly married | šinnin | trust |
| šinka | evolution | šimbi | appreciating beauty |
| šimpo | advance, progress | šintō | "way of the Gods" |
| šinkō | advance, drive | šinšin | mind |

**PROBLEM 1**

Based on Wonderly (1951a and 1951b), this problem is taken from Zoque, a language spoken in southern Mexico that belongs to the Mixe-Zoque group of languages. Among the sounds of Zoque are [c], a voiceless alveolar affricate (similar to the consonants in the word *tsetse* [fly]), and [ʒ], a voiced alveolar affricate. From the data given here—to be taken as representative of the language—are [c] and [ʒ] allophones of one phoneme (that is, are they in complementary distribution), or are they assignable to two different phonemes (that is, do they contrast)? Support your conclusion.

1. ʔakaʔŋʒʌhk- "to be round"
2. ʔaŋʒoŋu "he answered"
3. camʒamnayu "he chatted"
4. cap "sky"
5. caʔ "stone"
6. cima "calabash"
7. nʒʌhku "I did it"
8. nʒima "my calabash"

9. nʒin "my pine"
10. pac "skunk"
11. puci "trash"
12. wanʒʌʔyu "he quit singing"

**PROBLEM 2**

Czech is a West Slavic language of the Indo-European language family, spoken in the Czech Republic. In Czech, among the various stops (plosives) are two alveodental stops, [t] and [d], articulated by the tongue tip against the boundary between the upper incisors and the alveolar ridge behind them, and two palatal stops, [tʸ] and [dʸ]. To how many phonemes are these four sounds assignable? Consider the following data and support your conclusion.

1. dej "give!"
2. dʸedʸit "to inherit"
3. dʸej "action"
4. dʸelo "cannon"
5. kotel "kettle"
6. kotʸe "kitten"
7. tedi "hence"
8. tele "calf (animal)"
9. tʸelo "body"
10. teta "aunt"
11. tikat "to be on a first-name basis"
12. titul "title"
13. tʸikat "to tick (clock)"
14. vada "flaw"
15. vana "bathtub"
16. vata "absorbent cotton"

**PROBLEM 3**

Based on Echeverría and Contreras (1965), this problem is taken from Araucanian, a language spoken by Native Americans of Argentina and Chile. Is the main stress, marked by [ˊ], distinctive, or is it predictable by rule? Support your conclusion.

1. elúmuyu "give us!"
2. kimúfaluwulay "he pretended not to know"
3. kurám "egg"
4. nawél "tiger"
5. putún "to drink"
6. θuŋúlan "I do not speak"
7. wuyá "yesterday"

**PROBLEM 4**

Based on Postal (1969), this problem is from Mohawk, the Iroquoian language of a Native American people who live mainly in southern Ontario and extreme northern New York state. On the basis of the following data, what is the status of vowel length—is it predictable or is it distinctive? Length is indicated by doubling a symbol—that is, éé is a long *e*; [ʔ] is the glottal stop; [ˊ] marks stress; [ʌ] is an unrounded back lower mid vowel, as in the English word *bud*; and [ɔ] is a rounded back lower mid vowel.

1. ranahéézʌs "he trusts her"
2. ragéédas "he scrapes"

3. rayʌ́thos "he plants"
4. waháágedeʔ "he scraped"
5. wísk "five"
6. rehyááraʔs "he remembers"
7. wahrehyááraʔneʔ "he remembered"
8. ɔwadunizaʔáshegeʔ "it will be ripening repeatedly"
9. yékreks "I push it"
10. royóʔdeʔ "he works"

**PROBLEM 5**

Based on Fromkin and Rodman (1988), this problem is from Korean, a language whose affiliation is disputed. The sounds [l] and [r] are in complementary distribution. On the basis of the following data, what is the form of the suffix meaning "of (the)"? What change do noun stems undergo when the suffix is attached, and under what circumstances does the change occur? What are the two mutually exclusive environments (complementary distribution) in which the sounds [l] and [r] occur?

1. pal "foot"
2. paruy "of the foot"
3. kul "oyster"
4. il "day"
5. rupi "ruby"
6. ratio "radio"
7. mul "water"
8. muruy "of the water"
9. saram "person"
10. saramuy "of the person"
11. multok "water jug"
12. ipalsa "barber"

**PROBLEM 6**

Based on Fromkin and Rodman (1988), this problem is taken from a Bantu language spoken in Angola, Africa. This language is a member of the Niger-Congo language family. The alveolar segments [t, s, z] in complementary distribution with their palatal counterparts [č, š, ž] are assignable to three phonemes. What is the distribution of each of the corresponding pairs of allophones, that is, [t] and [č], [s] and [š], and [z] and [ž]? Which of the phonetic symbols from the first pair, [t, č], would you choose to represent the phoneme, and why?

1. tobola "to bore a hole"
2. tanu "five"
3. kesoka "to be cut"
4. kasu "emaciation"
5. kunezulu "heaven"
6. zevo "then"
7. zenga "to cut"
8. nselele "termite"
9. čina "to cut"
10. čiba "banana"
11. nkoši "lion"
12. ažimola "alms"
13. lolonži "to wash the house"
14. žima "to stretch"

**PROBLEM 7**

Desperanto is spoken in an as yet unexplored tropical forest. Among the Desperanto words are the following nouns and noun phrases (long vowels are represented by double letters, short vowels by single letters).

1. muumu "home fried potatoes"
2. kaka "scrambled eggs"
3. wowo "bikini swimsuit"
4. kakaa "used bicycle"
5. mumu "garlic ice cream"
6. woowoo "banana split"

Is vowel length phonemic? ___ yes ____ no.
In your answer (one sentence should suffice), justify your choice:

______________________________

______________________________

______________________________

**PROBLEM 8**

Among the sounds of Czech are [k] and [x] ([x] is the sound written *ch* in the name of the composer J. S. Bach). On the basis of the Czech words listed below, are these two sounds two separate phonemes or two allophones of one phoneme?

1. [prak] "slingshot"
2. [puk] "puck"
3. [xrxel] "spittle"
4. [krkoun] "cheapskate"
5. [prax] "dust"
6. [xroust] "June bug"
7. [kras] "limestone region with caverns"
8. [pux] "stench"

____ two separate phonemes or ____ two allophones of one phoneme. Justify your decision:

______________________________

______________________________

______________________________

## Answer Key

True-false test: 1-F, 2-F, 3-T, 4-T, 5-T, 6-T, 7-F, 8-T, 9-T, 10-F
Multiple-choice questions: 1-A, 2-D, 3-C, 4-C, 5-B
Completions: 1. tone, 2. phone, phonemes, allophones

*Problem 1.* The sounds [c] and [ʒ] in Zoque are allophones of a phoneme because they are phonetically similar (both are affricates) and in complementary distribution: the voiced alveolar affricate [ʒ] occurs after nasal consonants ŋ, m, and n (as in 1, 2, 3, 7, 8, 9, and 12), the voiceless alveolar affricate [c] elsewhere (as in 3–6, 10, and 11). The rule could be written as follows: /c/ → [+ voiced]/N___ (where N = any nasal).

*Problem 2.* All of the four Czech stops, [t, d, $t^y$, $d^y$], are separate phonemes, /t, d, $t^y$, $d^y$/, because they contrast, as is evident from the existence of minimal pairs in the sample (as in 1 and 3, 4 and 9, 11 and 13, and 14 and 16).

*Problem 3.* The main stress in Araucanian is on the second vowel of a word and hence is predictable.

*Problem 4.* Vowel length in Mohawk is predictable: All vowels are short except those that are stressed and followed by a single consonant (as in 1, 2, 4, 6, and 7). Vowel length is therefore not distinctive.

*Problem 5.* From the word pairs 1 and 2, 7 and 8, and 9 and 10, the form of the suffix meaning "of (the)" is *-uy*. Stem-final [l] changes to [r] before the suffix (as in 1 and 2 and 7 and 8). [r] and [l] are allophones of the same phoneme: [r] occurs initially (as in 5 and 6) and intervocalically, that is, between vowels (as in 2, 8, 9, and 10), and [l] occurs finally (as in 1, 3, 4, and 7) and before a consonant (as in 11 and 12).

*Problem 6.* The alveolar segments [t, s, z] occur before the vowels /e, a, o, u/ (as in 1–8); the palatal segments [č, š, ž] occur before /i/, that is, before a high front vowel (as in 9–14). The phonemic symbol /t/ would be preferable to /č/ because its occurrence is less restricted. It may be expected to occur before the four vowels /e, a, o, u/; in this small sample it occurs only before /o/ and /a/ (as in 1 and 2) and therefore more frequently than the /č/ that occurs only before /i/ (as in 9 and 10). (This choice also happens to be more practical because *t* is one of the standard keys on American keyboards, whereas č is not; if one were to choose č, the háček [ˇ] diacritical mark would have to be selected from a separate typeface menu, requiring extra steps, and added above the letter *c* whenever the č occurred.)

*Problem 7.* Vowel length is phonemic; there are minimal pairs that differ only by vowel length (as in 1 and 5, 2 and 4, and 3 and 6).

*Problem 8.* The Czech sounds [k] and [x] are two separate phonemes /k/ and /x/; two word pairs of the sample, 1 and 5, and 2 and 8, differ only by virtue of these two consonants.

## *Notes and Suggestions for Further Reading*

Textbooks of linguistics are numerous, and most carry some explanations of phonology and phonemics, often along with exercises. The two classics are Sapir (1921) and Bloomfield (1933). Two excellent postwar but pre-Chomskyan introductions to linguistics are Hockett (1958) and Gleason (1961). Some representative contemporary standard texts are Akmajian, Demers, Farmer, and Harnish (2010) and O'Grady, Archibald, Aronoff, and Rees-Miller (2009). An eclectic set of problems can be found in Bergmann, Hall, and Ross (2007) or Dawson and Phelan (2016). Zsiga (2013), Hayes (2008), and Reetz and Jongman (2009) are standard treatments from a mostly linguistics perspective. Vanderweide, Rees-Miller, and Aronoff (2010) is a problem book to accompany the O'Grady et al. text mentioned above but stands on its own. For general reference, one may wish to consult Crystal (1997) and especially the excellent Crystal (2010). For more specialized topics, see Ladefoged and Johnson (2010) on phonetics, Hayes (2008) on phonology, and Chomsky and Halle (1968) on the phonology of English. Small (2016) offers a good student introduction to phonology and phonetics. Bright's four-volume encyclopedia (1992) is an excellent and reliable source on all aspects of linguistics.

# 4

# The "Nuts and Bolts" of Linguistic Anthropology II: Structure of Words and Sentences

## LEARNING OBJECTIVES

- Describe the importance of linguistic formalism for studying culture and society
- Define morphemes, and explain the different kinds
- Explain some basic morphological processes such as case, aspect, and reduplication
- Gain some facility in approaching basic problems in morphology and syntax
- Describe some of the basic ideas behind Chomsky's generative project

We have not eaten all our linguistic vegetables yet! We are going to talk about some more technical nuts and bolts of linguistic anthropology in this chapter. To see why this is important and necessary, let's briefly discuss life and language in the Navajo universe. Navajo cosmology is quite different from Western cosmology in many ways, especially regarding assumptions about how the world works. First, for the Navajo, objects in the world are ranked in order of how they can control things. For example, humans can control large animals, large animals can control medium-sized animals, and medium-sized animals control small animals. Animals control insects. Next in the order are natural forces, plants, and inanimate objects. Abstractions come last. Also, within these categories, things in motion control things that are stationary. Things that speak control things that can't.

You might at first think that this hierarchy is not that odd. After all, we make our dogs sit, dogs chase cats, cats eat mice, mice chew on cheese, and so on. But for the Navajo, when we say control, we really mean *control.* In the Navajo worldview, it is absurd and almost inconceivable for, say, mice to control cats, cats to control dogs, or dogs to control humans. But in the world, this actually happens all the time. For example, dogs escape from their owners, horses kick their riders, and a cornered mouse might bite the careless cat. These things are natural in the English-speaking universe; that's part of life. But how might a Navajo explain these things? In the case of the cat, "careless" might be the key word here. The Navajo believe the cat is really more controlling than the mouse, but the cat through its own volition—carelessness, playfulness, kindness, or whatever—somehow allowed itself to get bitten.

But how do we know this? These kinds of questions are not easy for informants to answer, because most people in most cultures rarely reflect on everyday life in such an abstract and philosophical way (or using the objective "etic" scientific terms). And how would anthropologists even begin to know to ask a question about how things are controlled in the Navajo universe unless they already had some idea about it? Perhaps surprisingly, one way would be through a look at Navajo syntax. To simplify things greatly, the Navajo language can have these two sentence types: (1) A B *yi*-VERB, and (2) A B *bi*-VERB. The first sentence translates as "A VERBs B" or "A does VERB to B" (like the "[The] HORSE KICKS [the] MULE"). The second sentence (which we awkwardly will call "passive" for the moment) translates as "A was VERB-ed by B" (as in "[The] HORSE WAS KICKED BY [the] MULE"). The only difference in the actual Navajo sentence is the prefix attached to the verb. Now it turns out that not just any noun can go in any place in the sentence. A man can kick a horse and a horse can kick a man—these things happen in real life, after all—but they must be phrased in certain ways in Navajo. Thus, a better way of describing the two sentences might be like this:

A → B *yi*-VERB "A VERBs B"
A ← B *bi*-VERB "A was VERB-ed by B" or "B VERB-s A"

where the (unspoken, of course) arrow shows the direction of control or agency. But we must add this important qualification: the more animate or controlling noun must occur in the first, or A, place in the sentence. This is an example of what linguists call **animacy**, the grammatical or semantic category of nouns based on how sentient or alive they are in their language's hierarchical scheme. So in order to say things like "The horse kicked the man" or "The mouse bit the cat," they must be said in the "passive," with "man" or "cat" appearing first: "The man was kicked by the horse" or "The cat was bitten by the mouse" (i.e., in the A <—B *bi*-VERB form). The other "active" "A—> B *yi*-VERB" form is not only ungrammatical, it sometimes sounds completely absurd in the Navajo view of things, as Gary Witherspoon explains in Box 4.1.

So we see, then, that some technical knowledge of Navajo grammar—AND English grammar, too—is necessary to fully understand the culture. For example, Westerners put value on various abstractions, for example, "truth" or legal technicalities. This is because these notions have a high degree of animacy in the English speaker's view of things. Westerners say things like "Ye shall know the truth, and the truth shall make you free" (as mentioned in the Bible). But to the Navajo, as we saw, abstractions lie low on the list of controlling objects. So in the rest of the chapter we will look at some of these formal tools that can help us understand how cultures think about, and talk about, their world.

### BOX 4.1 CLASSIFYING INTERACTION THROUGH LANGUAGE

The sentence "the girl drank the water"

| *At′e´e´d* | *to´* | *yoodla´$^{2}$a´$^{2}$′* |
|---|---|---|
| (girl) | (water) | (it-it-drank) |

is acceptable, but the sentence "the water was drunk by the girl"

| *To´* | *at′e´e´d* | *boodla´$^{2}$a´$^{2}$′* |
|---|---|---|
| (water) | (girl) | (it-it-drank) |

is unacceptable and absurd in the Navajo view of the world. . . .

It is rather evident . . . that we need some nonlinguistic data or information in order to interpret these rather unusual linguistic patterns properly. They are not generated by a set of operations at the deep structural level of Navajo grammar; they are generated by a set of cultural rules which are ultimately derived from more fundamental metaphysical propositions which the Navajo take to be axiomatic.

Taking a cultural approach to the explanation of this pattern in Navajo syntax, some years ago I asked my wife why it was so absurd to say *tó at′ééd boodla´$^{2}$a´$^{2}$′* "the water was drunk by the girl." She thought long and hard about this matter, unable to see why it was not absurd to me. Finally, she said, "The sentence attributes more intelligence to the water than it does to the girl, and anyone [even you—was the implication] ought to know that human beings are smarter than water." Therein I had a lead to solve this riddle, but I was not sure what to make of it. She went on to say that the water does not think, so how could it have the girl drink it. But, I insisted, the water was not acting or thinking, it just got drunk. She countered by saying that the way I had constructed the sentence made it appear that the water was the cause of the drinking action, not the girl.

From the discussion above I later surmised that maybe the sentence should be translated "the water caused the girl to drink it." I tried this translation out on several Navajos who knew English. They said it was much closer to the Navajo meaning of the sentence than "the water was drunk by the girl" but they were still a little uncomfortable with it. After some further thought and discussion, we came up with the translation "the water let the girl drink it." Therein we had captured in English not just the covert meaning of the Navajo sentence but the overt absurdity that the meaning expressed.

From Gary Witherspoon, *Language and Art in the Navajo Universe* (1977), 65–67

## COMBINING SOUNDS INTO LARGER FORMAL AND MEANINGFUL UNITS

Let's begin by seeing how the sounds we studied in the last chapter become combined to form words and other meaningful units. Because many of the languages they encounter have only been spoken and never written, anthropologists must adequately identify all the sounds before they can transcribe and later analyze what speakers of these languages have said. Because accurate transcription cannot be made at the speed at which people talk, magnetic tape recorders have been of great help in modern fieldwork. When ethnographic reports are published in which native words or texts are to be cited, a reliable method of writing down the language must be devised. Phonemic transcription is the most economical and at the same time accurate way of recording utterances ranging from short comments to long ceremonial speeches.

A good transcription is essential for an analysis because only with a reliable text in hand can the linguistic anthropologist determine a language's grammatical structure and exact meaning. Full understanding requires the identification of even the smallest meaningful segments (**morphemes**) that make up the text. Every language has its own stock of morphemes and arranges them into words, phrases, and sentences in a particular way, and every language has its own grammatical categories that vary from one language to the next.

In what units do people communicate? The answer depends on the approach one takes to the study of speech. An important unit of linguistic analysis is the sentence, which is in turn subdividable into smaller constituents—for example, noun phrases and verb phrases or the subject, verb, and object. The principal analytical unit of communicative behavior in linguistic anthropology is **discourse**. The concept of discourse is not easy to define because individual scholars use it differently. Discourse may be as short in duration as a greeting or as long as a protracted argument or the telling of a traditional narrative; it can be oral or written, planned or unplanned, poetic or businesslike, and it can be exemplified by any one of the genres characteristic of the speech behavior of a particular culture. A great deal of any culture is transmitted by means of discourse, and discourse may be said to constitute a significant part of any culture. As Joel Sherzer put it:

> Discourse is the broadest and most comprehensive level of linguistic form, content, and use . . . [and] the process of discourse structuring is the locus of the language-culture relationship. . . . It is in certain kinds of discourse, in which speech play and verbal art are heightened, as central moments in poetry, magic, politics, religion, respect, insult, and bargaining, that the language-culture-discourse relationship comes into sharpest focus and the organizing role of discourse in this relationship is highlighted. (Sherzer 1987:305–306)

Linguistic theories and methods underwent great changes during the twentieth century, the transformational-generative approach of recent decades rapidly gaining followers. And although linguistic anthropologists are more concerned with the relationships among language and culture and society than with linguistic structure in and of itself, they nevertheless follow current linguistic research with interest and when applicable use its results in their own work.

## MORPHEMES AND ALLOMORPHS

An overview of phonetics and the fundamental principles of phonemic analysis was presented in the previous chapter. Let us now shift to the level of analysis conventionally referred to as grammar or syntax. Consider the phrase *shockingly disgraceful acts*, which can be subdivided into the following meaningful segments (to simplify matters, conventional spelling instead of phonemic transcription is used below):

shock, meaning "to startle, offend, distress,"
*-ing*, an adjectival segment meaning "causing to, . . . "
*-ly*, an adverbial segment meaning "in a . . . manner,"
*dis-*, meaning "not, opposite of,"
*grace*, meaning "propriety, decency,"
*-ful*, meaning "characterized by,"
*act*, meaning "deed," and
*-s*, meaning "more than one," that is, marking the plural.

It appears that the three-word phrase consists of eight meaningful segments of English, none of which can be further subdivided without the loss of the original meaning (it cannot be claimed, for example, that the word *grace* is made up of *g-* plus *race*). Linguistic units that have a meaning but contain no smaller meaningful parts are termed *morphemes*. To put it differently, a morpheme is the smallest contrastive unit of grammar. The search for such units in a particular language is called morphemic analysis. And the study of word structure, including classification of and interrelationships among morphemes, is referred to as **morphology**.

### *Free Versus Bound Morphemes*

There are many thousands of morphemes in any language. The large majority are commonly **free morphemes** because they may occur unattached to other morphemes; that is, they can stand alone as independent words—in the example above, *grace*, *shock*, and *act*. Some morphemes, but usually relatively few, are bound morphemes because they normally do not occur on their own but only in combination with another morpheme—for example, *dis-*, *-ing*, *-ly*, and *-s*. The stem is that part of the word to which inflectional affixes (such as the plural) are attached.

In English and other languages, bound morphemes occur in limited numbers. There are languages, though, in which most morphemes are bound; Inuit (Eskimo) is usually cited as an example of such a language. In still other languages, those noun stems that stand for objects that are typically possessed do not occur as free morphemes. This is true, for example, of Arapaho nouns referring to body parts, kinship relationships, and a few other referents. (In Arapaho, the acute accent [ ′ ] marks stressed vowels with higher pitch; long vowels are written doubly.) Examples of dependent nouns are *bétee* "(someone's) heart," *wonotóno*ʔ "(someone's) ear," *notóóne* "my daughter," *béíteh*ʔéí "(someone's) friend," and *betéí* "louse, flea," because there is no such thing as a heart or an ear apart from a human or an animal, a daughter without a mother or father, a friend unattached to another by affection, or a louse or flea that could survive without deriving benefits from a host. The forms *bétee*, *wonotóno?*, *notóóne*, béíteh?éí, and *betéí* consist of either the first-person possessive morpheme *n-* in *notóóne* or the indefinite personal possessor morpheme *b-* or *w-* in the other four nouns. None of these four or some two hundred other nouns ever occurs as a free (unpossessed) stem.

### *Affixes*

Some but not all bound morphemes in a language are affixes; attached to other morphemes, they modify meaning in some way and make more complex words. If an affix is attached before a stem, it is called a **prefix**; if it follows a stem, it is a **suffix**; and if it is placed within another morpheme, it is called an **infix**. In English, only the first two types of affixes occur. Examples of prefixes are *be-*, *de-*, *in-*, *pre-*, *re-*, and *un-*, as in *befriend*, *debug*, *inlay*, *prewash*, *rewrite*, and *undo*; examples of suffixes are *-en*, *-er*, *-hood*, *-ish*, *-ize*, and *-ward*, as in *oxen*, *smaller*, *childhood*, *bookish*, *equalize*, and *skyward*. An example of an infix may be taken from Chontal, a language spoken by a people in southern Oaxaca, Mexico: *akán'ö?* "woman," *kón'í?* "grandchild," *sewí?* "magpie," and several other stems form the plural by inserting an infix in the form of -ɬ- (a voiceless lateral continuant) before the second consonant, yielding *akáɬn'ö?* "women," *kóɬn'í?* "grandchildren," and *seɬwí?* "magpies." Infixation is fairly common in Native American, Southeast Asian, and African languages.

What about such "irregular" plurals in English as *feet*, *geese*, *men*, and *mice*? Rather than adding a suffix to the stems *foot*, *goose*, *man*, and *mouse*, the plural is formed by changing the stem vowel—for example, in *foot* → *feet* and *goose* → *geese*—by fronting and unrounding it. Pluralization in such words is effected by what is sometimes referred to as a process morpheme and is quite different from the addition of a suffix after the stem (as in *cat* plus *-s*).

### *Allomorphs*

A particular morpheme does not have to have the same shape every time it occurs. The plural of English nouns offers an excellent example of the considerable variation in the phonemic shape of a morpheme. Noun stems ending in a so-called sibilant (an *s*-like or *sh*-like fricative) form their plural by adding a vowel plus a *z* sound, very commonly [əz], as in *box-es*, *pass-es*, *buzz-es*, *bush-es*, *garage-s*, *patch-es*, and *judge-s*. The great majority of noun stems ending in voiced nonsibilant sounds add a voiced [z], whereas those ending in voiceless nonsibilant sounds add a voiceless [s], as in *bear-s*, *can-s*, *comma-s*, *lathe-s*, *pad-s*, *pill-s*, *rib-s*, *rig-s*, and *song-s*, on the one hand, and *cat-s*, *laugh-s*, *lip-s*, and *tick-s*, on the other. But a number of noun stems form the plural differently—among them *alumna*, *alumnus*, *child*, *crisis*, *criterion*, *datum*, *kibbutz*, and *ox*; their plurals are, respectively, *alumnae*, *alumni*, *children*, *crises*, *criteria*, *data*, *kibbutzim*, and *oxen*. And then there are a relatively few noun stems the plurals of which are not overtly marked, for example, *sheep* and *swine*. These and other such nouns are said to have their plurals marked by a *zero* (written as Ø), that is, by the absence of an overt linguistic feature. The variant forms of a particular morpheme are referred to as its **allomorphs** (just as the varieties of a phoneme are called allophones), or morpheme alternants. Allomorphs of a given morpheme, therefore, are different forms of the morpheme, depending on the context in which they occur.

In summary, then, one may say that the plural morpheme in English has a number of allomorphs, ranging from the most common ones of /-z/, /-s/, and /-əz/, through several others associated especially with loanwords, to zero. And in the case of pluralizing the noun *man* to *men*, one would represent the plural allomorph as /æ/ →/ɛ/. The plural morpheme in English is by no means an exception in that it has morpheme alternants. For example, the stem *child* has a different phonemic shape in its plural form (*children*) from when it occurs by itself or when it is suffixed by *-hood*, *-ish*, and *-like* (in *childhood*, *childish*, and *childlike*).

Morphemes also vary considerably in length. Some consist of a single phoneme; for example, the three English morphemes marking the plural, the possessive, and the third-person singular (as in *apes*, *ape's*, and [*he*] *apes* [*someone*]) have /s/ as one of their several allomorphs. Others, like *caterpillar* or *hippopotamus*, consist of several syllables. Words, too, in English vary in length: *a* is the shortest, but it is impossible to list the longest. Suppose you wish to refer to a lineal paternal male relative from the sixteenth century: He would be your great-great- . . . great-grandfather.

## MORPHOLOGICAL PROCESSES

Just as languages differ in their phonemic systems, they differ in their morphologies. Some morphological processes, however, are quite common throughout the world, even though they may be applied differently in specific languages. One such process is **derivation**, by means of which new words are formed from existing ones, frequently by changing them from one word class to another. In English, this process of word formation is frequently accomplished by the use of derivational affixes. For example, affixes change the adjective *modern* to the verb *modernize*, the noun *friend* to the adjective *friendly*, the verb *speak* to the noun *speaker*, and the adjective *abrupt* to the adverb *abruptly*. They also produce such words as *kingdom*, *outbid*, and *despite*.

The other common morphological process is **inflection**, the use of affixes to indicate grammatical relationships (number, case, person, tense, and others). In English, all inflectional affixes are suffixes and are limited to the plural and possessive markers in nouns (as in *mothers* and *mother's*), comparative and superlative markers in adjectives (as in *taller* and *tallest*), and the third-person singular present-tense marker and the past-tense, progressive, and past-participle markers in verbs (as in *waits*, *waited*, [*is*] *singing*, and *beaten*).

Derivational and inflectional morphemes may have the same phonemic shape: One *-ing* in English serves as the derivational suffix changing a verb into a noun, as in "Excessive eating is harmful," whereas another *-ing* is an inflectional suffix marking the progressive verb form, as in "They were eating voraciously." In English, inflectional suffixes always follow derivational suffixes, as in *reader's*, *organizers*, and *friendliest* (*read-er-'s*, *organ-iz(e)-er-s*, and *friend-li-est*).

As languages go, English has very few inflectional affixes compared with, for example, Latin. As against the handful of different forms of an English verb (*speak*, *speaks*, *speaking*, *spoke*, and *spoken*), a Latin verb has scores. Regarding number, English distinguishes formally only between the singular and the plural, whereas some languages have special forms also for the dual to refer to two of a kind, and even forms to refer to three and four of a kind. Old English marked the dual number in its personal pronouns: besides *ic* "I" and *wē* "we," there was *wit* "we two"; besides *mē* "(to) me" and ūs "(to) us," there was *unc* "(to) the two of us"; and so on. These dual forms gradually disappeared during the second part of the thirteenth century, halfway through the Middle English period. However, derivational suffixes in English are plentiful: *-able* (as in *reasonable*), *-ade* (*blockade*), *-age* (*breakage*), *-al* (*coastal*), *-ance* (*assistance*), *-ant* (*servant*), *-ar* (*linear*), *-ard* (*drunkard*), *-ary* (*budgetary*), *-ate* (*activate*), *-atic* (*problematic*), and scores of others.

Some languages distinguish nouns according to several genders, each of which may require corresponding forms in pronouns, adjectives, and even verbs. Frequently there is no correlation between grammatical and natural gender. In English, all inanimate objects are referred to by the pronoun *it*; in German, however, *der Löffel* "spoon" is masculine, *die Gabel* "fork" is feminine, and *das Messer* "knife" is neuter, as are also *das Weib* "woman" and *das Mädchen* "girl." (We will have more to say about this in Chapter 13.) In Old English, *stān* "stone" and *wīfman* "woman" were masculine, *duru* "door" and *sunne* "sun" feminine, and *word* "word" and *wīf* "woman, wife" neuter. The substitution of natural for grammatical gender also took place during the Middle English period.

Another grammatical category that may serve as an example is *case*. Although Old English had three **case forms** for, say, *stān* "stone" in the singular (nominative and accusative *stān*, genitive *stānes*, and dative *stāne*) and three in the plural (*stānas, stāna*, and *stānum*, respectively), Modern English manages quite well with only two forms, namely, *stone* and *stones*. It has retained case forms only in the interrogative pronoun *who* (that is *whom*) and in several personal pronouns: *me*, the objective case form of *I*, and *him, her, us*, and *them*. In other languages, however, cases are an important and elaborate grammatical feature. For example, the Czech language has seven cases in both singular and plural, applied not only to nouns but also to pronouns, adjectives, and numerals.

Finnish has a particularly rich case system. What in English is usually expressed by means of prepositions, Finnish does with cases. Among these cases modifying, for example, the noun *talo* "house," is the adessive (case), meaning "at, near (a place)," as in *talolla* "at the house"; elative, meaning "out of (a place)," as in *talosta* "from (inside) the house"; inessive "in, within (a place)," as in *talossa* "in the house"; illative "into (a place)," as in *taloon* "into the house"; allative "to(ward) (a place)," as in *talolle* "to(ward) the house"; and several others.

**Aspect** is a grammatical category expressing how activities denoted by verbs are related to time. This category is particularly well developed in Slavic languages, as some of the following examples from Czech will show. Czech verbs are perfective, expressing action as complete or concluded, as in the suppletive *přišel* "he has come, arrived" from the infinitive *přijít*, or imperfective, expressing action as incomplete or repeated, as in šel "he went" from *jít* "to go." The multiplicity of verbal action is expressed in the iterative form *nosil* "he carried" and the more intensive frequentative form *nosíval* "he used to carry." A particular phase of a verbal action may be specified as an initiatory one, as in *vyběhl* "he ran out," a completed one, as in *doběhl* "he reached [a place] by running," and a terminative one, as in *proběhl se* "he had run." The extent of a verbal action may be momentary, as in *střelil* "he took a shot," or durative, expressive continuity, as in *střílel* "he fired away"; or the extent is small, as in *usmál se* "he gave a smile," or large, as in *nasmál se* "he had a good laugh."

An interesting morphological process is reduplication, the doubling or repetition of a phoneme or phonemes. In Isthmus Nahuat, a dialect of Nahuatl spoken by Native

Americans in eastern Mexico, verb stems are derived by reduplication to mark different kinds of repetitive action: *-kakalaki-* "enter a house many times" from *-kalaki-* "enter"; *-pahpano-* "pass by many times" from *-pano-* "pass by"; *-poposteki-* "break many times" or "break into many pieces" from *-posteki-* "break"; *-papaka-* "wash many times" and *-pahpaka-* "wash many things" from *-paka-*"wash"; and the like. The compounds *goody-goody, helter-skelter, teeny-weeny,* and *wishy-washy* are reduplications of sorts, but the process in English is quite limited.

One could go on illustrating various other grammatical categories found in the world's thousands of languages (aspect, mood, tense, voice, and so on) and the processes by which they are marked, but the examples already given should suffice. However, one important point must be made. Whether or not a language formally marks a particular grammatical category does not make it superior (or inferior) to others. If it were so, Old English would have to be rated as much superior to Modern English—something no one can seriously maintain. All languages are fully adequate because they enable native speakers to express all that they wish to say about the society and culture in which they live.

## MORPHOPHONEMICS

Sound alternations like the one between /f/ and /v/ in *knife* and *knives, life* and *lives, loaf* and *loaves,* and *wife* and *wives* are common in English and other languages. Alternations of this kind are changes in the phonemic shape of the allomorphs of a morpheme, and as such they represent important processes in the structure of language. The study of the relations between morphology and phonology or, to put it in other words, the study of the phonemic differences among allomorphs of the same morpheme, is referred to as **morphophonemics** or morpho(pho)nology, and the generalizations concerning the occurrence of the various shapes of morphemes are called morphophonemic rules. To formulate such a rule one usually selects a particular allomorph as the base form and then describes the conditions under which other allomorphs of the same morpheme occur. To refer to an example used earlier in this chapter, nouns in English (except for those specifically exempt) form the plural by adding /z/ to their stem (as in *leg, legs*) but insert /ə/ before the plural suffix if the stem ends in a sibilant (/s/, /z/, /š/, /ž/, /č/, or /ǰ/ (as in *kiss, kisses*) or change the voiced /z/ to voiceless /s/ if the stem terminates in a voiceless nonsibilant (as in *neck, necks*).

Morphophonemic rules in any language are stable even if they are fairly complex. For example, in Arapaho, an Algonquian language spoken by Native Americans in Wyoming and Oklahoma, the word *néíʔibéheʔ* "my grandmother" is regularly changed to *hiníʔiiwóhoʔ* to mean "his/her grandmother." (The explanation of why this change takes place is fairly complex, but to satisfy the curious, here it is: in addition to the two common word-initial prefixes marking possession ["my" and "his/her"], the differences between the two forms are also regular. The final *-oʔ* in *hiníʔiiwóhoʔ* is the obviative suffix [a morpheme that marks the so-called fourth person when two third persons are referred to, in this case a grandmother and the person who claims her as grandmother]. The vowel of the obviative, *o*, influences the selection of a like vowel in the diminutive suffix before it, and *b* regularly changes into *w* before a back vowel [in this case *o*]. The word apparently means "his/her little one [mother]"—a rather gentle way of referring to one's grandmother.)

## SHOWING GRAMMATICAL RELATIONSHIPS: INFLECTIONS VERSUS WORD ORDER

To indicate grammatical relationships between words in a sentence, languages draw on one of two general strategies: **word order** or **inflections**. Chinese (and to a large extent, English) uses the word-order strategy. For example, the English sentence "I like Linda" would be *Wǒ xǐhuan Linda* in Beijing Mandarin, and "Linda likes me" would be *Linda xǐhuan wǒ*. The forms of the words in the two sentences are identical, but the order is different to indicate who likes whom. Notice that in both the English and Chinese examples it is the word order that indicates the grammatical relationships at work. "John loves Jane" is not necessarily the same thing as "Jane loves John."

Languages that use inflections take a different tack. Here we see grammatical relationships are not indicated by where they appear in a sentence, but by *inflections:* suffixes, prefixes, or other markers that indicate what grammar-school teachers used to call "parts of speech." For example, suppose in English we had a suffix *-a* that was applied to the subject of any sentence (or the "doer of the action" in the old grade-school parlance). And let's say the receivers of the attention (or the "direct objects" in linguistic-ese) always took the suffix *-u*. So to say "John loves Jane" it would be *John-a loves Jane-u*. Notice that the word order now really does not matter because we always know that whoever has the -a suffix is the subject/lover and whoever has the -u suffix is the beloved. Thus, *Jane-u loves John-a, John-a Jane-u loves,* and *Loves John-a Jane-u* would all mean the same thing. And if we wanted to talk about Jane loving John, we would have to switch the inflections—*not* necessarily the word order—to indicate this (as in *Jane-a loves John-u*).

There are many languages that use this strategy (such as Latin, the exemplar case below), just as there are many languages that indicate grammar through word order. Most languages, however—while generally stressing one approach—will use a little bit of both. For example, in English if we want to invert the sentence *She left him*, we don't say *Him left she* (that is, only change the word order). We have to say *He left her.* That is, we have to change or inflect the subject and the object words. For historical reasons that need not concern us here now, these become manifested as "she" and "he" (subjects) and "her" and "him" (objects) in modern English. However, as we saw in Chinese, which is more strictly word-order based than English, the forms did *not* change (*wǒ* was the subject "I" in the first sentence about Linda, as well as the object "me" in the second).

To see how inflections actually work in natural language, consider two English sentences and their following translations into Latin and Czech:

| | | | |
|---|---|---|---|
| English: | (1) A hunter tracks a lion | *and* | (2) A lion tracks a hunter. |
| Latin: | (1) Venator leonem vestigat | *and* | (2) Leo venatorem vestigat. |
| Czech: | (1) Lovec stopuje lva | *and* | (2) Lev stopuje lovce. |

Although the meanings of the two English sentences are quite different, the five words of each sentence are exactly the same. Whether the hunter or the lion is the grammatical subject or the grammatical object (that is, the goal of the action of the word "tracks"), the same five words are all that are needed. who is tracking whom is fully indicated by the word order—that is, the arrangement of words.

Of the two other languages, Latin and Czech are richly inflectional, that is, changing the form of the words to mark various grammatical categories. In Latin, the form of the word for the hunter as a grammatical subject is *venator*, and as a grammatical object it is *venatorem*. Unlike in English, the word order does not indicate the grammatical relationship of the words of a sentence, but instead can be used to show emphasis. As words can really come in any order, the most important or interesting focus might be mentioned first. For example, if a Roman had said *Venator leonem vestigat*, he would have meant something like *It is the HUNTER who tracks the lion*, but if a Roman had said *Leonem venator vestigat*, he would have meant something like *It is the LION whom the hunter tracks* (rather than, say, a *DEER* or a *HORSE*).

To show the richness of the inflectional system in Latin, here are the forms of the noun (often called **cases**) for *venator* in the singular: *venator* (nominative, indicating the subject of a verb); *venatoris* (genitive, indicating possession, like "of" in English); *venatori* (dative, indicating the indirect object of a verb, like "to" as in "throw the ball to him"); *venatorem* (accusative, indicating the direct object of a verb); *venator* (vocative, indicating the person being spoken to; the form is the same as the nominative); and *venatore* (ablative, indicating the instrument or method by which something is done, like "by" or "with" in English). (These descriptions have been simplified.)

## CHOMSKY AND TRANSFORMATIONAL-GENERATIVE GRAMMAR

The study of languages and linguistics has been documented for ancient Greece as early as two and a half millennia ago. At about that time, the earliest preserved scientific grammar was compiled in India. The work is Pāṇini's grammar of Sanskrit, written around the fifth century BCE, or even earlier, and described by a distinguished American linguist as "one of the greatest monuments of human intelligence" (Bloomfield 1933:11). Not a great deal is known about the development of linguistics during the Middle Ages, but both pedagogical and philosophical studies of languages continued. In Europe, attention was given almost exclusively to classical Latin rather than to the living languages spoken by the various peoples. By contrast, Arab grammarians furnished excellent descriptions of their own language.

Although the roots of modern linguistics go back to the end of the eighteenth century, most of the revolutionary developments did not come about until the beginning of the twentieth, around the same time anthropology was coming into its own (as we saw in Chapter 1). To simplify matters considerably, one may say that the first half of the 1900s was characterized primarily by structural and descriptive approaches in the study of language: *structural* because language—any language—was considered to be a complex system of elements that were interrelated and could be studied and analyzed only as such; *descriptive* because the aim was to describe actual usage rather than what, according to a traditionalist view, usage ought to be. During the second half of the 1900s, linguistics departed radically from these earlier approaches as a result of the contribution of the American linguist Noam Chomsky, whose theoretical perspective and methodology are referred to as **generative** or **transformational** (or transformational-generative) **grammar**.

Using the descriptive approach, linguistic analysts would begin by writing down words and phrases of a language phonetically, and when sufficient phonetic data had been collected, proceed to determine the phonemes of the language. Once they had completed phonemic analysis and devised transcription, the analysts would phonemically transcribe words, phrases, sentences, and entire utterances in order to understand the morphology of the language as well as the meanings of its different morphemes. Sentence structure would usually receive only secondary attention.

One of the early techniques structural linguists *did* use to examine sentences and morphemes was **constituent analysis**. Basically, constituent analysis provides various tools to allow us to try to find the smallest linguistic elements. Grammatical analysis consisted of dissecting forms until the ultimate smallest units were arrived at. For example, the term *unhelpfulness* could be bracketed by steps into (unhelpful+ness), then (un+[(helpful)+ness]), then (un+[([help]+[ful])+ness]). This demonstrates two things: the constituent parts of this example are *un*, *help*, *ful*, and *ness*, and (2) there are only certain ways these parts can co-occur; *unhelp*, for example, is precluded. This is a simple (and obvious) example, of course, but constituent analysis can be very useful when working on more complex cases or with unknown languages. Such devices also did things earlier techniques could not do. For example, constituent analysis could clarify a phrase like *old men and women*, seeing if it meant "old men and women of any age" or "old men and old women": ([old men] and women) versus (old [men and women]).

But problems remained, and many sentences could not be clarified this way. *Visiting relatives can be a nuisance* became a famous commonly cited example. This sentence remains ambiguous because the elements are not contiguous, so no amount of constituent analysis will help. Cutting and bracketing will never reveal whether it is the relatives who are a pain to have around, or it is our having to go visit them that is bothersome. So, in contrast to this way of thinking, linguists doing transformational-generative grammar would proceed the other way around, going from the sentence back to its various constituents.

Let us consider the following pair of sentences: "Father is eager to please" and "Father is easy to please." The structure of both sentences appears to be the same, and in an analysis concerned with listing morphemes and their arrangements the two would be considered very much alike. Yet they are fundamentally different: in the first one, it is Father who is doing the pleasing and is the subject of the sentence, whereas in the second Father is the person being pleased and therefore the underlying object. If one changes the sentences from active to passive voice, "Father is easily pleased" is acceptable as grammatical and meaningful, but "Father is eagerly pleased" is clearly not. Although the superficial, or surface, structure of the two original sentences is much the same, there is a basic difference between them, and it can only result from differences in their deep structure. It appears, then, that the mere listing of morphemes and their arrangement in sentences is not enough to account for the differences that may obtain between them.

To write the generative grammar of a language, then, is to develop a finite device—a limited set of rules, the fewer the better—capable of generating an infinite number of correct and well-formed grammatical sentences in that language. For example, generating the sentence *The stream carries the boat* can be viewed as applying a successive series of **rewrite rules**. Generative grammar assumes the existence of several basic categories and conventions to modify and change them. Some of these categories are NOUNs, VERBs, and ARTICLEs. The grammar consists of a series of these rules, which expand in a formal way the basic categories and phrases. Consider this "grammar":

1. S → NP VP
2. VP → V NP
3. NP → Art N
4. N → {*stream*, *boat*}
5. Art → {*the*}
6. V → {*carries*}

What this gives is a set of steps to show how the sentence *The stream carries the boat* came about. Rule 1 says that all sentences in English consist of an NP and a VP—that is, a noun phrase and a verb phrase, similar to the "subject" and "predicate" in old grammar books. Rule 2 says a VP can be rewritten as a verb (V) and a noun phrase (NP). Rule 3 says a noun (NP) can be rewritten as an article (Art) and a noun (N). At this point we add the lexicon, the actual words our grammar can use. Here in the simple example, we say nouns can be *stream* or *boat*, the verb is *carries*, and the article is *the*. The elegance of the system comes through when we start adding to the lexicon or modifying or adding rules. For example, if we add another Art, *a*, the grammar already expands rapidly: *The stream carries a boat*, *A stream carries the boat*, and so on. If we add a few more nouns (e.g., *car*, *people*) and verbs (e.g., *capsizes*), we have already created the possibility of generating hundreds of new sentences just by following the few simple rules: *The stream capsizes a boat*, *The car carries the people*, *A steam capsizes a car*, and so on.

Our grammar is not yet finished. For example, we must add a few rules to make sure certain ill-formed sentences won't be generated (e.g., *The car carries the stream*). This is not hard to do, at least initially. Also, we will no doubt want to add a few more rules—often called **transformational rules**—to make our grammar do even more things (like create interrogative sentences, commands, or passives). We call these *transformational* rules because we take some simple or basic sentence (e.g., *He walks to the store*) and apply one of these rules to it to derive some other kind of sentence. Our rule, for example, might be "Take the final *-s* of a verb and transform it into *-ed* to get the past tense." That would make our sample sentence *He walked to the store*. Transformational rules are productive; that is, they can be used repeatedly, and in many new cases (e.g., *Joe talked about this every day* can come from *Joe talks about this every day* or *She touched the cat* from *She touches the cat)*. In formal linguistic analysis these rules are formed more precisely than is presented here, but the idea is fundamentally the same.

Although modified greatly since its introduction in the 1960s, Chomsky's generative project has remained true to its initial principles, as we saw in Chapter 2. But to write a complete generative grammar for a language is a very tall order even for professional linguists, and it is one reason our coverage of this type of grammar has been so brief. Another reason is that at this point, transformational-generative grammar is not a tool that most linguistic anthropologists are able to use or would profit from using. For example, this type of analysis would likely not lend itself well to the examination of the Navajo cosmology we described in the beginning of the chapter. Nor would many generative grammarians be as excited about studying the language-in-use problems that Witherspoon addressed in Box 4.1. The semantic component in transformational-generative grammar has not yet been fully charted. However, if lexical semantic structure can be significantly related to the structure of the corresponding culture, then future research in this area could be of special interest to linguistic anthropologists.

## SUMMARY AND CONCLUSIONS

Morphology is the study and description of word formation. The principal unit of morphology is the morpheme, the smallest meaningful part of language. There are thousands of morphemes in any language: Those that may be used by themselves are termed free; those that occur only attached to other morphemes are termed bound. Many morphemes have more than one phonemic shape; the variant forms of a morpheme are its allomorphs. Grammar—the various rules that govern the workings of a language and the processes that implement these rules—varies from one language to the next. Some languages are characterized by many inflectional forms (for example, Latin), others by relatively few (for example, English). The complexity of grammar, however, does not add to the prestige of a language. The study of the phonemic differences among allomorphs of the same morpheme is referred to as morphophonemics. The plural morpheme of English nouns has a variety of allomorphs; one may therefore speak of the morphophonemic rules of English noun pluralization.

Sentences are the largest structural units of a language, and their study in the traditional conception is called syntax. In transformational-generative grammar, syntax refers not only to sentence structure but to word structure as well. In this approach, the syntactic component is one of three major organizational units of a grammar, the others being the phonological and the semantic components. Having to do with the structure of meaning, the semantic component has been the last to be studied in modern linguistics and the one worked out in least detail.

The interest of structuralists and descriptivists in linguistic variety the world over has long been shared by linguistic anthropologists, many of whom deal with unwritten languages of little-known peoples. Before the introduction of transformational grammar, the approach to the study of language was somewhat mechanical because it was concerned primarily with items (units) and their arrangement. Chomsky, the founder of transformational-generative grammar, has both posed and attempted to answer new questions concerning language, many of which are of great importance. For example, how is it possible that already at an early age individuals know as much about their native languages as they do without any formal learning? According to Chomsky, one must assume that children are born with a knowledge of what can be termed

**Photo 4.1 Gary Witherspoon and his wife, Nellie, at their Navaho wedding. Courtesy of Gary Witherspoon.**

universal grammar, in other words, that universal grammar is part of our human biological endowment. What the speakers of a particular language must learn, of course, are the specifics of the language they are acquiring (for example, the lexicon).

Linguistic anthropologists are primarily interested in understanding language within the overall matrix of culture, and speech as an inseparable link to social behavior. But even though they are not so much concerned with linguistic structure as such, they are obviously influenced by the latest developments in linguistic theories and methods because of their interest in the speech of those whose cultures they study.

## RESOURCE MANUAL AND STUDY GUIDE

### Questions for Discussion

1. The relationship between phonemes and morphemes of a language could be likened to the relationship between the atoms of naturally occurring elements and the molecules of compounds formed by their chemical union. Explain the nature of the similarity.
2. English has become the language of the world not only because it is the native or official language of many millions of people, but for structural reasons as well. Explain this assertion.
3. Explain the basic differences between the descriptive and generative (or transformational) approaches to analyzing languages.

### Objective Study Questions

**TRUE-FALSE TEST**

T F 1. Native speakers who do not observe the proper grammatical rules (they may say, for example, "I ain't" or "he don't know nothing") are not used as informants by linguists and linguistic anthropologists.

T F 2. The study of phonemic differences between various forms of a morpheme is termed *morphophonemics*.

T F 3. Morphology is the study of the origin of words.

T F 4. Linguistic units that have a meaning but contain no smaller meaningful parts are called morphemes.

T F 5. One major advantage that transformational/generative grammar has over a purely descriptive grammar is that it can show how new sentences can be derived from basic ones.

**MULTIPLE-CHOICE QUESTIONS**

____ 1. How many different morphemes (not how many morphemes) are there in the following sentence: "She cooks tasty soups and stews."? (A) 7 (B) 8 (C) 9 (D) 10.

____ 2. What is the total number of morphemes in the preceding sentence? (A) 7 (B) 8 (C) 9 (D) 10.

____ 3. The English word undesirable contains (A) one prefix. (B) one suffix. (C) two affixes. (D) three affixes. (E) Two of the above choices apply. (F) Three of the above choices, A–D, apply.

____ 4. Which of the English words listed below has a zero allomorph of the plural morpheme? (A) syllabus. (B) mouse. (C) ox. (D) sheep. (E) zero.

____ 5. The sentence "Dogs bite thieves" contains (A) three free morphemes. (B) one bound morpheme. (C) two bound morphemes. (D) Only one of the three choices above applies. (E) Two of the three choices above, A–C, apply.

**COMPLETIONS**

1. What kind of morpheme (allomorph) is exemplified by a change rather than an addition, as in the pluralization of *mouse* to *mice*? It is a __________ morpheme (one word).
2. In Latin, the arrangement of words in a sentence does not indicate which noun is the subject and which is the object, but rather is used to show ______________ (one word).

## *Problems*

### SOME TECHNIQUES FOR SOLVING MORPHOLOGY PROBLEMS

Below we show how one might go about doing morphemic or syntactic analysis. This is an area in which experience and intuition count for much, and one gets much better with practice, which is why we have included the problems here. There usually is no right or wrong answer—just better or more judicious ways of accounting for the data at hand. And that also means that any conclusion will be tentative; the next set of data we see may force us to change our previous hypotheses.

There is no recipe for solving the kind of problems at the end of the chapter. Maybe think of them as a game—a glorified crossword puzzle, and something to do for fun.

**Sample Problem 1**: Let's start with this small data set from Indonesian. How are plurals formed?

| *orang* | person | *orangorang* | people |
|---|---|---|---|
| *buku* | book | *bukubuku* | books |
| *kucˇing* | cat | *kucˇingkucˇing* | cats |
| *babi* | pig | *babibabi* | pigs |

It seems pretty straightforward to see that reduplication is how plurals are constructed. One just says the singular form a second time. Note, however, that more data would indicate that reduplication here only implies plurality. For example, *orangorang* means "two or more people." Saying the noun a third time (e.g., *orang orang orang*) would not mean "three people."

**Sample Problem 2**: Here are some data from Bontok, a language spoken in the Philippines (Gleason 1967:29). Recall, we saw some examples from Bontok in Chapter 2.

| *fikas* | strong | *fumikas* | he is becoming strong |
|---|---|---|---|
| *kilad* | red | *kumilad* | he is becoming red |
| *bato* | stone | *bumato* | he is becoming a stone |
| *fusul* | enemy | *fumusul* | he is becoming an enemy |

How do we say "he is becoming . . . "? Brief inspection shows that *fikas* and *fumikas* only differ by the *-um-* being inserted after the first sound of the word: *fikas* → *f-um-ikas*. This hypothesis holds for all the other cases in the data set. This type of morpheme is called an infix, because it occurs inside the root form (just as PRE-fixes occur at the beginning, and SUF-fixes occur at the end, of words).

**Sample Problem 3:** This Hebrew example (Hockett 1958) is a little harder but can be worked through methodically.

| *zəkartiihuu* | *zəkarnuuhuu* |
|---|---|
| I remembered him | We remembered him |
| *zəkartiihaa* | *zəkarnuuhaa* |
| I remembered her | We remembered her |
| *zəkartiikaa* | *zəkarnuukau* |
| I remembered them | We remembered them |

Find the English glosses, and state how a Hebrew sentence might be constructed. How do we start? We could begin by noticing that the sentences in the first group to the left differ only in their final forms *-huu*, *-haa*, and *-kaa*. Our initial hypothesis, then, might be that these three forms represent the English direct objects "him," "her," and "them," respectively. Assuming this is true, and including now the second group of sentences, we see that the top two sentences differ only by the infix *-tii-* versus *-nuu-*. Thus we might hypothesize that *-tii-* refers to the first-person pronoun ("I") and *-uu-* to the second-person pronoun ("we"). Checking the other two pairs gives us no reason to alter this hypothesis. So that leaves us with *zəkar-* as the verb form, "remembered." So we can also hypothesize that sentences are structured as

VERB FORM + SUBJECT PRONOUN + OBJECT PRONOUN

Because our data set is small, we have to be ready to change things in light of new information. But if we heard a sentence like *qətaltiihuu* and were told it meant "I killed him," we would have good reason to suspect that our initial hypothesis was correct, and that *qətal-* meant "killed."

**PROBLEM 1**

Based on Langacker (1972), this problem is taken from Luiseño, a Uto-Aztecan language spoken in southwestern California. [ʔ] is the glottal stop; [q] is a postvelar voiceless stop (similar to [k] but articulated farther back in the mouth); long vowels are written as a sequence of two vowel symbols; the stress, [ˊ], is marked only on the first of two adjacent vowels. From the following data—to be taken as representative of the language—isolate Luiseño morphemes and provide each with an English gloss (a brief translation to indicate meaning).

| | | |
|---|---|---|
| 1. | nóo wukálaq | "I am walking" |
| 2. | nóo páaʔiq | "I am drinking" |
| 3. | nóo páaʔin | "I will drink" |
| 4. | temét čáami páaʔivičunin | "The sun will make us want to drink" |
| 5. | nóo póy wukálavičuniq | "I am making him want to walk" |
| 6. | nóo páaʔivičuq | "I want to drink" |
| 7. | temét póy wukálavičuniq | "The sun is making him want to walk" |

**PROBLEM 2**

Based on Zepeda (1983), this problem is from Tohono O'odham (formerly referred to as Papago), a Uto-Aztecan language spoken in southern Arizona and northwestern Mexico. [ʔ] is the glottal stop and [ñ] is pronounced like the ñ in the English word piñon, also spelled pinyon. On the basis of the third-person singular verb forms in Column A and the plural forms in Column B, how would you describe in general terms the process of pluralization of the verb forms in Column A?

| | A | | B |
|---|---|---|---|
| 1. | ñeok | "speaks" | ñeñeok |
| 2. | ʔul | "sticks out" | ʔuʔul |
| 3. | helwuin | "is sliding" | hehelwuin |
| 4. | him | "walks" | hihim |
| 5. | dagkon | "wipes" | dadagkon |

**PROBLEM 3**

The regular English past tense morpheme has three allomorphs: /-d/ as in *begged*, /-t/ as in *chirped*, and /-əd/ as in *guided*. The third-person singular morpheme also has three allomorphs: /-z/ as in *goes* or *begs*, /-s/ as in *chirps*, and /-əz/ as in *houses*. Describe the environments in which the allomorphs of each of the two morphemes occur.

## PROBLEM 4

Based on Merrifield et al. (1967), this problem is taken from Sierra Popoluca, a Mixe-Zoque language spoken in about two dozen villages and settlements in the state of Veracruz, Mexico. The raised dot [·] after a vowel marks vowel length; [ʌ] is a central unrounded vowel; [ʔ] is the glottal stop; [ŋ] is a velar nasal (similar to *ng* in *sing* or *king*); and [$t^y$], [č], [š], [ñ], and [y] are palato-alveolars—a voiceless stop, an affricate, a fricative, a nasal, and a semivowel, respectively. From the following data, list the allomorphs of the morpheme marking that corresponds to the English gloss "my" and then state the rules that govern the morphophonemics of this prefix.

| | | | | | |
|---|---|---|---|---|---|
| 1. | co·goy | "liver" | 21. | anco·goy | "my liver" |
| 2. | čikši | "itch" | 22. | añčikši | "my itch" |
| 3. | ha·ya | "husband" | 23. | anha·ya | "my husband" |
| 4. | he·pe | "cup" | 24. | anhe·pe | "my cup" |
| 5. | kawah | "horse" | 25. | aŋkawah | "my horse" |
| 6. | kʌ·pi | "firewood" | 26. | aŋkʌ·pi | "my firewood" |
| 7. | me·me | "butterfly" | 27. | amme·me | "my butterfly" |
| 8. | me·sah | "table" | 28. | amme·sah | "my table" |
| 9. | nʌc | "armadillo" | 29. | annʌc | "my armadillo" |
| 10. | nʌ·yi | "name" | 30. | annʌ·yi | "my name" |
| 11. | petkuy | "broom" | 31. | ampetkuy | "my broom" |
| 12. | piyu | "hen" | 32. | ampiyu | "my hen" |
| 13. | suskuy | "whistle" | 33. | ansuskuy | "my whistle" |
| 14. | suuŋ | "cooking pot" | 34. | ansuuŋ | "my cooking pot" |
| 15. | sapun | "soap" | 35. | añšapun | "my soap" |
| 16. | siʔmpa | "bamboo" | 36. | añšiʔmpa | "my bamboo" |
| 17. | tʌk | "house" | 37. | antʌk | "my house" |
| 18. | $t^y$aka | "chick" | 38. | añ$t^y$aka | "my chick" |
| 19. | wʌčo·mo | "wife" | 39. | aŋwʌčo·mo | "my wife" |
| 20. | yemkuy | "fan" | 40. | añyemkuy | "my fan" |

## PROBLEM 5

Based on Fromkin and Rodman (1988), this problem is taken from Samoan. Samoan is a member of the Austronesian language family.

| | | | | | |
|---|---|---|---|---|---|
| 1. | manao | "he wishes" | 8. | mananao | "they wish" |
| 2. | matua | "he is old" | 9. | matutua | "they are old" |
| 3. | malosi | "he is strong" | 10. | malolosi | "they are strong" |
| 4. | punou | "he bends" | 11. | punonou | "they bend" |
| 5. | atamaki | "he is wise" | 12. | atamamaki | "they are wise" |
| 6. | savali | "he travels" | 13. | pepese | "they sing" |
| 7. | laga | "he weaves" | | | |

Given the preceding data, what Samoan words would you expect for the following:
he sings ________________________, they weave ________________________ they travel ____________________?

## PROBLEM 6

The following data are from the Aztec dialect heard in Veracruz, Mexico:

| | | | | | |
|---|---|---|---|---|---|
| 1. | ničoka | "I cry" | 5. | timayana | "you (sing.) are hungry" |

| | | |
|---|---|---|
| 2. ničoka? "I cried" | 6. nimayanas | "I will be hungry" |
| 3. nimayana "I am hungry" | 7. tičoka | "you (sing.) cry" |
| 4. nimayana? "I was hungry" | 8. ničokas | "I will cry" |

Consider the morpheme marking the first person singular: Is it a prefix? ______ Or a suffix? ______ What is its form? ______ What is the form of the morpheme marking the present tense? _______ The past tense? _________ The future tense? _________What is the form of the stem meaning "cry"? _________ Consider the morpheme marking the second-person singular: What is its form? ________________

**PROBLEM 7**

Here are ten English words, written in traditional orthography:

| | | | | |
|---|---|---|---|---|
| 1. rewriting | 3. tasteless | 5. illegally | 7. carefully | 9. immobile |
| 2. fearfully | 4. carelessly | 6. hopelessly | 8. irretrievable | 10. immorally |

How many *different* (not how *many*) prefixes do these ten words display? ___ (give the number)
How many allomorphs of one particular prefix are shown? ___ (give the number)
How many *different* suffixes are shown? ___ (give the number)
How many *different* stems are shown? ___ (give the number)

## Answer Key

True-false test: 1-F, 2-T, 3-F, 4-T, 5-T
Multiple-choice questions: 1-C, 2-D, 3-F, 4-D, 5-E
Completions: 1. process, 2. emphasis

*Problem 1.* Morphemes are obtained by comparing words or sentences that appear to differ only by a single difference in meaning (as judged from the English glosses)—for example, 2 and 3 (they differ only in the tense—present as against future). Morphemes representing grammatical meanings (in this case present tense and future tense) are usually glossed in capital letters.

| *Luiseño Morphemes* | *English Glosses* |
|---|---|
| nóo | I |
| póy | him |
| čáami | us |
| q | PRESENT |
| n | FUTURE |
| ni | make |
| viču | want |
| wukála | walk |
| páa?i | drink |
| temét | sun |

*Problem 2.* The Tohono O'odham verb forms are pluralized by adding a prefix to the singular; the form of the prefix is the initial consonant and the following vowel of the singular verb form.

*Problem 3.* Allomorphs of the past tense morpheme: /-əd/ if the base ends in /t, d /; /-t/ if it ends in /p, k, č, f, θ, s, š/; and /-d/ if it ends in any other sound. Allomorphs of the third-person singular morpheme: /-əz/ if the base ends in /s, z, š, ž, č, ǰ /; /-z/ if it ends in any voiced sound except /z, ž, ǰ/; and /-s / if it ends in any voiceless sound except /s, š, č/.

*Problem 4.* The stems or roots are listed under 1–20. The first-person singular possessive uses the prefix *an-*. The morphophonemics of this prefix may be stated as follows: the *n* of the prefix *an-* becomes *m* when the initial consonant of the stem or root that follows is *m* or *p*. Concisely written:

n→m/__ m, p (that is, *n* becomes *m* before *m* or *p* [bilabials]) (as in 27, 28, 31, and 32)
n→ñ/__ y, č, š, $t^y$ (palato-alveolars) (as in 22, 35, 36, 38, and 40)
n→ŋ/__ k, w (as in 25, 26, and 39)
n→n/__ t, c, s, n, h (= elsewhere) (as in 21, 23, 24, 29, 30, 33, 34, and 37)

*Problem 5.* The third-person singular of Samoan verbs is pluralized by a morpheme whose form is derived from the singular form by reduplication (repetition) of the penultimate (next to the last) vowel and the preceding consonant. (This may be a better way of stating the rule than using the phrase "penultimate syllable" because one should then define the term "syllable" for Samoan.) Under this rule, "he sings" would be *pese,* "they weave" *lalaga,* and "they travel" *savavali.*

*Problem 6.* By comparing words 1–4, 6, and 8, we see that they all share the prefix *ni-*that corresponds to "I" in the English glosses. By comparing words 1 and 7, we obtain the prefix *ti-* "you (sing)," and by comparing words 1, 2, and 8, we obtain the suffixes *-ʔ* PAST TENSE and *-s* FUTURE TENSE; it appears that PRESENT TENSE is not marked, that is, it is marked by a zero (Ø) morpheme (absence of a sound). If one detaches all prefixes and/or suffixes from words 1, 2, 7, and 8, what is left is čoka, the stem of the word meaning "cry."

*Problem 7.* This problem is somewhat simplified. In order not to confuse students by using phonemic transcriptions, all words are written in the traditional orthography. The ten English words display two *different* prefixes, *re-* and *iC-* (*C* stands for a consonant). The prefix (morpheme) *re-* means "again" (as in 1) and the prefix *iC-* "not" (as in 5, 8–10). The latter prefix occurs in this sample in three allomorphs (forms of a morpheme): as *-im* in 9 and 10, *ir-* in 8, and *il-* in 5. The most common allomorph of this morpheme, *in-* (as in "indecent," "incapable," or "inimitable"), is not represented in this sample.

Four suffixes are shown: *-ing, -ly, -less,* and *-able.* The sample contains ten different stems: *care, fear, full, hope, taste, write, legal, mobile, moral,* and *retrieve.* (Note: *re-* in *retrieve* cannot be considered in the *synchronic* analysis of Modern English as a prefix, because there is no stem *trieve*; diachronically, it comes from the Anglo-French *retrueve-* "to find again.")

## Notes and Suggestions for Further Reading

There are numerous excellent texts on linguistic anthropology (e.g., Bonvillain 2013; Ottenheimer 2013a; Ahearn 2017) and linguistics (e.g., Fromkin, Rodman, and Hyams 2010; Yule 2010; Akmajian, Demers, Farmer, and Harnish 2010; O'Grady, Archibald, Aronoff, and Rees-Miller 2009; McGregor 2010) dealing with the topics of this chapter. Most of these books have problem sets that can be quite useful. Other excellent samples of problems and exercises are found in Merrifield, Naish, Rensch, and Story (2003); Mihalicek and Wilson (2011), or Dawson and Phelan (2016); Ottenheimer (2013b); Farmer and Demers (2010); and Bickford (1998). Other references to textbooks of linguistics may be found in the notes to Chapter 3. Those seeking a kinder, gentler introduction can look at Burton, Dechaine, and Vatikiotis-Bateson (2012); though ostensibly for *Dummies*, its treatment is sound if a bit light.

The Chontal examples are from Waterhouse (1962), the Isthmus Nahuat examples from Law (1958), and the Samoan examples from Fromkin and Rodman (1988).

The publication by Chomsky that proved to be a turning point in modern linguistics is *Syntactic Structures* (1957). Other writings by Chomsky include *Aspects of the Theory of Syntax* (1965), *Language and Mind* (1972), and *Lectures on Government and Binding* (1993). A good introduction to Chomsky's contributions to linguistics and transformational grammar is Lyons (1978), as are Radford (1988, 1997, and 2006). Carnie (2011); Adger (2003); and Cook and Newson (2007) discuss some of the newer directions Chomsky has taken in his syntactical analysis. For the ambitious, *Chomsky's Linguistics* (2012), edited by Peter Graff, gives over seven hundred pages of Chomsky in all his flavors (plus commentary); the less ambitious can consult McGilvray's 2005 edited collection. Although technical, beginning students will still find much of interest. For a delightful introduction to Chomsky's views on language, in which his philosophy is most approachable, see Chomsky and Chomsky (2012).

# 5

# Communicating Nonverbally

## LEARNING OBJECTIVES

- Explain how and when writing developed in different parts of the world
- Describe various strategies people have used to put speech down on paper (or other medium)
- Clarify how alphabets and syllabaries differ
- Discuss how extra "nonverbal" features contribute to communication
- Notice how different cultures/languages think about space, posture, and gestures
- Argue that deaf sign languages are as "real" as a spoken language

Spoken language—speech—is by far the most common and important means by which humans communicate with one another, but it is not the only one. The many different writing systems used throughout the world are of tremendous importance for communication, having in some respects an advantage over spoken language, especially their relative permanence.

The term **nonverbal communication**, taken literally, refers to the transmission of signals accomplished by means other than spoken words. Not everyone agrees on what the term encompasses, and some even question whether nonverbal communication is definable. Used broadly, the term includes bodily gestures, facial expressions, spacing, touch, and smell, as well as whistle, smoke-signal, and drum "languages," and such optional vocal effects as those that accompany spoken utterances and can be considered apart from actual words. In this chapter we will examine these features of communication, as well as looking at various written forms of language, in particular the origins and types of orthographies found throughout the world.

Nonverbal systems of communication may be divided into those that are derived from spoken language and those that are independent of it. With only a few exceptions, writing systems belong to the first category, representing as they do the sounds of speech. In turn, writing systems may serve as the source of other systems. The English word written as *tree* can be transmitted in the International Morse Code by audible or visual signals as –·–· · ·, with –, ·–·, and · representing, respectively, the letters *t*, *r*, and *e*.

Some sign languages are independent of speech. Because some *are* independent, it was possible for the Plains Indians to use sign language as a means of effective communication among tribes speaking different, and many times even unrelated, languages.

For the most part, human communication is a multichannel affair operating on verbal and nonverbal levels. Regardless of the society, it is not only how people talk and what they say but also how they present themselves to others that seems to make a difference as to how they are perceived. The study of the properties of signs and symbols and their functions in communication is referred to as **semiotics**. Because of the increasing attention given to all modes of communication in humans and other animals, the field of semiotics has been steadily growing in volume and popularity. Among the subfields of semiotics are biosemiotics, the semiotic study of living systems; semiotics of food, because the preparation of food transforms its meaning and also because certain foods can be symbolic of specific social codes; and social semiotics, which includes the interpretation of such cultural codes as fashion and advertising.

## PARALINGUISTICS

Characteristics of vocal communication considered marginal or optional and therefore excludable from linguistic analysis are referred to as **paralanguage**. The most common paralinguistic features are usually assigned to three categories.

**Voice qualifiers** have to do with the tone of voice and pacing of speech, and they include variations in volume or intensity (for example, overloud, oversoft), pitch (noticeably high, noticeably low), tempo (overly fast, overly slow), and articulation (for example, drawling, clipping, or rasping).

Besides these and other voice qualifiers, there are various **voice characterizers** that accompany speech or, more precisely, through which one talks. These range from laughing and giggling to crying and sobbing to yelling, moaning, groaning, whimpering, and whining.

And then there are the so-called **vocal segregates**, represented for the most part by such extralinguistic sounds (that is, sounds not part of the phonemic system) as the ones graphically represented in English texts as *uh-huh* to indicate agreement or gratification, *uh-uh* to indicate disagreement, *tsk-tsk* to express mild disapproval, and other graphic approximations of different kinds of snorts and sniffs.

Here are some concrete examples of paralinguistic behavior: highly controlled articulation produces the crisp, precise pronunciation expected of formal pronouncements addressed to large audiences; by contrast, speech so relaxed as to become slurred is heard from those who are very tired, sleepy, or under the influence of alcohol or other drugs. Speakers of English and other languages tend to associate extreme pitch variation with happiness and surprise; high pitch level or fast tempo with fear, surprise, or anger; and low pitch level or slow tempo with boredom and sadness. The rounding of lips imparts to the voice the cooing quality that is frequently used by adults when talking to a baby.

As an additional example, consider whispering. A person may whisper to avoid waking up others who are napping or sleeping (an example of thoughtful behavior); to avoid being overheard (consideration of privacy); to convey a secret or a conspiracy; or to spread rumors of an intimate nature about someone (hence the phrase "whispering campaign").

In the discussion of speech, one may be tempted to consider silence, or forbearance from speech, not worth mentioning. However, that would be a mistake. Depending on the context, silence can indicate a variety of meanings or feelings. In a tense situation, silence can be threatening if it is used deliberately instead of an appeasing remark; by contrast, it may help to lessen tension by withholding a comment that could worsen a situation. Silence may also express one's uncertainty about an issue or help to avoid an argument. It may be a gentle substitute for saying "no," as when a young man asks "Will you marry me?" and no response is forthcoming. Some of these and other uses of silence are by no means universal; they may vary somewhat, or even quite deeply, from culture to culture.

## KINESICS

Just as any speech that is not neutral tends to be accompanied by one or more paralinguistic features, it is also likely to be supplemented by visual gestures. This is the subject of **kinesics**, the study of **body language**.

There is no question that bodily gestures (in the broadest sense) serve as an important means of communication. Comedians are notably adept at slanting, canceling, or completely turning around the meaning of their spoken lines with a well-chosen grimace or gesture of different communicative content, and professional mimes know how to move their audiences to tears or laughter without uttering a single word. But speech-related body motions are by no means limited to performers—they are an integral part of everyone's daily communicative activity.

The basic assumption that underlies kinesics is that no body movement or facial expression is likely to lack meaning because, just like other aspects of voluntary human behavior, body movements, posture, and facial expressions are patterned and occur together. For example, accidental meetings of good male friends are commonly characterized by a brief raise of hand first, then a firm handshake, a brief raising of eyebrows, and a smile.

Influenced by structural linguistics, Ray L. Birdwhistell (1918–1997) in the 1950s developed a method of studying and describing the body-motion aspects of human communicative behavior by means of units that parallel those employed in linguistic analysis. One such unit, the **kineme** (analogous to the phoneme), has been defined as the smallest discriminable contrastive unit of body motion.

Students of kinesics take note of several basic components, all of which are associated: facial expression, eye contact, body posture, and hand gestures. Facial expressions signal a wide range of emotions from pleasure, happiness, and pleasant surprise to suspicion, sadness, fear, anger, disapproval, or disgust—to list only the most common feelings.

The nature of eye contact between people in face-to-face interaction varies not only from culture to culture but also within the same society (particularly such a large society as our own) from one individual to the next according to the experience, age, self-confidence, and intentions of the communicator. Eye contacts therefore range all the way from avoidance to the look of a person who is in love.

Types of hand gestures are too many to classify in this brief survey, and only two are mentioned for illustration. First, emphatic use of arms or wrists in the air can serve to emphasize what is being said. Second, handshakes are very common cross-culturally as a sign of greeting; but this can be accomplished in a variety of ways. The hands can be combined together, and one's second hand can be used to impart emphasis to the handshake. Handshaking may be elevated to hand clasping, arm clasping, shoulder clasping, or shoulder embracing. All these gestures involve touching behavior, and that is culture-specific.

Body posture conveys the individual's attitude to the face-to-face interaction he or she is participating in: it can signal feelings ranging from interest, concern, or anticipation to boredom, depression, or impatience. During some ritual occasions, of course, specific body postures are expected or required—for example, kneeling, standing, or bowing.

Observant travelers noticed centuries ago that members of societies along the Mediterranean Sea used many more bodily gestures and facial expressions than, say, those living in Scandinavia or Japan. However, not all Italians, for example, use the same "body language," just as they do not all speak the same dialect of Italian. Birdwhistell offered an interesting example in support of the expectation that kinesic behavior is likely to be just as culture-specific as the corresponding language. He reported that even when the sound is removed from films made back in the 1930s and 1940s of the speeches of the late politician and mayor of New York City Fiorello La Guardia, it is possible to tell whether he is speaking English, Yiddish, or Italian, as characteristic body motions are associated with each language (Birdwhistell 1970:102). Although the holistic and contextual approach to communication that Birdwhistell advocated has been uniformly accepted, the extent to which "body language" can be analyzed in terms of his units remains controversial, in part because the detailed transcription he designed is far too complicated and time-consuming.

## PROXEMICS

In the early 1960s, the interdependence between communication and culture stimulated Edward Hall to develop **proxemics**, the study of the cultural patterning of the spatial separation individuals maintain in face-to-face encounters. The term has subsequently come to embrace studies concerned with privacy, crowding, territoriality, and the designing of buildings, private as well as public, with the view of meeting the different cultural expectations of their prospective users.

According to Hall, the distances individuals maintain from one another depend on the nature of their mutual involvement and are culture-specific. For example, under normal circumstances, middle-class American adults of northern European heritage make regular use of four **proxemic zones**, or distances, ranging from intimate to public, each of the zones consisting of a close and a far phase.

In the close phase of the intimate distance, the individuals are close enough to be encircled by each other's arms. all senses are engaged: Each individual receives the body heat as well as any odor or scent emanating from the other individual, and the other person's breath is felt; because of the closeness, vision may be blurred or distorted and speaking is at a minimum. As is obvious, this narrowest of all interpersonal distances is suited to lovemaking, protecting, or comforting.

By contrast, business is transacted at the social-consultative distance: The close phase is characteristic of contact among people who work together or are participants at casual social gatherings; the far phase characterizes more formal business transactions, such as interviews or situations in which two or more people find themselves in the same space and do not want to appear rude by not communicating. For instance, receptionists who are also expected to type and manage a switchboard must have enough space between them and the visitors to permit them to work rather than to feel they must engage in polite conversation with those waiting to be seen.

The manner in which members of different societies space themselves in each other's presence varies along a contact-noncontact continuum. For example, Arabs, other Mediterranean peoples, and Latin Americans prefer spatially close interactions; northern Europeans prefer to keep their distance, literally and figuratively.

However, some differences in proxemic and **haptic behavior** (haptic behavior relates to the sense of touch) may be noticeable even among members of societies that live in close proximity. According to a recent study, Dutch dyads (two individuals) maintain greater distances than French and English dyads. And one would be justified in undertaking a study to determine whether people born and raised in southern France have the same proxemic and haptic behaviors as those who have grown up and made their homes in northern France.

Without being acquainted with Hall's proxemic matrix, people are aware when someone encroaches into their personal zone, or into the zone of someone on whom they think they have a special claim. An example of the latter would be a young male seeing his girlfriend being spoken to by another young male who is using the close personal zone that touches the intimate zone. The male who feels "threatened" is likely to join the talking couple to alter the proxemic situation.

Finally, it should be mentioned that personal space is occasionally modified by the conditions imposed by the physical situation in which people find themselves. For example, the fixed spacing of classroom desks may not be the most proxemically satisfactory for the thousands of foreign students who study in the United States.

## SIGN LANGUAGES

Signing, that is, communicating manually by **sign language** of some kind, is undoubtedly at least as old as speech. From the writings of ancient Greeks and Romans, we know that their deaf made use of signs. It is, however, reasonable to assume that even among the earliest humans, those who were not able to communicate orally would have used their hands to make themselves understood. Sign languages used to the exclusion of spoken language—for example, by people born deaf—are referred to as **primary**. Sign languages found in communities of speaker-hearers as regular or occasional substitutes for speech are termed **alternate sign languages**.

### *Sign Languages as True "Languages": The Style and Scope of Signing*

For many years, scholars neglected the study of sign languages, considering them as little more than crude substitutes for speech. Serious attention to sign languages dates back to the late 1950s; it was accompanied by renewed interest in the sign language of the Indians of the Great Plains.

In the United States, the hearing impaired use a combination of two signing systems. One is the manual alphabet, which is made up of signs representing the twenty-six letters of the English alphabet and the ampersand (&). It is finger spelled, using one hand only, and both the sender and receiver must be acquainted with the orthography of the language. (By contrast, the signs of the manual alphabet used in Great Britain and Northern Ireland are made with both hands.) In the other signing system, sign language proper, a particular sign stands for a concept, or, to put it in terms of spoken language, a word or a morpheme. A number of sign languages are in use in English-speaking countries, most involving some modification of either American Sign Language (ASL, or Ameslan) or British Sign Language (BSL). Ameslan offers its users more than 5,000 signs, with new ones coined as needed. It makes use of three-dimensional sign space that forms a "bubble" about the signer, extending roughly from the waist to the top of the head and outward from the extreme left to the extreme right as far as the signer can reach. Within the sign space, the user can specify time relationships, distinguish among several persons being signed about, signal questions and embedded clauses, and express a variety of grammatical categories such as plurality and degree (as in *good, better, best*) as well as aspectual differences of a verbal action such as habituality, repetition, intensity, and continuity. Head tilt, eyebrow and lip configuration and other body motions are frequently used to add to the expressive capacity of manual gestures.

Fluent use of signs can match the speed of an unhurried conversation, as can be seen from television programs in which speech is being translated into ASL for viewers who are hearing impaired. Finger spelling is considerably slower, but it is indispensable for proper names or concepts for which there are no signs (for example, chemical substances).

There are many different manual alphabets, just as there are many different writing systems; further, sign languages proper vary internally and among themselves, just as do the dialects of a spoken language and as one spoken language differs from another (see Box 5.1). Regardless of the particular sign language used, the majority of signs are not transparently **iconic**; that is, they cannot be interpreted by those who have not first learned their meanings.

If primary sign languages function much like spoken languages, do they also have duality of patterning? That is, are they analyzable at two levels of structural units comparable to phonemes and morphemes? According to William C. Stokoe Jr. (1960), who devoted many years of study to the sign language of the American deaf, Ameslan grammar has the same general form as the grammars of spoken languages. It is characterized by a small set of contrastive units meaningless in themselves (**cheremes**, on the analogy with phonemes) that combine to form meaningful sign units, the morphemes. Chereme refers to a set of positions, configurations, or motions that function identically in a given sign language. And each morpheme of a sign language may be defined according to hand shape, orientation of the palm and fingers, place of formation, movement and its direction, point of contact, and other spatial and dynamic features. Users of Ameslan and other natural sign languages are no more aware of cheremes than users of spoken English are of phonemes.

To sum up, contrary to popular misconceptions, primary sign languages used by the deaf are highly structured, complete, and independent communicative systems, comparable in complexity to spoken and written languages; otherwise they could not substitute for spoken languages as effectively as they do. Furthermore, they are natural languages in the sense that their acquisition is the automatic result of interaction with others who depend upon signing.

Alternate sign languages take a variety of forms, ranging from occupational sign languages, such as the one developed by sawmill workers in the northwestern United States and western Canada, to the performance sign language employed in the classical Hindu dance tradition, to monastic sign languages that make it possible for the members of orders who use them to observe the self-imposed rule of silence. The best-known alternate sign languages, however, are those used by the aboriginal peoples of various parts of Australia, and especially the system of signing developed by the tribes of the North American Plains, the most elaborate in the New World.

### *Native American Sign Languages*

For the earliest mention of sign language in North America we are indebted to Pedro de Castañeda de Nájera, the most widely read chronicler of the 1540–1542 Coronado expedition to what is today the US Southwest. His report described an encounter of the Spaniards with what probably was a band of Apaches (he referred to them as Querechos) along the present-day New Mexico–Texas border:

> These people were so skillful in the use of signs that it seemed as if they spoke. They made everything so clear that an interpreter was not necessary. They said that by going down in the direction in which the sun rises there was a very large river, that the army could travel along its bank through continuous settlements for ninety days, going from one settlement to another. They said that the first settlement was called Haxa, that the river was more than one league wide, and that there were many canoes (Hammond and Rey 1940:235–236).

Although frequently mentioned in the travel accounts of the early explorers west of the Mississippi, Plains Indian sign language has not yet received the attention it deserves, particularly as there remain only a very few individuals who are still proficient in it.

For a score of nomadic tribes whose spoken languages were either completely unrelated or related but mutually unintelligible, Plains Indian sign language is known to have been an effective means of intertribal communication in trade and other negotiations. Moreover, it was commonplace for members of a tribe to recount their war exploits or to "narrate" a long traditional tale exclusively by means of manual signs, and it is a matter of record that the Kiowa Indians gave General Hugh Lenox Scott a detailed account of their sun dance ceremony by using signs. Plains Indian sign language consisted of a large repertory of conventionalized gestures performed with one or both hands. The hands were either held stationary in various configurations or moved between the levels of just above the ground to over the signer's head. For example, to sign *snow* or *snowing*, both hands were extended in front of the face, all ten fingers pointing downward, and then lowered in whirling motions. Abstract concepts were conveyed with equal facility. The concept of *cold* or *winter* was conveyed by clenched hands with forearms crossed in front of the chest, accompanied by shivering movements. The idea of *badness* was indicated by a motion suggesting something being thrown away: the right fist held in front of the chest was swung out and down to the right as the hand was opening up.

Although the bulk of the signs must have been shared by the tribes of the north-central Plains, there were no doubt "dialectal" differences similar to those found in widely extended spoken languages. Unlike the whistle "languages," however, sign languages are independent of speech even though they have occasionally been used in combination with it. Only in manual alphabets is there a connection: a manual alphabet represents the elements of a writing system that in turn derives from speech.

## WRITING

Writing is very new in the course of human history. Of course, "writing" itself is hard to define. For example, there are pictures and pictographs from the famous Ice Age caves in France that go back some 20,000 years. Although many of these designs are apparently intentionally abstract, we probably would not consider them writing as we usually use the term. Any definition of writing will be arbitrary, as John DeFrancis points out (1989:4),

### BOX 5.1 INCLUDING SIGN LANGUAGES WITH THE WORLD'S OTHER 7,000 LANGUAGES IN THE *ETHNOLOGUE* DATABASE

Sign languages are not in the same category as all the other languages in *Ethnologue*, people say to me. What is the reason they are included right along with spoken languages? It's a fair question. And in fact, up until the eleventh edition, *Ethnologue* did not include any signed languages. But it might be surprising to learn how similar these languages are to "spoken" languages as they are often called. . . . For example: complexity. It will surprise some to learn that a fully developed sign language has a grammar that is just as complex as any other. . . . Can they truly be languages? People say, we don't read and write sign languages. Well, . . . [o]n the other hand, sign languages are not so different in this regard since in fact the majority of spoken languages have not been reduced to writing either. Some ask, aren't sign languages just hand motions that stand for words in the person's national language? No, signs stand for concepts just as words in a spoken language do. But they don't match up one for one. Some signs will have a range of meaning that covers several words; some words will need different signs depending on the context in which the word is used. And while there is a system for signing English, for example, and it uses quite a few of the same signs as American Sign Language, it's not a natural language. ASL has an entirely different grammar that is more natural, streamlined and fine-tuned for use in a visual medium. . . . Why so many sign languages then? . . . [And] how do we know that one sign language is different from another and deserves a separate entry? A good test is whether people can understand a video, or can understand a discussion going on in the other language variety when they are not part of the conversation. Another concern is whether there is an attitude of acceptance toward the other's signing. If so on both points, we count them as using dialects of the same language deserving only a single entry. . . . Often each country has its own, unique sign language. This comes about because a sign language develops

*continues*

because there will always be inclusivists who claim that writing is *any* system of graphic symbols that conveys *some* thought—like a mathematical formula—whereas exclusivists will say that writing must be a set of symbols that can convey *any and all* thought—like an alphabet for a language. Others claim that a writing system must not be independent of a particular language. We will not debate the issue here and will just say that for our purposes, writing is some form of "visible speech."

It is really impossible to say exactly when and where writing first began, but it appears to have diffused more than having been created independently. That is, writing systems developed in many parts of the world, but more cultures borrowed them than invented them. This shows that the connection between spoken sound and some arbitrary symbol placed on some medium is quite an abstraction, one not readily apparent to our distant ancestors, no matter how much we take it for granted today.

*continued*

naturally when deaf people come together, and because schools are not standardized across the world. Many schools for the deaf have been started by missionaries or other foreigners so there is often a link to the foreign sign language in the new. However as time goes by, new words and other innovations are added and now the challenge is to find out how much mutual intelligibility still exists between a new sign language and its source, and what attitudes exist. The sign language used in the Philippines is based on American Sign Language and is still very similar to it, for instance, but due to national pride, Filipino Sign Language is given a separate entry. Things like this happen in spoken languages too; Danish and Norwegian are mutually-intelligible but have separate entries. . . . Some countries have more than one signed language. The west of Panama signs differently from the east. In Nepal, besides Nepali Sign Language there are three "village sign languages" that we know about. Village sign languages are ones typically used by deaf and hearing alike when the population in a small region has a significantly high number of deaf people. . . . The eleventh edition listed 69 and the thirteenth edition has 136 living sign languages. We know there are many more, but research is needed to document attitudes and which varieties are separate languages and not dialects of another language. Research on signed languages of the world lags far behind most other language families. . . . In short, signed languages, of which there are many, truly deserve to be considered real languages in every way, and that's why they are included in *Ethnologue*.

Reprinted from "Why are Sign Languages Included in the Enthnologue?" by Ted Bergman, JULY 31, 2013, www.ethnologue.com, SIL International Publications."

## *Types of Writing Systems*

### Pictures, Protowriting, and Rebuses

Classifying writing systems and their origins is also problematic. Figure 5.1 shows a simplified scheme. We start with the assumption that all writing somehow grew out of pictures and their representations of the natural environment. Then, too, probably every ancient culture had some form of **protowriting**, with doodles, scratches, knots, scribbles, or marks of various kinds that could be used as mnemonic devices (number of "kills" on a hunt, for example).

It is likely, too, that all writing systems went through a "**rebus**" stage as the relationship between sound and orthography was worked out in each particular case. What does this mean? Traditionally, a rebus is a device in which pictures are used to represent words or their parts. For example, someone named "Smith" might put a picture of a farrier or a blacksmith on his mailbox. Because of the possibility of allusions and verbal puns, rebuses have been popular. For example, probably everyone has seen a T-shirt with this on it: I♥NY. Of course, the intention is supposed to be "I love New York." In fact, this is so commonplace that "I heart . . . " phrases have now become almost cliché. The important thing to notice, however, is that we are to *read* the heart symbol on these T-shirts for its *semantic* value, "love," and not its phonetic value, "heart." However, suppose we replaced the "I" with a symbol for a stylized eyeball, rendering the phrase on the T-shirt something like this: 👁♥ NY. Here the first symbol stands for its phonetic value, "eye," while the second symbol stands for its semantic value, "love." Saying—or reading—"eye" now results in the spoken form of the first-person pronoun, "I." The point of this is that most ancient writing systems probably went through a stage when their units consisted of meaning + sound in some form. These could include cases in which some units were used for their phonetic value and others for their semantic value. Or it could be that within each unit itself there are semantic and phonetic elements.

### The Development of Chinese Characters: Scripts, Sounds, and Semantics

We have a few well-documented cases in which we can trace the origin of modern orthographic units back to their pictorial source. For instance, the origins of most of today's ideographic characters in Chinese are well known. For example, the sun was originally drawn as a fairly transparent picture like ✳ . Over the course of time, this picture became abbreviated to a circle with a mark in the middle, like ◉. Eventually this became written as 日, meaning "sun" or "day" in contemporary Chinese or Japanese. (Japan borrowed Chinese writing around the year 550 CE.) Another example is the character for "mountain," 山, which was supposed to depict three peaks of a mountain range in the distance (something like ♒). Over time, the peaks were reduced to just three vertical lines as the character became written quickly and often (much like reducing the picture of a person to a "stick figure" drawing). A river was drawn as ≀≀≀ and became 川 . A half-moon was drawn as ☽ becoming today's 月, meaning "month" or "moon." Some pictures were less iconic, as in a "rice field" being depicted by the outline of its plots (田). Today's horse (馬) is a little harder to visualize, but there are its four feet and long tail on the bottom, and its flowing mane on top. Characters can also have component parts, some of which determine meaning. For example, if we put the character for "sun" (日) together with the character for "moon" (

**FIGURE 5.1** A POSSIBLE CLASSIFICATION OF WRITING, INCLUDING THE MAJOR LANGUAGES MENTIONED IN THIS CHAPTER

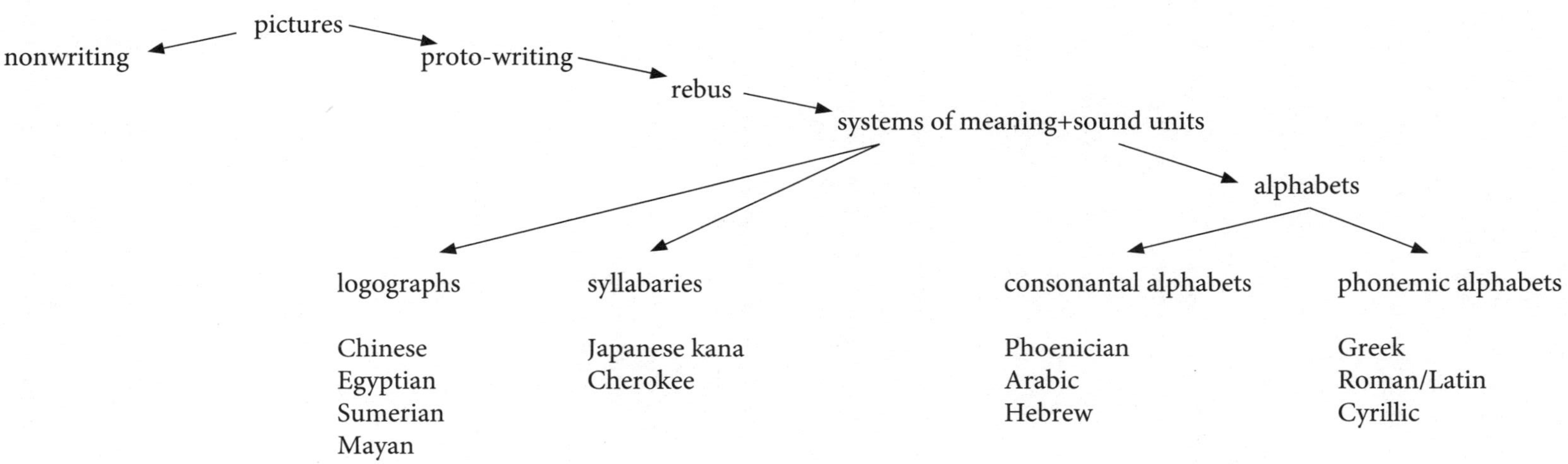

**TABLE 5.1** COMPONENTS OF SOME CHINESE CHARACTERS PRONOUNCED MA

| *English Gloss* | *Character* | *Semantic Part* | | *Meaning* | *Pronunciation* | *Phonetic Part + Pronunciation Guide* | |
|---|---|---|---|---|---|---|---|
| horse | 馬 | 馬 | ---- | horse | mǎ | 馬 | mǎ |
| mother | 媽 | 女 | on left | woman | nǔ | 馬 | mā |
| to scold | 罵 | 口 | on top | mouth | kǒu | 馬 | mà |
| question-tag | 嗎 | 口 | on left | mouth | kǒu | 馬 | ma |

月) the result is something really "bright" (明). Notice, then, that this single compound character has two semantic components.

But what of the sound components of the apparently semantic-nature of Chinese characters? They exist in several ways, which are obvious to native speakers but probably not to Americans. The most famous example of phonetic components in Chinese characters is *ma*, as seen in Table 5.1. (We discussed the tones of this *ma* syllable in Table 3.6.) The Chinese character for "horse," as we have seen, is 馬 and is pronounced mǎ. If the character for horse is combined with the character for "woman" (女) the resulting new character is 媽. This is also pronounced with this syllable, mā, and means "mother." If the character for horse is combined with the character 口 for "mouth"—repeated several times across the top—the resulting new character is 罵 and is pronounced mà. This means "to scold," as several mouths can be critical! If this "mouth" part is placed on the left instead of the top, we get a kind of spoken question marker put at the end of interrogative sentences (also pronounced *ma*), as "the mouth makes inquiries." Thus, we see that these characters have both a phonetic and semantic component. There is nothing "horsey" about mothers and scolding and questions; its presence is just a way to remind us of how this character might be pronounced.

## Cuneiforms and Hieroglyphics

Chinese writing is of great antiquity, at least going back to the famous Shang dynasty oracle bones of some 3,000 years ago. Even older than Chinese characters are the famous Sumerian **cuneiforms**, which apparently followed a similar developmental path. Around 3500 BCE, at the meeting of the Tigris and Euphrates Rivers in Mesopotamia (today's southern Iraq), wedge-shaped marks made by a stylus in tablets of soft clay, which were then either baked or allowed to dry in the sun to harden, were used to keep economic records for temples and other religious and official purposes. Sumerian civilization ended around 2000 BCE, and little was known of its writing system until serious work in the mid-nineteenth century—by a combination of bookish university scholars and adventurer-explorers—revealed its pattern and nature.

Several other systems of writing developed in the area at about the same time or somewhat later. The Akkadians, who conquered the Sumerians, adopted its cuneiforms, as did the Babylonians, Assyrians, and Hittites. In Egypt another pictographic writing system developed beginning about 3000 BCE. These famous **hieroglyphics** fascinated generations of European scholars and the general public and were long considered indecipherable. However, the discovery of the Rosetta Stone in 1799, which included text in Greek, Demotic Egyptian, and Egyptian hieroglyphics, was the key to solving the mystery. The polyglot

**Photo 5.1 Egyptian hieroglyphs. Fedor Selivanov/Shutterstock.com.**

Jean-François Champollion (1790–1832)—he knew Latin, Greek, Hebrew, Arabic, Persian, and Chinese—used his knowledge of Coptic (similar to Demotic Egyptian) to discover that there were sound elements inherent in the hieroglyphic signs, thus allowing for their eventual decipherment. All of these and other ancient Old World writing systems were eventually abandoned and replaced by others. In the New World, the **Mayan glyphs** were also based on a similar system (close to Japanese, as we will see, which uses a combination of sound and meaning elements). The earliest inscriptions date from the third century BCE. Although not all glyphs are known completely, the majority of most texts can now be read while assuming a relatively high level of accuracy.

We saw that the Chinese, the Sumerians, the Egyptians, and the Mayans took their orthographies of meaning+sound units and eventually developed them into functioning logographic systems; indeed, the Chinese orthography is still used by a quarter of the world's population today. The word **logograph** can be misleading, however, if taken too literally. Usually people use the term *logograph* to refer to a system in which there is one word corresponding to one idea, concept, or spoken form. However, as we saw with Chinese, that is not exactly the case, as Chinese writing has phonetic or morphemic components built into it. But what of the choices available (see the bottom of Figure 5.1)? Next we will discuss syllabaries.

## Syllabaries

Probably most English speakers think that the alphabet—in which one symbol stands for one sound—is the most natural and convenient next step in the growth and development of writing. They might be surprised to find that syllabaries—in which one symbol stands

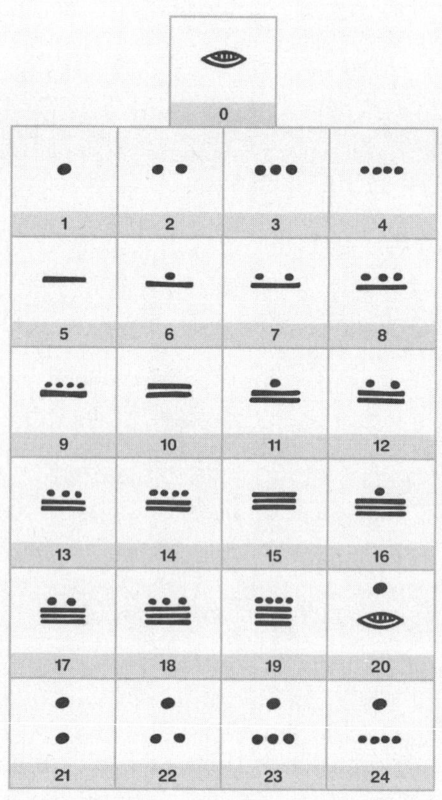


**Photo 5.2 Mayan writing. peterhermesfurian/ 123RF.**

for more than one sound—rival alphabets in terms of popularity. Perhaps the best way to see why this is so is to look at the development of the syllabary system in Japan.

Around 560 BCE Japan borrowed the Chinese writing system, having no indigenous orthography of its own. It soon became clear, however, that the two languages were quite mismatched, and the Chinese writing system was very difficult to apply to Japanese. The Chinese characters worked well for a language like Chinese, which was uninflected for tense and most other features, had a word-order-based syntax, and had a monosyllabic vocabulary. In contrast, Japanese was polysyllabic, highly agglutinative, and case-marked, with complex honorific and tense-based verbs. Also, the Chinese and Japanese phonological systems were quite different, with Chinese being tonal (the pitch accent of a word could determine meaning). This has caused centuries of difficulties, and even in modern times there have been periodic efforts to make the Japanese writing system more straightforward, because to make things work, even badly, much work was needed.

One of the first changes was the development of a **syllabary**, an orthography making use of signs representing syllables rather than ideas (as supposedly in Chinese) or single sounds (as in alphabets). Two syllabaries were actually created, one favored and used by women and the other by men. This was accomplished in the 700s CE by taking components of the borrowed Chinese characters and using them for their phonetic value only. This resulted in two sets of about fifty signs, each of which was derived from a Chinese character. For example, in the so-called angular *katakana* system, the syllabary sign ル was taken from the bottom part of the character 流. In the more cursive *hiragana* syllabary, the sign る was taken from the top part of the character 留 (and then stylized to be written quickly). In both cases, these two signs are to be pronounced as *ru*. The rest of the syllabary signs in Japanese are shown in Tables 5.2 and 5.3. Basically, in these two tables (based on older Indian traditional descriptions) the possible vowels are listed across the top and possible consonants are listed vertically at the left (and the "zero" symbol Ø meaning there is no consonant paired with that vowel for that symbol). If one wanted to, say, write the syllables "a," "ka," and "sa" using the *hiragana* system, they would be あ, か, and さ (the first three symbols in the left column of Table 5.2).

At the time the two syllabaries were invented—or more, accurately, finally agreed upon—there was a remarkable degree of linguistic sexual dimorphism in Japan. Men

**TABLE 5.2** HIRAGANA SYLLABARY (GOJŪ-ON, IN TRADITIONAL ORDER)

| | -a | -i | -u | -e | -o |
|---|---|---|---|---|---|
| Ø | あ<br>a | い<br>i | う<br>u | え<br>e | お<br>o |
| k- | か<br>ka | き<br>ki | く<br>ku | け<br>ke | こ<br>ko |
| s- | さ<br>sa | し<br>shi | す<br>su | せ<br>se | そ<br>so |
| t- | た<br>ta | ち<br>chi | つ<br>tsu | て<br>te | と<br>to |
| n- | な<br>na | に<br>ni | ぬ<br>nu | ね<br>ne | の<br>no |
| h- | は<br>ha | ひ<br>hi | ふ<br>fu | へ<br>he | ほ<br>ho |
| m- | ま<br>ma | み<br>mi | む<br>mu | め<br>me | も<br>mo |
| y- | や<br>ya | | ゆ<br>yu | | よ<br>yo |
| r- | ら<br>ra | り<br>ri | る<br>ru | れ<br>re | ろ<br>ro |
| w- | わ<br>wa | | | | |
| -n | ん<br>-n | | | | |

operated in the public sphere, socially and politically; often knew some Chinese; and wrote using the borrowed Chinese characters (*kanji*). Women operated in the private sphere, were discouraged (if not forbidden) from learning Chinese or *kanji*, and wrote interior thoughts and feelings in the vernacular, using the *hiragana* syllabary. Ironically, in the Japanese medieval period, it was women who wrote some of what is today considered the world's best literature (like the *Tale of Genji*, the world's first novel, a millennium ago). In modern times these syllabaries now serve different functions. The *hiragana* is used for

**TABLE 5.3** KATAKANA SYLLABARY (GOJŪ-ON, IN TRADITIONAL ORDER)

| | -a | -i | -u | -e | o |
|---|---|---|---|---|---|
| Ø | ア<br>a | イ<br>i | ウ<br>u | エ<br>e | オ<br>o |
| k- | カ<br>ka | キ<br>ki | ク<br>ku | ケ<br>ke | コ<br>ko |
| s- | サ<br>sa | シ<br>shi | ス<br>su | セ<br>se | ソ<br>so |
| t- | タ<br>ta | チ<br>chi | ツ<br>tsu | テ<br>te | ト<br>to |
| n- | ナ<br>na | ニ<br>ni | ヌ<br>nu | ネ<br>ne | ノ<br>no |
| h- | ハ<br>ha | ヒ<br>hi | フ<br>fu | ヘ<br>he | ホ<br>ho |
| m- | マ<br>ma | ミ<br>mi | ム<br>mu | メ<br>me | モ<br>mo |
| y- | ヤ<br>ya | | ユ<br>yu | | ヨ<br>yo |
| r- | ラ<br>ra | リ<br>ri | ル<br>ru | レ<br>re | ロ<br>ro |
| w- | ワ<br>wa | | | | |
| -n | ン<br>-n | | | | |

**TABLE 5.4** SAMPLE JAPANESE SENTENCE WITH FOUR SCRIPTS

| Japanese sentence: | JAL | の | フライト | ナンバー | は | 何 | 番 | です | か |
|---|---|---|---|---|---|---|---|---|---|
| Japanese script: | Roman letters | *hiragana* | *katakana* | *katakana* | *hiragana* | *kanji* | *kanji* | *hiragana* | *hiragana* |
| transliteration: | ***jaru*** | *no* | ***furaito*** | ***nambaa*** | *wa* | *nan* | *ban* | *desu* | *ka* |
| glosses: | "Japan Air Lines" | Possessive marker | English loan: "flight" | English loan: "number" | topic marker | "what" | numerical classifier | "is" | question marker |
| English translation: | "What is the Japan Air Lines flight number?" | | | | | | | | |

**TABLE 5.5** FIVE WAYS OF WRITING "JAPAN" IN JAPANESE

| | | |
|---|---|---|
| *Kanji*: | 日本 | |
| *Hiragana*: | にっぽん, | にほん |
| *Katakana*: | ニッポン, | ニホン |
| *Rooma-ji*: | *Nippon*, | *Nihon* |
| English: | Japan | |

adverbs and modifiers for which there are no *kanji* (which are mostly nouns and verbs). The *katakana* acts as a kind of italics and can be used to write foreign names and places.

The legacy of all this is that Japanese today is written in four scripts, because the Japanese have avidly borrowed many English words and are facile in the roman alphabet. These scripts can be seen in many places every day, from newspapers to product names (e.g., as in Photo 5.1). Table 5.4, for example, shows how these four scripts—*kanji*, *hiragana*, *katakana*, and roman letters—might appear in a typical sentence. Because "pure" English is also often used, it could be argued that a fifth script—pure English—is present as well. For example, Table 5.5 shows how the name "Japan" can be written in five ways.

Another example of a syllabary system is one used to write Cherokee, the language of an Indian group of the American Southeast. Unlike Japanese and most other syllabaries, we know exactly when this system appeared: it was invented by a half-Cherokee Indian named Sequoya (ca. 1760–1843) in 1821. This syllabary is shown in Table 5.6 (in the chart, the /ə̃/ represents a nasalized version of the schwa vowel ə). A cursory examination shows that it is an interesting mixture of roman letters and fonts of apparently arbitrary design. The Cherokee syllabary was used not only by the Cherokee but also by missionaries working with them. It immediately became popular and was used in tribal newspapers throughout the nineteenth century.

**Photo 5.3 A photo of typical Japanese product packaging shows how ubiquitous this use of five orthographies has become.**

**TABLE 5.6** THE CHEROKEE SYLLABARY SYSTEM

| | a | e | i | o | u | ə̃ | |
|---|---|---|---|---|---|---|---|
| Ø | Ꭰ | Ꭱ | Ꭲ | Ꭳ | Ꭴ | Ꭵ | |
| g- | Ꭶ | Ꭸ | Ꭹ | Ꭺ | Ꭻ | Ꭼ | ka = Ꭷ |
| h- | Ꭽ | Ꭾ | Ꭿ | Ꮀ | Ꮁ | Ꮂ | |
| l- | Ꮃ | Ꮄ | Ꮅ | Ꮆ | Ꮇ | Ꮈ | |
| m- | Ꮉ | Ꮊ | Ꮋ | Ꮌ | Ꮍ | | |
| n- | Ꮎ | Ꮑ | Ꮒ | Ꮓ | Ꮔ | Ꮕ | hn = Ꮏ; nah = Ꮐ |
| qu- | Ꮖ | Ꮗ | Ꮘ | Ꮙ | Ꮚ | Ꮛ | |
| s- | Ꮜ | Ꮞ | Ꮟ | Ꮠ | Ꮡ | Ꮢ | s = Ꮝ |
| d- | Ꮣ | Ꮥ | Ꮧ | Ꮩ | Ꮪ | Ꮫ | |
| t- | Ꮤ | Ꮦ | Ꮨ | | | | |
| tl- | Ꮭ | Ꮮ | Ꮯ | Ꮰ | Ꮱ | Ꮲ | dl = Ꮬ |
| ts- | Ꮳ | Ꮴ | Ꮵ | Ꮶ | Ꮷ | Ꮸ | |
| w- | Ꮹ | Ꮺ | Ꮻ | Ꮼ | Ꮽ | Ꮾ | |
| y- | Ꮿ | Ᏸ | Ᏹ | Ᏺ | Ᏻ | Ᏼ | |

Today, the Cherokee number about 140,000. There are 10,000 speakers of the language, with 130 being monolingual (http://www.ethnologue.com/language/chr). However, they are rather dispersed, residing in reservations in Oklahoma, Arkansas, and North Carolina. Thus, compared to other Native American groups, the Cherokee have fared better than most linguistically, but *Ethnologue* still classifies the language as "6b threatened" (see Chapter 16). The Cherokee syllabary has no doubt been helpful in language maintenance; it has become a symbol of pride and identity, and it is used in Cherokee language-immersion schools. There is a press that publishes literature and songbooks in the Cherokee syllabary.

## Alphabets

The next logical step in writing development would seem to be the **alphabet**, in which each different distinct sound of a language is represented by a single separate sign, or "letter." The advantage of such a system is obvious: Despite the spelling inconsistencies in English, any one of its thousands of words can be written down using no more than the twenty-six letters of the English alphabet. This is an advantage compared to Chinese, whose dictionaries have up to 50,000 characters (though in real life only about 10 percent of these are commonly used). Japanese—even augmented with its two systems of syllabaries—still has 2,000 "daily use" characters all students are required to learn. The Cherokee syllabary uses eighty-five signs. Alphabetic writing, then, is the easiest and most economical system and has become the means of writing the majority of languages today.

However, unlike syllabaries, relatively few alphabets have been invented, probably fewer than twenty, compared to the dozens of syllabaries. (Of course this depends on how one counts, because many systems are blends of several devices, and much borrowing and diffusion has taken place.) Nonetheless, the invention of an alphabet is not something that has happened often. This is sometimes attributed to the great insight or singular intelligence of the cultures that have invented them. That said, however, psycholinguistically it appears that syllables are favored over phonemes (and therefore, single "letters"). It seems cross-culturally, for example, that in terms of ease of learning to read and other measures, awareness of syllables precedes phonemic awareness (Goswami 2006). This is probably the real reason most invented systems were syllabaries or logographs, or some hybrid (Daniels and Bright 1996). The evidence from writing systems, then, "suggests that syllables are if anything more linguistically real than segments, despite the fact that early generative phonology ignored them. . . . Such an oversight can be attributed to an unconscious alphabetic bias in Western phonologists, conditioned by their script into perceiving the segment as the most important phonological unit" (Gnanadesikan 2008).

The first alphabetic system was probably used by a Semitic-speaking people, perhaps as early as 1700 BCE in ancient Syria, and the earliest preserved alphabetic text, in cuneiform, comes from the site of the ancient city-state of Ugarit on the present-day Syrian coast. With only consonants represented, the early alphabets were designed for the writing of Arabic, Hebrew, and Phoenician. Around 1000 BCE, ancient Greeks came into contact with the Phoenician system and somewhat later used it as a basis for developing their own, adding vowel symbols to adapt the alphabet to the different structure of their language. About two centuries later, the Greek alphabet in turn served as a model for the Etruscans of central Italy, whose alphabet influenced the Romans to develop their own Latin, or Roman, alphabet. Although the so-called Latin alphabet is used today for the writing of the great majority of European languages, the Cyrillic alphabet, current in parts of Eastern Europe and the former Soviet Union, was derived directly from the Greek alphabet, which in many ways it still resembles.

This orthographic journey is depicted in the top of Table 5.7. In the second column, arrows tracing right from "Phoenician" lead to "Greek" (and thus, "Cyrillic" and "modern Latin" via Etruscan, which is not shown), "Hebrew," and "Arabic." There we also find alphabet signs for these six languages—modern Latin (roman letters), ancient Phoenician, modern Greek, modern Cyrillic, modern Hebrew, and modern Arabic. For each language, a letter is given, along with its name and approximate phonetic value. Of course, such a table simplifies many complex issues (such as there being more than one alphabet in use in Greece). We can also see how many of the letters are related or derived.

We should also mention an important difference between the two kinds of alphabets depicted in Table 5.7. The Greek, Cyrillic, and modern Latin orthographies are sometimes called "pure" or **phonemic** alphabets, in that every sound in the language, including the vowels, has a letter. On the other hand, Phoenician, Hebrew, and Arabic are sometimes called **consonantal** alphabets because their letters for the most part only represent consonants. Vowels are represented by using other symbols/letters in combination, or with

**TABLE 5.7** THE ORIGINS AND DEVELOPMENT OF SEVERAL WESTERN ALPHABETS

| Modern Latin | PHOENICIAN | | | Greek | | | Cyrillic | | | Hebrew | | | Arabic | | |
|---|---|---|---|---|---|---|---|---|---|---|---|---|---|---|---|
| **letter** | **letter** | **name** | **phon. value** | **letter** | **name** | **phon. value** | **letter** | **name** | **phon. value** | **letter** | **name** | **phon. value** | **letter** | **name** | **phon. value** |
| A a | 𐤀 | 'alēph | ' | Α α | alpha | a | А а | ah | a | א | alef | silent | آ | alif | ' |
| B b | 𐤁 | bēth | b | Β β | beta | b | Б б | beh | b | ב | beit | b,v | ب | bā' | b |
| | | | | | | | В в | veh | v | | | | | | |
| C c | | | | | | | | | | | | | ت | tā' | t |
| D d | 𐤃 | dāleth | d | Δ δ | delta | d | Д д | deh | d | ד | dalet | d | ث | thā' | th |
| | | | | | | | | | | | | | د | dāl | d |
| | | | | | | | | | | | | | ذ | dhāl | dh |
| | | | | | | | | | | | | | ض | ḍād | ḍ |
| E e | 𐤄 | hē | h,e | Ε ε | epsilon | e | Е е | yeh | ye | ה | hei | h | ج | jīm | j |
| | | | | | | | Э э | eh | eh | | | | | | |
| F f | | | | Φ φ | phi | f | Ф ф | ehf | f | | | | ف | fā' | f |
| G g | 𐤂 | gīmel | g | Γ γ | gamma | g | Г г | geh | g | ג | gimel | g | غ | ghayn | gh |
| H h | 𐤇 | ḥeth | ḥ | Η η | eta | e | Ж ж | zheh | ǰ | ח | cheit | ḥ | ح | ḥā' | ḥ |
| | | | | | | | | | | | | | خ | khā' | kh |
| I i | 𐤉 | yōdh | y | Ι ι | iota | I | И и | ee | ee | י | yud | y, j, I | ي | yā' | y, i |
| | | | | | | | Й й | ee krahtkoʸeh | y | | | | | | |
| | | | | | | | Ы ы | i | i | | | | | | |
| J j | 𐤑 | ṣādē | ṣ | --- | san (early Gk) | | | | | ץ | tzadi | tz, ṣ | | | |
| K k | 𐤊 | kaph | k | Κ κ | kappa | k | К к | kah | k | ך | khaf | k, kh | ك | kāf | k |
| | | | | | | | | | | | | | ق | qāf | q |
| L l | 𐤋 | lāmedh | l | Λ λ | lamda | l | Л л | ehl | l | ל | lamed | l | ل | lām | l |
| M m | 𐤌 | mēm | m | Μ μ | mu | m | М м | ehm | m | מ | mem | m | م | mīm | m |
| N n | 𐤍 | nun | n | Ν ν | nu | n | Н н | ehn | n | ן | nun | n | ن | nūn | n |

| | | | | | | | | | | | | | | |
|---|---|---|---|---|---|---|---|---|---|---|---|---|---|---|
| O o | O | ’ayin | ‘ | O o | omicron | o | O o | o | o | ע | ayin | silent | ع | ‘ayn | ‘ |
| P p | 7 | pē | p | Π π | pi | p | П п | peh | p | ף | pei | p, f | | | |
| Q q | Φ | qōph | q (k) | --- | qoppa (early Gk) | | | | | ק | kuf | ḳ | | | |
| R r | 4 | rēš | r | Ρ ρ | rho | r | Р р | her | r | ר | reish | r | ر | rā’ | r |
| | | | | | | | Я я | $^{y}$ah | ya | | | | | | |
| S s | W | šin | š/s | Σ σ | sigma | s | С с | ehs | s | ש | shin | sh,s | س | sīn | s |
| | | | | | | | | | | | | | ش | shīn | š |
| | | | | | | | | | | | | | ص | ṣād | ṣ |
| T t | † | tāw | t | Τ τ | tau | t | Т т | the | t | | | | ط | ṭā’ | ṭ |
| U u | Y | waw | w, | --- | digamma (early Gk) | | | | | | | | | | |
| V v | | | | Υ υ | upsilon | y | | | | | | | | | |
| W w | Y | wāw | w | | | | | | | | | | و | waw | w, u |
| X x | ǂ | sāmekh | s | Ξ ξ | chi | x | Ш ш | shah | š | ס | samech | s | | | |
| | | | | | | | Щ щ | shch$^{y}$ah | šč | | | | | | |
| Y y | | | | --- | --- | | **У у** | oo | oo | | | | | | |
| | | | | | | | **Ю ю** | $^{y}$oo | u | | | | | | |
| Z z | Z | zayin | z | Ζ ζ | zeta | z | З з | zeh | z | ז | zayin | z | ز | zayn | z |
| | | | | | | | | | | | | | ظ | ẓa | z |
| | ⊕ | ṭēth | ṭ | **Θ θ** | theta | th | | | xs | ט | teit | t | | | |
| | X | | | Χ χ | chi | ch,kh | Х х | khah | x | ת | tav | t,s | ه | hā’ | h |
| | | | | | | | Ч ч | ch$^{y}$ah | č | | | | | | |
| | | | | | | | Ц ц | tseh | c | | | | | | |
| | | | | Ψ ψ | psi | ps | | | | | | | | | |
| | | | | Ω ω | omega | o, ō | | | | | | | | | |
| | | | | | | | Ъ ъ | ty$^{y}$ordiyznahk | | | | | | | |
| | | | | | | | **Ь ь** | m$^{y}$akhkeey znahk | | | | | | | |

diacritics. For example, to write the syllable *lâ* in Hebrew we would use ל (i.e., *l*) followed by ה (i.e., *he*) to get לה (remember, Hebrew is read right to left). To write *lê* or *lî* we would use ל followed by י (i.e., *i* ) to give לי. To write *lô* or *lû* we would use ל followed by ו (i.e., w) to give לו. To write *bā* we would use כ (i.e., *b*) with a ָ mark directly under it, as in כָ.

Despite the complicated development of the many writing systems over the past five or six millennia, the main tendencies in the general evolution of writing have been fairly straightforward. One has been toward increasing abstractness (from readily recognizable pictograms to letters—of which Latin *S*, Greek Σ, and Cyrillic *C*, all representing the "*s*" sound, are examples). The other tendency has been toward simplicity (from a great many

### BOX 5.2 WRITING AS THE UNIFYING CULTURAL FORCE IN EAST ASIA

The Chinese writing system has certain drawbacks when compared with the simpler phonetic systems of the West. It obviously takes a great deal more time and effort to master. Many characters are extremely complex, some being made up of more than twenty-five strokes. At least two or three thousand characters must be memorized before one can read even simple texts. The writing system thus has been an increasing handicap in modern times, when the need for widespread literacy has sharply risen. The emphasis on rote memory work to learn all these characters may also have had a limiting influence in Chinese education, putting a premium on memorizing abilities but giving less scope for creative talents. Moreover, even though the Chinese invented printing, has made printing<cl>much more complicated. . . .

On the other hand, the Chinese writing system has certain values that our Western systems lack. The very complexity of the characters and their graphic qualities give them a vitality that is entirely absent in the Latin alphabet. Once the characters are learned, who can forget that "peace" is a woman under a roof or that "bright" is made up of "sun" and "moon"? By comparison our written words . . . are as dull as numbers in a phone book. No one who has learned Chinese characters can ever free himself of the notion that somehow the written word has richer substance and more subtle overtones than the spoken word it was originally designed to represent. Chinese characters thus lend themselves to a terse vividness in both prose and poetry that is quite unattainable in our phonetically-bound writing systems. . . .

The magic quality of writing is perhaps one of the reasons why the peoples of East Asia have tended to place a higher premium on book learning and on formal education than have the peoples of any other civilization. It is no mere accident that, despite their extremely difficult systems of writing, literacy rates in East Asia run far higher on the whole than in the rest of the non-Western world (and in the case of Japan even surpass those of the West). . . .

*continues*

pictograms, ideograms, or phonograms to two to three dozen letters that can be easily drawn).

But if a simple alphabetic system has such an advantage over a logographic one in which thousands of different morphemes need to be learned and kept apart in their graphic representation, then why have languages like Japanese and Chinese not adopted one of the several romanizations (transcriptions using the roman alphabet) devised over the past several centuries? The answer is simple. A number of different languages are spoken in China, each in several dialects. The present system of characters is used for writing by all Chinese citizens even though they speak mutually unintelligible languages, with the result that the

> Another tremendous advantage of the Chinese writing system is that it easily surmounts differences of dialect or even more fundamental linguistic barriers. All literate Chinese, even if they speak mutually unintelligible "dialects," can read the same books and feel that classical written Chinese is their own language. If they had had a phonetic system of writing they might have broken up into separate national groups, as did the Italians, French, Spanish, and Portuguese. The stature of China as the largest national grouping in the world is to be explained at least in part by the writing system. It may also explain the extraordinary cultural cohesiveness of the Chinese abroad. The millions of Chinese who have migrated to Southeast Asia are actually divided from one another and from the mass of Chinese at home by the different languages they speak; yet even after generations abroad they have not, for the most part, lost a sense of identity with the homeland. The same is often true of the smaller communities which have migrated to the cities of the West. . . .
>
> The larger unity of East Asian civilization has also depended greatly on the writing system. A love and veneration for Chinese characters has been a binding link between the various countries. Until the last century, virtually all books written in Korea and Vietnam and many of those written in Japan were in Chinese, not in the national languages. Even today any educated Japanese or Korean and until recently any educated Vietnamese could pick up a Chinese book and read its title at a glance. In fact, it is impossible to tell from the titles of many contemporary books, as printed in Chinese characters, whether these books are actually written in Chinese, Japanese, or Korean. If the Chinese had had a phonetic system of writing, East Asia would certainly not have been so distinct a unit in world civilization.
>
> From Edwin Reischauer and John Fairbank,
> *East Asia: The Great Tradition* (1960), pp. 42-44

same newspaper, for example, can be read by China's citizens across the length and breadth of the country. If romanization of Chinese writing were to be officially adopted, books and newspapers would have to be published in as many different alphabetic systems as there are different languages spoken in the country (see Box 5.2).

For several millennia, the skill of writing was possessed by relatively few individuals, as the vast majority of the world's population was illiterate. By the end of the Middle Ages, however, the demand for copies of the growing number of manuscripts was such that it was not uncommon for well-known booksellers to employ several dozen copyists to satisfy the demand of reader-customers. The time had clearly come for inventing a method of multiplying book pages mechanically. Although block printing was apparently known in Europe by the end of the fourteenth century, it seems not to have threatened the patient work of the copyists. The major innovation, in about 1450, was the printing press and movable type, an invention attributed to the German Johannes Gutenberg (ca. 1390–1468). But even though Gutenberg apparently did invent printing independently, he was not the first to develop it; movable-type printing was used in China as early as the first half of the eleventh century. Moreover, the earliest known book, which was block printed, also comes from China and bears a publication date, when converted to our calendar, of May 11, 868.

Both writing and printing have raised communication to great efficacy. Without the permanence of the printed word, civilization could not have grown as rapidly and to the extent that it has. The impersonal messages encoded in writing, though, are generally not as effective as face-to-face communication. For power, the spoken word remains unsurpassed.

## SUMMARY AND CONCLUSIONS

Although spoken language is undoubtedly the oldest and most efficient means of human communication, there are many other ways in which people transmit or exchange information. Information, emotions, and feelings, in addition to writing, can be transmitted nonverbally. Nonverbal systems of communication are based on either spoken or written language, or are independent of it.

The Morse Code and Braille derive from the written representation of a language; whistle "languages," by contrast, are based on certain acoustic features of speech. Vocal communication is invariably enhanced or modified by so-called paralinguistic features, such as extra loudness, whispering, or sounds other than those of normal speech. Body language includes facial expressions, hand gestures, and other body motions. Hearing-impaired individuals make use of sign systems that are very nearly as efficient and expressive as spoken languages. The Plains Indians of North America used an elaborate sign language to communicate with members of other Plains tribes whose languages they could not understand; and by means of signs, they were even able to tell very long and elaborate traditional myths.

We have traced some of the history of the development of writing systems, a very long and complicated journey, to be sure. However, there are still many questions to ask. For example,

> How . . . is the ability to write distributed among the members of a community, and how does the incidence of this ability vary with factors such as age, sex, socioeconomic class and the like? . . . What kinds of information are considered appropriate for transmission through written channels? . . . Who sends written messages to whom, when, and for

what reasons? . . . In short, what position does writing occupy in the total communicative economy of the society under study and what is the range of its cultural meanings? (Basso 1974:431–432)

These questions need to be seriously addressed, and we tackle them in more detail in Chapter 15. Interestingly, we will see that they apply even more to "hyper-literate" modern industrial societies (for example, those who use Twitter, texting, and emojis).

## RESOURCE MANUAL AND STUDY GUIDE

### *Questions for Discussion*

1. Some nonverbal systems of communication derive from spoken language. Which particular features of spoken language might these be?
2. Can paralinguistic features be represented in writing, for example, in novels, and if so, how?
3. Observe another person at close range—a teacher, a visiting neighbor, or shop clerk—for a period of several minutes in order to learn how he or she has strengthened what he or she is saying by body motions (hand gestures, facial expressions, and the like).

### *Project*

The world-famous matriarch of anthropology, Margaret Mead, said we should develop an international writing system that could be used as an auxiliary form of communication (much like Esperanto advocates claim regarding spoken language). As an example, in the West, at least, we all use a series of "Arabic" numerals (e.g., *1*, *2*, *3*), even though we pronounce them differently, depending on our native language. That is, these numbers are a written form of communication independent of any one language. Wouldn't it be good if we could do this not only for numbers, but for other topics such as science, philosophy, and politics? Obviously, we would need a set of abstract graphic symbols to do so. Mead and Modley suggest that Chinese might be a good starting point, being "the most complete model" (1968:62). Is this a great idea, or is it another one of Mead's well-intended but impractical proposals (for which she was noted)? Using what you know of Chinese and Japanese writing in this chapter, give three reasons such a thing would not work. Be technical and specific, not just saying, "Well, no one would do it." After you have presented your case for why the Mead proposal would not work, then redo the task, this time finding ways to address the problems you just mentioned, and create a plan to make the international writing system work! Good luck. A Nobel Peace Prize is on the line.

### *Objective Study Questions*

**TRUE-FALSE TEST**

T F 1. Ameslan (American Sign Language) has two signing systems that complement each other.

T F 2. In theory, proxemic behavior varies from society (culture) to society; however, the proxemic behaviors of some societies do not appreciably differ.

T F 3. Plains Indian sign language developed to supplement the relatively poor vocabularies of languages of the tribes in this culture area.

T F 4. What is being said, and the kinesic behavior accompanying it, can be in conflict.

T F 5. The four zones of interpersonal space discussed by Edward Hall in his study of proxemics are universal.

T F 6. True writing is believed to go back no more than 5,000 to 6,000 years.

T F 7. There are a number of different languages and dialects spoken in China, but the same newspapers published in Beijing serve all Chinese citizens.

**MULTIPLE-CHOICE QUESTIONS**

____ 1. The use of gestures to accompany speech is referred to as (A) kinesics. (B) proxemics. (C) paralinguistics.

____ 2. Ordinary business transactions are customarily performed at what proxemic distance? (A) Personal. (B) Public. (C) Social-consultative.

____ 3. Finger spelling is employed in (A) Plains Indian sign language. (B) American Sign Language. (C) kinesic behavior.

____ 4. During an exchange between two people, the use of silence by one of them may turn out (A) to be threatening. (B) to be a means of relaxing potential tension. (C) to mean "no." (D) Depending on the circumstances, it may serve any of the three functions.

____ 5. The channel(s) used in kinesic behavior is (are) (A) olfactory. (B) acoustic. (C) visual. (D) Two of the preceding choices are applicable.

____ 6. The main tendencies in the general evolution of writing have been (A) from concrete to abstract and from complex to simple. (B) from concrete to abstract and from simple to complex. (C) from abstract to concrete and from simple to complex. (D) from abstract to concrete and from complex to simple.

**COMPLETIONS**

1. The study of the cultural patterning of the spatial separation individuals maintain in face-to-face encounters is called ________________ (one word).
2. Features of vocal communication that are considered marginal or optional, such as tempo or intensity, are referred to as ________________ (one word).
3. The study of the properties of signs and symbols and their functions—for example, the social symbolism of certain foods—is referred to as ________________ (one word).
4. Several centuries before Johannes Gutenberg discovered movable-type printing, it was already being used in ________________ (one word).

## Answer Key

True-false test: 1-T, 2-T, 3-F, 4-T, 5-F, 6-T, 7-T
Multiple-choice questions: 1-A, 2-C, 3-B, 4-D, 5-C, 6-A
Completions: 1. proxemics, 2. paralanguage, 3. semiotics, 4. China

## Notes and Suggestions for Further Reading

For a discussion of paralanguage and paralinguistics, see Trager (1958) and Crystal (1974); the latter source has an extensive bibliography appended. For a selection of essays concerning kinesics, see Birdwhistell (1970). A very readable introduction to proxemics is Hall (1966); a much shorter account, with comments by a number of scholars and Hall's reply to them, is in Hall (1968). For a discussion of gestures and cultural differences in gestures, see Kendon (1997).

An excellent introduction to American Sign Language can be found in Klima and Bellugi (1979). A nontechnical but reliable source for Plains Indian sign language is Tomkins (1969).

For sign language and theories, see Brentari (2010); for cross-cultural studies of sign languages, see Mathur and Napoli (2010), Nakamura (2006), and the articles in the collection of Monaghan, Schmaling, Nakamura, and Turner (2013). Mattingly (1972) is still a classic on the relationship between reading and writing, though a whole field has bloomed since.

A book of readings concerning nonverbal communication, with commentary, has been edited by Weitz (1974); the topics in the anthology include facial expression, paralanguage, body movements and gestures, and spatial behavior. A survey by specialists of paralinguistics and proxemics is included in Sebeok (1974).

A number of books and articles have been written on the origins and development of writing in general or of a particular writing system, especially the alphabetic. The most comprehensive source on the subject is Diringer (1968), consisting of one volume of text and one of illustrations. A shorter but informative treatment of the subject (some 130 pages) is Trager (1972). The several aspects of the interface between cultures with and without writing, and between written and oral traditions, on the one hand, and the use of writing and speech, on the other, are dealt with in Goody (1987). For an early review of the relation between written and spoken language and a bibliography on the subject, see Chafe and Tannen (1987). For newer general overviews of writing see Gnanadesikan (2009), Coulmas (2002), Daniels (1996), Daniels and Bright (1996), and Woodard (1997). Other classic studies of writing systems include Gelb (1963) and Harris (1986). Interestingly, Chapter 4 of Peterson (2015) gives a very entertaining overview of possible writing systems written by the man who constructed the languages for the HBO series *Game of Thrones*. The calligrapher Ewan Clayton (2015) gives a good history of the origin and growth of writing and literacy in the West.

Sources for Table 5.7 include Robinson (2009:101, 105), DeFrancis (1989:85, 76, 89–121, 166–169), and Crystal (2010:210–212).

For Mayan, see Schele and Mathews (1999) and Coe and Van Stone (2005). For Cherokee, see Holmes and Smith (1976) and Scancarelli (1996). For Chinese and Japanese, see the classic works by DeFrancis (1984 and 1989), as well as Williams (2010), Hadamitzky and Spahn (1981), Mair (1996), and Taylor and Taylor (1995).

# 6

# The Development and Evolution of Language: Language Birth, Language Growth, and Language Death

### LEARNING OBJECTIVES

- Name and describe some of the groundbreaking ape-language experiments
- List and define the design features of language
- Explain when a generalized communication system can become a language
- Be familiar with the causes of language death, and some of the ways it might be ameliorated

It is now generally accepted that communication among members of animal species is widespread and that most vertebrates transmit information by acoustic signals. The variety and ingenuity of these communicative systems have stimulated a great deal of research in animal communication and its comparison with human speech. If we accept the single modern human species (*Homo sapiens*) as a very recent result of the evolution living organisms have undergone for more than a billion years, then we may also be likely to assume that human speech is the end result of a long, cumulative evolutionary process that shaped communicative behavior throughout the animal kingdom. But how this happened is not easy to discover. In this chapter we will examine how the evolution of language might have taken place.

## COMMUNICATION AND ITS CHANNELS

Communication among members of animal species is universal because it is important to their survival; it takes place whenever one organism receives a signal that has originated with another. An early (from the 1940s) but serviceable model of communication uses five components: the sender (or source), the message, the channel, the receiver (or destination), and the effect. These components take into account the entire process of transmitting information, namely, who is transmitting what by what means to whom and with what effect. The model appears to be rather simple and straightforward, but because communication is by no means uniform, some discussion is in order.

Although communication among members of any particular species is to be expected, interspecific communication—that is, transmission of signals between members of different species—is far from rare. An experienced horseback rider transmits commands to a horse and expects them to be received and followed. A dog whining outside its owner's door conveys its wish to be let in. Communication between people, on the one hand, and their pets or work and farm animals, on the other, is very common and not limited to sounds. Touching (stroking, patting, holding, and grooming) animals is frequently more effective than talking to them, and the dog that wags its tail and vigorously rubs its muzzle against a human knee leaves no doubt about its feelings of satisfaction and pleasure. The means of sending messages clearly vary and are not limited to sounds (as in speech) or visible signs (as in looks or hand gestures), although these two channels, or media selected for communication, are the means humans most frequently employ.

The most common and effective channel of human communication is the *acoustic channel*, used whenever people speak to each other as well as in so-called whistle speech (discussed in Chapter 5). Writings, gestures, and pictorial signs make use of the *optical channel*, relating to vision. Braille, a writing system for the blind that uses characters consisting of raised dots, is received by the sense of touch, the *tactile channel.* The *olfactory channel* is chosen whenever one wishes to communicate by the sense of smell: people sometimes use room deodorizers before receiving guests and put perfume or deodorant on themselves when they expect to spend time with other individuals at an intimate distance. By the same token, most Americans consider garlicky or oniony breath to be a signal that reflects unfavorably on its senders.

The olfactory channel is especially important among social insects, which do much of their communicating by means of odors in the species-specific substances they secrete known as pheromones. Regardless of the channel used, animals send out messages for a variety of reasons, such as to guide individual organisms of the same species to one another or to help synchronize the behaviors of those who are to breed. In other words, communication enables organisms to maintain certain relationships that are of advantage to them individually as well as to their species as a whole.

Members of any animal species may use several kinds of signaling behavior. The signals familiar to humans are patterns of behavior known as **displays**. They may take the form of birdsongs, croaking (among frogs), chirping (among crickets), spreading fins or changing color (among certain fish), chest beating (among gorillas), and so on. Some signal units are cooperative, involving at least two individuals; others are rather formalized. A male hawfinch touches bills with a female, and during courtship the male bowerbird builds a chamber or passage decorated with colorful objects that will attract a mate. Some animals (for example, dogs and wolves) use urine marking as a chemical signal delimiting territory, whereas others (skunks and bombardier beetles, to mention just two) use chemical signals for defense. Some of the unexpected findings in the field of animal communication have stimulated continued research.

## COMMUNICATION AMONG NONHUMAN PRIMATES

The greatest amount of research on animal communication since World War II has been devoted to nonhuman primates, especially the chimpanzees. Table 6.1 lists some of the most important ape-language experiments, giving the name and species of the animal, the name of the investigator, the experimental technique used, and the alleged achievement of the ape in terms of number of signs learned or other measures of language ability. In the wild, besides visual and other signals, apes use a variety of vocal sounds, including grunts, pants, barks, whimpers, screams, squeaks, and hoots. Each vocalization is associated with one or several circumstances. The physical similarity between the great apes and humans has long intrigued observers, suggestions that apes could be taught to speak having been made several centuries ago. Of the various experiments to teach chimpanzees to talk, the best documented was the one begun by Keith J. Hayes and Catherine Hayes in the late 1940s. They adopted a newborn female chimpanzee, Viki, and brought her up in their home as if she were a human child. Despite all the Hayeses' efforts to teach Viki to speak, after six years she had learned to approximate only four words (*mama*, *papa*, *cup*, and *up*), and poorly at that. It appears from the disappointing results of this and similar experiments in home-raising chimpanzees that the ability to speak is unique to humans and that the principal channel of communication for apes is the optical one—postures, facial expressions, and gestures.

In a more recent experiment, Washoe, an infant female chimpanzee, was taught the form of gestural language used by the American deaf. Toward the end of the second year of the project, Washoe was reportedly able to use more than thirty signs spontaneously. After five years of training, she was said to be actively proficient in about 150 hand signs, was able to understand more than twice that many, and could use combinations of several signs. At about the same time, another chimpanzee, Sarah, was taught to write and read by means of plastic tokens of various shapes, sizes, and colors, each token representing a word. According to a report published in 1972, Sarah acquired a vocabulary of about 130 terms that she used with a reliability of between 75 and 80 percent. Her performance included the use of a plastic symbol that stood for the conditional relation *if-then*, as in "If Sarah takes a banana, then Mary won't give chocolate to Sarah" (Premack and Premack 1972).

Studies of communicative behavior among the great apes are continuing, and important new findings have been reported. Some of these studies concern the pygmy chimpanzees (*Pan paniscus*), whose habitat is the dense equatorial forest south of the Congo (Zaire) River in Zaire. Because their population is relatively small, the species may be considered endangered. The behavior of the pygmy chimpanzee is noticeably different from that of the common chimpanzee (*Pan troglodytes*). Pygmy chimpanzees appear to be more intelligent and more sociable and are faster learners; there is also evidence that they are more bipedal, less aggressive, and more willing to share food. Adult males and females associate more closely, and those in captivity seem to enjoy contact with humans. Of interest is a study by E. S. Savage-Rumbaugh (1984) based on two pygmy chimpanzees observed at the Language Research Center of the Yerkes Regional Primate Research Center in Atlanta,

**TABLE 6.1** SOME FAMOUS LANGUAGE-LEARNING APE EXPERIMENTS

| *Name* | *Year* | *Species* | *Investigator(s)* | *Technique/language* | *Ability* |
|---|---|---|---|---|---|
| Gua | c. 1931 | chimp | Kellogg & Kellogg | vocal exposure | 70 spoken words understood |
| Viki | c. 1950 | chimp | Hayes & Hayes | vocal mimicry | 4 words produced |
| Washoe | c. 1970 | chimp | Gardner & Gardner | ASL | 160 signs |
| Lucy | c. 1973 | chimp | Foutes & Termerlin | ASL | 100 signs |
| Sarah | c. 1972 | chimp | Premack & Premack | plastic chimps | 120 chips |
| Azak | 1973–1975 | orangutan | Gary Shapiro | plastic chimps | similar to Premack |
| Lana | c. 1979 | chimp | Rumbaugh & Savage Rumbaugh | "Yerkish" | 75 items |
| Nim Chimpsky* | c. 1979 | chimp | Terrace, Petito, et al. | ASL | 125 signs |
| Koko | c. 1979 | gorilla | Patterson | ASL | 600+ signs |
| Kanzi | c. 1990 | bonobo | Greenfield | "Yerkish" variant | 650 signs, grammar |
| Ai | c. 1990 | chimp | Kyoto U. Primate Res. Inst. | cognitive tasks | notable cognitive skills |
| Panbanisha | c. 2000 | bonobo | Savage-Rumbaugh | lexigrams | 250 symbol keyboard |
| Ayumu* | c. 2000 | chimp | Kyoto U. Primate Res. Inst. | cognitive tasks | notable cognitive skills |

***Note:* * = male; "chimp" = *Pan troglodytes*; "bonobo" = *Pan paniscus*; "gorilla" = western lowland gorilla, *Gorilla gorilla gorilla***

Georgia. When the study was conducted, the center had two pygmy chimpanzees, a twelve-year-old female born in the wild and her "adopted" son, Kanzi, then one and a half years old. When Kanzi wanted something, he intentionally used a combination of gestures and vocal sounds to draw the attention of a staff member. His wishes included being taken from one area to another, being helped with a task he could not perform alone (for example, opening a bottle), and the like. He would point to strange objects with an extended index finger, sometimes accompanying such pointings with vocal signals and visual checking; he would also lead his teachers by the hand to where he wanted them to go, pulling on their hands if he wanted them to sit down. On occasion, Kanzi expressed frustration by fussing and whining. If we judge from the behavior of the small sample of pygmy chimpanzees at the center and elsewhere, they appear to be better able to comprehend social situations than common chimpanzees can, and communicate correspondingly. In other words, their behavior is more reminiscent of human behavior than is the behavior of other species of apes.

In another project, research assistants were requested to teach signs for objects to the young chimpanzee Nim; they were to reward him for correct responses but not treat him like a human child. In contrast to a human child, Nim preferred to act upon his social environment physically rather than communicatively and was little interested in making signs simply for the sake of contact. Several years later, an experiment was performed to test the hypothesis that social context can influence the communicative performance of a sign-using chimpanzee. The results of the experiment established that Nim adjusted his conversational style according to whether the interaction with humans was social or instructional (as in drill sessions). For example, in a social context, Nim made more than four times as many spontaneous contributions in sign language as he did when he was being trained. Apparently chimpanzees, just like children, tend to interact spontaneously when the situation is relaxed; in testing situations they are repetitive and imitative, and do not elaborate their contributions. If the communicative behavior of chimpanzees does indeed vary according to context, earlier reports on the cognitive capacities of signing chimpanzees may not tell the whole story.

Another noteworthy finding, made at the Institute for Primate Studies at the University of Oklahoma, involved Loulis, the young male that Washoe adopted when he was ten months old. Although staff members were requested to refrain from signing to Loulis, or even to other chimpanzees when Loulis was present, Washoe and several chimpanzees in contact with Loulis freely used signs they had learned earlier from their human teachers. Five years and three months later, when Loulis's "vocabulary" consisted of fifty-one signs, the restriction on human signing was lifted. During the subsequent two years, Loulis learned to use an additional nineteen signs. Independent observers acquainted with American Sign Language (ASL) were able to recognize the signs Loulis had learned from the other chimpanzees and could identify more than 90 percent of them (Fouts, Fouts, and Van Cantford 1989; Fouts and Fouts 1989).

Some of the great apes have also been observed to indulge in generalization; that is, they made a response to a stimulus similar to but not the same as a reference stimulus. To give a few examples: Washoe extended the sign for "dirty" from feces and dirt to a monkey who threatened her and also to Roger Fouts, who had raised her, when he refused to accede to a request. The female gorilla named Koko generalized "straw" from drinking straws to hoses, plastic tubing, cigarettes, and other objects of similar shape. And Lucy, a

**Photo 6.1 Koko, the Famous Signing Gorilla, and her kitten, and trainer, Penny Patterson, signing "think." Bettmann/Getty Images**

chimpanzee, signed "cry hurt food" to mean radishes (Hill 1978).

These and other experimental results are naturally of considerable interest, but one must keep in mind that the chimpanzees were learning to communicate in an artificial setting and for the most part were carefully directed by humans. It would have been of greater significance if some of the human-trained chimpanzees had subsequently been able, on their own, to add new signs to their "vocabulary" and to understand conversational turn-taking. Scholars have argued that at least some of the reported animal responses may have been due to unconscious nonverbal cueing by those who studied them. Although this may be true, there is little doubt that apes can learn the communicative behavior researchers have described. But even at that, the nearly sexually mature chimpanzee is quite limited in what it can sign compared to a human child of six, who is capable of communicating verbally about a large variety of subjects. In short, the proficient use of the repertory of gestural signs of which chimpanzees are highly capable is a far cry from the conscious linguistic processing common to all humans from childhood on.

## WHEN DOES A COMMUNICATION SYSTEM BECOME LANGUAGE?

The question, When did language originate? is altogether too vague unless one first specifies what is meant by the term *language*. If it stands for a set of discrete vocal sounds, meaningless by themselves, that can be strung together to produce higher-order units ("words") endowed with conventional but arbitrary meanings, and, further, if such a system makes it possible for its users to generate an unlimited number of unprecedented comments about events removed in time as well as space, then most of the several million years of hominid existence would have been languageless.

Members of all animal species have a way of transmitting information among themselves, and before the **hominids** branched off from other hominoids—the gorillas and chimpanzees in particular—from 5 to 8 million years ago, they undoubtedly possessed a means of communicating similar to that of their closest primate relatives. Judging from what is now known about the behavior of the great apes in the wild, the communication system of the earliest hominids likely employed signals that were both visual and acoustic (or auditory) as well as olfactory (connected with the sense of smell) and tactile (especially grooming).

The visual signals, or gestures, would have been made by various parts of the body, including the face; the auditory signals no doubt consisted of a variety of vocalizations—grunts, roars, barks, moans, hoots, howls, and the like—but also of such nonvocal sounds as chest beating or ground stamping. The overall repertory, however, must have been rather modest, with the signals employed only when the stimuli that provoked them were present. The significance, or meaning, of these signals would have been limited to very basic "comments" concerning the immediate environment (for example, sudden danger or the discovery of food) or the individual's emotional state (annoyance, surprise, distress, assertion of dominance, fear, and the like).

It is clear that a vast distance had to be bridged between some such limited means of communication—a mere call system—and full-blown language that modern humans have been making use of for thousands of years. One may refer to the communication system that preceded full-fledged language as **prelanguage**. But even this differentiation into language and prelanguage is extremely rough because it suggests an evolutionary leap from one stage to the next rather than a long series of countless incremental changes that would have been imperceptible to the evolving hominids as they were occurring. Some anthropologists have attempted to reconstruct the evolution of human communication in some detail. For example, Roger W. Wescott (1974) postulated hand waving and vocal synchronization among the members of a group for the australopithecines, finger-pointing and vocal imitation for *Homo erectus*, and manual signing and unintelligible "speech" involving the use of meaningless syllables for the Neanderthals; writing and fully developed language he reserved for later *Homo sapiens*. Most anthropologists would probably find this scheme too conservative; its virtue is in its attempt to correlate the development of two communicative channels, the visual and the acoustic.

## DESIGN FEATURES OF LANGUAGE

If human language is unique among the many known systems of communication that exist in the animal kingdom, then it must possess some features of design not to be found elsewhere. In the 1960s, Charles Hockett (1916–2000) and others proposed a set of "**design features" of language**—properties that characterize human speech.

This was a radical shift in thinking in linguistics, and even to a certain extent in anthropology. Although there was general agreement on the biological affinity between humans and other animals, language was thought to be unassailable in that it was assumed to be exclusively human. Even through the 1970s and 1980s, many structural linguists refused to entertain the possibility that incipient linguistic behavior might be found, say, in chimpanzees or gorillas. They often defined language at the very beginning as something possessed only by humans (e.g., Trager 1972).

Hockett originally proposed seven design features but soon increased the number to sixteen. (In light of new findings from linguistics and cognitive science, we could even propose four more shortly.) The following are the properties that Hockett argued characterized human language:

1. *Vocal-auditory channel.* Some sounds produced by animals are not vocal (for example, the chirping of crickets), nor are they received auditorily (as with bees, having no ears). (Writing, of course, is excluded because the channel used for written messages is optical rather than vocal-auditory.) Among mammals, the use of the

**vocal-auditory channel** for communication is extremely common, though they often use other means of communication (for example, a dog "marking" its presence against a tree). One important advantage of using the vocal apparatus to communicate is that the rest of the body is left free to carry on simultaneously various other activities.

2. *Broadcast transmission and directional reception.* Speech sounds move out from the source of their origin in all directions, and the sender and the receiver need not see each other to communicate, nor do they have to "aim" their speech in a narrow direction. Binaural reception (involving both ears) makes it possible to determine the location of the source of sounds.
3. *Rapid fading.* Speech signals immediately disappear to clear the channel for new messages to come. This is more important than might appear at first glance. If we communicated olfactorily, as many animals do, we would have to wait for old messages to dissipate. This would be very time-consuming. Human sounds, on the other hand, are heard only at the time they are being produced. After that they are irretrievably lost, and the channel is ready for new messages.
4. *Interchangeability.* Speakers of human languages can be speakers and hearers—that is, speech signals can be transmitted or received interchangeably by all adult members (and most child members) of a community. In theory, at least, human beings are capable of uttering what others say (if, of course, the language used is familiar). This is not true of many animal species, in which the nature of messages varies between males and females or according to other natural divisions. For example, in some species of crickets only the males chirp by rubbing together parts of their forewings, and the dance language of worker honeybees is not understood nor can it be performed by a queen or the drones of the same colony.
5. *Complete feedback.* Speakers of any language hear what they themselves are saying and are therefore capable of monitoring their messages and promptly making any corrections they consider necessary or appropriate. By contrast, a male stickleback (a fish) cannot monitor the changing of the color of his eyes and belly that serves to stimulate the female of the species. It also "makes possible the so-called internalization of communicative behavior that constitutes at least a major portion of 'thinking'" (Hockett 1960:90).
6. *Specialization.* Human speech serves no other function than to communicate. By contrast, the primary purpose of, say, the panting of a dog is to effect body cooling through evaporation, even though panting produces sounds that carry information (for example, the location of the dog or the degree of its discomfort). In other words, the communication system of many animals transmits signals only as a by-product of some other biological function.
7. *Semanticity.* Speech has meaning. "Salt" means salt and not sugar or pepper. Some features of honeybee dance language denote the distance of a food source from the beehive, and others give the direction in which the food is to be found. However, in no system other than human language is there such an elaborate correlation between the vast number of words and possible sentences and the widely different topics humans talk about.
8. *Arbitrariness.* There is no intrinsic relationship between the form of a meaningful unit of a language and the concept for which the unit stands. The common domestic

animal that barks—*Canis familiaris,* by its scientific Latin name—is referred to as *dog* in English, *Hund* in German, *chien* in French, *perro* in Spanish, *pes* in Czech, *cîine* in Romanian, *sobaka* in Russian, *köpek* in Turkish, *kutya* in Magyar, *pohko* in Hopi, *heu* in Arapaho, and *inu* in Japanese. But there is nothing about canines that makes English speakers call them "dogs," and there is nothing inherent in the sounds D-O-G that make them necessarily apply to canines.

9. *Discreteness.* Messages in human languages do not consist of sounds that are continuous (like a siren, for example) but are made up of discrete—that is, individually distinct—segments. The difference between the English questions "Would you care for a piece of toast?" and "Would you care for a piece of roast?" is due solely to two discrete sounds at the same place in each sentence, one written and pronounced as *t* and the other as *r.* By contrast, bee dance language is continuous; it does not make use of discrete elements.
10. *Displacement.* Humans can talk about (or write about, for that matter) something that is far removed in time or space from the setting in which the communication occurs. One may, for instance, describe quite vividly and in some detail the military campaign of the Carthaginian general Hannibal against ancient Rome, even though the Second Punic War took place more than 2,000 years ago on another continent. Or people may talk about where they plan to live after retirement some twenty or thirty years in the future. Displacement of this kind exists nowhere else in the animal kingdom as far as we know.
11. *Productivity/openness.* Humans can say things that have never been said before, and they can understand things they have never heard before. Thinking up a novel sentence is not difficult (as, for example, "Our two cats argue about approaches to linguistic anthropology whenever they are left at home alone"). Good poets quite regularly use language in innovative ways. When a new thing is invented, we make up a new name for it. Other animal communication systems have limited repertoires, which can be used only in limited ways.
12. *Duality of patterning.* This is perhaps the most subtle design feature proposed by Hockett. This feature tells us that human language is organized on two distinct levels: (a) a level of *meaningless* sounds and (b) a level of *meaningful* parts of a language. Both have their own largely independent patterns (rules for creating combinations). For example, consider just these three sounds: /t/, /æ/, and /k/. On the phonemic (sound) level, they have no meaning, but they can be combined to form words like "tack," "cat," or "act" (here written in the conventional English orthography). That is, the units on the first level—the level of sound—are used to construct units on the second level—the level of words. The obvious advantage of duality of patterning is that a limited number of linguistic units of one kind make up a vast number of units on another level, much as the atoms of only about ninety naturally occurring elements make up the molecules of millions of different compounds.
13. *Cultural* (or *traditional*) *transmission.* Although there are biological predispositions for humans to acquire language, linguistic information is not passed on genetically, but culturally. One does not inherit a particular language; children learn language from parents or others with whom they speak. Speaking a particular language is therefore a part of one's overall cultural behavior, that is, behavior acquired through learning.

14. *Prevarication.* What a person may say can be completely and knowingly false (as if someone asserts that the moon is made of green cheese or that Washington is an hour's leisurely walk from St. Petersburg). Admittedly, an opossum may feign death (play possum) if surprised on the ground, or a bird may pretend to have a broken wing to lead predators away from her nest, but these behaviors are probably instinctive and do not reflect a cognitive decision or an intent to deceive. On the whole, attempts at deception are not common among animals.
15. *Reflexiveness.* Humans can use language to talk about language, or communication in general, and indeed do so all the time. Nonhuman animals do not appear to be capable of transmitting information about their own or other systems of communication.
16. *Learnability.* Any human speaker can potentially learn any human language. Speakers of one language can learn a second language, or even several languages, in addition to their mother tongues. Some communicative behavior among nonhuman animals is also the result of learning, either by experience or from humans. No other animals, however, possess the ability to learn one or several systems of communication as complex as language.

**Photo 6.2 Charles Hockett. Courtesy of Photo Services, Cornell University.**

Human languages possess all these design features, whereas the communicative systems of other animals possess only some. For example, according to Hockett (1960), calls produced by gibbons are characterized by the presence of design features 1 through 9 but lack displacement, productivity, and duality of patterning (Hockett is unsure about traditional transmission). Knowing that none of these design features is a completely either-or proposition, Hockett and Altmann (1968) called for examining design features using five frameworks: the social setting, the behavioral antecedents and consequences of communicative acts, the channel or channels employed, continuity and change in communication systems, and the structure of messages and their repertories in specific systems. Accordingly, if one is to study a particular communicative system or transaction, one should include inquiries concerning who the participants are and where and under what circumstances they communicate, what channel or channels they use, what the structure of their messages and of the code as a whole is, and so on.

These and related concerns not only are necessary for a fuller understanding of subhuman communication but are equally important for the study and appreciation of human language in the context of society and culture.

## LANGUAGE AS AN EVOLUTIONARY PRODUCT

Like all aspects of the human condition, language must also have been a product of evolution. However, unlike items of material culture, language leaves no physical traces of its evolutionary past. Until recently, many anthropologists, linguists, and biologists believed that there was little that could be said about the origins of language.

Although no definitive answers can be given at present, recent studies in human genetics, behavioral biology, anatomy, and artificial intelligence give us reasons to be optimistic about solving some of the mysteries of the origin and development of language. Two sets of related issues must be addressed. The first "big" question is, Did language suddenly develop all at once, or was it a gradual process? The second is, Did language develop under selective forces directly acting upon it, or was it a secondary by-product of evolutionary processes?

### *Continuity Versus Discontinuity*

In his book dealing with the biological foundations of language (1967), Eric H. Lenneberg (1921–1975) included an extended discussion of language in the light of evolution and genetics. Language development, he pointed out, may be viewed from two sharply differing positions. One, which Lenneberg called the *continuity theory*, holds that speech must have ultimately developed from primitive forms of communication used by lower animals and that its study is likely to reveal that language evolved in a straight line over time. According to this view, human language differs from animal "languages" only quantitatively, that is, by virtue of its much greater complexity. Although the proponents of a variant version of this theory argue that differences between human and animal communication are qualitative rather than merely quantitative, they also believe that all communicative behavior in the animal kingdom has come about without interruption, with simpler forms from the past contributing to the development of later, more complex ones.

The second theory, referred to as the **discontinuity theory of language evolution** and favored by Lenneberg, holds that human language must be recognized as unique, without evolutionary antecedents. Its development cannot be illuminated by studying various communicative systems of animal species at random and then comparing them with human language. One statement concerning the antiquity of language, however, can be made with some assurance: Because all humans possess the same biological potential for the acquisition of any language, the capacity for speech must have characterized the common ancestors of all humans before populations adapted to different environments and diversified physically.

Lenneberg rejected the continuity theory of language development for several reasons. Even though the great apes are the animals most closely related to humans, they appear to have few, if any, of the skills or biological prerequisites for speech. Frequently cited examples of animal communication have been drawn from insects, birds, and aquatic mammals, but the evolutionary relationships of these animals to humans vary greatly. That only a few species within large genera or families possess particular innate communicative traits indicates that such species-specific behavioral traits have not become generalized and therefore are likely to be of relatively recent date. In the following discussion, human speech and the several representative communicative systems of other animals should therefore be viewed as having no evolutionary continuity. There is, in short, no evidence to suggest that human speech is an accumulation of separate skills throughout the long course of evolution. If it were so, gibbons, chimpanzees, orangutans, and gorillas would not be as speechless as they are.

### *Language as Emergent Versus Language as Innate: Spandrels, or Language as an Evolutionary By-Product*

The paleontologist Stephen Jay Gould (1941–2002) argued that evolutionary biology needed a term for features that arose as by-products of, rather than actual, adaptations. He called such features *spandrels* (Gould and Lewontin 1979; Gould 2002:1249–1253), by analogy with the curved areas of supporting arches found in Renaissance architecture. Although pleasing to the eye, and usually covered with beautiful decorative art, spandrels served another purpose: they were necessary to provide needed support to a square frame of the archway. Likewise, for example, the feathers of birds may have originally evolved as a mechanism for regulating heat and body temperature (as seen, say, in modern-day penguins). Over time, however, feathers seem to have taken on another use—flight. If true, this co-opting of feathers for use in flight would be an example of a spandrel.

The question is: Did language evolve directly or was it a spandrel? Noam Chomsky and some others who subscribe to the existence of a universal "language faculty" believe that language itself evolved as a by-product (Hauser, Chomsky, and Fitch 2010). Steven Pinker (Pinker 2009; Pinker and Bloom 1990) argues that natural selection played a more direct role in language evolution. The processes of natural selection designed a "language acquisition device" module in the protohuman mind, and evolutionary forces increasingly made it more sophisticated over time. Talmy Givón (2002:123), however, believes that modern neurology supports the claim that "human language processing is an evolutionary outgrowth of the primate visual information processing system." The key question, he argues, is, Does the neurology that supports language processing involve any language-specific mechanisms or is it just a collection of preexisting modules that have been recruited to do so? To put things in extremes, we could phrase these two positions as:

> 1. *Language as something that emerges:* "All language-processing modules continue to perform their older prelinguistic task and reveal no special language-dedicated adaptations."
>
> or
>
> 2. *Language as something that is innate*: "All language-processing modules are either entirely novel, or at the very least have been heavily modified to perform their novel linguistic tasks." (Givón 2002:123)

## MONOGENESIS VERSUS POLYGENESIS

One other question arises when discussing language origins: Did the potentialities and traits required for the development of language originate in separate places at different or approximately the same times (polygenesis), or did they come into being just once (monogenesis)? Although one can never expect a conclusive answer to this question, a reasoned discussion of the alternatives is in order.

The theory of polygenesis, with its implication that languages spoken today ultimately derive from several unrelated sources in the remote past, is not easy to defend. For one thing, the process leading to prelanguage and language must have consisted of a long chain of transformations, structural and functional. That two or more parallel developments of such complexity took place independently of each other cannot be taken for granted. Derek Bickerton (1990) posited that the transition from "protolanguage" (referred to here as prelanguage) to true language was abrupt and the result of a single crucial mutation. However, it is difficult to accept that a system of communication as unique and complex as human language could have been the consequence of a single mutation. Then, too, the capacity of all normal children, regardless of ethnic background, to acquire any one of the several thousand natural languages with the same degree of mastery and according to approximately the same timetable is a strong indication that speech is innate throughout the human species and that all languages are simply variations on a common basic structural theme.

The theory of monogenesis may take two forms: radical (or straight-line) or, to use Hockett's term, fuzzy. Of the two, the fuzzy version of monogenesis appears more realistic. Although it presupposes a single origin of traits essential for language, it allows for the further development of the incipient capacity for speech to take place in separate groups of hominids within an area. The resulting differentiation could have been bridged by gene flow among the groups or brought to an end by the eventual dominance and survival of that early human population whose communicative system was most efficient. If, instead, several varieties of prelanguage managed to persist, then there would be more than one "dialect" ancestral to all those languages that developed subsequently.

## THE LIFE AND DEATH OF LANGUAGES

We have looked at the birth and growth of language in general and a few languages in particular. But another issue we must confront is **language death**. This occurs, obviously, when the last of its speakers die. Language death has been just as much a part of the evolutionary process as language expansion and language growth. According to the Multi-Tree (2009), a project sponsored by the National Science Foundation and the LINGUIST List, there are some 1,400 languages that we know about that have become extinct (http://multitree.org/codes/extinct.html). How many others there have been is impossible to know. As linguistic diversity was probably many times greater in the past than in modern times, at least an equal number more probably have become extinct.

Of course we must distinguish "normal" language death through natural development from the kind of linguistic extinction we are referring to in this section. For instance, consider Old English, a language that no native English speakers living today could fathom unless they studied it as a foreign language. Old English is technically dead, but via Middle English and Shakespeare's Early Modern English, it is alive and well in most places in Britain and North America (to name only a few). We would not consider Old English to be really extinct in the same way as we would Gaagudju in Australia, when its last native speaker, Big Bill Neidjie, died in May 2002. Language change does not equal language death.

A look at a source book such as *Ethnologue* (Gordon 2005; Lewis 2009) shows that there is great linguistic diversity all around us: The world's 6 billion people speak some 7,000 languages. On the surface this seems healthy, as this averages out to about 850,000 speakers per language. However, Tables 6.2 and 6.3 show what the problems are—things are not evenly distributed. Table 6.2 shows that eight languages are spoken by 2.5 billion

**TABLE 6.2** DISTRIBUTION OF THE WORLD'S LANGUAGES AND NUMBER OF SPEAKERS

| | *Living Languages* | | | *Number of Speakers* | | |
|---|---|---|---|---|---|---|
| POPULATION RANGE | NUMBER | PERCENT | CUMULATIVE % | TOTAL NUMBER | PERCENT | CUMULATIVE % |
| 100,000,000 to 999,999, 999 | 8 | 0.1% | 0.1% | 2,614,031,200 | 40.2% | 40.2% |
| 10,000,000 to 99,999,999 | 84 | 1.2% | 1.3% | 2,608,411,777 | 40.1% | 80.3% |
| 1,000,000 to 9,999,999 | 306 | 4.3% | 5.6% | 917,412,798 | 14.1% | 94.4% |
| 100,000 to 999,999 | 944 | 13.3% | 18.9% | 297,092,808 | 4.6% | 98.9% |
| 10,000 to 99,999 | 1,808 | 25.5% | 44.4% | 61,213,595 | 1.0% | 99.9% |
| 1,000 to 9,999 | 1,979 | 27.9% | 72.3% | 7,614,348 | 0.12% | 99.99% |
| 100 to 999 | 1,070 | 15.1% | 87.3% | 469,345 | 0.007% | 99.99980% |
| 10 to 99 | 337 | 4.7% | 92.1% | 12,753 | 0.0002% | 99.99999% |
| 1 to 9 | 132 | 1.9% | 94.0% | 536 | 0.00001% | 100.00000% |
| 0 | 220 | 3.1% | 97.1% | 0 | 0.00000% | 100.00000% |
| **UNKNOWN** | **209** | **2.9%** | **100.0%** | | | |
| **TOTALS** | **7,097** | **100%** | **100.0%** | **6,506,259,160** | **100%** | **100%** |

From Simons, Gary F. and Charles D. Fennig (eds.). 2017. *Ethnologue: Languages of the World, Twentieth edition*. Dallas, Texas: SIL International. Online version: http://www.ethnologue.com. Used by permission, © SIL.

**TABLE 6.3** DISTRIBUTION OF THE WORLD'S LANGUAGES BY DEGREE OF ENDANGERMENT OR STATUS

| | | *Living Languages* | | | *Number of Speakers* | | | |
|---|---|---|---|---|---|---|---|---|
| DESCRIPTION | SCALE CODE | NUMBER | PERCENT | CUMUL. % | TOTAL | PERCENT | CUMUL. % | AVERAGE |
| international | 0 | 6 | 0.1% | 0.1% | 1,910,305,410 | 29.4% | 29.4% | 318,384,235 |
| national | 1 | 96 | 1.4% | 1.4% | 1,944,722,578 | 29.9% | 59.3% | 20,257,527 |
| provincial | 2 | 68 | 1.0% | 2.4% | 627,218,790 | 9.6% | 68.9% | 9,223,806 |
| wide comm. | 3 | 166 | 2.3% | 4.7% | 584,974,240 | 8.9% | 77.9% | 3,523,941 |
| education | 4 | 236 | 3.3% | 8.1% | 252,622,839 | 3.9% | 81.8% | 1,070,436 |
| developing | 5 | 1,619 | 22.8% | 30.9% | 677,113,264 | 10.4% | 92.2% | 418,229 |
| vigorous | 6a | 2,462 | 34.7% | 65.6% | 448,099,167 | 6.9% | 99.1% | 182,006 |
| threatened | 6b | 1,061 | 14.9% | 80.5% | 50,831,670 | 0.8% | 99.8% | 47,909 |
| shifting | 7 | 463 | 6.5% | 87.0% | 9,535,479 | 0.1% | 99.987% | 20,595 |
| moribund | 8a | 279 | 3.9% | 91.0% | 765,298 | 0.01% | 99.998% | 2,743 |
| near extinct | 8b | 423 | 6.0% | 96.9% | 70,425 | 0.0011% | 100.000% | 166 |
| dormant | 9 | 218 | 3.1% | 100.0% | 0 | 0.0% | 100.0% | 0 |
| **TOTALS** | | **7,097** | **100.0%** | | **6,506,259,160** | **100.0%** | | |

From Simons, Gary F. and Charles D. Fennig (eds.). 2017. *Ethnologue: Languages of the World, Twentieth edition*. Dallas, Texas: SIL International. Online version: http://www.ethnologue.com. Used by permission, © SIL.

people, or 40.5 percent of the world's population. Only seventy-seven languages (about 1.2 percent of the 7,000) are spoken by more than 78 percent of the world's population. Around 94 percent of the world's languages are spoken by only 6 percent of the population. More than half the world's population speaks just twenty languages. The 4,000 least common languages are spoken by only a total of 8 million people; the 2,000 least common languages, less than half a million.

But in addition, this diversity is threatened even more because languages are dying at an alarming rate. David Crystal (2004:47) claims that, on average, one language dies every two weeks. At that rate, half the world's languages will become extinct within this century. We are witnessing language death at rates unprecedented in human history. In this section we will look at why so many languages are dying and what—if anything—can be done about it.

### *Endangered Languages*

According to the US Fish and Wildlife Service, in 2017 more than 2,300 species of plants and animals worldwide were considered threatened with extinction or seriously endangered, and citizens of the United States and other countries are frequently reminded of this fact by the media. On the other hand, very few people are being made aware that some of the world's languages are facing a similar threat at an ever-increasing rate. Table 6.2 shows that more than six hundred languages have fewer than one hundred speakers, and more than 1,700 languages have 1,000 speakers at most.

Table 6.3 shows the status of the world's languages using *Ethnologue*'s Expanded Graded Intergenerational Disruption Scale (EGIDS). Basically this is a 0-to-10 scale estimating the overall health versus endangerment of a language (http://www.ethnologue.com/about/language-status). An "international" language like English gets a 0. Languages used "nationally" and "provincially" are 1 and 2. Languages at least used in "education" are 4, and so on, down to "nearly extinct" (8b) or "extinct" (10). Of the 7,000 languages used in the world today (keeping in mind that by the time you are reading this book, the number will have been reduced by as many as several dozen), only about fifteen are higher than "threatened" (6b), and probably only six hundred can be considered safe, meaning that the number of their speakers will have become larger, or will at least maintain a necessary critical mass. (In theory, very small societies could maintain their languages if they were both viable and isolated from large societies around them, but such isolation is less and less possible. And if there still are such societies, say, in New Guinea or near the Amazon, their isolation will not last much longer.)

Why do languages die? A fairly common reason in the past could be that very small societies did not survive epidemic diseases against which they had no resistance, or they perished in warfare or in such natural disasters as earthquakes, floods, volcanic eruptions, and drought. The most common reason during the twentieth century was the economic and cultural influence of large nation-states that encompass small tribal societies within their borders. Unable to provide for themselves by their traditional means of subsistence, they become dependent on the dominant society and must learn to communicate with that larger society in its own language. Quite frequently there is a phase of bilingualism during which members of the small society have command of both languages; but this phase usually does not last long because the next generation becomes monolingual in the language of the larger society.

This has happened with many of the Native American languages spoken in the United States. For example, toward the end of the nineteenth century and in the early years of the twentieth, an aggressive effort was made on the part of public schools and mission schools on Western reservations to teach young Native American students English. School administrators used such punishments as not allowing pupils in residential schools to spend weekends with their families if they forgot themselves and spoke to each other in their native language. Less than one hundred years later, the situation has been practically reversed: The US government has financed efforts to preserve languages on the verge of disappearing. Unfortunately, for most languages the demise can be postponed only for a generation, if that long.

### *Language Death*

"Why should we care [if a language dies]?" This query was asked by noted linguist David Crystal. He devoted a full chapter of his popular book (2000:27–67) to discussing five reasons we should care: 1. because we need diversity in order to preserve our traditional cultural wealth; 2. because a language constitutes the primary symbol of ethnic identity; 3. because languages, whether written or unwritten, are repositories of history; 4. because languages contribute to the sum of human knowledge; and 5. because languages are fascinating in themselves. As one fieldworker observed, "To fight to preserve the smaller cultures and languages may turn out to be the struggle to preserve the most precious things that make us human before we end up in the landfill of history" (cited in Crystal 2000:67). And as Kenneth Hale, a linguist at MIT who devoted himself to preserving languages of small tribal societies, once said, "When you lose a language, it's like dropping a bomb on a museum."

This situation poses important questions: Should anthropological or linguistic fieldworkers make special efforts to maintain or revitalize an endangered language? Should they try to persuade the remaining speakers of such an endangered language to make sure that the youngest members learn it as their mother tongue (along with the language of the dominant society as their second language)? And should linguistic anthropologists wonder whether they have a moral obligation to try to save a language even if its speakers are ambivalent about its practical value and future usefulness? Answers to such questions are not easy to come by. Not only has very little debate taken place on this subject, but the resources for the study of endangered languages are still far from adequate. In the meantime, languages are dying out at a faster pace every year.

### *Language Maintenance and Reinforcement: An Arapaho Example*

Since the mid-1960s, increasing efforts by linguists and Native American tribal leaders have been devoted to language maintenance and reinforcement in communities where the traditional transmission of oral skills from parents to children is no longer functioning effectively. Although perhaps as many as two hundred Native American languages are still spoken at least to some extent in the United States and Canada, ever-increasing numbers of them are in danger of being completely replaced by English. Only a relatively few Native American languages (for example, Navajo, some of the Siouan languages of the northern Plains, and Inuit) continue to play a vital role in Indian community life; they are the languages serving larger populations in the less densely inhabited parts of North America. Language maintenance and reinforcement typically include linguistic analysis (on all levels—phonological, morphological, syntactic, and lexical), a writing system (usually the Latin alphabet with a few additional symbols and diacritics if necessary), and the production of instructional materials for the use of Native American pupils.

For the Northern Arapaho of the Wind River Reservation in Wyoming, who are eager to maintain, and even reinforce, their ethnic identity and cultural heritage, the present situation is nothing short of critical. Several factors contribute to the gloomy outlook:

1. With few exceptions, the only individuals who have full command of Arapaho—even if they no longer use it habitually and even if English has come to influence it—are members of the oldest generation.
2. Parents no longer teach Arapaho to their children in the home.
3. The numbers of active speakers and of those who have at least some passive knowledge of Arapaho are declining rapidly.
4. The bulk of the population is for all practical purposes monolingual; English is preferred in essentially all situations, including even some traditional ceremonial contexts.
5. Arapaho is losing its communicative viability—its capability to adapt successfully to new situations.

It is sad that young Arapaho parents can no longer be expected to pass along to their children the rich cultural heritage of the tribe, the Arapaho language in particular. As a result, the task has fallen to the reservation schools.

The most significant step taken to arrest the language decay was to formalize the teaching of spoken Arapaho to the youngest pupils. Thanks to the foresight and energy of the administrators of one of the schools, two weeklong workshops were organized in March and September 1984 to experiment with videotaping lessons in spoken Arapaho for use in reservation classrooms. So much was learned from the work of those two weeks that at a January workshop the following year, it was possible to approach the task with a greater degree of professional skill and, aided by the administrators of another school, to produce the first formal set of lessons in spoken Arapaho. The Spoken Arapaho Curriculum Development Project team set its goal for the two weeks rather ambitiously at forty lessons, but the enthusiasm of the participants was such that forty-two were completed and are still in classroom use. To spare young pupils from having to learn how to write two languages (Arapaho spelling happens to be much simpler than English spelling because it is phonemic), Arapaho-speaking classroom aides teach the students spoken Arapaho with the help of the videotapes. Forty-odd lessons will not reverse the declining fortunes of the Arapaho language on the reservation, but their completion and use in the lower grades have the great symbolic value of a last-ditch stand and a hope for things to come.

Also, the end of 1983 saw the completion of the *Dictionary of Contemporary Arapaho Usage*, made possible by a grant from the National Endowment for the Humanities. It was a source of great satisfaction to the Arapaho that the very same government that only a few generations ago prohibited the use of Native American languages in schools has become seriously concerned with their preservation.

While the work on the dictionary and the videotaped lessons was taking place, one of the schools continued to add to the growing series of booklets designed to aid the teaching of Arapaho language and culture in the upper grades. Overall, the body of instructional materials produced under various auspices for use with Arapaho students in the reservation schools is quite impressive—more than one hundred items, not counting the videotaped lessons. Not to be outdone by the other schools, staff members of a third school came up with an idea to further help revitalize the efforts made on behalf of Arapaho: an annual Arapaho language bowl for the most accomplished students of the reservation schools, with prizes and diplomas to be awarded.

Since the first edition of this book came out in 1993, further developments have occurred. Stephen Greymorning, director for several years of the Arapaho Language and Culture Project among the Northern Arapaho of Wyoming, began an Arapaho-language immersion project for kindergarten children and then expanded it through the addition of a preschool program. For use with the children, Greymorning arranged for the Disney film *Bambi* to be dubbed in Arapaho by Disney Studios, using Greymorning's translation and with Arapaho elders and children from the immersion program speaking the roles. The dubbed film became available in several thousand copies, and young children were said to watch it repeatedly, learning the speaking parts of their favorite characters. Although these and other revitalization efforts are not likely to save the Arapaho language in the long term, they are a welcome step forward at a time when so many languages are becoming seriously endangered or extinct.

This brief account of one example of language maintenance and reinforcement would not be complete without emphasizing that many additional steps must be taken to expand the program in the future. The following steps are worth mentioning here (the list is meant to be merely suggestive, not complete): workshops designed to develop new Arapaho curricular materials and improve the existing ones; in-service training of current Arapaho studies teachers and teacher aides; an internship program for future teachers of Arapaho studies; tribal scholarships for Arapaho high school students who have shown exceptional intellectual capacity as well as interest and skill in learning Arapaho to allow them to study linguistics and anthropology at the college level; adult education programs featuring elders narrating, in Arapaho or English, traditional tales or life histories and other reminiscences; and an Arapaho-language summer camp for preschoolers and elementary pupils, staffed in part by those Arapaho elders, women and men, who have command of the language and a willingness to share it with the young members of the tribe.

In the initial stages of any language maintenance programs, linguistic anthropologists provide useful advice and help (see Box 6.1), but it is preferable and important that, as far as possible, such programs and activities be further developed, organized, and administered by members of the societies concerned.

## SUMMARY AND CONCLUSIONS

Speech is only one of several means by which humans communicate, but it is the most common and efficient one. Besides the acoustic channel employed in speaking, people

## BOX 6.1 WHAT LINGUISTIC ANTHROPOLOGISTS HELPED ACCOMPLISH

It is the policy of the United States to—

(1) preserve, protect, and promote the rights and freedom of Native Americans to use, practice, and develop Native American languages; . . .

(3) encourage and support the use of Native American languages as a medium of instruction in order to encourage and support—

(A) Native American language survival,
(B) educational opportunity,
(C) increased student success and performance,
(D) increased student awareness and knowledge of their culture and history, and
(E) increased student and community pride;

(4) encourage State and local education programs to work with Native American parents, educators, Indian tribes, and other Native American governing bodies in the implementation of programs to put this policy into effect;

(5) recognize the right of Indian tribes and other Native American governing bodies to use the Native American languages as a medium of instruction in all schools funded by the Secretary of the Interior; . . .

(7) support the granting of comparable proficiency achieved through course work in a Native American language the same academic credit as comparable proficiency achieved through course work in a foreign language . . .

Public Law 101-477 of 1990, Title I, Native American Languages Act

make use of other channels, especially the optical one; they do so whenever they make gestures or facial expressions and, of course, when they write.

Communication is common among animals of all species and in some cases is surprisingly elaborate. To a considerable extent, animals are genetically endowed with communicative behavior; that is, they do not have to learn it. Although the capacity for speech is also a part of human genetic makeup, the particular language or languages an individual happens to speak must be learned. Among the design features that distinguish speech from the communicative behavior of other animals, the most striking are productivity, displacement, and reflexiveness.

The emergence of the order of primates, to which humans belong, dates to some 60–70 million years ago, only a small fraction of the 3–4 billion years since life on Earth began. Most of the early primates were arboreal, but in the course of time, as a result of changes in the natural environment, some of them became adapted to existence on the ground.

One of the subdivisions of primates is the superfamily of **hominoids** (Hominoidea), which in turn comprises three families: the lesser apes (siamangs and gibbons), the great apes (gorillas, orangutans, and chimpanzees), and the hominids (Hominidae) (humans and their immediate ancestors). Current evidence suggests that the earliest hominids came from East African sites in Tanzania, Kenya, and Ethiopia and go back about 3–4 million years. The best-known specimen among them, referred to as Lucy, and fossil bones of a similar type have been assigned to the genus *Australopithecus* (southern [African] ape) and the species *afarensis*, named for the Afar badlands in Ethiopia, where the discovery was made in 1974. Small-brained, with cranial capacity estimated at about one pint (473 cubic centimeters), these early hominids were bipedal; that is, they used only their lower limbs for locomotion.

There is not complete agreement on the intermediate link between *Australopithecus afarensis* and the first representatives of the human genus, although most experts would probably choose another **australopithecine** species, *Australopithecus africanus*. This man ape, whose fossil remains in South Africa date to about 3 million years ago, was quite likely an ancestral form of *Homo habilis*, with whom it may have shared parts of Africa for several hundred thousand years. As the term suggests, *Homo habilis* is considered to be the first human, though still far removed from the modern species. The remains of *Homo habilis*, found in Tanzania and Kenya and dated between 1.9 million and 1.6 million years old, came from individuals with a braincase capacity equal to about one-half that of modern humans. These early humans were correspondingly shorter in stature but more capable of making and using simple tools than the australopithecines may have been before them. Members of this species undoubtedly began to depend to an ever-increasing degree on group activity and a culturally patterned means of subsistence rather than on behavior governed solely by instinct.

With the appearance of *Homo habilis*, the pace of human evolution accelerated, producing a new species, *Homo erectus*, close to 2 million years ago. Members of this species spread from Africa to Asia and Europe, enduring for more than 1 million years until some 400,000 to 300,000 years ago. The tool kit of *Homo erectus*, best known for the multipurpose hand ax, included a variety of other implements used for cutting, piercing, chopping, and scraping. Evidence indicates that these ancestors of modern humans possessed the skills needed to become proficient large-game hunters. They also learned to use fire to keep warm, to prepare food, and to drive animals to locations where they could more easily be dispatched. The greater complexity of their culture was associated with an increased size of the brain, the average volume of which in *Homo erectus* approached about one quart (1,000 cubic centimeters). The last major stage in human evolution took place about 300,000 years ago with the transition from *Homo erectus* to *Homo sapiens*, the species to which all contemporary humans belong.

Communication among early hominids such as the australopithecines undoubtedly involved several modes, with a combination of the visual channel (manual gestures or facial expressions) and the vocal-auditory channel (simple vocalizations) predominating over touch and smell. Adaptations that made speech possible very likely coincided with the initial stages of hominization—the evolutionary development of human characteristics—some 2 to 3 million years ago. The process was exceedingly slow, but in the course of time the early hominids came to rely primarily on the vocal-auditory channel, probably as a result of the increasing employment of hands for making and using tools. The steadily expanding repertory of calls eventually led to blending, which may have had its beginnings with *Homo habilis* and reached the limits of serviceable complexity (prelanguage) in late *Homo erectus* times. At that point, the stage was set for the development of duality of patterning, and the efficiency of full-fledged language was completed by *Homo sapiens* some 50,000 to 70,000 years ago at the latest, and likely even earlier.

Of necessity, this has been a very brief and oversimplified account of how language may have come about; the reader should bear in mind the length of time the process took and the countless changes, both behavioral and anatomical (and hence genetic), required for the attainment of full humanness.

At the same time, death is part of the cycle of human language development and growth. In this chapter we also examined a major trend in what David Crystal calls the world's linguistic ecology: simply put, most of the world's languages are dying out—quickly—and our linguistic diversity is, for good or bad, rapidly disappearing. However, there are also many pressures working to maintain linguistic diversity. Revitalization programs and language maintenance efforts have been undertaken by many cultures worldwide whose members realize the importance of retaining their knowledge and traditions in their indigenous tongues.

## RESOURCE MANUAL AND STUDY GUIDE

### *Questions for Discussion*

1. All animals communicate, that is, transmit information between organisms by means of different kinds of signs. Discuss those characteristics of human languages that are *not* found in the communicative behavior of any other species in the animal kingdom.
2. Chimpanzees communicate, but their means (channels) of communication are different (as is also the scope) from those used by humans. Discuss the differences and the reasons for them.
3. What is the difference between prelanguage and protolanguage? On what basis do we judge the transition from prelanguage to full-fledged language to have taken place?

### *Projects*

**PROJECT 1**

The following are some real comments made by ten people, taken off the Web, in response to the question: "Do you think the world's linguistic diversity should be preserved?" I am sure you have an opinion on this matter. Respond to at least four of the arguments made below (pro or con, your choice; you are not necessarily obligated to support saving endangered languages). You may respond in either essay form or a student-discussion format.

1. At least we have come a long way from the times when languages were repressed and forbidden in favor of the language of the dominant political or colonial power. But I believe that the matter of preserving declining languages should best be left to private initiative among those who have a personal interest in seeing them preserved.
2. I believe that all languages are unique and help identify who we are as a people and as an individual. It is unfortunate that most languages are on the verge of dying, but that's the price of progress.
3. The utility of a single global language, spoken by everyone as their mother tongue, would surely outweigh any loss of cultural heritage.
4. It's sad when a language dies out, but it is unavoidable, isn't it? If not by suddenly no longer being used, it will happen simply due to the language changing slowly over time. The "English" that exists today is very different from a thousand years ago and from what will be in a thousand years. History is littered with languages that no longer exist.

5. I think that the reduction in the number of languages spoken is also a great way to help unify the world and humans in general. How can we expect cultures to keep peace between each other when they cannot understand each other? Having one or a few global languages will make things much more convenient and seamless. Also, languages isolate communities, which are most likely to be economically weak. "Our heritage" is only history, and history will never and can never be more important than the present or the future.
6. Professor Salikoko Mufwene is absolutely right when he says that asking groups to hold onto languages they no longer want is more for the linguists' sake than for the communities themselves. Communities are best served by a language that can be used to communicate intelligibly with the greatest number of people. It would seem to me that the fewer the number of languages, the fewer the chances for misunderstanding one another. The revival of dead or minority languages such as those mentioned in the article is an affectation at best and insular at worst. Even if people no longer communicated with one another using these minor languages, that does not mean that knowledge of these minor languages would be gone. After all, no one now speaks Latin, but the language itself is not lost.
7. Most of the problems in the world stem from a lack of communication. If we all spoke English then these problems might disappear. It may be sad to lose other languages, but we must strive for one universal language.
8. Not only is the death of languages a natural thing, it's also a good thing. "Whereof one cannot speak, thereof one must be silent" wrote Wittgenstein. By that he meant if you can't describe an object or a concept in a language, then you can't think about it or engage with it. Concepts of parliamentary democracy, the liberal economy, or multicultural societies cannot be expressed in Mayan or Navajo or even Latin. It's one of the reasons they're dead, while English-speaking societies thrive and prosper around the world.
9. A good proverb: a house divided against itself cannot stand. The earth is the home of humans, plants, animals, various forms of life. Right now we humans have divided this home of ours into divided nations, languages, religions, and so on. In this time and age we need unity more than divisions. What is the point of having hundreds of languages that will make it difficult for people from different places to communicate?
10. Languages that are dying out should just be catalogued for the interests of linguists, but communities shouldn't be forced to use it, and at the very most it should be taught to the next generation as a secondary language, much like Welsh is in Wales.

**PROJECT 2**

Consider these two "conversations." The first is between a signing gorilla, Gogo, and her trainer. The second is between one of our graduate students, Dan, and his three-year-old daughter, Ally.

***Conversation 1***

*Trainer:* *[OK, can] you tell me how gorillas talk?*
*Gorilla:* *pounds chest*
*T:* *What [do] gorillas say when [they're] happy?*
*G:* *Gorilla hug*
*T:* *What [do] gorillas say to [their] babies?*
*G:* *pounds chest*
*T:* *What [do] you say to your [doll] baby?*
*G:* *Love Gogo . . . give me nut*
*T:* *gives nut*
*T:* *What [do] you say to Mike (another gorilla) when you play?*

G: *Mike Gogo love*
T: *What scares gorillas?*
G: *Hat . . . dog*
T: *Hats [and] dogs scare gorillas?*
G: *Gorilla*
T: *What [do] gorillas say [when] tired?*
G: *Gorilla sleep*
T: *What [do] gorilla think [is] funny?*
G: *Clown . . . bug*
T: *Enough?*
G: *Gogo love . . . Gogo love*
T: *What?*
G: *Drink apple*
T: *[How about a] grape drink?*
G: *Gogo love drink*
T: *You [are] very smart [Are] all gorillas smart?*
G: *no response*
T: *[Are] gorillas smart [or] stupid?*
G: *Smart Gogo*
T: *What [do] you hate?*
G: *Love*
T: *[That's] nice, you love everything.*
G: *Candy . . . fruit*
T: *Where do gorillas go when they die[?]*
G: *Old hole die*

***Conversation 2***

Dan: *Can you tell me how people talk?*
Ally: *Like this: baa baa here baa baa there Old MacDonald had a farm Do you want something . . . please may I be excused*
D: *What do people say when they are happy?*
A: *Um . . . pick up the toys . . . love (gives a big hug)*
D: *What do people say to their babies?*
A: *Don't cry*
D: *What do you say to your doll?*
A: *It'll be OK*
D: *What do you say to Thor when you play?*
A: *She did not understand, got tired of the questions and answers, and left.*
D: *What scares people?*
A: *Alligators!*
D: *What do you say when you are tired?*
A: *Nothing else . . . I don't have any more words*
D: *What do you think is funny?*
A: *You!*
D: *Are people smart or stupid?*
A: *Smart*
D: *What don't you like, Ally?*
A: *Alligators!*
D: *How do people feel when they die?*
A: *Nothing*
D: *Where [do] people go when they die?*
A: *Goats . . . daffodil . . . her went to see the mens*

*D: When do people die?*
*A: Jesus died . . . in my Bible*
*D: Where do babies come from?*
*A: In people's tummy and the hospital too*
*D: What is the meaning of life?*
*A: Laying down?*

Comment on these two conversations. Argue that they support the ape language hypothesis OR ELSE criticize the dialogue by arguing that it does not support the ape language hypothesis.

## *Objective Study Questions*

### TRUE-FALSE TEST

T F 1. Honeybees are able to communicate the location and approximate distance of an abundant source of nectar immediately after hatching; they do not have to learn how to do it.

T F 2. Young chimpanzees can learn to say several dozen words, but when they become adult they do not teach their young to speak.

T F 3. The discontinuity theory of language evolution holds that human language must be recognized as unique, without evolutionary antecedents.

T F 4. Interspecific communication—that is, transmission of signals between members of different species—is far from rare.

T F 5. The design feature of displacement is unique only to humans and some of the higher apes.

T F 6. One amazing thing about languages is that in each, a limited number of contrastive sounds—only several dozen on the average—make up tens of thousands of individual words.

T F 7. It is reasonable to assume that the Cro-Magnons, who lived some 30,000 years before the present and were known for their cave art, had a full-fledged language or nearly so.

T F 8. The term prelanguage refers to the stage in the development of language that preceded full-fledged language; protolanguage refers to an assumed or reconstructed fully developed language.

T F 9. It is safe to assume that the australopithecines had some sort of a multimodal system of communication.

T F 10. It appears that the ability of the higher primates to communicate must have been an important evolutionary step toward the development of speech in humans.

T F 11. The mother tongue of Arapaho schoolchildren today is English.

### MULTIPLE-CHOICE QUESTIONS

____ 1. Of all the design features of language, the one that appears to be most distinctly and uniquely human is (A) broadcast transmission and directional reception. (B) rapid fading. (C) vocal-auditory channel. (D) openness (productivity).

____ 2. The fact that the four-legged domestic animal that barks is called dog in English, Hund in German, pes in Czech, and heu in Arapaho is the design feature referred to as (A) duality of patterning. (B) displacement. (C) arbitrariness. (D) complete feedback.

____ 3. Which of the following statements having to do with communicative behavior among the great apes is not acceptable? (A) The pygmy chimpanzees of central Africa appear to be more intelligent, sociable, and eager to learn than common chimpanzees. (B) Despite the well-known experiment of the Hayeses with the female chimpanzee Viki, it appears that the ability to speak is unique to humans. (C) Sarah, a chimpanzee, had a plastic-token vocabulary of about 130 terms and used them with a surprisingly high

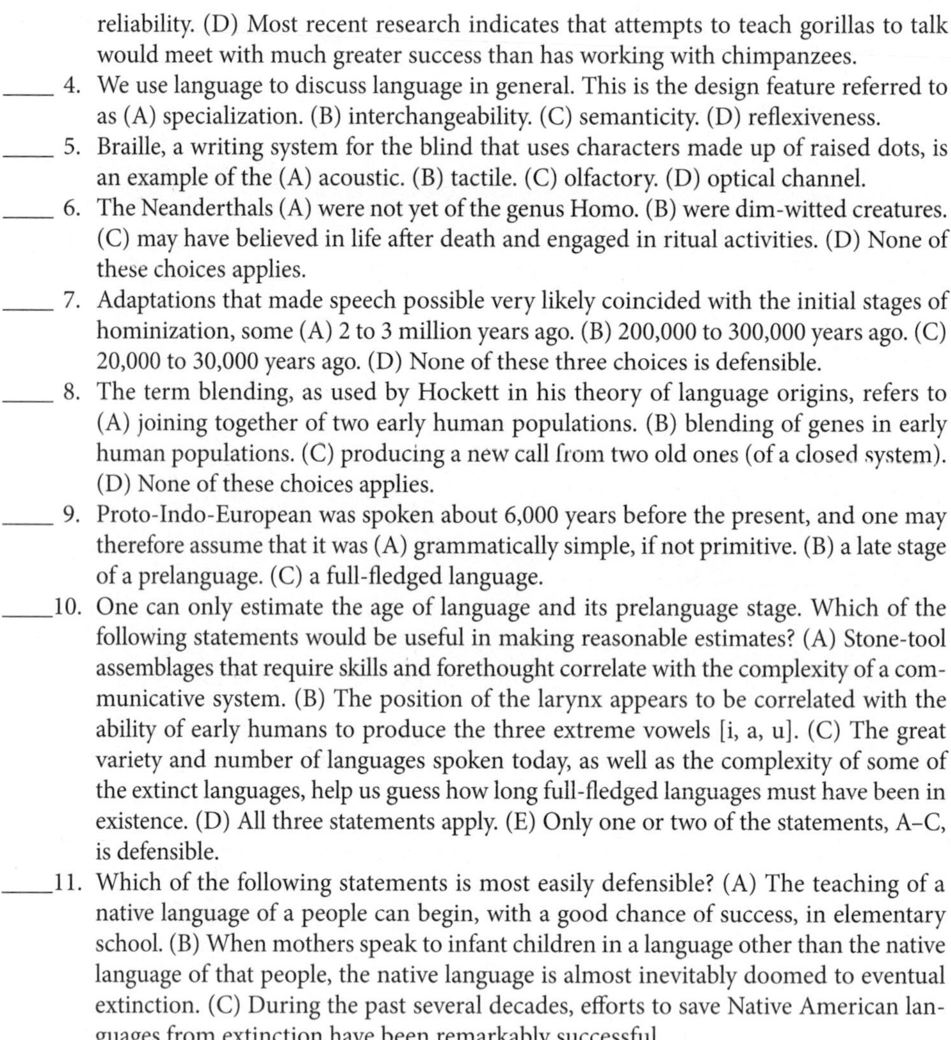

reliability. (D) Most recent research indicates that attempts to teach gorillas to talk would meet with much greater success than has working with chimpanzees.

____ 4. We use language to discuss language in general. This is the design feature referred to as (A) specialization. (B) interchangeability. (C) semanticity. (D) reflexiveness.

____ 5. Braille, a writing system for the blind that uses characters made up of raised dots, is an example of the (A) acoustic. (B) tactile. (C) olfactory. (D) optical channel.

____ 6. The Neanderthals (A) were not yet of the genus Homo. (B) were dim-witted creatures. (C) may have believed in life after death and engaged in ritual activities. (D) None of these choices applies.

____ 7. Adaptations that made speech possible very likely coincided with the initial stages of hominization, some (A) 2 to 3 million years ago. (B) 200,000 to 300,000 years ago. (C) 20,000 to 30,000 years ago. (D) None of these three choices is defensible.

____ 8. The term blending, as used by Hockett in his theory of language origins, refers to (A) joining together of two early human populations. (B) blending of genes in early human populations. (C) producing a new call from two old ones (of a closed system). (D) None of these choices applies.

____ 9. Proto-Indo-European was spoken about 6,000 years before the present, and one may therefore assume that it was (A) grammatically simple, if not primitive. (B) a late stage of a prelanguage. (C) a full-fledged language.

____10. One can only estimate the age of language and its prelanguage stage. Which of the following statements would be useful in making reasonable estimates? (A) Stone-tool assemblages that require skills and forethought correlate with the complexity of a communicative system. (B) The position of the larynx appears to be correlated with the ability of early humans to produce the three extreme vowels [i, a, u]. (C) The great variety and number of languages spoken today, as well as the complexity of some of the extinct languages, help us guess how long full-fledged languages must have been in existence. (D) All three statements apply. (E) Only one or two of the statements, A–C, is defensible.

____11. Which of the following statements is most easily defensible? (A) The teaching of a native language of a people can begin, with a good chance of success, in elementary school. (B) When mothers speak to infant children in a language other than the native language of that people, the native language is almost inevitably doomed to eventual extinction. (C) During the past several decades, efforts to save Native American languages from extinction have been remarkably successful.

## Answer Key

True-false test: 1-T, 2-F, 3-T, 4-T, 5-F, 6-T, 7-T, 8-T, 9-T, 10-F, 11-T
Multiple-choice questions: 1-D, 2-C, 3-D, 4-D, 5-B, 6-C, 7-A, 8-C, 9-C, 10-D, 11-B

## Notes and Suggestions for Further Reading

An excellent critical evaluation of and guide to early works concerning language origins was published by Hockett (1978). There has been a heightened and renewed interest in the origin and evolution of language in the past decade, probably due to greater attention being paid to this topic by such noted autonomous linguists as Noam Chomsky (e.g., Berwick and Chomsky 2016). Regardless, much discussion has been generated, and some of this can be found in places like Burling (2005) and Dessalles (2007); and as expected, Everett (2017) contradicts Chomsky. Destined to be the new standards are Fitch (2010) and Larson, Déprez, and Yamakido's edited collection (2010). But the definitive summary to date is the useful Oxford handbook edited by Tallerman and Gibson (2012). Jackendoff (2002) ambitiously tries to tie in formal linguistics, neuroanatomy, and language evolution.

Of the many books, book chapters, and articles dealing with the evolution of speech, the following may be of interest to readers who seek less technical treatment: Kenneally (2007),

Campbell (1979), Hockett and Ascher (1964), Stross (1976), and Time-Life Books (1973). More technical accounts may be found in de Grolier (1983); Harnad, Steklis, and Lancaster (1976); and Wescott (1974). Two Pinker works (1992 and 2009) have been bestsellers. The work of Bickerton (1990) is full of stimulating ideas and interesting speculations, but reviewers tend to consider many of Bickerton's specific claims indefensible and even contradictory (see Pinker 1992 and Burling 1992). For contrary views concerning the evolution of modern humans, see Wilson and Cann (1992) and Thorne and Wolpoff (1992).

There are many excellent treatments of human biological evolution; one of the most thorough yet accessible—as well as richly illustrated—is Cartmill and Smith (2009).

Informative sources concerning communication among animals include Sebeok (1977), Bright (1984), and Roitblat, Herman, and Nachtigall (1992). The dance language of bees is described in Frisch (1967). For communication of nonhuman primates, see Schrier and Stollnitz (1971), which contains articles by Keith J. Hayes and Catherine H. Nissen, Beatrice T. Gardner and R. Allen Gardner, and David Premack, who trained Viki, Washoe, and Sarah, respectively. For an extensive and richly illustrated report on the chimpanzees of Gombe National Park in Tanzania, see Goodall (1986), and for a book-sized discussion of Nim, see Terrace (1979). Savage-Rumbaugh (1986) discusses at length the various projects, including her own, to teach chimpanzees to communicate, and Susman (1984) deals with the evolutionary biology and behavior of pygmy chimpanzees. For a survey of works and bibliography concerning apes and language prior to 1978, see Hill (1978).

On endangered languages and language extinction, start with the overviews in Nettle and Romaine (2000) and Crystal (2000). Their points have remained unchallenged. But for further information and the latest statistics, go to the resources of *Ethnologue* written versions, Gordon (2005) and Lewis (2009). Of interest may be the contributions to the symposium "Endangered Languages" by Hale et al. (1992); for a contrary view of endangered languages, see Ladefoged (1992); and for a response to Ladefoged, see Dorian (1993). The standard text on the subject is now Thomason (2015).

The discussion of language maintenance and reinforcement among the Northern Arapaho of the Wind River Reservation is based on Salzmann's personal involvement in such a project during the 1980s. For the latest report on Arapaho language maintenance efforts, see Greymorning (2001).

# 7

# Acquiring and Using Language(s): Life with First Languages, Second Languages, and More

## LEARNING OBJECTIVES

- Name and describe three theories of language acquisition
- Describe the basic neurological structures of the brain that relate to language
- Clarify the different ways "bilingualism" is used
- Explain and give examples of code-switching
- Explain and give examples of diglossia

As most students know only too well, learning to speak a foreign language is a demanding undertaking that means coping with unfamiliar sounds and sound combinations, mastering grammatical rules different from those of one's native language, and learning a new vocabulary containing thousands of words. But if for most adults learning a foreign language is a major task, and only relatively few attain fluency in a second language, how is it that small children learn a language, or even two or more, as effortlessly as they do? Is first-language acquisition different from second-language acquisition? Is learning a third language easier than learning a second? Do **polyglots**—people who can speak several languages fluently—possess a special kind of innate intelligence the rest of us lack? Are the brains of **bilingual** and **multilingual** people somehow different from monolingual brains?

## THE FIRST STEPS OF LANGUAGE ACQUISITION IN CHILDHOOD

For the most part, children are not taught to speak their native language. They learn it by exposure to people who talk to them. They do not go to language labs, and they are given no pattern drills to memorize. In fact, children seem to pick up the language spoken around them with very little effort, and, indeed, often with little input. Actually, many of the examples they are presented are poor approximations of correct speech, as anyone who has ever heard a grandmother talk "baby talk" to a child knows. Yet by about age two or three, most children are usually communicating well enough for parents and most others to understand them.

The first step for the infant is to find some way to learn the phonological system. To reproduce the speech sounds of any particular language when they begin to talk, infants must learn to discriminate among sounds that may be quite similar. Among the sounds in English considered to be alike or to closely resemble each other are the initial consonants of such pairs of words as *bill* and *pill* or *thin* and *sin*, the final consonants of *sin* and *sing* or *dose* and *doze*, and the vowels of *pet* and *pat*, *pen* and *pin*, or *mill* and *meal*.

How soon and how well do infants discriminate among similar speech sounds? One of the techniques to test infants' acuity of sound perception is high-amplitude sucking. A pacifier connected to a system that generates sounds when a child sucks records the rate of sucking. When infants begin to hear sounds, they suck energetically, but they gradually lose interest if the sound stays the same. When the sound changes, however, vigorous sucking is resumed. Infants only one month old appear to be able to distinguish two synthetic consonant-vowel syllables different only in the initial consonants *p* and *b*. Other tests have established that infants are born with the ability to differentiate between even closely similar sounds, but that this ability diminishes or disappears by the age of about one year in favor of perceiving only the differences crucial to the native language. The acuity of voice perception in newborn babies has also been attested. It has been established that three-day-old infants are able to distinguish their mothers' voices from among other female voices. And it has also been shown that newborn infants prefer to listen to their mother tongue rather than another language.

Although the rate of speech development in normal children varies somewhat, it is possible to generalize about the stages that characterize language acquisition. Only **reflexive** (basic biological) **noises** such as burping, crying, and coughing are produced during the first eight or ten weeks; these are supplemented by cooing and laughing during the next dozen or so weeks. **Vocal play**, consisting of the production of a fairly wide range of sounds resembling consonants and vowels, becomes noticeable by about the age of six months. The second half of an infant's first year is characterized by **babbling**. According to some observers, sounds made during this stage are less varied and tend to approximate those of the language to be acquired. Babbling appears to be largely instinctive because even children who do not hear go through the babbling stage. In general, even before the onset of babbling, infants show eagerness to communicate and begin to process the information they are receiving through various channels. It also appears that regardless of the language they are acquiring, children learn to use the maximally distinct vowel sounds of their language (usually *a*, *i*, and *u*) before other vowels, and the consonants articulated with the help of the lips and teeth (commonly *p*, *b*, *m*, *t*, and *d*) before those produced farther back in the mouth (Jakobson 1968). Although subsequent research has indicated that the order in which the sounds of languages are acquired is not universal, Roman Jakobson (1896–1982) must be credited with the discovery of significant statistical tendencies.

**Intonational contours** (such as those characteristic of questions) begin to appear around the end of the first year, at about the same time as the one-word stage (for example, *mama*, *cup*, and *doggie*). This stage is succeeded around the age of two by the multiword stage. At first the child combines two words (for example, *see doggie*, *baby book*, *nice kitty*, and *daddy gone*) but soon expands such phrases to short sentences. On the average, the spoken vocabulary of two-year-olds amounts to two hundred words or more, although they understand several times that many. Initial consonants of words tend to be pronounced more distinctly by this age group than the consonants toward word ends. By the age of five or so, all normal children the world over are able to ask questions, make negative statements, produce complex sentences (consisting of main and subordinate clauses), talk about things removed in time and space, and in general carry on an intelligent conversation on topics they are able to comprehend (but they have yet to learn to tie their shoes). Even though much of the speech to which children are exposed is quite variable and casual, they gain command of the many sounds, forms, and rules so well that they are able to say, and do say, things they have never before heard said—and all of this without the benefit of formal teaching.

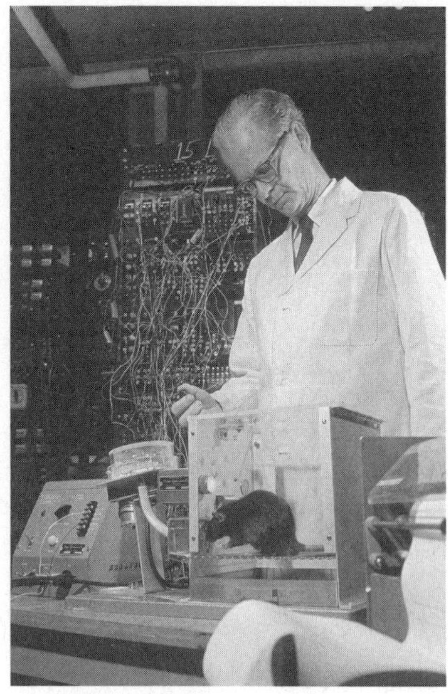

**Photo 7.1 B. F. Skinner. Nina Leen / Getty Images**

## SOME THEORIES OF LANGUAGE ACQUISITION

### *Behaviorist Psychology Theory*

Behaviorism is a school of psychology popular in the mid-twentieth century that made a major impact on learning theory. Probably its best-known proponent was B. F. Skinner (1904–1990), who argued for his view of language acquisition in his book *Verbal Behavior* (1957). Behavioral psychology theory is based on the stimulus-response-reward formula and is not unlike the popular view of language acquisition. According to this theory, the human environment (parents, older peers, and others) provides language stimuli to which the child responds, largely by repetition of what he or she is hearing. If the response is acceptable or commendable, the learner is rewarded (by praise or in some other way).

### *Innatist Theory*

Among the most influential approaches to language development is innatism. Where behaviorism argues that all of language is acquired through different types of learning (stimulus-response, classical conditioning, etc.), innatist theory argues that there are at least some aspects of language that must already be present in the child at birth. This point of view received great support when Noam Chomsky (1959), in a lengthy review of Skinner's book, convincingly undermined all of its assumptions and claims. For example, some things—like an equilateral triangle—are only products of the imagination and do not actually exist in the real world. Such things cannot be learned, then, in the behaviorist sense. And it is true that children do imitate, of course, but not as consistently as is generally thought. If children only imitated what they heard, how could we account for such forms

### BOX 7.1 CHOMSKY ON LANGUAGE ACQUISITION

We can think of every normal human's internalized grammar as, in effect, a theory of his language. This theory provides a sound-meaning correlation for an infinite number of sentences. . . .

In formal terms . . . we can describe the child's acquisition of language as a kind of theory construction. The child discovers the theory of his language with only small amounts of data from that language. . . . Normal speech consists, in large part, of fragments, false starts, blends, and other distortions of the underlying idealized forms. Nevertheless, as is evident from a study of the mature use of language, what the child learns is the underlying ideal theory. This is a remarkable fact. We must also bear in mind that the child constructs this ideal theory without explicit instruction, that he acquires this knowledge at a time when he is not capable of complex intellectual achievements in many other domains, and that this achievement is relatively independent of intelligence or the particular course of experience. These are facts that a theory of learning must face. . . .

. . . It is unimaginable that a highly specific, abstract, and tightly organized language comes by accident into the mind of every four-year-old child.

From Noam Chomsky, "Language and the Mind," *Psychology Today* 1(9)(1968):66

they produce as *sheeps*, *gooses*, and *taked*? There is no way behaviorism, Chomsky argued, could account for such analogical but ungrammatical forms. Such forms as *sheeps*, *gooses*, and *taked* in fact show that rather than imitating others, children derive these forms on the assumption of grammatical regularity—by extending the "regular" plural and past-tense markers to words to which they do not apply.

In Chomsky's view, children are born with a capacity for language development (see Box 7.1). However, the nature of the innate hypothetical **language acquisition device**, with which all infants are equipped, cannot at present be specified. According to some, it consists only of general procedures helping the child to discover how to learn any natural language; according to others, this device provides children with a knowledge of those features that are common to all languages. Chomsky (1986), for example, speaks of a genetically built-in "core grammar" that besides a number of fixed rules also contains various optional rules; it is up to the child to discover which of these options apply to a particular language. This would help to explain how children manage to overcome what is referred to as "poverty of stimulus"—that is, their ability to learn to speak a language effectively in a relatively short time, regardless of how complex it may be grammatically, even if much of what they hear happens to be largely fragmentary or repetitious.

It would probably oversimplify the explanation of how young children are able to acquire so rapidly the knowledge of such a complex symbolic system as language if one were to accept any one of these or other theories to the exclusion of the others. There is little doubt that children do imitate, but certainly not to the extent some claim, and it is also quite likely that the earliest phases of language learning are not completely divorced from the child's mental development. However, many of the aspects of the innatist theory are quite convincing, and the theory has received much acceptance. It is indirectly supported by the somewhat controversial critical-period (or **critical-age**) **hypothesis** that language is acquired with remarkable ease during brain maturation, that is, before puberty. By this time the brain has reached its full development, and the various functions it performs have been localized in one side or the other (**lateralization**). According to recent research, though, lateralization may already be complete by the end of the fifth year, by which age children have acquired the grammatical essentials of their mother tongue.

### *Sociocultural Theory*

Until recently, language acquisition was treated as if it were unaffected by sociocultural factors; correspondingly, the process of children's learning their culture was usually studied without giving attention to the role language plays in the process. Among those linguists and anthropologists who have called for the integration of the two approaches are Elinor Ochs and Bambi B. Schieffelin. In one of their works concerning language acquisition and socialization (1982), their view of the subject was expressed in the following two claims: "The process of acquiring language is deeply affected by the process of becoming a competent member of a society [and] the process of becoming a competent member of society is realized to a large extent through language, through acquiring knowledge of its functions . . . i.e., through exchanges of language in particular social situations" (Ochs and Schieffelin 1982:2–3). In the main body of the article, the authors made use of their fieldwork experiences in Western Samoa and Papua New Guinea (among the Kaluli) and for comparative purposes drew on data pertaining to the communicative development of children of the Anglo-American white middle class. To simplify matters, we present only the comparison between the Kaluli and the Anglo-American children.

According to Ochs and Schieffelin and others (e.g., Ochs and Schieffelin 1982, 2006; Ochs and Taylor 2001; Schieffelin 2005), these kinds of acquisition patterns can be found cross-culturally. For example, Anglo-American white middle-class infants interact mainly with their mothers. This dyadic (two-party) interaction is in part the consequence of the typical family form, postmarital residence, and physical setting characteristic of American middle-class apartments or houses—nuclear family, separate home for the young married couple, and a separate bedroom for an infant. Mothers (or caregivers) hold infants face to face and treat them as social beings and communicative partners, frequently taking the perspective of the child or displaying interest in what may have been meant by a child's incomplete or unintelligible utterance.

To accommodate young children and protect them from injury, the environment is adapted to their needs. Consider the availability of baby food, high chairs, and baby walkers as well as books and toys designed for specific ages, and the parental concern shown for the safety of the child by the cushioning of sharp edges, the placing of protective gates at stairs, and the like. The gap between the caregiver's and the child's verbal competence is reduced by a generous interpretation of the child's utterances or is masked by attempts to elicit stories from the child by posing questions he or she can answer with brief responses. In short, the child is the focus of attention and quite frequently the starting point of social interaction.

Among the Kaluli, a small, nonliterate, egalitarian society, the process of language acquisition and socialization is different. Kaluli babies are considered helpless and unable to comprehend the world around them; their unintelligible utterances tend to be ignored and no attempt is made to interpret them. Infants' needs are of course attended to, and a mother nurses her child even if she is involved in other activities. Nor are infants ever left alone: Mothers carry babies with them in netted bags whenever they happen to be gathering wood, gardening, or simply sitting and talking with others.

But despite the physical proximity of a mother and her child, there is little communicative interaction between them. Infants are carried facing others, not their mothers. When infants approaching the age of one year do something they should not, they are reprimanded with such questions as "Who are you?" or "Is it yours?" meaning, respectively, "You are not someone to do that" and "It is not yours." Not until a child begins to use the words *nɔ* "mother" and *bo* "breast" is the child considered ready to be "shown how to speak." Because adult men and women are involved in extensive networks of obligation and reciprocity as they organize their work and manipulate social relations, the primary goal of socialization at the time when children begin to talk is to teach them how to talk effectively. Among the conventions of adult speech is avoiding gossip and indicating the source of information by noting whether something has been heard or seen and by quoting others directly. Children are expected to follow these conventions. Very little language is directed to Kaluli children before they begin to talk, but the verbal environment in which they grow up is rich, and children acquire verbal skills from listening to others. Although the one large village longhouse, where all villagers once lived together, is no longer in general use, at least two or more extended family groups share living space. The presence of a dozen or more individuals in one semipartitioned dwelling leads to frequent multiparty interaction. To teach the Kaluli language as spoken by adults, mothers constantly correct children for faulty pronunciation, grammar, and use of words so that they bypass the stage of baby talk.

In evaluating the available information about how children develop their communicative skills for functioning in different societies or subcultures, the authors were led to assume that "infants and caregivers do not interact with one another according to one particular 'biologically designed choreography' . . . [but] there are many choreographies within and across societies . . . that contribute to their design, frequency and significance" (Ochs and Schieffelin 1982:44). This means, for example, that dyadic exchanges are accorded a varying degree of significance in different societies: Among the Kaluli, children are exposed to multiparty interaction much more frequently than to dyadic interaction.

The authors further proposed that the "simplifying features of caregiver speech that have been described for white middle class speakers are not necessary input for young children to acquire language," and on the basis of these two proposals, the authors suggested that "a functional account of the speech of both caregiver and child must incorporate information concerning cultural knowledge and expectations . . . [and] generalizations concerning the relations between behavior and goals of caregivers and young children should not presuppose the presence or equivalent significance of particular goals across social groups" (Ochs and Schieffelin 1982:46, 50).

Without language, no child could adequately learn all aspects of the culture and worldview of his or her society. It follows, then, that normal communicative exchanges in which caregivers and small children engage must in some way relate to the behavior patterns expected of adult members of a society. Are situations adapted to the child, or must the child adapt to situations? And if there is a shift from one to the other of these two orientations in any given society, when does it take place?

The authors made clear that their model does not exclude the role biological predisposition may play at the expense of culture and that they did not view socialization as a process that is inflexible over time or during an individual's lifetime. But they insisted that "our understanding of the functional and symbolic interface between language and culture" can be furthered only through studies of "how children are socialized through the use of language as well as how children are socialized to use language" (Schieffelin and Ochs 1986:184).

## LANGUAGE AND THE BRAIN

Even though our understanding of how the human brain operates is steadily increasing, our knowledge of its functions is still far from complete. Among the reasons for this are that the brain is tremendously complex and that experimentation with the brain is still somewhat limited. Some of what is known about its functions has been learned from the location and extent of brain injuries; however, a great deal of information has recently been gained from new experimental techniques (for example, neuroimaging and the stimulation of the cerebral cortex or nerve centers below it by electric current).

**Neurolinguistics**—the branch of linguistics concerned with the role the brain plays in language and speech processing—explores questions regarding which parts of the brain control language and speech; how the brain encodes and decodes speech; and whether the controls of such aspects of language as sounds, grammar, and meaning are neuroanatomically distinct or joint.

In relation to body mass, the human brain is not only the largest in the animal kingdom but also the most complexly organized. The largest part is the **cerebrum**, situated at the top of the brain and consisting of two lobes—the left and right cerebral hemispheres—and connecting structures. Each of the two hemispheres fulfills different functions. For example, the left is specialized for associative thought, calculation and analytical processing, the right visual field, temporal relations, and other functions; the right hemisphere for tactile recognition of material qualities, visuospatial skills, nonlinguistic auditory stimuli (including music), the left visual field, some use of language in social context, and others. In an overwhelming majority of right-handed individuals, the left hemisphere controls language, speech, writing, and reading. In more than one-half of left-handed people, it is also the left hemisphere that either controls language or is significantly involved; in other left-handers, language specialization is located in the right hemisphere. Apart from the cerebral cortex—the surface layer of gray matter of the cerebrum—several other parts of the brain contribute to language processing. One such part is the left thalamus, the largest subdivision of the posterior of the forebrain.

Injuries to specific areas of the language-dominant hemisphere from such causes as gunshot wound, tumor, stroke, or infection result in different aphasias or other impairments of linguistic capabilities. To give a few examples, Broca's aphasia, also referred to as expressive or motor aphasia, is caused by a lesion in what is known as **Broca's area** (see Figure 7.1) and is characterized by omission of function words (such as articles, prepositions, demonstratives, and conjunctions) and past-tense and plural endings, as well as by

**FIGURE 7.1** THE HUMAN BRAIN

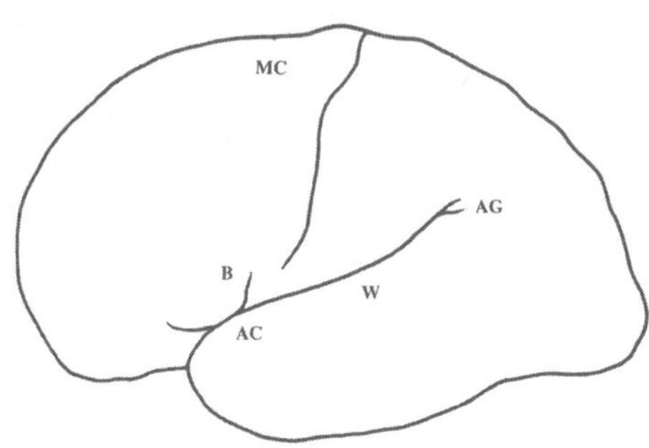


Side view of the left hemisphere of the human brain, with its front on the left. The locations of the areas mentioned in the text are indicated as follows: AC = auditory cortex; AG = angular gyrus; B = Broca's area; MC = motor cortex; W = Wernicke's area. The thalamus is not seen from this view.

faulty word order and distortions of sounds. Wernicke's aphasia, also known as sensory or receptive aphasia, results from a lesion in **Wernicke's area**; it is characterized by circumlocutions, impaired ability to understand written and spoken language, and occasional substitutions of inappropriate words, leading in severe cases to nonsensical utterances. Individuals affected by anomic aphasia have difficulty naming objects presented to them. Impairment of this type is associated with lesions in the dominant angular gyrus, one of the characteristic ridges of gray matter at the surfaces of the hemispheres.

Wernicke's area appears to generate the basic structure of sentences, which are then encoded in Broca's area; the articulation of sounds is directed by certain motor areas of the cortex. Comprehension of speech takes place in Wernicke's area after acoustic signals are transferred there from the ear by the auditory cortex. In general, speaking and writing are more likely to be affected by damage to the front part of the brain, listening and reading by damage to the rear part.

From what is now known, lesions in different parts of the language-dominant hemisphere result in different language and speech impairments. But much is yet to be learned about the human brain, both in general and concerning its role in communicative behavior.

## BILINGUAL AND MULTILINGUAL BRAINS

In the past, it was often assumed that competence acquired in the first language (L1) was qualitatively different from that in a second language (L2) or any subsequent language. This privileging of the "native language" led to many popular misconceptions, such as believing that children of bilingual parents would never fully acquire either language, remaining somehow linguistically disadvantaged. Such claims are made in the belief that monolingualism is the norm, and they are held by many in the United States and other countries where a single language is politically or socially dominant. That this view must be wrong can easily be seen from the fact that many people in the world speak more than one language. In fact, it is **bilingualism** or **trilingualism**, rather than monolingualism, that

**TABLE 7.1** SOME CRITERIA OF BILINGUALISM

| *criterion* | *the native language is* | *a speaker is bilingual who* |
|---|---|---|
| *origin* | the one first learned (and established first earliest contacts) | has learned two languages in the family from native speakers from the beginning |
| | | has used two languages simultaneously as a means of communication |
| *competence* | best known | has complete mastery of two languages |
| | | has native-like control of two languages |
| | | has equal mastery of two languages |
| | | can produce meaningful utterances in the other language |
| | | has knowledge and control of the grammar of the other language |
| *function* | mostly used | can use two languages in most situations regarding one's individual wishes and the demands of the community |
| *attitudes* | internal definition | identity by self<br>identifies oneself as bilingual and/or bicultural |
| | external definition | identity as is given by others as bilingual, or native speaker of two languages |

**From cf. T. Skutnabb-Kangas, 1984. Bilingualism or Not. Clevedon, UK: Multilingual Matters. p. 91.**

is most common. Even in supposedly monolingual nations such as the United States, US census figures show that at least 20 percent of Americans regularly speak a language other than English, and 53 percent of these people also speak English.

Another matter that must be considered is definition. "Bilingual" or "multilingual" can mean a variety of things. Some people may learn two languages natively as children and be equally proficient and comfortable in both. Others may have only full competence in one language and just get by in the other. Some people may be passive or receptive bilinguals, having the ability to understand a second language but not being able to speak it. There is also the issue of order. Are we dealing with simultaneous bilingualism, in which a child learns two languages at the same time, or sequential bilingualism, in which a person becomes bilingual by first learning one language and then another? And probably everybody understands at least a little of some other language, whether it is the leftovers from high school Spanish class, the words and phrases from neighbors, or words picked up on a job working with foreign-born employees. Bilingualism, then, should be viewed as a continuum from the relatively monolingual speaker to the highly proficient speaker of two languages (see Table 7.1).

For our purposes here, speaking in very broad terms, the childhood bilingual acquisition process may be considered as three developmental stages (Crystal 2007:409–415; 2010:374–375). First, the child builds up a set of words from both languages but usually keeps them separate, not as translations of each other. Second, as sentences begin to appear, words from both languages can be used. This mixing rapidly declines, however, dropping almost completely by the end of the third year. After this, vocabulary in both languages grows, but a single grammatical pattern is used. Usually by the fourth year, however, the syntax of each language becomes distinct as the child becomes more cognizant that the two languages are not the same. It is then that the child becomes aware of the sociolinguistic power of each language—the ways each language is to be used, and for what purposes.

## CODE-SWITCHING, CODE-MIXING, AND DIGLOSSIA

Probably all speakers of every language have a variety of linguistic resources available to them. For example, the prewar Russian literary theorist Mikhail Bakhtin (1981) wrote of the illiterate peasant who prays to God in Old Church Slavonic, speaks to his family in their local village dialect, sings hymns in Standard Russian, and attempts to petition the local government in what he thinks is the high-class speech of officialdom. In most places in the world, there are not only dialects but several languages present in a community, the speakers possessing varying degrees of facility. In these multilingual situations, the codes—that is, language varieties or languages—often become blended. This is so common that linguists have special terms for this blending: **code-switching** and **code-mixing**.

### *Code-Switching*

This nomenclature has had a long history in linguistics. Einar Haugen (1956:40), who most likely coined the term *code-switching*, defined it as "when a bilingual introduces a completely unassimilated word from another language into his speech." Carol Myers-Scotton (1993:3) broadened the definition by saying that code-switching "is the selection by bilinguals or multilinguals of forms from an embedded variety (or varieties) in utterances . . . during the same conversation." Eyamba Bokamba (1989:3) distinguishes code-switching and code-mixing: "Code-switching is the mixing of words, phrases and sentences from two distinct grammatical (sub) systems across sentence boundaries within the same speech event . . . [while] code-mixing is the embedding of various linguistic units such as affixes (bound morphemes), words (free morphemes), phrases and clauses from a co-operative activity where the participants, in order to infer what is intended, must reconcile what they hear with what they understand." An example of the former would be the Spanish-English bilingual who says: *Sometimes I'll start a sentence in English y termino en español* ["and finish it in Spanish"] (Poplack 2000:221). An example of the latter would be the Japanese-English bilingual who says *Kawai-sō sono-bug!* ("That *bug* is so pitiful" or "Oh, that poor *bug*"), incorporating the English word for insect into the Japanese sentence.

These distinctions are not always separated by all scholars, and some use code-switching to refer to all types of combined languages. The important thing in these situations is that a person capable of using two languages, A and B, has three systems available for use: A, B, and C (a combination of A and B). Mixing and switching probably occur to some extent in the conversations of all bilinguals. Code-mixing and code-switching can serve a variety of functions, such as building or reinforcing solidarity among speakers who share these languages. For example, two Czechs in the United States conversing in Czech may use English words, phrases, or sentences whenever they feel more comfortable doing so—as

**TABLE 7.2** SOME EXAMPLES OF DIGLOSSIA: HIGH AND LOW FORMS OF SPEECH

| *Language* | *High(er) Form Name* | *Low(er) Form Name* |
|---|---|---|
| Arabic | 'al-fuṣḥ (Classical) | 'al-'āmmiyyah (Colloquial) |
| Greek | Katharévousa ("puristic" Greek) | Dhimotiki (Demotic vernacular Greek) |
| Swiss German | Hochdeutsch (High German) | Schweizerdeutsch (Swiss German) |
| Hatian French | Standard French | Creole |
| Javanese | Krama (polite/formal style) | Ngoko (informal style) |
| Tamil | ceniltamil̲ (literary and formal Tamil) | kọtuntamil̲ (colloquial Tamil) |

*Note:* **These categories are often a continuum, and prescribed usages are variable. Some forms, like Katharévousa, are becoming increasingly less common. Languages like Javanese also have devices such as honorific and humble forms that can be used within different categories.**

in *"Víš co? Popovídáme si pěkně u mě doma u piva. Ale než si vlezeme do subwaye, let's buy some pastrami and potato chips!"* (Here's an idea! Let's talk over beer at my place. But before we get on the subway, let's buy some pastrami and potato chips!)

### *Diglossia*

The use of two distinct varieties of a language for two different sets of functions is called **diglossia**. The common language is the colloquial, or the "low," variety (L). A second, "high" variety (H), is used in formal circumstances: It is taught in schools and assumes administrative, legal, religious, and literary functions. Charles Ferguson (1921–1998) coined this term in reference to the Classical Arabic based on the standards of the *Quran* (Koran) used in formal settings against the local or regional dialects of colloquial Arabic found throughout the Middle East (1959).

Of the two varieties, the colloquial typically is learned first and is used for ordinary conversation with relatives and friends or servants and working persons, in cartoons, on popular radio and television programs, in jokes, in traditional narratives, and the like. The formal variety, which carries prestige, is taught in schools and assumes most of the literary, administrative, legal, and religious functions.

Instances of diglossia are fairly common. Those Swiss who use Standard German as their formal variety are fluent in the Swiss German dialect (Schwyzertütsch), the low variety, in addition to the other national languages they may have learned. Similarly, in Greece colloquial Greek is in use side by side with the literary form derived in large part from its classical ancestor. In actual speech, however, neither the two diglossic varieties nor the languages of a bilingual community are always kept strictly apart (see Table 7.2).

## SUMMARY AND CONCLUSIONS

Learning to speak a foreign language is a formidable task, and most adults fail to achieve fluency even after many years of trying. Children, however, learn their native language with no apparent effort and without instruction before they reach school age. One widely accepted theory concerning language acquisition holds that infants are born with an abstract language model already programmed into their brains. Endowed with such a language acquisition device, they apply it as they learn the particular mother tongue they hear spoken around them. Acquisition of language should not be studied without considering the sociocultural context in which it takes place. Knowing how to use their native language effectively helps individuals cope with their culture, and learning to use it appropriately is an important part of enculturation (the process of learning one's culture).

Among the many activities the human brain controls are speech, writing, and reading. Even though much is still to be learned about the workings of the brain, it has long been known that different parts of the brain contribute to different aspects of language processing. Injuries to these areas result in corresponding language and speech impairments.

Competency in one language only, typical of most Americans with English as their mother tongue, is uncommon in the rest of the world, where hundreds of millions of people are able to speak several languages or language varieties—that is, they are multilingual or diglossic. Even though many people speak only one language, they are actively, or at least passively, acquainted with several dialects and speech styles of that language. Their own speech patterns differ from those of others, even if only slightly. All speakers have their individual idiolects.

## RESOURCE MANUAL AND STUDY GUIDE

### *Questions for Discussion*

1. By the age of five or six, all normal children everywhere have a good command of their mother tongue (even though, of course, their vocabularies are still limited). However, college students, and adults in general, find learning a foreign language quite difficult, and most learn to speak a second language only haltingly at best. How do you explain this phenomenon?
2. Should English be chosen by law to become the official and national language of the United States? Discuss the pros and cons of such a law.
3. What are the advantages and disadvantages of the United States becoming a bilingual nation?

### *Projects*

**PROJECT 1**

1. The following is part of a dialogue between two professional, bilingual, Hispanic women (whom we will Ms. A and Ms. B). We step into the middle of their conversation as they are talking about their various attempts to quit smoking. You will notice that they use both English and Spanish in this conversation. Spanish is in italics, and English is in plain text. Translations of the Spanish appear below in smaller type. Ellipses ( . . . ) indicate pauses or thinking in the discourse. Your task in this exercise is to try to determine when and why English is used, and when and why Spanish is used. Which language do you think is their first language? Why? Assuming this little dialogue might be typical of many speakers with these sociolinguistic variables, what might you say about language choice, topic of discourse, and so on, among bilinguals in these situations?

*A: . . . I'd smoke the rest of the pack myself in two weeks.*
*B: That's all you smoke?*
*A: That's all I smoked.*
*B: And how about now?*
*A: Estos . . . me los halle . . . estos Pall Malls me los hallaron. No, I mean that's all the these . . . I found these they were found for me*
*cigarettes . . . that's all. They're the ones I buy.*
*B: Oh really.*
*A: . . . They tell me, 'How did you quit, Mary?' I don't quit, I . . . I just stopped. I mean, it wasn't an effort that I made que voy a dejar de fumar por que me hace daño o this or*
*that I am going to stop smoking because it is harmful to me or*
*that, uh uh. It's just that I used to pull butts out of the wastepaper basket. Yeah. I used to go look in the . . . se me acababan los cigarros en la noche. I'd get desperate*
*my cigarettes would run out on me at night*
*y ahi voy al basarero a buscar, . . . a sacar, you know.*
*and there I go to the wastebasket to look for some, to get some*

**PROJECT 2**

2. Comedian Dave Chappelle says, "Every black American is bilingual. All of them. We speak street vernacular and we speak 'job interview.'" What does he mean by this? Discuss this claim in light of the chapter descriptions on code-switching or diglossia. (Also see multimedia links below.)

## Objective Study Questions

**TRUE-FALSE TEST**

T F 1. Most countries in the world are monolingual, like the United States.
T F 2. Usually children cannot learn to discriminate speech sounds until the age of eighteen months or more.
T F 3. According to Noam Chomsky, it is unimaginable that a highly specific, abstract, and tightly organized language comes by accident into the mind of every four-year-old child.
T F 4. From what is now known, all speech impairments are traceable to lesions in one particular part of the language-dominant hemisphere of the human brain.
T F 5. The most widely accepted theory concerning language acquisition holds that all infants are born with some kind of language acquisition device that enables them to learn whatever their mother tongue happens to be.
T F 6. The use of two distinct varieties of a language for the same functions is called diglossia.

**MULTIPLE-CHOICE QUESTIONS**

____ 1. Basic biological (reflexive) noises such as burping, crying, and coughing are produced during the first (A) eight or ten days. (B) eight or ten weeks. (C) eight or ten months.
____ 2. Intonational contours, such as those characteristic of questions, begin to appear around the end of the (A) first week. (B) first month. (C) first year. (D) second year.
____ 3. The country with the most stable bi- or multilingualism is (A) Greece. (B) the United States. (C) Mexico. (D) Switzerland.

____ 4. The area of the brain that seems especially associated with language is (A) the spinal cord. (B) the thalamus. (C) Broca's area. (D) the angular gyrus.

**COMPLETIONS**

1. A sentence such as "Sometimes I'll start a sentence in English *y termino en español* ["and finish it in Spanish"]" is an example of English-Spanish ________________________ (one hyphenated word).
2. __________ theory argues that there is a capacity for rapid language development present in the child at birth (one word).
3. The ___________ theory of language acquisition argues that humans acquire language through successive stimuli and reinforcements (one word).
4. It is _________ that more than anything else serves as a people's badge of ethnic identity and uniqueness (one word).
5. _____________ is the de facto second language of the United States (one word).

## Answer Key

True-false test: 1-F, 2-F, 3-T, 4-F, 5-T, 6-F
Multiple-choice questions: 1-B, 2-C, 3-D, 4-C
Completions: 1. code-switching, 2. Innatist, 3. behaviorist, 4. language, 5. Spanish.

## Notes and Suggestions for Further Reading

Useful surveys of child language acquisition and the neurological basis of language can be found in Crystal (2007 and 2010). See Chomsky (1959) for an extensive and now classic review and critique of the book *Verbal Behavior* by the influential advocate of behaviorist psychology, B. F. Skinner. Jakobson (1968) is an English translation of Jakobson's German original published in Sweden in 1942. For a detailed account of language socialization of Kaluli children, see Schieffelin (1990). More information on language development, language disorders, and language and learning may be found in Menyuk (1988) and Gleason and Ratner (2008). For a classic (though no longer the latest) account of the biological foundations of language, see Lenneberg (1967). Later sources on biological foundations include Newmeyer (1989); Christiansen and Kirby (2003); Fitch (2010); and Larson, Déprez, and Yamakido (2010). For discussion of the linguistic features of Broca's area, see Grodzinsky and Amunts (2006). The procedures used to measure mutual intelligibility among Iroquoian languages are described in an article by Hickerson, Turner, and Hickerson (1952). The term *diglossia* was coined by Ferguson (1959) describing the social place of the Arabic language. Sayahi (2014) and Albirini (2015) show the latest work done in this area. Wei Li's edited *The Bilingualism Reader* (2007) includes many of the classic articles in the discipline. For multilingualism, see the collection in Martin-Jones and Martin (2016). For code-switching and code-mixing, see Heller (1988) or Gardner-Chloros (2009); Stell and Yakpo (2015) is good collection of advanced essays. Saville-Troike (2006) is a good general introduction to second-language acquisition.

# 8

# Language Through Time

## LEARNING OBJECTIVES

- Explain the various ways languages are classified.
- Name some of the features of language typology.
- Describe some of the regularities of sound changes.
- Describe some of the processes of vocabulary change.
- Be able to do reconstructions of some protolanguage forms.

The structure of a language may be analyzed and described as it exists at some point in time, either in the present or the past. The approach that considers a language as though it had been sliced through time, ignoring historical antecedents, is referred to as **synchronic linguistics**. But it is also possible to study the historical development of a language by giving attention to the changes that occurred in the language over a period of time. Such an analysis or approach is **diachronic**, or **historical**, **linguistics**. This chapter shows some of the ways a diachronic approach can benefit anthropologists.

## HOW LANGUAGES ARE CLASSIFIED

Anyone who knows Spanish will tell you that other languages, such as Portuguese or Italian, seem to be related to Spanish. This is due to their common origin from Latin. Traditionally, one of the most common activities in historical linguistics has been to classify languages according to these genetic relationships. It is difficult to give the exact number of languages spoken in the world at present, but the total undoubtedly approaches 6,000 (Krauss 1992:5–6), possibly 7,000. It is impossible to guess how many languages must have become extinct in prehistoric times. We do know that during the historical period for which we have written records, a great many languages have died out.

### *Language Families*

A **language family** includes all those languages that are related by virtue of having descended from a single ancestral language. The concept of the language family is somewhat conservative: it is generally employed only if the relationship and the correspondences among the languages have been firmly established by careful comparative work and a

CHART 8.1 THE INDO-EUROPEAN LANGUAGE FAMILY

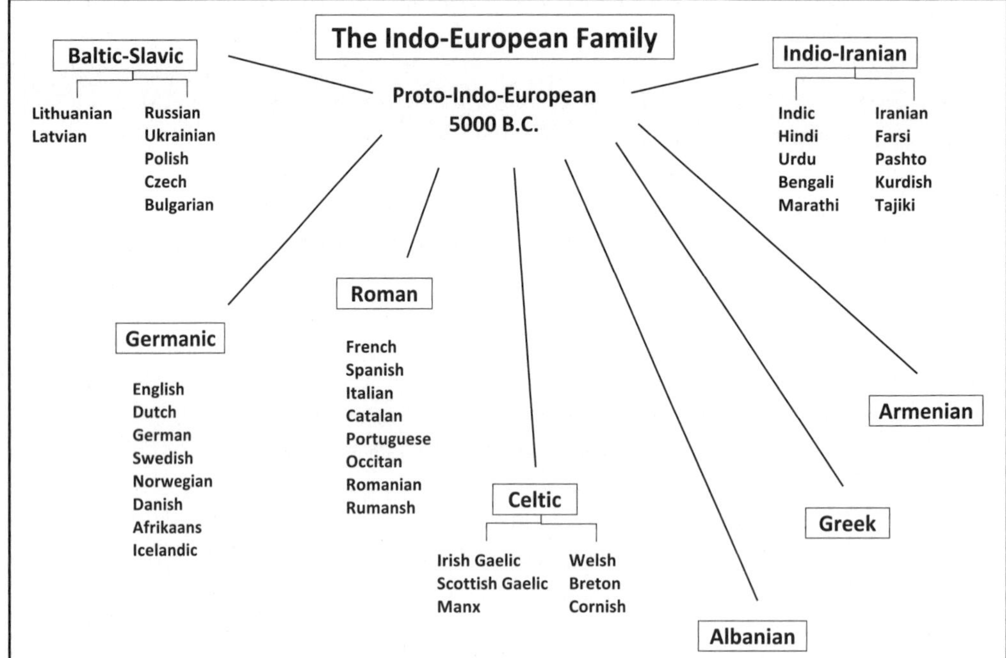


convincing number of cognates. Subdivisions of a language family are usually referred to as branches. The **Indo-European** language family (see Chart 8.1), for example, consists of almost a dozen branches (some of which have sub-branches; note: not all the languages and subfamilies are given in this simplified chart). Some branches are Germanic (with about a dozen languages, including German and English), Celtic (with four languages), Romance or Italic (with about a dozen languages, including French and Spanish), and Balto-Slavic (with more than a dozen languages belonging to either the Baltic or Slavic sub-branches—including Russian and Polish). Some branches are represented by a single language, for example, Albanian, Armenian, and Hellenic or Greek. Indo-Iranian, with its Indic and Iranian sub-branches, consists of several hundred languages and dialects spoken mostly in southwestern Asia. Some branches of Indo-European, for example, the Tocharian and Anatolian branches, are no longer represented by spoken languages.

The number of languages that make up a language family varies greatly. The largest African family, Niger-Congo, is estimated to consist of about 1,000 languages and several times as many dialects. Yet some languages do not appear to be related to any other; these are referred to as **language isolates**. The Americas have been more linguistically diversified than other continents; the number of Native American language families in North America has been judged to be more than seventy, including more than thirty isolates. The numbers for South America have been even larger, but they are only estimates because our knowledge of the Indian languages of South America is still incomplete.

Several attempts have been made to simplify the apparent linguistic diversity of the New World. In 1929, Edward Sapir proposed a major reduction in the number of language families, assigning all Native American languages north of Mexico to only six "major linguistic groups" (superfamilies), later referred to as phyla. Consequently, a phylum in linguistic classification is a grouping that encompasses all those languages judged to have more remote relationships than do languages assigned to a family. Except for the Eskimo-Aleut "group," which is considered to be one family, each of the other five groups of Sapir's proposed classification included several families and one or more language isolates. A similar simplification of South American language families was proposed in 1960 by Joseph H. Greenberg (1915–2001), who subsumed the hundreds of native South American languages under three "families" (using the term not in the older conservative sense but more in the sense of superphylum or macrophylum). In another classification, Greenberg (1987) assigned all native languages of the New World to only three "families," of which the Amerind "family" covers all native languages of the two continents except for those belonging to the Na-Dene and Eskimo-Aleut groups (spoken for the most part in the northern half of North America). Most specialists in Native American languages are not ready to accept the validity of Greenberg's huge Amerind genetic unit, or family. In any event, a family of this size has little in common with the earlier conservative concept of language family. (Most of the objections to this classification are discussed in the lengthy review of Greenberg's work by Campbell 1988.) In 1964, two comparative linguists in the Soviet Union produced evidence that six major language families of the Old World—Indo-European, Afro-Asiatic, Altaic, Dravidian, Uralic, and Kartvelian (South Caucasian)—were remotely related. To this macrofamily, referred to as Nostratic, some scholars subsequently added other language families and languages, among them Eskimo-Aleut, Nilo-Saharan, and Sumerian (Kaiser and Shevoroshkin 1988). And still another proposed macrofamily links together many languages from both the Old and the New Worlds (one of the names of this macrofamily is Dene-Caucasian).

The ten largest conventional language families, ranging from more than 2 billion speakers to about 60 million, are Indo-European, Sino-Tibetan, Niger-Congo, Afro-Asiatic, Austronesian, Dravidian, Japanese, Altaic, Austroasiatic, and Korean (Japanese and Korean are frequently considered language isolates but may be distantly related to each other and to the Altaic family).

### *Language Typologies*

Less frequently used are typological classifications, based on structural similarities of languages regardless of their history—that is, regardless of genetic relationship. Typological classifications take various structural features into consideration. For example, some scholars have classified languages according to their sound systems, basing their grouping on how many and which distinctive vowels and consonants are used and whether tones are employed. Others have classified languages according to word order, that is, the sequence of subject (S), verb (V), and object (O) in simple declarative sentences (in English the typical arrangement is SVO, as in "I love you").

#### Typology-Based Grammatical Techniques for Displaying Semantic Relationships

Recently, semantic typology has been proposed; its proponents compare languages, for example, according to how much specificity relating to meaning a language requires. The best-known language classifications are based on morphological characteristics; the most widely used assigns languages to one of four types—isolating, inflecting, agglutinative, and polysynthetic—although frequently a language combines features of more than one type. Actually, the first two we have already encountered in Chapter 4 in a different context with slightly different terminology.

We saw in Chapter 4 that to indicate grammatical relationships between words in a sentence, languages draw on one of two general strategies: **word order** or **inflections**. Chinese (and to a large extent, English) uses the word-order strategy. Word order indicates the grammatical relationships at work: "John loves Jane" is not the same thing as "Jane loves John." Word-order languages are called **isolating** languages in this typology. (NOTE: We should mention that is an unfortunate choice of terminology: these "isolating languages" described here are *not* the same thing as "language isolates" described a few paragraphs ago, which referred to those relatively rare languages that do not seem to fit into any of the well-known language families.) Languages that use **inflections** take a different approach. Here we see grammatical relationships not indicated by where they appear in a sentence, but by inflections: suffixes, prefixes, or other markers.

In **agglutinative languages**, each component of grammatical meaning is expressed by a separate piece of morphemic structure. Usually these are prefixes, suffixes, and/or infixes. For example, in the Turkish word *yazmalɨymɨšɨm* "I should have written," the stem *yaz-* "write" is followed by three suffixes here taking the forms of *-malɨy-mɨš-ɨm*, meaning, respectively, "obligative" (expressing obligation), "perfective" (implying completion), and "I." Turkish, Finnish, Swahili, and Japanese are among languages that are agglutinative.

Also in agglutinative languages, there may be long strings of numerous prefixes or suffixes, but generally they can be parsed out and the individual meanings and functions determined. This is not so simple in the case of **fusional** languages. In these languages these individual prefixes and suffixes and infixes sort of disappear, or at least become hard to detect because they have "fused" together through phonological assimilation, or have no clear boundaries within the word. And often these morphemes encode several meanings at the same time—for example, tense and person and aspect—making things even harder to discern.

## Typology-Based Morphological Techniques for Displaying Words or Concepts

We can also type languages on the basis of how their morphemes create words. The three main types are **analytic**, **synthetic**, and **polysynthetic**. An analytic language is a language in which one word consists of only one morpheme (like Chinese, where there is a verb but no special markers attached, say, to indicate tense). In a synthetic language, words can consist of more than one morpheme (like English *talked,* which has two morphemes, though the *-ed* cannot exist independently but must be attached to a verb). A polysynthetic language is a language in which the words consist of many morphemes all bound together. Actually, these "words" are more like phrases or little sentences. Most polysynthetic languages are fusional (see paragraph above). And polysynthetic languages are considered by many linguists to be a combination of agglutinative and inflectional features. The words in polysynthetic languages are long and morphologically complex.

**TABLE 8.1** LANGUAGE TYPOLOGIES FOR SEVERAL LANGUAGES

| | *Analytic*<br>a word = 1 morpheme | *Synthetic*<br>a word = more than 1 morph. | *Polysynthetic*<br>a word = clause or phrase |
|---|---|---|---|
| ISOLATING<br>(one word/one morpheme, using word-order grammar) | Chinese | English | |
| INFLECTING<br>(suffixes with several meanings) | | Latin | |
| AGGLUTINATIVE<br>(affixes and groups of affixes) | | Japanese | |
| FUSIONAL<br>(morphemes hard to identify; can encode several meanings simultaneously) | | | Inuit (Eskimo) |

***Note:*** **The horizontal axis—left to right—shows three ways words or concepts relate to the number of morphemic parts that compose them (one word is composed of one morpheme, several morphemes, or many morphemes). The vertical axis—top to bottom—shows *how* the morphemes do this (via word-order grammar; inflectional suffixes; compound groups of prefixes, infixes, and suffixes; and complex compound affixes that are hard to detect because they "fuse" together through phonological assimilation or have no clear boundaries within the word; and often these morphemes encode several meanings at the same time—e.g., tense and person and aspect).**

An example is the single Inuit (Eskimo) "word" *a:wlisa-ut-issʔar-si-niarpu- ŋa,* which translates "I am looking for something suitable for a fishing line" (the hyphens in the Eskimo word are used to indicate morpheme boundaries). None of these parts really can exit by themselves independently.

These two typology systems are actually describing two different properties: morphology and semantic relationships. That is, one explains how concepts can relate to morphemic parts, and the other explains how grammatical/semantic techniques can be used to create words. Therefore, it might be useful to arrange them in a table, as we have done in Table 8.1. Note that the horizontal axis—left to right—shows three ways words or concepts relate to the number of morphemic parts that compose them (one word is composed of one morpheme, several morphemes, or many morphemes). The vertical axis—top to bottom—shows *how* the morphemes do this (via isolating word-order grammar; inflectional suffixes; compound groups of prefixes, infixes, and suffixes; and complex compound affixes that are hard to detect because they "fuse" together through phonological assimilation or have no clear boundaries within the word).

## INTERNAL AND EXTERNAL CHANGES

Languages change not only internally from within but also as a result of external influences. The reasons for such changes vary; here we will illustrate them by discussing sound changes known as assimilation, dissimilation, and metathesis, and a grammatical change by means of which certain irregular forms become regularized.

### *Sound Changes*

**Assimilation**

**Assimilation** is the influence of a sound on a neighboring sound so that the two become similar or the same. For example, the Latin prefix *in-* "not, non-, un-" appears in English as *il-*, *im-*, and *ir-* in the words *illegal, immoral, impossible* (*m* and *p* are both bilabial consonants), and *irresponsible* as well as in the unassimilated original form *in-* in *indecent* and *incompetent*. Although the assimilation of the *n* of *in-* to the following consonant in the preceding examples was inherited from Latin, English examples that would be considered native are also plentiful: in rapid speech, native speakers of English tend to pronounce *ten bucks* as though it were written *tembucks*, and in anticipation of the voiceless *s* in *son* the final consonant of *his* in *his son* is not as fully voiced as the *s* in *his daughter*, where it clearly is [z].

**Dissimilation**

Another process of this type is **dissimilation**, which works the other way around: one of two identical or very similar neighboring sounds of a word is changed or omitted because a speaker may find the repetition of the same articulatory movement difficult in rapid speech. This is why it is so common to hear *February* pronounced as if it were written *Febyuary*, with the substitution of [y] for the first [r] in anticipation of the [r] toward the end of the word. People are asked to repeat a tongue twister (for example, "The sixth sheik's sixth sheep's sick") to test their ability to pronounce similar neighboring sounds rapidly without making any errors.

### *Metathesis*

Still another process producing sound change is **metathesis**, the transposition of sounds or larger units; for example, the antecedent of Modern English *bird* is Old English *bridd* "young bird." A spoonerism, involving the transposition of the initial sounds of several words, is a slip of the tongue based on metathesis, as when *dear old queen* becomes *queer old dean*.

An example of a grammatical change is the regularization of a number of strong (irregular) Anglo-Saxon verbs: Old English *fealdan* "to fold" and *helpan* "to help" had the first-person singular past-tense (preterite) forms *feold* and *healp* and the past-participle forms *fealden* and *holpen*. In Modern English, these verbs are regular: *fold, folded* and *help, helped*. As for semantic change, Old English *mete* referred to food in general (usually solid), not just to animal flesh, as does Modern English *meat*.

As long as they are being used, all languages change. Today, no members of any society and no speakers of any language are completely isolated from speakers of other languages and dialects, and these contacts between speakers of different languages cause external language changes. The most common instances of external language change are borrowings, which can be of various types. The letter *b* in the word *debt* apparently has been borrowed for the sake of prestige from Latin (*dēbitum* "debt") even though the Middle English antecedent of the word was *dette*, without a *b*, from Old French *dette* "something owed."

## *Changes in Vocabulary*

### Loanwords and Borrowing

Much more common than orthographic borrowings are lexical borrowings, known as **loanwords**. Not all languages adopt foreign words to the same extent. Even though Icelandic serves a modern industrial society, for two centuries now Icelanders have resisted borrowing words from other languages and instead coin new words from their native linguistic resources for the many things and concepts that come to Iceland from other cultures. In grammar, too, Icelandic is highly conservative, having changed only a very little since the Old Norse period.

English has always been very hospitable to words of foreign origin. The vocabularies of the Angles, Jutes, and Saxons were enriched by words from Celtic (for example, the word ancestral to Modern English *bin*), Latin (*pipe* and *angel*), Old Norse of the Vikings (*take*), and Anglo-Norman French (*journey*). From the sixteenth century forward, during the Modern English period, the English lexicon borrowed from a great many of the world's languages, ranging from Afrikaans (for example, *aardvark*) to Czech (*robot*) to Yiddish (*chutzpa[h]*) to Japanese (*kamikaze*) to Dakota (*tepee*) to one of the native Australian languages (*boomerang*) to one of the native languages of Africa, probably related to Twi (*okra*). The many thousands of loanwords that have been incorporated into English since earliest times would not recommend English to misguided purists who think a language should be protected from the use of foreignisms, but such borrowings have certainly made the English vocabulary one of the richest in the world.

Some languages borrow selectively. In one of his studies of Native American languages of California, William Bright investigated the origin of words for those domestic animals introduced by European American settlers. Borrowing from Spanish was considerable, but there appears to have been a resistance to borrowing from English. In Bright's opinion, this disparity may well have been due to the benevolent (if condescending) treatment of Native American peoples in California under the Spanish mission system and, by contrast, the inhuman treatment they received from Anglo-Americans (Bright 1960:233–234). In this instance, then, the nature of the sociocultural contact between the native peoples and the newcomers was reflected in the vocabularies of the Native American languages.

### Neologisms: Newly Coined Vocabulary Items

In addition to borrowing, languages enrich their vocabularies in two other ways: neologisms and semantic extension. One way is to coin new words from native resources. Newly coined words—called **neologisms**—are added to English (and many other languages) every year: Among thousands of such coinages are the blend *brunch* (from *br*eakfast and l*unch*), for a late-morning meal usually combining menu items from both breakfast and lunch; *vaporware*, for new software that has been announced but is not yet available; and *wannabe* (from the phrase *want to be*), for a person who aspires to be or tries to act or look like someone else.

### Semantic Extension

Vocabularies also adjust to new inventions or ideas and objects introduced through intercultural contact by extending the meaning of existing words to include a new referent—**semantic extension**. For example, during the 1930s when the Western Apache in east central Arizona began using automobiles and pickup trucks and needed terms in their language for the various parts of these vehicles, they chose to extend many anatomical terms referring to the human body to the "corresponding" parts of the automobile: The meaning of the word *biyedaaʔ* "chin and jaw" was extended to mean "front bumper," *bigan* "hand and arm" to "front wheel," *bizéʔ* "mouth" to "gas pipe opening," *bidááʔ* "eye" to "headlight," *bitaʔ* "forehead" to "windshield," *bizig* "liver" to "battery," *bijíí* "heart" to "distributor," *bikeeʔ* "foot, feet" to "tires, rear wheels," *bibid* "stomach" to "gas tank," *bijííʔizólé* "lung" to "radiator," *bitsʔǫǫs* "veins" to "electrical wiring," *bichíh* "nose" to "hood," and so on (Basso 1990:20–21). The sense of the word that applies is invariably clear from the context. Similar extensions of anatomical terms to parts of the automobile have been recorded for other Native American languages.

That no confusion results from the use of words that have several senses—unless one indulges in punning—should be evident from the example of the English word *horse*, which has designated the quadruped *Equus caballus* from Old English (before the twelfth century) to the present, but later gained additional senses: "trestle" or "sawhorse," "pommel horse" or "vaulting horse," "horsepower," and "heroin" (in slang).

## HOW AND WHY SOUND CHANGES OCCUR

Characteristically, sound changes are gradual. Only some speakers of a dialect or language adopt a particular speech innovation to begin with; others do so later, and ultimately all or most speakers accept the change. To put it differently, a particular sound change initially affects words that are frequently used, and only later is the change extended to other words. The modern view concerning how sound changes operate—namely, that they gradually spread, or diffuse, through the words (the lexicon) of a language—is referred to as **lexical diffusion**. Pioneered by William Labov and others during the 1960s, this view differs from the **neogrammarian hypothesis** of the 1870s, according to which sound laws admit no real exceptions, operating across the board within any given language.

An example of linguistic change proceeding from speakers enjoying higher prestige was provided by Labov (1966) in his famous study of English used by salespeople in three New York City department stores. According to this study (discussed in more detail in Chapter 13), the use of [r] after a vowel in such words as *car, card, four*, and *fourth* tended to characterize careful lower-class speech once the usage had become associated with higher prestige. For an example of linguistic change proceeding from below, one may refer to Labov's study of the speech in Martha's Vineyard, an island several miles south of Cape Cod, Massachusetts. This study dealt with the progressive change in the quality of the first vowel of the diphthongs /ay/ and /aw/ in such words as *firefly* and *outhouse*. During the 1930s, when data for the *Linguistic Atlas of New England* were being collected, and for a long time before that, the diphthong /aw/ was not centralized, whereas /ay/ was (that is, its pronunciation resembled [əi]). During Labov's fieldwork in the early 1960s, the centralization of both diphthongs was most noticeable in the speech of thirty-one- to forty-five-year-old fishermen in the rural parts of the island, especially the Chilmark area in the west. According to Labov (1963:297, 304–305):

> [The] high centralization [of the two diphthongs] is closely correlated with expressions of strong resistance to the incursions of the summer people [who at the time outnumbered the native Vineyarders by a ratio of seven to one]. . . . It is apparent that the immediate meaning of [centralization] is "Vineyarder." When a man [uses the centralized diphthongs], he is unconsciously establishing the fact that he belongs to the island. . . . [The] younger members of the English descent group [of Vineyarders] . . . recognize that the Chilmark fishermen are independent, skillful with many kinds of tools and equipment, quick-spoken, courageous and physically strong. Most importantly, they carry with them the ever-present conviction that the island belongs to them. If someone intends to stay on the island, this model will be ever present to his mind.

Sound changes, then, clearly are neither random nor do they operate without exception. Careful studies of the conditions under which sound changes take place reveal not only the direction and rate of linguistic change but the motivation behind it as well.

And why do languages change? One reason is a strong tendency in languages to maintain a definite pattern of organization. *Analogy* is another factor: regular forms tend to influence less regular forms. Many Latin loanwords, for example, are now made plural almost exclusively by using the suffix *-s* (as in *auditoriums*) rather than their original Latin plural ending (as in *auditoria*). At least in some instances, more easily articulated sound sequences replace those that require greater effort (the principle of least effort). Not only have short words (*prof*, *exam*, *dorm*, *math*, and the like) been coined to supplement the original longer ones, but sometimes the simplification has been phonetic, as in the word *clothes*, which is usually pronounced as if it did not contain the sound represented by *th*.

Changes even occur when a language is passed on from parents to children and when children's speech habits are influenced by those of their peers. Although typically small, especially in phonology and morphology, such changes are cumulative and are noticeable when the speech of grandparents is compared with that of their grandchildren.

As we have already seen, sociocultural factors also promote language change. Some individuals like to imitate the sounds, grammar, and words used by those who have social prestige. When such imitations are overdone, hypercorrection results. Someone who has learned that *it is I* is correct rather than *it is me* may then say *between you and I* instead of the correct *between you and me*. On the phonetic level, **hypercorrection** occurs when *singer* is made to rhyme with *finger* because the two words are orthographically similar. Speakers of any language coin new words continually in order to give names to new inventions or new concepts. By the same token, those words that stand for items or ideas that are going out of use become obsolescent and eventually obsolete. The vocabulary of any living language, then, is constantly changing. For written languages, new editions of dictionaries need to be published every ten years or so to record the changes that have come about.

The comparative method in phonology rests on the assumption that sound changes are regular and predictable (this is why these changes have been referred to as "sound laws"). But their regularity is not absolute because the conditions under which sound changes take place are not identical. For example, Latin *t* corresponds to the sound written as *th* in

English words cognate with Latin words (a **cognate** is a word related to another by descent from the same ancestral language): compare Latin *tenuis* and English *thin*, Latin *tongēre* "to know" and English *think*, Latin *trēs* and English *three*, and Latin *trāns* "across" and English *through*. But English words have retained *t* when it is preceded by *s* in the Latin cognate: Latin *stāre* "to stand" corresponds to English *stand*, Latin *stēlla* "star" to English *star*, Latin *stīpāre* "to compress, cram" to English *stiff*, Latin *stringere* "to clasp, tighten" to English *strain*, and so forth.

Or to give an example of a so-called regular sound correspondence from the historical development of English, consider Old English ā (that is, long *a*) as in *bāt*, gān, māwan, sāwan, *slāw*, and *stān* changing in Modern English to the respective vowel sound in the words *boat*, (*to*) *go*, (*to*) *mow*, (*to*) *sow*, *slow*, and *stone*; but in words in which Old English â occurred after a cluster containing *w*, the sound correspondence was different: Thus *hwâ* and *twâ* changed in Modern English to *who* and *two*, respectively.

Sometimes an expected correspondence is not found because the words that are being compared are not cognate despite their having similar forms. For example, this is why Latin *d*, which in English cognates corresponds to *t* (as in *two*, *duo* in Latin, and *ten*, *decem* in Latin), does not appear as *t* in *day* because the words *day* and *diēs* "day" are not related. Another example: the first consonant of the word *tooth* shows the expected correspondence to Latin *d* in *dēns* (*dentis*) "tooth," but the word *dental* does not because it was borrowed from medieval Latin at the end of the sixteenth century, too late to be subject to the regular change of Latin *d* to English *t*.

The force of analogy may also interfere with the regularity of sound changes. The inflection of the strong Old English verb *helpan* "to help," which had among its various forms *hilpst* (second-person singular), *healp* (the first- and third-person singular of the preterite), *hulpe* (the second-person singular of the preterite), *hulpon* (the plural form of the preterite), and *holpen* (the past participle), was simplified by analogy with weak verbs to Modern English forms *help* and *helped*.

In short, then, sound changes are regular, provided they occur in like circumstances, but given the complexity of languages and the many different influences on them (regional, social, and others) as they are spoken century after century, it seems more appropriate to refer to such so-called laws as tendencies. Concerning the conflict between "phonetic laws" and analogy, one of the most outstanding American comparative linguists, Edgar Sturtevant (1875–1952), noted: "Phonetic laws are regular but produce irregularities. Analogic creation is irregular but produces regularity" (1947:109).

## RECONSTRUCTING PROTOLANGUAGES

It is generally accepted that the beginning of modern linguistics, historical linguistics in particular, dates back to 1786. It was then that Sir William Jones (1746–1794) observed in his presidential address to the Royal Asiatick Society of Bengal that Sanskrit, Greek, and Latin "have sprung from some common source, which, perhaps, no longer exists [and that] there is a similar reason . . . for supposing that both the *Gothick* and the *Celtick* . . . had the same origin with the *Sanscrit* [and] the old *Persian* might be added to the same family" (Salus 1969). As early as the sixteenth century, it had been suspected that many European languages were related and that their parent language might be Sanskrit, an ancient language of India. Jones, however, went still further; according to him, Sanskrit, ancient Greek, Latin, and other European languages were the descendants of a language spoken in prehistoric times. During the first half of the nineteenth century, a number of major works were published to demonstrate in some detail that relationships existed not only among the several ancient languages that were no longer spoken but also between them and Germanic, Slavic, Romance, Baltic, and other languages spoken in Europe and southwestern Asia. During the same period, reconstructions were begun of words of the ancestral language, assumed to have been spoken before the invention of writing and therefore never documented. These reconstructions proceeded so rapidly that in 1868, the German philologist August Schleicher (1821–1868) was able to "translate" into the prehistoric ancestral language a short fable about a sheep and three horses.

What can be reconstructed, and how are such reconstructions accomplished? It is possible to reconstruct the sounds and meanings of words as well as the grammar and syntax of an earlier undocumented state of a language, but usually the ultimate goal of linguistic reconstruction is the assumed ancestral language, or protolanguage, of all those languages derived from the same source. Reconstruction of a protolanguage requires thorough knowledge of historical grammar and good acquaintance with the daughter languages. The procedure is intricate, but the two main assumptions underlying it are not difficult to explain. The first assumption is that recurring similarities between words from different languages or dialects indicate that these languages or dialects are related to each other and must therefore have descended from a common ancestral language. The second assumption is that, as discussed above, sound changes are regular under like circumstances.

For example, we know from written records what the forms of the word meaning *cloud* were in the three ancient languages assumed to be related: *nábhas* in Sanskrit, *néphos* in ancient Greek, and *nebo* in Old Church Slavonic. There is a similarity among the three words, and the sound correspondences may be represented as follows:

| Sanskrit | Ancient Greek | Old Church Slavonic |
|---|---|---|
| n | n | n |
| a | e | e |
| bh | p | b |
| a | o | o |
| s | s | |

If these three words for *cloud* are found in the daughter languages of the protolanguage, in this instance **Proto-Indo-European** (PIE), what would the PIE word most likely have been? The first sound, the nasal consonant *n*, presents no problem; one would reconstruct a PIE **n* (the asterisk marks a reconstructed form, one that has not been attested or is unattestable). An alternative reconstruction, using the nasal **m*, is much less probable because the presumption would then be that all three daughter languages independently made the same change, from **m* to *n*. The second sound, a vowel, was *a* in Sanskrit and *e* in both ancient Greek and Old Church Slavonic. Here one would reconstruct the PIE sound as **e* because it is more logical to assume that only one of the daughter languages innovated while the other two kept the original sound than to assume that two of the daughter languages independently effected the same change. The medial consonant, which is different in each of the three words, is reconstructed as **bh* because the reconstructed sound has something in common with each of the three sounds derived from the earlier one—bilabial articulation in all three cases, a voiced sound with Sanskrit and Old Church Slavonic, and aspiration (*h*) with Sanskrit and ancient Greek. The second vowel and the final consonant pose no new questions. Consequently, the reconstructed PIE word for cloud is **nebhos*. This is not to assert, however, that this very word must actually have existed in Proto-Indo-European times but rather that there must have been such a word, or a very similar one, to have given rise later to the three words attested for Sanskrit, ancient Greek, and Old Church Slavonic.

Historical linguists have further established that Proto-Indo-European was a highly inflected language. For example, its nouns had three genders (masculine, feminine, and neuter), three numbers (singular, plural, and dual for objects occurring in pairs), and eight cases, and its verbs had three persons, three numbers, and a variety of tenses, moods, and other features. Those who assume that the grammatical systems of prehistoric languages must have been rather simple (primitive) could scarcely be further from the truth. The grammatical system of Modern English is an example of simplicity when compared with that of Proto-Indo-European.

For several Indo-European languages, written records (some on clay tablets) exist from as far back as the second millennium BCE, and for many others the earliest records are on the order of 1,000 years old. Documentation of such time depth provides invaluable information about the changes that occur over time and aids historical linguists in their efforts to make reliable reconstructions. But for most other groups of related languages, such documentation is the rare exception rather than the rule. Some scholars were convinced, in fact, that comparative reconstruction was feasible only in the case of related languages whose history was known at least to some extent.

That the comparative method is just as applicable to unwritten languages, provided that some reliable sketches of their contemporary structures are available, was demonstrated in 1946 by Leonard Bloomfield (1887–1949), a well-known American linguist. His reconstruction of the sounds and grammar of the ancestral language of Native Americans speaking Algonquian languages was based on four of the so-called Central Algonquian languages—Fox, Cree, Menomini, and Ojibwa. Through his fieldwork begun in the early 1920s, Bloomfield was well acquainted with three of them. Basing his judgment on his knowledge of Algonquian languages, Bloomfield believed that the "reconstructions will, in the main, fit all the [Algonquian] languages [including the divergent Blackfoot, Cheyenne, and Arapaho in the West] and can accordingly be viewed as Proto-Algonquian" (1946:85). Research by others during subsequent decades has shown that except for some details, Bloomfield was correct. The reconstruction of protolanguages on the basis of their modern descendants is now a fairly common linguistic undertaking. Some of the protolanguages reconstructed for North and Central America are Proto-Athapaskan, Proto-Mixtecan, Proto-Otomian, Proto-Popolocan, Proto-Salishan, Proto-Siouan, Proto-Uto-Aztecan, and Proto-Zapotecan.

## RECONSTRUCTING THE ANCESTRAL HOMELAND

People—individuals, families, bands, and still larger groups—have always migrated to new places from localities in which they were born and raised, frequently as far away as to

**MAP 8.1 THE SPREAD OF THE INDO-EUROPEAN LANGUAGES–HERE]**

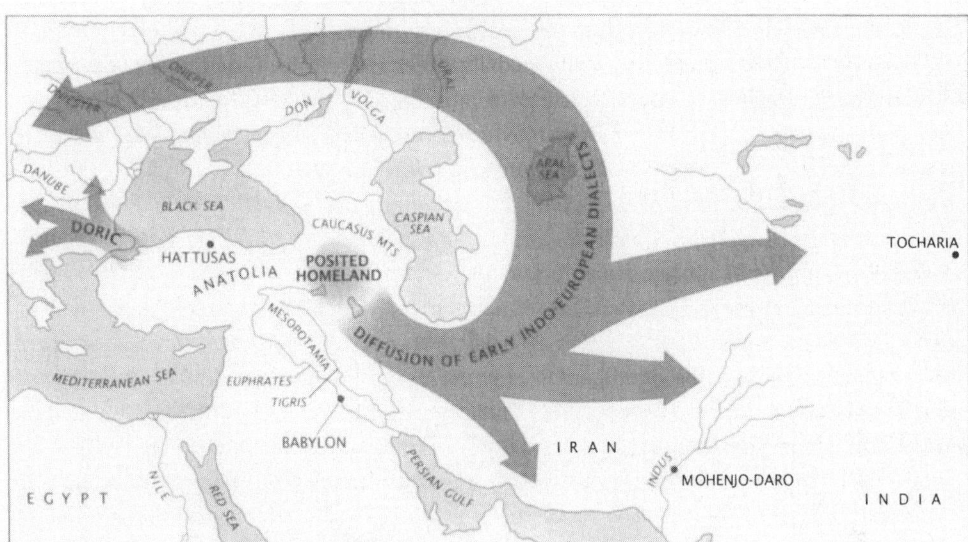


**From "The Early History of the Indo-European Languages," by Thomas V. Gamkrelidze and V. V. Ivanov (*Scientific American*, March 1990:110)**

another continent. And they take their languages with them, of course. For example, Map 8.1 above, shows the hypothesized spread of the early Indo-European language speakers from their presumed homeland in the Caucasus Mountains to much of South Asia and Europe.

The main reason for such migrations has been population pressure: whenever the natural resources of an area have become insufficient to support the local population, some of its members have had little choice but to move away. Moving from one locality to another was already true of early humans, who were hunters and gatherers—foragers for game, wild plants, and water. But once animals and plants were domesticated in the Middle East about 10,000 years ago, the need for hunting and gathering diminished in many parts of the world as permanent settlements became established. In modern times new situations caused people to migrate. The institution of slavery was responsible for the forced removal of large numbers of people not only from region to region but even from one continent to another (by the middle of the nineteenth century, the slave population in America had surpassed 4 million). Others migrated voluntarily, attracted to a particular area or country by the news of better living conditions as reported by acquaintances or relatives who had already resettled there (chain migration). Many of the 17 million or so people from various European countries who entered the United States between 1880 and 1910 were following compatriots who had pioneered the transatlantic migration. During the twentieth century, much migration occurred for political reasons. Immediately following World War II, more than 10 million Germans were either transferred to a reduced German territory from countries that had suffered under the Nazi regime or chose to resettle there on their own initiative. At about the same time (in 1947), the Indian subcontinent was partitioned between India and Pakistan, and more than 15 million Hindus from Pakistan and Muslims from India moved from one of the two new countries to the other in order to live among peoples of the same religion. According to the United Nations Refugee Agency, at the start of 2016, there were more than 65.3 million "forcibly displaced" persons (http://www.unhcr.org/576408cd7), up 5.8 million from the previous year.

For those time periods and parts of the world long characterized by the use of writing, information is available in more or less detail concerning the historical migrations that took place. However, such information is very shallow where written language has been in use for only several centuries, the Americas and Australia in particular. For example, in North America, speakers of more than two dozen languages and major dialects of the Algonquian language family (along with enclaves of other language families, of course) extended from Tennessee and eastern North Carolina in the Southeast, to northeastern Newfoundland and the southern coast of Hudson Bay in the North, and to Colorado, Wyoming, Montana, Saskatchewan, and southeastern Alberta in the West. In the absence of historical records extending several thousand years into the past, is it possible to discover where the speakers of Proto-Algonquian, the language that must have been ancestral to the present Algonquian languages, originally lived? It is, and the method of investigation involves the careful use of linguistic data as well as information pertaining to the natural history of the North American continent. This method of reconstruction was illustrated by Frank Siebert Jr. (1912–1998) in his well-known article, "The Original Home of the Proto-Algonquian People" (1967).

Let us summarize the working assumptions on which reconstructions of this kind are based. First, the territory occupied at some time in the past by speakers of an ancestral language would have been rather limited in extent when compared with the area in which the daughter languages are (or were) spoken. The fairly large part of North America that the Algonquian-speaking peoples inhabited at the time of their initial contact with the European immigrants was the result of many centuries of movements by their ancestors away from wherever their ancestral home may have been. Second, the vocabulary of the ancestral group must have included words designating the main features of the surrounding natural environment—among them the words for the various kinds of mammals, fish, birds, trees, and the like. To be able to refer fairly specifically to such features of the environment would have been essential for their survival. The families and groups that wandered off from the population in the ancestral homeland began their independent existence using the speech of the parent group. In the course of time, however, the speech habits of those who moved away began to show the inevitable changes to which all living languages are subject. The method for locating the ancestral homeland of linguistically related peoples is based on the justifiable assumption that one can reconstruct from certain cognates in the descendant languages the portion of the ancestral vocabulary that reveals the original location of the parent population.

Drawing on more than a dozen available vocabularies of modern Algonquian languages and their dialects, Siebert reconstructed fifty-three Proto-Algonquian (PA) words referring to particular features of the natural environment. Of these words, eighteen are bird names, nineteen mammalian names, twelve tree names, and four fish names. All these reconstructed words of the ancestral vocabulary are regularly derivable from the corresponding words of the modern Algonquian languages. For example, PA **a·skikwa* "(harbor) seal" (*Phoca vitulina concolor*), one of the fifty-three words, is reconstructible from the Swampy or Woodland dialect of the Cree word *a·hkik*, the Lake St. John dialect of Montagnais *a·hčok*, Ojibwa *a·skik*, and the Penobscot dialect of Abnaki àhkikw; PA **aʔšikanwa* "smallmouth black bass" (*Micropterus dolomieu*) is reconstructible from the Fox word *ašikanwa*, Menomini word *aʔsekan*, Ojibwa word *aššikan*, Shawnee word *aʔšika*, and the Penobscot dialect of the Abnaki word ásikan; and PA **a·kema·xkwa* "white ash" (*Fraxinus americana*), a compound of PA **a·kem-* "snowshoe" and PA *-*a·xkw-* "(hard)wood," from the modern cognates obtained from Swampy or Woodland dialect of Cree, the Lake St. John dialect of Montagnais, Ojibwa, and the Penobscot dialect of Abnaki. (In Ojibwa and Penobscot, the original meaning has been preserved, whereas in the Cree and Montagnais dialects the name came to be applied to the black ash after the speakers of these two dialects migrated north of the white-ash range.) Of the approximately fifty reconstructible species terms, about a score contributed significantly to the solution of the problem.

The data Siebert used consist of the reconstructed Proto-Algonquian words designating the following natural features: for mammals, bear, beaver, bison or buffalo, buck (male of moose, deer, elk, caribou), fawn, flying squirrel, fox, lynx or bobcat, mink, moose, muskrat, porcupine, raccoon, (harbor) seal, skunk, squirrel, weasel, woodchuck or groundhog, and woodland caribou; for birds, blue jay, bobwhite or quail, common loon, golden eagle, great horned owl (two terms), greater yellowlegs, gull, hawk, heron or crane, kingfisher, merganser, nighthawk, old-squaw, pileated woodpecker or logcock, raven, ruffed grouse or partridge, and large edible game bird; for fish, brown bullhead, lake trout, northern pike, and smallmouth black bass; and for trees, (speckled) alder, basswood, American beech, conifer or evergreen, elm, quaking aspen, sugar maple, tamarack, white ash, white spruce, willow, and a kind of tree whose species could not be determined.

Because all these animals and trees—the names for which are reconstructible for the Proto-Algonquian language—must have been present in the environment surrounding the speakers of the ancestral language, the task that next confronted Siebert was to locate the corresponding area on this continent. But finding it was not as easy as it might seem. The distribution of individual animal and plant species had changed considerably over the past several centuries as a result of the rapid settlement of the continent by immigrants from the Old World. Some forestlands had been converted to fields and pastures, some species of fish had been eliminated by pollution while other fish species may have been introduced into streams and lakes in which they were not native, and some species of mammals had been greatly reduced or virtually exterminated by indiscriminate hunting (for example, the buffalo) or urbanization. What Siebert therefore had to establish was the earliest possible ranges of the fifty-odd species. He consulted nearly a hundred sources containing information about the natural history of North America, some dating as far back as 1625. Trees served as particularly reliable guides because they are fixed and their ranges are governed by soil, moisture, and long-term climatic patterns. Bird species contributed much less to the investigation because seasonal migrations tend to make their geographic ranges quite extensive. Once the geographic distributions had been established, Siebert plotted the ranges on a map of the continent. The earliest homeland of speakers of Proto-Algonquian would have had to be in the area that all the significant species shared in common, or at least touched. For Siebert's ingenious reconstruction of the location of the original home of the Proto-Algonquian people, we can refer to the author's own discussion and conclusion (Siebert 1967).

## TIME PERSPECTIVE IN CULTURE

How linguistic data can aid the reconstruction of cultural history was discussed at length and exemplified in one of the early works of Edward Sapir, a brilliant American linguist and anthropologist, and probably the greatest specialist on Native American languages until World War II. *Time Perspective in Aboriginal American Culture: A Study in Method* (1916) was his longest monograph in ethnology and is testimony to his methodological prowess. The few examples that follow illustrate Sapir's discussion of inferential linguistic evidence for time perspective.

The relative age of a culture element can be determined with some reliability from the form of the native (not borrowed) word that refers to the element. Such simple and not further analyzable words as *bow*, *plow*, *spear*, and *wheel* are as a rule much older than words that can be broken down into smaller constituent parts—for example, *airplane*, *battleship*, *railroad*, and *spaceship*. Irregular grammatical forms also indicate the great age of those words with which they are associated and, by implication, of those entities to which they refer; hence the plurals *geese*, *kine* (archaic plural of *cow*), *lice*, *oxen*, and *sheep*, on the one hand, but *elephants*, *lions*, *parrots*, and *tigers*, on the other.

Loanwords, which usually designate elements of foreign cultures, can frequently be identified by their different phonetic structure (we would now say "phonemic"). Thus, although /z/ and /ǰ/ occur in old words of the native English vocabulary in medial or final position (as in *frozen*, *rise*, *bridges*, and *ridge*), initially these two sounds are found only in loanwords, for example, in *zeal* (adapted from Late Latin) or *just* (adapted from Middle French). Similarly, some combinations of sounds betray the foreign origin of words in which they occur, as /ps/ does in *apse* and *lapse* (both from Latin) and *rhapsody* (from Greek via Latin). But the final /-ps/ in *lips*, *sleeps*, *ship's*, and other such words is not comparable, because the /-s/ represents other morphemes—the plural, the third-person singular, or the possessive, respectively. For societies with a long tradition of writing, inferential linguistic evidence may add little if anything to what is already known about their cultural history. This is not the case, however, with nonliterate societies.

The assignment of related languages to a language family implies the earlier existence of an ancestral language from which all modern languages of the family have descended. The more differentiated these descendant languages are, the longer the period of time one must allow for their development to have taken place; the time depth has important consequences for culture history.

Linguistic scholars have known for some time that phonetic (or phonemic) and morphological similarities sometimes exist among unrelated neighboring languages to an extent that could scarcely be due to chance. Such similarities are indicative of an extensive period of cultural contact between the respective societies, a circumstance the ethnologist must take into account.

In the concluding remarks of his monograph, Sapir made the point that, although direct evidence is much to be preferred to inferential evidence in the study of culture history and the establishment of culture sequences, anthropologists frequently face situations in which direct evidence is either insufficient or completely lacking. In such cases inferential evidence, linguistic in particular, becomes invaluable.

## SUMMARY AND CONCLUSIONS

Living languages change slowly but constantly. Old English is no longer intelligible to speakers of Modern English, and even words that rhymed in Shakespeare's time do not always rhyme today. The tendency of sound changes to be regular makes it possible to reconstruct the assumed ancestral language of daughter languages. Reconstructible words having to do with the natural environment of a prehistoric society facilitate determining the location of its ancestral homeland. Furthermore, the reconstruction of **protowords** may also throw light on features of a prehistoric culture not discoverable by other means. For example, the reconstructibility of certain kinship terms, such as those for in-laws, may provide clues to postmarital residence practices of the people who used them. Reconstruction of an ancestral homeland location and other protocultural features on the basis of linguistic data is not always a standard procedure, but, when the archaeological record is insufficient or lacking, it may be the only means of probing the prehistoric past.

When languages are classified genetically, those that are related by virtue of a common origin are assigned to one language family. The original concept of a language family was conservative, requiring the relationships among the member languages of a family to be close and well documented. The tendency since the 1960s has been to group together languages that are considered to be much more remotely related. Such languages are said to constitute a phylum or even a superphylum (or macrophylum). The difference between the older conservative unit of language family and the newer phylum can best be illustrated by comparing numbers: the several hundred language families of the New World are said to be reducible to only three superphyla.

Linguistic typology, on the other hand, is based on examining the similarities among languages that are not due to a common origin. Scholars engaged in finding common features or attributes in cross-linguistic diversity have taken various approaches as they attempt to assign to a relatively few basic types the many languages of the world.

## RESOURCE MANUAL AND STUDY GUIDE

### *Questions for Discussion*

1. Vocabularies of living languages change constantly to keep up with the changes in the cultures of their speakers. Is the rate of lexical change the same in all societies, or can it be expected to be much faster in some than in others? Why?
2. Can you also cite some English words that have gone out of fashion or have disappeared? Why did they disappear? What have they been replaced with?
3. Reconstructions based on linguistic data are sometimes the only way scholars can learn something about the distant past of a particular people. Explain and illustrate.

### *Objective Study Questions*

**TRUE-FALSE TEST**

T F 1. An inflecting language is one like Chinese, where many morphemic parts are *fused* together to make new words.

T F 2. The term *language family* refers to all those languages whose speakers belong to the same culture area, that is, have similar cultures.

T F 3. Languages change very slowly, so earlier versions of English (like that found, say, in Shakespeare) are still completely intelligible to modern English speakers.

T F 4. A language isolate is a language that, although related to other languages, is spoken some distance from them.

T F 5. Dealing with linguistic phenomena as they exist at a specific point of time, without regard to historical antecedents, is referred to as the synchronic approach.

T F 6. A protolanguage (the assumed or reconstructed ancestral language of a language family) *cannot* be reconstructed unless one has good records from the distant past of some of the languages making up that language family.

T F 7. The English words *illegal, immoral,* and *irresponsible* illustrate assimilation.

T F 8. English has never been very hospitable to words of foreign origin.

**MULTIPLE-CHOICE QUESTIONS**

____ 1. An exemplary case of reconstruction of the location of the ancestral homeland has been done for prehistoric speakers of which language family? (A) Siouan. (B) Uto-Aztecan. (C) Indo-European. (D) Algonquian.

____ 2. The word meaning "garlic" in language A is *mopan*, in language B *maban*, in language C *mapo*. What would likely be the reconstructed word (designated by *) in the ancestral (proto-)language of the related languages A, B, and C? (A) **mapan*. (B) **moban*. (C) **mopo*. (D) **mopon*.

____ 3. Cognate is a linguistic form related to another by virtue of (A) descent from an ancestral language. (B) borrowing from another language. (C) historical accident.

**COMPLETIONS**

1. English is a language that belongs to the ____________________ language family (one hyphenated word).
2. What reconstructible Indo-European word indicates that Proto-Indo-Europeans did not live near the equator? _____________ (one word).

## *Problems*

In order to enable readers to try their hand at some simple reconstructing, a few problems are included below. Solutions can be found following the answer section. Keep in mind that because language reconstructions are no more than brief statements concerning an earlier or the earliest stage of a language family or one of its branches, some reconstructions may need minor changes when additional data become available. The problems offered here have been simplified; they require only the most straightforward application of the techniques of reconstructing linguistic forms. Remember that the asterisk is used to mark a reconstructed form, that is, one that has not been attested or is unattestable.

**PROBLEM 1**

Based on Cowan and Rakušan (1998), this problem calls for the reconstruction of the initial Proto-Indo-European consonant on the basis of the following cognates (related words) in three Indo-European languages:

| *English* | *Latin* | *Ancient Greek* |
|---|---|---|
| father | pater | patēr |
| foot | pēs | pous |
| for | per | peri |
| flat | plānus | platos |
| fathom | patēre | atanē |

(The horizontal lines over certain vowels mark their length; for example, ā in *plānus* sounds like *a* in *father.*)

(Fill in the blanks: Initial Proto-Indo-European * ___ corresponds to ___ in Modern English, ___ in Latin, and ___ in Ancient Greek.)

**PROBLEM 2**

Based on Langacker (1972), this problem concerns the reflexes of Proto-Cupan *[l] in three languages of Cupan, a subfamily of Uto-Aztecan. (A reflex in this case is a sound derived from a prior [older] sound.)

| *Cahuilla* | *Cupeño* | *Luiseño* | |
|---|---|---|---|
| haal | hal | hal | "look for" |
| kiyul | qəyul | kiyuul | "fish" |
| laʔlaʔ | ləʔəl | laʔla | "goose" |
| qasilʸ | qəṣilʸ | qaaṣil | "sagebrush" |
| puul | puul | puula | "doctor" |
| mukilʸ | mukʔilʸ | muukil | "sore" |
| silʸi | silʸi | ṣiili | "pour" |

Proto-Cupan *[l] corresponds to ___ in _________, ___ in _________, and ___ in _______ under what circumstances?

**PROBLEM 3**

Based on Cowan and Rakušan (1998), this problem calls for the reconstruction of whole Proto-Austronesian words from the following cognates of several Austronesian languages:

| *Sundanese* | *Old Javanese* | *Modern Javanese* | *Malay* | *Madurese* | |
|---|---|---|---|---|---|
| manis | manis | manès | manes | manes | "lovely" |
| taman | taman | taman | taman | taman | "garden" |
| kuraŋ | kuraŋ | kuraŋ | kuraŋ | kòraŋ | "reduction" |
| damar | damar | damar | damar | dhámar | "lamp" |
| bantal | bantal | bantal | bantal | bhántal | "pillow" |
| tanjuŋ | tanjuŋ | tanjóŋ | tanjoŋ | tanjhuŋ | "flower" |
| qupah | qupah | upah | opah | òpa | "reward" |

Example: Proto-Austronesian word for "lovely" is reconstructible as *manis.

**PROBLEM 4**

According to Watkins 1992, among the reconstructible Proto-Indo-European words are the following: *gr̥ə-no- "grain," *bhar(e)s- "barley," *yewo- "grain," *mel(ə)- "to grind," *sē- "to sow," *yeug- "to join, to yoke," *gʷou- "cow, ox," *weik- "village," *owi- "ewe, sheep," *ekwo- "horse," *dem- "house(hold)," and *dhwer- "door(way)." What conclusions can one draw from these Proto-Indo-European words about the livelihood of members of old Indo-European society?

## Answer Key

True-false test: 1-F, 2-F, 3-F, 4-F, 5-T, 6-F, 7-T, 8-F
Multiple-choice questions: 1-D, 2-A, 3-A
Completions: 1. Indo-European, 2. snow

*Problem 1.* On the basis of the cognates listed, the reconstructed initial Proto-Indo-European consonant would be **p*; it corresponds to *f* in Modern English and *p* in both Latin and Ancient Greek.

*Problem 2.* After the vowel [i], Proto-Cupan *[l] is represented as [lʸ] in Cahuilla and Cupeño and as [l] in Luiseño; in all other environments it is represented as [l] in all three languages.

*Problem 3.* The reconstructed Proto-Austronesian words are *manis, *taman, *kuraŋ, *damar, *bantal, *tanjuŋ, and *qupah.

*Problem 4.* This is an open-ended question; the answer should be limited to what a reasonable interpretation of the data presented would allow.

## Notes and Suggestions for Further Reading

Crowley and Bowern (2009), Hale (2007), Millar (2007), and Schendl (2001) are standard recent texts in historical linguistics. Burridge and Berg (2017) is a new, approachable entry-level text.

For classic technical introductions to, and survey of, historical linguistics, see Anttila (1989) or Hock (1991). The collection of articles in Bowen and Evans (2014) is broad and very useful.

Several thematic sections on the subject of this chapter are included in Crystal (2010). Most of the Japanese examples come from Inoue (1979), and hundreds of others can be found in Stanlaw (2004a).

The fascinating story of the Indo-Europeans and their spread throughout Europe and Asia is told in several well-researched and accessible accounts, including Mallory (1991) and Fortson (2010). The award-winning *The Horse, the Wheel, and Language* by Anthony (2007) gives a nice blend of archaeology and Proto-Indo-European linguistics. Voyles and Barrack (2009), though not for beginners, is an exhaustive look at Indo-European grammar and culture. A good Indo-European reference grammar is Quiles and López-Menchero (2009). A classic dictionary of Indo-European terms is Buck (1988).

Campbell (2000) and Silver and Miller (2000) are probably the two most popular and standard texts on the history of Native American languages. Although Sapir (1916) is not easily available, the entire monograph is reprinted in Sapir (1949:389–462). The number of North American language families and isolates is based on Voegelin and Voegelin (1966). Sapir's reduction of North American Indian language families to six "major linguistic groups" was published in 1929 in the *Encyclopaedia Britannica* (14th ed.) and was reprinted in Sapir (1949:169–178).

# 9

# Languages in Variation and Languages in Contact

## LEARNING OBJECTIVES

- Explain the different criteria used to define dialects
- Explain the differences between dialect and style
- Provide examples of language contact
- Discern the differences between pidgins and creoles
- Appreciate the variety and distribution of the world's languages, and their numbers

Strictly speaking, the speech pattern of one individual is somewhat different from the speech pattern of the next, even though the two speak the same language, and regional varieties of language differ from each other by features of vocabulary, grammar, and pronunciation.

## IDIOLECTS

It is possible to identify over the telephone people we know well without their having to say who they are; similarly, we recognize familiar television newscasters even when we cannot see the screen. The recognition of individuals by voice alone is possible because of their idiosyncratic combination of voice quality, pronunciation, grammatical usage, and choice of words. Voice quality, or timbre, is determined by the anatomy of the **vocal tract** (the tongue, the nasal and oral cavities, the vocal cords, the larynx, and other parts), over which the speaker has little or no control. Other voice features—for example, tempo, loudness, and to some extent even pitch range—can be controlled fairly simply. But none of these features of an individual's speech pattern is constant. Voice quality changes with age as muscles and tissues deteriorate and the dentition undergoes modification. Over a lifetime, changes tend to occur in the choice of words, grammar, and pronunciation as well.

An individual's speech variety is referred to as an **idiolect**. Almost all speakers make use of several idiolects, depending on the circumstances of communication. For example, when family members talk to each other, their speech habits typically differ from those any one of them would use in, say, an interview with a prospective employer. The concept of idiolect therefore refers to a very specific phenomenon—the speech variety used by a particular individual.

## DIALECTS

Often, people who live in the same geographic area, have similar occupations, or have the same education or economic status speak relatively similar idiolects compared to those from other groups. These shared characteristics may entail similarities in vocabulary, pronunciation, or grammatical features. When all the idiolects of a group of speakers have enough in common to appear at least superficially alike, we say they belong to the same dialect. The term ***dialect***, then, is an abstraction: It refers to a form of language or speech used by members of a regional, ethnic, or social group. Dialects that are mutually intelligible belong to the same language. All languages spoken by more than one small homogeneous community are found to consist of two or more dialects.

Mutual intelligibility, of course, can vary in degree. In the early 1950s, a number of men and women from eight reservations in New York and Ontario were tested in an experiment designed to determine which of their local dialects were mutually intelligible and therefore dialects of one language, and which were not and therefore could be classified as individual languages of the Iroquoian language family. Even though the investigators arrived at percentages of intelligibility between any two of the Iroquoian speech communities, the question of where the boundaries lay between intelligibility and unintelligibility remained unresolved. If the boundaries between language and dialect had been drawn at 25 percent of mutual intelligibility, there would have been four different languages, of which one would have consisted of two dialects and another of three. If set at 75 percent, there would have been five languages, two of which would have consisted of two dialects each.

Because it is spoken in so many different areas the world over, English is particularly diversified dialectally. Speakers' home countries may be guessed from their pronunciation and from the use of certain words that are characteristic of specific varieties of English. For example, included in the vocabulary of Australians is *bludger* "loafer, shirker"; of Canadians *to book off* "to notify an employer that one is not reporting for work"; of the Irish *spalpeen* "rascal"; of the Scots *cutty sark* "short (under)garment"; and of the British to *knock up* "to wake up (someone), as by knocking on the window." A speaker of any dialect of American English is likely to find it quite difficult to understand a cab driver in London who speaks cockney, the dialect of London's East End, even though both speak dialects of the same language.

English was brought to North America during the seventeenth century by colonists from England who settled along the Atlantic coast from Maine to Georgia. The language of these colonists consisted of dialects reflecting the social stratification and geographic division of their former home country. Today, despite regional differences (especially along the East Coast and in the South), American English exhibits a remarkable degree of uniformity. Historically, this uniformity resulted from the mingling of settlers from various parts of the East as they pushed westward; since World War II it has been because of the ever-increasing mobility of Americans. Today, few people live in the communities in which they were born; most move from one place to another when they change jobs, marry, or retire. Nevertheless, certain regional dialects in the United States are well known and readily recognizable when heard—for example, those of Boston, Virginia, or Texas. Vocabulary may be just as helpful in identifying where older speakers from rural areas have come from. For example, the dragonfly is referred to in most of Virginia as *snake doctor*, in southwestern Pennsylvania as *snake feeder*, in eastern North Carolina as *mosquito hawk*, in New England as *(devil's) darning needle*, in coastal New Jersey as *spindle*, in northern California as *ear sewer*, and so on (see Table 9.1, an excerpt from the Harvard Dialect Survey).

Earlier nineteenth-century migration patterns are still in some ways seen in the United States. One of the biggest cultural divisions can be seen as we travel along the fault line that runs up from Texas through Arkansas, along the Ohio River, across northern Kentucky, until the Mason-Dixon line. This also coincides with one of the great linguistic dividing lines in the United States: the split over how to say the second-person plural pronoun. In theory, "you" can be both singular or plural, so we really do not need to have another way of saying this. But for most people this is unsettling, and there are a variety of choices available: *you guys* (said by about 50 percent of Americans), *y'all (*28 percent*), you all* (10 percent), *you (*10 percent*),* or *yins* (less than 1 percent). However these terms are not dispersed uniformly: for example, *y'all* is mostly found in the deep antebellum South and *you guys* is found in most other places (New England, the upper Midwest, and West, and the West Coast); *you all* goes along the line from Missouri through the hills of Kentucky, to Washington, DC. *Yins* is restricted to the Pittsburgh metropolitan area, and *yous/youse* is found in New York City, New Jersey, and parts of the Pocono Mountains in Pennsylvania. Taylor Shelton (2014), looking at geotagged tweets (see Chapter 15) from 2012 to 2014, finds basically this same distribution on Twitter (see Map 9.1)

The way individuals speak varies not only according to their regional and social dialects but also according to context. The distinctive manner in which people express themselves in a particular situation is referred to as style. Speech styles are thus comparable to styles of dress. One would feel out of place and uncomfortable going on a hiking trip in formal attire or attending a traditional wedding reception in sneakers, jeans, and a sweatshirt. Similarly, a person who might use the vulgar expression "I'm pissed" when talking with former schoolmates would probably substitute the colloquial phrase "I'm mad" under other circumstances and use such words as "angry" or "aggravated" under more formal conditions.

## STYLES

Stylistic variations are not only lexical but also phonological (for instance, the casual pronunciation of *butter* with the flap [ɾ] rather than the dental [t]), morphological (as in the casually styled "Who are you taking to lunch?" as against the formal "Whom are you taking to lunch?"), and syntactic (as in "Wanna eat now?" as against "Do you want to eat now?"). A stylistic or dialectal variety of speech that does not call forth negative reaction,

**TABLE 9.1** SOME AMERICAN DIALECT DIFFERENCES BASED ON VOCABULARY DIFFERENCES

73. **What is your *general* term for the rubber-soled shoes worn in gym class, for athletic activities, etc.?**
  a. sneakers (45.50%)
  b. shoes (1.93%)
  c. gym shoes (5.55%)
  d. sand shoes (0.03%)
  e. jumpers (0.01%)
  f. tennis shoes (41.34%)
  g. running shoes (1.42%)
  h. runners (0.17%)
  i. trainers (0.23%)
  j. I have no general word for this (0.89%)
  k. other (2.95%)
  (10,722 respondents)

85. **What is the thing that women use to tie [back] their hair?**
  a. (hair) elastic (12.46%)
  b. rubber band (32.01%)
  c. horsetail (0.09%)
  d. hair thing (14.97%)
  e. hair tie (18.77%)
  f. other (21.71%)
  (10,241 respondents)
  (10,665 respondents)

96. **What is the distinction between dinner and supper?**
  a. Supper is an evening meal while dinner is eaten earlier (lunch, for example) (7.79%)
  b. Supper is an evening meal; dinner is the main meal. (7.76%)
  c. Dinner takes place in a more formal setting than supper. (12.12%)
  d. There is no distinction; they both have the same meaning. (34.56%)
  e. I do not use the term supper. (33.14%)
  f. I don't use the term dinner. (0.82%)
  g. other (3.83%)
  (10,661 respondents)

97. **Which of these terms do you prefer?**
  a. trash can (35.53%)
  b. garbage can (27.38%)
  c. rubbish bin (0.41%)
  d. waste(paper) basket (1.06%)
  e. These words refer to different things. (33.26%)
  f. other (2.36%)
  (10,676 respondents)

100. **Do you cut or mow the lawn or grass?**
  a. cut the grass (18.38%)
  b. cut the lawn (0.64%)
  c. mow the grass (5.75%)
  d. mow the lawn (66.79%)
  e. other (8.43%)
  (10,553 respondents)

103. **What do you call the thing from which you might drink water in a school?**
  a. bubbler (3.84%)
  b. water bubbler (0.30%)
  c. drinking fountain (33.16%)
  d. water fountain (60.97%)
  e. other (1.74%)
  (10,656 respondents)

111. **What do you call the end of a loaf of bread?**
  a. end (17.29%)
  b. heel (59.15%)
  c. crust (15.21%)
  d. nose (0.17%)
  e. butt (3.53%)
  f. shpitzel (0.05%)
  g. I have no word for this. (1.97%)
  h. other (2.63%)
  (10,665 respondents)

***Note:*** **An excerpt from the Harvard Dialect Survey, a Linguistics project by Bert Vaux and Scott Golder (http://www.tekstlab.uio.no/cambridge_survey/)**

**MAP 9.1** HEY Y'ALL GEOGRAPHIES

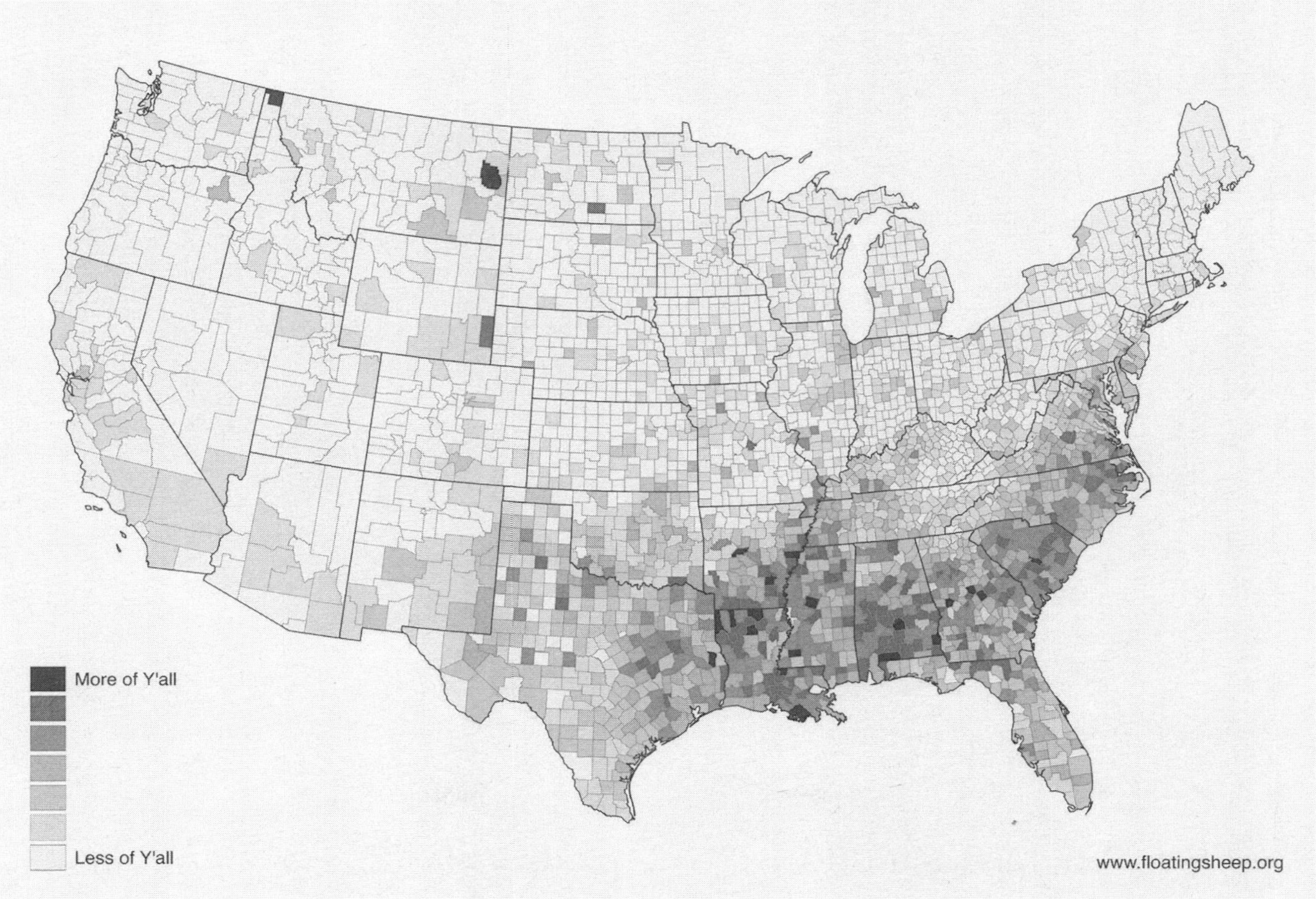

Courtesy of floatingsheep.org

that is used on formal occasions, and that carries social prestige is considered **standard speech**; varieties that do not measure up to these norms are referred to as nonstandard or substandard. Standard British English, often referred to as Received Standard (and its pronunciation as Received Pronunciation), is used at English public schools (private secondary boarding schools); is heard during radio and television newscasts; and is used when circumstances call for a serious, formal attitude (sermons, lectures, and the like). In less formal situations, there has been an increasing tendency to use a style that deviates from or falls short of the standard. Informality in dress, behavior, and speech is a sign of the times both in the United States and elsewhere.

How many different styles do speakers of English use? According to Martin Joos (1907–1978), five clearly distinguishable styles were characteristic of his dialect of American English (spoken in the east-central United States); he termed them frozen, formal, consultative, casual, and intimate (Joos 1962). Today, very few speakers of American English ever use the frozen style except perhaps occasionally in formal writing. The assumption that the exact number of speech styles can be determined for a language serving millions of speakers does not seem to be warranted. No two native speakers of English talk alike, and just exactly what use each person makes of the various stylistic features, ranging all the way from a pompous formality to an intimate or even vulgar informality, is up to the individual speaker.

## LANGUAGE CONTACT

Languages must have been in contact as long as there have been human beings. From what can be ascertained from the current and historical ethnographic record, people have also often been in close proximity with those who spoke languages that were mutually unintelligible. Trade, travel, migration, war, intermarriage, and other nonlinguistic causes have forced different languages to come into contact countless times throughout history. When this occurs, several things can happen over time: languages can die, new languages can develop, or languages in contact can become mixed in various ways. We will now explore some of the consequences of mixing and see how it can sometimes lead to the development of drastically different linguistic structures.

When a new physical item or concept is borrowed from another culture, the name for that new item in the donor language is often just directly taken over. For example, Hawaiian gave English *ukulele*; Bantu, *gumbo*; Czech, *polka*; Cantonese *wok*; Arabic, *algebra*; German, *pretzel*; and Malay, rice *paddy*. Of course, English has contributed hundreds of words to other languages as well, such as *weekend* to French, *boyfriend* to Russian, *aerobic classes* to German, and *beefsteak* to many languages.

This exchange can go both ways. As most native English speakers know, many words of French origin have been borrowed into the language. In return for *le weekend*, English received *rendezvous* and *lingerie*. One of the reasons for this was the introduction of Old French during the Norman conquest of England in 1066, which replaced Old English as the language of the ruling classes in England (and which held prominence until well into the fourteenth and fifteenth centuries). During these centuries of French linguistic dominance, a large proportion of English vocabulary drastically changed. Some words disappeared, others acquired different meanings. For example, consider the words in this table:

| MODERN ENGLISH | OLD ENGLISH | MODERN GERMAN | MODERN ENGLISH | OLD FRENCH | MODERN FRENCH |
|---|---|---|---|---|---|
| **cow** | *cū* | *Kuh* | **beef** | *boef* | *boeuf* |
| **calf** | *cealf* | *Kalb* | **veal** | *veel* | *veau* |
| **swine** | *swīn* | *Schwein* | **pork** | *porc* | *porc* |
| **sheep** | *scēap* | *Schaf* | **mutton** | *moton* | *mouton* |
| **chicken** | *cicen* | *Küken* | **poultry** | *pouletrie* | *volaille* |
| **deer** | *dēor* | *Tier* | **venison** | *venesoun* | *venaison* |

Here we see two columns of Modern English terms in bold: cow, calf, swine, sheep, chicken, and deer on the far left (followed by Old English and modern German equivalents), and beef, veal, pork, mutton, poultry, and venison (followed by their Old French and modern French equivalents) from the middle to the right. In both instances, it is fairly easy to see the relationships (e.g., "cow" and *cū*, etc.). What are the connections between these two sets of Modern English terms? The column on the far left names the live animal. The column in the middle labels the food derived from that animal (e.g., "beef" from a "cow"). We might say that the Anglo-Saxon terms became restricted for the names of animals and the more prestigious French terms were applied to the cooked and prepared animal brought inside the house (Jackson and Amvela 2007).

## PIDGINS

A common way in which individuals and groups interact across language boundaries is by means of a **pidgin**. Typically, a pidgin originates when speakers of two or more mutually unintelligible languages develop a need to communicate with each other for certain limited or specialized purposes, especially trade. Because pidgins have a much narrower range of functions than the languages for which they substitute, they possess a limited vocabulary, and because they need to be learned rapidly for the sake of efficiency, they have a substantially reduced grammatical structure. From a sociocultural perspective, an important characteristic of a pidgin is that it does not serve as the native, or first, language of any particular group.

A pidgin is not the result of the same kind of development true languages are subject to: it tends to come about suddenly, as the need arises, and ceases to exist when no longer called upon to perform its original function. It may last as little as a dozen or so years; only infrequently does it outlast a century. In its phonology and morphology, a pidgin is invariably simpler than the first languages of those who use it, and the bulk of its lexicon is based on, or derived from, one of the languages in contact.

Although customarily associated with European colonialism, pidgins have developed whenever speakers of different languages have been in regular but limited contact. Among the examples that abound are the English-based China Coast Pidgin, which may have originated as early as the seventeenth century but became especially widespread during the course of the nineteenth; the English-based Maori Pidgin, current during the early years of British colonization of New Zealand; Trader Navajo, the Navajo-based pidgin used by traders in the Southwest; and the various Congo pidgins that facilitate contacts among the speakers of a variety of African languages used in the Congo River basin. Reflecting the impact of European colonialism during the eighteenth and nineteenth centuries, many of the former pidgins as well as those still in existence are English-, French-, Spanish-, Portuguese-, or Dutch-based.

A good illustration of the origin, succession, and demise of pidgins can be drawn from recent Vietnamese history. When Vietnam was ruled by the French as part of Indochina, a French-based pidgin was used by those French and Vietnamese who lacked command of the other's language. After the defeat of the French at Dien Bien Phu in 1954 and the evacuation of French forces from Vietnam two years later, the pidgin was no longer needed and became almost extinct. With the introduction of US combat forces into the Republic of Vietnam in the early 1960s, an English-based pidgin rapidly developed to assume the role of its French-based predecessor. After the US soldiers were withdrawn in 1973, and political events in 1975 brought the influence of the United States in Vietnam to an abrupt end, the new pidgin, too, all but disappeared.

Although it is true that pidgins can be simplified versions of any language, the most common are those based on English. The reason for this is the widespread contact that English-speaking people have had with non-Western nations. The British Empire not only spread the Union Jack but also its language over much of the world. Thus, English-based pidgins were found from the coasts of Africa to the New World to the South Pacific. For instance, here is an example of the first lines of Shakespeare's *Julius Caesar* (Act 3, Scene 2) in Melanesian Tok Pisin compared to the original English (Murphy 1980:20):

> *Pren, man bolong Rom, Wantok, harim nau.*
> *Mi kam tasol long plantim Kaesar. Mi noken beiten longen.*
> Friends, Romans, countrymen, lend me your ears;
> I come to bury Caesar, not to praise him.

We can see here many of the typical devices pidgins (and later creoles) use that allow them to communicate effectively with a limited set of grammatical and lexical resources. Words such as *pren*, *mi*, and *kam* are simply nativized forms of English "friend," "me," and "come." "Romans" comes out as *man bolong Rom* (lit, "man/men belong(ing) to Rome"). Countrymen is *Wantok*—those of us who all speak "one talk." Although "lend me your ears" loses some of its power when rendered as *harim nau* ("hear 'em now"), it still makes its point; but *plantim* ("plant 'em") meaning "bury" is almost a poetic metaphor. The pidgin *tasol* ("that's all") acts as a conjunction (such as "but") or adverb (such as "only"). The word *noken* ("no can") is a verbal negative auxiliary. There are no inflections, case markers, or tenses in pidgin; therefore, certain words must do a multiplicity of tasks. One such word is *long*. This word serves many uses, as a preposition ("to," "at," "with," "under"), a comparative marker ("than . . . "), an indirect object sign, or an indication of duration. For example, *lukluk long* (lit. "look look long") can mean to seek, to watch, to look for, to take care of, or to protect. *Beten* or *beiten* is "prayer," and *beiten longen* ("prayer belong 'em") is a way of saying "praise."

Although they characteristically lack inflection and possess a limited vocabulary, pidgins have a structure of their own and readily adapt to changing circumstances. The structural simplicity of pidgins is to their advantage, allowing cross-cultural communication with a minimum of effort. The reduction or total elimination of inflectional affixes, the use of morphemic repetition for intensification, and simplified syntactic constructions make geographically separated pidgins look remarkably similar—so much so that some scholars have argued that in their basic structure, all modern and recent pidgins may well go back to some such protopidgin as Sabir, the original lingua franca, a medieval pidgin based on Romance languages and used in Mediterranean ports until the beginning of the last century. As similar as pidgins may be structurally, though, they differ according to the languages that have lexified them (that is, supplied them with the bulk of their word-stock).

Finally, it is important to remember that pidgins are not "broken" languages, a kind of "primitive" speech or manifestations of "corrupt" thought processes of simple peoples. They are quite the opposite: "[P]idgins are demonstrably creative adaptations of natural languages, with a structure and rules of their own. Along with creoles, they are evidence of a fundamental process of linguistic change . . . [and] they provide the clearest evidence of language being created and shaped by society for its own ends, as people adapt to new social circumstances" (Crystal 2010: 344).

## FROM PIDGINS TO CREOLES

The process of grammatical and lexical reduction of a language such as English or Navajo to a pidgin, referred to as *pidginization*, reflects a limitation on functions the pidgin is expected to serve. But it would be wrong to assume that the role pidgins are destined to play is invariably humble. In many instances, a pidgin has come to be used by a growing number of people over an increasingly large area, especially when none of the native languages can claim priority by virtue of population size or the prestige of a written tradition. In short, a pidgin may become widely recognized and depended upon as an indispensable means of interethnic communication. Under such circumstances, the growing demands placed on the pidgin cause an expansion of its vocabulary and elaboration of its syntax—a process opposite to pidginization. It may be furnished with a writing system and used in the mass media, it may acquire a semiofficial status, and it may even become the mother tongue of those children in whose families it is habitually used. This process of expansion of a pidgin to other language functions is referred to as **creolization**, and the end result is termed a **creole**. A creole, then, is a pidgin that has become the first language of a speech community.

Among the many places in the world where this process has taken place is Papua New Guinea. There what once was an English-based pidgin of limited utility has been elevated over the past several decades to one of the official languages of the now independent country. Known as Neo-Melanesian, or Tok Pisin (from talk pidgin), it has become the lingua franca of about 1 million people who speak some seven hundred languages native to Papua New Guinea and the first language of some 20,000 households (Mühlhäusler 1987:178). Tok Pisin has acquired such prestige that more parliamentary debates are now conducted in it than in English, and most recently it has been heard even in the country's university lecture halls.

At least three-fourths of the Tok Pisin vocabulary derives from English; some 15 percent from indigenous New Guinea languages, especially Tolai (Kuanua); and the remainder from various other languages, including German. For example, in the singular, Tok Pisin personal pronouns *mi* "I, me," *yu* "you," and *em* "he, him; she, her; it" remain the same whether they serve as subject or object. In the first-person plural, the distinction is made between the inclusive form *yumi* "we, us (including the hearer)" and the exclusive form *mipela* "we, us (excluding the hearer)," and in all three persons of the plural the exact number (up to three) is usually indicated, as in *yutupela* "you two" or *yutripela* "you three"; the form *ol* for the third-person plural occurs in addition to the expected form. Possession is indicated by *bilong*, the predicate is commonly marked by the particle *i*, and transitive verbs have the suffix *-im*, which also converts adjectives into causative verb forms. Accordingly, *Mi kukim kaikai bilong mi* translates as "I cook my food," *Wanpela lek bilong mi i bruk* as "One of my legs is broken," *Em i krosim mi* as "He scolded me," and *Ol i kapsaitim bensin* as "They spilled the gasoline."

A New Guinea road safety handbook (*Rot Sefti Long Niugini*), which instructs readers in three languages, contains the following English paragraph and the Tok Pisin equivalent (Crystal 2010:345):

> If you have an accident, get the other driver's number, if possible, get his name and address too, and report it to the police. Don't fight or abuse him.
>
> *Sapos yu kisim bagarap, kisim namba bilong narapela draiva, sapos yu ken, kisim naim bilong em na adres tu, na tokim polis long em. Noken paitim em o tok nogut long em.*

Even though creoles are languages in their own right and have in some instances found their way into the mass media as well as into primary school instruction, they nevertheless tend to carry less prestige than the standard European languages beside which they are used and from which they derive the bulk of their vocabulary. Consequently, some speakers of creoles, especially those who live in cities and hold semiprofessional jobs, try to "improve" their speech by using the standard language as a model. When this happens, creoles undergo a change, moving in the direction of the standard language in a process known as **decreolization**. Such a change is currently taking place, for example, in English-based Jamaican Creole, giving rise to a continuum ranging from the **basilect**, the variety most differentiated from the standard and used by members of the rural working class, to the **acrolect**, an urban variety approaching the standard and therefore seen as more prestigious.

The great majority of pidgins and creoles are found in coastal areas of the equatorial belt where contacts between speakers of different languages, including those of former European colonialist nations, have been a common occurrence because of trade. Some recent pidgins, however, have been developing under different circumstances—for example, the Gastarbeiter Deutsch spoken in the Federal Republic of Germany by several million guest workers from southern and southeastern Europe.

Pidgins and creoles have received the serious attention they deserve only since the fourth quarter of the last century. Some of the most stimulating (but also controversial) contributions to their study were made by Derek Bickerton. One important concept based on the study of creoles is Bickerton's bioprogram hypothesis (1981), that is, the assumption that the human species must have a biologically innate capacity for language. In support of this hypothesis, Bickerton linked pidgins and creoles with children's language acquisition and language origins. Because the syntax of Hawaiian Creole English, which Bickerton knew well, has many features in common with other creole languages, the cognitive strategies for deriving creoles from pidgins are so much alike as to be part of the human species-specific endowment. Furthermore, the innate capacities that enable children to learn a native language are also helpful to children as they expand a pidgin into a creole. According to Bickerton, some basic cognitive distinctions (such as *specific* versus *general* and *state* versus *process*) must have been established prior to the hominization process (development of human characteristics), and these distinctions are evident in the structure of creoles as well as in the earliest stages of language acquisition.

Some of the recent research concerning pidgins and creoles has resulted in the "blurring" of these two types of speech (Jourdan 1991). It is now accepted that pidgin and creole varieties of a particular language can exist side by side and that a creole can become the main language of a speech community without becoming its native language. In other respects, however, our understanding of pidgins and creoles has improved because greater attention is being paid to the historical and socioeconomic contexts in which pidgins and creoles come into being.

## LANGUAGE CONTACT IN THE CONTEMPORARY WORLD

In spite of the dominance of English, or the effects of electronic mass media and the Internet that are supposedly diluting some of the linguistic differences among us, languages are still in contact in very complex ways. As an example of what might happen in current contact situations, we can consider Japanese. English has been very much a presence in the country ever since a Japanese infatuation with English began in the nineteenth century. Almost every Japanese takes some six years of formal English instruction in school, yet Japan is hardly a bilingual nation. In fact, Japanese critics and English language instructors alike often lament the poor English abilities of most Japanese, especially conversationally.

Nonetheless, the number of English loanwords is extensive. Estimates of the number of *commonly* used loanwords in modern Japanese range up to 5,000 terms, or perhaps as high as 5 to 10 percent of the ordinary daily vocabulary (Stanlaw 2004a, 2010). Table 9.2 shows the most frequent two dozen loanwords for magazines, television shows, and newspapers. All of them are from English. The presence of some of these loanwords is not surprising: *terebi* for "television," *tabako* ("tobacco") for cigarettes (a word that is so commonly accepted that it is not even written as a loanword), and many baseball terms (e.g., *battā* for "batter" or *pitchā* for "pitcher") all came as these things were imported. Many words, however, are *wa-sei-eigo* terms, or "made in Japan" English—vocabulary created using English words as building blocks to coin words that have no real correspondents in the United States or England. Examples include *famikon* ("FAMIly COMputer") for a Nintendo Entertainment System; *furaido poteto* ("fried potato") for french fries; *purasu-doraibā* ("plus driver") for a Phillips screwdriver; *sukin-shippu* ("skin-ship") for bonding through physical contact of the skin, such as between a mother and a child; *uinkā* ("winker") for an automobile turn signal; *handoru* ("handle") for the steering wheel of a car; *romansu-gurē* ("romance gray") for the silver hair of an older virile man who is still sexually attractive;

and the ubiquitous *pokemon* ("POCKEt MONster") for the Pokémon game and anime franchise. Probably most of these vocabulary items are not immediately transparent to native English speakers.

Often English loanwords reflect changing Japanese cultural norms. For example, the very productive English loanword possessive pronoun *mai* ("my") apparently is indicative of a new view held in Japan that the values of corporate allegiances or group loyalty, which were thought to be the mainstay of Japanese society, are now being questioned. Terms such as *mai-hoomu* (owning "my home"), *mai-waifu* (adoring "my wife"), *mai-peesu* (doing things at "my pace"), *mai-puraibashii* (valuing "my privacy"), or being a member of the *mai-kaa-zoku* (the "my own car tribe") suggest that individual interests and goals can compete on an equal footing with the traditional priority given to collective group responsibilities. In the mass media this prefix is found on a vast array of products or their advertisements: *my juice*, *my pack*, *my summer*, *my girl calendar* (Stanlaw 2004a:17–18). Nonetheless, not everyone is happy with the presence of so much English in Japanese. Japanese purists say it pollutes the language, and English-language teachers often lament the fact that their students believe—incorrectly—that they know the meaning of a term because they know the Japanese loanword. But this practice shows no signs of letting up soon.

Besides pidginization, mixing, or one language dominating another, there are other possibilities that can occur when speakers of different languages come into contact. Speakers of mutually unintelligible languages who wish to communicate with each other have a variety of means available to them. One widespread method of bridging the linguistic gap is to use a **lingua franca**, a language agreed upon as a medium of communication by people who speak different first languages. In present-day India, for example, the English that spread with British imperialism frequently serves as a lingua franca among speakers of the many different languages native to the subcontinent. In the United States, the language used for communication with members of the many different Native American tribes has been English, the speech of the dominant society. And in Kupwar, a southern Indian village with speakers of four separate languages—Marathi, Urdu, Kannada, and Telugu—where almost all male villagers are bilingual or multilingual, the speakers of the first three languages have been switching among them for so long that the structures of the local varieties of these languages have been brought very close together, making it easier for their speakers to communicate (Gumperz and Wilson 1971).

We should mention another possibility when discussing how people who speak different languages try to communicate. Besides choosing a lingua franca or a pidgin, some have proposed adopting an **artificial** or **auxiliary language** to facilitate international communication. Although several hundred are known to have been devised over the past several centuries, only a few have achieved any measure of acceptance and use, with Esperanto, already more than one hundred years old, the most widespread. Despite efforts to make Esperanto the official international language, however, English, the mother tongue of some 400 million speakers and the official or semiofficial language serving well over a billion people in the world, appears today to have little, if any, serious competition (Crystal 2010:371).

**TABLE 9.2** RANKINGS OF THE TWENTY-SEVEN MOST FREQUENTLY USED LOANWORDS IN JAPANESE IN A NATIONAL NEWSPAPER, VARIOUS MAGAZINES, AND VARIOUS TELEVISION PROGRAMS, C. 2000

| | *Mainichi Newspaper* | | | *Magazines* | | | *Television Programs* | | |
|---|---|---|---|---|---|---|---|---|---|
| 1 | タイプ | *taipu* | type | メートル | *mētoru* | meter | テレビ | *terebi* | TV |
| 2 | サイズ | *saizu* | size | キロ | *kiro* | kilogram | ニュス | nyūsu | news |
| 3 | セット | *setto* | set | ドル | *doru* | dollar | アイアイ | ai-ai | aye aye[1] |
| 4 | エンジン | *enjin* | engine | リーグ | *riigu* | league | ゲーム | gēmu | game |
| 5 | スキー | *sukii* | ski | チーム | *chiimu* | team | ピtチャー | pitchaā | pitcher |
| 6 | デザイン | *dezain* | design | テレビ | *terebi* | TV | チャンス | chansu | chance |
| 7 | コース | *kōsu* | course | グループ | *gurūpu* | group | ファン | fan | fan |
| 8 | レース | *rēsu* | race | プロ | *puro* | professional | セクシー | sekushii | sexy |
| 9 | モデル | *moderu* | model | メダル | *medaru* | metal | スポンサー | suponsā | sponsor |
| 10 | カラー | *karā* | color | システム | *shisutemu* | system | イメージ | *imēji* | image |
| 11 | メートル | *mētoru* | meter | センター | *senta* | center | ホームラん | hōmu ran | home run |
| 12 | シリーズ | *shiriizu* | series | ユーロ | *Yūro* | Euro | ボール | bōru | ball |
| 13 | チーム | *chiimu* | team | メーカー | *mēkā* | maker | バッタ | battā | batter |
| 14 | ホテル | *hoteru* | hotel | サッカー | *sakkā* | soccer | ヒット | hitto | hit |
| 15 | ポイント | *pointo* | point | サービス | *sābisu* | service | ピラシ | purasu | plus |
| 16 | テレビ | *terebi* | TV | スラート | *sutāto* | start | チーム | *chiimu* | team |
| 17 | ビル | *biru* | building | センチ | *senchi* | centimeter | ビデオ | bideo | video |
| 18 | プレゼント | *purezento* | present | テーマ | *tēma* | theme | リズム | rizumu | rhythm |
| 19 | システム | *shisutemu* | system | トップ | *toppu* | top | カーブ | kābu | curve |
| 20 | ページ | *pēji* | page | ミサイル | *misairu* | missle | ファースト | fāsuto | first[2] |
| 21 | イメージ | *imēji* | image | カレー | *karē* | curry | ジーパン | jii pan | jeans[3] |
| 22 | シャツ s | *shatsu* | shirt | ケース | *kēsu* | case | コーナー | kōnā | corner |
| 23 | バス | *basu* | bus | ポイント | *pointo* | point | スラート | *sutāto* | start |
| 24 | クラス | *kurasu* | class | マイナス | *mainasu* | minus | レース | *rēsu* | race |
| 25 | メーカー | *mēkā* | maker | メンバー | *menpā* | member | テーマ | *tēma* | theme |
| 26 | バランス | *baransu* | balance | インターネット | *intānetto* | Internet | パパ | *papa* | papa |
| 27 | プロ | *puro* | professional | データ | *dēta* | data | ポイント | *pointo* | point |

[1] An aye-aye is a small primate

[2] First means "first base"

[3] (blue) "jeans" or "G-pants"

*Note:* Tabulated by the Kokuritsu Kokugo Kenkyūjo [National Language Research Institute]; cf. Scherling (2012:80–87)

## THE WORLD OF LANGUAGES

It may come as a surprise to learn that no one knows exactly how many languages are spoken in the world today. One standard source suggests the total is more than 6,900 (Gordon 2005). This number includes creole languages but excludes pidgins, as well as the thousands of languages in the course of history and prehistory that must have disappeared without a trace. There are several reasons for the lack of precision in gauging the world's linguistic diversity. A few languages are likely to be discovered in those regions of the world still only partly explored, especially the equatorial rain forests of South America, Africa, and New Guinea. Some languages are on the very verge of extinction, currently used by as few as a handful of speakers and not even habitually, at that. Then, too, it is not always easy to determine whether two dialects are sufficiently divergent to become mutually unintelligible and therefore merit the status of two separate languages. In this respect, sociocultural considerations sometimes override the linguistic criterion of mutual intelligibility. For example, Czechs and Slovaks communicate with one another in their respective languages without the slightest hindrance, although Czech and Slovak have separate standards and literary traditions as well as dictionaries and textbooks. If these two languages were to be spoken in nearby villages somewhere in New Guinea, they would unquestionably be classified as two dialects of one language. As for the number of dialects of the languages currently spoken in the world, the total would reach tens of thousands if anyone were interested in making such a count.

The figure of some 6,900 languages is an impressive number when one considers that each language represents a distinct means of communication with its own elaborate structure and unique way of describing the cultural universe of its speakers. However, in terms of the numbers of speakers, the great bulk of today's world population makes use of relatively few languages. It is obvious that at this point in human history, speakers of some languages have been more successful than speakers of others, whether by conquest, historical accident, or some other circumstance. The greatly uneven distribution of speakers of the world's languages is graphically represented in Figure 9.1.

## SUMMARY AND CONCLUSIONS

Although about 6,900 languages, assignable to several hundred language groups (families), are currently spoken, the overwhelming majority of people speak languages that belong to only a dozen or so families, with Indo-European at the top of the list for most speakers. The worldwide spread of English and various other European languages dates back to the beginning of the Age of Discovery in the mid-fifteenth century.

Among the great variety of languages, pidgins occupy a special place. Although structured and efficient as a means of communication, their vocabularies are limited because they are not called upon to perform the broad range of functions that characterize full-fledged languages.

Competency in one language only, typical of most Americans with English as their mother tongue, is uncommon in the rest of the world, where hundreds of millions of people are able to speak several languages or language varieties—that is, they are multilingual or diglossic. Even though many people speak only one language, they are actively or at least

**FIGURE 9.1** THE WORLD'S LANGUAGES AND THEIR SPEAKERS

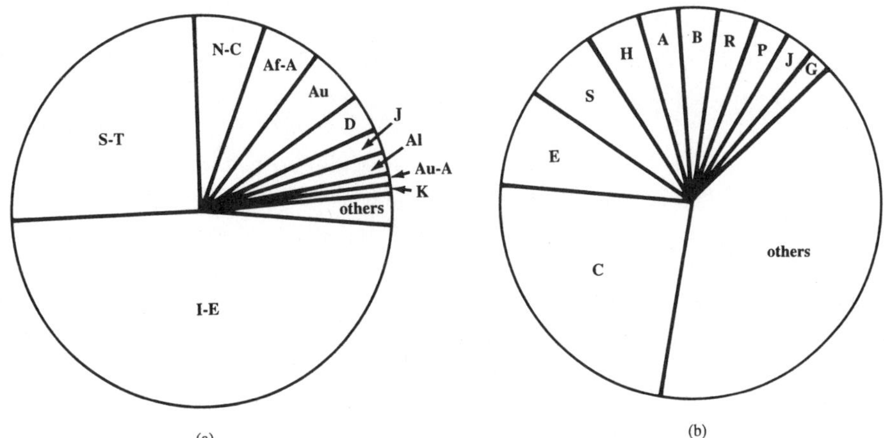


(a) (b)

The estimated relative numbers of speakers belonging to the top ten language groups (families) are graphically represented in (a). The following abbreviations are used:

I-E Indo-European: most of the languages spoken in Europe, several of which have spread to other parts of the world, as well as some languages spoken in India and southwestern Asia

S-T Sino-Tibetan: various Tibetan, Burmese, and Chinese languages spoken in southeastern Asia

N-C Niger-Congo: most of the languages spoken in western, central, and southern Africa, including the Bantu languages

Af-A Afro-Asiatic: various Semitic, Berber, Cushitic, and Chadic languages spoken in northern Africa and southwestern Asia, as well as extinct (Ancient) Egyptian

Au Austronesian: languages spoken in the vast area extending from Madagascar eastward through the Malay Peninsula to Hawaii and Easter Island

D Dravidian: languages spoken primarily in southern India and parts of Sri Lanka

J Japanese: the language of Japan, considered by some scholars to be distantly related to the Altaic family

Al Altaic: languages spoken from Turkey in the west across central Asia into Siberia

Au-A Austroasiatic: languages spoken for the most part in southeastern Asia (Laos, Vietnam, and Cambodia) but also in some parts of India

K Korean: the language of the two Koreas, considered by some scholars to be distantly related to Japanese or the Altaic family

Others: a great variety of languages belonging to numerous language groups and spoken in Eurasia, Africa, and Australia as well as all native languages of the New World—altogether nearly 3,000 languages, or half of the world's total

The estimated relative numbers of speakers of the top ten mother tongues are graphically represented in descending order in (b). The following abbreviations are used: C = Chinese (languages or dialects); E = English; S = Spanish; H = Hindi; A = Arabic; B = Bengali; R = Russian; P = Portuguese; J = Japanese; G = German; the others include the remaining 6,000 to 7,000 languages of the world.

The top ten official or semiofficial languages serving the largest number of speakers are, in descending order: English, Chinese, Hindi, Spanish, Russian, French, Arabic, Portuguese, Malay (including Indonesian), and Bengali.

Based on data provided in David Crystal, *The Cambridge Encyclopedia of Language* (Cambridge, UK: Cambridge University Press, 2010: 294–297; 465–484).

passively acquainted with several dialects and speech styles of that language. Their own speech patterns differ from those of others, even if only slightly. All speakers have their individual idiolects.

But the number of languages spoken in the world today is rapidly diminishing. According to one estimate, of the 6,900 languages, only six hundred can be considered safe from extinction during the twenty-first century. The primary reason for languages of small-sized societies becoming extinct is that, in order to survive, small tribal populations must adapt to the economic and cultural influence of the nation-states that encompass them, and one of the vital adaptive processes is the use of the language of the larger society.

## RESOURCE MANUAL AND STUDY GUIDE

### Questions for Discussion

1. Do you use a different term for some of the following items when you refer to them informally at home?

| | |
|---|---|
| *baby carriage* | *dry streambed* |
| *cottage cheese* | *earthworm (fishermen's term)* |
| *doughnut* | *pancake* |
| *dragonfly* | *trough along the eaves to catch and carry off rainwater* |

2. It has been said that a language is dialect with an army. What do you think this means? Is there any wisdom to such a claim?
3. One of the authors was in New Guinea and heard two local pidgin speakers looking at a Land Rover with a broken headlight. One said to the other, "*Eye belong 'em bugger up pinis.*" What do you think he was trying to say? HINT: *Pinis* is the pidgin form of English "finish."

### Projects

**PROJECT 1**

Here are some English words and their corresponding equivalents in Kamtok, Cameroon Pidgin English:

| | | |
|---|---|---|
| I | = | *a / mi* |
| he/she/it | = | *i* |
| you | = | *yu* |
| we | = | *wi* |
| they | = | *dem* |
| eat | = | *chop* |
| know | = | *sabi* |
| come | = | *kom* |
| go/will go | = | *go* |
| (past) | = | *bin* |
| be | = | *bi* |
| who | = | *hu* |
| many | = | *penti* |
| home, house | = | *haus* |
| for, to | = | *fo* |
| now | = | *nau* |
| tomorrow | = | *tumro* |

Translate the following Cameroon Pidgin English sentences into English, and the English sentences into Cameroon Pidgin English.

(1) ____________________ *yestadei a bin chop*
(2) ____________________ *tumro a go chop*
(3) ____________________ *a bin chop penti*
(4) ____________________ *a bin chop nau nau*
(5) ____________________ *dem bin go fo haus*
(6) He just came. ____________________
(7) We will eat. ____________________
(8) I know. ____________________
(9) I will go. ____________________
(10) I know them. ____________________

Write three other sentences in Cameroon Pidgin English.
(1) ____________________
(2) ____________________
(3) ____________________

**PROJECT 2**

Identify at least a dozen words that have been borrowed into English from other languages. Try to find out what they mean in their original language. What kind of modifications do you see taking place?

**PROJECT 3**

Examine the data on English loanwords found for different media presented in Table 9.2. What kinds of words are being used? For what purpose do you think they are being used? How might you account for the differences and similarities among the media found in the table?

**PROJECT 4**

On June 27, 2013, the *Japan Times* reported that a seventy-one-year-old man, Hoji Takahashi, was suing NHK, Japan's public broadcasting network (similar to America's PBS), for "mental distress allegedly caused by the broadcaster's excessive use of foreign words." He was asking for damages of about $15,000. Some loanwords that particularly irked him were *risuku* (risk), *toraburu* (trouble), and *shisutemu* (system). Takahashi's attorney said that "with Japanese society increasingly Americanized, Takahashi believes that NHK, as Japan's national broadcaster, shouldn't go with the trend, but remain determined to prioritize the use of Japanese, which he thinks would go a long way toward protecting Japanese culture" (http://www.japantimes.co.jp/news/2013/06/27/national/gifu-man-71-sues-nhk-for-distress-over-its-excess-use-of-foreign-words/#.UdhmGVOr84Z).

Do one of the following: (1) Write a letter of apology to Mr. Takahashi about the many loanwords English speakers have sent over to Japan. (If you are not a native English speaker, we have just made you one for the purposes of this project!) Brainstorm with him on how you can make this stop. (2) Write a letter to Mr. Takahashi explaining as best you can why English loanwords are beneficial to the Japanese people and culture as a whole.

## *Objective Study Questions*

**TRUE-FALSE TEST**

T F 1. Accent and dialect are terms that generally refer to the same linguistic phenomenon.
T F 2. An idiolect is the speech variety of an individual.
T F 3. A creole that has become the first language of a speech community (that is, the mother tongue of the members of a community) is referred to as a pidgin.
T F 4. Today more people in the world speak Indo-European languages than speak languages of any other language family.
T F 5. There are about 3,000 known languages in the world today, and only a handful are pidgins or creoles.

T F 6. There are a number of instances when two languages are mutually intelligible but not considered to be dialects of one language.

**MULTIPLE-CHOICE QUESTIONS**

____ 1. Tok Pisin is spoken in which of the following countries/places (A) Papua New Guinea. (B) Australia. (C) New Zealand. (D) Tahiti.

____ 2. The differentiation between a language and a dialect is based on (A) mutual intelligibility. (B) the sociocultural relationship of the two communities (groups, peoples). (C) Both of these criteria, A and B, must be taken into account.

____ 3. Although pidgins can be based on any language, the most common—or at least the most well-known—pidgins have been based on (A) French. (B) Spanish. (C) English. (D) Japanese.

**COMPLETIONS**

1. The process of expansion of a pidgin to other language functions is referred to as ____________________ (one word).
2. The linguist Martin Joos claims there are _________ clearly recognizable styles in his dialect of east-central American English (one word).
3. The theory of the linguist Derek Bickerton that tries to explain the similarities found in all pidgins and creoles is the ______________ hypothesis (one word).
4. A language that people who speak different languages agree upon to use as a neutral medium of communication is called a ____________________ (two words).
5. The best known artificial language is __________________ (one word).

## Answer Key

True-false test: 1-F, 2-T, 3-F, 4-T, 5-F, 6-T
Multiple-choice questions: 1-A, 2-C, 3-C
Completions: 1. creolization, 2. five, 3. bioprogram, 4. lingua franca, 5. Esperanto.

**PROBLEM 1**

| | |
|---|---|
| 1. I ate yesterday. | *yestadei a bin chop* |
| 2. I will eat tomorrow. | *tumro a go chop* |
| 3. I ate a lot. | *a bin chop penti* |
| 4. I just ate. | *a bin chop nau nau* |
| 5. They went back home. | *dem bin go fo haus* |
| 6. He just came. | *i bin kom nau nau* |
| 7. We will eat. | *wi go chop* |
| 8. I know. | *a sabi* |
| 9. I will go. | *a go go* |
| 10. I know them. | *a sabi dem* |

## Notes and Suggestions for Further Reading

The literature on dialectology is vast. Chambers and Trudgill (1998) is a standard introductory text. See Wolfram and Schilling-Estes (2005) or Labov (2005) for discussions of English dialects and sound change. Labov's three *Principles* works (2010a, 2010b, and 2010c) will likely be the new standards on language variation and change for some time.

The origin of the word *pidgin* is not known for certain, although it is usually considered to be a Chinese mispronunciation of the English word *business.* A recent survey (Crystal 2010:348–349) has identified more than one hundred pidgins and creoles the world over, including some that are now extinct, but there have undoubtedly been more. For example, the fifteenth edition of the definitive language resource *Ethnologue* (Gordon 2005) cites about four hundred pidgins and six hundred creoles, though of course problems of definition abound. Any figure should be viewed as a conservative estimate, as many pidgins must have ceased to exist without any record, and some of the creoles of the past are no longer identifiable as such.

The definitive resources on current pidgins and creoles are Michaelis (2013a, 2013b, and 2013c). Going along with this set is Michaelis (2013d), an atlas of dozens of linguistic features clearly mapped out, a companion volume to this three-volume collection. Using these four books as a basis, Velupillai (2015) is textbook version for students. An excellent recent guide to the study of pidgin and creole languages is Romaine (1988); a shorter and more popular introduction to pidgins is Hall (1959), as well as the later Todd (1990). The theory and structure of pidgins and creoles are the subject of the two volumes of Holm (1988–1989), though students new to the topic should start with Holm's standard introductory text (2000). The new theoretical standard, however, will likely be Siegel (2008). For a brief and more popularly written article on creole languages, see Bickerton (1983). A critical, partly negative evaluation of Bickerton's bioprogram hypothesis is to be found in Mühlhäusler (1986) and Romaine (1988).

The Tok Pisin examples are from Woolford (1979) and Murphy (1980); the short text is taken from Todd (1984:65). See Scherling (2012) for how to get access to the latest Japanese language corpuses. The Harvard Dialect Survey is explained by Vaux and Golder (2003).

The procedures used to measure mutual intelligibility among Iroquoian languages are described in an article by Hickerson, Turner, and Hickerson (1952).

# 10

# The Ethnography of Communication

## LEARNING OBJECTIVES

- Discuss why and how linguist anthropologists like Hymes and Gumperz differ with Chomsky
- Define what a speech community is
- Be able to articulate the units of speech behavior
- Name and explain the different components of the SPEAKING model

In some ways, what is often termed the "ethnography of communication" can be thought of as a combination of the techniques of linguistic anthropology and classical sociolinguistics (Kaplan-Weinger and Ullman 2015:15–28). This is because the two names that have historically been most associated with the ethnography of communication—Dell Hymes and John Gumperz—were seminal founders of these respective fields.

In an article written in 1966, Dell Hymes (1927–2009) observed that it used to be customary to consider languages as different from each other but the uses to which they are put as closely similar if not essentially the same. Hymes then noted that the opposite view was beginning to prevail: languages are seen as fundamentally very much alike but the social uses of speech as quite different from one culture to the next. In the earlier period, distinct division of labor existed between linguists and cultural anthropologists. With few exceptions, linguists studied languages to discover the structural differences between them and to learn about their historical development, whereas anthropologists studied human societies in order to understand the workings of their cultures. But culture and the use of language are not easily separable. People must use language to accomplish a wide variety of culture-specific goals. If societies are to function smoothly, their members must have not only *linguistic competence*—the knowledge of the grammatical rules of their mother tongue, acquired well before adulthood—as Chomsky argued (see Chapter 2 ); they must also have **communicative competence**—the knowledge of what is and what is not appropriate to say in any specific cultural context. That is, this communicative competence is very much action-oriented; what you *do* is emphasized more then what you theoretically *know*. In other words, where autonomous linguists like Noam Chomsky stressed linguistic competence, linguistically oriented anthropologists found that the more interesting questions lie in performance.

And just because any native speaker has the same potential to say anything that anyone else can at any given time, we simply just *don't* say anything anytime. As Hymes put it, "A child from whom any and all of the grammatical sentences of a language might come with equal likelihood would be . . . a social monster" (Hymes 1974:75). Some parents occasionally learn this from their own experience when a child who is not yet fully communicatively competent makes an embarrassing comment in front of guests, such as saying to a guest who praises the coffee cake being offered, "My mom said it was lousy, but it was good enough to give to you."

The nature and function of communicative behavior in the context of culture are the subject of **ethnography of communication**. In its modern form, ethnography of communication dates back to Hymes's 1962 article "The Ethnography of Speaking." John Gumperz (1922–2013) is also widely recognized as the co-founder (though sometimes his approach is termed *interactional sociolinguistics*). Inasmuch as this relatively new field focuses on those aspects of human behavior in which communication meets culture, research in ethnography of communication contributes to the interdisciplinary studies that are proving to be of increasing value in modern scholarship. Some scholars consider ethnography of communication one of the several fields of inquiry within the scope of sociolinguistics. Others argue that ethnography of communication, as the study of communicative behavior in relation to the sociocultural variables associated with human interaction, is broader and more encompassing than sociolinguistics. Be that as it may, sociolinguistics and ethnography of communication are fields of inquiry that have been gaining in importance and attracting significant research.

## SPEECH COMMUNITY AND RELATED CONCEPTS

The terms *society* and *culture* in anthropology are useful as general concepts, but no society's culture is uniform for all its members. Any complex of learned patterns of behavior and thought that distinguishes various segments of a society (minorities, castes, and the like) is referred to as a subculture. By extension, this term is also used to refer collectively to all those who exhibit the characteristics of a particular subculture (for example, the homeless as well as the so-called beautiful people). Language and speech, too, are characterized by lack of uniformity. In general, any particular society is associated with a specific language, and multinational societies are associated with several. But no language is ever uniform for all speakers of a society (people, community, tribe). As we have already seen, certain ways of speaking the same language may differentiate men from women, the young from the old, the poor from the rich, and the like. All those who share specific rules for speaking and interpreting speech and at least one speech variety belong to a **speech community**. However, it is important to remember that people who speak the same language are not always members of the same speech community. On the one hand, speakers of South Asian English in India and Pakistan share a language with citizens of the United States, but the respective varieties of English and the rules for speaking them are sufficiently distinct to assign the two populations to different speech communities. On the other hand, Muriel Saville-Troike (1982:20) identified even monolingual speakers of either Spanish (the official language) or Guarani (the national language) as belonging to the same speech community in Paraguay because the social roles of the speakers of the two languages are complementary—both groups are mutually dependent for services or employment.

Most members of a society, even if they happen to live in the same town, belong to several speech communities. For example, an elderly person may have considerable difficulty following the monotonous chant of an auctioneer or comprehending what students talk about among themselves. But an auctioneer and a college student can easily make the adjustment necessary to engage in a conversation with the elderly person and be fully understood; all they have to do is to share enough characteristic patterns of pronunciation, grammar, vocabulary, and manner of speaking to belong to the same speech community.

It may also be that peoples live in different countries and speak different languages but share some rules for speaking, as do the Czechs and the Austrians (and for that matter some of the other peoples who until World War I were part of the Austro-Hungarian Empire or lived in adjacent areas). As an example, the commonly used phrase for greeting or taking leave of a woman who is economically and socially well situated was (and to some extent still is) "*Rukulíbám, milostivá paní!*" in Czech and "*Küss' die Hand, gnädige Frau!*" in German. The English translation, "I kiss your hand, gracious lady," clearly indicates how different such rules of speaking are from those used, say, in Britain or the United States. Linguists refer to an area in which speakers of different languages share speaking rules as a **speech area**.

Less frequently employed terms for related concepts include *language field*, *speech field*, and *speech network* (Hymes 1972:55). The first of these (language field) refers to all those communities in which an individual is able to communicate adequately by virtue of knowing the languages and language varieties serving the communities. The concept of speech field parallels that of language field but involves the knowledge of rules for speaking rather than knowledge of languages. Speech network refers to linkages between persons from different communities who share language varieties as well as rules for speaking. To give an example, in addition to her mother tongue, a woman knows four languages well enough to read books and newspapers published in them; a total of five languages make up her language field. However, the same woman is able to communicate easily in only one foreign language in addition to her native language; the speech communities within which she functions effectively in the two languages make up her speech field. Within that speech field, the woman has special rapport with those persons, regardless of where they may come from, who share with her the two languages, rules for speech, and a professional interest in, say, archaeology; the linkages with these people make up her speech network.

## UNITS OF SPEECH BEHAVIOR

To distinguish among different levels of speech activity, Hymes made use of three terms for the ethnographic analysis and description of speech behavior—**speech situation**, **speech event**, and **speech act** (Hymes 1972:56–57). (If one were to include nonverbal communication as well, these three terms would need to be broadened and the word *speech* replaced by *communicative*; after all, a hand gesture or the wink of an eye can be just as effective as an entire sentence.)

A speech situation is the context within which speaking occurs—that is, any particular set of circumstances typically associated with speech behavior (or its absence). A speech situation may be a family meal, birthday party, baby shower, seminar meeting, campus beer party, auction, fishing trip, Quaker meeting, or any one of a large number of situations that take place in a society and are definable in terms of participants and goals and are therefore distinguishable from other speech situations.

The minimal unit of speech for purposes of an ethnographic analysis is the speech act. A speech act may be a greeting, apology, question, compliment, self-introduction, or the like. Although normally attributable to a single speaker, collective speech acts also exist, such as, for example, the "Amen" said by a congregation or the reciting of the Pledge of Allegiance by young pupils. In size, a speech act may range from a single word ("Scram!" or "Thanks") to a five-minute shaggy-dog story or a long harangue on conduct. Speech acts that follow each other in a recognized sequence and are governed by social rules for the use of speech combine to form a speech event, the basic unit of verbal interaction. Examples of speech events are conversation, a confession to a priest, an interview, dialogue with a salesperson, a telephone inquiry, and so on. Boundaries between successive speech events are marked by a change of major participants, a noticeable silence, or some remark designed to introduce another topic of conversation, for example, "If I can change the subject . . . " or "By the way, have you heard that. . . . " Under special circumstances, a speech act may become a speech event, as when someone shouts "Fire!" in a crowded movie theater.

An alumni reunion can be used to illustrate the three units of speech behavior. The gathering itself is an example of a speech situation: It has a beginning and an end and lasts usually only part of one day; the participants are restricted to former members of a class and their spouses or partners. Within such a speech situation, a number of speech events invariably take place: for example, one group may be reminiscing about favorite teachers and classroom antics, those in another group may be giving brief accounts of what they have been doing since graduation or the last reunion, and still others may be simply swapping jokes and stories. Within these speech events, the telling of a single joke or personal experience is a speech act.

Just as native speakers of any language are expected to produce sentences that are grammatically acceptable and meaningful, speech acts are judged according to how appropriate they are to any specific speech situation or speech event. It would be considered odd if one were to say to a stranger in the street, "My name is John Smith; what time do you have?" Similarly, at a baby shower it would be out of place to bring up the increasing infant mortality rate. When inappropriate speech acts do occur, participants in the speech event or situation are later likely to comment on them: "Did you hear what she said? How inconsiderate!" or "What a crazy thing for Bill to say. Has he lost his mind?"

## COMPONENTS OF COMMUNICATION

Dell Hymes and John Gumperz are generally recognized as the founders of the ethnography of communication. We might think about the ethnography of communication as having three broad components:

## *Participants and Setting*

Describing a language with emphasis on its function as the primary means of communication requires more than simply describing its sounds (phonology) and grammatical structure (morphology and syntax). Careful field research is necessary to discover how members of a society use their language under differing circumstances to satisfy the goals they set for themselves.

### Participants

Traditionally, speech behavior was said to involve a speaker and a hearer and include the message transmitted between them. Modern ethnographic descriptions and analyses have shown that many more components need to be taken into account if any particular instance of communicative behavior is to be fully understood. Which of these components assumes a crucial role depends on a given speech situation and the particular community in which it takes place.

The component termed *participants* includes not only the sender of a message (also referred to as the speaker or addresser) and the intended receiver (hearer, addressee) but anyone who may be interested in or happens to perceive (hear, see) the message—the audience. The number of participants can vary from only one to many thousands. For example, a person who has a job interview scheduled may practice for it by posing potential questions and then answering them, thus assuming the role of both sender and receiver. But at an outdoor political rally, one or more charismatic leaders may not only address several hundred thousand followers but also succeed in mobilizing them.

In some cultures, the ability to communicate is not perceived as limited to ordinary humans. Among the Ashanti, a West African people on the Gulf of Guinea, a midwife may direct a question to a fetus concerning its father's identity, and recently deceased persons are believed to be able to inform their surviving relatives who or what was responsible for their deaths. The Ashanti also believe that forest fairies and monsters are able to instruct young men in medicine; these beings are said to communicate in a whistle language but are able to understand Twi, the language in which humans pray to them.

As indicated earlier in the discussion of language in its social context, a thorough ethnographic account of communicative behavior must carefully note the characteristics of the participants. Age, gender, ethnic affiliation, relationship (kinship) among participants, their relative social status, the degree to which they are acquainted, and other factors can influence how communication proceeds. Who talks to whom and in whose presence tends to determine not only how one talks (casually or respectfully) but also whether or not one can interrupt the other participant, how long speech acts should be, what additional channels one should use to enhance the presentation, and so on.

### Settings

Any communicative act or event happens at a particular time and place and under particular physical circumstances—that is, it is characterized by a particular *setting*. Settings are likely to vary somewhat from one instance to the next even if the events are of the same kind, but the variation has culturally recognized limits. Small college classes normally meet in classrooms, but on warm spring or autumn days they may be conducted in the shade of a tree outside the classroom building; to meet in a nearby tavern or the lobby of the administrative building would be considered inappropriate. On April Fools' Day, practical jokes are accepted by people who would consider them presumptuous on any other day. Hymes distinguished between setting and scene, the latter designating the "psychological setting." It is true that the mood pervading a given setting may invite or inhibit certain communicative acts or events, and in this sense the scene contributes to the definition of setting. One can easily imagine the identical setting and participants but completely different scenes: compare, for example, the atmosphere surrounding the announcement of across-the-board wage increases with the announcement of the company's going out of business.

## *Purpose, Channels, Codes, and Message Content and Form*

### Purpose of Communication

The purpose of speaking is not always to transmit information or to exchange ideas. Sometimes it is to establish an atmosphere of sociability and is the equivalent of a hug or a hearty handshake. Speech behavior with the goal of bringing about such an emotional effect is referred to as phatic communion.

### Channels

The motivation for communicative behavior varies from one occasion to the next. An individual may make an offer or a request, threaten or plead, praise or blame, invite or prohibit some action, reveal or try to conceal something, and so on. One's goal or purpose quite frequently determines the manner in which one speaks or acts. Even an aggressive person may speak meekly and deferentially when stopped for speeding by a police officer, hoping that polite and apologetic speech behavior will influence the officer to issue a warning instead of a ticket.

Although the acoustic channel, best exemplified by spoken words, is the one most commonly employed, other channels of communication should not be overlooked. To do so would be to ignore that communicative behavior that makes primary use of one channel frequently depends on other channels for reinforcement. To hear a play read aloud or to see it professionally performed can mean the difference between experiencing boredom or enjoyment. Quite commonly, too, one channel offers an effective substitute for another: the military salute, using the optical channel, substitutes a visual expression of respect or honor for what could otherwise be orally recited, and photojournalists strive to present news events pictorially because "a picture is worth a thousand words."

The most common form of the acoustic channel is oral, as in singing, whistling, and of course speaking. If human language is to be considered as a general language code, then it is manifested in several thousand specific codes, of which English, Russian, Navajo, and Japanese are examples. Each of these codes subsumes a number of subcodes. English has not only several national varieties, such as American, British, and Australian but also regional dialects such as those of New England, the English Midlands, and South Australia, and a number of slangs peculiar to particular groups.

Among the Ashanti, the acoustic channel is quite diversified. The principal verbal code is Twi, a language characterized by five distinctive tones. The ceremonial language priests and priestesses use is a subcode; it is identified as an earlier form of Twi that Ashanti laypeople apparently cannot understand. The so-called language of the ghosts, consisting of cooing noises and said to be intelligible only to unborn babies and toothless infants, is an example of an oral but nonverbal form of the acoustic channel. Other nonverbal codes of the Ashanti include the drum code to convey messages and signals; the horn code, used for similar purposes; the gong code, employed for public summonses; and whistling, used not by the Ashanti themselves but by the forest fairies and monsters who instruct their medicine men. Some parts of the ceremony at which ancestral spirits are propitiated are conducted in complete silence; other parts permit the chief to communicate only by gestures.

### Message Content and Form

Message form and message content are closely related, or as Hymes (1972:59) put it, "It is a truism . . . that *how* something is said is part of *what* is said." A paraphrase may be sufficient to indicate the message content, but only the quoting of the exact words can represent adequately the message form of a speech act. To paraphrase the statement "Like hell I'm kidding; I've warned you—now get out, fast!" as "I told him in no uncertain terms that he was no longer welcome" does away with so much color and feeling that the changed form no longer has much in common with the original content.

Here it is appropriate to mention the term **register**, referring to a variety of language that serves a particular social situation. In American linguistics the term is used to differentiate between broad varieties of a language—for example, between the vernacular (everyday, casual spoken form) and the standard (prestige form) in English. In Great Britain, *register* is used for any of a number of specifically defined varieties, such as legal, scientific, religious, intimate, and so on.

## *Genres, Key, Rules of Interaction, and Norms of Interpretation*

### Genres

The term **genre** refers to speech acts or events associated with a particular communicative situation and characterized by a particular style, form, and content. Ritual or religious occasions, for example, regularly call for such special genres as prayers and sermons. Both sermons and prayers make use of a ceremonial style of speech with special attention to form. This is why thou, thee, thy, and thine for "you," "your," and "yours" have survived to the present in prayers and the language of the Friends (Quakers).

A good storyteller of Old World fairy or wonder tales would customarily begin the telling by some such phrase as "Once upon a time" and signal the end of the tale by the formula "And they lived happily ever after" or, more elaborately, "The festivities lasted nine days and nine nights. There were 900 fiddlers, 900 fluters, and 900 pipers, and the last day and night of the wedding were better than the first." Important incidents in Old World tales usually take place three times (that is, the formulaic or magic number is three), whereas in Native American tales things happen four times.

Myths represent another genre, one found in the traditions of all the world's societies. Arapaho stories concerning *nihʔóóθoo* "Whiteman," a popular character of Arapaho trickster tales, almost invariably have him walking down (or up) the river in the initial sentence of the story. The end is signaled by the formula "This is the end of the story." In Upper Chinook, a Native American language spoken in Oregon, myths are characterized by features not found elsewhere in the language (Hymes 1958). The diagnostic features of

Upper Chinook myths are phonological (for example, the doubling of a consonant word-finally to indicate stuttering from fright or excitement), morphological (limiting the use of certain noun prefixes to the speech of characters appearing in myths), lexical (reserving the use of certain names for myths only), and syntactic. Other linguistic features of Upper Chinook are limited to casual speech.

A "war talk" genre was employed among the Navajo (Hill 1936) and other Native Americans. Upon entering enemy territory, the leader of a Navajo war party would instruct the group to use words different from the ones commonly used to refer to the livestock, captives, and whatever else they hoped to bring back; members of the war party spoke this warpath language until they turned toward home.

### Keys

Perhaps more than genre or other components, key varies widely among cultures. By the term *key*, Hymes referred to the "tone, manner, or spirit in which an act is done" and added that "acts otherwise the same as regards setting, participants, message form, and the like may differ in key, as, e.g., between *mock* [and] *serious* or *perfunctory* [and] *painstaking*" (Hymes 1972:62). Key may even override another component, such as when a speaker who is presumably praising someone becomes slowly but increasingly so sarcastic that the person spoken of feels hurt or ridiculed. A particular key may be used so frequently by members of a group that it loses much of its effect, whereas another key may be so rarely employed that it may require some effort on the part of hearers to identify it and comprehend its social meaning.

### Rules of Interaction

Communicative activity is guided by **rules of interaction**. Under normal circumstances, members of a speech community know what is and what is not appropriate. Among members of the middle class in the United States, for example, interruptions are not considered appropriate except among close friends or family members, but if someone monopolizes a conversation, there are acceptable ways of breaking in. A compliment addressed to another person is usually gratefully acknowledged, or some remark is made to the effect that the compliment may not be fully deserved. When rules of interaction are broken or completely neglected, embarrassment results, and unless an apology is offered, future contacts between the parties may be strained or even avoided.

### Norms of Interpretation

The judgment of what constitutes proper interaction is of course subject to interpretation. The **norms of interpretation** (just as the rules of interaction) vary from culture to culture, sometimes only subtly but usually quite distinctly or even profoundly. And within a single society, if that society is socially or ethnically diversified, not all members are likely to use the same rules of interaction and the same norms of interpretation.

If the norms of interpretation are shared by the interlocutors, their relations are likely to be marked by understanding and harmony. Deborah Tannen (1982:219) gave an example of shared norms of interpretation that differ subtly from those employed by most Americans. (Reference is to a Greek family.) Before marriage, a Greek woman "had to ask her father's permission before doing anything. . . . If she asked, for example, whether she could go to a dance, and he answered, '*An thes, pas* (If you want, you can go),' she knew that she could not go. If he really meant that she could go, he would say, '*Ne. Na pas* (Yes. You should go).'" In addition to the manner in which the father phrased his answer, his intonation (a rise on the *if* clause) reinforced his meaning of disapproval.

In an interethnic conversation, even though carried on in English between husband and wife, subtle differences in the norms of interpretation may lead to a misunderstanding. The following example is also from Tannen (1982:220–221). The reconstructed conversation between a native New Yorker wife and her Greek husband runs as follows: "Wife: John's having a party. Wanna go? Husband: OK. (Later) Wife: Are you sure you want to go to the party? Husband: OK, let's not go. I'm tired anyway." Tannen's commentary (given here only in part):

> In discussing the misunderstanding, the American wife reported she had merely been asking what her husband wanted to do without considering her own preference. Since she was about to go to this party just for him, she tried to make sure that that was his preference by asking him a second time. She was being solicitous and considerate. The Greek husband said that by bringing up the question of the party, his wife was letting him know that she wanted to go, so he agreed to go. Then when she brought it up again, she was letting him know that she didn't want to go; she had obviously changed her mind. So he came up with a reason not to go, to make her feel all right about getting her way. This is precisely the strategy reported by the Greek woman who did what her father . . . wanted without expecting him to tell her directly what that was.

Misunderstandings may be expected when individuals interpret cues generated by others according to rules that are different. US citizens of Mexican origin may well have norms of interpreting communicative behavior that differ from those adhered to by fellow citizens of Japanese ancestry. Awareness of these differences and a need for understanding and adjustment are particularly crucial in intercultural communication. In a study conducted at the University of Colorado among male students from Arabic-speaking countries and male students from the United States, Michael Watson and Theodore Graves (1966:976–979) found, much as they had hypothesized, that "Arabs confronted each other more directly than Americans when conversing. . . . They sat closer to each other . . . [and] were more likely to touch each other. . . . They looked each other more squarely in the eye . . . and . . . conversed more loudly than Americans. . . . Persons from the various Arab countries [appeared to] be more similar to each other than to any regional group of Americans." Interpretation of American communicative behavior by foreign visitors to the United States according to their own norms, and vice versa, can only result in misunderstanding rather than the appreciation of different cultures.

## *SPEAKING*

In discussing the various components of speech, Hymes used as a mnemonic device the word S P E A K I N G, whose letters stand for *s*ettings, *p*articipants, *e*nds (discussed previously as "purpose"), *a*ct sequences (the arrangement of components), *k*eys, *i*nstrumentalities (discussed previously as "channels," "codes," and "message form"), *n*orms (of interaction and interpretation), and *g*enres.

A concept frequently used in recent years is termed **frame** (or, to endow it with some dynamic, *framing*). It is closely related to what Hymes called "key" and to what is referred to in modern folklore as performance. A particular performance—that is, what the participants in a face-to-face interaction (or discourse) are doing when they speak—commonly determines the frame of reference in which the exchange is to be interpreted and understood. Authentic frames are culture-specific and vary, somewhat or a great deal, from one society to another. A short list of frames (or framings; the list could be greatly expanded) might include bargaining, complaining, congratulating (someone), consulting, excusing (oneself), insinuating (something), interviewing (someone), joking, mimicking (someone), and reporting (something). These and other speech situations have meanings that participants are familiar with, except in situations of wide difference in age or socioeconomic status. A lack of common frame could be extreme if two (or several) individuals of strikingly different cultural backgrounds were to interact. The purpose of such a discourse might be poorly served, or a serious misunderstanding could even result.

A sample list of means by which discourses are framed includes such stylistic devices as rhyme; prosodic devices—for example, tempo or intonation; such figures of speech as metaphor and metonymy; genre formulas such as conventional openings or closings of fairy tales; special codes—for example, the use of archaic words or obscenities; and a distinctive manner of speech such as a very formal style or an intimate one.

Suwako Watanabe's account of American and Japanese university students' group discussions (Watanabe 1993) addressed the cultural differences in framing. To give an example: Whereas the American students entered and exited the discussion frame immediately and directly, the Japanese students began their participation deliberately and made their points gradually. Moreover, the American students accepted a potential confrontation as a given, whereas the Japanese students tried to avoid confrontation, considering both supportive and opposing arguments. This particular characteristic was perceived by the Americans as too indirect and ambiguous. According to Watanabe (1993:205):

> [W]hen Japanese and Americans are to discuss a controversial issue, the Japanese may experience frustration, being unable to participate in the argument because they find the one-at-a-time argumentation of the Americans too fast [the reference here is to the fact that American participants presented one position at a time and drew a conclusion each time]. At the same time, the Americans may perceive the Japanese as illogical and elusive because they give both supportive and contradictory accounts.

## RECENT TRENDS IN THE ETHNOGRAPHY OF SPEAKING

The methods of the ethnography of speaking are increasingly applied even in what is essentially linguistic (rather than linguistically anthropological) inquiry. When fieldworkers so apply these methods, they make use of recorded narratives, monologues, or dialogues to show, for example, how the syntactic patterns of a language are adjusted to principles of culture-specific discourse. Jeffrey Heath discussed this approach in his article about clause structure in Ngandi, a language now spoken by only a very few aborigines in southeastern Arnhem Land (northern Australia). For his analysis, rather than using a text corrected and refined with the help of an informant after a more or less spontaneous first recording had been made, Heath preferred "the original text, warts and all" or at least kept "editorial emendations . . . to a minimum" (Heath 1985:90). Furthermore, he liked to obtain texts that are stylistically diverse rather than uniform. Having such texts made it easier to match different styles with corresponding grammatical (or even "ungrammatical") forms.

To cite (in a simplified form) one of the several examples with which Heath illustrated his discussion: Among many speakers of English, such fillers as *er*, *uh*, *um* used to fill pauses or gaps in discourse carry a stigma. Not so among speakers of Ngandi. The most common of what Heath termed a "whatchamacallit" element in Ngandi, the noun *jara*, is fully acceptable in all styles, and its syntactic prominence is attested by its having derivational forms (as in *man-jara* "group associated with whatchamacallit" and *bicara* "whatchamacallit [place-name]") and a full set of noun-class prefixes and suffixes. The word *jara*, usually heard after a pause, is used while a speaker searches his or her memory for a specific noun, and when a second such element is used in the same utterance, ŋuni is added to express impatience and self-irritation, as in *bulukiʔ bicara ba-ga-ṇ-i:, bicara ŋuni* "they also sat (lived) at whatchamacallit place—what the hell was the name of that place?" (Heath 1985:107). To linguists who would most likely be analyzing unwritten languages spoken by very small, out-of-the-way societies, Ngandi discourse structure might well appear as highly fragmented and unpredictable. What struck Heath in particular "about the differences between English and such Australian languages as Ngandi . . . is that most of them relate closely to 'psycholinguistic' aspects of speech production" and that the underlying clear-cut grammar and the psycholinguistic component concerned with memory limitations, surface ambiguities, and the like "are far more tightly welded to each other than it seems at first" (Heath 1985:108). To make some sort of sense of this connection, the investigator must attach due significance to language as it is used. Here we have a good example of the recognition of the contribution that ethnography of speaking can make to linguistics.

In papers dealing with language use, the term *context* has been commonly employed to denote the interrelated conditions under which speech and other forms of communicative behavior occur. There has recently been a tendency to employ the term *contextualization* instead. Many linguistic anthropologists believe that it is preferable, at least in some instances, to view context as a process—as something that develops and perhaps even changes significantly while two or more individuals are interacting rather than as something that is given, or fixed. Those features of the settings that are used at particular stages of the interaction to aid in the interpretation of the content are signaled by contextualization cues.

To put it differently: When two (or more) individuals interact for even a relatively short period of time, the nature and purpose of their verbal exchange may abruptly change as well as the message content and form, rules of interaction, and so forth. Such a situation is easy to imagine. For example, two neighbors are chatting casually about the weather and their gardens until one happens to make a remark about the other's child and the remark is taken as a criticism of parenting skills. The casual atmosphere surrounding the conversation changes instantly. The tone of the person whose child's behavior has been found wanting may suddenly turn cool, indicating that the conversation is about to end, and on a very different note from the way it began, or the tone may become angry, with a countercharge launched against the child of the one making the original criticism. In the latter case, the contextualization cue could well be some such remark as "My child is fine—why don't you concentrate on your own, who is always leading our boy astray!"

## SUMMARY AND CONCLUSIONS

Ethnography of communication is an important recent development supplementing the already well-established study of cultures by anthropologists and languages by linguists. The goals of this new field are first to give as complete an account as possible of the social uses of speech in different societies and then to produce historical and comparative studies on the subject (ethnology of communication). Thus far the scope of ethnography of communication has been largely descriptive and synchronic, but cross-cultural comparisons of the social uses of speech as well as studies of how speech uses change over time are forthcoming.

Because their purpose is to discover how humans interact under the many different circumstances of the real world, anthropologists who specialize in the ethnography of communication obtain their data from direct observation of communicative performances. The social unit to which studies in ethnography of communication refer is the speech community—that is, all those people who share at least one speech variety as well as specific rules for the social uses of speaking and for interpreting what is being communicated.

An understanding of the diversity in the ways of communicating is of course of great interest to linguistic anthropologists, but we need to look beyond the merely intellectual satisfaction derived from the study of the subject. There is reason to hope that the application of the growing body of information in the field of ethnography of communication may contribute to the solution of some of the social problems of societies in which many peoples live side by side but do not always share the same ways of speaking.

## RESOURCE MANUAL AND STUDY GUIDE

### *Questions for Discussion*

1. Whenever we communicate with someone face to face, we tend to couch what we say in a style to fit the given situation. What form would your speech behavior take if you were stopped by the state police for speeding? If you were falsely accused of cheating? If you were reprimanded for not having finished an assignment on time? How and why might these forms differ?
2. Describing a language with emphasis on its function as the primary means of communication requires discussing a number of communicative components. Discuss these components and, whenever possible, offer an illustration from your own experience.
3. Different peoples have different attitudes toward the use of speech. Support this statement with examples that show how different these attitudes can be.

### *Objective Study Questions*

**TRUE-FALSE TEST**

T F 1. The rules (not grammatical) for speech behavior in different societies are the same.

T F 2. Today, linguistic anthropologists hold that languages are different from each other, but the uses to which they are put are similar if not essentially the same.

T F 3. The purpose of speaking is not always to transmit information; sometimes it is to establish a sociable atmosphere.

T F 4. If the norms of interpreting speech behavior are shared by speakers, their relations are always harmonious.

T F 5. In every language, speech fillers such as *er, uh, um*—which are used to fill pauses or gaps in discourse—carry a stigma.

**MULTIPLE-CHOICE QUESTIONS**

____ 1. The minimal unit of speech for purposes of an ethnographic analysis is the (A) speech situation. (B) speech act. (C) speech event.

____ 2. All those who share specific rules for speaking and interpreting speech as well as at least one speech variety belong to a (A) speech network. (B) speech area. (C) speech community. (D) None of these three choices applies.

____ 3. Which of the following figures is not especially associated with the ethnography of communication? (A) Dell Hymes. (B) John Gumperz. (C) Noam Chomsky. (D) Deborah Tannen.

**COMPLETIONS**

1. The study of the nature and function of communicative behavior with emphasis on linguistic interaction is called ________________________________ (three words).
2. Recently, there has been a tendency to use the term ____________________ (one word) to replace the term *context*; the new term denotes a *process* rather than something that is given or fixed.

## *Answer Key*

True-false test: 1-F, 2-F, 3-T, 4-F, 5-F
Multiple-choice questions: 1-B, 2-C, 3-C
Completions: 1. ethnography of communication, 2. contextualization

## *Notes and Suggestions for Further Reading*

The information concerning the Ashanti has been drawn from a study by Helen Marie Hogan (n.d.), who based her account on a thorough review of published data. Because most of her sources appeared between the 1920s and 1960s, some of the information may no longer conform to the current communicative behavior of the Ashanti. The examination of the essential components of communicative behavior draws on Hymes (1972) and Saville-Troike (1982).

The standard resource on the ethnography of communication is Saville-Troike (2002). Other articles and books dealing with the ethnography of speaking include Bauman and Sherzer (1974, or 1989); Gumperz and Hymes (1964 and 1972); Hymes (1974 and 1989); Sherzer (1977); Kroskrity (1988); and Sherzer and Darnell (1972). For a survey of literature on the subject, see Bauman and Sherzer (1975 and 1989) and Duranti (1988); for a bibliography, see Philipsen and Carbaugh (1986). The latest work is summarized in Kaplan-Weinger and Ullman (2015).

# 11

# Culture as Cognition, Culture as Categorization: Meaning and Language in the Conceptual World

### LEARNING OBJECTIVES

- Explain the importance of semantics, and why it has defied linguistic analysis for so long
- Explain the notions behind concepts, words, and categories
- Evaluate "ethnoscience" and its various techniques (taxonomies, componential analysis, and so on)
- Understand that meaning emerges from conversation

We have already seen that minimal units of sound (phonemes) are used to compose morphemes, the smallest units of grammatical or lexical function. These morphemes combine to make up the words of our vocabulary. Words form into sentences, and these sentences make up conversation and discourse. But when does language cease to be self-contained? At some point language must make contact with the outside world. As the noted twentieth-century linguist Dwight Bolinger said, this point of contact is what we call meaning, and the study of meaning is generally referred to as *semantics* (1975:185).

## THE SCOPE OF SEMANTICS

But this connection is hardly foregone or obvious. Probably no two things are more unlike than utterances of sounds and things in the world (though through force of habit, these connections come to seem only natural and unquestionable to us). But what some word or sentence means is hardly transparent (see Box 11.1). For example, one of the first words a child learns is the word for mother, but this is done only in the context of a single case—one's own maternal parent—and it is not easy to see how this meaning can be extended to all the other mothers in the world. Often we call our own biological mother "Mama," but why can't we do this for other "mothers," such as the head of a Catholic convent? It is doubtful that the nun who won the 1979 Nobel Peace Prize would ever be called "Mama Teresa." But sometime "Mamas" can indeed be found in other places, such as the names of blues singers (Big MamaThornton), or in the popular *Big Momma's House* movie series starring Martin Lawrence. But why do we say that necessity is the mother—not the father—of invention, and that it is not nice to fool Mother—not Father—Nature? (cf. Macnamara 1982; Lyons 1977; Weinreich 1980; Riemer 2010).

### BOX 11.1 AN EXAMPLE OF HOW MEANING IS DISCOVERED

It is still not definitively clear how we as children learn what words mean. For the most part, words are never explicitly defined for us, even though many times specific examples are pointed out ("Look, there's a 'puppy' coming!"). Still, this process is often equally mysterious, even to adults, when things are explained to them and they have the intellectual maturity to know what to look for and the tools to do so. A case in point is when one of the authors (Stanlaw) was studying Japanese. The first week of language class he learned two important survival words: "eat" (*taberu*) and "drink" (*nomu*). When Japanese people would consume tea, beer, or water they would *nomu*; when they would consume sushi, hamburgers, or pizza they would *taberu*. There were a few oddities, however (as seen below). Japanese people would *nomu* chicken soup or aspirin, while Americans would "eat" the soup or "take" the aspirin. If something was dropped on the floor, a dog could "eat" it—or *taberu* it—in both languages (even if it was an aspirin). Stanlaw chalked this up to just some of the inevitable exceptions to the rules in learning a foreign language and never thought much more about these peculiarities, as about 90 percent of the time he ate and drank in Japanese just fine.

| | ENGLISH | JAPANESE |
|---|---|---|
| water, beer | "drink" | *nomu* |
| hamburger, sushi | "eat" | *taberu* |
| chicken soup | "eat" | *nomu* |
| aspirin | "take" | *nomu* |
| dog's stuff on the floor | "eat" | *taberu* |

On his first trip to Japan, Stanlaw went to the zoo one day to people-watch and noticed a grade school class on one of its ubiquitous field trips getting a guided tour in the reptile house. After being shown a number of snakes,

*continues*

Modern linguistics has begun to study semantics in a rigorous and systematic way only relatively recently. Part of the reason for this has to do with the influence psychological behaviorism had on the social sciences until the 1960s. *Behaviorism* sought to reduce most of human activity to conditioning and reinforcements. The seminal American structural linguist Leonard Bloomfield viewed meaning as a kind of connected series of speakers' and hearers' stimuli (S) and responses (R): A person is hungry and, seeing food (S), tells another to bring it, which he does (R). Presenting the food to the hungry person (S) elicits a "thanks" in return (R). Meaning arises from the events that accompany an action.

*continued*

someone asked the zookeeper, "What do pythons *nomu*?" Assuming he was smarter than a Japanese fifth grader, Stanlaw thought the answer would be obvious. Even snakes sometimes probably had to "drink" water. He was surprised at the zookeeper's reply, "Pythons *nomu* mice and rats." Pondering how pythons could "drink" mice, it finally dawned on him what *nomu* really meant: "to ingest something without chewing." Pythons, of course, swallow their prey whole, so they don't "ingest by moving the jaws," which is what *taberu* refers to. This is why Japanese can *nomu* soups or aspirin tablets, as these are generally not chewed. Dogs, however, will chew something they pick up off the floor, even an aspirin, so the right verb is *taberu* in this case.

Stanlaw went to his Japanese teachers with his new insights: First, in English the world of consumables is divided into liquids (which are "drunk") and solids (which are "eaten"). Second, the Japanese divide the world into actions—whether or not something is chewed (*taberu*) or not chewed (*nomu*). His teachers looked at him as if he had just discovered that the sky is blue or dogs have tails. This fact about the cultural universe was so self-evident to the Japanese teachers that they were at a loss to even know that it had to be pointed out (and in fact, at the time, most Japanese-English dictionaries didn't).

Stanlaw also realized a third thing: In the English world, speakers "take" medicines, regardless of whether they are solids or liquids. So there is another distinction English makes—that between consumables and medicines. It is the *intent* behind the ingestion that is as significant as either the act itself or the item ingested. Dogs snatching up the dropped aspirin are not really "taking" it; they are just eating it as they would any stray scrap of food they find. But a veterinarian might prescribe baby aspirin for a sick dog, which the owner would be instructed to have the dog "take" at certain times. These were aspects about the meaning of the English words "eat," "drink," and "take" that Stanlaw had never been explicitly taught. Nor had he really noticed their usage before, even though he had been using these words—presumably correctly—for decades.

James Stanlaw

For structural linguistics through the 1950s, such notions were generally sufficient. They relied on these kinds of "differential meaning" to do their phonemic and morphological analysis. For example, to determine phonemes of a language, they would ask informants to differentiate between two words of a minimal pair, say [*art*] and [*ark*]. If the two words did not mean the same thing, it would be concluded that [*t*] and [*k*] were different phonemes.

Most linguists of the first half of the twentieth century saw little reason to go much further than this. Even the great pioneer Edward Sapir failed to include a chapter on semantics in his influential classic *Language* (1921). But the limitations of this kind of analysis were apparent to linguists, anthropologists, and philosophers even during the height of structuralism's popularity. Such a narrow semantics precluded explanations of figurative language, metaphorical uses of words, or language change—to say nothing of having little to offer about simple concepts such as **synonyms**, **antonyms**, or **homonyms**.

Modern linguistics and philosophy now have a more nuanced view of semantics, realizing that meaning is not something isolated from the rest of language but is intrinsic to it. If Chomsky is right in claiming that we should study linguistic competence—that is, what speakers know of their language—then semantics must be as important to its description as syntax or phonology. Nonetheless, semantics is quite multifaceted and diverse, being influenced by many different disciplines—from modern computer scientists working on artificial intelligence to classical scholars studying Greek rhetoric.

In the rest of this chapter, we will examine meaning from the point of view of the linguistic anthropologist. That is, we will seek to see how meaning emerges through the interactions of culture, cognition, and categorization. We start with some issues of nomenclature—how we might formally define words, concepts, and categories—and we will make some remarks on how such terms have been thought about in the past. We will then look in some detail at how language meets the real cultural world by examining the lexical, grammatical, and social nature of concepts.

## CONCEPTS, WORDS, AND CATEGORIES

A commonly held view of meaning is that it entails the names of things in the world: "Bill" standing over there, or this "tree" here. These are sometimes called ostensive definitions. But there are many problems with such a view, and we'll mention just three. First, there are many words for which it is hard to see what they refer to in the world (e.g., abstract nouns such as "truth" or "beauty"; properties such as "big," "terrible," or the "redness" of an apple; or verbs such as "thinking" or "doing"). Second, there are some things that are named but do not exist (e.g., "unicorns" or "Godzilla"). Third, when we say the word "tree" we might not be talking about just this particular tree in front of us, but of treeness (the quality or nature of trees).

### *Signs and Symbols*

Some early rhetoricians argued that the things in the world (**referents**) and the words (**symbols**) that refer to them are mediated by concepts in the mind that underlie them (thought). This is reflected on the left in the diagram that follows, the famous "semiotic triangle" of Ogden and Richards (1923:99). For example, seeing an actual physical referent, such as a "tree," conjures up thoughts about trees, giving rise to the spoken symbol, that is, the word T-R-E-E. Of course, things can go the other direction: hearing someone say the word "tree" puts all these same processes in reverse motion. There have been dozens of varieties of the semiotic triangle—all emphasizing different aspects of the connections between objects in the world, the words used to symbolize them, and the thoughts these words generate—and we will use the version depicted on the right for our discussion here.

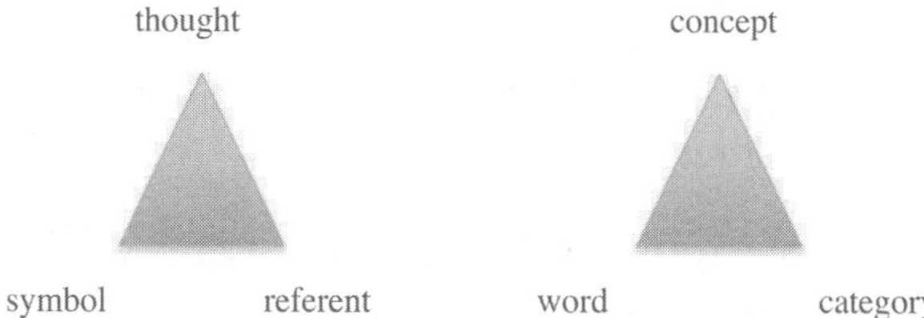


"Concepts" and "words" are often not distinguished, and much of the literature uses the terms interchangeably. By concept we mean a nonlinguistic psychological representation of a category or class of entities in the world (Murphy 2002:385). A word is the linguistic—usually spoken—manifestation of that representation. Concepts, then, are the mental glue (Murphy 2002:1) that ties past experiences—our knowledge of some category or class of objects in the world—with our present experience in labeling them by means of words.

## *Categories and Concepts*

Categories are subtle. We can begin thinking about categories by realizing that no two objects in the real world are exactly the same. No matter how close they may seem, given enough time and attention to detail, we can always find some differences between them. If the differences do not matter, the two items are placed in the same category. If these differences *do* make a difference, then they are not. Categories, then, are the bridge between the necessity of making generalizations (and ignoring differences that don't matter) and the necessity of making distinctions (and attending to differences that do make a difference). This has some important implications.

First, perception is just as much about ignoring stimuli as it is about responding to them. We have an infinity of stimuli coming into our brains at any given moment. A language or culture's categories allow us to filter out the unimportant from the important. Second, the human brain allows us to react to the world using categories instantaneously. If we had to look at, and uniquely respond to, every desk in the classroom as we walked in, it would take us an hour to take a seat. Classifying them all together as "desks"—where presumably one is the same as any other—allows us to get on with more important things, such as today's quiz or the person sitting next to us.

Both perceptual devices—editing out and taking in stimuli—are necessary to apprehend the world, and presumably most, if not all, of this is conducted through the medium of the categories of one's language. But getting at these categories is not an easy thing to do. How and when we create categories is rather complicated and will be discussed in more detail in the next sections. For now, we can think of a category as a set of referents that are somehow grouped together.

Sometimes the terms *categories* and *concepts* are used interchangeably, and other authors use them in somewhat different ways. At any rate, there are five points to notice:

(1) Categorization by itself is not necessarily useful, but it is our ability to apply our knowledge *about* the category that makes categorization useful. (2) Here we are not talking about a single referent, as in the classic semiotic triangle (see Diagram 11.1) but of classes or kinds of referents. This is analogous to the notion of the phoneme; that is, a group of sounds that are psychologically thought of as being the same (in spite of certain phonetic differences between their allophones). (3) The essential aspect of cognition is the ability to categorize: to judge whether or not a particular thing is an instance of a particular category (*Rover* is a "dog"; *Garfield* is a "cat"). (4) The ability to apply categories successfully is "indispensable in using previous experience to guide the interpretation of new experience: without categorization, memory is virtually useless" (Jackendoff 1983:77). (5) We should remember, however, that although categories are indispensable for living, not all çategorization is necessarily linguistic. Animals must do so all the time—this is "eatable," this is "harmful"—without using *linguistic* categories.

Finally, we should note that some semanticists and linguists use the term *lexeme* or *lexical item*—rather than *word*—when they want to distinguish a word as an abstraction from any of its specific forms or parts of speech. For example, there is some underlying notion of "runningness" in the terms *run, ran, running, runs*, and so on that would be missed if we considered them to be different terms entirely. We will now look at how concepts become incorporated into language by way of words, grammar, and discourse.

## THE RISE AND (RELATIVE) FALL OF ETHNOSCIENCE

The well-known anthropologist Ward Goodenough claimed (1964:39), "We learn much of a culture when we learn the system of meanings for which its linguistic forms stand. Much descriptive ethnography is inescapably an exercise in descriptive semantics. . . . [However,] relatively little [systematic] attention [has been] devoted . . . to isolating the concepts or forms in terms of which the members of a society deal with one another and the world around them, and many of which are signified lexically in their language." Goodenough was writing at a unique time in the history of anthropology. The Allied victory after World War II made the United States an economic and military superpower. Turning away from its prewar isolationism, American foreign policy became increasingly proactive and internationalist. At universities and colleges, area studies programs proliferated; anthropology departments and their students increased exponentially. Thus, more Americans were becoming professional anthropologists than ever before, and more fieldwork was being conducted.

Several other things happened in the 1950s and 1960s that caused some anthropologists to reevaluate certain prewar assumptions about the discipline. For one thing, anthropologists rediscovered that culture was not only encoded *in* language; it was encoded very much *like* language. This entailed three points (Stanlaw 2004b): (1) Culture appeared to be rule-bound, as consistent and replicable behaviors were easily found. (2) The natives knew these rules well, as children acquired them very early and most adults made few mistakes. (3) As much as these rules were internalized, the natives were always hard-pressed to explain them adequately.

### *The "New" Ethnography of "Ethnoscience"*

All these contradictions came together in the 1960s and 1970s into what was called at the time the **new ethnography**, and later **ethnoscience**. The new approaches focused on lexical classification of the social and physical environments of speakers of a language by means of its vocabulary rather than the relationships of grammatical categories. This was definitively an emic rather than an etic approach. But an important motivation was to try to make anthropology more scientific. As more fieldwork was being done, concerns over ethnographic *validity*—that is, how do we know we found out what we thought we were looking for?—and *reliability*—if I did this study again, or if you did it instead of me, would the same conclusions be drawn?—became a nagging problem.

Ethnoscience addressed both the problems of covert rules and reliability (or replicability) directly. The intent was to find a way to extract accurate information from the minds of informants, despite the fact that much of this knowledge was overtly unknown to them. It was thought that finding the appropriate methodology was critical, and several related techniques were proposed. The most influential were the study of folk taxonomies and componential analysis. In both methods, however, the assumption was that in general the words in a language reflect the mental categories and the cultural elements held by the speakers. However, this idea, as we will see, is problematic.

### *Folk Taxonomies*

In doing a folk taxonomy, the fieldworker tries to uncover how natives conceive of the structure of a particular domain. As a simple example, consider the concept of "cars" in the United States. Americans love their cars, so it is not so surprising that they have hundreds of names for them. But how is this knowledge of cars structured in their heads? One thing we might do is first elicit as many car terms as possible. We might ask someone, "What are all the different kinds of cars you know?" and write all these words down. We would elicit names like "Fords," "Chevys," "hatchbacks," "Mitsubishis," "Corvettes," and so on (Stanlaw 2004b). The result of data concerning foreign cars obtained from an informant may then be represented as in the following diagram.

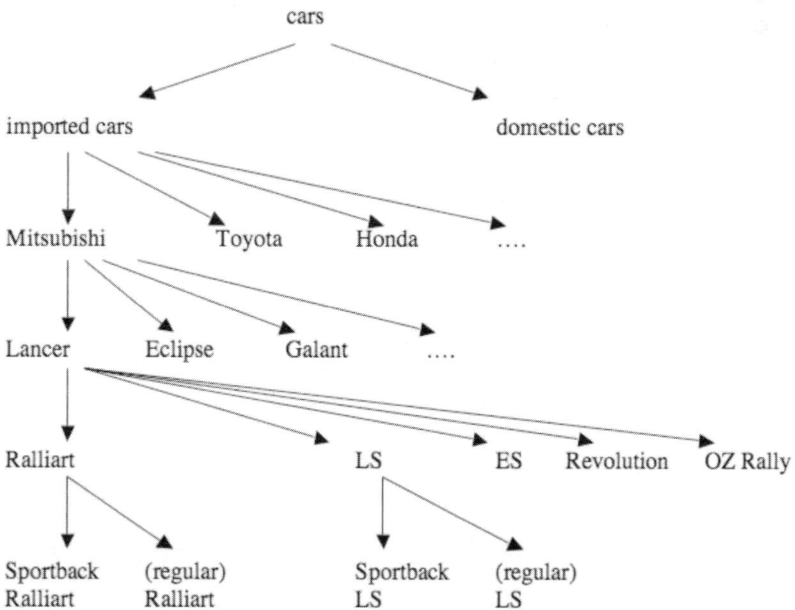

### *Componential Analysis*

**Componential analysis** has similar techniques and goals. Here the focus is on the necessary and sufficient features that are used to distinguish all the terms in the domain. For example, let's assume we're anthropologists from Mars, and our Earthling informant gives us the following set of terms when asked to name the kinds of bottled coffees Starbucks offers: *Vanilla Frappuccino*, *Vanilla Light Frappuccino*, *Doubleshot Energy Vanilla*, and *Doubleshot Energy Vanilla Light*. For the sake of our Martian anthropologists and those few Earthlings still in the dark, a Frappuccino is a sort of chilled coffee milk shake. Doubleshot Energy is a chilled coffee with the addition of guarana, ginseng, and B vitamins; it is supposed to be the coffee equivalent of an energy drink—"It's all zap, no nap," according to the Starbucks website (http://www.starbucks.com/menu/drinks/bottled-drinks/starbucks-doubleshot-energy-coffee-drink?foodZone=9999). In the following chart we see how the properties of *light* versus *regular* (basically, diet versus non-diet) and type of beverage (*Frappuccino* versus *Doubleshot Energy*) account for all the different kinds of Starbucks bottled beverages in our data.

type of beverage

| | | |
|---|---|---|
| regular | *Vanilla Frappuccino* | *Doubleshot Energy Vanilla* |
| light | *Vanilla Light Frappuccino* | *Doubleshot Energy Vanilla Light* |

However, as all good coffee drinkers know, this hardly exhausts the possible bottled coffees from Starbucks. Let's say we find these terms given to us by our informant: *Vanilla Frappuccino, Vanilla Light Frappuccino, Doubleshot Energy Vanilla, Doubleshot Energy Vanilla Light, Mocha Frappuccino, Mocha Light Frappuccino, Coffee Frappuccino, Doubleshot Energy Coffee, Doubleshot Energy Mocha.*

Now we have to take into consideration different flavors (which we didn't have to do before, as the dimensions of "type" and "regular-light" were enough to distinguish our data from each other). So we have to modify our table to account for this third dimension, "flavor." These new data might be accounted for in a chart like the following.

type of beverage

<table>
<tr><td></td><td></td><td>Frappuccino</td><td>Doubleshot Energy</td></tr>
<tr><td rowspan="2">coffee</td><td>regular</td><td>Coffee Frappuccino</td><td>Doubleshot Energy Coffee</td></tr>
<tr><td>light</td><td></td><td></td></tr>
<tr><td rowspan="2">mocha</td><td>regular</td><td>Mocha Frappuccino</td><td>Doubleshot Energy Mocha</td></tr>
<tr><td>light</td><td>Mocha Light Frappuccino</td><td></td></tr>
<tr><td rowspan="2">vanilla</td><td>regular</td><td>Vanilla Frappuccino</td><td>Doubleshot Energy Vanilla</td></tr>
<tr><td>light</td><td>Vanilla Light Frappuccino</td><td>Doubleshot Energy Vanilla Light</td></tr>
</table>

The appealing thing about an analysis in terms of components, as shown in these charts, is that such a tool is economical and can readily be changed or expanded in light of new information. For example, decaffeinated Frappuccinos were present when they were invented in the late 1990s but discontinued in 2008. However, they were made available again in 2010. Thus, if necessary we could add the dimension of "+/-caffeine" to our analysis if we were to find such data. Also, there are many new flavors being added, especially during the holidays. (And there are many other Starbucks bottled coffees that we have not considered. Any of this new information can be easily incorporated into the chart by adding new component features.)

Initially, using the standard questions (called **elicitation frames**) to uncover the underlying properties of various domains was thought to be productive. It seemed to offer recipes that would ensure anthropologists would get pretty much the same data if they were working on the same topic at the same place. It also seemed to offer a way to get at some of the cognitive patterns used by informants themselves to structure their world, even if they didn't articulate them—or could not articulate them.

### *Ethnoscience Highs and Lows*

Optimism was high, and two special issues of the *American Anthropologist* (Romney and D'Andrade 1964; Hammel 1965) offered legitimacy to what came to be called cognitive anthropology. Important edited volumes (e.g., Tyler 1969; Spradley 1972) saw cognitive anthropology being fruitfully applied to the study of kinship systems, as well as to a number of special domains such as disease terminologies, categories of beer in Germany, and spatial concepts of the homeless. Plant terminologies (e.g., Berlin, Breedlove, and Raven 1974), zoological classifications (e.g., Brown 1984), and ceramics and material culture (Kempton 1981) were also extensively analyzed in this way, with good success.

By the 1980s, however, it was clear that ethnoscience as initially conceived was not fulfilling its promises (Stanlaw 2004b). Although the specifics of certain domains were elucidated, many anthropologists began to wonder whether it wasn't just "hocus pocus," as one early critic alleged (Burling 1964), or a "paradigm lost" (Keesing 1972). Part of the problem was that the notion of classification itself needed rethinking (e.g., Kronenfeld 1996). Some argued that the idea that a domain could be defined by just discovering its necessary and sufficient features was proving simplistic or ethnographically inadequate. Such analysis ignored, for example, the fact that cultural knowledge is interlocking and organized on the basis of principles relevant to, and emergent from, experience (Stanlaw and Yoddumnern 1985:152). And it soon "became evident that there is a problem inherent in determining core meanings in a vastness of meaning-influencing contexts" (Shaul and Furbee 1998:166).

It would be incorrect to think that ethnoscientists were the first cultural anthropologists to insist on the importance of discovering how a culture is seen from the perspective of the society's members. Such a view has had a long tradition in American anthropology. Nevertheless, the practitioners of these recent approaches have made some valuable contributions to the study of culture; they have elicited helpful data by making the language of those they study a rich source of information rather than merely the means of communicating. The main shortcoming of the ethnoscientific method is that its emphasis on understanding culture through language results in the neglect of nonverbal behavior and those aspects of culture that lie outside the domains accessible through terminological sets.

## MEANING IN DISCOURSE AND CONVERSATION

### *Deriving Meaning from Pragmatic Presuppositions*

Traditionally, those who begin a study of semantics—the branch of linguistics devoted to **meaning**—will begin by noticing a distinction between **denotation** and **connotation**. Denotation (sometimes called the referent) is the thing in the real world that a word refers to: "That is a *dog*." Connotation is the personal emotions and feelings that get associated with a word: "A *dog* is a man's best friend." Most quickly realize that things are more complicated than this.

When people speak they are not just playing a chess game, manipulating abstract symbols that have importance only in that they contrast with each other. People have beliefs and vested interests that they bring to the conversation. Presuppositions are the assumptions or beliefs implied by using a certain word or phrase. These are often of two kinds. **Semantic presupposition** is concerned with certain kinds of presuppositions among sentences. A famous example (Levinson 1983:170–173) is *The king of France is wise*, requires as a prerequisite a sentence like *There is at present a king of France.* **Pragmatic presupposition**, however, deals with the relationships between speakers and the appropriateness of their statements in context. The famous punch line, *Do you still beat your wife?* is an example. This is really an unanswerable question because even if you adamantly deny it using all the linguistic resources at your disposal, the meaning of the discourse has already been established: you are a wife-beater, and the only question at issue is whether you have done so lately. In a similar vein, we probably wouldn't say *Jane Doe was assassinated in Dallas* unless we think she was a noted person, nor would we say *John F. Kennedy was murdered in Dallas* because we know Kennedy was a famous past president of the United States. Pragmatic presuppositions, then, are those assumptions that speakers make about what their listeners will accept without challenge. Consider these two snippets of conversation:

*Person A: Did I tell you, my wife was Canadian?*
*Person B: Oh, yeah? When did you get divorced?*

*Person X: Did I tell you, my wife was a teacher?*
*Person Y: Oh, yeah? When did she quit?*

In the first case, A did not go on to explain the woman he used to be married to is indeed still a Canadian citizen, and B could make this assumption for himself. Likewise, in the case of X and Y, the listener could also assume that X's wife had a new occupation. If we add a phrase to A's and X's initial comment, however, the assumptions B and Y change, and the answer is the same in both cases.

*Person A: I was married to Sally for twenty years. Did I tell you, my wife was Canadian?*
*Person B: No, I never knew that.*

*Person X: I was married to Sally for twenty years. Did I tell you, my wife was a teacher?*
*Person Y: No, I never knew that.*

Subtle presuppositions are made all the time in every conversation. Consider the difference in assumptions the speaker makes of his listener as he phrases his sentence as either of the following:

*Person A: My girlfriend is coming to visit me tomorrow.*
*Person A: I have this girlfriend who is coming to visit me tomorrow.*

No doubt the young lady would prefer to have A utter the first sentence to his friends.

### *Deriving Meaning from Speech Acts*

The famous philosopher J. L. (John Langshaw) Austin (1962) claimed that another thing we must also take into account during any conversation is how the speaker's intention—or **illocutionary force**—relates to the listener's response—the **perlocutionary effect**. This is often called **speech act theory**. Speech act theory has been a major influence not only in philosophy but also in linguistics and anthropology (e.g., Enfield, Kockelman, and Sidnell 2014:1–25, 128–157, 343–447; Hanks 1995, 2010; Agha 2007; Duranti 2006, 1994; Wilson and Sperber 2012; Tambiah 1970). Searle (1969, 1979) argues that a speaker's actions can be reduced to just five types:

1. *Commissives,* where the speaker commits to some future action (as in promising, threatening, or guaranteeing).
2. *Directives,* where the speaker tries to get the listener to do something (such as begging, commanding, requesting).
3. *Expressives,* where speakers indicate their psychological state (such as apologies, congratulations, welcomings).
4. *Declarations,* where the speaker's utterance brings about a new state of affairs (such as christening, firing, resigning, marrying, excommunicating).
5. *Representatives,* where the speaker conveys beliefs about the truth of some proposition (such as asserting, concluding, or hypothesizing).

A representative sentence such as *It is raining* is different than a declaration such as *I now pronounce you man and wife*. Performative sentences like this last example prompt linguists and philosophers to ask two key, interrelated, questions (Godby 1982). First, which sentences can change the state of the world? Second, how do performative sentences regulate social relationships? When a priest or minister "performs" a marriage ceremony, the world is no longer the same as it was before, and the roles between the two people now have a new social meaning. Indeed, they are thought about by others differently. Of course, the social context under which pronouncements are made are critical. The words must be stated while fulfilling an unspoken social contract: the persons must want to get married, there must be the appropriate ceremony, the speaker of the words must have the recognized social authority to conduct the ceremony, and the appropriate words must be spoken at the appropriate time.

Still, most usages of speech are indirect (Levinson 1983:264). For example, the imperative form *Close the door!* is rarely used to make a request. Instead, we would usually say something like:

*Can you close the door?*
*Would you mind closing the door for me?*
*I'd like to close the door, please.*
*We ought to close the door, don't you think?*
*Could I ask you a favor? Could you close the door, please?*

These **indirect speech acts** show that grammatical form and social function do not necessarily correspond. *Can you close the door?* is technically an interrogative, but it may function as a command. The implicit social contract among the parties involved must therefore be inferred from context. Consider the old joke where Person A asks Person B, *Do you know what time it is?* and Person B nods *Yes!* and then walks away. In such a case we can probably infer that Person A does not know the time and that his true motive for asking was not simply to find out *if* B had knowledge of the hour, but was a true inquiry: if you know the time, then tell me. The joke is, Person B violates these indirect expectations and answers as if A were asking a yes/no question. The social context in which a sentence is uttered is as important to its meaning as its syntax or formal semantic properties.

### *Deriving Meaning from Conversations and Discourse*

We might define conversations as linguistic structures and patterns beyond the sentence. Conversational structure is often examined in two ways, by conversational analysis and discourse analysis. Both approaches strive to explain how the coherence and sequential organization of conversations are produced and understood (Levinson 1983:286, Brown and Yule 1983, Sacks 1992a and 1992b). Levinson (1983:286–287) claims that **conversational analysis** is characterized by the following:

1. Methodologically, conversational analysis examines conversations minutely in great detail; it is rigorous and empirical, and avoids grandiose theory construction.
2. The method is highly inductive.
3. A search is made for recurring patterns in large numbers of naturally occurring conversations (and not just based on single texts).
4. Instead of positing a set of rules that all conversations must theoretically follow, emphasis is placed on the choices and alternatives available to speakers in differing types of conversations, and their interactional and inferential consequences.
5. Emphasis is placed on what is actually in the data rather than on what intuition might tell us about what is or is not acceptable.
6. As many instances as possible of some phenomena under consideration are found across texts. These examples are used to discover the systemic properties of conversations, their structure and organization, and the ways in which utterances are designed and used to manage the sequences of talk.

On the other hand, **discourse analysis** is typified by adherence to the following:

1. Methodologically, in discourse analysis you (a) isolate the set of basic categories or units of discourse, (b) form rules concatenating and linking these basic categories,

and (c) determine the well-formed sequences (coherent discourse) from the ill-formed sequences (incoherent discourse).

2. Discourse analysis attempts to adopt the methods of autonomous linguistics to levels beyond the sentence and employs its theoretical principles and concepts (e.g., rules, well-formedness).
3. An appeal to intuition determines what constitutes a well-formed sequence.
4. Only a few texts are analyzed in depth (or perhaps only a single one), examining all the interesting features of this limited sample.

Both discourse analysis and conversational analysis have had major impacts on linguistic anthropology (e.g., Wortham and Reyes 2015; Enfield, Kockelman, and Sidnell 2014; Duranti 2006). Both approaches offer different ways of examining a conversation, and each has its own strengths and insights. However, we also need a way to draw inferences during a conversation about what is meant, but *not* really said. This unspoken information is called **conversational implicature**, and the philosopher Paul Grice (1975, 1991) has done much work in this area. Grice posits a set of rules that he believes people use to regulate and structure conversations:

1. Maxim of cooperation.
   a. You should speak at the appropriate time, in the appropriate order.
   b. You should follow the general direction of the talk.
2. Maxims of quantity.
   a. Make your contribution as informative as needed, but . . .
   b. Do not make your contribution more informative than needed.
3. Maxims of quality.
   a. Do not say anything you know to be false.
   b. Do not say things for which you lack evidence.
4. Maxims of manner.
   a. You should avoid being too obscure.
   b. You should avoid ambiguity.
   c. You should be brief.
   d. You should be orderly.
5. Maxim of relevance.
   a. Be relevant.

These are the unwritten rules people are using when playing the conversation "game." Thus, if Person A says *Hey, I'm hungry*, and Person B says *I've got ten bucks*, A probably perceives this exchange as invitation to go out to eat. Person B might also conclude that Person A is a little short on cash. The second person's statement is taken as an offer of loan. If not, B would be violating several conversational maxims, such as being relevant and avoiding ambiguity. Person B would not tell the first person he or she had ten dollars if indeed he or she did not, or if he or she did not intend to share a meal with Person A. Nor would money be mentioned at this point in the conversation if he or she was just informing the other person about finances.

In a similar manner, British linguist Geoffrey Leech offered a set of politeness maxims (Brown and Levenson 1987) that complement the conversational maxims above. These are:

1. The tact maxim: "Minimize the expression of beliefs which imply cost to other; maximize the expression of beliefs which imply benefit to other."
2. The generosity maxim: "Minimize the expression of beliefs that express or imply benefit to self; maximize the expression of beliefs that express or imply cost to self."
3. The approbation maxim: "Minimize the expression of beliefs which express dispraise of other; maximize the expression of beliefs which express approval of other."
4. The modesty maxim: "Minimize the expression of praise of self; maximize the expression of dispraise of self."
5. The agreement maxim: "Minimize the expression of disagreement between self and other; maximize the expression of agreement between self and other."
6. The sympathy maxim: "Minimize antipathy between self and other; maximize sympathy between self and other."

Information is exchanged when all these tacit rules of various kinds are followed in an orderly fashion, but information is also conveyed when they are ignored or broken. For example, consider this hypothetical conversation between two college students in a residence-hall dining center:

*Joe: Hey, Jane, I'm going to see Beyoncé in concert next weekend!*
*Jane: Really! I would just die to see her!*
*Joe: Well, actually, I was wondering if you'd like to go with me . . . I've got two tickets.*
*Jane: Wow, next weekend? I'm kinda tied up, but thanks anyway.*
*Joe: Well, how about the weekend after? I'm sure someone good will be playing downtown. I could get tickets and . . .*
*Jane: Well, why don't we just wait for a while. Maybe give me a call later or something. Maybe check my Facebo—*
*Joe: Well, do you want to study together for the anthropology midterm this Monday? I've heard . . .*
*Jane: Oh, sorry, Joe, but tonight I have to wash my hair.*
*Joe: OK, well how about tomorrow night?*
*Jane: Hey, sorry . . . laundry, you know.*

Most native English speakers would assume that Jane was not especially interested in seeing Joe. Some reasons, among others, are that Jane is being deliberately ambiguous (being *kinda tied up* next weekend) or evasive. The tone of the conversation would change if instead of saying she was tied up, Jane said, *Wow, next weekend my sister is getting married in New York, but thanks a lot anyway*. Unless this was a case of prevarication, and Joe found out about it, he probably would ask her out again.

No doubt similar conversational maxims apply to other languages, but probably not in the same ways. That is, there are conversational rules, to be sure, but they are often very different. For example, Keenan (1976) claims that on Malagasy, a large island off the east coast of Africa, the maxim of quantity is constantly violated. New information is hoarded as a form of prestige, and direct questions are avoided, or given incomplete or evasive replies. If asked about the specific number of people in the market, for instance, a person might simply reply "many." Certainly politeness maxims are vastly different from culture as well. In Japanese, it is not felt to be prying to ask someone their age or marital status upon meeting them for the first time, or where someone specifically is going when confronting them on the street. At the same time, Japanese people feel very reluctant to say no to someone, and sometimes might even end up doing things they don't want just because they could not find a way to decline in a face-saving way for both parties.

## SUMMARY AND CONCLUSIONS

In this chapter we have dealt with the lexical, grammatical, and social nature of meaning and conceptualization. We have found several ways that meaning and concepts appear to be similarly manifested across languages. First, there is a tendency for people to think in terms of linguistic and sociocultural **binary oppositions**. Second, all languages and cultures classify at least certain aspects of the world through labeled domains that are hierarchical (as in taxonomies) and consist of identifiable components available for formal analysis. These universally demonstrate many of the same properties (e.g., numbers and levels of superordinate terms). Third, there are apparently some direct nonarbitrary associations between form and meaning found in all languages (sound symbolism). Fourth, all languages have rules that govern social discourse and conversation, and these encode the roles of the participants, their points of view, and their presuppositions. Violations of these accepted—though unarticulated—patterns, presumptions, and regulations result not only in miscommunication but also in social sanction.

## RESOURCE MANUAL AND STUDY GUIDE

### *Questions for Discussion*

1. In this chapter we saw many sets of English terms using similar sounds that seem to share certain feelings or meanings. Why might this be the case? Could this phenomenon be universal?
2. If onomatopoeic terms are supposed to imitate sounds, why are the various onomatopoeic expressions different across languages (e.g., *bowwow* in English, *wan wan* in Japanese, or *aw aw* in Tagalog)?

### *Projects*

**PROJECT 1**

You are doing an ethnoscientific analysis of soft drinks in the United States. When presented with the elicitation frame, "Tell me the kinds of Pepsi-Colas there are," your informants give you the following data:

*Pepsi*: the regular cola-flavored brand name soft drink
*Diet Pepsi*: a low calorie version of Pepsi (using the artificial sweetener aspartame)
*Pepsi ONE*: a diet Pepsi, with one calorie per serving
*Caffeine-Free Pepsi*: Pepsi with no caffeine
*Caffeine-Free Diet Pepsi*: a diet Pepsi with no caffeine
*Crystal Pepsi*: a clear version of Pepsi
*Pepsi Lime*: lime-flavored Pepsi

*Christmas Pepsi*: a nutmeg and cocoa Pepsi
*Pepsi Strawberry Burst*: strawberry-flavored Pepsi
*Pepsi Twist*: lemon-flavored Pepsi
*Pepsi Light*: a lemon-flavored diet Pepsi
*Cherry Vanilla Pepsi*: cherry-vanilla-flavored Pepsi
*Wild Cherry Pepsi*: a cherry-flavored Pepsi
*Diet Wild Cherry Pepsi:* low-calorie Wild Cherry Pepsi
*Pepsi Jazz, Diet Black Cherry French Vanilla*: a multiflavored diet Pepsi
*Pepsi Jazz, Diet Strawberries and Cream*: a multiflavored diet Pepsi
*Pepsi Jazz, Diet Caramel Cream*: a multiflavored diet Pepsi
*Pepsi AM*: Pepsi with extra caffeine
*Diet Pepsi Max*: Diet Pepsi with extra caffeine
*Pepsi Natural*: Pepsi made with only natural ingredients
*Pepsi Edge*: a diet Pepsi containing the artificial sweetener Splenda instead of aspartame

Try to analyze these data to find the native emic categories. Can you use the chart on page 220? If so, does it have to be modified? How?

**PROJECT 2**

Make a taxonomic analysis of American-made automobiles (Ford, Chevrolet, etc.), following the example in the chapter.

**PROJECT 3**

Provide a rationale for why the following pairs might (or might not) be considered to be binary oppositions:

(1) dog/cat
(2) hen/chick
(3) heaven/hell
(4) raw/cooked
(5) black/white

Do the following words have binary oppositions? Why or why not?

(1) red
(2) animal
(3) handsome
(4) Pepsi
(5) skirt

**PROJECT 4**

In the chart on sound symbolism, we saw, besides the first row discussed in the text, two other rows of sets of English words depicting possible cases. What do you think the words in each column (i.e., all the words in the *sl*-column, the words in the *pr*-column, and so on) have in common?

## Objective Study Questions

**TRUE-FALSE TEST**

T F 1. Edward Sapir was one of the first anthropologists to be explicitly concerned with semantics.

T F 2. In many ways, the so-called "New Ethnography" developed out of an attempt to make anthropology more scientific, empirical, and replicable.

T F 3. Lévi-Strauss believed that all languages have binary oppositions, and that for the most part, these binary oppositions are very much alike.

T F 4. Sometimes some researchers use the term *lexeme* rather than *word* when they want to distinguish a word as an abstraction from any specific forms or parts of speech.

**MULTIPLE-CHOICE QUESTIONS**

____ 1. We find that concepts become manifested in a language through (A) lexicalization. (B) grammaticalization. (C) socialization and discourse. (D) All of the above.

____ 2. One of the historical reasons that semantics was the last area in linguistics to receive attention was because (A) anthropologists generally cared more about social structure than meaning. (B) behavioral psychologists and structural linguists believed meaning could be reduced to stimuli and responses. (C) Chomsky and other linguists in the last half of the twentieth century dismissed meaning in favor of studying the ethnography of communication. (D) philosophy had generally solved most problems concerning meaning.

____ 3. Which of the following terms is not associated with a semiotic triangle? (A) Symbols, or words. (B) Thoughts, or concepts. (C) Referents. (D) Idioms.

____ 4. The emotional feeling tied to a word is referred to as (A) synonymy. (B) connotation. (C) reference. (D) denotation.

**COMPLETIONS**

1. When we look at a word as an abstraction rather than just as spoken sounds, we often use the term ____________________ (one word).
2. Words that have the opposite meaning are called __________________ (one word).
3. Perception is just as much about ____________________ stimuli as it is about responding to stimuli (one or two words).
4. The term ______________ refers to the things in the real world, whereas ____________ is concerned with how a word contrasts with, or is related to, other words (one word each).

## *Answer Key*

True-false test: 1-F, 2-T, 3-T, 4-T
Multiple-choice questions: 1-A, 2-B, 3-D, 4-B
Completions: 1. lexeme, 2. antonyms, 3. filtering out/ignoring, 4. referent/sense

## *Notes and Suggestions for Further Reading*

The study of meaning and conceptualization has a vast literature. Probably for the linguistic anthropology student almost anything by George Lakoff, Brent Berlin, William Labov, Ray Jackendoff, Leonard Talmy, Charles Fillmore, Wallace Chafe, Ronald Langacker, or John Searle would be of great interest (as well as being generally accessible). Modern formal introductions to semantics include the comprehensive Riemer (2010) (excellent for undergraduate students) or the also good Hurford, Heasley, and Smith (2007). For a book of readings in cognitive anthropology, see Tyler (1969). It supplements two special issues of *American Anthropologist* devoted to cognitive studies and formal semantic analysis; one was edited by Romney and D'Andrade (1964), the other by E. A. Hammel (1965). Later books include Spradley (1972), Dougherty (1985), D'Andrade (1995), and Shore (1996). For good overviews of pragmatics, see Levinson (1983) and Huang (2007); for discourse analysis, see the excellent Wortham and Reyes (2015), or Gee (2011) and Johnstone (2008); for conversational analysis, see Sidnell (2010) and Hutchby and Wooffitt (2008); for speech acts, see Martínez-Flor and Usó-Juan (2010). Cutting's (2008) *Pragmatics and Discourse: A Resource Book for Students* (and its accompanying website), although primarily intended for English-language and linguistics students, offers extensive data—and many examples—for anthropologists to examine. The collections in Enfield, Kockelman, and Sidnell (2014) and Duranti (2006) are all excellent and highly recommended.

# 12

# Language, Culture, and Thought

## LEARNING OBJECTIVES

- Describe the Sapir-Whorf hypothesis and its components, linguistic determinism, and linguistic relativity
- Explain basic color nomenclature theory and why it is important
- Provide some philosophical and theoretical alternatives to linguistic relativity
- Compare universalism and cultural determinism to the Sapir-Whorf hypothesis

The nature of the relationship between language, thought, and culture was under consideration long before anthropology became recognized as a scholarly field in its own right. Wilhelm von Humboldt (1767–1835), a well-known German diplomat and scholar, was one of those who had very definite ideas on the subject. He wrote, "The spiritual traits and the structure of the language of a people are so intimately blended that, given either of the two, one should be able to derive the other from it to the fullest extent. . . . Language is the outward manifestation of the spirit of people: their language is their spirit, and their spirit is their language; it is difficult to imagine any two things more identical" (1907:42). Not only did the Danish linguist Otto Jespersen declare (1955:17) that language and "nation" (i.e., culture) are synonymous, he even believed that one language—English—was superior to, say, French, because it is a more "methodical, energetic, business-like and sober language, that does not care much for finery and elegance, but cares for logical consistency."

To modern anthropologists these statements are unacceptable in the forms in which they were made. But such quotations show the concern people historically have had about how language reflects the culture of the society it is spoken in, and the thought processes of those who speak it. In this chapter we will look at some of the relationships between language, thought, and culture, in particular, the so-called Sapir-Whorf hypothesis. The Sapir-Whorf hypothesis argues, first, that the language one speaks determines how one perceives the world, and, second, that the distinctions encoded in each language are all different from one another. Thus, in its strong form this hypothesis claims that each society and culture lives in its own "linguistic world," perhaps incommensurate with the linguistic worlds of other societies and cultures. If true, this has profound philosophical, social, and even political implications.

## THE DOUBLE-EDGED SWORD OF THE SAPIR-WHORF HYPOTHESIS: LINGUISTIC DETERMINISM AND LINGUISTIC RELATIVITY

Whereas Boas's and Sapir's ideas concerning the relationship between language and culture primarily influenced only their students and other scholars, the writings of Benjamin Lee Whorf (1897–1941) caught the attention of the educated public. Whorf, a chemical engineer by training, was a fire-prevention inspector and later an executive in the Hartford Fire Insurance Company in Connecticut. Although he continued to work for the company until his untimely death in 1941, he enrolled in a course at Yale University to do graduate work under Sapir, who had just been awarded a professorship at Yale. Among Whorf's numerous subsequent publications, the best known are those in which he expounded on what some have referred to as the Sapir-Whorf hypothesis (see Box 12.1).

### *The Sapir-Whorf Hypothesis (Not So) in a Nutshell*

Expanding on Sapir's ideas, Whorf wrote that

> the background linguistic system (in other words, the grammar) of each language is not merely a reproducing instrument for voicing ideas but rather is itself the shaper of ideas. . . . We dissect nature along lines laid down by our native languages . . . organize it into concepts, and ascribe significances as we do, largely because we are parties to an agreement to organize it in this way—an agreement that holds throughout our speech community and is codified in the patterns of our language. . . . [Not] all observers are . . . led by the same physical evidence to the same picture of the universe, unless their linguistic backgrounds are similar. (Whorf 1940a:231)

He further asserted that "users of markedly different grammars are pointed by their grammars toward different types of observations . . . and hence are not equivalent as observers but must arrive at somewhat different views of the world" (Whorf 1940b:61). In these passages Whorf set forth a double principle: **linguistic determinism**, namely, that the way one thinks is determined by the language one speaks, and **linguistic relativity**, that differences among languages must therefore be reflected in the differences in the worldviews of their speakers.

### *Whorf and the Hopi Language*

Many of the examples Whorf used to support his contention came from Hopi, a language spoken by Native Americans in the pueblos of northeastern Arizona. Although Whorf briefly visited the Hopi villages in 1938, the data for his grammatical sketch of the language (1946) were obtained from a native speaker of Hopi who lived in New York City. In an article dealing with grammatical aspects of Hopi verbs, Whorf put forth the claim that

### BOX 12.1 HOW WORDS AFFECT BEHAVIOR

It was in the course of my professional work for a fire insurance company, in which I undertook the task of analyzing many hundreds of reports of circumstances surrounding the start of fires, and in some cases, of explosions. My analysis was directed toward purely physical conditions, such as defective wiring, presence or lack of air spaces between metal flues and woodwork, etc., and the results were presented in these terms. . . . But in due course it became evident that not only a physical situation *qua* physics, but the meaning of that situation to people, was sometimes a factor, through the behavior of the people, in the start of the fire. And this factor of meaning was clearest when it was a LINGUISTIC MEANING, residing in the name or the linguistic description commonly applied to the situation. Thus, around a storage of what are called "gasoline drums," behavior will tend to a certain type, that is, great care will be exercised; while around a storage of what are called "empty gasoline drums," it will tend to be different—careless, with little repression of smoking or of tossing cigarette stubs about. Yet the "empty" drums are perhaps the more dangerous, since they contain explosive vapor. Physically the situation is hazardous, but the linguistic analysis according to regular analogy must employ the word "empty," which inevitably suggests lack of hazard.

From Benjamin Lee Whorf, *Language, Thought, and Reality* (1956), 135, Published by The MIT Press.

the Hopi "have a language better equipped to deal with such vibratile phenomena [that is, phenomena characterized by vibration] than is our latest [English] scientific terminology" (1936:131). Among his examples are the verb forms *wa´la* "it (a liquid) makes a wave, gives a slosh," *tï´rï* "he gives a sudden start," and ʔï´mï "it explodes, goes off like a gun." These and others can be changed from their punctual aspect (a term used to refer to a verb action concentrated into a very short period of time) to the segmentative aspect by repeating (reduplicating) their last two sounds and adding the ending *-ta* to produce the forms *wala´lata* "it is tossing in waves," *tïrï´rïta* "he is quivering, trembling," and ʔïmï´mïta "it is thundering."

Whereas in English the difference between something happening once briefly and something occurring repeatedly over time may call for different phrases (for example, "it explodes" as against "it is thundering," or "it makes a wave" as against "it is tossing in waves"), the Hopi express it by the use of a simple grammatical device. In Whorf's words, the example illustrates "how the Hopi language maps out a certain terrain of what might be termed primitive physics . . . with very thorough consistency and not a little true scientific precision" and "how language produces an organization of experience" (1936:130–131).

In another article, written in the mid-1930s but not published until nine years after Whorf's death, the author stated that "the Hopi language is seen to contain no words, grammatical forms, constructions or expressions that refer directly to what we call TIME, or to past, present, or future . . . or that even refer to space in such a way as to exclude that element of extension or existence that we call TIME" (1950:67). Instead, the grand coordinates of the universe for the Hopi are manifest, objective experience and the unfolding, subjective realm of human existence.

Whorf illustrated his notion of linguistic relativity by using as an example the Apache equivalent of the English utterance "It is a dripping spring" (referring to a source of water): "Apache erects the statement on a verb *ga:* 'be white (including clear, uncolored, and so on).' With a prefix *nÄ*-the meaning of downward motion enters: 'whiteness moves downward.' Then *tó*, meaning both 'water' and 'spring,' is prefixed. The result corresponds to our 'dripping spring,' but synthetically it is: 'as water, or springs, whiteness moves downward.' How utterly unlike our way of thinking!" (Whorf 1941a:266, 268).

### *Comparing Hopi to the Typical Western Language*

Following up on the hypothesis that a language and the culture it serves mirror each other, Whorf compared the Hopi language with western European languages (labeled SAE for "Standard Average European"). According to him, the differences in linguistic structure between Hopi and SAE are reflected in "habitual thought" and "habitual behavior." For example, "the Hopi microcosm seems to have analyzed reality largely in terms of *events* (or better[,] 'eventing'), referred to in two ways, objective and subjective" (1941b:84); the emphasis is on being in accord, by means of thoughtful participation, with the unfolding forces of nature. Speakers of SAE, in contrast, conceive of the universe largely in terms of things and of time in terms of schedules. SAE languages use tense to mark the time at which an action takes place (as in the past, present, future, or, even more specifically, as in "I had eaten," to express the completion of an action before a specific past time). No wonder, then, that speakers of western European languages tend to be preoccupied with "records, diaries, book-keeping, accounting . . . calendars, chronology . . . annals, histories . . . [and] budgets" (1941b:88).

The implications of Whorf's ideas concerning linguistic relativity and determinism are quite serious. If the worldview and behavior of a people are significantly affected by the structure of the language they speak, and if languages differ in structure, then cross-cultural communication and understanding are likely to be noticeably impaired, if not impossible to achieve. This is why Whorf's ideas received a great deal of attention and stimulated much discussion for a number of years after World War II.

## THE SAPIR-WHORF HYPOTHESIS RECONSIDERED

From a contemporary standpoint, however, it appears that Whorf overstated his case. According to a strong version of this proposition, lexical and grammatical categories of a language completely determine how its speakers perceive the world around them. This is undoubtedly not true. That we can translate from one language to another belies the correctness of the hypothesis in its strongest form: Humans do *not* live in incomparable linguistic worlds. But according to a weaker version, there is some sort of correlation between a language and its speakers' worldview (the philosophical dimension of a society's culture).

### *Whorf's Views of Lexical Differences in Language*

There is no question that the lexicon of any language mirrors whatever the nonverbal culture emphasizes; that is, those aspects of culture that are important for the members of a society are correspondingly highlighted in the vocabulary. For example, words conveying the various characteristics of camels (age, breed, gender, function, condition, and so on) are undoubtedly more plentiful in a language spoken by Bedouins who depend on camels than they are in English; the vocabulary of American English, for its part, is replete with the names of makes and models of automobiles, with new names of models of the various makes being added every year. In Pintupi, one of the aboriginal languages of Australia, there are at least ten words designating various kinds of holes found in nature or in manufactured objects: *mutara* is a special hole in a spear, *pulpa* is a rabbit burrow, *makarnpa* is a burrow of a monitor lizard, *katarta* is the hole left by a monitor lizard after it has broken the surface after hibernation, and so on.

This example also shows that even though a language may not have a one-word equivalent for a word of another language, it is possible to provide an adequate translation by a descriptive phrase (for *katarta* this may take as many as fifteen English words). To avoid wordiness or the use of borrowed words, many languages coin new words. Some years ago, an American anthropologist thought a kinship term was needed to include the meanings of *nephew* and *niece* and coined the word *nibling*, using the word *sibling* (brother or sister) as a model. However, to conclude that the absence of equivalent terms between different vocabularies must always be associated with a different perception of the world would be far-fetched.

Whorf's examples from Hopi also call for comment. According to Voegelin, Voegelin, and Jeanne (1979), the relationship between the punctual and segmentative aspects is not as straightforward as Whorf described it: For example, not all nonreduplicated (not doubled) stems without the ending *-ta* can be said to express the punctual aspect. Furthermore, although speakers of Hopi make little of the division between future and nonfuture, they do indicate tense by temporal adverbs, the suffix *-ni* (future), and the gnomic suffix –ŋwɨ (meaning that something is generally true).

Whorf claimed that the Apache way of thinking is "utterly unlike" that of speakers of English because the utterance "It is a dripping spring" translates literally from Apache into English as "As water, or springs, whiteness moves downward." But suppose that speakers of a foreign language were to interpret literally *breakfast* as "breaking the fast (abstinence from food)," *bonfire* as "a fire of bones, bone fire," and *spinster* as "a woman whose occupation is spinning" and as a result saw a profound difference between their own way of thinking and that of English-speaking people. But some lexical differences between languages may have some consequences as to how speakers view the corresponding parts of their environment. Pronominal usage and kinship will serve as examples.

### *The Power of Pronouns*

Speakers of English use the personal pronoun *you* whether they are addressing one or several children, adults, old persons, subordinates, or individuals much superior to themselves in rank. Only when addressing God in prayer or in certain very limited contexts—for example, in the language of the Friends (the Quakers) or in poetry—does one use the pronoun *thou* (which is singular only). The typical situation in other languages, including most of those spoken in Europe, is more complex. When addressing someone, speakers of Dutch, French, German, Italian, Russian, Spanish, and other languages must choose between the "familiar" personal pronoun (T form) and the "polite" personal pronoun (V form) and/or the corresponding verb form. (The symbols T and V are derived from the French *tu* and *vous*, the familiar and polite second-person pronouns, respectively.) In Czech, for example, to address an individual who is closely related, someone socially close and of long acquaintance, or a child below the age of puberty, one commonly uses the personal pronoun *ty.* But in addressing a casual acquaintance, a stranger, or a person deserving respect, one uses the pronoun *vy*, which also serves as the plural of *ty.* A speaker may occasionally wonder, for example, which of the two forms to use when addressing an adult whom the speaker knew as a child and referred to repeatedly as *ty*. A translation from Czech into English, or vice versa, that involves these pronouns (and/or the corresponding verb forms) is therefore not equivalent. The Czech phrases "*ty a já*" and "*vy a já*" both translate into English as "you and I," even though the first one makes use of the informal, familiar—even intimate—pronoun and would not be used in situations in which the formal, polite pronoun of the second phrase would be appropriate. The English translation, then, can only be approximate, as it cannot fully convey the nature of the relationship between the speaker and the addressee.

Pronoun usage in Japanese is more complex than in the Indo-European languages, as other dimensions beside familiarity must be considered. Pronouns must be selected depending on differing levels of intended formality and the gender of the speaker. For example, consider some of the various ways of saying "we" in Japanese:

| **for female speakers** | **for male speakers** |
|---|---|
| watakushi-domo | watakushi-domo |
| watakushi-tachi | watakushi-tachi |
| watashi-tachi | watashi-tachi |
| watashi-ra | watashi-ra |
| atashi-tachi | — |
| — | boku-tachi |
| atashi-ra | boku-ra |
| — | ore-tachi |
| — | ore-ra |

From top to bottom, the terms become less formal. Although there are no exact rules, the levels depicted above probably correspond to intuitions most Japanese native speakers have of how these pronouns should be used. Some of the factors affecting levels of politeness and use of **honorifics** are:

- familiarity (e.g., stranger, family member, friend),
- age (older or younger than speaker),

- professional relations (e.g., boss, salesperson, customer),
- gender (same or different from speaker),
- in-group/out-group (e.g., same family, school, department, company), and
- context (e.g., request, command, greeting).

### *Other Lexical Differences: Kinship Terminology*

The Japanese kinship and pronominal systems reflect fine nuances of meaning or social distance. Japanese social structure—at least linguistically—follows what anthropologists call an "Eskimo" kinship terminology. What this means is that the kinship system in Japanese is similar in many ways to the American one, but with three important exceptions:

- Terms of address are different from terms of reference,
- older siblings are distinguished from younger siblings, and
- terms for relatives of the speaker are different from terms for others' relatives.

For example, if I were talking to my older brother, I would call him by the kinship term *o-nii-san* ("elder brother" with the honorific *-san* suffix attached)—rather than using his name. If I were talking about my older brother, I would use the term *ani*. If I were addressing someone else's older brother, I would use the family name (with the *-san* suffix being obligatory) or a title. To talk about him, I would use *o-nii-san*. When talking to my younger brother, I would use his first name (without the *-san* suffix, or possibly adding the diminutive suffix *-chan*). I would refer to him as my *otōto*. When introducing my wife, I would use the term *tsuma* (neutral), *nyōbō* (colloquial), or *kanai* (polite) but would need to use *oku-san* (polite) or *oku-sama* (very polite) for someone else's wife. There are some two dozen terms for wife in Japanese, each reflecting different emotional connotations, social attitudes, and levels of respect. Common these days is even the English loanword *waifu*, which some have claimed entered the Japanese language precisely to *avoid* some of the cultural baggage carried by these other terms.

Let us consider another example, one with even more significant consequences. Among the Arapaho, a Native American tribe of the Great Plains, the term for "my mother" is *néínoo* (Salzmann 1959, 1983). This term also applies to ego's mother's sister, a person referred to in the American kinship system as "my aunt" (**ego** is the person of reference to whom others are shown to be related). However, the term by which ego calls his or her mother's brother is *nési*, roughly equivalent to "my uncle." Similarly, the term for "my father," *neisónoo*, also refers to ego's father's brother, whereas father's sister is referred to as *nehéi*, roughly equivalent to "my aunt." Now if ego's father's brother is termed *neisónoo*, as is also ego's father, it follows that father's brother's wife would be referred to by the same term as ego's father's wife, that is, *néínoo*. And by the same token, ego's mother's sister's husband is referred to in Arapaho as *neisónoo* "my father." Whereas in American kinship terminology biological parents are distinguished from uncles and aunts, the Arapaho and many other peoples lump together lineal relatives with some of their **collateral relatives**—the biological mother, her sister, and father's brother's wife, on the one hand, and the biological

**FIGURE 12.1** PARTIAL COMPARISON OF THE AMERICAN AND ARAPAHO KINSHIP SYSTEMS

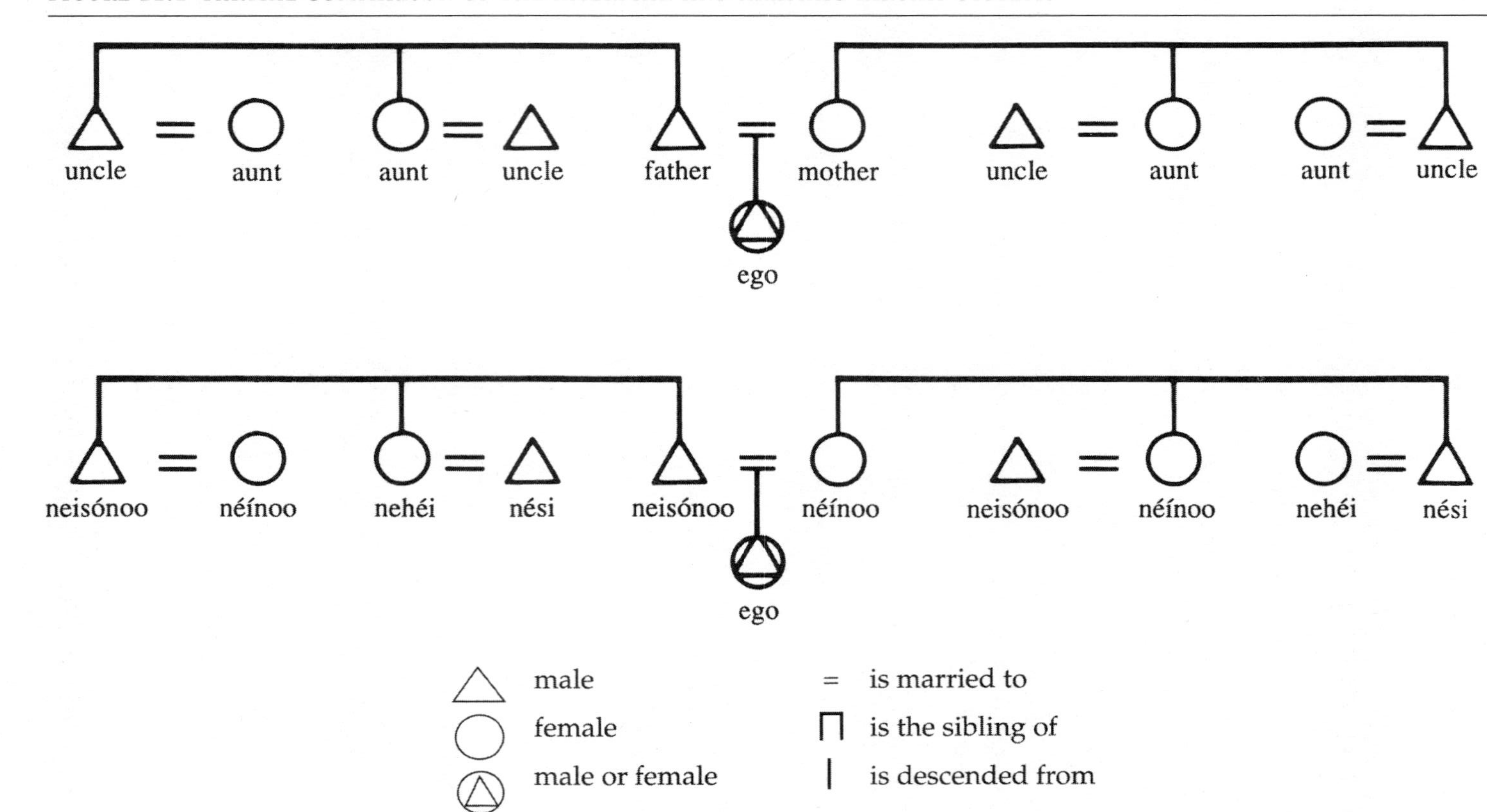

father, his brother, and mother's sister's husband, on the other (see Figure 12.1). It follows, then, that anyone who calls some relatives of the parental generation by terms that apply to the biological mother and father is in turn called by all these relatives by terms that apply to biological sons and daughters.

Is one to conclude from the Arapaho kinship terminology that the Arapaho are unaware of the difference between a biological mother (or father) and her sister (or his brother)? Of course not. What it means is that the extension of the Arapaho kinship terms *neisónoo* and *néínoo* from ego's biological parents to additional relatives is paralleled by an extension of ego's behavior toward his or her biological father and mother to all those relatives who are referred to by the same kinship terms. All Arapaho terminological "fathers" and "mothers" have the same obligations toward their terminological "sons" and "daughters" and vice versa, even though opportunities to fulfill them may sometimes be limited by circumstances. Among those "parents" and "children" whose interaction is limited by distance, the emphasis is on extending the relevant attitudes rather than behavior. It is clear that the kinship terminology by which one classifies relatives also governs the type of behavior patterns and attitudes applied to them.

## *Shape, Color, Space*

Several studies indicate that grammatical features may indeed have some influence on memory and nonverbal behavior. Among the best-known studies of this type is the report on an experiment administered to Navajo and white American children by John B. Carroll and Joseph B. Casagrande (1915–1982) in the late 1950s. A speaker of Navajo must choose from among several forms of Navajo verbs of handling according to the shape or some other characteristic of the object being handled—for example, solid roundish (rock), slender and flexible (rope), flat and flexible (cloth), slender and stiff (stick), noncompact (wool), and so on. Even though the use of the appropriate forms is obligatory, the selection operates below the level of conscious awareness on the part of the speakers, and even children as young as three or four make no errors. (In a somewhat similar fashion, in English one *shrugs* one's shoulders and *nods* one's head, and no native speaker would ever use one term for the other.) One of the hypotheses of the investigators was that this feature of Navajo affects the perception of objects and consequently the behavior of speakers.

Ten pairs of objects were used, each pair differing significantly in two characteristics. The 135 Navajo children who took part in the experiment included some who spoke only Navajo, some who were more proficient in Navajo than in English, some who were balanced bilinguals, some who spoke predominantly English, and some who spoke only English. Each of these children was presented with one of the pairs of objects, shown a third object similar to each member of the pair in one characteristic only (for example, a pair represented by a yellow stick and a piece of blue rope of comparable length, with a yellow rope as the third object), and then asked to match one of the paired objects with the third. The matching on the part of the Navajo-dominant children was predominantly on the basis of shape rather than color, this tendency increasing with the age of the child. Among the English-dominant Navajo children, color appeared to be more important among the youngest, but by the age of ten the two groups had almost converged, with the selection dominated by shape.

The performance of white children in the Boston area was more similar to that of the Navajo-dominant than the English-dominant Navajo children. According to the two investigators, this result may be due at least in part to the early and continued play of white children with toys of the form-board variety, stressing form and size rather than color. On the basis of the difference between the Navajo-dominant and English-dominant groups of Navajo children, the investigators concluded:

> The tendency of a child to match objects on the basis of form or material rather than size or color increases with age and may be enhanced by . . . learning to speak a language, like Navajo, which because of the central role played by form and material in its grammatical structure, requires the learner to make certain discriminations of form and material in the earlier stages of language learning in order to make himself understood at all. (Carroll and Casagrande 1958:31)

In general, those examining the relationship between language and culture in recent years have advocated more experimental rigor. They have argued that research concerning this relationship must be comparative, that is, contrast two or more languages, preferably widely differing; that it must use some "external nonlinguistic reality" (stimulus) as a standard for determining by comparison the content of linguistic and cognitive categories; that it must contrast the languages of the respective speech communities to determine how they differ in understanding a common stimulus; and that it must make plain the implication of differences in language for differences in thought between the members of these speech communities (summarized from Lucy 1992a).

For example, some assumptions that notions of space (that is, a three-dimensional area in which events and objects occur and have relative direction and position) are universal—are being reexamined. Stephen Levinson (1996:353) showed that "systems of spatial reckoning and description can in fact be quite divergent across cultures, linguistic differences correlating with distinct cognitive tendencies." More specifically, languages vary in their use of spatial concepts and, in some instances, determine the cognitive categories relating to space concepts; also, the speakers of a number of languages do not use spatial terms corresponding to the bodily coordinates of left-right and front-back. One example comes from the Tenejapa Tzeltal of Mexico: Their language uses no relative frame of reference and therefore has no terms for spatial reference that would correspond to *left*, *right*, *front*, and *back*. Although terms exist for *left hand* and *right hand*, they do not extend to other parts of the body or to areas external to it (Levinson 1996).

## COLOR NOMENCLATURE AND OTHER CHALLENGES TO LINGUISTIC RELATIVITY

As intriguing as the linguistic relativity hypothesis is, it is difficult to test objectively. After all, its claims lie in the realm of subjective experience, and it is hard to get inside people's heads. Early on, it was thought that one of the areas where linguistic relativity might be empirically examined was color. Around the turn of the twentieth century, Franz Boas anticipated much of this later work, stating:

> Differences of principles of classification are found in the domain of sensations. For instance: it has been observed that colors are classified in quite distinct groups according to their similarities, without any accompanying difference in the ability to distinguish shades of color. What we call green and blue is often combined under a term like "gall-color," or yellow and green are combined into one concept which may be named "color of young leaves." In course of time we have been adding names for additional hues which in earlier times, in part also now in daily life, are not distinguished. The importance of the fact that in speech and thought the word calls forth a different picture, according to the classification of green and yellow or green and blue as one group can hardly be exaggerated. (Boas 1938:210)

Color terminologies, then, have been a source of fascination for anthropologists ever since early ethnographers noticed that "non-Western" peoples often have very different ways of dividing up the color spectrum. For instance, some languages, it was found, would blend the colors blue and green under a single term (as Boas noted above); others would break up the English reds using three or four separate names. It was puzzling to find that so natural and neutral a stimulus as the color spectrum could be divided up in hundreds of different ways. Such findings supported the notions of the linguistic relativity hypothesis that the distinctions a language makes are arbitrary, and that there is no a priori way to predict what distinctions a language might, or might not, make.

## *Aspects of Formal Color Nomenclature Theory*

One of the most important—though also somewhat neglected—studies in color was conducted by Eric Lenneberg and John Roberts (Lenneberg and Roberts 1956). Their idea was to use an array of 320 scientifically calibrated color chips—similar to those you might see on display at a hardware store—from *The Munsell Book of Color*, varying in the dimensions of hue and brightness, and put them together in a physical chart. A more modern version, including ten shades of gray on the left, is shown in the following diagram (Stanlaw, Arrigo, and Anderson 2006). You can find the full-color version at the Virtual Anthropology Color Lab (The Mind Project, Illinois State University: http://www.mind.ilstu.edu/curriculum/modoverview.php?modGUI=207).

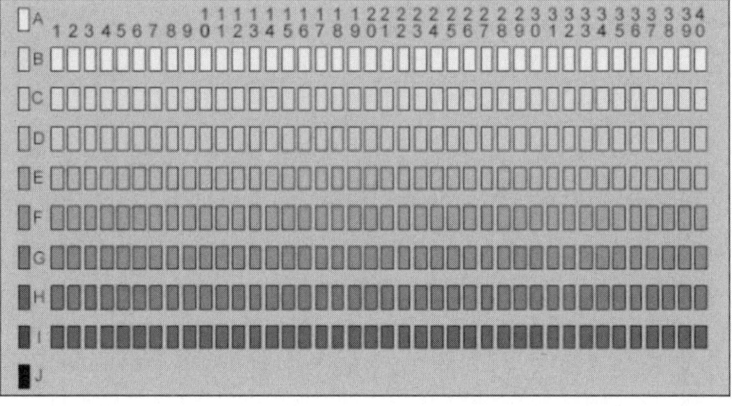

Lenneberg and Roberts worked with the Zuni from the American Southwest and native English speakers and asked them to circle on this chart all the chips of some color category (e.g., "please circle all the *red* colors").

### Zuni Data Supporting Linguistic Relativity

Lenneberg and Roberts immediately found significant differences between the Zuni and English speakers, both in the number of color terms found in each language and in the ranges informants marked off for these color terms. For example, they found that whereas English speakers distinguished *yellow* and *orange* colors—and circled them on the chart as two separate groups—Zuni informants circled all the yellows and oranges together as one group (and gave it a single name). Also, they discovered that for speakers of English, the color categories varied greatly in size (e.g., *red* being very small and *green* being very large). For Zuni speakers, the categories were generally about the same size. Although the main intention of Lenneberg and Roberts was to provide a tool, and a comparable methodology, that could be used for further research, most anthropologists and linguists through the 1960s felt this was sufficient evidence to provide support for the linguistic relativity hypothesis.

### Berlin and Kay's "Basic Color Terms": Refuting Linguistic Relativity

However, two researchers from Berkeley, anthropologist Brent Berlin and linguist Paul Kay (1969, 1991), expanded the Lenneberg and Roberts experiments to twenty languages and examined written materials on seventy-eight others. Both studies revealed several similar findings. For example, although Lenneberg and Roberts found that not every language uses the same color terms—and their number was apparently arbitrary—Berlin and Kay concluded that languages tend to use less than a dozen basic color terms. They also found that the chips chosen by informants to represent the ideal example of a color category (e.g., "Which is the best *red*?") were often quite similar across languages.

The critical theoretical insight made by Berlin and Kay was that color terms need to be operationalized. Many local colors in every language mostly depend on the particulars of the environment, for example, "the color of the so-and-so plant" or this or that animal. Such color terms are useful if everyone in the area is familiar with the particular referent. Every language has thousands of these "secondary color terms" as well, including English (*denim blue*, *fire-engine red*, or *olive green*). But are there some more general abstract colors that all cultures seem to have? It was this question that Berlin and Kay realized needed to be addressed before any real cross-cultural comparisons of color nomenclature could be attempted. They decided to define abstract "basic" terms using the following criteria (1969:5–7):

1. A basic color term should be *monolexemic* and *unanalyzable*. Compounds and terms that are lexically or morphologically modified will not be basic. Thus, "red" and "blue" are basic colors in English, but "reddish," "blue-green," or "light red" are not. Also, a term's meaning should not be predictable from the meaning of its parts (thus excluding such words as "olive green" as basic in English).

2. The meaning of a basic color term should *not be included* in the range of any other term. Thus, because "khaki" is "a kind of brown" it would not be an English basic color term. This means that subsets of colors are not basic colors. "Navy blue" is a kind of blue and therefore not a basic color term in English.
3. The term in question must have *wide applicability*, and not be restricted to any single—or just a few—referents but should exist as an abstract label widely applicable to all objects. Using this criterion, a term such as *blonde* is not basic in English because it usually only refers to hair color. The same applies to *peach*, which generally refers only to the light pink of peaches.
4. The term in question must be *psychologically salient* with respect to the number of speakers who use the term, and the number of occasions it is used. That is, the term must be conspicuous either in terms of frequency of usage or extensive occurrence and acceptability in a speech community. Thus, "sepia" in English would not qualify as a basic color term because it is not well known to all speakers. Common terms such as *white*, *red*, *blue*, and *black* would be.
5. Basic color terms are *consistently productive* using various morphemes in the language. Thus, "red-d*ish*" and "green-*ish*" substantiate the status of "red" and "green" as basic color terms in English because it makes sense to use them. However, the problematic status of "crimson-*ish*" confirms that *crimson* is not a basic term.
6. Terms for basic colors should *not name objects*. Thus, terms such as *gold* or *ash* are not basic color terms in English.
7. Recent foreign *loanwords* are suspect and probably not basic color terms.
8. *Morphological complexity* can be given some weight in determining a lexeme's status, particularly in questionable instances. Basic color terms are the less morphologically complex terms.

A common methodology was now established, as researchers knew what they were looking for to compare: salient abstract colors that had no specific ties to any referent. A list of basic colors would be elicited, and informants then asked, on the Munsell color array, to pick out the one chip that best corresponded to a term (focal color). They would then be asked for the range of each term (e.g., "circle all the chips that you think are *color X*"). Although later work altered the steps somewhat, this general idea has been used for investigating color terms in many studies for the past four decades.

The results of Berlin and Kay's carefully designed experiments were quite surprising, and they stimulated new types of research. In brief, they concluded that:

1. In all languages, there were at least two, but no more than eleven or twelve, color terms that could be considered as basic. Not every language has the same number of basic color terms, though all languages have many sets of culture-specific secondary color terms.
2. These basic color terms label universal perceptual categories ("psychological referents") of which there are probably no more than eleven.
3. These basic color categories are historically encoded in a given language in one of two possible orderings, as shown in the following diagram.

| | | | | | | |
|---|---|---|---|---|---|---|
| | | | | | | pink |
| white | | green --> | yellow | | | and/or |
| and | --> red --> | or | or | --> blue --> | brown --> | orange |
| black | | yellow --> | green | | | and/or |
| | | | | | | purple |
| I | II | III | IV | V | VI | VII |

This last finding is most intriguing and very important. Languages seem to develop color categories in strictly limited ways—in seven steps or stages (as labeled in Roman numerals in the diagram). All languages in the world have at least the terms for *white* and *black* (Stage I). If a language has only three basic color terms (Stage II), these color categories would always cover *white, black*, and *red*. Next is *green* followed by *yellow,* or *yellow* followed by *green* (Stages III and IV). The next terms to appear are *blue*, and then *brown* (Stages V and VI, respectively). At Stage VII, *pink*, *orange*, or *purple* could appear in any order or combination. *Gray* was thought to be a wild card that could appear any time after Stage III.

In the decades since the original Berlin and Kay work (1969), many studies have generally supported their original findings, albeit with some modifications. Today, their account is considered to be the standard model of color nomenclature against which all data and other models are evaluated. Although modified and refined, the universalist arguments of Berlin and Kay have remained principally substantiated for the past forty years.

### *Linguistic Relativity and Gender*

Do grammatical features have any influence on how speakers of a language perceive and categorize the world around them? In some instances they do, at least to some extent, but often the influence is negligible, if any at all. To give just one example, consider grammatical gender. In English the word *teacher* refers to a person who teaches, whether it is a woman or a man. From a pupil's remark "Our teacher is too strict," there is no indication of the teacher's gender, though in subsequent conversation, gender may be disclosed by the use of the teacher's name or the gender-specific personal pronoun (*she* or *he*). Such ambiguity is not so likely to occur, for example, in German, which distinguishes between the masculine form of *teacher* (*Lehrer*) and the feminine form (*Lehrerin*). Similarly, the suffix *-in* in German changes *Arzt* "male physician" to Ärztin "female physician" and *Professor* "male professor" to *Professorin* "female professor." English clearly differs from German in that what is optional in the former is obligatory in the latter. But the claim that this and similar distinctions between the two languages have an influence on the outlook of their speakers would be hard to prove: no one would argue, for example, that sexism is more or less common in countries that speak German, in which the marking of gender is more common (but in these and most other languages, the feminine form is derived from the masculine, as in *lioness* from *lion*, and *Löwin* "lioness" from *Löwe* "lion" in German).

Like some other Indo-European languages, German has three genders—masculine, feminine, and neuter—that for the most part have nothing to do with maleness, femaleness, or absence of sexual characteristics. In German, for example, window (*das Fenster*) is of neuter gender, as are girl (*das Mädchen*) and woman (*das Weib*); blackboard (*die Tafel*) is feminine, as is crowbar (*die Brechstange*); and bosom (*der Busen*) is masculine, as are the season spring (*der Frühling*) and skirt (*der Rock*). Do German-speaking people believe that crowbars and blackboards are feminine in the same way that mother (*die Mutter*) or a woman with whom someone is in love (*die Geliebte*) is? Clearly the answer is no. (However, we will see in Chapter 13 that this question is not as simple as it may appear at first glance, and that perhaps a more nuanced answer is required.)

### *Theoretical and Philosophical Counterarguments to Linguistic Relativity*

It was not only the Berlin and Kay work that discredited various forms of the linguistic relativity and determinism; other experiments, and examples such as grammatical gender above, contribute as well. There are also serious theoretical and philosophical challenges. We mention here eight of the more persuasive counterarguments:

1. *Translatability*. Simply put, translation across languages is possible and occurs every day, even between quite diverse languages. This should not be possible if we are experiencing different "realities." Thus, at least a strong Whorfian position—that speaking different languages causes us to live in different perceptual worlds—is questionable.
2. *Mutual linguistic comprehension*. Likewise, even if we grant the possibility that translations can never completely capture what was said in the original, we can still usually get at least the general idea. And even if we cannot know what it is like to be a Navajo or a Japanese—or to think their thoughts or have their experiences—we can at least entertain the possibility of guessing what another cultural system might be like.
3. *Language and thought*. It is not clear that all thinking is linguistic in nature. For example, Keller and Keller (1998) demonstrated that creating a physical artifact is a very different process than verbally describing it to someone. If this is true, how can Whorfian effects manifest themselves in a nonlinguistic realm?
4. *Multilingualism*. What does the Sapir-Whorf hypothesis say about a person who grows up learning to speak several different languages at the same time? In which "linguistic world" does such a person live? A strong Sapir-Whorfian position does not seem to allow for the possibility of a person being able to go back and forth between two different "realities" depending on the language being spoken. Nor does it seem to allow for some sort of mixed mental structure combining these two or more linguistic worlds.
5. *Language change*. One of the problems of the extreme linguistic determinism of the Sapir-Whorf hypothesis is that of change. Languages and cultures change over time. Both the English and the physics of Newton's day are different from today. How did the replacement of Newtonian physics with the theory of relativity occur? Or did the change come about because of the change in language? Unfortunately, the Sapir-Whorf hypothesis is hard-pressed to answer these questions.

6. *Untestability.* One of the main criticisms leveled against the Sapir-Whorf hypothesis is that it is untestable, and therefore vacuous no matter how intriguing it may sound (Black 1962). Many philosophers of science require that a useful theory be falsifiable—that is, one should be able to state what kinds of evidence would be needed to either support or refute it. Until recently, the possibility of finding experimental evidence for the Sapir-Whorf hypothesis was rare.
7. *Language and perception.* It appears that at least some aspects of perception are beyond the reach of language-influence or interpretation. For example, cross-cultural psychologists found certain basic colors—such as pure "fire engine" red—are easier to remember and recall than other colors, even if a language has no name for them. It is not yet clear if such findings are due to anatomical universals (for example, neurology) or other factors. Whatever the cause, it seems that at least some concepts are not perceptually arbitrary, and some categories—for example, certain vowels and consonants—are more "natural" than others.
8. *Language universals.* Since the 1970s, linguists have—with great success—become increasingly absorbed in the search for those aspects all languages have in common. For example, all languages are spoken in sentences and seem to have some notion of subject versus predicate. Most languages have many sounds in common. The existence of these linguistic universals seems to suggest that languages, and the construction of linguistic categories, may not be as totally arbitrary as Sapir and Whorf have implied. In fact, it was the strength of the universalist arguments by linguists such as Noam Chomsky that led to a gradual decline in interest in linguistic relativity.

## THEORETICAL ALTERNATIVES TO LINGUISTIC RELATIVITY

In the last section we saw that linguistic relativity, at least in unmodified form, is facing some serious challenges. In this section we will look at two theoretical alternatives to linguistic relativity—the commonly accepted universalism of Noam Chomsky, and the approach of cultural determinism (such as proposed by Gary Witherspoon and Daniel Everett).

### *Chomsky and Universalism*

In the mid-twentieth century, the intellectual climate underwent a substantial change in attitude toward languages and their structures. Until the 1950s, scholars were relativists. They were most fascinated by the tremendous linguistic diversity found throughout the world. Non-Western languages had some features that the Indo-European languages did not: time was counted in different ways, and words were found for concepts about which Europeans had no inkling. And in many ways this was a holdover from the days of Franz Boas, who made passionate arguments for relativism, mostly in a valiant attempt to undermine some of the racist claims popular even until World War II. To Boas, a belief in universalism usually led to comparisons that left the non-Western world wanting. And such beliefs were only one small step away from dangerous biological reductionism: Peoples and their languages are the way they are because of their biology (that is, their race).

But in the 1960s, a brilliant young linguist, Noam Chomsky, wrote a series of books and monographs showing that grammar across all the world's languages is very much the same if you examine them thoroughly. Chomsky has made a compelling case that there is much more linguistic similarity in the world than previously thought. But, more important, his so-called transformational grammar movement has swayed the court of scholarly opinion to a rejection of relativism in favor of universalism. Simply put, universalism is the current standard model in many of the social sciences:

> The dominant view among contemporary linguists is that language is primarily an instinct; in other words, that the fundamentals of language are coded in our genes and are the same across the human race. Noam Chomsky has famously argued that a Martian scientist would conclude that all earthlings speak dialects of the same language. Deep down . . . all languages share the same universal grammar, the same underlying concepts. . . . The only important aspects of language, therefore, or at least the only ones worth investigating, are those that reveal language as an expression of innate human nature. (Deutscher 2010:6)

Chomsky turned around some of the questions asked by the early structural linguists. Instead of trying to descriptively analyze sentences that an informant had uttered, Chomsky argued that we needed to find the mental rules that would generate these sentences. Over the course of several decades, Chomsky's formal approaches have gone through several revisions, each refining universalist arguments in more subtle ways. Perhaps Chomsky's most compelling claim for universalism was what he calls the "poverty of stimulus" argument" (1980). According to him, there is simply no way for a child to infer all the complex rules of grammar from mere exposure to its speakers. There must be some knowledge or predispositions already present in the child's brain to enable it to make sense of what it is exposed to. Children, after all, are never really taught their native language.

## *The Claims of Cultural Determinism*

There are several ways to view the relationships between language, thought, and culture. As we have seen, linguistic relativists such as Whorf and Sapir claim that languages influence culture, thought, and perception. Universalists such as Chomsky argue that language is an innate human property and that language, culture, and thought have no connections (except insofar as dictated by the limitations and psychobiological structure of the human mind). We might ask if there are those who argue for **cultural determinism**—where culture determines to a large degree grammatical patterns and modes of thinking. Such claims have been made, and we will examine two cases, the Navajo in the southwestern United States and the Pirahã in South America.

### Controlling the World Through Language Among the Navajo

The Navajo are among the most extensively studied Native American peoples, and the depth of our understanding of Navajo culture is due in large measure to those individuals who were exposed to the culture for an extended period of time. One such person is the anthropologist Gary Witherspoon, who made the Navajo country his home for more than ten years. Prior to his academic career, he worked for Navajo communities and local boards of education and became an interested and concerned participant in the life of the local communities. He learned the Navajo language by listening to Navajos and talking with them.

In *Language and Art in the Navajo Universe* (1977), Witherspoon shared some of the results of his unique experience with the Navajo language and culture. "In the Navajo view of the world," noted Witherspoon (1977:34), "language is not a mirror of reality; reality is a mirror of language." Ritual language in Navajo culture is powerful, its primary purpose being to maintain or restore *hózhǫ́* (the symbol [ ́] marks high tone; ǫ́ is nasalized *o*). Although this word refers to the central theme of Navajo worldview and religious thinking, its use is not restricted to ritual contexts—the word is heard frequently in everyday speech. What is *hózhǫ́*? The stem *-zhǫ́* refers to a state characterized by goodness, peace, order, happiness, blessedness, health, beauty (of the natural surroundings), satisfaction, perfection, well-being, deliberation, care, success, and harmony in one's relations with others (the list is not exhaustive but should serve). The form therefore refers not only to aesthetic but also to moral, emotional, and intellectual qualities, and it is difficult to translate into English by a single word or even a phrase. The verbal prefix *hó-*, which is part of *hózhǫ*, adds to the meaning of the stem the idea of "total environment"—the whole, the general, the abstract, the indefinite, the infinite. As Witherspoon put it, "Navajo life and culture are based on a unity of experience, and the goal of Navajo life—the creation, maintenance, and restoration of *hózhǫ*—expresses that unity of experience" (Witherspoon 1977:154).

### The Immediacy of Experience Among the Pirahã

Linguistic anthropologist Daniel Everett (2005, 2008) has offered some serious formal challenges to Chomskyan universalist grammar. A much-discussed article in *Current Anthropology* that captured the attention of many linguists and anthropologists soon after it appeared was called a "bomb thrown into the party" by the noted psycholinguist Steven Pinker (Colapinto 2007:120).

The Pirahã—as described by Everett (2005)—are one of the most interesting peoples in the linguistic and ethnographic literature. Their language supposedly has no concept of counting or ordinal numbers; few, if any, terms for color; a poverty of kinship terms; no tradition of art or drawing to speak of; and one of the simplest pronoun inventories ever documented. For example, for counting, there appear to be only three terms: *hói* ("small size or amount"), *hoí* ("somewhat larger size or amount"), and *ba-a-gi-so* ("cause to come to together"). A single term, *baíxi*, is applied to both one's biological mother and father, and generally there are no gender distinctions in the Pirahã kinship system.

But it is perhaps culturally that the Pirahã are especially intriguing. They have no tales or creation myths, and their discourse almost always consists of descriptions of immediate experience or interpretations of experience. Stories of the past go back only a few generations. Also, the Pirahã continue to be monolingual in spite of more than two centuries of regular contact with Brazilians and other peoples. In fact, Everett argues that there is striking evidence for the influence of culture on major grammatical features of the Pirahã language. Everett hypothesized that the Pirahã embody a living-in-the-present cultural ethos—an "immediacy of experience" principle (2008:115)—that affects every aspect of the language.

For example, consider the cultural notion *xibipíío*. As a mere gloss, it might translate as "just now," as in someone arriving, but it really encapsulates a condition whereby an entity comes into sight or goes out of sight (2008:128). It delimits a boundary of direct experience: "When someone walks around the bend in the river, the Pirahã say that the person has not simply gone away, but *xibipíío*—'gone out of experience.' They use the same phrase when a candle flickers. The light 'goes in and out of experience'" (quoted in Colapinto 2007:130). Thus, "The Pirahã language and culture are connected by a culture constraint on talking about anything beyond immediate experience. The constraint, as I have developed my conception of it, can be stated as follows: *Declarative Pirahã utterances contain only assertions related directly to the moment of speech, either experienced by the speaker or witnessed by someone alive during the lifetime of the speaker*" (emphasis in the original; Everett 2008:132).

To be sure, Everett has his detractors, as noted in the commentary to the *Current Anthropology* article itself and other places. Best-selling novelist Tom Wolfe, in his recent book on language evolution and the "language wars" surrounding it, talks about the snarky comments Everett attracts (2016:121). He quotes Andrew Nevins, "a young linguist at Harvard" and defender of Chomsky, who said of Everett, "You, too, can enjoy the spotlight of mass media and closet exoticists. Just find a remote tribe and exploit them for your own fame by making claims nobody will bother to check." Says Wolfe: "He couldn't hold it in any longer! Nobody in the used-to-be seemly field of linguistics or any other discipline had ever seen a performance like this before."

Everett, then, questions many of the tenets of the supposed innate structure of universal grammar proposed by Chomsky; but in addition, he also questions a Whorfian approach, arguing in essence that it is culture that dictates how language and thought become manifested rather than that language determines thought, perception, and culture. His work therefore offers different perspectives that universalists and relativists alike might wish to take into account.

## FUTURE TESTS OF LINGUISTIC RELATIVITY AND LINGUISTIC DETERMINISM

In this section we examine a few of the latest experimental findings concerning the Sapir-Whorf hypothesis. We saw that the Berlin and Kay color experiments seemed to cast doubt on the whole enterprise of linguistic relativity. We will see this time, however, that there is also some experimental evidence for the claims of the Sapir-Whorf hypothesis, at least in somewhat weakened forms.

### *Yucatec Mayan and English Number*

John Lucy has examined the Sapir-Whorf hypothesis in several domains other than color. For example, he compared Yucatec (a Mayan language) and American English. The focus of his study has been on the marking of the grammatical category of number (for example, the pluralization of nouns): Is there any correspondence between the grammatical treatment of number and the habitual thought (cognition) of the speakers of Yucatec, on the one hand, and those of American English, on the other?

For example, in English, the marking of the plural is obligatory for numerous "thing" nouns, or countables, such as *child*, *horse*, or *chair*; the only exceptions in nontechnical contexts are mass and abstract nouns, or uncountables, such as *sand*, *water*, *butter*, and *honesty*.

By contrast, speakers of Yucatec mark plural optionally and for a relatively small number of nouns. The two languages also differ fundamentally in the use of numerals. In English, numerals modify a noun, as in *one candle* and *two baskets*. In Yucatec, numerals must be accompanied by a special piece of structure, a classifier, that identifies the counted object as to its material properties, as in *un-tz'íit kib'* "one long thin wax," referring to a candle.

In nonverbal experimental tasks, speakers of English and Yucatec were responsive to the number of objects presented to them according to how the objects were treated grammatically in the respective language. Speakers of English were aware of the number of animate entities and objects but not of the substances represented by mass nouns; speakers of Yucatec were sensitive to number only for animate entities. In classifying three test objects as to which two of the three were more similar (a small cardboard box, a plastic box similar in form, and a piece of cardboard), speakers of English preferred to classify them according to shape (selecting the cardboard box and the plastic box), whereas the speakers of Yucatec preferred to classify them according to material (selecting the cardboard box and the small piece of cardboard). Although Lucy considered his study exploratory in nature, his findings suggest that "language patterns do affect cognitive performance" or, in other words, that "there is good preliminary evidence that diverse language forms bear a relationship to characteristic cognitive responses in speakers" (Lucy 1992b:156, 158).

### *Theoretical Considerations*

We have looked at three ways to describe the relationships between language, culture, and thought. At the risk of oversimplifying, we might summarize them as follows (with the arrow sign meaning "determines," "affects," "predisposes," or "influences," depending on how strong a claim one wants to make):

| *Label* | *Proponents* | *Claim* |
|---|---|---|
| linguistic determinism | Whorf, Sapir, Lucy | language —> culture, thought, perception |
| universalism | Chomsky, Pinker | "thought" —> language, culture, thought |
| cultural determinism | Witherspoon, Everett | culture —> language, thought |

Here, under "thought" for the universalism row, we are actually referring to the psychobiological structures of the human mind. And we should note, too, that probably some of these individuals might not be comfortable being placed in the same pigeonhole on a table. For example, although both Chomsky and Pinker believe that language is innate—a biological instinct—each differs in his view of how this came about. For Pinker (2009), language was an evolutionary adaptation and was selected for by itself. For Chomsky (2010), language was a biological by-product of other evolutionary adaptations and was not necessarily selected for on its own.

Are all these positions irreconcilable? Perhaps not, if we view Sapir and Whorf's position in a more nuanced way. Sapir suggested that the lexicon and syntax of a language might compel a speaker to attend to certain environmental features and presumably pay less attention to others. For example, when using pronouns in English we must know something about the sex of the referent we are talking about, as we have to choose among "he," "she," or "it" when speaking. Another way of stating the Sapir-Whorf hypothesis is this:

- Languages have categories.
- These categories are encoded in linguistic features.
- These linguistic features affect cognition and behavior.

However, what Sapir and Whorf believed was that the most important part of these compulsory linguistic choices was not the particular syntactic feature itself but the categorization that was the underpinning of this feature. But where did these categories come from? Categories are not given to a language out of thin air. They must be motivated and come from somewhere. It is most likely that this underpinning or conceptual framework is largely culturally dependent.

Thus, there is another way of looking at the Sapir-Whorf hypothesis that is often neglected, namely, the cognitive or mental schema that underlie the categories, and ultimately the language itself. Instead of viewing language as modifying perception by way of grammar or vocabulary, another way is to look at the conceptual system that must be underlying it. We see this not as turning the Sapir-Whorf hypothesis around but as extending it. This extended version of the Sapir-Whorf hypothesis, then, might look something like this:

- Culture, society, and environment interact to produce physical-psychological reality.
- People handle this reality through mental models and cultural schemas.
- These mental models and cultural schemas are instrumental in the creation of categories.
- Languages obtain these categories from the above models and schemas.
- Therefore languages have categories.
- These categories are encoded in linguistic features.
- These linguistic features affect cognition and behavior.

The reason we pay attention to an object's sex when speaking English, therefore, is not because we use the word "he," "she," or "it" when choosing a pronoun, but because we know ahead of time that we must be making a gender-based pronoun choice and that we will be looking at the sex of things as we speak. What this means is that we must have a mental construct or schema in our heads for how reality works—in this case, a world where gender is important, indeed so important that it is encoded in our particular language.

Noting that speakers of a particular language might neglect objects or events that speakers of another language normally take into account, John Carroll also restated the hypothesis of linguistic relativity and determinism in a more modest but more acceptable form: "Insofar as languages differ in the ways they encode objective experience, language users tend to sort out and distinguish experiences differently according to the categories provided by their respective languages. These cognitions will tend to have certain effects on behavior" (Carroll 1963:12).

## SUMMARY AND CONCLUSIONS

Today, people from a variety of disciplines are coming together to study some of the most basic problems of humanity: What is the nature of knowledge? What is the nature of thought? How is the mind structured? What, if anything, is innate or biological? What is cultural or environmental? Just what *can* we think about—or can we *not* think about? Linguistic anthropology has much to contribute to these discussions.

There is no question that languages differ—if only superficially, as contemporary universalist linguists would add. But linguists would agree that any nontechnical utterance can be expressed with reasonable accuracy in any language, although usually not on a word-by-word basis. When it comes to technical subjects, some languages have highly specialized terminologies that may be lacking in others—one could hardly expect to give a report on quantum chromodynamics in, say, Hopi. Yet Hopi has specialized areas in its lexicon that are not matched in English. In general, the aspects of any culture that are worked out in some detail receive corresponding attention in the vocabulary of the language so that the speakers of the language can discuss them with ease and accuracy.

Whorf concerned himself with the important question of language-culture dependency, but he overstated his case. Some of his evidence is anecdotal, that is, short and amusing but not necessarily representative of a specific language taken as a whole. One may also wonder how reliable for the purposes of Whorf's illustrations was his Hopi informant, who resided in New York City and must have been nearly or fully bilingual: If the perception of one's environment is affected by the particular language one speaks, then fluency in Hopi and English alike might obscure the contrast between the two. According to Whorf, "the Hopi language contains no reference to TIME, either explicit or implicit" (Whorf 1950:67). Hopi may indeed not have tenses in the same sense that English has (as in *I go, I went, I will go, I had gone*, and so on), but speakers of Hopi are able to refer to the time at or during which an action takes place by using morphemes or words that pertain to such time references as "today, late morning, noon, last night, towards evening, yesterday, tomorrow, day after day, once in a while, from tomorrow on until the next day" and "next year" (Voegelin and Voegelin 1957:24).

We have seen that the breakthroughs of the Berlin and Kay color research established some important universal constraints on the way color categories can operate in a language system and culture. These universal constraints seemed to be so strong—and the evidence presented so overwhelming—that many believed positions such as the Sapir-Whorf hypothesis could be discarded. But we have also found in the experiments discussed in this chapter that there still seems to be much life left in the linguistic relativity hypothesis. Can the two extremes be united, without contradiction? It might be possible.

Sapir was not only a linguist and psychologist but also an anthropologist and poet. He asked questions about the relationships between language, culture, and thought that in many ways were years ahead of their time. The "cognitive anthropology" revolution in America, which began in the mid-1960s, would have disappointed him in several ways. First, many anthropologists simply equated cognitive categories with linguistic categories. The assumption was that if we were looking at language, we were looking at the mind. Second, many anthropologists believed that formal devices such as "elicitation procedures" would ensure cross-informant, cross-researcher, and cross-cultural replicability. Sapir understood that things were not that easy.

Today, linguistic anthropologists are more sophisticated, and most are quite sensitive to such philosophically naive assumptions. So a more nuanced way of viewing the Sapir-Whorf hypothesis does not make the claim that language determines behavior or thought in a simple or reductionist way. What we must consider is where the categories and schema that underlie language come from. That is, there is room for culture in the explanation as well, as Witherspoon and Everett remind us. And we must always remember that "language, culture, and meaning have inextricably contaminated each other" (Hill and Mannheim 1992:382–383).

## RESOURCE MANUAL AND STUDY GUIDE

### Questions for Discussion

1. English kinship terminology, as used by Americans, varies somewhat from person to person. Some kin terms are used by everyone—*father, mother, son, daughter*—whereas other kin terms are not so well understood and therefore not so commonly used—*second cousin, third cousin, first cousin once removed*, and the like. Examine those kin terms that *you* use and determine which distinctive variables they employ (for example, gender, generation level, and relationship by marriage rather than by blood). A hint: the kin term *cousin* applies to both males and females, but *niece* only to females.
2. Benjamin Lee Whorf's articles published at the time of World War II stimulated much interest in the relationship between language and culture, but he overstated his case and in some instances his examples were only anecdotal. Explain and illustrate.
3. Do you agree with the criteria Berlin and Kay proposed regarding basic colors? What is the status of the English term *orange* by these criteria?

### Projects

#### PROJECT 1

*Japanese kinship and pronouns.* In this chapter there were some data presented on the Japanese kinship and pronominal system. It was argued that these "reflect fine nuances of meaning or social distance." Using information given in the chapter, find three examples that show how the Japanese kinship system or its pronominal system reflects social relations in ways other than in English (or some other language). What cultural implications, if any, might this have? How would Sapir or Whorf explain these results? How would Noam Chomsky do so?

#### PROJECT 2

*Relativism versus universalism.* Try to find three arguments that support or refute this statement:

> I would argue that one of the most important things that cognitive science has done in recent years is show that the chasm between relativists (that is, those who focus on linguistic or cultural constraints on the mind) and universalists (those who are more concerned with innate psycho-biological constraints) has now become narrower, if not closed. To put things in other terms, it seems that human beings, and their cultures, can be quite creative and imaginative—almost limitless, it would appear at first glance—but we cannot think about anything without restraint.

How might a linguistic determinist (e.g., Whorf, Sapir, or Lucy), a universalist (e.g., Chomsky), and a cultural determinist (Witherspoon or Everett) respond to your arguments?

### Objective Study Questions

#### TRUE-FALSE TEST

T F 1. Every language in the world basically has the same set of color terms.

T F 2. Cultural determinists believe that environment and culture determine the structure of the human mind.

T F 3. There are no areas in the world where societies have very similar cultures but speak completely unrelated languages.

T F 4. In anthropology, the term *society* always refers to a homogeneous population, that is, a population of uniform ethnic composition.

T F 5. Because the Hopi language—according to Whorf—does not have tenses in the same sense that English does, the Hopis have no way of expressing that something took place last night or is taking place today, or the day after.

T F 6. According to Edward Sapir, easily analyzable words (for example, words that are descriptive [*battleship*, *ironware*]) are more recent than words whose origin is obscure (for example, *hammer*, *horse*).

T F 7. There is very little correlation between the vocabulary of a language and the material culture of the society whose members speak that language.

T F 8. Arapaho kinship makes no distinction between some lineal and some collateral relatives.

T F 9. Gender is not a distinctive component of cousin terminology in English.

**MULTIPLE-CHOICE QUESTIONS**

____ 1. Which of the following is not one of the components of the Sapir-Whorf hypothesis? (A) cultural determinism. (B) linguistic relativity. (C) linguistic determinism.

____ 2. Ego in anthropology refers to: (A) the person of reference to whom others are shown to be related. (B) any person who has an exaggerated sense of self-importance. (C) the oldest male of an extended family.

____ 3. From the point of view of a native speaker of English, a peculiar feature of the Arapaho kinship system is the fact that (A) both ego's father and mother are referred to by the same term. (B) there are no kinship terms comparable to the English aunt and uncle. (C) ego's father's brother's wife is referred to by the same kinship term as ego's mother.

____ 4. One reason English grammar is much easier to learn than the grammars of some of the other major languages spoken in Europe is that (A) the gender of nouns is natural. (B) the personal pronoun of the second person singular (with very few exceptions) has only one form. (C) the subject form of a noun is the same as the direct-object form. (D) All three choices above apply.

____ 5. Which of the following statements would be impossible to defend? (A) For technical subjects, some languages may have highly specialized vocabularies that are lacking in other languages. (B) Major sociopolitical revolutions tend to change profoundly not only the structure of the societies in which they occur but also the structure of the languages spoken by the members of such societies. (C) No correlation has yet been established between certain types of cultures and certain types of languages.

## Answer Key

True-false test: 1-F, 2-T, 3-F, 4-F, 5-F, 6-T, 7-F, 8-T, 9-T
Multiple-choice questions: 1-C, 2-A, 3-C, 4-D, 5-B

## Notes and Suggestions for Further Reading

The citation from Humboldt is from *Wilhelm von Humboldts Werke* (translation by Salzmann). The references to the linguistic affiliation of the Native American languages of the Great Plains are according to Voegelin and Voegelin (1966). For representative selections from the writings of Sapir and Whorf, see Sapir (1949) and Whorf (2012). The Pintupi examples are from Crystal (2010) and the Arapaho examples from Salzmann (1983). The acute accent over an Arapaho vowel marks prominent stress and higher pitch; long vowels are written doubly. For additional discussion of the interrelationships of language and other aspects of culture, see Hoijer (1954);

Fishman (1960); Gumperz and Levinson (1996); Lucy (1992a, 1992b, and 1997); and Pütz and Verspoor (2000). And for a survey of early works on language and worldview and the relevant bibliography, see Hill and Mannheim (1992). John Leavitt (2011) will be a new standard. Goodenough's comment made in 1957 is quoted here from Hymes's reader (1964). For work on color and color nomenclature theory see Kay, Berlin, and Merrifield (1991); Hardin and Maffi (1997); MacLaury (1997); Biggam and Kay (2006); Pitchford and Biggam (2006); MacLaury, Paramei, and Dedrick (2007); and Deutscher (2010). For data from the World Color Survey see Kay, Berlin, Maffi, Merrifield, and Cook (2009).

For an entertaining review of the current controversy over Daniel Everett's dispute with Chomsky, see Wolfe (2016). Everett's own case, made accessible to a popular audience, can be found in Everett (2008 and 2012). The debate over the Sapir-Whorf hypothesis continues. A historical summary of its theoretical development is found in Lee (1996). Current thinking finds McWhorter (2014) coming out nay, with Taylor (2016) and Deutscher (2010) siding with yea.

# 13

# Language, Identity, and Ideology I: Variations in Gender

## LEARNING OBJECTIVES

- Describe the characteristics that supposedly mark women's language as special
- Identify examples of men's and women's speech from several cultures
- Identify and compare the various theories of women's language
- Understand the relationship–if any–between grammatical gender and biological gender
- Understand the linguistic practices of LGBTQI communities and individuals

In any particular speech community, differences in language are readily apparent. These differences can be based on context and situation, as we have seen in previous chapters. In Chapter 9, in the discussion of dialects, we saw how geography can also be a factor in differentiating people's speech. There are also variations based on "properties" of people, including things like one's age or generation, social status or economic class, "race" or ethnicity, and nationality or citizenship. In this chapter we will examine some of the complex interactions of gender and language. (We discuss the other factors in the next chapter.)

Of course such discussions by their very nature are always going to be somewhat artificial because it is impossible to isolate these factors. First, nobody is just one thing, and these properties are generally continuums. Second, we must remember that people do not always choose the speech variety that will bring them the most benefit in any given social situation. Sometimes people may be quite aware of this—such as when students in a classroom maintain their informal street vernacular in order to keep up their image or "cred" among their peers. Or maybe I want to maintain my foreign accent in order to show my allegiance to my family and homeland. We and our in-group often have certain expectations about how we should talk. But again, as Sapir noted when he described the habitual use of language (as seen in Chapter 12), at other times it may be hard for us to even notice how our use of language is determined by our individual background and experience. We might not always be aware of how our speech variety "sounds" to others around us. Does our "normal" speech make us appear educated or uneducated, smart or unintelligent, clever or pretentious, experienced or naïve, rich or poor? Such questions deal with language ideology: the beliefs held by people in a community regarding their conceptualization of the nature and function of language. In other words, language ideology is the mediating link among social structure, **language variety**, and forms of speech.

In this chapter we examine language and gender, a big topic on which thousands of books have been written. In this overview, we will start by looking at the social and biological aspects of "gender" and "sex." We will then examine the relationship—if any—between grammatical gender and biological gender. We will then ask if women and men speak differently—and if so, what these differences are, and whether they are the same across cultures. We will then examine some theories about language and gender that have been proposed to explain how and why men and women speak differently. We then return to some of the issues brought up in Chapters 11 and 12: Does grammatical gender have an effect on thinking? Conversely, do speakers of languages that are more gender-neutral experience the world in different ways than those whose languages are highly marked for gender? We then ask if language, gender, and power are related, and, if so, should we take steps to make language more gender-neutral? We then turn to language use in gay subcultures. We end with a cautionary note, noticing that although language gender differences are exciting topics enthusiastically embraced in the popular media, perhaps these differences are not as pronounced in the ways they are often presented.

## "GENDER" VERSUS "SEX"

Before we begin a discussion on gender and language, we need to address the distinction that is often made between **gender** and sex. Because sex roles vary from culture to culture, and time and place, how any given male or female might behave is predicated upon numerous cultural expectations, biological options, and individual personalities. Thus, social scientists often restrict the use of the term *sex* to a person's biological physiology, while using *gender* to refer to someone's social or cultural identity as a male or female.

But the simplistic equations "sex = biology" and "gender = culture" are fraught with many problems and inconsistencies (Ahearn 2012:189). First, though it may seem natural and obvious to place a person in either male or female categories, "intersexed" individuals are more common than is often assumed. By some estimates, at least 1 percent of the human population has some degree of anatomical or hormonal sexual ambiguity (http://www.isna.org/faq/frequency). How such persons live their lives varies greatly. Some people may decide to undergo anatomical or social reassignment, through surgery, dress, or other means. The term **transgender** is often used to describe the condition in which a person's social gender identity does not match the person's assigned biological sexual identity. But it should be pointed out that transgenderness does not necessarily imply any preconceived sexual or romantic attraction a person might have—heterosexual, homosexual, bisexual, or otherwise. **Sexual orientation** is something different. It ranges along a continuum from exclusive attraction to the opposite sex to exclusive attraction to the same sex. Although "straight" is generally taken as the default role, gay people—and most scientists—point out that sexual orientation is probably not a lifestyle choice but rather the result of a complex interaction of genetic, hormonal, and environmental influences. Therefore, we may need to add a third variable to the "sex = biology" and "gender = culture" equations mentioned previously: "sexual identity." But this once again shows how oversimplified this dichotomy is.

This dichotomy suggests that "gender" is something built upon a set of cultural and social practices that "amplify, simplify, and give meaning to perceived or actual biological differences" (Ahearn 2012:190). Gender is a social construct that is likely to vary from one society to the next, or even from one social group to another within a society or culture. Here we are concerned with the concept of gender as a status ascribed to certain individuals or groups by members of a particular culture or society. For us, some pertinent questions are: Do members of a community differentiate gender in their speech behavior? If so, what forms does this differentiation take, under what culturally authentic circumstances does it occur, and does it have any effect on the nonverbal behavior of a society's members? To what extent is any differentiation of gender in speech the result of socialization, and, more specifically, how does the expression of gender in speech relate to such aspects of social identity as ethnicity, "race," age, and socioeconomic class? Under what circumstances do men and women interact as equals (or nearly so), and under what circumstances do they not?

## GRAMMATICAL VERSUS BIOLOGICAL GENDER

Even if you have never studied linguistics or a foreign language, you are probably aware that many languages make distinctions that are clearly based on biology. This is common in lexical elements like pronouns (e.g., she, hers versus he, his) and nouns (e.g., Latina and Latino in Spanish, or French *chat* for "male cat" and *chatte* for "female cat"). But many languages also make distinctions based on **grammatical gender**. That is, words fall into certain classes or categories—generally exclusively—based on some property or feature assigned to them.

We should mention here that the origin of the word *gender* comes from the Latin "genus" ("class" or "sort"). So in linguistics, gender refers to a grammatical category based on certain properties a word has, including—but hardly restricted to—the common "masculine," "feminine," and "neutral" genders found in some Indo-European languages. And even then, in Indo-European languages these assignments are often arbitrary. For example, in German "knife" (*das Messer*) is neutral, "fork" (*die Gabel*) is feminine, and "spoon" (*der Löffel*) is masculine. Common kinds of gender classes include "masculine versus feminine," "masculine versus feminine versus neutral," and "animate versus inanimate," though many others actually exist. For example, George Lakoff titled his well-known book on cognition *Women, Fire, and Dangerous Things* (1987), based on the four gender classes found in the Australian language Dyirbal: *bayi* (human males and animals), *balan* (women, fire, dangerous things, water, fighting), *balam* (nonflesh foods), and *bala* (all other nouns). Although uncommon, some languages, such as Bantu in Africa, can have more than a dozen gender classes. For example, Ganda has sixteen, Lozi has eighteen, and Venda has twenty.

The consequence of a word being in a particular gender category is that it is required to match or co-occur with other grammatical categories such as number or case. For example, in Spanish, gender agreement is required between nouns and definite articles (as in *la muchacha*, "the girl" versus *el muchacho*, "the boy"), where feminine definite articles (*la*) must precede feminine nouns and masculine definite articles (*el*) must precede masculine nouns. There is no direct mapping of biological sex or social gender onto grammar or thought, however. It is unlikely that Germans conceptualize forks as having female characteristics, or spoons as somehow being male, just because these nouns are "feminine" and "masculine," respectively. Nonetheless, it is still an empirical issue whether or not grammatical gender affects thought and behavior, or if grammatical gender categorizations are arbitrary. We return to this question later in this chapter.

## DO MEN AND WOMEN SPEAK DIFFERENTLY?

Although we may not always think about it, we are well aware that men and women perform the act of speaking differently. We would probably disagree if someone argued otherwise, even if we could not readily find examples to the contrary. In everyday popular culture we find all kinds of instances, at least in North America. Books such as *Men Are from Mars, Women Are from Venus: The Classic Guide to Understanding the Opposite Sex* (Gray 2012) and *You Just Don't Understand: Women and Men in Conversation* (Tannen 2007) are perennial bestsellers, spawning whole cottage industries of sequels, talk-show rounds, and workshops. On afternoon television, it is almost assumed by default that compared to women, men are either the strong and silent type or emotionally arrested children unable to adequately express themselves—depending on the show. Sometimes "sensitive New Age men" who try to show some sympathy for women's issues or communicate effectively are ridiculed as being overemotive or unmanly. These are generalizations, of course, but it shows that people are quite aware that men and women can speak quite differently and apparently often do.

### *Gender and Speech in American Society*

In American English, some differences have been noted in intonational patterns between male and female speakers. If one analyzes intonational contours as four relative pitch levels, then men tend to use only three, hardly ever reaching the highest one. Consider, for example, how men and women say the phrase "Oh, that's terrible!" Women's range frequently includes all four. Among the contours very rarely heard from men is the full downglide from the highest to the lowest pitch level, as when expressing surprise, excitement, concern, and the like. In general, women's speech appears to be more dynamic, making greater use of paralinguistic features and extending over a broader pitch range.

Some of these differences in gender can be seen at an early age. For example, in a sample of children in a semirural New England village studied by Fischer (1958), the girls were more likely to pronounce the present-participle suffix *-ing* [iŋ] more "correctly" than the boys, who more frequently used the *-in'* [in] form.

#### **Vocabulary and Word Choice**

Scholars have described a variety of other gender differences in speech, as the choice of words used by men and women varies according to the occasion, the type of audience present, and various other circumstances. Profane or coarse speech is less likely to be heard when children or people held in respect are within earshot, and a job interview calls for a more considered vocabulary than a casual conversation between two close friends. Nevertheless, some lexical differences between the speech of men and women are fairly common and can be illustrated from American English. Certain words are used by women much more frequently than by men. Among such words are expressive adjectives that convey approval or admiration—for example, *delightful, spectacular, charming, divine, lovely, fascinating,* and *sweet*—and fashionable color names—for example, *beige, chartreuse, fuchsia, magenta,* and *mauve.*

Men are much more likely to phrase their approval or liking for something by using a neutral adjective, such as *fine, good,* or *great,* and reinforcing it, if necessary, with such an adverb as *damn,* as in "That was a damn good show." As a rule, men's color vocabulary is much less discriminating, and hence somewhat poorer, than women's. But in the United States, differences between men's and women's word choices seem to be steadily growing smaller. For example, until a decade ago, *sweet* and *awesome* were slang terms exclusively used by young women, but now these adjectives are commonly used by both genders. And profanities are now casually used by many young women whose mothers and grandmothers not only would never have uttered them but would probably have been embarrassed even to hear them. Nonetheless, on the whole, as several authors have noted, in careful speech women are likely to use fewer stigmatized words than are men.

### Tag Questions

One of the characteristics of women's speech—particularly of older women—is the use of a "tag question" in certain contexts. The term refers to a question attached to an utterance to obtain the assent of the addressee, as in "*That was a silly thing for them to do, wasn't it?*" Seeking confirmation or validation of a statement may indicate the speaker's desire to avoid assertiveness. A "tag" in the form of a question may also be attached to an order or a criticism to soften it, as in "*Answer the phone, would you?*" or "*You are drinking a bit too much, don't you think?*" Another purpose of the tag question is to include the person spoken to in friendly conversation by offering the opportunity to respond, as in "*It's a beautiful day, isn't it?*" Today, younger women use tag questions much less frequently. When men use tags, they do so to obtain or confirm information, as in "*To get this work done, I would have to leave the car here until sometime tomorrow, wouldn't I?*" On the subject of tag questions, some scholars have argued that "a more sophisticated view of the complexity of both linguistic and social behaviour" is needed (Cameron, McAlinden, and O'Leary 1988:92).

### Hedges

Another way women may try to avoid assertiveness is to use so-called hedge words or phrases, such as *maybe, rather, perhaps, I guess, sort of, I am wondering,* and others. A sentence using a hedge word may even be combined with a tag question, as in the first of the following examples: "*You are rather tired, aren't you?*"; "*I have been kind of wondering if I should go*"; "*Well, I guess I might have been right*"; and "*Maybe we could try adding some seasoning.*" Once again, young American women tend to use less of this type of speech behavior or to be free of it altogether.

### Other Alleged Differences

Other differences between the speech behavior of men and women have been suggested. For example, some investigators found that when women talk with other women on a social basis, favored topics are relationships, social issues, house and family, the workplace, and personal and family finances. When men talk with other men, the favored topics have been work, recreation and sports, and women. In other studies of speech behavior, women interviewees were found to be more cooperative and polite and offered more information than did men.

With respect to any society, the following issues may be considered: what counts as a *turn* (rotation of speakers) in a discourse, how turns and interruptions are handled, to what extent culture-specific gender differences may be overridden by culture-specific socioeconomic and other hierarchies, what cues male and female speakers use to allocate turns, and so on. In short, important as the male-female distinction may be in a particular society, one should never assume that it is the only, or the main, criterion for how the various aspects of communicative behavior are chosen and employed.

Some scholars have approached the topic of speech behavior of the genders with the view that women's language reflects men's dominance over them. They note that in American society men tend to control conversations. Furthermore, their talk is usually blunt (sometimes even tough), straight, and colloquial in style. Others have pointed out that women are usually better conversationalists, raising the level of discourse by striving for more harmonious relations with their face-to-face interactants.

To sum up, in American English there are no pronunciations, grammatical forms, words, or sentence constructions that are employed exclusively by men or by women. Rather, what differences there are between male and female speech have to do with the *frequency* with which some usages are employed by one sex or the other and the use of certain lexical items. That these differences are decreasing rather than maintaining themselves or growing is an indication that long-standing social differences between women and men are in the process of breaking down.

## Gender and Speech in Japan

Perhaps one of the most famous examples of how women and men speak differently in Japanese is found in the classic overview of the language by one of the West's leading scholars of Japanese historical linguistics, Roy Andrew Miller. Here in translation is an excerpt he gives of a conversation between two women about a garden (1967: 289–290):

A: *My, what a splendid garden! The lawn is so nice and big, it certainly is wonderful, isn't it[?]*

B: *Oh no, not at all. We don't take care of it anymore, so it simply doesn't look as nice as we would like it to.*

A: *Oh, not at all. It is just because it is such a big garden that it is so hard to take care of by yourself. Still, . . . it always looks beautiful every time someone sees it.*

B: *Oh no, not at all.*

This same discussion by two Japanese men might come out something like this:

*A: Pretty garden, eh?*
*B: Yeah.*

As Miller suggests, the dialogue between these two women was in every sense a special kind of discourse. The conveying of information is less important than the way it is said, the feelings that are exchanged, and the emphatic communication taking place. At the same time, "Japanese men would not carry on in this way about anything, particularly about gardens" (1967, 290). To be sure, Miller has been accused of exaggerating, and this example is indeed perhaps a bit skewed. Nonetheless, it certainly captures assumptions that many have about how women's and men's speech can be quite different in Japanese. In fact, it is often claimed that Japanese is one of the world's languages that shows remarkable linguistic sexual dimorphism, and many books have been written about this (e.g., Takahashi 2013; Takemaru 2010; Inoue 2006; Okamoto and Shibamoto Smith 2004).

### Sentence Final Particles as Gender Markers in Japanese

One of the most conspicuous features of the Japanese language is the use of **sentence-final particles**—markers that come at the end of sentences to indicate things like mood, intent, and identity. There are literally dozens of them, as well as many regional and dialectal variants. The frequent *ne* is roughly a tag-question marker asking for the listener's confirmation (similar to " . . . , right?" in English). This particle also carries with it an attempt to soften requests and generally to solicit empathy and agreement from the listener. As one might expect, this particle is used more often by women than men, whereas assertive sentence-final particles like *-yo* (similar to " . . . , I tell you!) are more commonly used by men. Some particles, like *-wa*, really reflect little except to indicate that a female is speaking. Sentence-final particles are conspicuous and unambiguous markers of gender.

### Honorifics and Polite Language

The Japanese language is noted for having an extremely complex system of honorifics to indicate in various ways differing degrees of politeness, formality, humility, distance, and hierarchy (e.g., Wetzel 2004; Mizutani and Mizutani 1987; O'Neill 1966; Niyekawa 1991). Consider the following Japanese sentences:

| | | | |
|---|---|---|---|
| *Are-ga* | *toshokan* | *da-yo.* | informal |
| *Are-ga* | *toshokan* | *desu.* | polite |
| *Are-ga* | *toshokan* | *de gozaimasu.* | more polite |
| "there" | "library" | "is" | |

All translate grammatically as "That's the library over there" but differ from top to bottom in formal level of politeness. Notice the level of politeness (underlined) is expressed in the different forms of the verb "is." In general, Japanese differs from English in that, in Japanese, politeness is encoded in the grammar, whereas in English it is generally encoded in words or phrases. Polite forms in Japanese are rather complex and appear in many grammatical forms, usually with more levels than those mentioned above. But the sociolinguistic consequence is that in most contexts women should always use more polite speech than men. If they do not, there are likely to be social consequences (e.g., giving offense, insulting someone, or sounding unfeminine).

There are numerous other ways to be courteous in Japanese. For instance, the prefix *o-* or *go-* can be attached to many nouns or adjectives to create polite expressions. These generally reflect politeness to the addressee. Some examples are *o-genki* ("health") and *go-kekkon* ("marriage"). Again, women are expected to use these forms more frequently than men. There are even whole sets of nouns that women tend to almost always use, regardless of whether or not they are being polite. These include many domestic items. For instance:

| | |
|---|---|
| *o-hashi* | "chopsticks" |
| *o-sushi* | "sushi" |
| *o-senbei* | "rice crackers" |
| *o-bentō* | "lunch box" |
| *o-tofu* | "tofu" |
| *o-shōgatsu* | "New Year's Day" |

Men and women can even have different sets of terms, at least in certain domains and the more colloquial registers. Examples of this are shown in Table 13.1.

Honorifics, humble forms, and other markers of politeness abound in Japanese, and these can reflect subtle and fine nuances of meaning or social distance. But there are also special sets of terms that can show particular attitudes toward women in Japanese. There are many "wife" terms, and each conveys special shades or details; no two are quite the same. That this is so, of course, can be seen in the component characters that make up these terms. (Note, however, that Sino-Chinese character compounds are not precisely "syntactic" in the sense that, say, the pair of characters for "house" and "inside" together do not necessarily make up the phrase "the one who is inside the house"). Although the history of Sino-Japanese characters is complex, some emotional connotations and attitudes are likely revealed by their examination. In fact, it has been argued (Stanlaw 1992) that a loanword such as the common term *waifu* entered the language precisely to avoid some of the social baggage carried by these other terms.

## *Gender and Speech in Some Native American Societies*

In Native American languages, differences between the speech of men and women are fairly common. Some are morphophonemic (that is, some morphemes of a language have a slightly different phonemic shape when used by women or by men), whereas others are lexical (sometimes men and women use different words for the same thing or concept).

### Koasati

Among the languages in which certain morphemes have a different phonemic shape depending on whether women or men are speaking is Koasati, a Muskogean language spoken in southwestern Louisiana. According to Haas (1944), the speech of middle-aged and older Koasati women in the late 1930s differed from that of men in certain indicative and imperative verb forms. Because in a few instances the speech of women appeared to be older and more basic, Haas described the men's forms as derived from the women's forms. For example, verb forms ending in a nasalized vowel—such as ą·in *lakawwą*—"he will lift

**TABLE 13.1** SOME DIFFERENCES OF USAGE BETWEEN MEN AND WOMEN FOR SELECTED TERMS IN JAPANESE

| | *Men* | *Women* | *Both* | *Dictionary Form* |
|---|---|---|---|---|
| stomach | *hara* | *o-naka* | *o-naka* | *o-naka*<br>*fukubu* |
| meal | *meshi* | *go-han* | *shokuji* | *meshi*<br>*go-han*<br>*shokuji* |
| delicious | *umai* | *oishii* | *oishii* | *umai*<br>*oishii* |
| flatulence | *he* | *o-nara* | *o-nara* | *o-nara* |
| money | *kane* | *o-kane* | *o-kane* | *kane*<br>*o-kane* |
| toilet | *benjo* | *o-tearai*<br>*toire* | *tearai* | *o-tearai* |
| eat! | *tabero* | *tabete* | *tabena* | *tabenasai* |
| get up! | *okiro* | *okite* | *okina* | *okinasai* |

**Note:** **"Dictionary form" is what is found in most dictionaries and is a rough measure of politeness or formality. These differences in usage are not always strictly enforced, and some of these forms are colloquial.**

it [woman speaking]," add an s after the corresponding oral vowel, yielding *lakawwa̜·s* "he will lift it [man speaking]." Similarly, the women's word *lakawhôl* "lift it! [addressed to second-person plural]" yields the men's form *lakawhós*. In other instances, a vowel is lengthened, and the final *n* becomes an *s*, and in still others the men's form simply adds an *s* to the form occurring in women's speech (see Table 13.2, based on Haas 1944:144). One may summarize the changes at the end of certain Koasati verb forms as follows: W = women's form, M = men's form, v = any vowel, v́ = high pitch, v̂ = falling pitch, v̜ = nasalized vowel, C = any consonant, and (·) = short or long:

| W | M |
|---|---|
| v̜(·) | v (·)s |
| v̂l | ·s |
| v̂n | v̂·s |
| v(·)C | v(·)Cs |
| v(·)CC | v(·)CCs |

Haas further reported that in telling traditional narratives, Koasati women used men's forms when quoting male characters, and conversely.

### Atsina

For the language of the Atsina (also referred to as Gros Ventre) of Fort Belknap Reservation in north central Montana, now spoken by a rapidly decreasing number of tribal members, we have both fairly recent information (Allan Taylor 1994) and an account from

**TABLE 13.2** EXAMPLES OF MEN'S AND WOMEN'S FORMS OF SPEECH IN KOASATI

| *Women's Form* | *Men's Form* | *English Gloss* |
|---|---|---|
| lakáw | lakáws | "he is lifting it" |
| lakáwwitak | lakáwwitaks | "let me lift it" |
| mól | móls | "he is peeling it" |
| lakáwwilit | lakáwwilits | "I lifted it" |
| í·p | í·ps | "he is eating it" |
| ta·ł | ta·łs | "he is weaving it" |
| tačílw | tačílws | "you are singing" |
| iltolí·hn | iltolí·hns | "we are not working" |
| mí·sl | mí·sls | "he is blinking" |

1945 (Flannery 1946). According to Taylor, before the vowels *i*, *e*, and *a*, men often use the sound č (as in the word *church*), where women have a k-sound; for example, ʔanáákyaaʔ "buffalo bull" in the speech of women would be ʔanááčaaʔ in men's speech. In addition to differences in pronunciation, Flannery mentioned lexical differences—the use of two completely different words having the same meaning, depending on the sex of the speaker. Of interest are some of her findings concerning the attitudes of the Atsina toward gender differences in speech:

> A much older woman said that if a member of either sex "talked like the other" he or she was considered bisexual. This she illustrated by telling of the mortification suffered by the parents of a boy who persisted in acting like a girl in every way. The boy's mother was so sensitive that "she never went about and she just bowed her head in shame when her son was heard talking like a woman." It is recognized, however, that one Gros Ventre man who at present uses woman's pronunciation and expressions does so because he had the misfortune of having been reared in a household consisting of women only. (Flannery 1946:135)

## Other Cases of Differences Between Women's and Men's Speech

Boas, whose anthropological fieldwork was initiated among the Inuit (Eskimo), reported (Boas 1911:79) that the men of some groups pronounced the final consonants *p*, *t*, *k*, and *q* (a back velar stop) quite distinctly, but that the women substituted for these four sounds the corresponding nasals *m*, *n*, ŋ, and ṅ (a back velar nasal). He added that in some dialects the men adopted the women's pronunciation, favoring the female speech forms.

A few lexical differences between male and female speech have been recorded for the Pueblo peoples of the Southwest—specifically among the Hopi of the Third Mesa; the Arizona Tewa; and the Tiwa, Laguna, and Acoma of New Mexico. With the exception of the Hopi words, some formal similarity appears to exist between the two gender forms. It is interesting that the languages listed above belong to three different language families (Uto-Aztecan, Kiowa-Tanoan, and Keresan). We may be dealing here with an areal feature. Although the number of gender-specific pairs of words is small, they occur in kinship terminology according to the sex of the ego, as well as in responses given during ceremonial observances, and they must therefore be judged as culturally significant (Kroskrity 1983; Sims and Valiquette 1990).

An interesting case was reported in 1912 by Alexander F. Chamberlain. According to him, the men's language of the Caraya, a people of eastern Brazil, differs from the women's language by the addition or change of a consonant. If the information is correct, this is another of the relatively rare cases in which men's forms are derived from women's forms.

Douglas Taylor (1951) reported on a more complex situation in Central American Carib, a modern dialect of Island Carib. Two genders, masculine and feminine, are distinguished in this dialect. Gender is in part natural (assigned as a rule in accordance with the sex of a living thing), in part grammatical (for example, the words for *sun*, *milk*, *river*, and *maize* are masculine, whereas those for *star*, *liver*, *knife*, and *snake* are feminine). However, words denoting qualities, states, actions, and the equivalent of the pronoun *it* in such English sentences as "it is raining" tend to be assigned to the feminine gender by men but to masculine by women. The equivalent of "the other day," for example, is *ligíra buga* when said by women but *tugúra buga* when said by men (buga is a past tense particle).

Such differences as those described thus far are found the world over. For example, in North Africa, Arabs who speak French as a second language articulate the French (r) according to the speaker's gender: In men's speech it is an apical consonant (produced with the tip of the tongue serving as the active articulator); in women's speech it is a uvular consonant (made by the back of the tongue with the aid of the uvula). Because both of the (r)s occur and are phonemically distinct in the Arabic dialects native to these people, the two variants are easily pronounceable by men and women alike. According to a survey of French dialects by Henriette Walter (1988), North African men would now prefer to approach the contemporary French norm, which happens to be the uvular *r*, [R]. What prevents them from doing so is a fairly rigid convention, according to which the uvular articulation of *r* in North African French is a social characteristic of women.

## GENDER AND LANGUAGE: THEORETICAL MOVEMENTS

Perhaps the first modern linguist who theorized on language and gender was Otto Jespersen, in his famous book *Language: Its Nature, Development, and Origin* (1922). But the name of the germane chapter ("The Woman") reflects the attitude of the time. Jespersen, though he tried to seriously examine how women and men spoke in various languages, ended up saying some things that in retrospect sound incredibly silly. He believed that women's language developed because of their "almost exclusive concern with the care of the children, cooking, brewing, baking, sewing, washing, etc., things which for the most part demanded no deep thought, which were performed in company and could well be accompanied with a lively chatter. Lingering effects of this state of things are seen still" (1922:254). Thus even today women talk more than men; leave sentences half-finished; use adverbs, adjectives, and hyperbole excessively; avoid "gross and coarse expressions"; and have a "preference for veiled and indirect expressions" (p. 246). "Men will certainly with great justice object that there is a danger of the language becoming languid and insipid if we are always to content ourselves with women's expressions. . . . Men thus become the chief renovators of language, and to them are due those changes by which we sometimes see one term replace an older one, to give way in turn to a still newer one, and so on" (p. 247). Unfortunately, such claims for the most part went unchallenged for some fifty years.

In the last quarter of the twentieth century, the study of language and gender really became recognized as a discipline in its own right (or a subdiscipline of linguistics, sociolinguistics, or linguistic anthropology). Historically, the field has often been viewed as being shaped by three major paradigms or frameworks: deficit theory, difference theory, and dominance theory. In actuality, there have always been more approaches than these, and viewing things only through these three lenses is essentialist and myopic (cf. Eckert and McConnell-Ginet 1992, 2013; Henley and Kramarae 1991). And current research has gone beyond work in just the three "big Ds." In this section we will discuss a variety of historic and current approaches that have been used to examine gender and language, though of course this oversimplifies things because there is much overlap, and not every research project fits nicely in a heuristic pigeonhole.

### *Deficit Theory*

In brief, deficit theory views women's language as deficient or ineffective in comparison to men's language and explains "women's manner of speaking as being a reflection of women's insecurity and powerless place in society" (Freed 2003:701). In the mid-1960s and early 1970s, when phonological differences as markers of social class were being investigated by William Labov and his students (as described in the next chapter), Labov also suggested that gender might be marked in a similar fashion. Probably the most influential work at that time was Robin Lakoff's *Language and Women's Place* (1975). She found not only phonological differences but also subtle differences in lexicon and syntax. Compared to men, she found that women demonstrated a

greater use of tag questions (" *. . . , right?*"; " *. . . don't you think?*")
greater use of polite forms ("*If you don't mind, could you . . .* ")
greater use of wh- words ("*Why don't we go to the store*?")
greater use of hedges ("*I kinda like it*")
greater use of qualifiers ("*I think that might be true*")
greater use of apologies ("*Sorry to bother you, but . . .* ")
greater use of intensifiers ("*That's so so adorable*!")
greater use of certain "women's vocabulary" (e.g., colors)
greater use of modal auxiliaries ("*We ought to/should/might . . .* ")
wider range of intonation ("*That dress JUST looks SO adorable on you! . . .* ")
greater use of adjectives expressing admiration ("*She wore a divine dress*")
greater use of euphemisms ("*I'm going to the bathroom and powder my nose*")

greater use of diminutive forms or reduplication (*itsy bitsy*)
less use of swear words or profanity ("*Darn it, all!* . . . ")
less use of threats and insults
less acute sense of humor

In some ways, Robin Lakoff's approach was a nuanced response to Jespersen, who in essence argued that male language is the norm, and female language is an—often failed—attempt to emulate it. Lakoff's work began at a time when the feminist movement in the United States was gaining strength, and her book was widely read in both popular and academic circles. Much of her evidence, however, was from "introspection" (1975:4)—a common technique used by Chomsky and others at the time (see Chapter 2)—which led many to question her generalizations like those listed above. Nonetheless, the book broke new ground, and it inspired many subsequent studies empirically testing her claims.

### *Difference Theory/Subculture Theory*

**Difference theory**—or **subculture theory**—argues that men and women live in different linguistic worlds basically because they live in different subcultures. "[W]omen and men use specific and distinct verbal strategies and communicative styles which were developed in same-sex childhood peer groups" (Freed 2003:701). Subculture theory claims that the social lives of women lie in a subculture somewhat apart from the mainstream. Women and women's language are marked as different from men and men's language. As we will see in a later section, this is why we find certain marked terms for women, such as *actress*, *waitress*, *woman*, *bachelorette*, and *female*, derived from the masculine forms. In other words, men's language is thought to offer the normative forms from which women's terms are derived.

The linguist Deborah Tannen is perhaps the most notable proponent of the subculture theory, and she advocated this notion in a series of professional and popular best-selling books such as *You Just Don't Understand: Women and Men in Conversation* (2007), *Talking from Nine to Five: Men and Women at Work* (1994b), and *That's Not What I Meant! How Conversational Style Makes or Breaks Your Relations with Others* (1986). Tannen calls gender-associated varieties of language **genderlects**. According to Tannen, each gender has different means of accomplishing conversational goals, and perhaps ultimate ends as well. The goal for men in communication is to send factual information, which Tannen calls the *report style*. On the other hand, women want to build and maintain relationships among participants in the conversations, which she calls the *rapport style*. "Researchers who adhered to this framework believed that by focusing on language difference instead of power difference (or male dominance), the antagonistic comparison between women and men could be avoided and the positive values of each language style could be celebrated" (Freed 2003:701). Nonetheless, many felt that power differentials should be at the theoretical forefront.

### *Dominance Theory/Social Power Theory*

**Dominance theory**—or **social power theory**—focuses on patriarchy and male power. Researchers using dominance theory characterize the "social and political arrangement between the sexes as one in which women were viewed and treated as unequal to men because the norms of society" have been established by men; the "division of labor between women and men was seen to include a division of language practices, one belonging to the powerful and the other belonging to women" (Freed 2003:701). Language differences, then, are manifestations of an unequal social structure, wherein men and women do not compete on a level playing field of economic opportunity, access to social perks, or influence.

Social power theory goes back to the 1980s, when William M. O'Barr and Bowman K. Atkins (1998) studied how witnesses speak in court. In several important ways, their work challenges the approaches of Lakoff's and Tannen's views of women's language. O'Barr and Atkins studied courtroom witness testimony for two and half years, looking at the ten speech differences between men and women proposed by Lakoff and others. They concluded that speech patterns were "neither characteristic of all women nor limited only to women." Instead, they found that women who used the lowest frequency of women's language traits had unusually high social or economic status (e.g., being well-educated professionals with middle-class backgrounds). A similar pattern was found for men (i.e., men with high social or economic status spoke with few women's language traits). O'Barr and Atkins argued that it was power and status, rather than gender, that accounted for these differences. A powerful position that "may derive from either social standing in the larger society and/or status accorded by the court" allowed speakers—both male and female—certain linguistic advantages. Thus, what so-called women's speech is really manifesting is difference in power within mainstream society, where women typically are at a disadvantage.

Other studies have also examined the position of power of women in society as it is reflected in language. For example, Bonnie McElhinny did a year of fieldwork in 1992 with the Pittsburgh police department, observing the effects of gender, race, and age on police officers' language. She found that female officers tried to portray themselves as competent beyond question, as well as rational, efficient, and professional beyond reproach. They neither adopted the accommodating and empathetic manners typically associated with women nor demonstrated the commanding physical presence and emotional aggression often associated with the police. Instead, they chose to adopt a communicative style more typical of the "middle-class masculine norm" (1995:220). Thus, although the female police officers had no intention of acting as social workers, their presence and language served as an implicit challenge to the "hegemonic masculinity" found on the police force, replacing it with a definition of policing centered around mental ability and coolness under pressure (1995:238).

And Deborah Tannen (1999), too, modified some of her early ideas in her study of conversations in the workplace by incorporating some of the work of Erving Goffman (1974) on frames and the presentation of self. She showed how speakers simultaneously balance the dimensions of status and connection, arguing that gender patterns of behavior are class-linked as well as sex-linked. In other words, women's and men's subcultures are each deeply associated with social status.

### *Communicative Strategy Theory*

Some scholars argue that women's language is also significantly shaped by the style of **communicative strategy**. For example, Jane Hill (1987) studied the social expectations, gender roles, power differences, and language in the Malinche Volcano communities near Mexico City. She found that local women changed their native language, Nahuatl, to be "more Spanish." By the mid-1970s, many Nahuatl-speaking men were earning relatively good wages in Mexico City, where Spanish was the elite language. The men saw Spanish as the language of capitalism and hegemonic power, but they used Nahuatl to maintain local social solidarity. The women remained behind to take care of the farm fields. They had the responsibility to pass the Nahuatl language on to the children. They saw the Spanish language as a modern and elite language and Nahuatl as a traditional language. Understanding the importance of maintaining the language of their ethnic group, but also wishing to show their appreciation of modern things and education, the women began to speak a form of Nahuatl highly influenced by Spanish pronunciation. Hill argues, however, that this was largely unconscious. To maintain Nahuatl, they intentionally did not use Spanish loanwords, but less obvious features such as Spanish phonology influenced the use of their native language.

Another example can be seen in the use of English and English loanwords by Japanese women. The anthropologist Karen Kelsky (2001) claims that English (and other foreign languages) are thought to be the most valuable weapon (*buki*) in the women's war for equality in the Japanese workplace. The feminist critic Junko Matsubara says that "business comes first for men and English only second, but for women English is always first. . . . [I] f you cannot speak English, you have no chance of even getting your foot into the business world" (Kelsky 2001:101). For example, more than 90 percent of interpreters for the Japanese national broadcasting corporation—and 90 percent of all other interpreters—are women (Kelsky 2001:101). Monopolizing fields such as interpreting, translating, or bilingual guiding gives women powerful—though often unacknowledged—clout in many domains. The various Japanese male attacks on the current worldwide hegemony of English—for example, *eigo byō* ["English mania"] as Tsuda (1994, 1996, 1997) calls it—might be caused by their inadequacy in the language. To be fair, many of these scholars speak very good academic English, and their theoretical and political criticisms of English should be taken seriously. But articles in popular magazines with titles such as *Nihonjin no Eikaiwa Shijō-shugi no Gu* ["The Stupidity of the Japanese Worship of English"] do give one pause.

However, English can be more than a mere tool for career advancement. Foreign languages might be the "means by which women enter bodily into alternative systems of thought and value" (Kelsky 2001:101). As Matsubara says, "English is not just a language. . . . [I]t is something that has the power even to transform women's lives." As one of her interviewees argues, "In my case, if you took away my English, there would be nothing left. I can't imagine myself existing without English." Another stated, even more plainly, "I had so many opinions I wanted to express. I felt I couldn't possibly say them in Japanese. I wanted to learn this new vocabulary to express myself better. So I worked really hard. The average Japanese doesn't have any opinion! Even in Japanese! But I had loads of opinions, and because of that I learned English fast" (Kelsky 2001:101–102).

English loanwords also offer the Japanese a chance to avoid some of the constraints imposed upon them by the gender requirements of speaking the Japanese language, as we saw in the discussion of terms for "wife." Not only does the use of English loanwords help them change their images of themselves, English allows Japanese women to speak about social issues or problems in ways they otherwise might not be able to do comfortably. For example, the Japanese term *gōkan* ("rape") carries some social stigma because it suggests an act of physical intercourse instead of a crime. As a result, victims of *gōkan* in Japan are often thought to be less desirable marriage partners, and the women and their families often hide such incidents. However, because the modern English loanword *rēpu* focuses on the crime and on being a victim of a crime—rather than being considered as complicit—more women are now reporting *rēpus* to the police. Women are often making an effort to effect social change by using English loanwords that do not carry the traditional "linguistic baggage" associated with native Japanese terms (Stanlaw 2004a and 2014; Hogan 2003).

## *Identity Theory*

*Identity* can be defined as the "linguistic construction of membership in one or more social groups or categories"; though other factors may be significant, "language and communication often provide important and sometimes crucial criteria by which members both define their groups and are defined by others (Kroskrity 2001:106). As Bucholtz (1999:4) has pointed out, if language and gender scholarship is to explore issues of identity, it must engage feminist theory, which has discovered that identity is much less static than previously believed. That is, identity is a dynamic construct—a multifaceted assemblage of racial, ethnic, class, social, cultural, *and* gender properties, each also in a state of flux. We never belong to just one category, and at any given moment these identities emerge, disappear, mutate, and mix—either through our own intention, performance, or presentation of self, or as a reaction to those imposed upon us. No aspect of our identity is privileged, nor is any language associated with these identities (1999:6). "When we come into possession of a voice, we sometimes have to choose *with which voice* (the voice of the dyke, the Chicana, the professor, the master) *in which voice* (first person, third, vernacular, formal) or *in which language* (Black English, Tex-Mex, Spanish, academese) to speak and write in" (Anzaldúa 1990:xxii; emphasis added).

An example of these identity and language issues is seen in Marcyliena Morgan's work on African American women's speech (1999:27–45). As we will see in the next chapter, research on "Black (African American) English" has had a long history in the United States—at least a half century of formal investigation. However, much of the generalization of this work—in essence, defining what "Black English" is—has been based until recently on young, urban, lower-class, vernacular-speaking males. The speech of female or middle-class or upper-class African Americans has been marginalized as being somehow less "authentic" (Bucholtz 1999:12). But Morgan describes how African American girls and young women "grow and function as core social actors in their communities [demonstrating] that they are part of rather than peripheral to vernacular culture" (1999:41). Part of this is maintaining one's cool—being "current and trendsetting, calm, detached, yet in control" (p. 31).

## *Community of Practice Theory*

One of the problems of much of the older research in language and gender studies is that categories such as "male" and "female" or "men's language" and "women's language" are tacitly assumed to be real, given, and taken for granted. As we will explore later on in this chapter, this starting point is not as obvious as one might think at first glance. Also, earlier investigators were interested in making broad pronouncements about what constituted "women's speech" and how "women" talked—often making generalizations that were unwarranted, especially cross-culturally. Today, most gender-based research in linguistic anthropology is more localized, with an emphasis on specific practices. Penelope Eckert and Sally McConnell-Ginet, in their seminal article "Think Practically and Look Locally: Language and Gender as Community-Based Practice" (1992), argued for ethnographically grounded, in-depth investigations of particular activities or "practices."

The notion of a **community of practice** is an influential alternative to the speech community concept favored by ethnographers of communication (as described in Chapter 10). The main difference between them is that although both are interested in shared rules and norms of language use, the idea of a community of practice entails examining the social relations among members, as well as being cognizant of the differences among members. "A community of practice is an aggregate of people who come together around mutual engagement in an endeavor" (Eckert and McConnell-Ginet 1992:464). By doing so, practices—ways of doing things—emerge. Note that this construct is a little different from the way community is traditionally defined—for example, "Irish Americans"—because it also includes the practices and activities in which the membership engages. This makes boundaries porous and in flux, as news headlines such as these show: "The Irish-American Politicians Have Long Dominated Chicago Politics . . . "; "Irish American Fiddlers Did Well in the Contests in Dublin . . . "; "More Irish-Americans Favor Birth Control. . . ." A community of practice, then, "is a social grouping which is constituted by engagement in some joint endeavor: a language class would be an example" (Cameron 2005:488).

Thus, instead of taking some predefined speech community as a starting point, Eckert and McConnell-Ginet argue that various "communities" emerge—not through sameness but in diversity, "made up of individuals who are temporarily unified through shared engagement in activity, and thus are able to shift identities from moment to moment" (Bucholtz 2001a:77). In other words, masculinities and femininities are produced in specific contexts—that is, communities of practice—with no assumption that these same patterns will be found universally. In addition, the relationships between and among various communities of practice, and the relationships between communities of practice and institutions, are important: "Individuals typically negotiate multiple memberships (in families, on teams, in workplaces, etc.), many of them important for understanding the gender-language interaction" (Eckert and McConnell-Ginet 1992:464).

An example of this approach is Mary Bucholtz's work with white high school nerds in California. Nerds are typically viewed as intellectual overachievers, but also as those who lack the social skills and the coolness-capital necessary to be popular. However, to be a nerd is not an "inevitable social death sentence" but instead is often a "purposeful choice that allows those who embrace this identity to reject locally dominant social norms" and current trends of coolness in American society (2001b:85).

In many urban high schools in the United States, there is a delicate balancing act students must perform between coolness and race. As many have noted, African Americans are the arbiters of student coolness, the visible force that sets the standards for everything from which musical styles are popular to what the latest slang terms are (Stanlaw and Peshkin 1991). European American students must decide how "black" they want to be: too little, and they risk being ostracized from high school youth culture; too much, and they risk offending African Americans or alienating other European Americans. The acts or "performances" need to be carefully calculated. The nerds in Bucholtz's study rejected both the normative whiteness of the mainstream majority and attempts to be cool by emulating certain aspects of African American culture. They did this through the use of hyper-correct super-standard English. For example, they intentionally avoided using trendy slang terms and were careful to pronounce the final syllables of words (not replacing *going to* with *gonna*, for instance). "Anthropological research has shown that identities that are 'not white enough' may be racially marked. Yet marking may also be the result of being 'too white.' California high school students who embrace one such white identity, nerds, employ a superstandard language variety to reject the youth culture norm of coolness. These practices also ideologically position nerds as hyperwhite by distancing them from the African American underpinnings of European American youth culture" (Bucholtz 2001b:84).

### *Agency Theory*

There are several other theories of language and gender, but we will end with a brief discussion of **agency theory**. Simply put, linguists and philosophers use the term *agency* to mean the human capacity to act, especially for oneself (Ahearn 2001b). Marxist scholars remind us that human beings make society as much as society makes them, a notion sometimes called practice theory (as previously discussed). "The riddle that practice theorists seek to solve is how social reproduction becomes social transformation—and they believe agency is the key" (Ahearn 2001a:7).

The theoretical construct of agency has direct applicability to the study of language and gender. For example, "[a] focus on the construction of gender in activities seems to accord speakers a great deal of agency in their language choice, and in their construction of social identity" (McElhinny 2003:31). Laura Ahearn (2012:284–289) describes such a case, in which her informants explicitly wanted to talk about agency. She studied how economic and social changes in a Nepali village affected how the people conceptualized causality or responsibility for events. More and more villagers attributed events to individuals rather than fate—especially particular individuals. Shila and Vajra at first seemed an unlikely couple, as she was vivacious and outgoing and he painfully shy. Nonetheless, they began courting in the early 1990s. The usual theory of love among these villagers was that it starts with infatuation via an exchange of glances. As in America, it was assumed that love just happened. "No one has to *do* anything . . . love is something that happens to people rather than something for which they themselves are responsible" (2012:286).

But an analysis of their love letters showed a difference in their conception of love, both through "their explicit talk about agency . . . and their implicit grammatical choices. While they both mix individualist and fatalistic notions of action in their letters . . . [the woman] Shila tends to emphasize the more fatalistic notions and tends to claim that it is not possible to achieve what one wants to achieve in life. Vajra, on the other hand, often states that any and all obstacles can be overcome" (2012:287). In her analysis of the Nepali love letters, Ahearn attributes this difference to gender.

## DOES GRAMMATICAL GENDER AFFECT HOW WE THINK?

At the beginning of this chapter we stressed the difference between biological and grammatical gender. There we said that the use of masculine, feminine, or neutral genders to classify words does not require their speakers to conceptualize these words as necessarily having male- or female-like properties. Again, there is nothing male about a German "spoon" (*der Löffel*). Just as English speakers are not supposed to exclude women when they read a book called *The History of Man*, real biological properties are supposed to mentally disappear when engendered words in a language like German are actually used.

But do they? There is nothing biologically male, say, about spoons, after all. Thus, the only information about a spoon's possible or alleged "maleness" comes from one's language. In Chapter 12 we saw how the Sapir-Whorf hypothesis argued that language can influence thought in subtle ways. It is useful to ask, then, if speakers of languages with grammatical gender differ from speakers of gender-neutral languages in the ways they think about inanimate objects.

## Spanish and German

In a series of provocative studies, Lera Boroditsky (e.g., Boroditsky, Schmidt, and Phillips 2003) argues that distinctions in grammatical gender between languages can bias people's memory, description of pictures they have seen, and ability to notice or replicate similarities between pictures. For example, a group of native German speakers and a group of native Spanish speakers were shown the same set of twenty-four objects. Proper names were assigned to each of these items (e.g., an apple might be labeled "Patrick" or "Patricia"), and subjects were asked later to recall what this name was for that item. For each group, half the time the proper names assigned were consistent with the grammatical gender given in the language, and half the time they were inconsistent. The prediction was that German speakers would be better at remembering a proper name for "apple" if the name was "Patrick" than if it was "Patricia," because apple is masculine in German. The opposite was expected for Spanish speakers, because "apple" is a feminine noun in Spanish. These hypotheses were experimentally supported.

In another study, German and Spanish native speakers were asked to write the first three adjectives that came to mind to describe a presented object. The question was whether or not the grammatical gender of an object in one's native language influences the choice of adjectives used to describe it. For example, German speakers described "key" (masculine in German) with words like *hard, heavy, jagged, metal, serrated*, and *useful*. Spanish speakers ("key" is feminine in Spanish) said keys are golden, intricate, little, lovely, shiny, and tiny. On the other hand, bridges (feminine in German; masculine in Spanish) were described by German speakers as beautiful, elegant, fragile, peaceful, pretty, and slender. Spanish speakers said "bridges" were big, dangerous, long, strong, sturdy, and towering. Several other similar protocols led the researchers to conclude that objects do appear to have conceptual gender and are consistent with the grammatical gender in one's language. How does gender actually make its way into the representations of objects?

> But what does it mean for a turnip to be conceptually feminine or for a toaster to be conceptually masculine? . . . [O]ne possibility is that, depending on grammatical gender, different (stereotypically masculine or feminine) aspects of objects may become more or less salient in the representations of those objects. For example, if the noun that names a toaster is masculine, then perhaps its metallic and technological properties may become more salient; but if the noun is feminine, then perhaps its warmth, domesticity,

> and ability to provide nourishment are given more importance. (Boroditsky, Schmidt, and Phillips 2003:70)

## *Other Evidence*

Do such findings for German and Spanish hold up in languages other than Indo-European ones? Prewitt-Freilino, Caswell, and Laakso (2012) investigated data from 111 countries and divided their language sample into three groups: (1) grammatical-gender languages (which use grammatical classes, as we have been discussing), (2) natural-gender languages (such as English, which have pronouns that correspond to both biological sexes, but in which most nouns are not marked for gender), and (3) genderless languages (in which there is a complete lack of grammatical-gender distinctions in the noun and pronoun system). They argued that

> language not only reflects the conventions of culture and particular patterns of thought, but systems of language can actually shape our cognitive understanding of the world . . . around us. Specifically, the gendering of language (even that which appears mundane and purely grammatical, such as the use of *la* versus *le* in French) can actually impact our perceptions. . . . [O]ne could infer that when language constantly calls attention to gender distinctions by discriminating between masculine and feminine nouns and pronouns—as is the case in gendered languages—that individuals may be more apt to draw distinctions between men and women. If, in fact, language plays a role in how people organize their beliefs about gender, then it stands to reason that differences in the gendered language systems across different cultures could play a role in societal differences in beliefs, attitudes, and behavioral practices about the role and status of men and women. (2012:268–269)

Indeed, as might be predicted from the preceding comments, these researchers found that countries in which languages with grammatical-gender distinctions are spoken did show less social and economic gender equality than countries where natural-gender languages or genderless languages are spoken. However, it was not the case that the greatest social equality was found in countries in which people speak genderless languages. Instead, the greatest social equality was found where natural-gender systems are used. They suggest two reasons for this. First, even if there is no grammatical gender per se in a language, it is often the case that "gender neutral terms can continue to connote a male bias in the mind of the audience" (Prewitt-Freilino, Caswell, and Laakso 2012:278). Second, they propose that in a natural-gender system it is relatively easy to revise the language where clear instances of sexism or inequality are found. They claim (p. 279) that

> natural gender languages may be the most successful at promoting gender-inclusive language, because unlike genderless languages they are able to include gender-symmetrical forms in pronouns and nouns (thus increasing the visibility of women), but compared to gendered languages they do not depend upon gendered structures that would limit the legibility or intelligibility of symmetrical revisions.

These are certainly intriguing findings. If substantiated, they have important implications for the relationships between men and women, language, power, and ideology.

## LANGUAGE AND GENDER: HEGEMONY, POWER, AND IDEOLOGY

Clearly there are differences in how men and women speak, and there is even some evidence suggesting that grammatical gender might influence thought and conceptualization, at least in subtle ways. The various theories of language put forth in a previous section all seemed to take for granted the linguistic power differential between males and females. The question now is: If we assume this premise to be true, how great a part does language play in the social conditions of women? Does the less aggressive and less linguistic stance taken by most women cross-culturally reflect—or cause, or reinforce, or reify—their alleged subservient social status? If a society's language is "gender-neutral," would there be social equality between men and women? Should we intentionally try to change a language to eliminate prejudice or chauvinism? As these are all philosophical questions about **ideology** as much as language, even asking them can make some people uncomfortable.

### *The Struggle for a Gender-Neutral Third-Person Pronoun*

A prime example of these ideological issues is the perennially contentious problem of the search for a **gender-neutral third-person pronoun** in English. Generally, *he* is taken as the default, as in *If someone thinks this linguistic anthropology book is brilliant, he should write a nice letter to each of the authors!* There is no easy choice if someone wants to avoid this. *He or she* is long and cumbersome, and constructs like *s/he* or *(s)he* or *he/she* have never really caught on, probably because they sound artificial (and how would you even pronounce them?). *They* is plural and not singular. And *one* (as in *One should write a nice letter*) sounds literary or stilted. Of course to change the default to *she* would be unthinkable! If it is any consolation to us poor English speakers, other places—even a progressive country like Sweden—face similar dilemmas (see Box 13.1).

Professional authors have struggled with this problem, too. The award-winning science fiction novelist Ursula K. Le Guin's *The Left Hand of Darkness* is about the Gethenians, a race of people who are neither male nor female, but change their gender randomly once a month during estrus. Needless to say, pronoun choice here is difficult, but Le Guin initially used the default *he* and defended it against much feminist criticism:

> But the central failure in this area [of depicting the hermaphrodite characters in the book more as "men" rather than "menwomen"] . . . arises in part from the choice of pronoun. I call [the hermaphrodite] Gethenians "he" because I utterly refuse to mangle English by inventing a pronoun for "he/she." "He" is the generic pronoun, damn it, in English. (I envy the Japanese, who, I am told, do have a he/she pronoun.) But I really do not consider this very important. (1989 [1976]:14–15)

However, after a decade's reflection, she had second thoughts:

> This "utter refusal" . . . collapsed, utterly, within a couple of years more. I still dislike invented pronouns, but I now dislike them less than the so-called generic pronoun he/him/his, which does exclude women from discourse; and which was an invention of male grammarians, for until the sixteenth century the English generic singular pronoun

### BOX 13.1 THE *HEN-DEBATTEN*: LANGUAGE AND GENDER PRONOUN-WARS IN SWEDISH

Currently, there is a debate in Swedish regarding the use of pronouns. The Swedish language has gendered pronouns—*hon* ("she") and *han* ("he")—but in an effort to promote gender equality the pronoun *hen* ("she," "he," "him," or "her") was introduced as one means to close the social gender gap. For example, a popular children's book was released in 2012 using the *hen* pronoun, starting a controversy that has yet to subside. The pronoun wars have divided the Swedish population—not only the general public, but also institutions and the authorities. In all domains and parts of society, there are avid *hen*-opponents and *hen*-supporters.

Common arguments against the use of *hen* concern not only its supposedly artificial-sounding usage, but also issues related to human biology. Many opponents state that a gender-neutral pronoun is unnecessary, arguing that if human beings are born as men and women, distinguished by different biological features, these differences should also be reflected in the language through the use of gendered pronouns.

On the other hand, *hen*-supporters make two arguments. First, they say that linguistically marking gender is unnecessary and draws attention to differences that are irrelevant, perhaps even reinforcing gender stereotypes already in place. Second, forcing speakers to make a binary male-female sexual distinction using *hon* or *han* excludes certain individuals who do not clearly identify themselves as men or women. Thus, *hen* allows for a third identity and gender option, challenging the gender dichotomy and beliefs about biological sex, and by extension, highlighting the socially constructionist views on gender.

Although the debate is still ongoing, *hen* is more accepted today than before. But even though the prestigious Swedish Academy has come out in support, not everyone is convinced. As the arguments from both sides illustrate, the debate is not necessarily about the word itself; rather, it is about what the word *does* and what implications it has. The addition of *hen* means that old social structures are questioned, identities and identity options are contested, and lastly, it means that the social structures in the future could be different and unfamiliar.

Su Yin Khor

> was they/them/their, as it still is in English and American colloquial speech. It should be restored to the written language, and let the pedants and pundits squeak and gibber in the streets.(1989 [1987]:15)

Over the past two centuries there have been dozens of proposals for gender-neutral third-person pronouns in English. None has gained acceptance. But even if one of these had become common, there are still many other cases of subtle gender bias in the English lexicon: for example, policeman, department chairman, salesman. These can be changed with relative ease (police officer, department chairperson, sales associate). But other cases are more problematic, even in our own discipline: anthropology is the holistic study of man; most of the Peking Man skulls were lost during World War II; Stone Age Man had few sophisticated tools. Here something like humankind could substitute, but not with ease.

Since the 1970s, the feminist movement has had an impact in changing at least some of the subtle sexism in English. The title *Ms.* is now widely accepted, and numerous books have been written on how to write in a nonsexist way. But the biggest impact has been in the written language. For some forty years *The Associated Press Stylebook* (2013) has been quite conscientious in advocating for nonsexist English. For example, it says that "[c]opy should not gratuitously mention family relationships when there is no relevance to the subject, as in: Golda Meir, a doughty grandmother, told the Egyptians today. . . . " Likewise, "Copy should not express surprise that an attractive woman can be professionally accomplished, as in: Mary Smith doesn't look the part but she's an authority on. . . . " And: "Use the same standards for men and women in deciding whether to include specific mention of personal appearance or marital and family situation."

The state of Washington passed a gender-neutral language bill in April 2013. In state statutes every effort must now be made to eliminate gender bias. *Ombudsman*, *freshman*, *penmanship*, and *watchmen* are now replaced by *ombuds*, *first-year student*, *handwriting*, and *security guard*. However, the bill's sponsor, Senator Jeanne Kohl-Wells, has received a fair bit of backlash, being called a femi-Nazi among other more colorful terms, even though the legislation referred only to statutes, not personal conversations or any other venue. Her response is indicative of how contentious these issues still are:

> The legislation simply reflects society's steady progression to update outdated or insensitive terms. Words matter, and language that accurately references genders should not be threatening to anyone. If anything, the hysterical and misogynistic reactions to my bill suggest the need for intelligent, reasoned discussion that advances mutual respect for gender and common courtesy. (Kohl-Wells 2013)

Linguistic gender bias is more pervasive and nuanced than just following formulaic recipes or passing laws. For example, linguist Deborah Cameron (n.d.) points out that the sentence, "The man went berserk and killed his neighbor's wife" seems unobjectionable at first. But why do we not find this as the default: "The man went berserk and killed his neighbor"? After all, both the husband and the wife are equally his neighbors. For all the progress that has been made, English still has a way to go in terms of eliminating gender bias.

### *Gender Bias and Modern Digital Technology*

Another example in which language appears not to have influenced social conditions very much is the area of what Herring (2003:202, 205) calls **computer-mediated communication**, or CMC. This includes the use of the Internet, Twitter, e-mails, online discussion groups, Instagram, Facebook, instant messaging—in other words, all the communicative possibilities offered by modern digital technology. It was assumed—perhaps over-optimistically—that CMC would change the social order. The Internet, for example, would level "traditional distinctions of social status, and creat[e] opportunities for less powerful individuals and groups to participate on a par with members of more powerful groups" (2003:202). For example, the lack of physical and auditory cues on the Internet would make gender irrelevant (as opposed to face-to-face conversation, in which gender is obvious and cannot be ignored). Also, it was assumed that the Internet would enable dispersed individuals, and those with less access to capital or the usual channels of power, to find ways to organize politically.

In her review of the literature, Herring argues that for the most part, however, this has not happened. At least in American society, men still dominate online "conversations" or discussions, control the "talk" and the direction of discourse, and get more replies and responses. Moreover, the "conventionally masculine value on agonism [sic] and the conventionally feminine value on social harmony" tends to discourage women's participation (2003:209). Women tend to do better in environments where the norms of interactions are monitored by a moderator.

Why has CMC not been especially beneficial in changing social norms? For one thing, the Internet simply reproduces the greater social status quo. Control of Internet access and resources is exercised by the more privileged in the community. Also, the single largest activity on the Internet—pornography—is "not only controlled by men, but casts women as sexual objects for men's use" (Herring 2003:218). Also, the notion that CMC would erase biological gender differences has, for the most part, not been realized:

> [T]raditional gender differences carry over into CMC, in discourse style and patterns . . . in images, content, and patterns of use. At the same time, women themselves choose to reveal their gender when they could remain anonymous . . . and choose to frequent commercial Web sites that offer mainstream, gendered stereotyped content. (Herring 2003:218)

This is certainly puzzling. Why do women appear to maintain traditional and disadvantageous gender arrangements when new technologies like CMC allow them to avoid them? Herring (2003) and O'Brien (1999) suggest that it is because these traditional arrangements are not really seen as disadvantageous at all:

> Positive motivations for signaling (and even exaggerating) gender difference include gender pride, the social approval accorded to individuals for behaving in gender-appropriate ways, and the pleasure that can be derived from flirting, which often invokes binary gender stereotypes, in the relative safety of on-line environments. (Herring 2003:219)

Also, even on places like Twitter, where there are no gender indications per se, Tyler Schnoebelen, Jacob Eisenstein, and David Bamman (Schnoebelen 2012) have found clear differences between male and female tweets that were fairly easy to detect. Women were found to use more pronouns, emotional adjectives, emoticon symbols, Internet acronyms and abbreviations, and "backchannel sounds" like *ah* and *hmmm*. The researchers believe they can predict the gender of an author almost 90 percent of the time. It is likely that the average user, then, is probably able to determine the gender of a tweet's author as well, though perhaps not always as accurately. This, of course, weakens the supposed leveling of the playing field that CMC was thought to provide.

### *Marking Gender*

Another common way differences in power and prestige between men and women are reflected in English is through marked forms. In marking theory, there is an asymmetrical relationship between pairs of terms—one of them the "normal," default (or the unremarkable "unmarked" case); the other the special, "marked" case. For example, *honest* is assumed to be the normal unmarked term, whereas *dishonest* is the derivative or marked term. Marked terms do not always have to have a special prefix or suffix: We ask, "*How old are you?*" (using the unmarked term *old*) rather than "*How young are you?*" (using the marked term *young*)—unless there is some reason marking the event as special, like asking a potentially underage drinker for ID. Common sex-markers in English are suffixes like -ette, -ess, -ness, -ine, or -trix—as in *prince* versus *princess*. There are many instances of deriving nouns designating females from nouns designating males—for example, *aviator -aviatrix*, *duke -duchess*, and *waiter -waitress*. (Instances of derivation in the opposite direction are few; only two come readily to mind: *widow -widower* and *bride -bridegroom*.) These terms are not necessarily of equal emotional or social value. Consider these examples:

> He is a master of political intrigue.
> She is a mistress of political intrigue.
> Let me introduce you to the governor.
> Let me introduce to the governess.
> He is a war hero.
> She is a war heroine.
> Jane wants to meet an eligible bachelor.
> John wants to meet an eligible spinster/bachelorette.
> John has a real cool bachelor pad!
> Jane has a real cool spinster pad/bachelorette pad!

The second sentence in each pair above probably strikes at least some native speakers as being somehow odd—or least uncommon. And if it is uttered, it carries a meaning different from the first. Regardless, it is clear that the forms in the second sentences are derivative of the first; "bachelorette" makes no sense unless one knows what a "bachelor" is. This is the reason that some terms, like *waitress*, *stewardess*, *authoress*, or *actress*, are thought by some to be demeaning. As Whoopi Goldberg said, "An actress can only play a woman. I'm an actor; I can play anything" (https://www.brainyquote.com/quotes/quotes/w/whoopigold113538.html).

Also, some lexical items in English apparently have implicit gender associations built into them. This is especially true for occupational titles. Again, the second sentence in each pair below is marked for gender:

He is a tramp (i.e., a wandering homeless person).
She is a tramp (i.e., a woman of questionable morality).
Careful! He's professional (i.e., someone who knows what he is doing).
Careful! She's a professional (i.e., a prostitute).
Give this to the secretary; she will sign it for you.
Give this to the secretary; he will sign it for you.
Give this to the CEO; he will sign it for you.
Give this to the CEO; she will sign it for you.
Give this to the doctor; he will sign it for you.
Give this to the doctor; she will sign it for you.
You need to give your specimen to the nurse. She'll give you a cup.
You need to give your specimen to the nurse. He'll give you a cup.
She's a real beauty, isn't she? (referring to a sports car)
He's a real beauty, isn't he? (referring to a sports car)
John sure knows how to handle his clients (e.g., he is a lawyer).
Jane sure knows how to handle her clients! (e.g., she is [also] a prostitute).

Some of these examples are probably more obvious than others. Differences between male and female "tramps" and "professionals" probably are found in the casual speech of most dialects of English. Likewise, even though occupational roles are rapidly changing in the United States, there is still an expectation—albeit less pronounced than previously—that secretaries and nurses will be females, whereas CEOs and doctors will be male. And there is still an assumption that many high-end luxury commodities—for example, sports cars or yachts—are female and therefore can be "beautiful." Finally, in the last example, we see how terms can be used—especially by men attempting in various ways to be clever or funny—as double entendres (figures of speech that could be interpreted in two ways). Generally the targets of these expressions are female. In the last pair of sentences above, even if both John and Jane were accomplished attorneys, John would probably never be the butt of a joke in the way Jane might be.

## LANGUAGE IN GAY, LESBIAN, AND TRANSGENDER SUBCULTURES

When we think of "gender," we often think in the usual default male-female biological dichotomy. But gender, as we have seen, is not sex. Because sexuality and sex roles are as equally complex as gender roles, sexual orientation is another area that could affect language use. In the past two decades, linguistic anthropologists and other scholars have been paying increasing attention to the language found in gay, lesbian, and transgendered communities. Sometimes this field of study is termed lavender linguistics (e.g., Leap

1995), named for the (stereotypical) color associated with gay and lesbian civil-rights activism since the 1960s. At the risk of oversimplifying a very complex topic, two theoretical questions immediately come to mind: (1) Are the language practices of gay, lesbian, and transgendered individuals and communities significantly different from those of "straight" individuals and communities? (2) Are these differences the same cross-culturally?

As we will explore more fully in the next chapter, twentieth-century linguistic researchers found that besides gender, things like "race," ethnicity, geography, education, and social class were clearly reflected in language, and this had tremendous social consequences in myriad areas, from jobs and financial success to marriage patterns and residency. Since the 1980s, gay, lesbian, and transgendered individuals and communities have increasingly been viewed as another group facing marked social discrimination and stereotyping. For example, gay American men were thought to act effeminately, using elaborate gestures inappropriate to their sex, and often speaking with a lisp (especially for sibilant sounds like /s/, /z/ or /š/). Words like "faggot" became slurs, and "gay" increasingly became appropriated as an **endonym** and self-identifier. There were enumerable cases—some of them high-profile—of violence against people who "acted like a fag," and nationwide attention began to be paid to gay issues.

### *Terminology Issues: Language and Culture*

For researchers, some of the early discussions concerned terminology, as this was also an issue in the community itself. There were heady debates about what kind of language was used in the gay community—and the origins of various terms supposedly common to it—and numerous glossaries and dictionaries were compiled. Even what to call people whose sexual identities do not follow "normal" heterosexuality was problematic. Which words to use to label the community was contested, and in some ways this is still problematic for both insiders and outsiders. As anthropologist Don Kulick (2000:243–244) mentioned:

> For a very short while, in the late 1960s, "gay" seemed to work. Then, in the early 1990s, it seemed that "queer" might do the trick. Queer, however, has never been accepted by a large number of the people . . . [because of its] activist contexts. . . . [T]he latest acronym, which I encountered for the first time at a queer studies conference . . . was LGBTTSQ. When I . . . inquired what this intriguing, sandwich-sounding clot of letters might mean, I was informed . . . that it signified "Lesbian, Gay, Bisexual, Transgendered, Two-Spirit, Queer, or Questioning."

The 1980s saw attempts at theorizing the language found in gay, lesbian, and transgendered communities by analyzing the performative aspects of these lexical items. For example, in his analysis of the language of gay American men, Hayes (1981a, 1981b) claimed that it had three functions: (1) to act as a secret code to protect against exposure (by, for example, switching the gender of pronouns); (2) to enable one to take on a variety of roles and behaviors (e.g., playing a drag queen); and (3) to empower gays to politicize social life (by, for example, co-opting pejorative terms like *fag* or *dyke* and turning them into symbols of defiance) (Kulick 2000:259). However, there are limits to how far such approaches can go. As Kulick (p. 259) says, the fact that gays do X or Y does not make X or Y gay. Nor are those who do X or Y necessarily gay, either.

Problems begin, then, when things are taken cross-culturally. The biggest difficulty is that constructs like "gay language" might be "meaningless outside particular Western contexts, because it is far from certain that elsewhere people like 'gays' even exist as a social and ontological category in the way they have come to do" in the United States (Kulick 2000:268). One solution is to turn to language philosopher J. L. Austin's (1976) notion of **performance**. Austin was one of the founders of **speech act** theory, the analysis of how utterances affect speakers and hearers, their behavior, and the social conditions resulting from these utterances (see Chapter 10). For example, when a religious official says, "I now pronounce you husband and wife," the world is a different place than it was just moments before. Such statements Austin called **performatives**, in contrast to **constative** sentences, which just convey information.

Livia and Hall (1997a) believe Austin's notion of performativity solves this problem. They suggest that "by looking at the way in which language performs actions on the world and calls identities into being through its own felicitous pronouncement" (Kulick 2000:268), this allows performativity to be a tool to study how language is used by sexually and gender-variant people. And in the process, this also calls them into being, creating "its own object of research" (Livia and Hall 1997a:12). For example, some members of the gay men's community might use stylistic or rhetorical devices—such as using female pronouns or terms of address for other men, as in "*Hey, girlfriend, how are you doing!*"—to both establish, and reinforce and reify, particular categories of identity and sexual orientation.

### *Bahasa Binan*

There are apparently variations in language based on sexual orientation found throughout the world, but the dynamics and specifics can be quite different from those in the United States. For example, in his discussion of Indonesia, *The Gay Archipelago* (2005), Tom Boellstorf described Bahasa Binan, Bahasa Bencong, or Bahasa Gay, the language of the gay community. One common device gay Indonesian men use is to build a sense of solidarity by resemanticizing many everyday terms, or giving them special meanings. Two examples of this semantic shift are the Indonesian word *goring* ("to fry"; "fried"), which refers to sodomy in Bahasa Binan, and *kucing* ("cat"), which means a male prostitute.

But several other morphological properties are also used in Bahasa Binan. For instance, there are a number of ways to render a normal Indonesian word into Bahasa Binan using various prefixes, suffixes, or replacements. Replacing the final syllable of a word with *-ong* is one such device: the Indonesian word *polis* ("police") becomes *polesong* in Bahasa Binan. When used consecutively, the changes can become rather drastic. The simple everyday sentence *Aku tidak mau* ("I don't want [it], I don't want [to]") might transform into *Akika tinta mawar*. The question is, what is the function of this language variety? Is this an insider's language used by members to protect themselves from the scrutiny of outsiders, or is it a language intended to foster a sense of community?

Boellstorf saw that, if asked, many Indonesian gay men would claim that Bahasa Binan was really a "secret language" (*bahasa rahasia*). Individuals' use of this gay slang allowed men to speak freely about their desires, and perhaps negotiate liaisons, without having to worry about others knowing what they were talking about. In a Muslim country where sex outside of marriage—to say nothing of homoerotic encounters—is a major transgression, this no doubt serves a useful purpose.

Many times, however, the changes in a sentence are fairly simple or transparent (something on the order in English of saying, "I've been Hungarian for two hours" to mean "I've been hungry for two hours"). Such transparency makes the secret language hypothesis harder to defend. But then what is its purpose?

> But if *bahasa gay* so rarely serves the cause of secrecy, why should it exist at all? It appears to act most often to invoke a sense of *gay* community in a context where many *gay* men can socialize extensively in civic spaces such as parks, but where they have almost no institutional infrastructure—no places to call their own beyond the corner of a town square, no social recognition beyond the occasional (and often lurid) gossip column. Language here works to stabilize social relations, creating a sense of similarity and shared community. Likewise, many languages in Indonesia, though not Indonesian itself, have honorific registers. The best-known example is Javanese, commonly described as having an overall distinction between High and Low variants. . . . The relationship between Indonesian and *bahasa gay* is somewhat parallel to the relationship between High and Low Javanese . . . substituting a single High Javanese lexeme in an otherwise Low Javanese utterance marks the entire utterance as High Javanese. Similarly, one or two *bahasa gay* lexemes move an Indonesian utterance into the register of *bahasa gay*. The key difference is that honorific registers invoke difference, whereas *bahasa gay* invokes sameness and belonging. (Boellstorf 2004:260)

In other words, it seems that Bahasa Binan functions in at least two ways: as a means to create group solidarity through the use of terminology and forms that might not be picked up easily by outsiders, and as a means of protection and secrecy by communicating in a way that others cannot perceive. Such situations are not restricted to Indonesia but are found in other parts of Southeast Asia as well. For example, Manalansan (1995:202) found a similar function of *gayspeak* or *swardspeak* in the Philippines.

The study of the language in gay, lesbian, and transgendered communities is still in its relative infancy, and it has had a number of growing pains to work out. For example, as Kulick says (2000:271):

> [T]he most curious thing about research on gay and lesbian language is that even though it ostensibly is concerned with understanding the relationship between sexual orientation and language, it has no theory of sexuality. That is to say, it has no real understanding of what sexuality is, how it is acquired, and what the relationship is between its "literal performance" and its unconscious foreclosures.

Also, this fixation on identity categories, like "gay" or "lesbian," is implicitly linked to other common identity categories like "woman" or "African American." This no doubt has held back theory and research. Until work is done on how language conveys sexuality and desire, and not just on how it conveys identity, research on language in the gay, lesbian, and transgendered communities will be stifled—though to be sure, some scholars (e.g., Don

Kulick, Mary Bucholtz, Kira Hall, and others mentioned here) are now expanding the field in new and interesting ways.

## SOME CURRENT THOUGHTS ON LANGUAGE AND GENDER DIFFERENCES

In her epilogue to the seminal *Handbook of Language and Gender* (Holmes and Meyerhoff 2003), the linguist Alice Freed argued that one of the weaknesses in language and gender research was that "there are still relatively few . . . discussions which criticize the approach that takes female-male difference as both a starting point and as an explanation for linguistic behavior" (2003:699). This has important implications for the **folk linguistic theories** average people carry with them:

> When I have queried my own American university students about how women and men talk, they have always quickly and easily provided predictable responses. . . . My students say that women curse less than men and that little girls are explicitly taught not to curse at all. Students report that men use obscenities quite freely, though in theory, not around women because boys are admonished from cursing in the presence of their mothers or sisters. [W]omen are less direct in their speech, though students find it hard to describe what it means to be verbally indirect. Women are consistently portrayed as more polite, friendlier in their use of language, and are said to use better grammar than men. Men make more sexual comments, my students report. Men use blunter language. Women are more hesitant in their speech than men. Women ask more questions than men. Men won't ask for directions when they are lost. (Freed 2003:707)

Little scientific research supports these claims, and even her students themselves, if queried, are hard-pressed to give even any anecdotal evidence for them.

At the same time, Freed believes that the media are stressing the differences between women and men with startling regularity, and perhaps this is a new, subtle strategy to discriminate:

> [T]he popular press, television programs, the self-help industry, books on popular psychology, relentlessly inform us that women and men are different. We are told that we shop differently, that we vote differently, that we think differently, that we process information differently, and that we speak differently. Some of the time, it is true, some women and some men do some things differently from some particular subset of other men and women. But we know with certainty that this is not simply based on sex. What we may well be witnessing in the press's obsession with sex difference is a new tactic to counter the changing tides. Instead of simply ridiculing women, as the press has done in the past, we may wonder if what we are observing is not a deliberate or perhaps unwitting intensification of the volume of the rhetoric of difference. The insistence on the authenticity and naturalness of sex and gender difference may be part of an ideological struggle to maintain the boundaries, to secure the borders, and to hold firm the belief in women and men as essentially different creatures. We will be watching as a new age dawns and

> as language and other social practices continue to reveal the real texture and complexity of people's everyday lives. (Freed 2003:717–718)

Likewise, Cameron (2005) suggests that the biological reductionism of **evolutionary psychology** is also helping to maintain and essentialize differences between men and women. Evolutionary psychology is the subfield of psychology that treats human behavior the same way that biology treats human physical characteristics: both are products of natural selection, and much of human behavior is assumed to be hardwired. "Language plays a special role in this argument: women are said to have superior language and communications skills because of the survival advantage conferred on human females if females were good at empathizing, social networking, and nurturing, whereas males had the spatial skills for hunting and the lack of empathy that would enable them to be aggressive in competing for resources" (Cameron 2005:500).

To take things to the extreme, then, perhaps the differences between men's and women's language are often exaggerated—for any number of ulterior purposes—and care should be taken when we hear them. Instead of claiming that all men (say, from Mars) speak like Martians, and all women (say, from Venus) speak like Venusians (Cameron 2008), we need to look at the specific contexts of how and why women and men are speaking, at that particular time and speech event. Simplistic and dualistic generalizations are just another form of linguistic ideology and should be considered suspect.

Perhaps linguistic "gender equality" does necessarily mean that men and women end up sounding alike. For example, Yu (2013) has reported some interesting results from her large corpus analysis of US congressional speeches from the 101st to 110th Congresses (1989 to 2008). In such a setting, both genders demonstrate a strong penchant for formality (e.g., a low frequency of pronoun usage, high percentage of articles and long words, and little use of informal or vernacular speech), and it is not surprising that there is strong pressure on women legislators to conform to a "congressional style" of speech. But "[w]hile conforming to the normative masculine language, female legislators seem to have formed a unique style that combines female characteristics and professional expectations. This study also found a new pattern of gender difference that has not been reported in the literature: female legislators used more possessive first-person pronouns (our and my), while males used more subjective ones (we and I)" (Yu 2013:13).

## SUMMARY AND CONCLUSIONS

Although we often think that language variation is largely attributable to geographically based dialects, much of the time there are other reasons for the differences in language use we hear around us. Many languages exhibit differences according to whether they are spoken by women or men. In some languages, these differences are limited to a few sounds; in others they are lexical, such as, for example, in Japanese, in which certain words are heard primarily from women and others primarily from men.

Research on language and gender traditionally has been dominated by three major themes: women's language as somehow being an inadequate approximation of standard—that is, men's—speech (deficit theory); women's language as a reflection of their living in their own subculture (difference theory); and women's speech being a result of, and reflection of, male patriarchy (dominance theory). Recent work, however, has shown that even categories like gender—supposedly natural and interminable—are context-bound and emergent within social interaction. Rather than striving to make broad generalizations—"Men speak like this; women speak like that"—current researchers are interested in looking at things like communities of practice, which are groups of people who come together around mutual engagement and activities and—at least in some ways—a shared linguistic repertoire. This theoretical construct helps us to examine how language is involved in the creation of identity, gender, and sexual orientation.

The topic of language and gender will inevitably involve discussions of ideology and prescriptive linguistics. Should a language be changed if it appears to some that certain features might be discriminatory—such as English using "man" generically, or its lacking a neutral third-person pronoun? If so, who decides? How would such a change be implemented? Should there be an official linguistic governing body in the United States (like France's Académie française), which would monitor English and issue pronouncements and decrees on what kind of language can be used? What about those who do not think certain features are inequitable, and find nothing wrong, say, with using "he" or "his" as default pronouns? Or, instead of being proactive, should we let language evolve at its own natural pace? After all, linguistically, great strides toward gender equality have been made in the last few decades in the United States. None of these are easy questions, and both language specialists and the general populace must provide input.

## RESOURCE MANUAL AND STUDY GUIDE

### Questions for Discussion

1. Explain this statement: "Gender is a status ascribed to individuals."
2. Even women often use the term *you guys* as a second-person inclusive pronoun regardless of the group's composition (as, for example, when a sorority sister says, "Hey, you guys want to go get something to eat?"). Comment!
3. Linguistically, are men really from Mars and women from Venus? Discuss!

### Projects

#### PROJECT 1: GENDERED LANGUAGE AND MAGAZINES

Go through a women's magazine and a men's magazine and compare their use of language. Are there any differences in vocabulary, phrases, and/or the structure of a sentence? What about pronoun usage? What about pictures and captions? Advertisements? And how would you show that a magazine was a women's or men's magazine?

#### PROJECT 2: GENDERED LANGUAGE AND TELEVISION

Commercials on television are presumably as self-segregated by gender as was the case for the magazines above. Repeat the exercise above, but for the commercials on three prime-time network television shows.

#### PROJECT 3: MEN'S AND WOMEN'S WORDS

Some words are used—or thought to be used—strictly by men, and others by women. Write down five adjectives, five adverbs, and five phrases you think are mostly used by men.

| adjectives | adverbs | phrases |
|---|---|---|
| a. | a. | a. |
| b. | b. | b. |
| c. | c. | c. |
| d. | d. | d. |
| e. | e. | e. |

Write down five adjectives, five adverbs, and five phrases you think are mostly used by women.

| adjectives | adverbs | phrases |
|---|---|---|
| a. | a. | a. |
| b. | b. | b. |
| c. | c. | c. |
| d. | d. | d. |
| e. | e. | e. |

## PROJECT 4: THIRD-PERSON GENDER-NEUTRAL PRONOUNS IN ENGLISH

*Problem:* Tom Utley complained in the British newspaper the *Daily Mail* (June 13, 2009) that because there is no third-person gender-neutral pronoun in English, "We're reduced to . . . verbose and clunking construction[s] [like]: 'If an MP steals taxpayers' money, he or she should be ashamed of himself or herself.' ('Themselves,' employed to stand for a singular MP, would, of course, be a grammatical abomination)."

*Solution:* If you look at *Webster's Second International Dictionary* of 1934 you will see an entry for *thon*, "a proposed genderless pronoun of the third person."

We have to ask, what happened? Why has there been no solution to this problem? You might even be surprised to learn that there have been dozens of proposals for a new third-person gender-neutral pronoun in English, some going back at least to the time of the American Revolution (*ou*, based on Old English, for example, was suggested in 1789).

There seem to be five possible ways to address the lack of a third-person gender-neutral pronoun in English:

1. Keep the generic "he," do nothing, and let things remain as they are.
2. Use combinations—as we often do already—like "he or she," or "s/he," and so on.
3. Allow the plural "they" to stand for "he or she," as it does in many registers of informal English.
4. Allow "it" and "one" to perform the function of a third-person gender-neutral pronoun (e.g., "A child will learn its native language by simple exposure. One does not need to be explicitly taught.").
5. Invent a new term or neologisms, such as *thon* or *ou*.

**Question:** Which choice do you prefer? Why? (You might want to check Dennis Baron (1986) or his blog [http://Illinois.edu/blog/view/25/31097] for more discussion of these issues and other proposed third-person gender-neutral pronouns.)

## PROJECT 5: GENDER IN GERMAN

The following is a brief excerpt from Mark Twain when he was trying to learn "The Awful German Language" (1879 [1921]:274). He is—supposedly!—translating a famous old German folktale, and in frustration, and for humorous effect, uses the pronouns that the German language actually uses depending on the gender of their noun. He capitalizes nouns in the German fashion:

Tale of the Fishwife and Its Sad Fate

> It is a bleak Day. Hear the Rain, how he pours, and the Hail, how he rattles; and see the Snow, how he drifts along, and oh the Mud, how deep he is! Ah the poor Fishwife, it is stuck fast in the Mire; it has dropped its Basket of Fishes; and its Hands have been cut by the Scales as it seized some of the falling Creatures; and one Scale has even got into its Eye, and it cannot get her out. It opens its Mouth to cry for Help; but if any Sound comes out of him, alas he is drowned by the raging of the Storm. And now a Tomcat has got one of the Fishes and she will surely escape with him. No, she bites off a Fin, she holds her in her Mouth,—will she swallow her? No, the Fishwife's brave Mother-Dog deserts his Puppies and rescues the Fin,—which he eats, himself, as his Reward. O, horror, the Lightning has struck the Fishbasket, he sets him on Fire; see the Flame, how she licks the doomed Utensil with her red and angry Tongue.

Choose ten nouns from the excerpt and determine their grammatical gender. We did the first one for you; for example, you can tell *Rain* is male because of the pronoun that follows: how *he* pours. What particular combinations do you find natural? What combinations do you find odd? Do we sometimes do similar things in English (e.g., for some sailors, a ship being a she)?

| Rain | male |
|---|---|
| ____ | ____ |
| ____ | ____ |
| ____ | ____ |
| ____ | ____ |
| ____ | ____ |
| ____ | ____ |
| ____ | ____ |
| ____ | ____ |
| ____ | ____ |
| ____ | ____ |

**PROJECT 6: HOTEL GUESTS IN GERMANY**

Consider the following note found in a hotel room in Germany (Sunderland 2006:38):

> Forgetful hotel guests: We will always have to reckon with the classic case that a wife may not know about her husband's stay in a hotel. Therefore we return lost property only at the guest's request.

**Question:** What does the gender-neutral term *guest* really mean? What does this say about the value of supposedly nonsexist terms in a language? What might this say about attempts to make languages gender-neutral (e.g., using *Ms.* in place of *Miss* or *Mrs.*, *chairperson* in place of *chairman*, etc.)? How you might you rewrite this card . . . assuming you wanted to?

**PROJECT 7: NEW LANGUAGE FOR INTERACTING WITH THE LGBTQI COMMUNITY**

Colleges and universities are trying to become more inclusive and sensitive to those in the LGBTQI community. For example, here is an excerpt from a list of guidelines one Midwestern university gave its faculty regarding interacting with LGBTQI students, teachers, and staff:

- Do not assume you can tell who is or is not LBGTQI.

- Avoid inaccurate, outdated, and/or pathologizing language to identify someone such as "homosexual" (instead: same-sex desiring, gay, lesbian), "hermaphrodite" (instead: intersex person), "transvestite" or "tranny" (instead: transgender person), "transgendered" (instead: transgender).
- Learn new language to discuss sex, gender, and sexuality: asexual, demigirl, demisexual, genderqueer, non-binary (NB), poly, pansexual, and so on.
- Ask for personal gender pronoun (PGP) preferences early in the semester on student info forms.
- Practice using "they/them/their" as singular gender-neutral pronouns.
- Use gender-neutral language when possible: "ladies and gentlemen" (people), "boys and girls" (kids), "his/her" (their or his/her/their).

What are your feelings about these suggestions? Are some more acceptable than others? If so, which ones? Why?

**PROJECT 8: CIS AND CISGENDER**

In June, 2015, the *Oxford English Dictionary* officially added the word "cisgender" (or cis), meaning a person whose gender identity matches the sex they were assigned at birth. Basically, it is the opposite of "transgender." What problem was the introduction of this new term supposed to solve? Has it done so? Has it created new ones? For example, consider this comment by Southern California gender studies professor Chris Freeman: "For me, 'cis' reifies something that is mostly a fiction. It creates—or re-creates—a gender binary, which is exactly what many scholars and activists have been fighting against for decades." (http://www.advocate.com/transgender/2015/07/31/true-meaning-word-cisgender). Or is it a matter of just getting used to new terminology? The authors of this text remember when the replacement of "Ms." for "Miss/Mrs." was as equally contentious. Is it just a matter of language catching up with a real shift in social norms?

## *Objective Study Questions*

**TRUE-FALSE TEST**

T F 1. So-called tag questions characterize the speech of young American women rather than of older ones.

T F 2. Both male and female speakers of American English use the same patterns of intonation.

T F 3. There is no evidence at all that grammatical gender and biological gender are connected in any language in the world.

T F 4. It was found that messages on computer-mediated communications effectively hide the user's gender, leveling the playing field when women and men communicate.

T F 5. In almost every language in the world, only grammatical systems that distinguish masculine from feminine forms are found.

T F 6. Much of what Otto Jespersen said in 1922 set the stage for how women's language was viewed for more than half a century.

**MULTIPLE-CHOICE QUESTIONS**

____ 1. Why did Mary Haas believe that certain men's forms of speech were derived from female forms of speech? (A) This was mentioned in the written sacred texts of the Koasati. (B) They appeared to be historically older, being present in the speech of middle-aged and old women, but not of men. (C) The forms seemed to have been borrowed from English. (D) These forms seem to have been borrowed from the Zuni.

____ 2. In her work with women police officers, Bonnie McElhinny found that they (A) tried to use reason and a "soft touch" to defuse problems among citizens or with the police.

(B) usually still let their male partners do the more aggressive tasks when on patrol.
(C) tried to emulate the commanding physical presence associated with male officers.
(D) tried to be super-competent and professional beyond reproach.

____ 3. In American English the differences between the speech of men and women have to do almost only with (A) morphology. (B) lexicon (choice of words). (C) phonology. (D) None of the three choices applies, as American men and women speak pretty much the same.

____ 4. Which of the following is not a common way in which sex is marked in Japanese? (A) Through sentence-final particles. (B) Through greater use of honorific forms. (C) Using the prefix o- or go-. (D) Having a special set of terms for "husband."

____ 5. Which of the following is generally not the purpose of a tag question? (A) To obtain the assent of the addressee. (B) To seek confirmation. (C) To set the stage for a disagreement. (D) To avoid assertiveness. (E) To include the listener in the conversation.

____ 6. The reasons for the use of Bahasa Binan in Indonesia included all of the following except which one? (A) It provided a secret language that outsiders could not understand. (B) It helped create group solidarity. (C) It allowed men to speak freely of their desires. (D) It helped men negotiate liaisons. (E) It was only used for economic exchanges.

### BOX 13.2 THE CONSTRUCTION OF LÁADAN: LANGUAGE BY LINGUIST AND SCIENCE FICTION WRITER SUZETTE HADEN ELGIN

In the fall of 1981, I was . . . asked to write a scholarly review of the book *Women and Men Speaking*, by Cheris Kramarae. . . . I had also been reading a series of papers by Cecil Brown and his associates on the subject of lexicalization—that is, the giving of names (words, in most cases, or parts of words) to units of meaning in human languages. Out of this serendipitous mix came a number of things. . . . I became aware, through Kramarae's book, of the feminist hypothesis that existing human languages are inadequate to express the perceptions of women. This intrigued me because it had a built-in paradox: if it is true, the only mechanism available to women for discussing the problem is the very same language(s) alleged to be inadequate for the purpose. . . . There occurred to me an interesting possibility within the framework of the Sapir-Whorf hypothesis (briefly, that language structures perceptions): if women had a language adequate to express their perceptions, it might reflect a quite different reality than that perceived by men. This idea was reinforced for me by the papers of Brown et al., in which there was constant reference to various phenomena of lexicalization as the only natural and self-evident possibilities. I kept thinking that women would have done it differently, and that what was being called the "natural" way to create words seemed to me to be instead the male way to create words.

—Suzette Haden Elgin, on her motivation for constructing Láadan

*continues*

____ 7. Which of the following is the unmarked form? (A) Unhelpful. (B) Misspelled. (C) Man. (D) Woman. (E) Short (versus tall).

**COMPLETIONS**

1. Beliefs about the social world as expressed by speakers through their language are called language ________________ (one word).
2. Terms such as *maybe*, *rather*, and *perhaps* are called ________________ words (one word).
3. Three differences between American women's and men's speech are a greater use of ___________________, ___________________, and ___________________ (three phrases).
4. The view that women's language is a manifestation not of genderlect differences but of women's traditionally weaker social position, is called ________________ ________________ theory (two words or one word).
5. "All women curse less than men, are less direct in their speech, are more polite and friendlier, use better grammar, and learn languages better." This is an example of ___________ ______________ (two words or three words).

*continued*

Some Láadan forms:

| | |
|---|---|
| *osháana* | to menstruate early |
| *lawida* | to be pregnant |
| ásháana | to menstruate joyfully |
| *lalewida* | to be pregnant joyfully |
| *elasháana* | to menstruate for the first time |
| *lewidan* | to be pregnant for the first time |
| *husháana* | to menstruate painfully |
| *lóda* | to be pregnant wearily |
| *desháana* | to menstruate early |
| *wesháana* | to menstruate late |
| *widazhad* | to be pregnant late in term, and eager for it to end |

"Evidence morphemes," which come at the end of sentences where speakers must make clear on what grounds they base their statements:

| | |
|---|---|
| *wa* | I know it because I perceived it myself. |
| *wi* | I know it because it is obvious to everyone. |
| *we* | I know because I perceived it in a dream. |
| *wáa* | I assume it is true because I trust the source. |
| *waá* | I assume it is false because I don't trust the source. |
| *wo* | I imagine it, it's hypothetical. |
| *wóo* | I have a total lack of knowledge as to whether it's true or not. |

From Arika Okrent, *In the Land of Invented Languages* (2009), 243–244, 246–247

6. In discussing language, gender, and social roles, it is sometimes said that sex = ____________ whereas gender = ______________, though this is an oversimplification (two words).

## Answer Key

True-false test: 1-F, 2-F, 3-F, 4-F, 5-F, 6-T
Multiple-choice questions: 1-B, 2-D, 3-B, 4-D, 5-C, 6-E, 7-C
Completions: 1. ideology, 2. hedge, 3. any three of the following: greater use of tag questions, greater use of polite forms, greater use of wh- words, greater use of hedges, greater use of apologies, greater use of intensifiers, greater use of "women's vocabulary," greater use of modal auxiliaries, greater use of question intonations in declarative sentences, 4. social power or dominance, 5. folk linguistics or folk linguistic theory, 6. biology/culture

## Notes and Suggestions for Further Reading

There are numerous articles and books about the speech of women and men, both popular and academic. Many are noted in the chapter. Perhaps the best starting points are the exhaustive handbooks by Ehrlich, Meyerhoff, and Holmes (2014), Holmes and Meyerhoff (2003), and Garcia and Flores (2016), all of which are quite useful; and the resource book for students, Sunderland (2006). Other general overviews include Talbot (2010); Coates (2004); Coates and Cameron 1988; Kramarae (1981); Philips, Steele, and Tanz (1987); Silverstein (1985); and Thorne, Kramarae, and Henley (1983). The last book includes an extensive early annotated bibliography (pp. 151–342), and a later bibliography is found in Sunderland (2006) (pp. 324–358). The literature on gender differences and language is reviewed in Philips (1980); McConnell-Ginet 1988; and Eckert and McConnell-Ginet (2013). McElhinny (2013) will likely become a standard text. Bucholtz (2004) is a reissue with commentary on Robin Lakoff's classic (1975) text.

Several other collections dealing with the topics covered in this chapter are Bergvall (1999); Kroskrity (1983, 1993, and 2000); Cheshire (2002); Mills (1995); Tannen (1994a); and Hall and Bucholtz (1992, 1996). For a feminist perspective on linguistic analysis, see Mills (2012) and Mills and Mullany (2011).

For additions and corrections pertaining to Mary Haas's classic work on gender-specific speech among the Koasati, see Kimball (1987); he has reevaluated several of her findings. The entire example from North African French has been drawn from Walter (1988).

For the long story of the search for a gender-neutral third-person pronoun, see Livia's *Pronoun Envy* (2001).

For further discussions of language in gay, lesbian, bisexual, or transgendered communities, see the classic set of articles in Livia and Hall (1997b), and later Cameron and Kulick (2006); Cameron and Kulick (2012) provide the latest theoretical assessments. Ziman, Davis, and Raclaw (2014) discuss the linguistic practices in non-binary communities and individuals.

For useful general surveys on language ideology, see Mooney and Evans (2015), Woolard and Schieffelin (1994), and Schieffelin, Woolard, and Kroskrity (1998), as well as articles in Holmes and Meyerhoff (2003) (others are mentioned in Chapter 14). In the context of schools, the relationships among language, gender, race, and class are discussed in Orelus (2011) (see particularly the interviews with Noam Chomsky, Pedro Noguera, and Antonia Darder).

Work on Japanese women's language includes Takahashi (2013); Takemaru (2010); Inoue (2006); Okamoto and Shibamoto Smith (2004); Shibamoto (1985); and Itoh, Adachi, and Stanlaw (2007).

See Bucholtz (2011); Hill (2008); Kubota and Lin (2009); and Baugh (2002) for discussions of language and race (as well as the references in the next chapter).

For popular and best-selling accounts of the complexities of communication between men and women, see almost anything by Deborah Tannen (e.g., 1986 and 2007). But note the cautions given by Cameron (2008).

Linguist and science fiction writer Suzette Haden Elgin's most famous novel dealing with language and gender is *Native Tongue* (available in numerous editions). Láadan, the language she started there, has spawned a cottage industry of fans and contributors. Her comments in Box 13.2 are found at https://laadanlanguage.wordpress.com. More about the intricacies of this language can also be found there. For more on constructed and invented languages—both feminist and otherwise—see Okrent (2009).

# 14

# Language, Identity, and Ideology II: Variations in Class, "Race," Ethnicity, and Nationality

## LEARNING OBJECTIVES

- Explain how class, ethnicity, "race," and nationality intersect in language
- Explain how language reifies and reinforces particular patterns of social behavior and institutions
- Define terms like *African American English* (AAE), *Spanglish*, and *Asian American speech*
- Understand the pros and cons of some of the proposals concerning the origin of African American English
- Explore how language can foster and maintain institutionalized forms of racism
- Analyze how language is utilized by nation-states and subcultures for their own purposes

It is obvious that people speak quite differently, even those who share the same native language. But there are many reasons people speak the same language in different ways. For example—to speak in broad generalizations—the speech at the reunion of graduates of a private university is different from the speech at a homeless shelter in California; in New York City, the sounds in Chinatown are different from those in Little Italy; until the smash hit *Hamilton*, the songs and lyrics of a classic Broadway musical typically had little in common with the songs and lyrics of a hip-hop artist. In Chapter 9 we looked at some ways geographic variation contributes to creating different "dialects" or "accents," and in the last chapter we examined how men and women might speak differently. In this chapter we will discuss some of the sources—and implications—of language variation based on social class, ethnicity, and "race."

As we saw in Chapter 1, during the nineteenth century most people thought that physical difference and language were closely connected. That is, people were thought to speak differently because of these physical differences (i.e., "race"). In the early twentieth century, Franz Boas vehemently argued that there is no relationship between race, language, and culture, though this assertion often fell on deaf ears. That children of immigrants learn to speak the language of the new country should be the obvious proof of this statement. However, even today this is forgotten at times. For example, Chinese Americans are sometimes complimented on their excellent English, even though they (and perhaps even their grandparents) were born in the United States and never learned to speak Chinese. Likewise, language ability is separate from religion, occupation, financial status, or other aspects of culture. Unlike many physical attributes, language and culture are subject to change from generation to generation. In one nuanced sense, then, one's language and culture is somewhat of an individual choice. Thus, differences in language can be readily observed among people in the same speech community.

Early sociolinguists and anthropologists thought that such variety was analogous to geographic dialects. That is, just as differences in speech could result from geographic isolation, social isolation due to **ethnicity**, **nationality**, or **race** could also create linguistic variation. For example, why don't people always choose the speech variety that would bring to them the most benefit in society? Answering such a question has to do with **language ideology**—beliefs about a language expressed by speakers as their conceptualization of the nature and function of language, as we spoke of in the last chapter.

## LANGUAGE, SOCIAL CLASS, AND IDENTITY

One of the most obvious manifestations of **social class** is found in language—perhaps more so than personal possessions, style, or place of residence. For our purposes, we will reduce class distinctions to differences in economics, education, familial prestige, and some other ways people might rank themselves in society. Speech differences can characterize different economic or social status. In the most extreme situations, such as the castes of India, hereditary social classes restrict the association of their members with members of other classes, and this is often reflected in language. For example, John Gumperz (1958), who spent two years in the Indian village of Khalapur, about eighty miles north of Delhi, reported that although the population at the time of his research was only about 5,000, it was divided into thirty-one endogamous castes, none of which had equal status. The linguistic differences were of several types. For instance, where the majority speech, or Standard, had a contrast between single vowels /a/, /u/, and /o/ and the corresponding diphthongs /ai/, /ui/, and /oi/ before consonants, this contrast was

**TABLE 14.1** VOWEL DIFFERENCES AMONG DIFFERENT CASTES IN INDIA

| | | | | | | |
|---|---|---|---|---|---|---|
| Standard | /a/ | / ai/ | /u/ | /ui/ | /o/ | /oi/ |
| Sweeper | /a/ | /a/ | /u/ | /u/ | /o/ | /o/ |
| Shoemaker | | | /ə/ | | | |

*Note:* From Gumperz (1958:668–682).

absent in the speech of the Sweeper caste, which had only the simple vowels. Where the speakers of the Standard had /u/ before a stressed vowel in the next syllable, the speech of most of the Shoemaker caste and many of the untouchable landless laborers had /ə/. And there were also some lexical differences between the vocabularies of the different castes. The larger castes had special words for items of their subcultures, such as food, clothing, and the like (see Table 14.1).

### *William Labov: Social Change and Social Status*

But even in places where the class differences are less pronounced, similar kinds of linguistic stratification can be found. In the United States, William Labov conducted a well-known study of **sociolinguistic change**—linguistic change understood in the context of the society in which it occurs. Labov's pioneering work was concerned with the relationship between the social status of speakers in New York City and their pronunciation of r-sounds. The study was conducted in some of the department stores of the city in 1962. The variation of the phonetic feature under consideration ranged from the absence of (r) altogether to its presence in postvocalic position, as in the words *car*, *card*, *four*, and *fourth*.

On the basis of exploratory interviews, Labov decided to test the following hypothesis: "If any two subgroups of New York City speakers are ranked in a scale of social stratification, then they will be ranked in the same order by their differential use of (r)" (Labov 1972b:44). Rather than simply comparing the pronunciations of occupational groups representing the city's social stratification, which would be difficult to operationalize and quantify, in an elegant experiment Labov chose to try to find out to what extent stratification is identifiable within a single occupational group. The population he selected for his study consisted of salespeople in the stores of Saks Fifth Avenue, Macy's at Herald Square, and S. Klein at Union Square. These three stores represented three status rankings, respectively—high, middle, and low—according to newspaper advertisements, the prices of their merchandise, the physical appearance of the store, and the socioeconomic status of their customers.

Assuming that salespeople in large department stores were likely to "borrow prestige" from their customers, Labov hypothesized that "salespeople in the highest-ranked store will have the highest values of (r); those in the middle-ranked store will have intermediate values of (r); and those in the lowest-ranked store will show the lowest values" (Labov 1972b:45). To elicit the relevant linguistic data, Labov asked a question that was best answered "[On the] fourth floor." Pretending not to understand the answer, he had the informant repeat the phrase in a more emphatic style of speech. As soon as he was out of view of his informants, Labov recorded the two words phonetically, noting not only the store in which the data were obtained but also the gender, function, race, and approximate age of the informant.

The results supported his hypothesis. At Saks, 30 percent of the salespeople interviewed always pronounced both r-sounds of the test phrase "fourth floor," whereas 32 percent pronounced them sometimes and sometimes not (as though "fourth floor" were written "fawth floah"), and 38 percent did not pronounce the r-sound at all. For Macy's, results were 20 percent, 31 percent, and 49 percent, and for Klein's 4 percent, 17 percent, and 79 percent, as shown in Table 14.2. Furthermore, at Saks the difference between casual and emphatic pronunciation was insignificant, whereas at the other two stores the difference

**TABLE 14.2 DISTRIBUTION OF (R)-SOUNDS BY SOCIAL CLASS**

| | *Saks (H)* | *Macy's (M)* | *Klein's (L)* |
|---|---|---|---|
| All (r) present | 30% | 20% | 4% |
| Some (r) presence | 32% | 31% | 17% |
| No (r) present | 38% | 49% | 79% |
| Number of subjects | 68 | 125 | 71 |

*Note:* **Based on Labov (1972b: 51).**

was considerable. Careful, emphatic speech appeared to call for the final (r) of *floor*, but casual speech did not.

Although prior to World War II certain r-sounds were "dropped" (except before a vowel) in the more prestigious pronunciation of New York City, in the years since then it had become one of the markers of social prestige. By the 1960s, its occurrence had increased, particularly in formal speech. In fact, some New Yorkers pronounced r-sounds even where they did not occur in spelling, as in the words *idea*, *Cuba*, and *saw* when the next word began with a vowel. Such a pronunciation or usage, which in an attempt to approach a presumed standard goes too far and produces a nonstandard form, is called *hypercorrection*. In short, as Labov's study showed, the pronunciation of r-sounds in the dialect of New York City was quite variable, depending on social factors such as status or class, and speech context such as casual versus emphatic speech.

Collecting authentic sociolinguistic data is not a simple matter because speakers are likely to adjust their manner of speaking if they are aware of being carefully observed or recorded. One way for the investigator to divert speakers' attention from their own speech is to lead informants into a relaxed dialogue. Natural speech also tends to characterize topics that help re-create emotions, such as when one asks an informant, "Have you ever been in a situation where you were in serious danger of being killed? . . . What happened?" The answer to such a question is likely to be spontaneous, that is, given in an unaffected manner (Labov 1972b:209–210). Recording data has a great advantage over writing out a phonetic transcription of speech. Recording conversation between two or more speakers, or recording one speaker long enough or often enough for the person to become unconcerned, is preferable to recording a more or less formal interview that may well keep the informant from relaxing into the **vernacular**—the casual, normal spoken form of the language or dialect of the person's speech community.

## *Quantitative Sociolinguistics*

In early sociolinguistic studies, scholars sought to identify language varieties and relate them to social differences among speakers. After the mid-1960s, largely because of the stimulus of Labov's work, linguists emphasized the use of the quantitative method in order to be able to describe with some accuracy the relationship between social differences and linguistic varieties. Peter Trudgill (1974) was one of them. He studied the covariation of phonological variables with social stratification in England in 1974. He investigated sixteen different phonological variables in an industrial city, Norwich. Considering England's

**TABLE 14.3** NG REPLACEMENT INDEX SCORES BY CLASS AND STYLE

| | *speech style* | | | |
|---|---|---|---|---|
| | WLS | RPS | FS | CS |
| *soc. class* | | | | |
| MMC | 0% | 0% | 3% | 28% |
| LMC | 0% | 10% | 15% | 42% |
| UWC | 5% | 15% | 74% | 87% |
| MWC | 23% | 44% | 88% | 95% |
| LWC | 29% | 66% | 98% | 100% |

*Note:* Based on Trudgill (1974:91–92)

social stratifications, Trudgill divided his social variables into five class-categories: middle middle class (MMC), lower middle class (LMC), upper working class (UWC), middle working class (MWC), and lower working class (LWC). He gathered speech for four contextual styles, similar to Labov; that is, he used word list styles (WLS), reading passage style (RPS), formal speech (FS), and casual speech (CS). One variable he analyzed was replacement of the /ŋ/ sound (for example, the -ng sound in walking and singing) by an /n/ sound.

According to Trudgill's analysis, middle-class speakers all used the ng-sound in word lists and reading passages, and only 3 percent in formal speech and 28 percent for casual speech. Although LMC speakers also used the ng-sound in word lists, 10 percent replaced it with the n-sound when reading, 15 percent in formal style, and almost half pronounced /ŋ/ with n-sounds in casual speech. As we can see in Table 14.3, this replacement became significant in the lower classes. In the casual speech of the upper working-class group, 87 percent of people used n-sounds instead of the ng-sound, although when the UWC people carefully read the word list, only 5 percent of people replaced -ng with n. In the case of the LWC reading word lists, there was still 29 percent replacement, but there was 66 percent replacement when they read the passage (see Table 14.3).

From the incidence and distribution of language variables in different social groups, scholars like Labov, Gumperz, and Trudgill expect not only to learn about the rate and direction of linguistic change but also to obtain valuable clues concerning the motivations that lead to such change globally. But it is important to remember that cross-culturally people are often unaware of their own speech habits (see Box 14.1).

In this connection, it may be appropriate here to introduce the concept of **social network**. Adding this concept gives us a deeper understanding of the variables examined in the studies mentioned above. Each speaker has a social network that includes all those people with whom the speaker interacts. A high-density network refers to a group of individuals who are in frequent contact and are therefore familiar with each other. A multiplex social network is one in which interacting parties share more than one role, often reciprocal—for example, employer/employee as well as father-in-law/son-in-law. The denser and more multiplex the network, the stronger it is (perhaps the father-in-law and son-in-law are also members of a chess club and a choral society). Members of a strong network tend to make use of what is referred to as **restricted code**—informal speech lacking in stylistic range

### BOX 14.1 LANGUAGE, PRESTIGE, AND MOTIVATION

If everyone shares the same norms and if users of generally disvalued speech dislike their own speech why does anyone speak in a nonprestigious manner? The answer is that people are not aware of how they are actually speaking. They think they sound different than they actually do. In fact, one sure way to get people angry is to tell them that they are using a particular pronunciation that they criticize in others.

Again, it was Labov who showed that people's evaluation of their own speech is not accurate. He played a tape with different pronunciations of seven words: *card, chocolate, pass, thing, then, her,* and *hurt*. Each word was pronounced four different ways, and subjects were asked to circle the number that correlated with their own pronunciation. In most instances, people reported themselves as using prestigious pronunciations even if they really used them no more than 30 percent of the time. They monitored their own speech according to the community norms. That is, they thought they were talking according to the community's standards of prestigious features. However, the way they actually talked correlated with their social class or ethnic group. In other words people talk according to their feelings of identity without realizing it.

From Elaine Chaika, *Language The Social Mirror* (1982), 174.


because the speakers share enough assumptions that some of the meaning of their messages is derived from context and gestures. By contrast, **elaborated code** refers to the variety of language use characteristic of relatively formal speech situations. In such situations little, if any, reliance is placed on extralinguistic context to make the message fully meaningful.

## LANGUAGE, "RACE," AND ETHNICITY

The study of the complex connections between language, "race," and ethnicity is theoretically still in flux, even though this has been on the research agenda of many scholars for several decades. However, much of the current work in contemporary linguistic anthropology focuses exactly on these topics, and many particular problems have been examined in great detail. These include language and nationality (which we will discuss later in this chapter), dialectology of multiethnic nations, language maintenance, code-switching, bilingualism and multilingualism in multilanguage nations, and language-politics and nationalism. For example, code-switching between French and English in Canada has been studied in relation to the political power and ethnic identity of Francophone and Anglophone Canadians (e.g., Heller 2013). Puerto Rican social discrimination, and Mexican American code-switching between Spanish and English, has been studied from the aspect of language and ethnic identity (Urciuoli 1996, Zentella 1997), which we will describe in more detail shortly. And, new research on Asian American language issues has now gone well beyond earlier work on language maintenance and heritage language issues. In this regard, then, ethnicity in its broadest sense is often looked at together with other variables such as age, gender, and social class.

In the United States, when people talk about "race" and ethnic groups, they are often talking about ethnic minority groups. Some people say that "race"—whatever the definition of that is—is based on physical phenotypical characteristics (like appearance or skin color), and "ethnicity" is based on social constructions (like someone's supposed ancestry or background). In reality, however, both are social constructs and emerge when they are used socially. Thus, when the connections between language, "race," and ethnicity are studied—especially when class is also factored in—the languages of minorities are often misconceptualized and misrepresented. In this vein, we will now examine three noteworthy cases that are particular to the United States: the language of African Americans, the speech patterns of Asian Americans, and Hispanic American speech and "Spanglish."

## *African American Vernacular English*

### Race and the Signifying President

Before we begin a discussion of the language of African Americans, we should mention at the beginning that most anthropologists today are suspicious of the notion of "race." It is obvious that human physical diversity is complex and genetically based. But modern genetics has also shown beyond all doubt that classifying people into neat standard racial categories is an arbitrary and unscientific exercise in futility. The way that the term *race* is commonly used in everyday life is simply not empirically justifiable and has little value. In short, for all practical purposes, "races" do not exist as a natural biological category (in the way that, say, "species" do). But there is an important caveat: everyone knows, races *do* exist as social categories (discrimination being just one manifestation). But these social categories are no more real or natural than any other arbitrary cultural construct (like having to wear a suit or dress to work in an office or believing the number thirteen to be unlucky). Nonetheless, linguistically, these social categories get manifested in various ways, the alleged uniqueness of African American speech being one example.

In 2007, a politician described then Illinois senator Barack Obama as "the first mainstream African American who is articulate and bright and clean and a nice looking guy." Later commenting on that quote, then president George W. Bush concurred, saying, "He's an attractive guy. He's articulate." Perhaps you have heard of that politician: he was Joe Biden, who later became Obama's running mate and vice president of the United States.

These comments caused an uproar in the greater African American community in the United States, as the word "articulate" entered the already racially polarized 2008 presidential campaign. Professors H. Samy Alim and Geneva Smitherman (2012:34–35) observed:

> As many Blacks noted, these remarks by two extremely high-profile White politicians merely echoed the numerous comments from many average, ordinary run-of-the-mill Whites. Why was everybody and they mama callin Barack Obama "articulate?"

Why *would* someone remarking that an accomplished young up-and-coming politician was "articulate" be so divisive? If the politician was a European American, the comment probably would have received little attention. But saying that an African American is articulate suggests he is an exceptional case—so unusual as to deserve comment. The unspoken implication is that African Americans are not usually articulate, and that their language—and maybe their way of thinking—is clouded, emotional, or even illogical. Such comments were all the more insidious and dangerous because it was likely neither Joe Biden nor George Bush was consciously aware of the nature of his casual remarks. They were implying, whether intended or not, that the everyday speech of African Americans is somehow deficient.

The other implication of such comments is that it is "obvious" European Americans and African Americans speak differently. Although linguists and anthropologists would say this is an empirical issue, it is clear that many African Americans and European Americans believe this to be true. People of all backgrounds can be accused of talking "too Black," "too White," "not Black enough," or "speaking to the crowd," and so on.

### Is There a "Black" English, and If So, What Features Define It?

In this section we look at some of the features of the English used by—at least some—African Americans. The language of African Americans in the United States is often given many names and acronyms: Black English (BE), African American Language (AAL). Black Language (BL), Ebonics, Black Vernacular English (BVE), **African American Vernacular English** (AAVE), **African American English** (AAE, the term we will use here), and Spoken Soul (see Box 14.3), among others. A word of caution is in order, however, as each of these can be problematic and contested terms. And we must remember that just because there is a label, doesn't mean that realistically there is a corresponding thing. There are some anthropologists, linguists, and sociologists who are not convinced that African American speech is any more unique than the speech of any other American ethnic group—or that it is somehow different from so-called standard American English. We will not enter into these arguments here, but AAE is heavily discussed both in textbooks and the popular media, so students of linguistic anthropology should have some awareness of the controversies and the facts regarding the speech of African Americans, as well as exposure to some of its history. It is important, however, to remember that when specific features are mentioned, it is done so to show their linguistic consistency and viability, and not as an example of a substandard characteristic when compared to some supposed normative style of speech. (The same thing applies in our later discussions of the speech of Asian Americans and Latinos.)

We might mention, too, that the linguistic features that are supposed to typify AAE are commonly seen more among working class than among middle-class speakers, more among adolescents than among the middle-aged, and more in informal contexts (like conversations on the street) than in formal ones. There are also some well-defined regional differences. One example of these differences is the possibility of finding **copula deletion** (dropping a form of the verb "to be," like *is* or *are*) in certain sentences, such as "He *is* a man" versus He Ø a man." As seen in Table 14.4, there is a fair degree of geographic and age variability.

Again, we must remember that the most prominent and common characteristic features supposedly found in AAE are not present in the speech of all African Americans. And they are mostly used in spoken rather than written registers. As with most rules of spoken language, no AAE speaker has ever been taught these things formally, and few speakers could articulate them (which is true for any speaker of any variety of speech). But

## BOX 14.2 THE SIGNIFYING PRESIDENT

"Playing the dozens" or "signifyin'" or "styling out" are names for various word games played in African American culture, especially by adolescent and young males. English professor Henry Louis Gates Jr. (1988:52) says that "signifyin' is a trope, in which are subsumed several other rhetorical tropes, including metaphor, metonymy, synecdoche, and irony (the master tropes), and also hyperbole." This is another way of saying that these are ritual insults or boasts—exchanged openly in contest-like form in banter back and forth, or given indirectly hoping to bait the intended victim. Sometimes insulting relatives is involved (e.g., "Your mama's so ugly . . . "), and humor and audience reaction is an important part of the game. Similar rhetorical devices are found in other ethnic groups (e.g., "Don't get mad. I'm just bustin' your balls" as heard in some Italian American communities), but this has become particularly formalized and stylized among African Americans. The following is a brief dialogue between President Obama and an employee at a fast-food restaurant in Washington, D.C. Here we see the informal speech patterns—and listener reaction—typical of signifying as he teases the employee about his supposedly not giving the president his full value for the chili dog he bought:

Barack: You just keep that [handing over money]. Where's my ticket? You got my ticket?

Cashier: [offering change]

Barack: Nah, we straight.

Customer[cashier?]: You got cheese fries, too?

Barack: Nah, nah, that's YOU man. . . .

Barack: [after getting his chili dog] Now, do y'all have some Pepto-Bismol in this place?

All present: [laughter]

Barack: Hey, how come he's got some cheddar cheese on and I don't have any on mine?

All present: [laughter, and collective "Woahhh!" indicating the signifying game is on]

Cashier: Whatever you like, sir.

Barack: We got some cheese, you can sprinkle on it? [Gesturing the sprinkling of the cheese, the signifying again] Not, not, not, not the Velveeta, but the . . .

Customers: [laughter]

Customer: The cheddar cheese!

Barack: The *cheddar* cheese!

Dialogue from *Articulate While Black: Barack Obama, Language, and Race in the U.S.* by Alim and Smitherman (2012) 126w from "Nah We Straight: Styleshifting From Ben's Chili Bowl to Ray's Hell Burger." By permission of Oxford University Press, USA.

**TABLE 14.4** COPULA DELETION BY GEOGRAPHY AND AGE

| AAE GROUP STUDIED | COPULA DELETION BEFORE NOUN ("HE Ø A MAN") | COPULA DELETION BEFORE ADJECTIVE ("HE Ø HAPPY") | COPULA DELETION BEFORE *GON(NA)* ("HE Ø GON GO") |
|---|---|---|---|
| New York City Thunderbirds (teenage gang) | 23% | 48% | 88% |
| Detroit working class (all ages) | 37% | 47% | 79% |
| Los Angeles (all ages) | 25% | 35% | 64% |
| Texas youngsters | 12% | 25% | 89% |
| East Palo Alto, California (all ages) | 27% | 45% | 83% |
| Ex-slaves (mainly from South, recorded in 1930s) | 12% | 29% | 100% |

**(Based on Rickford and Rickford 2000:116)**

some people outside the ethnic group view AAE as unsystematic, without rules or regularities—in short, a poor attempt at trying to speak standard English, or—even worse—an intentional disregard for the norms and rules of "standard" speech. However, AAE can be used not only by high school dropouts but also by African American intellectuals and religious and civil rights leaders, including President Barack Obama (see Box 14.2). Just as bilinguals can use **code-switching** in two languages, those from different communities—ethnic, racial, national, class, or otherwise—can shift styles (**style switch** or **style shift**) for various purposes.

And this brings up another issue concerning AAE: What are the necessary and sufficient features that should define it, or which features are the most prominent? If a grammatically "regular" English sentence is spoken using the phonological features of AAE, is it an example of AAE speech? What if the phonological features are largely absent, as in the case of a Signifying President in Box 14.2 mentioned above—does it still qualify as AAE? Can a European American legitimately speak in AAE, say, trying to emulate a favorite comedian or musician? These are questions that are as much political as anything else. This is because AAE entails notions of both language structure and language use. That is, AAE is not only an aggregate of structural features, but also a collection of language ideologies, communicative norms, and linguistic practices (Alim 2004:17).

AAE has often been looked at in relation to social class and education, sometimes even being seen as the incomplete language acquisition process of an undereducated minority group. But as Labov (1972a) and others (e.g., Burling 1973) since the 1970s have shown, the grammar of AAE is "a pretty complex set of rules and *restrictions*" (Rickford and Rickford

2000:115, emphasis ours). In this section, we will look at some of the most prominent and common features said to characterize AAE.

*Pronunciation.* One of the most noticeable cases of pronunciations of vowels in AAE is that some diphthongs (i.e., two-vowel sequences) in standard English—such as *my*, *I*, and *side*—are pronounced with a long monophthong or single vowel, like "*mah*," "*Ah*," or "*sahd*." The pronunciations of /e/ and /i/ before nasals like /m/, /n/, and /ng/ are similar, as in *pin* and *pen* and *find* and *found*. This phonological difference is also seen in southern European American speech, so it has been argued that AAE has been influenced by the social and regional dialects where the ancestors of today's African Americans were concentrated historically. Furthermore, the deleting vowel contrast is conditioned by the consonant /r,/ as in *fear* and *fair* and *sure* and *shore* (where the first two words and the latter two words may be pronounced alike). Other examples are shown in Table 14.5.

Reduction of word-final consonant clusters is also a well-known characteristic feature of AAE. They are also systematically deleted even if both (or all three) consonants are voiceless as in *test* or voiced as in *hand*. If one of the consonants is voiced and the other is voiceless, as in *jump* and *pant*, the final consonant cannot be deleted (Rickford and Rickford 2000:105). In the case of *th*, voicing is relevant because English *th* comes in both a voiced form as in *them* and a voiceless form as in *think*. Voiceless th-sound can be replaced by voiceless *t* or *f*. The *f* replacement is primarily at the end of the words like in *toof* ("tooth") or *Smif* ("Smith"), whereas the *t* replacement is almost anywhere, for example, *tink* for "think" and *nutten* for "nothing." The voiced *th* can be replaced by the voiced *d* or *v*. For example, the *th*-sound in the middle or at the ends of words often gets replaced by *d* as in *mudda* (mother) or *bade* (bathe) (Rickford and Rickford 2000:104). These and other features are shown in Table 14.6.

Finally, some claim that African Americans have a distinctive "inflection," "intonation," or "variation in pitch and rhythm." One example is where the stress is placed on the first rather than the second syllable, as in *PO-lice* and *HO-tel*. Furthermore, some African Americans supposedly delete the unstressed initial and medial syllables in words like *(a)bout*, *(be)cause*, *(a)fraid*, and *sec(re)t(a)ry* more often than European Americans do (Rickford and Rickford 2000:102).

*Some grammatical features.* The *-s* of the third-person singular present tense is frequently deleted in AAE, as in "*Johnny run*" or "*He eat meat*." In the case of the verb *be*, the invariant *be* is used without conjugation, becoming the *is* of the third-person singular. However, we should note that this usage of invariant *be* is used rather as a marker of habitual or durative aspect. In this case invariant *be* is used while being followed by *ing* as in *He be swimmin' every mornin'* ("He swims/is swimming every morning"). When an AAE speaker says, "He swim," this is the equivalent in standard English of saying "He swims occasionally" or "He has no problems with swimming."

There may be an absence of the copula and auxiliary conditions in forms like *She Ø tired* and *He Ø sleepin' right now*. However, the auxiliary verb cannot be deleted in the past tense, as in *He was swimmin' every morning*. The same rule applies when the auxiliary verb is used after *to*, *can*, *may*, *must*, *shall*, *should*, *would*, and *will*. The auxiliary verb cannot be

**TABLE 14.5** AAE VOWEL FEATURES

| VOWELS | |
|---|---|
| *Standard English* | *AAE* |
| **Diphthong such as /ai/ and /ei/** | **Long monophthong such as /ah/ and /ee/** |
| my | mah |
| I | Ah |
| side | sahd |
| eye | ah |
| **/e/ and /i/ before nasals like /m/, /n/, and /ng/** | **Similar pronunciation of /e/ and /i/ before nasal like /m/, /n/, and /ng/** |
| pin | pin/pen |
| pen | pin/pen |
| find | find/found |
| found | find/found |
| fear | fear/fair |
| fair | fear/fair |
| sure | sure/shore |
| shore | sure/shore |

**TABLE 14.6** AAE CONSONANT FEATURES

| CONSONANTS | |
|---|---|
| *Standard /Conventional English* | *AAE* |
| | **Reduction of world-final consonant cluster** |
| test | tes |
| hand | han |
| tooth | toof |
| think | tink |
| nothing | nutten |
| mother | mudda |
| *jump* | (X) *jum* |
| *pant* | (X) *pan* |
| **/r/** | Ø |
| after | afta |
| your | yo |
| **/l/** | Ø |
| help | he'p |
| wolf | wo'f |
| oil | ō |
| all | ō |
| | **Often described as deletion but actually is replacement of nasal sound** |
| walking | walkin' |
| singing | singin' |
| | **/k/ replacement in /t/** |
| street | skreet |
| stretch | skretch |
| | **/b/ replacement in /v/** |
| heaven | hebben |
| never | nebba |

deleted, as in *You can be sitting up in class an nex' thing you know, you Ø out of it* (Rickford and Rickford 2000:115). In the case of the present perfect tense, the verb *have* is deleted, as in *He Ø been swimmin' since he was six*. In the future tense the modal verb, *will* or *would*, may be deleted, as in *She be home for Christmas*.

There may be an absence of past-tense marking (of the suffix *-ed*, stem change, or other inflections) on semantically past verbs, as in *he walk Ø there yesterday*, *He pay me yesterday*, and *He tell Ø* before (Rickford and Rickford 2000:263). In this case, listeners know the past tense is intended because of other indications like "yesterday" or "before." When there is an option in standard English to use a contraction—for example, "He is going" becoming "He's going"—AAE offers the additional option of full deletion of the form of *be*, resulting in "He going." When the option to contract does *not* exist in Standard English, as in the latter part of the sentence "That's the way it is here" (one would never say "That's the way it's here"), the option to delete the form of *be* likewise does not occur in AAE, which would use "That the way it is [*or* be] here." The phrase *there is* that introduces a sentence or clause is replaced in AAE by *it is* or the contractions *it's* or simply *'s*.

The word *bin* (sometimes spelled as conventional English *been* when written) is used to form present and past perfect tenses, like *I bin playing cards since I was fou* ("four") and *We had bin married when tis ("this") lil' ("little") one came aon'* ("along") (Rickford and Rickford 2000:118, 119). The form *bin* could be used for the past tense before a verb stem like *We bin see dat ("that") man* instead of *We saw dat man;* this is used to exaggerate an action that took place or to state that the action came into being a long time ago (Rickford and Rickford 2000:118; Green 2002:93). The following sentence shows this: *He* [the dentist] *finish so quick. I aks him was he finished, and he say, "I bin finished!"* (Rickford and Rickford 2000:118). Although this usage has been a distinguishing feature of AAE, it is still seen in the speech of **Gullah** creole, which survives on the Sea Islands off the coasts of South Carolina and Georgia.

As for optional tenses, the situation of one particular variety of AAE has been described as follows:

> *I do see him* is just anterior to the present and intrudes upon it, and is therefore the *past inceptive tense. I did see him* is slightly longer ago, or the *pre-present tense. I done seen him* is still further ago, or the r*ecent past. I been seen him* is even farther ago and designated as the *pre-recent past.* Moving ahead from the present, if someone says *I'm a-do it,* he will do it in approximately 30 seconds, or in the *immediate future.* If someone says *I'm a-gonna do it,* he will do it soon, that is, in the *post-immediate future.* If he says *I gonna do it,* however, the execution may be indefinitely delayed. (Fickett 1972:19)

The verb conjugation of *do* (i.e., *done*) is used in present/past perfect sentences to emphasize the complete nature of an action and/or its relevance to the present or the past, as in *I done had enough* ("I have had enough") and *Even though he done took all the bullets out . . .* ("Even though he has already taken all the bullets out . . . ") (Rickford and Rickford 2000:120). However, *done* is not exactly identical to the present/past perfect tenses as used in conventional English. According to Rickford, in AAE *done* is used to express intense and forceful feelings. Furthermore, the major difference is that *has/have* can be used in a negative sentence like *He has not gone*, whereas *done* cannot be used in a negative sentence like *He ain't done gone.*

Since *be* can be used for the future tense, conditional or habitual meaning can be combined in sentences of "*be done*" with the completive sense of *done*, as in *He be done finished his work by the time they get back home* ("He has usually finished his work by the time they get back home"/"He'll finish his work by the time they get back home"). However, we need to note that *be done* is used most commonly with the future completive or future perfect (Rickford and Rickford 2000:120).

The critical thing to note from all these many examples is that things like indication of time duration, and completion, are often much more subtle and precise in AAE than the tenses typically used in conventional English. Thus, the argument that AAE is a poor approximation of standard English is again refuted.

*Negation*. There are a number of distinctive features for negation in AAE. One of the most common negative forms is *ain't*, which can be used for *am not, isn't, aren't, don't,* and *haven't*: for instance, *She ain't goin'*. In a negative sentence *anybody* and *anything* are used as "nobody" and "nothing" even when negation is marked with auxiliaries (i.e., doesn't, don't, isn't, and aren't). Thus, many negative sentences in AAE use double/multiple negation markers, as in *You don't do noting, I don' have no probem, He wasn' no boy, neite* ("neither"), and *I ain't neve seen nobody preach unde announcemen* (Green 2002:77).

*The lexicon, style, and ethnic identity: The "Man of Words."* As in any speech community, AAE has some unique vocabulary, variant stress patterns on certain words, and unique usages of certain words. Many of these are used to create intimate relationships among users or establish a certain stance. For example, as we saw in the last chapter, Marcyliena Morgan (1999:31) says that maintaining the speaker's social face by being cool is an important aspect of African American culture. We saw this, too, with the Signifying President playing the dozens in Box 14.2 at a fast-food restaurant.

Probably more than in typical European American discourse, in AAE there is an emphasis on style, the subtle turn of a word or phrase, or an unforgettable expression using all kind of tropes, allusions, and alteration—though of course this is a broad (and dangerous!) generalization. For example, people still remember O. J. Simpson's attorney, Johnnie Cochran, as he closed his arguments, saying, "If it doesn't fit, you must acquit!" as he held up as evidence the glove that was too small for O. J.'s hand. As writing teacher Kermit Campbell (2005:3) says, "[F]or most Black English Vernacular speakers it ain't about what you call it no way. It's about what you do with it, about making language—words, phrases, sentences, sounds—resonate with the tenor of your own voice and unique sensibility." Many scholars have said this ornate oratorical style of the "man of words" likely has its origins in Africa and the Caribbean (e.g., Abrahams 1972) and was brought to the New World during the Black Diaspora. We will now discuss the origins of AAE.

### The Origins of AAE

*The Origins of AAE I: Pidgin and Creoles.* We know that AAE is a language variant that has a set of systematic linguistic rules. But how did the African American vernacular style of English come about? Although no one knows for certain, there are three main theories: *the pidgin and creole approach*, *the dialect approach*, and the *African languages origin approach*. The pidgin and creole origin approach focuses on resemblances of the linguistic elements of AAE to those of Jamaican Creole and Gullah. Although AAE is today less divergent from conventional English than either Jamaican Creole or Gullah, there are a number of similarities between it and these two creoles. These include such features as the loss of the third-person singular *-s* and the possessive *'s*, multiple negation, and the zero copula (loss of forms of *be*, as in "*He rich*").

Pidgin and creole origin theorists believe these similarities are connected to the major migration periods when the ancestors of the majority of African Americans came to the New World as slaves. They believe the making of AAE dates back to the seventeenth century, when slave ships carrying cheap goods sailed from Bristol, Liverpool, and other English ports; the cargoes were exchanged along the West African coast for captured Africans who, in turn, were sold as slaves in the Caribbean and the North American South for work on plantations. The ships would then return to England loaded with sugar, tobacco, cotton, and other commodities, and the cycle would be repeated. To minimize the risk of organized uprisings, the cargoes of future slaves were assembled from a variety of tribes speaking different languages. According to the revealing testimony of one Captain William Smith:

> As for the Languages of *Gambia*, they are so many and so different, that the Natives, on either Side the River, cannot understand each other; which, if rightly consider'd, is no small Happiness to the *Europeans* who go thither to trade for Slaves; . . . the safest Way is to trade with the different Nations, . . . and having some of every Sort on board, there will be no more Likelihood of their succeeding in a Plot, than of finishing the Tower of *Babel*. (1744:28)

It is understandable that the need for a pidgin, or pidgins, had developed even before the ships left the African coast: The captives had to find a means of communicating, at least about the most vital matters, not only with each other but with their captors and overseers as well. Even after the captives had been sold into slavery in the New World, the need for pidgins continued for reasons similar to those that gave rise to them in the first place. In the Louisiana area, the pidgin was French-based; elsewhere in the South, it was English-based. According to J. L. Dillard, one of the exponents of the creole hypothesis, "When new generations grew up which used only the pidgin, the pidgin became creolized . . . [to] Plantation Creole" (1972:22).

Thus, a real possibility exists that the process of creolization contributed to the formation of modern AAE. Others view the same evidence in a different way. For them, AAE is just another dialect of American English, and just as rule-governed.

*The Origins of AAE II: Dialect Theory.* The dialect theorists point out that none of the features of AAE departs significantly from those found in other dialects of English or from the historical development of English as a whole. For example, multiple negation, commonly referred to as the double negative, which is frowned upon as one of the main sins against "good English grammar," was widely used in Elizabethan times; its retention in AAE can be interpreted as a conservative feature. By contrast, the loss of *-s* in the third-person singular can be viewed as the continuation of a tendency toward simplification that has characterized the English verb throughout its history. What AAE has done is to eliminate the last remaining suffix of the present tense verb paradigm, something that may well happen in Standard or conventional English in the next few hundred years. (Simplification of Standard English continues unabated, as can be seen from the ever-more-frequent substitution of *I* for the object form of this pronoun, *me*, as in "between you and I," that can now be heard even from major network television anchors and members of the US Congress.)

Also, many of the supposedly unique linguistic features of AAE are not unique in other natural languages (even though they are not common in English). For instance, the absence of a linking verb between subject and predicate, as in "He tired," is not a sign of corrupted speech or laziness on the part of AAE speakers; the same grammatical construction is found in many other languages of the world, Russian among them. And double negatives are seen in the "correct grammar" of many languages, including Spanish, Portuguese, and Japanese.

The negative attitude toward AAE in American society is in part reinforced by history, economic factors, and ethnic discrimination. Also, another contributing factor, oddly, is the pidgin and creole hypothesis, which linguistically unsophisticated people see as an academic way of saying AAE is inferior or inadequate. For example, the Oakland School Board in California, one of the worst-performing school districts at the time, thought that the stigma of AAE language could be an extra burden for their students, affecting academic success. The Oakland School Board then renamed AAE as Ebonics (combining the words *EBony* and *phONICS*, literally "Black sounds") on December 18, 1996. This was done for both social and pedagogical reasons: an unabashed attempt to connect language and ethnicity. Although this created a storm, both pro and con, the concept of tying ethnic identity and "Black sound" had political consequences and brought greater attention to AAE issues.

In the 1980s, Canadian multilingual educators even advocated AAE-speaking children be forced to learn "good" English in bilingual education classes. Cummins (1989, 1990) studied heritage-language education and reported that students working in an additive-bilingual environment (see Chapter 7) succeeded to a greater extent than those whose first language and culture are devalued by their schools and by the wider society.

Such attitudes, even if unspoken, leave their mark in social interaction. For example, in a widely known and frequently reprinted article, Labov (1970) reported that African American children will indeed respond defensively to a strange white interviewer (even when he or she is friendly), and they give monosyllabic answers if they find the setting or experience unfamiliar or intimidating. Once the sociolinguistic factors operating in this inherently asymmetrical situation have been removed, these same children produce a steady stream of speech, effectively using the various stylistic devices AAE has to offer.

In the same article, Labov quoted an interview conducted with Larry H., at the time a fifteen-year-old African American youth from Harlem. For someone who was put back from the eleventh grade to the ninth and who was also threatened with disciplinary action, Larry displayed a remarkable ability to think acutely and argue logically.

*The Origins of AAE III: African Languages Theory.* When ancestors of many of today's African Americans arrived in North America and learned English, their English was likely

**FIGURE 14.1 LANGUAGES THAT SHAPED AFRICAN-AMERICAN (BLACK) ENGLISH**

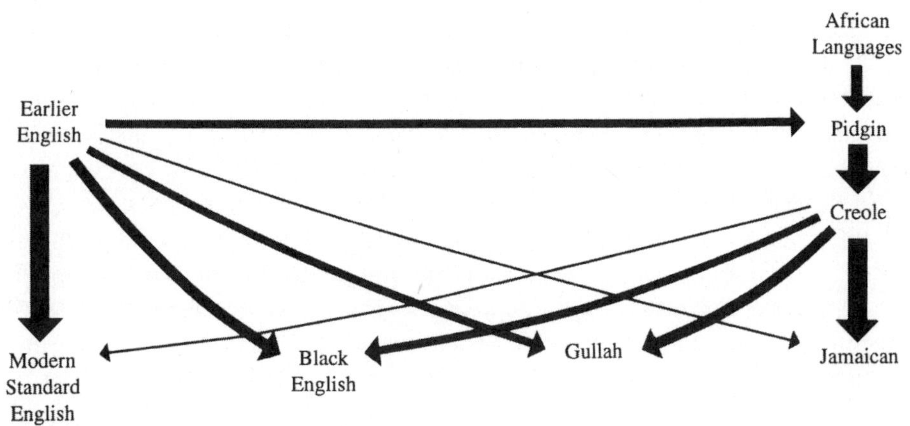


*Note:* From Robbins Burling, *English in Black and White*, (1973) 122.

highly influenced by their original languages. Some researchers see influences from several African languages, especially those of West Africa. These include the languages of the Niger-Congo, where the majority of the slaves came from. African languages origin theorists argue that the deletions of word-final consonant clusters (*pas'*) or omitting linking verbs like *is* and *are* (*He happy*) found in AAE could be from the influence of the Niger-Congo languages, which also omit word-final consonants often. Furthermore, use of habitual *be* and remote *bin* are also seen in Niger-Congo languages. However, there are some problems with this theory. Few actually specify which Niger-Congo languages had the biggest influence, and there are several that do not share many properties with AAE (Rickford 2013 [1997]:375).

Although each theory has its pros and cons, it is impossible to specify a single origin of AAE, as languages are always influenced by many social, political, and cultural factors throughout their history. It is possible, for example, that the current properties of AAE are a recent development, and that many of the early origins—be they Africanisms or creole residuals—have become diluted or have disappeared, or have become entwined with later social, cultural, and linguistic events (see Figure 14.1).

The most important thing to remember is that although AAE is the result of the meeting of numerous influences, it nonetheless manifests extremely complex and sophisticated forms. As Rickford reminds us (2013 [1997]:374; Rickford and Rickford 2000:119), AAE is not just slang (see Box 14.3). He points out how complicated its time and tense system is, as seen below (a configuration that would rival any aspect system):

1) *He Ø runnin'.* ("He is running.")
2) *He be runnin'.* ("He is usually running. Or he will/would be running.")
3) *He be steady runnin'.* ("He is usually running in an intensive, sustained manner," or "He will/would be running in an intensive, sustained, manner.")
4) *He bin runnin'.* ("He has been running—at some earlier point, but probably not now.")

5) *He BIN* (stressed bin) *runnin'*. ("He has been running for a long time, and still is.")

Today, attitudes toward AAE are changing. Hip-hop, a genre sung almost completely in AAE, is one of the world's most influential styles of music. An African American was elected president in 2008 and again in 2012, and millions of young people of all ethnic backgrounds try to emulate the style and verbal agility of famous AAE speakers, as well as even the regular African Americans around them (Stanlaw and Peshkin 1991).

This has had many positive influences in the United States, and not just for the black community. Other ethnic groups are developing a new pride in their heritage-languages, and mainstream society is beginning to see language issues in a new light. As we will see shortly, Chicano code-switching is not always seen as negatively as in the past, nor is it thought to represent Spanish-maintenance or symbolize Hispanic resistance to assimilation. Knowledge of Spanish does not mean an incomplete acquisition of English.

*The fate and future of AAE.* In discussing AAE in 1981, Nobel Prize–winning author Toni Morrison said, "It's a love, a passion. Its function is like a preacher's: to make you stand up out of your seat, make you lose yourself and hear yourself. The worst of all possible things that could happen would be to lose that language" (quoted in Rickford and Rickford 2000:4–5). William Labov (2010)—one of the early seminal researchers on the speech patterns of African Americans—claims that AAE is not an endangered language variety. This is hardly news to anyone who is into pop culture or loves contemporary music. But he thinks that increasing residential integration could dilute, or even eliminate, differences between AAE and other speech varieties, though he wonders about the possibility of this happening in the near future. He claims that residence, poverty, education, and AAE are inexorably interconnected.

In any case, it is undeniable that the notion of AAE is a source of controversy within the African American community and between the African American community and others in the United States. Lippi-Green (2012:209) says one reason for this is that a discussion of AAE sheds light on a very uncomfortable topic: racial equality in the United States. Clearly AAE speakers gain something from each other that is missing in mainstream culture, and missing linguistically in mainstream language practices. "The real trouble with Black English is not the verbal aspect system which distinguishes it from other varieties of U.S. English, or the rhetorical strategies which draw such a vivid contrast, it is simply this: [AAE] is tangible and irrefutable evidence that there is a distinct, healthy, functioning African American culture which is not white, and which does not want to be white . . . " and does not want to be measured by, as James Baldwin said, its "devotion to white people." "The real problem with [AAE] is a general unwillingness to accept speakers of that language and the social choices they have made . . . Instead we relegate their experiences . . . to spheres which are secondary and out of the public eye." Such comments no doubt are applicable to the language of Asian Americans and Hispanic Americans, to which we now turn.

### The Language(s) of Asian Americans

Reyes and Lo (2009:8) suggest there are at least four questions that might be asked regarding the existence of a supposed unique Asian American language: 1. In what situations and

## BOX 14.3 SPOKEN SOUL

For most people, languages and dialects are distinguished primarily by their words and expressions. French speakers say "*Bonjour*," English speakers "Hello." The British say "lorry" where Americans say "truck." Bostonians use "tonic" for what other northeasterners refer to as "soda" and Midwesterners call "pop." And so on. Similarly, for most casual commentators, what sets black talk apart is its distinctive word usage, particularly the informal and usually short-lived "slang" expressions known primarily to adolescents and young adults. The only examples of Black English in James Baldwin's 1979 tribute to the vernacular ("If Black English Isn't a Language, Then Tell Me, What Is?") are expressions, especially slang, that have crossed over into general American use, such as *jazz, sock it to me, let it all hang out, right on, uptight,* and *get down*. And for nine out of ten people who contributed to the American Online discussion of Ebonics in December 1996, Ebonics was "just a bunch of slang."

But Spoken Soul, like any other language variety, is much more than slang, and much more than the sum of its words. For linguists, the scientists who study human language, two other aspects of any language variety are as important as vocabulary, if not more so: its rules for pronouncing words, or pronunciation patterns, and its grammar—including its rules for modifying or combining words to express different meanings and to form larger phrases or sentences. African American vernacular has, for instance, a rule of grammar that allows speakers to move negative helping verbs such as *ain't* and *can't* to the front of a sentence to make the sentence more emphatic, so that "Nobody ain't going" can become "Ain't nobody going!" (This is an emphatic utterance, not a question, and usually such a phrase has the falling intonation of a statement or exclamation.) The verb can be moved to the front only if the subject of the sentence is a negative quantifier such as *nobody* or *nothing*. If the subject is not a negative quantifier—say, *John* or *the boy*—the rule does not apply. You can't convert "John ain't going" into "Ain't John going," at least not as an emphatic statement. (With rising intonation, of course, "Ain't John going?" would be [an] acceptable question.)

From John Russell Rickford and Russell J. Rickford, *Spoken Soul* (2000), 91–92.


with whom do Asian Americans speak a version of English that is different from Mainstream American English? 2. What are the features of this **Asian American English**? 3. Can this Asian American English, or Englishes, be identified with a particular group? 4. If so, who makes this attribution, and who recognizes this? And on what basis? We will see that unlike the case for AAE above, where at least a strong argument can be made for the existence of some distinctive dialectical features, Asian American identities are "locally constituted in conjunction with ideologies of race and ethnicity" (2009:8) and emerge during social interaction, such as speaking. That is, the key notion here is more on "identity" rather than "dialect" or "speech variety."

The language of Asian Americans is as diverse as the number of countries in Asia, because there are literally speakers in the United States from every one of them. Vietnamese, Korean, Tagalog and other Philippine languages, Japanese, numerous Chinese languages, Hindi and Urdu and dozens of other languages from the Indian subcontinent—these are just some of the languages of Asian America. According to the 2010 US census, there are over 17 million people who claim Asian or Pacific heritage, or 5.6 percent of the population; the Pew Research Center says, technically, "Asian Americans are the highest-income, best-educated and fastest-growing racial group in the U.S, with Asians now making up the largest share of recent immigrants" http://www.pewsocialtrends.org/asianamericans-graphics). Yet, as Reyes and Lo point out (2009:3), compared to AAE, Native American languages, and the language of Latinos in the United States, relatively little work has been done on their language practices.

There may be several reasons for this. First, the task is immense and daunting, as the **heritage languages**—the language of the family or natal household where one has grown up—that could influence the speech patterns of Asian Americans are so numerous and varied. For example, in spite of geographic proximity, no two languages could be more unalike than Chinese and Japanese.

Second, the English spoken by Asian Americans is often "interpreted in terms of an accent or interference from" a heritage language, rather than as "evidence of dialectical features of English" (Reyes and Lo 2009:8). However, it appears that heritage language seems to actually have little influence on a supposed Asian American style of speech. Research that has attempted to "delineate the contours of 'Yellow English' . . . along the lines of 'Black English' . . . has not been very productive"; that is, efforts to find a distinctive Asian American English have proven unsuccessful and "are often not recognizable as indexing a particular ethnic or racial group across a speech community" (Reyes and Lo 2009:5).

Third, both the general public—often intentionally—and some scholars—often inadvertently—have stressed the differences between mainstream American English and an imagined Asian American English. The mass media, for example, still often trade in stock characters who are either wise kung-fu sages or comic stereotypes. "**Mock Asian**" language (Chun 2009:261), like "Confucius say . . . " jokes or the pretend "Chinese accents" heard when Asian American children are teased on the schoolyard, abound. And sociolinguistics, which has long held to a "distinctiveness paradigm" can be said to be complicit in this (Reyes and Lo 2009:6).

An example of how ethnic identity can be established and reified through language can be seen in the following interview with Ellen, a self-identified "American" who was a counselor at a Korean American cultural camp in the Bay Area of northern California (Kang 2009:137–138):

> I have a similar story to Sara why I kept coming to camp and why I always come, you know? And like, I had the exact revelation she did cause I grew up with a white crowd, right? *And I think, every year that we have like—every year that we have camp, there's always conflict in what the emphasis is gonna be, more Korean, more Korean American, more American, you know?* And everyone comes with different ideas, right? And like, right

> now, I disagree with the *oppa ennui* ["older brother" and "older sister"], and I can hang with that, just, you know, whatever, and I'll do it? But it's like, I think we all have different ideas, you know? And like, as she said, no one's discussed the ideas? But it just comes out with our opinions? When we argue like this? You know? And it didn't like lay out, exactly what we're here for. *And I'm here . . . more on maybe the American side, not American side, but more of like a different angle than some other people come here for,* you know? And I think that . . . that doesn't show unless we argue about like this, but we never . . . just flat out said "I'm here because, this is what happened to me" as she just did right now.

We see that self-categorizations typically occur (as seen in the first set of italicized lines in the quotation above) after (1) laying out a field of oppositions within which the speakers can situate themselves, and (2) expressing a view about camp goals and motivations of everyone for participating. Whereas Ellen could have simply argued that merely stating opinions will only lead to strife—which she does in the next few lines—she approaches the issue by situating herself in terms of ethnic identity, as she does in the second set of bold lines. Clearly being in the category "American" is not so straightforward, as seen in her use of hedges. "Ellen's talk shows how claiming a 'more American' relational identity can also mean rejecting Korean modes of interaction that embrace social hierarchies, like showing respect for elders through the use of the kinship terms *oppa* 'older brother' and *ennui* 'older sister' . . . a practice 'she herself does not espouse'" (Kang 2009:139).

However, not all linguists and dialectologists agree that there is no real discernable Asian American English. In a dialect-identification task performed by New Yorkers, listeners were able to identify Asian American native English speakers from others (but could not distinguish Chinese Americans from Korean Americans). Newman and Wu (2011:152) conclude that Asian Americans "are indeed distinct pieces in the U.S. racial dialectal mosaic, instead of relatively minor variations on European American patterns. Perhaps the cues to racial identity are fewer and subtler than, say, for African Americans or Latinos in New York. Certainly, that lack of socio-phonetic saliency and idiosyncratic distribution of features among speakers suggests that this study does not provide sufficient evidence to refute Reyes (2005) and Reyes and Lo's (2009) assertion that there is no Asian American English along the lines of African American English. On the other hand, the features do exist, and therefore the Asian Americans' uniqueness seems to be best characterized in terms of an ethnolinguistic repertoire (Benor 2010). By selecting from a set of features, consciously or unconsciously, Asian American speakers can index their racialized group identity even though this crosses national heritage lines." Clearly, much more work on Asian American language awaits.

### *The Language(s) of People of Latin American Heritage in the United States*

*Hispanic, or Latino, or something else?* Another space where we see the complex intersection of race, ethnicity, and language is with people of Latin American heritage in the United States. First off, there is an almost insurmountable nomenclature problem. The terms *Hispanic* and *Latino* (or sometimes *Latino/Latina*) are common, but contested, **ethnonyms.** And do these labels mean "Spanish-speaking," "Spanish-surnamed," of "Latin ancestry," of "Latin ethnicity," or of a supposed "Brown" race? The US census defines "Hispanic" as "a person of Mexican, Puerto Rican, Cuban, South or Central American, or other Spanish culture or origin, regardless of race," though the Office of Management and Budget recommends using "Latino" and "Hispanic" interchangeably. However, the Mexican American performance artist and writer Guillermo Gómez-Peña believes "The term Hispanic, coined by technomarketing experts and by the designers of political campaigns, homogenizes our cultural diversity (Chicanos, Cubans, and Puerto Ricans become indistinguishable), avoids our indigenous cultural heritage and links us directly with Spain. Worse yet, it possesses connotations of upward mobility and political obedience" (http://www.azquotes.com/quote/670009). Indeed, often many younger people of Latin background often prefer to use a term referring to country of national origin rather than "Hispanic" or "Latino/a," especially if they are primarily Spanish speakers (Lippi-Green 2012:260).

*Speech communities.* Regardless, CNN has reported that there are now some 41 million Spanish-speakers in the United States, with another 11.6 million who are bilingual, making it the second-largest Spanish-speaking country in the world, second only to Mexico's 121 million. By 2050, the United States is projected to be the world's largest Spanish-speaking nation, with 132.8 million speakers (Melendez 2015). Clearly, Spanish and Spanish-speakers are an important presence in the United States.

Nonetheless, the speech communities of people of Latin background in the United States are diverse and varied. Some—as in the American Southwest—live in almost monolingual Spanish-speaking areas. Some live in largely monolingual English-speaking communities, where a Spanish accent is noticeable. Others—especially in the large US cities—"live in communities where multiple varieties of English co-exist in relative harmony, in which Spanish, English, and Chicano or other varieties of Latino English each have a place. Chicano English, Puerto Rican English, and Cuban English in Los Angeles, New York, and Miami are distinct from each other, with distinctive syntactical, morphological, and discourse markers" (Lippi-Green 2012:261),

There are no doubt many phonological features of various Hispanic Englishes that are marked, such as in the initial alveolar-palatal fricatives becoming affricates, as in the words "Chicago" (standard English šikƏgow versus čikƏgow) or "shower" (standard English šawer versus čawer) or "Chevy" (standard English ševiy versus čeviy). However, one of the most common features found in the speech of Hispanic-Latino/Latina Americans is *code-switching*. We saw in Chapter 7 that code-switching refers to the mixing of speech styles—or in the case of bilinguals, two languages—within a single sentence or speech event. In the following sentences we see examples of Spanish-English code-switching (Benevento and Dietrich 2015:407, 412; Orsi 2008:22):

| | |
|---|---|
| *Yo estaba bien* happy | I was very happy |
| I think, therefore *digo yo* | I think, therefore I am |
| *Yo perdi* a lot of that | I missed a lot of that |
| The water *esta boileando* | The water is boiling. |

In a community where many people are bilingual or there is an extensive presence of two or more languages, code-switching is ubiquitous. And the use of these forms often tends to build solidarity among the speakers. The problem is, to those who are not in the loop—those who do not know what is going on and why—such forms appear to be semi-lingual, or corrupted and poor attempts at trying to speak either language: That is, such stylistic or grammatical shifts and code-switching "may seem to an unsympathetic outsider [as] nothing more than a language hodge-podge." In the case of Spanish-English code-switching, this kind of speech is "often labeled ***Spanglish***" (Lippi-Green 2012:261).

*Spanglish.* Spanglish, of course, is a blending of the words "Spanish" and "English" and is a term loosely used to cover the wide variety of speech patterns that result from the interaction of these two languages. Whether one wants to consider Spanglish as a variety of Spanish with a heavy presence of English, or as English with a heavy presence of Spanish depends on one's politics and language ideology.

Regardless, Spanglish is highly localized and idiosyncratic. That is, depending on the individual or circumstance, Spanglish can vary greatly, and a single person's facility in it can be equally variable, though generally it is reserved for oral communication. There is a fair degree of freedom of choice even constructing sentences. For example, one way code-switching works in Spanglish is to consider how one might speak about a dress that is red (English, "the red dress"; in Spanish, "*el vestido rojo*"). In Spanglish one may prefer to use the Spanish NOUN + ADJECTIVE word order—*el dress rojo*—or the English ADJECTIVE + NOUN word order—*el red dress* (Orsi 2008:24).

In Spanglish, lexical items and grammatical forms from either language can be present, as well as idioms and **calques**—direct translations of a word or phrase from one language into another. For example, in Spanglish, the English phrase "to run for governor" might come out as *correr para gobernador* [lit. "run" "for" "governor"] compared to the standard Spanish *presentarse para gobernador* (Montes-Alcala 2009:107). Semantic extensions or reassignments are also common in Spanglish. For example, Spanglish *bizarro* (based on, and meaning, the English "bizarre") means "valiant" in Standard Spanish. Similarly *librería* (based on, and meaning, the English "library") means "bookstore" in Standard Spanish. (Montes-Alcala 2009:105).

Another way new words get introduced into Spanglish is through the addition of the productive verb-making morpheme *-ear* added to an English noun (Rothman and Rell 2005:522; Orsi 2008:29; Stavans 2003:97, 126, 236). For example:

| English noun | Spanglish verb | meaning |
|---|---|---|
| telephone | *telefonear* | to call |
| lunch | *lunchear* | to eat lunch |
| check | *chequear* | to check |
| watch | *watchear* | to watch |
| park | *parquear* | to park |

Stavans (2003:25) has said that "Spanglish is the encounter, perhaps the word is marriage or divorce of English and Spanish, but also of Anglo and Hispanic civilizations, not only in the United States, but in the entire continent and perhaps also in Spain." He adds (p. 27), "It is a very creative jazzy way of being Latino in the United States today." Some have also argued that Spanglish is accelerating the process of acculturation for newcomers to the United States, bridging the gap between Spanish and English:

> It is facilitating the transition, side-stepping the traditional process of abandoning the native language and slowly acquiring the one of the adopted land. As such, it is almost completely eliminating the transitional "broken English," and thereby shortening the time it takes for new arrivées to effectively communicate with those around them in their new surroundings. This unique phenomenon is, in all likelihood, the main factor distinguishing Hispanics from other immigrant groups. (Bazán-Figueras and Figueras 2014:264)

Bazán-Figueras and Figueras add (p. 265) that although Spanglish remains a controversial topic among many, over time its legitimacy will not be questioned either. After all, what we call the Romance languages today—French, Spanish, Italian, and so on—were all just "vulgar" versions of the classical Latin lingua franca of Western Europe a millennium ago. They were largely unwritten, "corrupted," and constantly in flux—just like Spanglish today. Maybe what we are witnessing is a very similar process of language development.

*Linguistic discrimination against Spanish speakers.* We cannot, however, leave a discussion of Spanish-speakers in the United States without addressing some of the covert racial discourse that has been leveled against them. (And, indeed, much of this applies to AAE and Asian Americans as well.) Jane Hill (2008) poses two very puzzling questions: How, taking American society as a whole, can racism still persist in a culture where to call someone a racist is a major insult? And, how can racism still persist in a culture where equal opportunity is a universally articulated—and highly subscribed-to—value? To be sure, explicit racial slurs are still made, but these are usually noticed, and generally challenged or rejected (at least in polite company). But perhaps much of our racism is encoded in subtle linguistic categories that we carry with us, and these are more insidious. In some real ways our own unexamined linguistic ideologies that we carry—which are often subtle and which we are often unaware of—can perpetuate a routine everyday use of language that helps racism survive in spite of our denying it is so.

An example of this is fake or "**Mock Spanish**." A while back, the Taco Bell fast-food franchise had a very popular ad campaign showing a Chihuahua saying ¡Yo Quiero Taco Bell! Was this just a cute little talking dog enticing customers to stop by for a Mexican lunch, or was it covert racist discourse reproducing negative stereotypes invisible—or at least deniable—for European Americans? Or what about Arnold Schwarzenegger in the *Terminator* films saying, "Hasta la vista, baby!" as he blows away a thousand people? Is this just a cool or colorful expression, or is it emblematic of something else?

A **folk theory**, or "common-sense" model about the world, is one that the mainstream community in general shares with little reflection or doubt—as opposed to a more empirically-based scientific theory that strives to be rigorous, predictive, replicable, and questioning. All of us who live in any kind of social group—even scientists, depending on the context—subscribe to our culture's various folk theories. Jane Hill (2008) contends that an "individualist" folk theory of racism is prevalent in America, and is one that still continues to impact everyday discourse in covert (and even sometimes overt) ways. That is, most individual Americans claim, "I am not a racist," and on one level, they are probably right.

**Photo 14.1 Taco Bell. An example of Mock Spanish used in a marketing campaign.**

But this commonsense belief—that racism is *only* based upon *individual* intentional feelings of prejudice or not—is something we might question. Much of our racism is encoded in subtle linguistic categories that we carry with us, and these are often quite sinister as they are largely unbeknownst to us. They can perpetuate a routine, everyday use of language that helps racism survive, in spite of individual actions to the contrary.

It is clear, then, that there has been—and continues to be—much prejudice against Spanish-speakers in the United States. Thus, we have to ask why Hispanics who were born in the United States and speak native English as their first language want to learn to speak Spanish or keep Spanish alive in a nation dominated by English. This is a question we will take up in the next sections.

## LANGUAGE AND NATIONALITY

In the last decades of the twentieth century, many scholars argued that "ethnicity is not always the survival of cultural diversity born of geographical and social isolation, but may be the outcome of intensive interaction, a constellation of practices that evolve to channel complex social relations" (Woolard 1989:3). Following this approach, Susan Gal (1979:3) studied language shift in Oberwart, a bilingual area in eastern Austria. After four hundred years of Hungarian-German bilingualism, German began replacing Hungarian in everyday conversation as well as in local business. She asked:

> By what intervening processes does industrialization, or any other social change, effect changes in the uses to which speakers put their languages in everyday interactions? How

BOX 14.4 THE EVERYDAY LANGUAGE OF WHITE RACISM

White Americans generally agree that things happen in the world because individuals with beliefs, emotions, and intentions cause them to happen. They consider this understanding to be the most obvious kind of common sense. Yet not everyone approaches the world from this perspective, and it is very interesting to try to think about racism from outside the framework that it imposes. Critical theorists do not deny that individual beliefs figure in racism. But we prefer to emphasize its collective, cultural dimensions, and to avoid singling out individuals and trying to decide whether they are racists or not. Furthermore, critical theorists insist that ordinary people who do not share White supremacist beliefs can still talk and behave in ways that advance the projects of White racism. [R] acist effects can be produced in interaction, in an intersubjective space of discourse, without any single person in the interaction intending discrimination.

From Jane Hill, *The Everyday Language of White Racism* (2008), 7. Used by Permission of John Wiley and Sons Inc.

does the social change affect the communicative economy of the group? How does it change the evaluations of languages and the social statuses and meanings associated with them? How does it affect the communicative strategies of speakers so that individuals are motivated to change their choice of language in different contexts of social interaction—to reallocate their linguistic resources radically so that eventually they abandon one of their languages altogether?

We might ask these questions even more broadly. Is speaking the same language sufficient grounds for people to establish a nation? Should all people in the same nation speak the same language? If the answer to both questions is no—and probably most people in the twenty-first century would agree—what should be the status of "minority" languages in multilingual societies? Because of the symbolic value of language—especially with regard to group solidarity and the ethnic identity of its speakers—language choice, maintenance, and shift are some of the most important personal and political social issues of any community.

In this section we will focus on language and the nation-state. We will look at how the symbolic value of languages is used by the people to pursue political power and ends and to foster consciousness among members of the group. We will look at four case studies: India, the Czech Republic, Canada, and Spain.

### *India*

Occupying an area only one-third as large as the United States but with the second-largest global population (of more than a billion people), India is one of the world's most multilingual countries. More than four hundred languages are spoken there (Gordon 2005:353), spanning at least four language families (Indo-European, Dravidian, Austroasiatic, and Tibeto-Burman), as well as some isolates. There are twenty-two officially recognized languages in the constitution. Although English is not a legally sanctioned language, the

Presidential Order of 1960 states that it "should be the principal official language and Hindi the subsidiary Official Language till 1965. After 1965, when Hindi becomes the principal official language of the Union, English should continue as the subsidiary official language."

How does India, a federal republic, deal administratively with such a vast collection of languages? On a regional basis, eastern India is dominated by three Indo-European languages (Bengali, Oriya, and Assamese), western India by two (Marathi and Gujarati), northern India by four (Hindi and Urdu, Panjabi and Kashmiri), and southern India by four languages of the Dravidian language family (Telugu, Tamil, Kannada, and Malayalam). The principal official language in six of the twenty-five states of the republic as well as of the country at the federal level is Hindi. However, as long as many non–Hindi-speaking citizens are reluctant to accept Hindi, it is English—the language of those who governed most of India as a British crown colony for nearly a century—that serves as the associate national language and as a lingua franca acceptable in both the Hindi-speaking north and the Dravidian-speaking south.

In a country where many languages are spoken but do not all enjoy the same degree of prestige, bilingualism, multilingualism, and diglossia are common. For interethnic oral communication of an informal nature, Hindi or Urdu is used to a varying degree throughout the country (the two are very similar in their colloquial forms, but Hindi is written in the Devanagari script, Urdu in a modified form of Arabic script). For reasons of cultural prestige, there has been some resistance to the use of Hindi as a contact language in the Dravidian-speaking part of the country and in Bengal. For formal and written communication, English (its South Asian variety) is used to a great extent. The importance of English can readily be seen: in 1977, although newspapers and periodicals in India were available in about seventy languages, Hindi- and English-language newspapers and periodicals accounted for, respectively, 26 and 20 percent of the total published, and those in English had the highest circulation. When India became independent in 1947, the official use of English was intended to be only temporary. But the need for English continues and in some respects has even increased. For example, to translate technical and scientific works into Hindi would be a nearly impossible task. Today, more than a half century after India gained independence, knowledge of English is still considered indispensable for high government positions, and although only a very small percentage of the population speaks and reads English, Indians with a knowledge of English tend to be the cultural, economic, and political leaders.

Such a large linguistic variety (in both languages and dialects) as exists in India poses a number of questions. Although it might be expected that having one official language would tend to promote unity in a multiethnic nation, such unity would be achieved at a considerable loss of prestige to other native languages spoken by many millions of people. This is why Hindi, the most widely used second language in India, has encountered resistance in many parts of the country. And this is also why a nonindigenous and formerly colonial language, English, has maintained itself surprisingly well as an associate official language since India's independence and will undoubtedly continue to do so in the future. A second language for many Indians, English does not give an advantage to speakers of one particular native language, as does Hindi. Another question has to do with determining the languages to be taught and used for instruction in Indian schools. What eventually became known as the three-language formula has resulted in secondary students being taught the regional language, Hindi, and English (and in many instances their mother tongue is yet a fourth language or local dialect).

Throughout much of the world, dialectal differences have tended to diminish rapidly in recent decades as a result of the mass media, education, and mobility. This has not happened in India, where caste differences are effectively symbolized by speech differences. As long as the old and well-established social hierarchy persists, linguistic differences serve a useful function and are likely to be retained.

### *The Czech Republic*

The Bohemian kingdom of the Czech people goes back to the end of the eleventh century, but the first Czechs settled in the area and made it their homeland no later than the sixth century. The development of a Czech national culture came to a temporary (though long) halt in 1620, when the Czechs possessing political rights and power were defeated in the battle of Bílá Hora (White Mountain). The Bohemian kingdom lost its independence, and its provinces were declared the hereditary property of the Hapsburgs. The area of the former kingdom had a fairly large proportion of German-speaking people, the descendants of German colonists who had been invited during the thirteenth and fourteenth centuries to settle in Bohemian cities and rural areas.

During the four censuses conducted between 1880 and 1910 in the western part of the multilingual Hapsburg Austro-Hungarian Empire, the Austrian census administration used the concept of *Umgangssprache* (language of use) rather than *Muttersprache* (mother tongue). The Czechs, who at the time were still citizens of the empire, resented this terminological practice because it underrepresented their numbers among the empire's nationalities, yielding a larger proportion of speakers of the higher-status German than was warranted.

How did this happen? For example, Czechs who were employed in German-speaking households or business enterprises were listed as users of German even though Czech was their mother tongue and the language they spoke with members of their own families.

Using language to establish ethnic identity continued a little over a decade later, but with a different goal. The people of some of the border areas of Czechoslovakia, an independent country established in 1918 at the end of World War I, belonged to two or even three different language groups. One such area was that of Teschen (*Těšín* in Czech and *Cieszyn* in Polish) along the Czechoslovak-Polish border. According to the final Austrian census of 1910, based on the concept of language of use, speakers of Polish accounted for 48.5 percent, of Czech for 39.5 percent, and of German for 12 percent. Percentages from the next census, in 1921, then conducted by Czechoslovak authorities, were quite different: The Czech-speaking population of the area was now given as 65.1 percent. Apparently the Czech administrators of the census assigned ethnic identity on the basis of mother tongue rather than language of use, and this they undoubtedly did to legitimize the hold of the new republic on at least a good part of an ethnically mixed border area.

### *Canada*

As in India and the United States, there is great linguistic diversity in Canada—some eighty-five languages being spoken (Gordon 2005:235)—but the biggest issue is the tension between the two official languages, French and English. Problems of bilingualism have always been the central issue in the nation's politics even before the Confederation of 1867. Jacques Cartier landed in current Quebec in 1534 and claimed the territory for King Francis I, eventually calling it New France. A century and a half later, British entrepreneurs, incorporated by royal charter, started fur trading in the Hudson Bay area in northern Canada. After that, animosity between France and Britain gradually increased, and as a result of the Seven Years' War (1756–1763), the British government took over lower Canada and New France (which was renamed Quebec). The differences between these two colonial populations were significant. French colonists spoke French, practiced Catholicism, and followed the French civil code; British colonists spoke English, practiced Protestantism, and followed traditional English common law. To avert further local conflict, the British passed the Quebec Act of 1774; this guaranteed the residents the use of the French language, Catholicism, and French civil law. This practice was reified several times, and in 1969 the Official Languages Act made English and French Canada's two official languages. According to 2007 government figures, about 60 percent of Canadians claim English as their native language, as do about 23 percent for French. The majority of these French speakers—about 85 percent—live in Quebec. More than 17 percent of the population of Canada is bilingual in French and English.

In spite of the unique characteristics and background of the original British and French settlers, Anglophone Canadians began to control most elite positions in business and industry, even in Quebec. By the 1960s, many Francophone residents began to feel that the French language was being overwhelmed by English. To maintain Canada's professed bilingualism, the federal and local governments created various departments and institutions to oversee the use of the languages in the province. For some Canadians, one of these—the Quebec Board of the French Language—has sometimes been draconian in its enforcement of language policies. For example, the board's "language police" (as labeled by some nationalist newspapers) gave tickets to shop owners in Quebec who neglected to provide signs in French. However, by the end of the twentieth century, such extreme policies were rescinded, and the laws were modified to make French just markedly predominant on exterior business signs, as suggested by the Supreme Court of Canada.

For the most part, the promotion of personal bilingualism in English and French is an important objective of the Canadian government (though one not always easily obtained or consistently supported). For example, in 2003 the federal government announced a ten-year goal to double bilingualism among Canadian college graduates from 24 percent to 50 percent by 2013. In 1970, the federal government launched the official languages in education program and supported French-language immersion education in many Anglophone public school districts. However, the influence of English still remains strong. According to Monica Heller (1988), because of the social and economic tensions between Francophone and Anglophone speakers in Quebec, how bilingual speakers of French and English see these two languages is highly charged. An awareness of the social value of the two languages reflects how they are used in daily conversations.

These language issues have important political implications. Some believe that the only way to protect the French language and Francophone rights is for Quebec to split off from the rest of Canada. This has been an issue in almost every election since the 1980s. Although it is unlikely that Canada will divide, the cultural and linguistic tensions remain.

### *Spain*

Although the official language of Spain is Castilian Spanish, some dozen other languages are spoken in the country. Catalan and Basque are two of the most important minority languages, and they are spoken by 15 percent and 1.4 percent of the population, respectively (Gordon 2005:559–560). Both are important because of the issues of nationalism and ethnic pride associated with each.

Euskara (Euskera), or Basque, is the language of the Basque people who inhabitant northeast Spain and southwest France. There are about 650,000 Basque speakers in Spain and some 100,000 in France. The language is an isolate, with only disputed affiliations with other languages. It has five major dialects. Under the language policy of the Franco regime (1939–1975), from 1937 until the mid-1950s it was prohibited to use the Basque language in public. After the Basques regained some political sovereignty, they were once again allowed to use their language in public (including in church services, education, and the mass media). The Royal Academy of the Basque Language created a standard form of Basque in 1964—called Euskara Batua—and established a standard orthography. Although many Basque speakers were reluctant to accept such standards at first, Euskara Batua gradually became accepted and is now used by the Basques at all levels of education.

Unlike Basque, Catalan is a Romance language of the Indo-European family and shares an 85 percent lexical similarity with Spanish. Its history goes back to the third century BCE, when the Catalonia area was ruled by Rome. Because of close contact with Rome, Catalan developed from a more modern and more popular form of Latin than did Castilian. Currently about 7 million people in Spain speak Catalan as their first language. It is also spoken in small areas in southwest France and in Sardinia in Italy.

Right after World War II, the Franco government took severe repressive measures against Catalan language and culture, partly because of the resistance put up by Catalonia during the Spanish Civil War. Barcelona, its capital, was then a center of revolutionary leftist activity. Much of Catalonia's prewar autonomy was lost, and public use of the Catalan language was prohibited. During the latter days of the Franco regime, some folk celebrations and religious observances in Catalan came to be tolerated. But because of the institutionalized language discrimination and its similarity to Spanish, today there are few, if any, monolingual Catalan speakers.

## SUMMARY AND CONCLUSIONS

Although we often think that language variation is largely due to geographically based dialects, much of the time the differences in language use we hear around us result from other causes. For example, one distinctive variety of English spoken in the United States is African American English, used primarily by African Americans in concentrated urban centers where ethnic minorities can form unified communities. Speaking the same way helps people identify themselves and develop social networks related to each other. Far from being deficient and its speakers verbally deprived, AAE has its own structure, related to but distinct from other varieties of American English, as well as a range of expressive styles. The stigma often attached to it is undeserved because it confuses the lower socioeconomic status of the many African Americans who use it with their speech—a good example of ignorance breeding prejudice.

Language is also an important marker at another level. Although not every language has a country, and few countries have only one language, for many people there is an almost visceral connection between a nation-state and some of the languages used within its borders. Should one language be privileged over the others, and if so, for what reasons? What does this mean for those who are its native speakers, and for those who are not? These are by no means trivial questions, as the world's many language wars have demonstrated. And as the world becomes more globalized and the borders of countries more porous, issues of language and nationality can only become more complex.

## RESOURCE MANUAL AND STUDY GUIDE

### *Questions for Discussion*

1. Discuss why the United States has no official language policy. Is this a good or bad thing? How might the United States be different if there *were* an official language?
2. In 1971, civil rights activist Bayard Rustin argued that "'Black English,' after all, has nothing to do with blackness but derives from conditions of lower-class life in the South (poor Southern whites also speak 'Black English')." But noted African American linguist John McWhorter disagrees, saying, "Yet while there is some obvious overlap between Black and southern English, few would say Jeff Foxworthy and Samuel L. Jackson speak the same dialect. . . . does anyone think black people in Pittsburgh would really feel a special connection to the speech style of Dolly Parton or Jim Nabors?" (McWhorter 2017:19). Defend or refute this claim, with arguments pro and con.
3. In our presentation of AAE in this chapter, we have suggested in places that there might not even be such a thing as "Black English." Keeping in mind that we authors are not African American, are we being overcautious—that is, that even acknowledging that there is a "black" way of talking is paramount to being racist? Discuss why believing in AAE might make some people, including professional linguistic anthropologists, uncomfortable.

### *Projects*

**PROJECT 1**

Go to a fast-food restaurant and one of the more expensive restaurants in your town (maybe just sit in the lobby, if you do not want to eat in the expensive restaurant!). Listen to people's talk and conversations for a while. Do you find any differences in language usage between the fast-food restaurant and the expensive restaurant? If so, are the differences found in vocabulary, or grammar, or pronunciation? Or some combination of these?

**PROJECT 2**

How have African American social and economic conditions changed since World War II? What role do you think language played in this? How has the language *changed*, if it all?

**PROJECT 3**

Listen to some blues songs and rap music and analyze their lyrics. What characteristics of AAE as described in this chapter do you find or *not* find?

**PROJECT 4**

Analyze the following stories using the features and properties of African American English as described in this chapter. In both cases give specific examples of African American English characteristics you find in each story.

***Story A***

I done made up my mind that if I did it I was gonna kill all's in the house. The old man, the old lady, the boys, everyone's there, I swear, I gonna kill everyone of 'em. And tell my own tale about it. Go to court, give myself up. "Well, why'd you kill the old lady?" "Well, she got in the way of a bullet." Ha ha ha ha. That's the way people get killed, get in the way of a bullet, you know.

***Story B***

That's the way I had it figured out. It's a bad thing, a man to have it figured out in his mind—I'm talking about *being get on it*, I was set on it. And there wasn't no nervous stuff, I'm not braggin' about it or nothing like that—that's the kind of person I *was*, and if a person do enough to me today, they'd cause me to kill them. They'd have to do an awful lot to me because I'm more settled, I got more understanding, and I know more about life, and I know more about what it's about than I did then. I was just a young fellow, I hadn't read much, hadn't traveled much, only I just didn't want to be run over and walked on. I'd as much as kill someone as to be walked on. Today I'd let a fellow walk on me a little bit before I'd kill 'im.

Here are the stories in more "standard" English:

I had made up my mind that if I did it, I was going to kill everyone in the house: the old man, the old lady, the boys, everyone who was there. I swear, I was going to kill everyone. And I would tell my own version of it. I would go to court. I would give myself up. They would ask me, "Well, why did you kill the old lady?" I would say, "Well, she got in the way of a bullet." Ha ha ha ha. That is the way people get killed; they get in the way of a bullet, you know!

That is how I had it figured out [that is how I understood it]. It is a bad thing for a man to come to such a place in his mind—to have decided to do such a thing, and be comfortable with it. I had decided, and I had come to terms with it. And I wasn't really nervous. I'm not proud of it, or anything like that. It's just that that was the kind of person I was back then. Now, if a person sufficiently provoked me today, I suppose I might still kill them. But they would have to do an awful lot to make me do that now because I am more settled; I understand things better, and I know more about life. I know more about what life is all about now than I did back then. I was just a young fellow. I hadn't read much and I hadn't traveled much. I just didn't want to be taken advantage of, and be disrespected. I would have just as soon killed somebody as lose respect. Today, I would give a person a little leeway before I would kill them.

## PROJECT 5

A discussion by college students of language and social class is found in (13 min.): http://www.bing.com/videos/search?q=language+and+social+class&&view=detail&mid=E8F5B66DF5423D59771BE8F5B66DF5423D59771B&FORM=VRDGAR.

And in this clip (10 min.) we see a discussion of various class symbols: https://www.youtube.com/watch?v=nU5MtVM_zFs&list=PLC6D871A2A8C3C8EF.

Here people are talking *about* the class system, how it is indicated, and what it measures. Summarize what is being said here. Besides the symbols, notice the accents! What can we conclude about language and social class from these clips?

## PROJECT 6

The US government's Office of Management and Budget in 1997 released a position paper, "Revisions to the Standards for the Classification of Federal Data on Race and Ethnicity." This paper is still in effect, and can be found here: https://nces.ed.gov/programs/handbook/data/pdf/Appendix_A.pdf.

What are the different arguments made for the use of the official race and ethnic categories in the US census and in other governmental activities? What are some of the assumptions and presumptions underlying this document? Is it satisfactory to you? What would you change? What would you say if you heard that in 2020 a new category is going to be added (South Asians, or those from the Indian subcontinent)?

## *Objective Study Questions*

### TRUE-FALSE TEST

T F 1. Some dialects are based on regional or geographical differences, but much less language variation is based on social or economic class, ethnicity, or race.

T F 2. Even though it covers a large geography and has many different ethnic groups, since it was the colony of England everybody in India speaks English.

T F 3. AAE is remarkably similar in pronunciation and form throughout the whole United States.

T F 4. In AAE the most stable consonants are those found at the end of words.

T F 5. Some varieties of AAE have more complicated tense rules than conventional American English and convey notions of time more subtly.

T F 6. AAE is just as rule-governed as other forms of English, though its rules of usage are somewhat different.

T F 7. Since bilingual education has been well established in Canada, all Canadians can switch back and forth between English and French easily; Anglophones and Francophones have little tension when they speak to each other.

T F 8. Basque is in the Indo-European language family.

T F 9. Catalan is spoken only in Spain today.

### MULTIPLE-CHOICE QUESTIONS

____ 1. William Labov found that some New Yorkers pronounced r-sounds in words that did not include them in the spelling. Such usage is called (A) hypercorrection. (B) prescribed pronunciation. (C) proscribed pronunciation. (D) a mistake.

____ 2. The most applicable comment concerning the AAE utterance "He eat meat" is: (A) AAE is less expressive than conventional American English. (B) AAE is a defective variety (form) of conventional American English. (C) AAE has carried the development of English verb morphology farther than conventional American English.

____ 3. How did AAE come about? Which of the following choices is most defensible? (A) AAE is one of the dialects of American English. (B) AAE is an English-based creole (similar to Jamaican Creole). (C) AAE shares some features with Standard English and others with creoles such as Gullah or Jamaican.

____ 4. Why do Chicanos code-switch? Choose the best answer from the following: (A) Chicanos lack an extensive English vocabulary. (B) Chicanos lack an extensive Spanish vocabulary. (C) They want to maintain their ethnic identity as Mexican Americans. (D) Their religion requires it.

____ 5. In Quebec, how do the people communicate? (A) Everyone speaks English. (B) Everyone speaks French. (C) Everyone speaks both English and French almost equally. (D) Some people speak French and others speak English, and the two groups are largely segregated.

____ 6. Which of the following countries is the most linguistically diverse? (A) the United States. (B) India. (C) Spain. (D) Canada. (E) the Czech Republic.

### COMPLETIONS

1. Beliefs about the social world as expressed by speakers through their language are called language ________________ (one word).

2. The official language of the Czech Republic is Czech; the languages with a major presence are Slovak, Polish, and ________________ (one word).
3. One of the well-known linguistic features of AAE is ________________, as in *I don't want nothing* (two words).
4. In northern Spain, the ________________ people have sometimes resorted to armed struggle for their linguistic and cultural rights (one word).
5. Basque language is not a member of any language family. It is a language ________________ like Japanese or Pirahã (one word).

## Answer Key

*Projects.* Actually, these stories were not told by an African American. They were told by Dock Boggs, a white rural banjo player from eastern Kentucky. These stories are taken from the liner notes accompanying the 1997 CD *Dock Boggs: Country Blues, Complete Early Recordings (1927–1929)* (Revenant Label, no number). What are some lessons that we can draw from this exercise? First, it makes us question the efficacy of the alleged properties of African American English that many scholars claim (as we reported in this chapter). That is, the presence or absence of, say, the double negative, does not necessarily indicate that the speaker is an African American. Conversely, it could also be argued—assuming AAE really exists—that at least some of its features are found in other geographic or ethnic dialects in the United States. In either case, we have to ask ourselves, is AAE something we *expect* to find—and then we do not disappoint ourselves by finding it? That is, is AAE the product of our own linguistic preconceptions?

True-false test: 1-F, 2-F, 3-F, 4-F, 5-T, 6-T, 7-F, 8-F, 9-F
Multiple-choice questions: 1-A, 2-C, 3-C, 4-C, 5-D, 6-B
Completions: 1. ideology, 2. German 3. double negatives 4. Basque 5. isolate

## Notes and Suggestions for Further Reading

Books and collections dealing with the topics covered in this chapter include Alim, Rickford, and Ball (2016); Fought (2006); Bergvall (1999); Kroskrity (1983, 1993, and 2000); Harris and Rampton (2003); Rampton (1995); Cheshire (2002); and Mills (1995). For particular problems concerning the United States, see the overviews in Tamasi and Antieau (2015), Lippi-Green (2012), Reyes and Lo (2009), and Macneil and Cran (2005). For a cross-cultural student-oriented discussion on language and power, see Mooney and Evans (2015).

The best general, linguistically accurate overview of AAE is McWhorter (2017), and is highly recommended for students. Our section concerning the origins of African American English draws heavily on Burling (1973). In comparing African American Vernacular English with Standard English, linguists use such expressions as *loss of* and *weakened* in their technical linguistic senses; they are not to be construed as carrying negative connotations. Weakening and losses have characterized the history of English inflections from Old English to the present, and no one has ever claimed that Modern English is the worse for it. For a survey of literature concerning the features of AAE, theories of its origins, and several related topics, see Morgan (1994) and Labov (1972a). On the future of AAE see Labov (2010). For a discussion of the Ebonics issue, see Fields (1997). A kind of anti-Ebonics prescriptive guide to English can be found in Garrard McClendon's (2004) humorous pamphlet *Ax or Ask? The African American Guide to Better English* (McClendonReport.com). But the best treatments of AAE are found in Rickford (2013 and 1999) and Rickford and Rickford (2000). An entertaining discussion, along with videos, on the use of "aks" in the African American community can be heard on the December 3, 2013, edition of NPR Radio's *The World* program: "Why Chaucer Said 'Ax' Instead of 'Ask,' and Why Some Still Do," by Shereen Marisol Meraji (which can be accessed at http://www.npr.org/blogs/codeswitch/2013/12/03/248515217/why-chaucer-said-ax-instead-of-ask-and-why-some-still-do).

For women and AAE, see Smitherman (1998) and Morgan (1999).

For an examination of the pejorative N-word in and out of AAE, see Asim (2007).

For issues of Spanglish, see Montes-Alcalá (2000) and Stavans (2003), which also includes a 185-page Spanglish-English dictionary.

For studies on language and nationalism, see Joseph (2004) and May (2008). Andresen and Carter (2016) take a very broad but very enjoyable approach on a wide range of topics concerning language, history, and politics. For specific countries, see Kachru, Kachru, and Sridhar (2008) (India); Kamusella (2009) (especially pp. 481–518) (Czech Republic); Woolard (1989) and Wright (1999) (Spain); and Heller (2011) and Edwards (2010) (Canada). Urla (2015) gives a good ethnographic perspective on the current state of Basque affairs.

Fought (2006) is a standard for language and ethnicity in general.

For useful general surveys on language ideology, see Woolard and Schieffelin (1994) and Schieffelin, Woolard, and Kroskrity (1998).

See Bucholtz (2011), Hill (2008), Kubota and Lin (2009), and Baugh (2002) for discussions of language and race.

For the role of AAE in politics—or not—see Alim and Smitherman's (2012) intriguing study of Obama and language. For the full story and a video on Joe Biden's comments about Barack Obama, see http://cnn.com/2007/POLITICS/01/31/biden.obama.

# 15

# The Linguistic Anthropology of a Globalized and Digitalized World

## LEARNING OBJECTIVES

- Describe the issues involved concerning language planning and national language policies
- Analyze the roles language plays in education and literacy
- Identify problems and solutions of intercultural communication and translation
- Describe how current digital communication and language affect one another
- Understand advantages and problems of "English hegemony" in a global world
- Understand ethical issues especially pertinent to linguistic anthropology

The year 2016 was quite an interesting one in terms of language. First, the editors of the *Oxford English Dictionary*—long held to be *the* definitive pronouncement on all matters regarding English—made an interesting choice as its Word of the Year (*OED* 2016):

> [T]he Oxford Dictionaries Word of the Year 2016 is *post-truth*—an adjective defined as "relating to or denoting circumstances in which objective facts are less influential in shaping public opinion than appeals to emotion and personal belief." . . . It has also become associated with a particular noun, in the phrase *post-truth politics*.

Other words on the shortlist included *Latinx*, a gender-neutral noun denoting a person of Latin American origin or descent, and *glass cliff*, describing a situation where a woman or minority "ascends to a leadership position in challenging circumstances where the risk of failure is high."

This choice was all the more interesting, seeing as in 2015 their selection was not even a word at all, but something else (*OED* 2015):

> [F]or the first time ever, the Oxford Dictionaries Word of the Year is a pictograph: 😂 officially called the "Face with Tears of Joy" emoji . . . was chosen as the "word" that best reflected the ethos, mood, and preoccupations of 2015. 😂 was chosen because it was the most used emoji globally in 2015 . . . [making] up 20 percent of all the emojis used in the UK in 2015, and 17 percent of those in the US.

And *Time* magazine, as it always does, made its choice for Person of the Year for 2016, Donald Trump. Yet Trump seemed not entirely pleased. *USA Today* reported on December 9 of his telling the crowd at a Des Moines, Iowa, rally, "They used to call it 'Man of the Year.' So they call it 'Person.' They want to be politically correct." He then added, "That's OK." The next day he told a Baton Rouge, Louisiana, crowd of the same honor, adding, "[T]hey were both nice and a little bit wise guy yesterday. . . . They're politically correct. They were very politically correct."

What might linguistic anthropology have to say about such things? It is these, and several other topics, we will take up in this final chapter. Linguistic anthropology is generally thought to be a field of research understood and practiced by only a relatively few specialists. Although the applications of anthropology to contemporary problems is generally seen as coming from the applied subfield of cultural rather than linguistic anthropology, many practical uses have been found for socially oriented linguistics, and linguistic anthropology expertise is being applied with increasing frequency to issues and problems having their roots in language use.

One of the most commonly used and best developed forms of applied linguistics and linguistic anthropology is in language planning. Language planning may be called for when the presence of several competing languages in a country has become divisive or when a particular language or dialect is to be elevated to serve as the official or national language of a multilingual or multidialectal society. The initial step in language planning is to define the nature of the problem. Linguists or linguistic anthropologists are best qualified to assume this task. Because the recommendation that a particular language or dialect be made the official language of a society affects everyone in that society, from elders down to elementary school pupils, such advice must be carefully considered. Once the society's leaders reach a decision, projects to facilitate the implementation of the new language policy must be initiated—for example, preparation of textbooks, grammars, and dictionaries and the development of a teacher-training program.

Linguistic expertise is often frequently and extensively applied in the field of education (for example, to enhance literacy), but it can also contribute to more effective communication in the fields of law, medicine, and business, and it plays an important role in language maintenance and language disorders. This chapter includes some specific examples of the application of linguistics and linguistic anthropology.

We will also look at how linguistic anthropology is involved with intercultural communication, and problems of translation. Here we also discuss the role of English in the global world, its place as a de facto lingua franca, and its potential hegemonic effects.

Much of this chapter, however, will be on new trends in digital and computer-mediated communication—e-mail, the Internet, **Twitter**, and other social media—and the new languages or styles they are inspiring (or perhaps, causing): Internet slang, emoticons, **emojis**, tweets, texting, orthographic changes—the list is almost limitless. What does it mean for us to be "always on" (Baron 2008) in an online mobile world, with messages potentially coming to us 24/7? The twenty-first century is not the first time humans have had to deal with "language at a distance" (Baron 2000)—the telegraph, telephone, radio, and television notwithstanding. But now we can make the discourse come to us. We no longer have to wait to be spoken to, to establish a dialog or conversation. We can seek out "speakers" of similar tastes or political persuasions with the click of a (wireless!) mouse or a finger on a trackpad. How might this have changed the way we communicate, and what might linguistic anthropology say about this?

Finally, we end the chapter with a discussion—albeit all too brief—on the ethical considerations about which all linguists, anthropologists, and other social scientists need to be aware when doing their work—and what the average citizen needs to know as well.

## LANGUAGE PLANNING

The most common form of applied sociolinguistics is language planning. The term refers to a deliberate attempt, usually at the level of the state, to affect language use to prevent or solve some problem of communication. The need for language planning and the formulation of language policies rapidly increased during the twentieth century and is continuing in the twenty-first. The two main reasons are the dislocation of millions of people as a result of wars and political persecution and the emergence of many new multiethnic states when colonial empires were dissolved after World War II.

In a very broad sense, language planning encompasses even the invention of artificial international languages such as Esperanto or Interlingua. Supranational languages such as these are expected to promote understanding and peaceful coexistence among people of different ethnic and linguistic backgrounds. More narrowly, language planning usually takes one of two forms. One form involves a change in the status of a language or a dialect—in other words, a change in language use. The other involves changes in the structure of a language—changes affecting its pronunciation, spelling, grammar, or vocabulary. Frequently, however, the two forms are combined. The following examples illustrate both forms of language planning in practice.

The nationalization of Swahili in Kenya is primarily an example of change in status. In 1974, the first president of independent Kenya, Jomo Kenyatta, decided that the country's national assembly should conduct its business in Swahili. When the members strongly objected, Kenyatta closed the assembly and announced: "Whether some people will like my decision or not KiSwahili will be spoken in our *Bunge* [Parliament], because it is the language of the *wananchi* [citizens, people]. English is not our language and the time will come when we will do everything in Swahili. I know many people will be annoyed but let them" (Hinnebusch 1979:290). Several dozen languages are spoken in Kenya, at least eight of them by more than 1 million speakers each. Kikuyu, the native language of more than 5 million people, is the language most frequently heard, whereas Swahili is a native language spoken by very few Kenyans and therefore is relatively neutral. To have selected one of the main languages of Kenya (for example, Kikuyu, Luo, Luhya, or Kamba) would have incited ethnic rivalry, and to have chosen English would have given preference to the non-African language of those who ruled Kenya from 1895 until 1963. At present, Swahili and English both serve as official languages, but Swahili is the national language. To promote and institutionalize Swahili as the national language of Kenya, a variety of government policies were called for; these ranged from the preparation of instructional materials to making sure that the Swahili used in official dealings is "good" Kenyan Swahili. The great variety of languages spoken in Kenya, the use of Swahili as a lingua franca and also as an important instrument of the country's detribalization, and the prestige that English still enjoys all indicate that language planning in Kenya will need to continue into the future.

Language planning of the second type has been fairly common, but usually not with the speed and to the extent carried out in Turkey after that country became a republic in 1923. When the Seljuk Turks became Islamized during the ninth and tenth centuries, they adopted Arabic script and borrowed many Arabic words, especially those having to do with religion, law, administration, and commerce. Later, when Persia (now Iran) became a part of the Ottoman (Turkish) Empire, the Turks also adopted Persian loanwords. Arabic and Persian influences affected not only the Turkish vocabulary but phonology and grammar as well. Often, then, three words—a native Turkish word and two loanwords, one each from Arabic and Persian—were available for a single referent. To make matters even more complex, the three words were not always subject to the same grammatical rules. Casual spoken Turkish and the literary language (Ottoman Turkish) were in a diglossic relationship, each with a distinct range of social functions. Ottoman Turkish (the high form), with its many loanwords, was virtually unintelligible to peasants and ordinary people, who spoke the low form.

To simplify and modernize written Turkish, Kemal Atatürk (1881–1938), the first president of Turkey, appointed a commission in 1928 to recommend a new system to replace the Arabic script that had been used for centuries even though it had never suited the structure of Turkish. The new writing system—the Latin alphabet with several diacritics—was ready within six weeks, and its use became law before the end of the year. The introduction of the Latin alphabet was later followed by a reform designed to rid Turkish of Arabic and Persian loanwords by substituting Turkish words taken from the popular language and the old Turkish texts, or coining new ones; to accomplish this demanding task, in 1932 Atatürk founded the Turkish Linguistic Society. The changing of the writing system and the simplification of Turkish grammar and the Turkish lexicon helped to modernize and Westernize Turkish society, but these measures also made much of classical Turkish literature, unintelligible to modern Turks in its original form.

## LITERACY, WRITING, AND EDUCATION

There is no doubt that there are significant social and cultural differences between literate and nonliterate peoples. Having a writing system, of course, expands the collective and historical memory of the group. In theory, in a literate community accurate historical records can be kept, scientific information accrued, and religious traditions maintained. Ideally, literacy allows for knowledge to be disseminated to everyone, not just held by a select few.

But things are not so simple. For one thing, we must ask, who controls the writing? What script or spelling or style is acceptable? It is commonly said that the pen is mightier than the sword, but is writing really power?

Members of complex industrial societies often underestimate the intellectual prowess and aesthetic sensibilities of nonliterates who do not make use of written language. The findings of anthropologists have demonstrated time and again how false such an assumption is. For example, there is startling imagery and intricate structure of interlocking repetitions in Navajo chants that invite comparison with the best in Western poetry, and many of the origin myths of Native Americans possess the terseness and dramatic quality characteristic of the Book of Genesis. Just as one expects the style of recognized writers in literate societies to rise above the level of everyday speech, it is common to find that demanding standards govern the performances of traditional narratives. And a reminder: oral folklore is also alive and well in Western societies such as the United States, where it takes the form of tall tales, ballads, jokes, counting-out rhymes, and riddles—to mention only a few genres—and varies from region to region according to occupation, ethnic background, and other characteristics.

Today, literacy is no longer considered simply the ability to read and write but is "increasingly conceived as a process of interpretation. Literacy is part of one's orientation to a lived reality made meaningful through the interpretation of text, that is, to written and oral descriptions and explanations of events that are endowed with sociohistorical value" (Baquedano-López 2006:246). In this sense, literacy allows us to reformulate existing knowledge to understand new knowledge: literacy is less a set of acquired skills than the acquisition of a new way of thinking—one that allows us to negotiate with the world in new ways. Literacy is learning to become competent in one's community.

Even though the term *communication* also includes writing, accounts of how writing is used in a particular society appear only rarely in ethnographic literature. This is because anthropologists have traditionally been interested in nonliterate societies (that is, societies without written language) and also because anthropological studies of complex industrial societies in which writing is important and widely used tend to concentrate on face-to-face interaction rather than the relatively remote contact established and maintained by writing. Anthropologists have always recognized the invention of true writing about 5,000 years ago as the starting point of a major cultural revolution in human history, and correspondingly their focus has been on the origins and diffusion of writing rather than on the functions of written language in particular societies. This is changing, however. And Keith Basso (1974:426) reminds us that "the ethnographic study of writing should not be conceived of as an autonomous enterprise . . . but as one element in a more encompassing field of inquiry which embraces the totality of human communication skills."

The same units and components that are employed in the ethnography of speaking might also apply to writing. Several related acts of writing (writing a letter, for example) combine to form a writing event (an exchange of letters on a particular subject or for a particular purpose). The sender(s) and the receiver(s) of letters are participants, and the circumstances under which a letter is sent or letters are exchanged provide a setting for an act of writing or a writing event (for example, the exchange of holiday greetings and New Year's wishes in December). The reasons for writing a letter vary greatly: personal letters range from bread-and-butter letters (to thank someone for hospitality) to love letters to letters of condolence; formal letters from letters of commendation to those threatening court action. The channel for writing is optical, but the codes vary: different languages make use of different writing systems, and preschool children sometimes "write" to their grandparents by drawing pictures.

The purpose and message content commonly determine the form of a letter: For example, on the one hand, a letter of application for a position is considered a formal letter and therefore would be carefully composed and typewritten or laser-printed on paper of good quality. On the other hand, a letter to a close friend is usually casual in style and can even be carelessly written, with the possible inclusion of slang or even an obscenity or two. To send someone who has just experienced a death in the family a card expressing wishes for a "Merry Christmas and a Happy New Year," or to type a letter of condolence rather than write it by hand, would be considered wholly inappropriate. Spoken utterances judged to be humorous even though somewhat risqué could well be considered insulting when committed to writing. In short, just as speaking is governed by rules of interaction and norms of interpretation, so is writing.

If we extend the term *writing* from true writing to any visual communication accomplished by the use of enduring marks or signs, we can then talk about various genres—road signs, pictorial advertisements, graffiti of various kinds, and many other forms. If studies in the ethnography of writing are to be complete and insightful, they need to include the sociocultural context in which they occur. Again, Basso posed some of the questions to be answered, among them:

> How . . . is the ability to write distributed among the members of a community, and how does the incidence of this ability vary with factors such as age, sex, socioeconomic class and the like? . . . What kinds of information are considered appropriate for transmission through written channels? . . . Who sends written messages to whom, when, and for what reasons? . . . In short, what position does writing occupy in the total communicative economy of the society under study and what is the range of its cultural meanings? (Basso 1974:431–432)

These questions have not yet been seriously addressed for more than a very few of the world's societies, though there has been some work in this vein. For example, Niko Besnier (1995) studied literacy, gender, and authority in Nukulaelae atoll in Polynesia. The Nukulaelae are now fundamentalist Christians. Sunday sermons are carefully scripted and circulated, often like a set of handouts of lecture notes, indicating the verses of the Bible to be studied, the remarks to be made about them, and various introductions and conclusions. Particular linguistic features characterize these sermons, including elaborate poetic alteration, special pronoun use, and other kinds of formal features. Women do not write sermons, and give few, claiming they do not have the aptitude for them. Besnier argues that this is a situation in which reading and writing are directly involved in the reproduction of inequality, and control over women's access to reading and writing contributes to their lower social position. On the other hand, women are allowed more freedom of emotional expression in the reading and exchange of letters, a primary means by which the Nukulaelae stay in contact with other islands or kinfolk who have moved away. Men are allowed to appear "feminine" (i.e., showing love or expressing vulnerability) in letter writing, but only within strict limits.

Where literacy comes directly in contact with culture is in education. But being "literate" is something not always easily defined. For example, among the Vai in Africa, one can be literate in three areas: in English for science, technology, and Western education; in Arabic for religious studies and the Koran; and in Vai for local government and social affairs (Scribner and Cole 1981). No one is equally literate in all three, and not all three are equally taught in school. Schools do much more than make their students literate, though writing is the medium through which most of this enculturation takes place. Schools impart values, attitudes, and standards, and a social awareness of one's place in society. Some radical critics argue (e.g., Bourdieu 1987, 1999) that learning one's social class and how to make appropriate class distinctions is introduced, reinforced, and reified through language and literacy in the classroom. It is well documented, for instance, that some ethnic groups in the United States do better in formal schooling because of their exposure at home to things that would most likely help them succeed in the classroom (for example, middle-class European American values, and language and literacy skills that are close to school practices).

## INTERCULTURAL COMMUNICATION

Today, when so many people frequently travel far away from home and encounter members of different ethnic groups and societies, interethnic and intercultural relations are continually being put to the test. Whether such relations are amicable or hostile, straightforward or confused, depends primarily on how individuals or groups with differing cultural backgrounds are able to communicate with each other. Even in languages or dialects that are closely similar or considered to be alike, specific words may have different senses or carry a different emphasis from one language to the other, resulting in occasional misunderstandings. A good illustration of a lack of equivalence between American and British English was provided by Margaret Mead when she pointed out that

> in Britain, the word "compromise" is a good word, and one may speak approvingly of any arrangement which has been a compromise, including, very often, one in which the other side has gained more than fifty per cent of the points at issue. On the other hand, in the United States, the minority position is still the position from which everyone speaks. . . . This is congruent with the American doctrine of checks and balances, but it does not permit the word "compromise" to gain the same ethical halo which it has in Britain. Where, in Britain, to compromise means to work out a good solution, in America it usually means to work out a bad one, a solution in which all the points of importance (to both sides) are lost. (quoted in Kluckhohn 1949:158)

Not always given sufficient attention but frequently of some consequence are differences in communicative styles among ethnic groups of a particular society. A number of research projects have been undertaken to determine the extent of such differences between Anglo-Americans, on the one side, and Latinos, African Americans, and members of other ethnic groups that make up the population of the United States, on the other. For example, according to one study, the ten- to fifteen-year-old recently arrived Latino pupils of several samples were found to be more interpersonally oriented and more inclined to attribute the feeling of shame to themselves or to others when compared with their Anglo-American peers. If teachers are aware of differences between members of differing ethnic groups that find expression in communicative behavior, they can better understand why under certain circumstances some pupils react differently than others (Albert 1986).

According to another study, black and white students at an eastern college differed in their handling of oral disagreements. The African American students tended to argue more persistently with each other for their positions and to take more control of the interaction than did white students, who appeared to prefer compromise or solution-oriented strategies in resolving their conflicts. Furthermore, all males in this sample, regardless of ethnicity, were more likely to engage in indirect, nonconfrontational strategies (for example, silence) than females, who tended to use more active strategies (Ting-Toomey 1986).

It is, of course, necessary to keep in mind that it would be inappropriate to extend the findings pertaining to a sample to an entire ethnic group. Any of a number of circumstances may invalidate such an extension—for example, setting (urban as against rural), the length of interethnic contact (a few years as opposed to decades as opposed to generations), amount of education, geographic location, socioeconomic status, and so on.

### *Communication Between Athabaskans and English Speakers*

Ronald and Suzanne Scollon (1981) published an informative account of the nature of interethnic communication between members of some of the Athabaskan tribes living in Alaska and northwestern Canada and Americans or Canadians having reason to interact with them. Most communication takes place in English, because good speaking knowledge of Athabaskan languages among Americans and Canadians is quite rare, and many Athabaskans (especially the younger ones) now speak only English. However, even those Athabaskans speaking only English have learned from their families and communities to use the communicative behavior characteristic of their ethnic background.

The Scollons analyzed several aspects of communicative behavior between Americans/Canadians and Athabaskans. In the presentation of self, the contrast between the two groups takes a diametrically opposite form: in a conversation between strangers concerning business, medical, legal, educational, or other matters, the Americans/Canadians talk freely and a great deal, hoping to learn from the exchange what is on the minds of the Athabaskans; the latter, on the other hand, say very little because they greatly respect each person's individuality and right to privacy, and they carefully guard their own as well. The Athabaskans gain the impression that their opposites are too talkative, and even boastful, whereas the Americans/Canadians tend to think of the Athabaskans as uncommunicative, unsure of themselves, and probably incompetent.

When two Americans/Canadians talk, they usually take turns speaking unless the relationship between them is so asymmetrical that one of them monopolizes the conversation. Several incongruities occur in turn-taking between Americans/Canadians and Athabaskans. One has to do with the length of pauses between turns. Athabaskan pauses may be somewhat longer, causing American or Canadian speakers to feel free to resume talking. The result is a conversation that is almost a monologue. Typically, a conversation is initiated by Americans/Canadians and is terminated by them with some such formula as "I'll see you later (tomorrow, soon)." But the Athabaskans consider it bad luck to make predictions about future events and do not reciprocate with a similar phrase. This lack of closure is interpreted by the Americans/Canadians as a failure of the communicative event.

Still other sources of misunderstanding have to do with the way information is coded. If Americans/Canadians want to emphasize certain aspects of their utterances, they usually do so by such means as stress, sentence intonation, and the like. In Athabaskan languages, emphasis is marked by special morphemes—for example, in Chipewyan, the morpheme *k*"´´, which expresses surprise. When Athabaskans use English, they do not mark emphasis by means of prosodic features. As a result, they may be only partly understood or, at worst, completely misunderstood.

This abbreviated account of the Scollons' research describes the confusion that is likely to occur in interethnic communication between Athabaskans and Americans/Canadians, but there are data to suggest that a similar situation exists whenever Americans communicate with other Native Americans. The differences in interethnic communicative behavior just described are easy to understand. The danger these differences lead to is ethnic stereotyping that may have as a consequence less than friendly and cooperative coexistence. The sources of problems in communication between Athabaskans and Americans/Canadians are summarized in Box 15.1. The table is culture-specific, but it applies to a great extent to communication between Anglo-Americans and Native Americans of other tribes as well (but keep in mind that the table lists *typical* behaviors).

## *Problems of Translations*

Translations can also be troublesome, as anyone who has ever studied a foreign language knows. The scholarly literature and personal anecdotes offer hundreds of examples of mistranslated words, phrases, or whole pieces of discourse. However, in our earlier discussions of the Sapir-Whorf hypothesis, we said that one of its refutations (at least of the strong version) was that anything in every language could be translated into any other. Although this is true, some caveats need to be made, as sometimes translations do not go smoothly. Often the problem is not just differences in grammar or vocabulary, even though the meaning and connotations of no pair of words in two languages are ever going to be precisely the same. Included in the whole package are also matters of context, cultural expectations, stylistic features, and personal interpretation.

As an example, consider a collision between a US spy plane and a Chinese fighter in spring of 2001 that almost caused an international incident. The contact occurred near the island of Hainan, a contested area, when two People's Republic of China jets scrambled to meet an American surveillance aircraft. The larger US plane and smaller Chinese jet collided (killing its pilot), forcing the damaged US plane to land in China, where the twenty-four-person flight crew was taken prisoner and held for eleven days, being released after a formal apology was made by the US ambassador to the Chinese foreign minister at the American embassy. What the apology said, and meant, almost immediately came under scrutiny.

Hang Zhang (2001:384) claims there are six levels of apology in Chinese, ranging from terms conveying a simple "sorry" to "feel regret" to "admit one's error and ask for punishment and humbly apologize." When the US letter was delivered, it was "carefully

## BOX 15.1 COMMUNICATION PROBLEMS BETWEEN ENGLISH SPEAKERS AND ATHABASKANS

| ***What's Confusing to English Speakers About Athabaskans*** | ***What's Confusing to Athabaskan Speakers About English Speakers*** |
|---|---|
| They do not speak. | They talk too much. |
| They keep silent. | They always talk first. |
| They avoid situations of talking. | They talk to strangers or people they don't know. |
| They only want to talk to close acquaintances. | They think they can predict the future. |
| They play down their own abilities. | They brag about themselves. |
| They act as if they expect things to be given to them. | They don't help people even when they can. |
| They deny planning. | They always talk about what's going to happen later. |
| They avoid direct questions. | They ask too many questions. |
| They never start a conversation. | They always interrupt. |
| They talk off the topic. | They only talk about what they are interested in. |
| They never say anything about themselves. | They don't give others a chance to talk. |
| They are slow to take a turn in talking. | They are always getting excited when they talk. |
| They ask questions in unusual places. | They aren't careful when they talk about things or people. |
| They talk with a flat tone of voice. | They are too indirect, inexplicit. |
| They don't make sense. | They just leave without saying anything, |

From *Cultural Communication and Intercultural Contact* by Donal Carbaugh, ed.
Ronald Scollon and Suzanne Wong-Scollon,
"Athabaskan-English Interethnic Communication" (1990), 284.

constructed in such a way that it said the most 'sincere' words possible without assuming any responsibility. At the lexical level it avoided the word *apologize*" (Zhang 2001:385):

*Dear Mr. Minister,*

*On behalf of the United States Government, I now outline steps to resolve this issue.*

*Both President Bush and Secretary of State Powell have expressed their sincere regret over your missing pilot and aircraft. Please convey to the Chinese people and to the family of the pilot Wang Wei that we are very sorry for their loss.*

*Although the full picture of what transpired is still unclear, according to our information, our severely crippled aircraft made an emergency landing after following international emergency procedures. We are very sorry the entering of China's airspace and the landing did not have verbal clearance, but very pleased the crew landed safely.*

*We appreciate China's efforts to see to the well-being of our crew.*

*In view of the tragic incident and based on my discussions with your representative, we have agreed to the following actions:*

*Both sides agree to hold a meeting to discuss the incident. My government understands and expects that our aircrew will be permitted to depart China as soon as possible.*

*The meeting would start April 18, 2001.*

*The meeting agenda would include discussion of the cause of the incident, possible recommendations whereby such collisions could be avoided in the future, development of a plan for prompt return of the EP-3 aircraft, and other related issues. We acknowledge your government's intention to raise U.S. reconnaissance missions near China in the meeting.*

*Sincerely,*

*Joseph W. Prueher [U.S. Ambassador]*

The media on both sides of the Pacific began interpreting the letter immediately—the Chinese literally and the Americans figuratively. The two instances of "sorry" in the English text were much discussed and analyzed, as well as the various back-translations. The translation from English to Chinese offered a translator a choice of at least six alternatives. In its own Chinese version, however, the United States chose the word *wanxi* (Zhang 2001:390), a word not normally used in Chinese when involving death (and not one of the typical six terms).

Zhang argues that this apology should be viewed not only as a simple speech act but also as a discourse event, extending beyond individual behavior to national behavior—one highly ideologically invested for both sides. Language became a field of combat of competing ideologies. It was not only an outcome of such negotiations but also the means to them.

## ALWAYS ON: NEW LITERACIES AND LANGUAGE IN AN ONLINE GLOBAL WORLD

It is likely that if you are a typical student reading this book, you will probably have some other task going on at the moment. Maybe you are watching television or checking your Facebook page. Maybe you are also instant messaging. Maybe you are checking some fact you have just read on your iPad. Perhaps you are listening to music. Undoubtedly your smart phone is charged, sitting on your desk. And when you use that cell phone, it is just as likely that you will send a text message as press the dial button. An obvious question is, "What are we, as speakers and writers, doing to our language by virtue of our new communication technologies, and how, in turn, do our linguistic practices impact the way we think and the way we relate to other people?" (Baron 2008:x). In other words, what is our linguistic life like now that we are "always on"? There are many ways to examine language and digital communication, but we will address the four most important ones in this section: We will look at sociolinguistic changes, formal syntactical and grammatical changes, changes in orthography, and possible cognitive impacts of these new literacies. Connecting with our discussions of English, we will also address the language of the international Internet. We will also examine emojis, Twitter, and visual language.

### *Sociolinguistic Changes from Being Always On*

As we have already said, the use of language is perhaps the most important reflection of one's personal and social identity. Simply put, language is who you are. Some fifty years ago, the well-known sociologist Erving Goffman (1959) introduced the theoretical construct of the "presentation of self in everyday life": although anticipated by Shakespeare four centuries earlier (all the world is a stage, after all), Goffman argued that much of social life—our face time—is spent managing how we want others to see us. And because we are in many ways what we pretend to be, as novelist Kurt Vonnegut said, this has important psychological implications as well.

In nondigital environments, our speech and dress are the most conspicuous presentations of ourselves. However, in day-to-day, face-to-face real life we are constrained in many ways. No matter how cool he talks and how baggy his pants are, a fifty-year-old male college professor still remains *that*, even if his ball cap is on backward. But on the Internet, these restrictions are diluted or nonexistent. On the Web, not only can we be anonymous, we can be anybody. All bets are off. Where previously the implicit rules of social politeness may have kept my language judicious, in a comment to a blog or an online news story, I can literally say whatever I please without fear of social consequences.

Likewise, in face-to-face communication, I am compelled to interact with people and conversations as they come up. You have to deal with meeting that old boyfriend on the quad; I have to deal with that problem student who comes to the office for hand-holding every day. We cannot avoid these encounters. But in the world of digital communications, we are all "language Czars," as Naomi Baron argues (2008). That is, we control whom we want to talk to and when, and on what terms. Although in the past, letters and telephones allowed some degree of management of whom we would communicate with, this complete control of accessibility we now have in the twenty-first century is unprecedented.

The types of communications have also radically changed. To take just one example, the anthropologist Bronislaw Malinowski (1923) proposed that some speech is **phatic communication**, small talk for its own sake rather than for conveying information. All people do it, everywhere, because it is both a bonding ritual and a way of regulating discourse. For instance, two negotiators may "get down to business" after they exchange pleasantries for a while, even though each may care little about the other's family or last night's ball game. But how these pleasantries are exchanged may set the stage for how the rest of the meeting will go. Digital communication offers both faster and more distant phatic communication. As any professor can tell you, the moment class ends, out come the cell phones. If it is a spoken conversation, invariably, it is brief and very phatic: "It's me. How you doing? I'm fine. Just got out of class. Yeah. Catch you later. Bye." Texting does the equivalent thing, with probably a similar message. Although these alternatives, such as Twitter and texting, offer another way of sending phatic signals, these are "away-messages" (Baron 2008:73) waiting to be read at the receiver's convenience. The 140-character limit makes Twitter almost intentionally designed for phatic communication. Combined with social network sites, we are never at a loss to know what our friends had for lunch or the latest cute thing Grandma's cat did. We will have more to say about Twitter shortly.

### *Are Instant Messages Speech? Formal Linguistic Changes*

Although it is obvious, we must remember that no matter how superficially it may appear to be the same as face-to-face interactions, digital communication is *not* exactly speech. David Crystal (2004) suggests that there are at least three major differences. First, for the most part, there is a lack of the simultaneous feedback found in an actual conversation. All the proxemic and paralinguistic features are missing. The feeling that the other person is not "getting" what we are saying would allow us to alter our conversational strategy in a face-to-face encounter. Second (unlike, say, at a party where we ourselves have to decide which of the many subconversations to attend to), in a chatroom or Facebook encounter, all messages are created equal. This is both a plus and a minus. "It has never been possible before in the history of human communication, to participate simultaneously in multiple conversations." Actually, you can now "contribute to as many as your mental powers and typing speed permit" (Crystal 2004:71). Third, the rhythm of communication is different. The lag between sending a message and getting a response in digital communication is very different in telephone or face-to-face encounters. This can cause a fair degree of ambiguity: Did Jane read my tweet yet? Did Professor Smith get my e-mail, or is he just not going to give me an extension? Did I get back to Joe when he friended me, or did I forget?

### *Changes in Orthography*

Converting spoken language into writing has never been easy, even though the school system tries to give us prescriptive rules and teach that they are absolute and unalterable. But even today there is not complete agreement about "correct" spelling and punctuation. Writing changes over time as fashions and opinions change. For example, what do you call that small permeable container that holds tea leaves (Baron 2008:177)? The *Oxford English Dictionary* cites *tea bag* in 1898, *tea-bag* in 1936, and *teabag* in 1977. And Shakespeare, the icon of all English courses, spelled his name a half-dozen different ways. That orthographic conventions are flexible is particularly true regarding digital communication. Is it *on-line* or *online*, or *e-mail* or *email*? Is the *Internet* supposed to be capitalized? What do we do about all those -s's that are now -z's, as in *Dawgz*, pirated soft *warez*, and shared *filez*? Is it *OK* or *okay*? Is it acceptable to use *btw* for "by the way" in an e-mail message—to anyone (even a professor)?

And does *lol* really even mean "laugh out loud" anymore? The *Atlantic*'s Megan Garber (2016) examined what several linguists had to say about this after seeing a picture of a disrobed Kim Kardashian that she posted on Instagram with the caption, "When you're like I have nothing to wear LOL." Garber says that Kim is doing many things in this picture, but laughing is not one of them. Indeed. Linguist Gretchen McCulloch argues "that LOL (commonly without caps) barely indicates an internal chuckle, never mind an uproarious audible guffaw." John McWhorter simply says, "LOL isn't funny anymore . . . LOL no longer 'means' anything. Rather, it 'does something'—conveying an attitude—just as the 'ed' doesn't 'mean' anything but conveys past tense. LOL is, of all things, grammar." So Kim's LOL—as are many of the LOL's of the rest of us mere mortals—is acting as a punctuation mark. As Garber says, "It is expressing the kind of meta-emotion that is very easy to make clear in in-person conversations and very difficult to make clear in other kinds." We will return to this shortly when we meet the next step on this linguistic evolutionary chain, the emoji.

Another question is, should we encourage or stifle creativity in digital communication orthography and style? Constance Hale and Jesse Scanlon in *Wired Style* (1999) argue that "no one reads email with red pen in hand" so we should "celebrate subjectivity" and "write the way people talk" (Baron 2008:172). Others feel that allowing such digital anarchy is a recipe for social and linguistic disaster. As Baron (2008:171) says, "Modern linguistic theory eschews passing judgment on any linguistic variant, and I am not about to do so now. Rather, I'm suggesting that should linguistic entropy snowball, we may discover that personally expressive, culturally accommodating, and clock-driven language users will find it increasingly difficult to understand one another's nuances." (One such example can be seen in Box 15.2.) Crystal argues that so far, at least, the pedagogical and "moral panic" surrounding e-mail and texting is overblown. The belief that the "highly deviant character" of digital communication is fostering poor literacy results has been shown by psychologists and educators to be largely an "urban myth" (2010:417).

### *Digital Communication, Literacy, and Cognition*

One other area in which it has been suggested that digital communication literacy is changing modern life is education and cognition. Donald Leu et al. (2007:41) argue that there are four defining characteristics of these new literacies. First, new information and communication technologies involving novel literacy tasks require new skills and strategies if they are to be used effectively. Second—though this is often resisted "overtly, by deliberate educational policies . . . or covertly, by educators who sometimes are not nearly as literate with the Internet as the students they teach (p. 38)"—new literacies are now a critical component for full participation in civic, economic, and social life in a global world. Third, these new literacies are deictic—that is, they change as new technologies emerge. Of course, literacy has always changed with technology (e.g., consider the intellectual and social revolutions brought about with the advent of movable type and the printing press). What is different about digital communication is its immediacy. It took centuries for the full impact of the Gutenberg press to be felt, but the Internet allows for the immediate and universal exchange of new ideas and technologies. Fourth, new literacies are "multiple, multimodal, and multifaceted," thus making them more complex to apprehend and understand. How this will be integrated into the twenty-first-century educational system remains to be seen.

Some also wonder how new digital communication literacy is changing human cognition and patterns of thought—and not just in ways of learning or how people relate socially to one another. The rise of book culture, of course, inexorably altered the way people conceived of the world and their place in it. The collective pool of human knowledge

BOX 15.2 1337 5P34K: 4N 31337 13350N F0R 4N O1D F4RT

In a class on Japanese linguistics I was teaching, I was describing some of the new orthographic games Japanese teenage girls play on their cell phones when they text-message using symbols, emoticons, and scripts from various foreign languages. "Oh, that's just like leet!" said a student. Seeing the puzzled look on my face, he went to the board and wrote *31337 sp34k,* as if this explained everything. It didn't. After a pregnant pause, with me unsuccessfully finding a way to appear both knowledgeable and cool, he said, "You really are a *newb*—a *newbie*—aren't you?" while writing *n00b* in big letters. It dawned on me that this was some kind of code. *0* replaced the letter o, *7* replaced t, *1* replaced l, *4* replaced A, *5* replaced S, and so on. So, *31337* was supposed to be "elite"—spelled *eleet,* and shortened to *leet,* in this strange argot. But this was not what cryptologists call a transposition cipher, where numbers simply encoded letters. Instead, what was going on was a kind of orthographic running joke. For example, *ph* was often used for any f-sounds, and words could be transcribed in several ways: "fear" might be rendered *ph34r, ph33r,* or *phear*. Phonetic and orthographic puns saturate *leet-speek,* and sometimes the uninitiated might miss the joke. I never would have guessed that *b7* is "banned," and the logic, such as it is, is something like this: The ampersand (&) is pronounced *"and,"* and the number *7* and the character *&* share the same key on the keyboard. Thus, *b* and *7* (i.e., and) make "banned." "Surely, even you . . . you who are . . . "—he wrote *4n o1d F4rt* on the board, as the class broke out into giggles—"can see this, right?" "But of course," I lied, trying to keep my composure. Later on, after class, I figured it out. I could console myself, however, that at least I was not an über g33k like my student.

James Stanlaw

exponentially multiplied, and people could travel vicariously to the far ends of the earth and time in travelogues or history books. However, as with anything, there were costs. Scholars at the start of the Renaissance lamented, for example, the decline of the power of human memory, and the reluctance of younger people to engage in daunting tasks of memorization. They were probably right, just as the spread of the hand calculator has impacted our ability to do even simple arithmetic in our heads. Already, for example, we see university libraries becoming places to network or centers for collaborative learning. Few go there to consult a journal article because often these are available in students' dorm rooms on computers. What kind of world will it be in the (very near) future when all the world's knowledge, music, and art are instantly accessible to everyone? With remarkable improvements in Web translations taking place daily, even problems in cross-cultural communication that result from people speaking different languages might gradually become less important.

## The Language of the Internet

If you ask most people what the language of the Internet is, they would probably say it is English. Even in places where English is not natively spoken, tweets and twitters are often sent out in English. English appears to be the default language of almost any site you hit. Even though operating systems now come in different language interfaces, many people still use an English version of Windows or a Mac operating system to more easily interact with the English-using computer sites.

### The Dominance of English?

In his book *Language and the Internet* (2001), the noted linguist David Crystal wondered whether the English-dominated Internet would contribute to the demise of other languages, at least on the Web. Perhaps he was being pessimistic. It appears that the use of English has gone down significantly, from 82 percent in 1997 to less than 57 percent in 2002 (Stanlaw 2005). German, French, and Japanese each now make up between 5 and 8 percent of all Web pages. If we look at PDF (portable document format) pages, these differences are even more pronounced. Chinese, Korean, Russian, and Dutch all went from almost nothing in 1997 to a noticeable presence ten years later. A similar trend appears if we look at the languages used to access the Google search engine. English went down 10 percent from June 2001 to May 2004.

However, we should not predict the waning of English as the dominant language on the Web yet because statistical data suggest that the drop in English is leveling off. For example, language access on Google since September 2003 has remained essentially the same for all languages. Also, if we look at the "penetration" levels—the percentage of the speakers of a given language that have access to the Web—we see that a great majority of speakers of many European languages (such as German, French, and Dutch) already use the Internet, so the number of these speakers going online might not be expected to grow very much. In contrast, only 59 percent of English speakers use the Web, so these numbers could increase (Stanlaw 2005).

But there is another, perhaps more significant, reason that English will still be a dominant presence in the digital world for some time to come. Political unrest and international and economic affairs will likely continue to be highly contentious in the near future, and digital communications will no doubt play an important role. For example, few could forget the vivid pictures and messages being sent out of Iran during the "Green Revolution" election protests in the summer of 2009. Because the Iranian government strictly monitors and censors such conventional media as radio, television, and newspapers, social networking sites, blogs, Twitter, and YouTube became the primary source of information for the outside world (which even news organizations such as CNN, the BBC, and the major print news agencies used when their personnel on the ground were quarantined). Not only were Western governments getting word of unrest taking place that they were not getting by the usual diplomatic means; the whole world's attention was drawn to these dramatic events. Reuters reported that these channels were so important that the Obama administration asked Twitter to postpone a scheduled network upgrade because it would have taken the service offline temporarily. According to Twitter's own blog, the company agreed to the State Department's request "because events in Iran were tied directly to the growing significance of Twitter as an important communication and information network."

### The Hegemony of English?

At first glance, it may appear a good thing that one language, English, is the world's de facto lingua franca, not only online but also in spoken and written communication. Everything from international air traffic control to publishing scholarly academic journals now becomes easier, using only one language. But we have to ask, is having English as *the* international language a good thing or not? Is there such a thing as the hegemony of English? The nature of hegemony implies an asymmetric relationship between two individuals, groups, or classes, with one being more powerful or in control, the other being more subordinate. This seems to be a shoe that fits the English foot.

Linguist Yukio Tsuda (2013:453) concurs, believing that both native-English speakers and non-native speakers suffer:

> One of the most influential factors that justify the use of English in international communication is the taken-for-granted assumption that English should be used. The English-speaking people unconsciously believe English to be used by all people; namely, they unconsciously hold linguistic imperialist consciousness, while the non-English-speaking people assume the use of English as the inevitable, indicating the colonization of the mind on their part.

Phillipson (1992:47) says that a "working definition of English linguistic imperialism is that the dominance of English is asserted and maintained by the establishment and continuous reconstruction of structural and cultural inequalities between English and other languages." By the very nature of Western/English-speaking countries' economic clout, English will be privileged. And in the United States, each political season finds new calls and attempts to eliminate bilingual education or to make English the only official language in some state or county. And having not all languages being created equal has important social and cultural consequences. For example, if an American—especially a "white" American—can speak more than one language, it is usually considered a good—though rather unusual—thing. This would be advantageous unless the person speaking the languages is a subordinate speaker (like an immigrant), in which case this would often be considered an impairment or handicap to learning English (Macedo et al., 2003:9). These issues are extremely divisive and political, and they cannot be solved here. But anyone with even a passing interest in linguistic anthropology needs to at least be aware of them.

## *Emojis: A New Writing System, a New Language, or Nothing New Under the Sun?*

Chances are, if you are reading this and you are under thirty, you use some kind of emoji to add visual spice to your written text, like the "grinning face" emoji here: 😀. Emojis have become so ubiquitous now that they appear across platforms, from cell phones to tablets and even to desktop computers (for those who still use them). They cover a wide range of—well!—emotions, and allow great digital orthographic creativity. We often spend a lot of time and energy thinking about them. What is the exact emoji I should use to ask a favor, but not appear I am begging? Does the 😍 emoji come off as too forward romantically? I want to appear interested but not desperate. Does the 😡 emoji or the 😠 emoji show just the right amount of anger I am feeling now?

## The Arrival of the Emoji

Emojis were invented by Shigetaka Kurita in 1999 while working as an engineer for NTT DoCoMo, Japan's largest mobile telephone network. He was said to be inspired by the *kanji* characters of the Japanese writing system (see Chapter 5) and the stylized symbolic representations of emotions found in Japanese *manga* comic books. For example, Thomas Wallestad (2013:5) argues that "Japanese manga have a large diversity of metaphorical figure symbols called *keiyu* ( 形喩 ) that are not considered as words or representational pictures, but act as symbolic adjectives or adverbs to events depicted. *Keiyu* consist of manga symbols (*manpu* 漫符 )"—for instance, like the stylized drawing of a person—"and effect symbols (*kōka* 効果 )"—for example, some stylized detail being drawn on that person. "*Manpu* tend to retain their meaning independent of a subject, whereas *kōka* need to be applied to a subject to be understood. In Japan's manga these symbols are applied to characters or subjects as representational indicators denoting their 'physical' states (*butsuriteki* 物理的 ) and/or as metaphorical indicators connoting their 'psychological' states (*shinriteki* 心理的 )" (romanization standardized and clarifications added).

In other words, these *kōka* are acting as sort of visual morphemes (see Chapter 4), as Neil Cohn (e.g., Cohn and Ehly 2016; Cohn 2010 and 2013) suggests. Figure 15.1 shows some of these visual morphemes. For example, the "vein" or "blood vessel" symbol called *kekkan* (💢) attached to the face or other parts of the body indicates anger. The "drop" (*suiteki*) sign 💧 has several meanings depending where it is placed. If applied to the eyes, the "tear bubble" (*namida*) indicates sadness. If the drop is applied to the mouth, the "drool" bubble (*yodare*) indicates distraction, hunger, lust or stupidity. The bloody nose (*hanaji*) indicates uncontrollable lust (Wallestad 2013:6, 8; Cohn n.d.:1).

## Visual Language

Those who argue for a special "visual language" paradigm in human communication say that "visual vocabulary is understood in cognitive terms: graphic patterns are stored as schemes of form-meaning mappings in the long-term memory of their creators, similar to the way that verbal patterns are stored as schemas (words) in spoken languages of the world" (Cohn and Ehly 2016:19). But there is no reason to assume these visual language units are necessarily going to be cross-culturally universal, just as gestures (see Chapter 5) are not. For example, the 🙏 emoji is often thought to mean "please do me a favor" or "thank you" in Asian cultures, whereas Westerners usually take it to mean "prayer/praying."

There is a difference, however, between visual and spoken language because visual language items are in some kind of print form (whether paper or electronic, or some other medium) and are thus free to cross geographic boundaries in ways that spoken language forms are not. It is not so easy for a spoken foreign language word or phrase or sentence to enter another language. But a sign or symbol—because of the permanence the medium offers—is more likely to enter and more likely to stay present.

Thus, even though many of the emoji were relatively specific to Japanese culture, as in manga and anime visual tropes, they were universal enough for others to catch on. Also, with Japanese pop culture being one of the arbiters of what is globally cute and cool (e.g., Yano 2013) many non-Japanese were not only accepting, they sought such things out.

Emojis, whether passing fad or permanent fashion, have left their mark, regardless. Maybe indelibly so. Thomas Dimson (2015:1–2, 9–10), a software engineer at Instagram says,

**FIGURE 15.1** SOME EXAMPLES OF JAPANESE VISUAL LANGUAGE "MORPHEMES"

| *Morpheme* | *Meaning* | *Type* | *Body Part* | *Example* |
|---|---|---|---|---|
| Vein | Anger | Affix | Forehead (flexible) |  |
| Bloody nose | Lust | Affix | Nose |  |
| Drool | Distracted, bored | Affix | Mouth |  |
| Vertical shadow | Fear, dread | Affix | Head |  |
| Cry streaks | Sadness | Affix | Eyes |  |
| Tear bubble | Sadness | Affix | Eyes |  |

**Cohn, Neil, and Sean Ehly. 2016. "The vocabulary of manga: Visual morphology in dialects of Japanese Visual Language." Journal of Pragmatics 92:17–29. doi: 10.1016/j.pragma.2015.11.008. www.visuallanguagelab.com/A/jvlmorphology.html**
**Graphic References:**
**Motomi, Kyousuke. (2007). Dengeki Daisy. Viz Media. Chapter 1, 1–47.**
**Oda, Eiichiro. (1997). One Piece. Viz Media. Chapter 1, 1–50.**
**Okubo, Atsushi. (2004). Soul Eater. Yen Press. Chapter 1, 1–59.**
**Toyama, Ema. (2009). Watashi ni XX Shinasai! Kodansha Comics. Chapter 1, 1–41.**
**Hoshino, Katsura. (2004). D.Gray-Man. Viz Media. Chapter 1, 1–54.**

> It is a rare privilege to observe the rise of new language. . . . [By] March of this year [2015], nearly half of [all] text contained the emoji . In the future will all text contain emoji? . . . [E]moji are becoming a valid and near-universal method of expression in all languages. . . . By observing words and emoji together we were able to discern representations of both.

Emojis often act as punctuation or sentence-final particles attached to word-based sentences. For example, one can add emotional flavor after making a verbal statement. "Taking the GRE's tomorrow ," indicating the tremendous pressure the writer is feeling. After finishing the tests and getting the results back, she might write, "Got the scores back ," indicating not only the joy of having finished the process, but perhaps also feeling relief from the pressure and maybe satisfaction with the scores. Or all these feelings.

### Just What Are Emojis? Their Linguistic Features

Corpus linguistics (Dimson 2015:4–5) show that the top three universal emojis—and their names, and some of their meanings—are

😂 (tears of joy): laughing out loud, too funny, hahaha, . . .
😍 (heart-shaped eyes): beautiful, gorgeous, hot, . . .
❤️ (heart): love, xoxo, love you, . . .

It is clear that these symbols, then, are not really words in the sense that Sino-Japanese *kanji* characters are words—logograms—which stand exactly for one lexeme in a language (see Chapter 5). Nor are *kanji* **polysemous** in the way emojis are, standing for so many ideas. Likewise, they are not really pictograms, either (for example, 💔 stands for the metaphor "broken heart," not an actual physiological condition). It seems that emojis are something we might call "semantigrams," symbols that carry meanings, probably multiple meanings, but cannot convey these meanings by themselves. The emoji's meaning only exists in connection to, or with, a lexical item or another emoji. And sometimes they have no real meaning at all, functioning only to provide phatic communication—as we saw, Malinowski's term for language that establishes and maintains social connections rather than exchanging actual information—as in "Sunny skies yesterday 😊" or "Lunch was good 😊."

But there is another interesting trend that is fascinating to linguists. Although expanding by the day, the number of emojis is finite, limiting the things that can be expressed with them. But users are expressing new thoughts by putting emojis together into sentence-like phrases. And the way this is done is remarkably similar, even though no one is taught the "correct" usage of emoji "grammar." For example, probably even the least facile emoji newbie can "interpret" this "sentence," which has appeared on the Internet in many places: 😊🙋😍❤️🙅😔🍷. It is the same old love story: boy meets girl, falls head-over-heels in love, gets rejected, is sad, becomes depressed, and turns to drink. The order of these emojis is not random. For example, these same emojis might tell a different story if presented differently: 😔🍷😢🙋❤️🙅😊😍. Here a guy is depressed, drinks too much and hits rock bottom, meets a girl who falls in love with him in spite of his drinking, gets him to stop, so he recovers and becomes normal again, and gratefully falls in love, too.

One reason for this consistency of word order is because emoji-use tends to respect linear time and action. For example, if you want to point a gun at a something, that something has to go to the left of the barrel (Steinmetz 2014:2): that is, 🐵🔫 and not 🔫🐵. Another rule is that the "agent" (the doer of the action) has to precede the action, and go to its left (Cohn 2015:6), hence the sad guy drinking in 😫🍷. Another convention might be the "stance first" rule (i.e., stance or attitude emojis come before actions or signals). For example, people weep and then—afterward—have a broken heart: 😢😢💔 and not the other way around: 💔😢😢. The stance-first rule may come from the more potent power of emojis to convey emotions that are easily expressed in spoken language—through such things as tone of voice, body language, gestures, or inflection—that are largely silent in text (Steinmetz 2014:2).

Another interesting linguistic feature of emojis is the tremendous creativity and productivity by their users. Our contributor Su Yin Khor claims her favorite emoji collocation is putting the "pizza" slice emoji together with the "turd" emoji, as in 🍕💩. To interpret the—spoken vernacular!—intention of this pair, remember the first symbol is used for its phonetic value "pizza" and the second for its semantic value, feces (recall the 👁❤ NY example in Chapter 5, where the first symbols was used for its pronunciation "eye" and the second for its meaning, "love").

These properties we have just mentioned—productivity, rules, grammaticality, and the ability to make an infinite number of messages with a limited number of units—all bring to mind the design features that were discussed in Chapter 6. So, should we consider this new use of emojis as a new kind of language, as several observers have suggested (Dimson 2015; Stockton 2015; Cohn 2015)? A first reaction says no. No less an authority than Leonard Bloomfield, one of the founders of American structuralist linguistics, still speaks for many in the discipline when he unequivocally says that "[w]riting is not language, but merely a way of recording language by means of visible marks" (1933:21). Thus, for many linguists, any writing system, with emojis or not, simply does not qualify as language.

But does this privilege the spoken word too much? Perhaps. Emojis and their users can be quite resourceful. For example, Matt Haughey (2015), a self-described "internet nerd writing about internet nerdery, mostly," posted a summary of the cult film *The Big Lebowski*, named fittingly enough "The Big Lebowskemoji." In conversation with blogger Samantha Lee (2016:1, 3–4, 8), Indiana University linguist Susan Herring claimed emojis have brought us into a "new phase of language development. More and more graphical representations, such as emojis, gifs, stickers, and memes are being incorporated into language use online." In many ways these act as incipient pidgins (see Chapter 9). "Pidgin basically comprises nouns and verbs strung together. That's what happens when you use emoji." But that said, "Text is never going away." Even "The Big Lebowskemoji" needed annotations as not every emoji sequence was transparent to the uninitiated. And retrieving the right emoji from the hundreds that are available on a device is still a problem. However, technology has solved so many other technical problems in the digital age, it is likely this will be solved as well.

### Twitter, Emojis, and the Linguistic Anthropologist

Can Twitter and emojis offer something in return to anthropology and linguistics? Undoubtedly, though these findings are still just at the beginning stages. For example, Ljubešić and Fišer analyzed a dataset of about 17 million geo-encoded tweets containing emojis and found interesting correlations between emoji usage and World Development indicators as defined by the World Bank. In particular, they asked (2016:82–83): 1. How popular are emojis in different parts of the world? 2. Does emoji usage vary from place to place? and 3. Does emoji usage reflect local conditions? They found emojis are most popular in South America and Southeast Asia, even though they were invented in Japan and propagated in the United States. And there were significant connections between emoji usage and development (see Table 15.1 below). In terms of frequency, "First World" emoji clusters tended to be rather descriptive and "emotionally empty" compared to "Second World" countries, which used emojis that had highly positive emotions. "Third World" nations used both positive and negative emotion emojis, whereas "Fourth World" nations used emojis that held negative emotions in addition to some rather basic concepts like fire 🔥, dance 💃, and

**TABLE 15.1** RANK ORDER EXAMPLES OF EMOJIS USED IN DIFFERENT DEVELOPING SPHERES

| | | | | | | | | | | |
|---|---|---|---|---|---|---|---|---|---|---|
| First World | ❤️ | 💕 | 👍 | 🌴 | 🎉 | 🎄 | 🏡 | 🍀 | 😴 | ☕ |
| Second World | 😘 | 🎉 | 😎 | 😍 | 👍 | 💕 | 💪 | 💖 | 💞 | 🍻 |
| Third World | 😍 | 😂 | 😁 | 😭 | 💔 | 🙏 | 😘 | 😔 | 👏 | 💃 |
| Fourth World | 😂 | 🔥 | 🙌 | 😭 | 😅 | 💃 | 🏃 | ✋ | 🙏 | 😩 |

**2016 A global analysis of emoji usage. Proceedings of the 10th Web as Corpus Workshop (WAC-X):82-89. https://www.aclweb.org/anthology/W/W16/W16-2610.pdf. Used by permission of Nikola Ljubesïć and Darja Fiser.**

hand gestures. They conclude (p. 89) that "emoji usage is indicative of the living conditions in different parts of the world."

In another case of how digital technology is helping language research, Bruno Gonçalves and David Sánches studied messages posted on Twitter and found "a major surprise about the way dialects are distributed around the world and provide a fascinating snapshot of how they are evolving under various pressures, such as global communication mechanisms" (Technology Review 2014). They sampled 50 million geo-encoded tweets in Spanish over a two-year period for vocabulary variability and dialect differences. For example, the Spanish word for "car" can be *auto*, *automóvil*, *carro*, *coche*, *concho*, or *movi*. What they found was the existence of two major "superdialects" of Spanish. The first used in the major cities of the world, particularly in Spain and America. "This is an international variety of Spanish that is similar across continents," likely due to the homogenizing effects of global communication systems like Twitter. The second superdialect was used only in rural areas, and there were three variations: one used exclusively in South America, one in Spain, and one in the Caribbean and Latin America. These kinds of findings would be next to impossible to discover if not for the advent of Twitter and powerful computational linguistic hardware and software tools.

## *The Age of Twitter*

There is no doubt that Twitter has changed the way human beings communicate, at least for the immediate future. In spite of messages having a 140-character limit, taken in aggregate they add up to something with a significant communicative impact. For example, several political commentators have said that one reason for Donald Trump's victory in the 2016 presidential election was because he won the Twitter wars—not just against Hillary Clinton, but against anyone who would engage him. Besides allowing friends to easily stay in contact with each other, teachers now use Twitter to communicate with students, and celebrities and the common folk get to talk and mingle with an intensity and immediacy never possible before in everyday face face-to-face speech.

## Hashtags

The development of the hashtag label—that is, placing a "pound" (#) sign before a particular word or phrase—was also a game-changer, making it easier for users to now find messages with a specific theme or with a specific subject, or allowing them to follow others with similar interests. The hashtag label also "intensifies a call to affiliate with the values expressed in the tweet by making it more searchable" (Dickinson 2013:11) for others with similar political or religious beliefs, or even prejudices.

But besides tagging messages, hashtags now can also be used to simply act as a contextualizing mechanism or self-reflexive meta-commentary on what is being written. In that sense hashtags can act much like paralanguage (see Chapter 5) in spoken language, that is, written versions of facial expressions, gestures, or body language that accompany speech. And as everyone knows, in spoken language, the paralanguage and the speech do not always agree, allowing for mixed or self-contradictory messages to be sent simultaneously. These hashtag expressions, often self-mocking or satirical, have spread from Twitter to Facebook to spoken language (where ironically now, saying the word "hashtag" allows the speaker to slip in some kind of aside remark or comment to what he or she has just said).

Regardless, the use of the hashtag is "indicative of a shift in computer-mediated discourse from online conversation to 'searchable talk'" (Dickinson 2013:11). This, combined with re-tweeting posts (and additional subsequent re-re-tweetings) make for a different kind of communication. Before, digitally, we may have been "always on," waiting for contact from some outside source. When that happened, we were free to either respond immediately or put that person or message on hold to be answered at our convenience. With Twitter, we no longer have to—only—wait. We can initiate communication about subjects on our own terms at a time of our own choosing.

## Have Twitter and Social Media Improved Human Communication or Hindered It?

The world's most famous linguist, Noam Chomsky, comes down on the latter position. When asked about his feelings concerning digital communication in an interview, he said, "Text messaging, Twitter, that sort of thing . . . I think it erodes normal human relations. It makes them more superficial, shallow, evanescent. One other effect is there's much less reading" (Jetton 2011:18). In an earlier interview (Ralon and Eljatib 2010) he was even more adamant: "Well, let's take, say, Twitter. It requires a very brief, concise form of thought and so on that tends toward superficiality and draws people away from real serious communication." These comments are typical of much of the criticism that has been leveled against Twitter.

However, many disagree, including *Salon*'s Nathan Jurgenson (2011), who posted a provocative piece, "Why Chomsky Is Wrong About Twitter." He argues that Chomsky doesn't realize that texting and tweeting is not just done by "wealthy kids and knowledge workers." Instead, he cites evidence (p. 4) that "nonwhites are much more likely to connect to the Web, communicate and create content on mobile phones than whites . . . [and] these so-called shallow ways of communicating are precisely the ways those in the Third World are connecting to and interacting" with the global world. And Chomsky shouldn't be submissive about the role social media plays in many current progressive social movements, from Arab Spring to Occupy Wall Street to Black Lives Matter. "When he defends *his* form of communicating (printed books and periodical essays) with claims that tweeting/texting lacks depth, he is implicitly suggesting that nonwhites and those in the Third World are inherently communicating less deeply." And even if we grant that social media is less deep and more instantaneous, "the important questions then become: is instant, digital communication less true? Less worthy? Less valuable? Less linguistically creative? Less politically efficacious? Chomsky, a political progressive linguist, should know better" (Jurgenson 2011:5).

**The Language on Twitter**

The language used on Twitter is in many ways similar to spoken language but in many ways is also quite different. For example, Dickinson (2013) argues that much of Twitter language is "formulaic." By this he means there are an extraordinarily high number of pat phrases or "morpheme equivalent units" (MEUs) found in most tweets. An MEU is a term used in psycholinguistics to describe lexical items—that is, a word or a string of words—that are processed together singly. Most idioms, for example, are MEUs. For instance, the meaning of *kick the bucket* makes no sense if one just looks at the meaning of the individual items; the meaning only makes when together as a whole morpheme-like indivisible unit.

In a concordance analysis of random Twitter posts, Dickinson found four main functions of these kinds of formulaic language: to manipulate the situation to the user's benefit, to convey individual identity, to convey group identity, and to connect meaning and structure the discourse. Each of these functions can be broken down into several types. Table 15.2 shows examples of some of these functions and types (based on Dickinson 2013:17).

When messages are limited to 140 typed characters, acronyms save both space and time, so it is no surprise that they abound in tweets. Dickinson (2013:25), following others, suggests that at least two acronyms—*lol* and *btw*—have identity-marking function and have become "conventionalized to serve as group membership markers among internet users." In fact, as we saw earlier in the chapter, *lol* has become lexicalized as something different from its "laugh out loud" origin and acts as a kind of uninflected discourse marker, appearing before or after clauses. If used at the beginning of a response, *lol* appears to indicate affiliation with the tweet being responded to. After a sentence or clause, *lol* is often used as a hedge, where writers indicate that their preceding statement should not be taken too seriously.

Internet-specific abbreviations also have a group-identifying—as well as space-saving—function: separating those in-the-know from those who are not in-the-know, and thus, don't belong. Such general abbreviations include *u* or *ur* or *yr* ("you"), *4* ("for"), *2* ("to" or "too"), *tho* ("though"), and *pls* ("please"). However, surprisingly, in all cases, the abbreviations were actually used much less frequently than their equivalent full forms (Dickinson 2013:27). However, if you think about it, this is not necessarily that unintuitive. A text with unusual abbreviations, too many abbreviations in total, would be hard to decipher, and thus take longer to read as well as write in the first place.

**Twitterology**

Twitter also has tremendous appeal to outside analysts, whether they be linguists looking for large corpuses of data to inspect or psychologists and advertisers trying to measure public feelings on everything from a political candidate's position on some topic, to product

**TABLE 15.2** EXAMPLES OF FUNCTIONS AND TYPES OF TWITTER FORMULAIC LANGUAGE

| FUNCTION | TYPE | EXAMPLE |
|---|---|---|
| **manipulate a situation to the user's benefit** | requests: | keep me posted |
| | complaints: | What's with . . . |
| | warning: | I hope you aren't . . . |
| | bargains: | I will tell you all about it if you promise to . . . |
| | apologies: | Sorry |
| | sympathy: | so sorry to hear this |
| | gratitude: | Thx so much |
| **to convey individual identity** | epithets: | I've always been a **Web 2.0** girl |
| | assertions: | As a smoker, I . . . |
| **to convey group identity** | inclusiveness: | aren't we all . . . |
| | acronyms: | lol, btw |
| **connect meaning and structure of discourse** | topic marker: | next up . . . ; Anyway, |
| | hedges: | as far as I know |
| | filters: | Hmmm, well, . . . |

preference, to the acceptance of a newly released film. People talk, and they talk—lots!—on social media. The relatively new science of **sentiment analysis** (or public opinion mining) is using the techniques of computational linguistics to extract subjective information from statements made by the people in these public arenas, like Facebook or Twitter. Twitter is, indeed, a natural data source for this kind of work, and some have even called this research "Twitterology" (Zimmer 2011).

At first glance, one might think this work would be blatantly obvious and terribly easy. In fact, in its most basic elements, it is: the computer scans millions of tweets, categorizes them, counts all the positive, negative, and neutral terms or statements about a subject, tallies them, and spits out an average. Many times this is simple: someone tweets "I liked *Star Wars,* go see it!" and that would be counted as a positive token, "I thought it was so-so," would be neutral, and "It is really sucks!" would be a negative. But much of the time it is not so easy for computers or software to code these attitudes accurately, both because of technical retrieval and coding problems as well as human complexity and ambiguity.

First, it is not always simple to tell a computer which concatenations in a text should be looked at, especially when the combinations are not contiguous. For example, how many terms—before and after a given target term or phrase—should a program look for before making a judgment about the overall statement? What do you do about emoticons? What about qualifiers, conditionals, and conjunctions like *but . . . , if . . . , in case . . .* (Chikersal et al. 2015)?

And second, sentiment analysis has been accused of having a naïve view of emotional states—that is, that people's true feelings can be discerned by simply examining their word choice (Zimmer 2011:2). After all, even two humans themselves might disagree about the polarity of a statement. And even the writer might be of two minds. Is the statement "I really want to ask her out to the Prom, but it is probably better if I don't get involved with her" positive, neutral, or negative? And tweets are full of sarcasm, innuendo, double entendre, and word play of all kinds.

In spite of all these problems, this kind of text analysis is producing results. Zimmer reports, for example, that "good" and "wonderful" sentiments were displayed across Arab-language tweets upon the death of Libyan dictator Muammar Qaddafi in 2011. The journal *Science* reported that positive terms fall off during the workday, hitting rock bottom in late afternoon. Georgia Tech computational linguist Jacob Eisenstein and his team investigated 107 million tweets authored by 2.7 million different authors between 2009 and 2012 and found "high-level patterns in diffusion of linguistic change over the United States.... Rather than moving toward a single unified 'netspeak' dialect, language evolution in computer-mediated communication reproduces existing fault lines in spoken American English" (Eisenstein et al. 2014:1). For example, they found *ikr* ("I know, right?") occurs six times more frequently in the Detroit metropolitan area than anywhere else in the United States. The emoticon ^-^ occurs four times more frequently in Southern California, and the phonetic spelling *suttin* (for "something") appears five times more frequently in New York City. They also argue that race and ethnic demographics, as much as geographic proximity, predict dialect variability. That is, two urban areas may have a similar dialect even though they may be far apart geographically, whereas two cities next to each other may have very different speech patterns if their demographics are different (see Box 15.3)

Initially, before technology of any kind, human communication was face-to-face. Or to put in information science terms, it was **synchronous** (or **synchronic**), a fancy way of saying back-and-forth. You talk, I listen, we then switch places, and we both know communication is taking place, and when. With the advent of the first wave of technology, communication became—again, in information science terms—**asynchronous** (or **asynchronic**). Here, the message is out there, and we retrieve it at our convenience. The book is on the shelf, I read it when I want. I can choose to ignore a phone call. I'll answer this e-mail when I have some time. No one except me knows when and where the "communication" is occurring. Now, with the advent of social media, things have changed. I can "talk" not only with thousands of people, but they can be anywhere on the planet. And with just a few judicious clicks and key presses, I can seek out and call to me any number of fellow like-minded brethren—and their messages—who share my interests, hobbies, proclivities, politics, and even prejudices. We might term this new communication style *meta-synchronous,* in that the message doesn't come to me, I go to the message.

The semiotician Marcel Danesi (2016:4) has said, "Unlike the Print Age, which encouraged, even imposed, the exclusive use of alphabetic writing in most message-making media and domains of literacy, the current Internet Age encourages different modes of writing (visual and audio) to be utilized in tandem with alphabetic (and non-alphabetic) scripts in the composition of messages. This new kind of 'blended writing' system harbors a broad range of implications within it, from the possible demise of the Print Age to a modern-day

### BOX 15.3 DEMOGRAPHICS AS A PREDICTOR OF DIALECT VARIABILITY: LINGUISTIC EVIDENCE FROM TWITTER

While geographical distance is prominent, the absolute difference in the proportion of African Americans is the strongest predictor [of dialect variability]: the more similar two metropolitan areas are in terms of this demographic, the more likely that linguistic influence is transmitted between them. Absolute difference in the proportion of Hispanics, residents of urbanized areas, and median income are also strong predictors. This indicates that while language change does spread geographically, demographics play a central role, and nearby cities may remain linguistically distinct if they differ demographically, particularly in terms of race. In spoken language, African American English differs more substantially from other American varieties than any regional dialect; our analysis suggests that such differences persist in the virtual and disembodied realm of social media. Examples of linguistically linked city pairs that are geographically distant but demographically similar include Washington D.C. and New Orleans (high proportions of African-Americans), Los Angeles and Miami (high proportions of Hispanics), and Boston and Seattle (relatively few minorities, compared with other large cities).

It is inevitable that the norms of written language must change to accommodate the new ways in which writing is used. As with all language changes, innovation must be transmitted between real language users, ultimately grounding out in countless individual decisions—conscious or not—about whether to use a new linguistic form. Traditional sociolinguistics has produced many insights from the close analysis of a relatively small number of variables. Analysis of large-scale social media data offers a new, complementary methodology by aggregating the linguistic decisions of millions of individuals.

Jacob Eisenstein, Brendan O'Connor, Noah Smith, and Eric Xing, *Diffusion of Lexical Change in Social Media* (2014)

manifestation of the unconscious forces at work in the evolution of human communication systems and practices." If anything, emojis, tweets, and the like are certainly that.

## ETHICAL QUESTIONS AND STANDARDS OF CONDUCT

In the introductory chapter we pointed out that "native" consultants make an essential contribution to studies in linguistics, cultural anthropology, and linguistic anthropology, and that every effort should be made to enable promising members of small ethnic groups to receive training in these fields. The insight into their cultures such individuals possess would be invaluable. One must realize, however, that it will take some years before members of small societies are reasonably well represented in the fields of linguistics and anthropology, both of which are dominated at present by white males.

Doing fieldwork in a foreign culture almost invariably gives rise to an asymmetrical relationship: On the one hand, there is the researcher (the word is used here to mean anyone who is an attentive and systematic observer and makes a study of something), and on the other hand, there are the subjects (that is, those who are being studied) or natives (those who are connected to a particular community or region by birth). The researcher, typically a cultural and linguistic outsider, lives for a number of months with those who are being studied, observes them and asks numerous questions, and now and then accompanies them when they do their chores or even helps with their daily tasks. Because much of the native consultants' time is taken up by the researcher's questions and requests for data concerning language and culture, it is customary to offer them modest but fair compensation (consultant fees usually come out of the grant the researcher has received for fieldwork).

Doing fieldwork in another country or in a foreign culture under physical conditions that are usually less comfortable than those at home, living among and depending on people who at least initially are complete strangers, having to eat unfamiliar foods, and trying to communicate with others who speak a different language all require both the will and the ability to make profound adaptations. For these reasons, a few anthropologists find fieldwork too taxing and, after their initial experience, engage in it only occasionally or not at all. But most anthropologists, linguistic and cultural alike, enjoy being in the field and return to fieldwork again and again.

And what about the people who are studied? An extended visit by an anthropologist is bound to have some effect on them, as every researcher needs to be aware. According to the code of professional ethics adopted by the American Anthropological Association, the responsibility of anthropologists to those they study is paramount. The aims of the anthropologists' activities should be communicated as clearly as possible to those among whom they work; consultants (informants) have the right to remain anonymous if they choose to, and their rights, interests, safety, and sensitivities must be safeguarded; consultants are not to be exploited but should receive a fair return for their services; and the results of research should be made available to the general public—clandestine research can potentially be used by others against the population under study. In short, prior to commencing research, the anthropologist should give serious thought to the possibility that the study of a group or community could at some future time negatively affect the people studied. If such an outcome seems possible, then the research project should be substantively redesigned or be abandoned.

A comment should also be made concerning the comportment of researchers in the field. Their expertise, educational background, and material advantages in no way entitle them to any feelings of superiority to those they study, who may live in conditions unaffected by modern technology and may be nonliterate. As guests in a foreign society, community, or home, fieldworkers should exercise even more sensitivity than they would be expected to use in their home environment. Asking for advice does not necessarily mean accepting it, but there are many instances when advice can be of great value and may even help determine whether a project succeeds or fails. Let us consider, for example, a group's need for educational materials designed to help pupils learn their own language and something about their culture in Western-style schools (such a situation can be encountered in schools in the United States serving primarily Native American students). If there are several adequate ways of writing down a language that has previously only been spoken, which method would be preferable to the potential users? And if an anthology of traditional narratives is to be compiled for the use of students, which of the many stories should be selected?

It occasionally happens, of course, that members of a tribe, a nomadic group, or a peasant village do not want their daily lives, religious beliefs, and traditional customs scrutinized by someone they do not know, who comes from another country and whose intentions they cannot fully comprehend. Reverse the situation: think of what the attitudes of members of a small community somewhere in the United States might be toward a foreigner of a different skin color, who has different religious beliefs and speaks a foreign language, announcing that he or she will live in the community for half a year or so to study the habits of the "natives."

In a world in which human communities and nations have become interdependent and in which respect for cultural diversity is essential, understanding other cultures is ever more important. This understanding is what anthropologists are committed to promote, and their behavior in societies other than their own must set an example.

Finally, we should mention one last ethical issue. Lately there has also been much discussion about the Human Terrain System (HTS) initiative of the US government in 2007, in which social scientists like anthropologists, linguists, sociologists, political scientists, and area studies specialists offer professional advice to the local American military presence in overseas deployments. The idea was that these social scientists would make for better interactions with the local population—the "human terrain"—because of their expertise of a nonmilitary nature. To put it in the vernacular of an earlier war, HTS was an attempt at winning hearts and minds. As expected, HTS was mired in controversy from the beginning. The American Anthropological Association stated:

> In the context of a war that is widely recognized as a denial of human rights and based on faulty intelligence and undemocratic principles, the Executive Board sees the HTS project as a problematic application of anthropological expertise, most specifically on ethical grounds. We have grave concerns about the involvement of anthropological knowledge and skill in the HTS project. The Executive Board views the HTS project as an unacceptable application of anthropological expertise. . . . The Executive Board affirms that anthropology can and in fact is obliged to help improve U.S. government policies through the widest possible circulation of anthropological understanding in the public sphere, so as to contribute to a transparent and informed development and implementation of U.S. policy by robustly democratic processes of fact-finding, debate, dialogue, and deliberation. It is in this way, the Executive Board affirms, that anthropology can legitimately and effectively help guide U.S. policy to serve the humane causes of global peace and social justice. (http://s3.amazonaws.com/rdcms-aaa/files/production/public/FileDownloads/pdfs/cmtes/commissions/CEAUSSIC/upload/CEAUSSIC_HTS_Final_Report.pdf)

What is the role of the linguistic anthropologist, then, in an increasingly chaotic and dangerous world? Indeed, what is the role of language training at all? (See Box 15.4.)

### BOX 15.4 DLAB AND ALAB: LINGUISTICS FOR DEFENSE

The Defense Language Aptitude Battery (acronymized to "Dee-Lab") is the test the US military uses to determine those likely to succeed in learning one of the fifty foreign languages taught at the Defense Language Institute. The DLAB is also said to statistically predict success in particular languages. If candidates score high enough, they can apply to study a language in one of four groups: Category I (with a score of 95 or better, for French, Italian, Portuguese, and Spanish); Category II (100+ for German or Indonesian); Category III (105+ for Dari, Hebrew, Hindi, Persian, Punjabi, Russian, Serbo-Croatian, Tagalog, Thai, Turkish, Urdu, and Uzbek); and Category IV (110+ for Arabic, Chinese, Japanese, or Korean). The University of Maryland's Center for Advanced Study of Language (CASL)—*"Language Research in Service to the Nation"*—has updated this test. DLAB 2 now incorporates "new cognitive measures, as well as non-cognitive measures such as personality and motivation."

No one is supposed to know what is on the DLAB ahead of time, and those who take it are not supposed to talk about it. Lately, however, more information has come out through the grapevine and the Internet. The navy, under its "cryptology" job description site, even has some sample questions, though some claim these are easier than the actual exam. The test is about two hours, consisting of both audio and visual portions. In the audio portion, test takers are asked to identify stress patterns in nonsense words. Next, an almost-English, pig-Latin-like language is presented in a foreign accent. (Many have said that earlier versions sounded Russian, while today some say it sounds Arabic.) You are told that rules for this language stipulate that nouns precede adjectives, nouns and adjectives will always begin and end in the same vowel, *o* and *a*, and that there are no articles. You are asked to select the correct translation for "red car" from the following choices (spoken only once): A. *ocara eredo*, B. *ocaro areda*, C. *areda ocaro*, D. *ovalore ogalori*. It is easy to see that the choice is B—or *o-car-o a-red-a*—when it is written, but this is not so easy to pick up aurally. Then new rules are added, like verbs begin and end in *-i*. Next, you may be asked to extrapolate a rule for tense by looking at example sentences such as these:

| | |
|---|---|
| The boy will sit on the chair | *oboyo isitiro ochairo* |
| The woman sat on the big chair | *owomano isitado ochairo abiga* |

*continues*

Here we see that when the suffix *-iro* is attached to the verb, this indicates future tense (*isit-iro* meaning "will sit"), while the suffix *-ado* indicates past (*isit-ado*, or "sat"). In the visual portion of the test, you are given a picture and asked to extrapolate some linguistic features of the item presented. You might be given these pictures and glosses: a black dog (*zimpan*), black cat (*zimbot*), and white dog (*sotpan*). You are then asked to give a gloss when shown a picture of a white cat.

However, in spite of all these efforts at recruitment, the number of American nationals in Afghanistan who speak Dari or Pashto is still quite small. The vast majority of translators are Afghanis who speak English—to varying degrees. The Western media have often questioned their English proficiency. For example, Brian Ross in a *Nightline* report in September 2010 claimed that more than one-fourth of Afghani translators in the battlefield could not speak passable English. CASL again has offered a solution. The agency is currently validating its ALAB (Afghan Language Aptitude Battery), designed to find Afghanis who will succeed in the Defense Language Institute's English language program. However, this test differs from DLAB in several significant ways. First, there is a range of nonlinguistic tests for general intelligence (like spatial reasoning). The language analysis test examines such skills as case marking, using an artificial language as in DLAB. For instance, given these examples—*zorit* ("farmer"), *volip* ("the worker"), *zorit volipu pigom* ("The farmer pushed the worker")—the test taker would be asked to translate "The worker pushed the farmer." But ALAB also tests for ability to be numerically and orthographically literate, as well as being able to transliterate scripts between Dari, Pashto, and the artificial language.

The predictive power of DLAB seems supported by several decades of testing by applied linguists. However, ALAB is still new. Never before has the military attempted such a vast and expensive undertaking—$1.5 billion to provide intensive English-language training from scratch to hundreds of locals during a war. As someone wrote on the *Economist* blog, "Yes, training competent linguists is hard. So is . . . training F-18 pilots. But the American military does [the latter] . . . in superlative fashion."

James Stanlaw

(an earlier version of this appeared in *Anthropology News* [December 2011])

## SUMMARY AND CONCLUSIONS

There are many different ways of applying expertise in socially oriented linguistics to the problems of the contemporary world. Knowledge gained from studying the ethnography of communication can be quite useful when individuals or groups of differing cultural and linguistic backgrounds are attempting to communicate. The informality of Americans (the ease with which they move to a first-name basis, for example) may be regarded by other societies as ill-mannered or even presumptuous; Americans, for their part, are likely to consider the formal behavior characteristic of some other societies stuffy and inflexible. If individuals or groups involved in intercultural contact know how to interpret each other's behavior, communication will proceed more smoothly.

Another area in which linguistic applications have been found useful is legal proceedings. Here the contributions of applied linguistics range from making the technical language of legal documents intelligible to the layperson to helping the judge, jury, witnesses, or litigants resolve problems resulting from misunderstandings caused by differing cultural and linguistic backgrounds. A policy adopted by the United States in 1990 encourages anthropologists to continue what they have been doing for some time now, namely, helping to preserve the languages and other cultural traditions of Native Americans.

Language problems in a pluralistic society are commonly due to the uneven status of competing languages or dialects. The question to be answered is not only which language (or languages) is to become the national or official language, but what the consequences of a particular choice are likely to be for the entire society. And if an unwritten language spoken by a small population in a pluralistic society is to be maintained by introducing it into the schools as a second language, the linguist may be called upon to devise a writing system and then to help in developing teaching materials.

With cultural differences around the world becoming less distinct as a result of communications media, modernization, and the volume of international travel, the language of a minority population may be the only prominent badge of its ethnic identity and pride. It goes without saying that the language concerns of such a group need to be handled not only with expert knowledge but also with understanding and tact.

In this chapter we have looked at three major trends in what David Crystal calls the world's linguistic ecology. First, simply put, most of the world's languages are dying out—quickly—and our linguistic diversity, for better or worse, is rapidly disappearing. As a consequence, more and more people are speaking fewer and fewer languages. Second, one language—English—appears to have become the de facto international lingua franca, the world's first global language. (And we have asked whether this is necessarily a good thing.) Third, the revolution in digital technology has been inescapable, and language has been tremendously affected. But even the name of this new kind of communication is uncertain. What do we call the language that results when people communicate using computers, cell phones, iPads, tablets, iPhones, Androids—using media such as Twitter, Facebook, and Instagram—which become a routine part of our lives? "Various technical and popular suggestions have been made, such as *cyberspeak*, *electronic discourse*, *Netlish*, *Weblish*, and *Netspeak*. None of these is satisfactory" (Crystal 2010:414). But no matter what its name, will this new method of "talking" break down barriers to communication, as many hope, or will it erect new, unforeseen gates that obstruct international tolerance and cooperation even more? Regardless, the tools of linguistic anthropology will help us analyze and understand the language problems involved, whatever the outcome.

## RESOURCE MANUAL AND STUDY GUIDE

### *Questions for Discussion*

1. Counter the argument that anthropology is of little consequence to life in modern, complex societies (such as the society of the United States) because anthropologists concern themselves with only "exotic" and "primitive" peoples marginal to modern civilization.
2. What ethical considerations should guide the anthropologist as a fieldworker, and why?
3. Almost daily, some commentator or media critic decries the corruption of English and predicts the collapse of the world due to the widespread use of social media, digital communication, video games, and the like. What do you think? Have these things caused a breakdown in human communication? Has English become degraded? Has literacy declined, and if so, is it because of new means of electronic communication? Have, indeed, critical thinking skills waned?
4. Noam Chomsky, whom we've discussed at length in earlier chapters, claims that the human condition is plagued by two interesting paradoxes. The first he calls "Plato's Problem": how can we know so much about the world, given our limited experience of it and so little available information? For example, no one has ever seen a perfect triangle (in the geometric sense) but everyone knows what one is. Likewise for Santa Claus, unicorns, or even truth. The second is called "Orwell's Problem": how can we know so little of the actual condition of the world—for example, our place in the political hegemony—given the availability of so *much* information? What, if anything, do the new forms of digital communication contribute to this dilemma?

### *Project*

Consider the following exchange of e-mail between two college instructors, Dr. Jane Doe and Dr. Ann Throwpologist at X University. What do you notice about style, tone, and orthography in these messages? What kind of conversation was taking place? Who wanted to do, or not do, what? How could you tell? Was a successful exchange taking place? What cues are missing? What cues *are* here? How might the conversation have been different had it taken place in person?

(first e-mail message). Quoting jdoe@x.edu:

> dear dr. throwpologist,
>
> i am jane doe and i teach commercial art at the school of business. i am teaching a special topics course on cultural identity in advertising this semester where students learn new research methodologies in advertising so they can create designs that are more meaningful for a multicultural audience.
>
> i am inviting guest speakers to talk about culture and identity. i would appreciate if you would be interested to be a guest speaker in my class. the class is held at Smith Hall 14 on M. and W. from 8 to 10. please let me know if this is possible.
>
> thanks for your time.
>
> sincerely,
>
> jane doe

(second e-mail message). Quoting annthrowpologist@x.edu:

Dear Dr. Doe,

Thank you very much for your invitation. I am very interested in culture and identity, as that is one of my linguistic specialties. However, I am also teaching on Mondays and Wednesdays this semester all day, so I am afraid I will not be able to be a guest speaker this Spring. Sorry. But again, thank you for your invitation.

Ann

(third e-mail message). Quoting jdoe@ x.edu:

dear dr. throwpologist,

thank you for responding. i do teach on fridays as well. please let me know if feb. 10th or 17th or 24th will work for you.

thank you,

jane

(fourth e-mail message). annthrowpoogist@x.edu:

Dear Dr. Doe,

Thank you for your offer again, but I am very sorry. This semester I need to finish a project so I will not be able to come to campus on Fridays. Perhaps I might be able to visit your class some other time. But thank you again.

Best,

Ann

(fifth e-mail message). Quoting jdoe@x.edu:

dear dr. throwpologist,

i am teaching this class again in fall please let know when you can come then.

thank you

jane

## *Objective Study Questions*

**TRUE-FALSE TEST**

T F 1. According to the code of professional ethics adopted by the American Anthropological Association, the first responsibility of anthropologists is to their country.

T F 2. Jomo Kenyatta, the first president of Kenya, chose the language spoken by the largest number of Kenyans to be the official language of the country.

T F 3. The mother tongue of Arapaho school children today is English.

T F 4. A conversation between Americans and Athapaskan Indians tends to be very asymmetrical: the Athapaskans are quite talkative and fill any pauses that may occur with speech.

T F 5. In courts, the specific phrasing of questions can and does influence the answers of witnesses.

**COMPLETIONS**

1. An imposed change in the status of a language or a dialect, and/or imposed changes affecting the structure of a language (its pronunciation, spelling, vocabulary, etc.) are referred to as ____________ ______________ (two words).
2. An examination, using corpus linguistics, of large blocks of texts (like tweets) that attempts to determine the public's feelings on some issue or product is called ____________ ______________ (two words).

## Answer Key

True-false test: 1-F, 2-F, 3-T, 4-F, 5-T
Completions: 1. language planning; 2. sentiment analysis

## Notes and Suggestions for Further Reading

Among the publications dealing with applied linguistics are Wardhaugh and Brown (1976), Crystal (1981), and Trudgill (1984). The *Annual Review of Applied Linguistics* (*ARAL*), first published in 1981, surveys research and comments on new trends in the field of applied linguistics. With several hundred new citations each year, *ARAL* is a good source of bibliographical references. For a survey of the uses of linguistics in medicine, law, and education, together with an extensive bibliography, see Shuy (1984). Linguistics and education are the subject of a survey article, Heath (1984); for an overview of the language of the law, see O'Barr (1981).

For sources on intercultural communication, see Scollon and Scollon 2001, Carbaugh (1990), and Samovar and Porter (1991). Language planning is discussed in Eastman (1983) and Kennedy (1983). A survey of American Indian language maintenance efforts is to be found in Leap (1981) and a guide to issues in Indian language retention in Bauman (1980).

International English (or Englishes) has now become an established and recognized subfield of linguistics with its own associations and journals. The literature is vast. Anything by Braj Kachru, Yamuna Kachru, Kingsley Bolton, Larry Smith, or Cecil Nelson would be intellectually rigorous and quite readable. A good overview of the field can be found in the six-volume collection of readings of Bolton and Kachru (2006) or the single volumes Y. Kachru and Smith (2008) or B. Kachru (1992). Good beginning student texts are Galloway and Rose (2015) and Jenkins (2015).

For book-length discussions of languages on the Internet, see Baron (2000 and 2008); and Crystal (2001, 2004, and 2009). For specific topics, see the references in the text. On visual language, and emojis, Cohn (2010, 2013) and Danesi (2016) are highly recommended.

There is much being written about how things like the Internet are corrupting English, often from either a hysterical or unconcerned point of view. John McWhorter (2003, 2016) takes a balanced, moderate position with witty insights and humorous examples. Anything by him is highly recommended. For a multilingual view of the Internet, see Danet and Herring (2007).

Stanlaw (2014), on Japanese slang (much of it influenced by English), shows one example of what can happen when orthographic innovation, language contact, and the hegemony of English meet.

The discussion of the principles of professional responsibility to those whom anthropologists study is abbreviated from the pamphlet *Professional Ethics*, published by the American Anthropological Association in 1983. Besides discussing relations with those studied, the statements on ethics also cover the anthropologists' responsibilities to the public, the discipline, anthropology students, sponsors, their own government, and host governments.

# GLOSSARY

**accent.** Refers to stress, as in, the pronunciation of a syllable (and words or phrases) and how it is emphasized. Commonly lumped together with *pitch.*

**acoustic phonetics.** Concerned with the physical aspect of sound produced by vocal organs, specifically the sound waves.

**acrolect.** The language variety closest to being a standard variety, seen as more prestigious in the post-creole continuum.

**African American English (AAE).** A variety of American English said to be spoken by many African Americans.

**African American Vernacular English (AAVE).** Refers to a variety of American English spoken by many African Americans. The term was popularized in the 1960s and 1970s by William Labov and was used to highlight the aspects of AAVE that diverged from what was seen as the standard American English, giving AAVE negative connotations. Today, the term *African American English* is to be preferred.

**agency theory.** The human capacity to act; for example, when making choices concerning language use and identity construction.

**agglutinative languages.** Morphemes are attached to a stem to form one longer "glued-together" unit, instead of using multiple words to form a long sentence. Each morphemic structure serves a specific grammatical function, e.g., the plural form, possessive form, or (grammatical) gender.

**allomorphs.** A variety of a particular morpheme. As the morpheme is used in different contexts, the pronunciation might also change. For example, the plural *-s* in English changes depending on which word it is attached to, as dog/z/, cat/s/, and bus/əz/. Other examples include internal changes like *man* to *men.*

**allophones.** For example, the unaspirated p-sound in "span" and the aspirated p-sound in "pan" are two allophones of the phoneme /p/.

**alphabet.** A writing system in which the distinctive sounds of a language are for the most part represented by a graphic symbol, or a letter, depending on the language.

**alternate sign languages.** Used by individuals in speaker-hearer communities to regularly or occasionally substitute speech, but not as their primary form of communication.

**American System.** The American System contains many symbols to represent sounds that the International Phonetic Alphabet (IPA) does not. Mainly used by anthropologists and some linguists, and was popular before World War II.

**analytic language.** In language typology, a language in which words consist mostly of a single morpheme. Some use the terms "isolating" and "analytic" synonymously.

**animacy.** A grammatical or semantic classification of nouns based on how sentient or alive the nouns are in a particular language and culture. This can influence other aspects of grammar, such as word order.

**anthropological linguistics.** An older term for linguisic anthropology, the study of the relationships between language and culture

**antonyms.** Words that have opposite meaning.

**archaeology.** One of the four subfields of anthropology in which the focus is on retrieving remains and material of past cultures.

**articulatory phonetics.** A subfield of phonetics concerned with the production of speech sounds by the vocal organs.

**artificial** (or **auxiliary**) **language.** A constructed language to facilitate international communication, such as Esperanto.

**Asian American English.** Commonly refers to the imagined variety of English that Asian Americans speak. As Asian Americans originate from different countries and speak different languages, it is not possible to discern a specific Asian American English variety.

**aspect.** The ability of verbs to express how activities relate time, as in when in time a specific action was completed

**assimilation.** A phonological process that refers to the change of a sound that makes it similar to another sound. In rapid speech, *ten bucks* sounds like *tembucks*.

**asynchronous/asynchronic.** Communication that takes place at the recipient's convenience.

**auditory phonetics.** The branch of phonetics concerned with how physical speech sounds are perceived by the ear and the brain.

**australopithecine.** A genus of several species of extinct hominids whose fossils are found in Africa and who are assumed to be ancestors of modern humans.

**babbling.** Early stage in children's speech development.

**basilect.** Language variety that is furthest away from being a standard and prestigious variety. Compare with **acrolect**.

**bilingual.** The ability to use two languages well in various domains and situations. The second language is either acquired after the first language has been developed, or in other cases, both the first and second language are acquired simultaneously.

**binary oppositions.** Antonyms; words with opposite meaning that are absolute and are not gradable, such as right versus left, or hot versus cold; a key part of anthropologist Claude Levi-Strauss's structuralist paradigm.

**biological anthropology.** A subfield of anthropology, also known as physical anthropology, that is concerned with the study of human evolution and physical variation.

**body language (kinesics).** Gestures and the non-verbal behavior part of communication.

**Broca's area.** Area of the brain that controls motor functions in speech production. Damage in this area is characterized by distortion of sounds and incorrect word order.

**calques.** Words or expressions that have been directly translated into a different language, such as the French word *gratte-ciel*, literally "scratch-sky," which is a calque on the English word for skyscraper.

**case forms.** Inflectional system used to mark a word's function in a sentence.

**cerebrum.** Largest part of the brain, consisting of two lobes, the left and right hemispheres.

**cheremes.** The basic form of communication in sign language, analogous to phonemes in spoken language. These are combined to form meaningful sign units, such as sets of positions, configurations, or motions.

**code-mixing.** The incorporation of elements of one language into another, as in using both English and Spanish words in a single sentence.

**code-switching.** The mixing of words, phrases, and sentences of two (or more) languages or varieties in a single larger speech event. The distinction between code-switching and code-mixing is often blurred or arbitrarily defined.

**cognates.** Words that have the same origin and come from the same ancestral language.

**cognitive linguistic anthropology.** The study of linguistic anthropology influenced by research in cognitive science.

**collateral relatives.** Relatives who are not in direct line of descent, such as aunts and cousins, as they are descendants of one's ancestor's brother or sister.

**communicative competence.** An individual's ability to effectively communicate in a specific language context (to avoid miscommunication); knowing *how* and *when* to use an utterance appropriately (but not necessarily *demonstrating* that knowledge perfectly all the time). See also **performance**.

**communicative strategy.** The idea whereby speakers tend to value a variety of a language that is seen as more useful and prestigious because it can help them advance in society in different ways, such as financially. This is not always a conscious choice.

**community of practice.** A focus on the social relationships and practices among members in a community. These members have a shared set of goals and endeavors.

**competence.** An individual's underlying knowledge of language. The knowledge refers to various aspects of grammar, such as morphology and syntax.

**complementary variation.** A technique of doing phonemic analysis: if sounds do not appear in the same phonetic environment in a set words, this implies they are likely the same phoneme.

**componential analysis.** The analysis of lexical units in a specific cultural domain to separate them into their component parts. The purpose is to understand the semantic differences of these words with respect to others, and to discern their cultural features.

**computer-mediated communication.** Human communication that occurs through the use of modern digital technology, such as through e-mail and texting.

**connotation.** Associations and emotional connections tied to a lexeme (word). For example, the word "dog" might conjure feelings of loyalty, besides just referring to the animal itself; and "cold" might be associated with winter rather than just temperature.

**consonant/consonontal.** A sound that is produced with the vocal tract closed or partially closed, as opposed to vowels, where the vocal tract is open.

**constative.** In speech act theory, statements which are descriptive, and thereby can be determined if they are true or false.

**constituent analysis.** A way to break down a (linguistic) unit to find its smallest linguistic elements, such as the morphemes, of a word. It is especially useful when studying unknown languages.

**contrasting distribution.** Minimal pairs that do not have the same meaning, indicating that the sounds in question are two different phonemes.

**contrasting variation.** A technique of doing phonemic analysis: two minimal pairs with different meanings.

**conversational analysis.** The study of how people engage in conversation, and rules, parameters, and underlying assumptions they use to do so; the emphasis is on how interlocutors experience and make sense of their interaction.

**conversational implicature.** The implications in a conversation that can be drawn from certain tacit principles in a speech community. For example, the parent saying, "The dog is loose again" to the children means they should go tie up the family pet.

**copula deletion.** Refers to the omission of the different forms of the verb to *be,* such as "He a man" instead of "He *is* a man."

**creole/creolization.** Creolization refers to the process in which a pidgin becomes a creole, meaning that it has become the first language of a speech community.

**critical-age hypothesis.** A claim that language is acquired with ease before puberty because of brain plasticity in childhood.

**cultural anthropology.** A subfield of anthropology that focuses on human culture.

**cultural determinism.** Refers to how culture, to a great extent, determines grammatical patterns and way of thinking in a language

**culture.** Learned—not instinctive or biologically based—behavior that involves a complicated relationship between beliefs and knowledge transmitted from one generation to the next; generally used only with respect to the higher primates; some restrict it to only humans.

**cuneiforms.** Early writing system used by Sumerians. Wedge-shaped marks were made on soft clay tablets that were then baked or dried.

**decreolization.** The process a creole goes through to assimilate with a standard language (one that it originates from).

**denotation.** The object that a word actually refers to, detached from its associations.

**derivation.** Refers to how new words are formed from existing ones by changing the word class, commonly accomplished by using derivational affixes: the noun *friend* can be changed to an adjective with the addition of *-ly*, creating *friendly*.

**design features of language.** A set of unique properties that supposedly characterize all human language and separate it from communication forms of other animals.

**diachronic (historical) linguistics.** The study of language change over a period of time.

**dialect.** A regional or social variety of a language that is often contrasted with a standard variety.

**difference theory.** Men and women live in different linguistic worlds, as they belong to different subcultures and have their own distinct communication styles.

**diglossia.** The use of two languages or two distinct varieties of a language that have different functions within the same society.

**diphthong.** A vowel change within a word such that the sound begins as one vowel but transitions into another vowel, as in *bite* and *boy.*

**discontinuity theory of language evolution.** The theory about human language that assumes that human language is unique and without evolutionary antecedents.

**discourse.** The main analytical unit of communicative behavior that varies in duration, such as a greeting or a conversation. Discourse can be spoken and written.

**discourse analysis.** The analysis of language at the level above the sentence; that is, the way people talk and what words or phrases they use.

**displays.** Signaling behaviors and patterns of any animal species, such as birdsong.

**dissimilation.** A change in pronunciation of two sounds that sound similar, in which one of them becomes less like the other; for example, the change of the [r] in *February* to *Febyuary*.

**dominance theory.** Also known as social power theory, this theory focuses on patriarchy, male power, and unequal power relations between men and women that are manifested as language differences.

**E-language.** Speech that is actually produced by speakers under specific external conditions.

**Ebonics.** A name sometimes given to "African American English," combining the words *ebony* and *phonics*, meaning "Black English."

**ego (in kinship terminology).** The person of reference to whom others are shown to be related: "my aunt" is the ego's mother's sister.

**elaborated code.** Language use that is typical of relatively formal speech situations.

**elicitation frames.** A set of structured questions used in componential analysis to undercover the properties of domains (e.g., "Tell me all the X's you can think of," or "Is Y a kind of X?").

**emic.** A research approach that investigates the variables from the "inside" perspective of the participants, rather than using supposed objective or "outsider" etic categories.

**emojis.** Electronic pictograms, like smiley faces, that can be added to electronic messages, websites, and other digital communications.

**endonym.** A word that is used as a self-identifier. For example, *gay* is acceptable, whereas *faggot* is a slur.

**ethnicity.** Commonly used to refer to a group of people with a common national or cultural tradition.

**ethnography of communication.** The study of the nature and function of communicative behavior among members within a speech community.

**ethnonym.** A name given to a group of people based on ethnicity.

**ethnoscience.** The study of culture by using more systematic ways of investigating it. Mostly done from the perspective of those who belong to the culture that is studied.

**etic.** A research approach that investigates the participants from an "outsider's" perspective, as in, from the perspective of the researcher rather than from "insider" emic categories.

**evolutionary psychology.** A subfield of psychology that assumes that human behavior is evolutionarily based and largely hardwired.

**fieldwork.** Researchers gathering linguistic and cultural data by talking to or observing those in their natural local environment.

**folk linguistic theories.** Beliefs that the average person has about language that may not be true, such as women curse less than men.

**folk theory.** A popular "commonsense" theory of how the world works, often unsubstantiated or stereotypical. For example, a folk theory of race might claim that prejudice is based solely on individual acts of discrimination rather that looking at the greater institutional forces that perpetuate it.

**frame/framing.** The culture-specific context shared by speakers, as in, they have the same frame of reference to understand and interpret the communicative event that is taking place.

**free morphemes.** Morphemes that are able to stand alone without losing their meaning, such as *car*, *house*, and *happy*. They can also be combined with other free or bound morphemes, for example, *cars*, *dollhouse*, and *unhappy*.

**free variation.** A technique of doing phonemic analysis: two minimal pairs with the same meaning.

**fusional.** In language typology, a kind of language where prefixes, suffixes and infixes disappear or become "fused" or blended together phonological assimilation.

**gender.** Someone's social and cultural identity as a male or a female. The traits associated with males and females are culture specific.

**genderlects.** A variety of speech that is used by a specific gender.

**gender-neutral third-person pronoun.** A third person pronoun that does not refer to a gender, such as *one thinks* . . . as opposed to *she thinks* . . . or *he thinks*. . . .

**generative/transformational grammar.** Chomsky's notion of the underlying grammatical rules of language that indicate what sentences are possible and not possible to generate.

**genre.** Speech acts or events associated with specific communicative situations are characterized by a specific style, form, and content.

**grammatical gender.** A grammatical category used in some languages to categorize words into separate classes, such as masculine, feminine, and neutral, or animate versus inanimate.

**Gullah.** An English-based creole with many West African language features, spoken in the coastal areas of the southeastern United States.

**haptic behavior.** Behavior and communication based on touch.

**heritage language.** A language that children learn at home in a society that speaks a different language. For example, in Quebec, children might learn French at home and speak it with family members, but they must use the dominant English language at school and at work.

**hieroglyphics.** Characters of the ancient Egyptian writing system.

**holistic.** A holistic approach means looking at different aspects of a system as an interconnected whole with the purpose of understanding the subject matter in its full complexity as opposed to looking at different units separately.

**hominids.** Members of the Hominidae family, which includes extinct and present-day species of humans and their direct fossil ancestors.

**hominoids.** A subdivision of primates that consists of three families: lesser apes (e.g., gibbons), the great apes (gorillas, chimpanzees, bonobos, orangutans), and hominids (humans)—excluding monkeys. Includes all extinct and contemporary species.

**homonyms.** Words that are spelled or pronounced the same but have different (or two or more) meanings, as in *right* [correct], *right* [appropriate], and *right* [not left]; or *bear* [animal] and *bear* [carry].

**honorifics.** Parts of language used to indicate politeness or respect. For example, when addressing someone, factors such as familiarity, age, and gender affect the choice of words and phrases that are used.

**hypercorrection.** A change in speech based on false analogy, such as making "singer" rhyme with "finger" as the spelling is similar; also, used when a form in one variety becomes used in another variety for sociolinguistic reasons (e.g., when speakers of one dialect "drop" their r-sounds in an effort, say, to sound more sophisticated or upper class).

**icon/iconic.** A sign that bears a direct similarity or analogy to its referent or meaning (e.g., a map of a state and the actual geographic shape of the state).

**idiolect.** Refers to an individual's own unique variety of language, in other words, one's personal dialect.

**I-language.** The internalized representation of language that speakers have, as opposed to E-language that is actually produced and visible.

**illocutionary force.** A kind of speech act—such as commanding, promising, giving an insult, or making an arrest—that reflects the speaker's intention in producing that utterance: "by saying something we *do* something," as when a minister joins two people together when saying, "I now pronounce you man and wife."

**indirect speech act.** Speech that performs a function in an indirect manner, such as asking, "Do you have the time?" instead of asking directly, "What time is it?"

**Indo-European.** A major language family which includes most of the languages in Europe, and many of the languages in India and southwestern Asia.

**infix.** An affix that is inserted within a root or stem of a word, as opposed to the beginning or end.

**inflection.** Refers to changes in the form of a word to mark different grammatical functions, such as number (singular and plural) or "inflecting" for tense (e.g., talk, talk*ed*, talk*s*, talk*ing*).

**intonational contours.** Refers to the pitches part of an utterance to indicate question or statement.

**isolating language.** In language typology, a language in which one word equals one morpheme, and grammar is depicted using word order. Some use the terms *isolating* and *analytic* synonymously.

**kineme.** The smallest unit of body motion and gestures.

**kinesics (body language).** The study of body language.

**language acquisition device.** A proposed neurological module made by Chomsky regarding the infant's innate ability to acquire language effortlessly without being taught.

**language death.** The loss of a language when its last native speakers die out.

**language family.** A classification system of languages in which related languages are grouped based on a common ancestral language.

**language ideology.** People's beliefs about language regarding the nature and function of language that link social structure, language variety, and forms of speech.

**language isolates.** Languages that are not related to other languages or to other language families.

**language variety.** Any form of language that is systematically distinct from others, such as varieties from different regions within a country, between countries (American English and British English), or those spoken by different social groups.

**lateralization (of the brain).** Refers to how certain brain functions are more dominant in one side or the other.

**length of sound.** The physical duration of a sound.

**lexical diffusion.** Refers to how sound changes operate; that is, through the gradual spread, or diffusion, throughout the words of a language.

**lexicon.** Another way to refer to vocabulary and words.

**lingua franca.** A language used for communication between groups of people who do not share a common first language.

**linguistic anthropology.** The study of the relationship between language and culture.

**linguistic determinism.** Refers to the notion that the way individuals think is determined by the languages they speak.

**linguistic relativity.** Refers to the notion that differences among languages are reflected in the different worldviews of their speakers; sometimes also meaning that all languages are equally complex, sophisticated, and so on.
**linguistics.** The scientific study of language.
**loanwords.** Words borrowed from another language that become a part of the borrowing language, such as *kindergarten* from German, or *spaghetti* from Italian, in English.
**logograph.** A written character that represents a word or a phrase.
**manner of articulation.** Refers to how different articulators are affected in the production of consonants.
**Mayan glyphs.** The writing system of the Mayan civilization.
**meaning.** What a linguistic form refers to, both substantively (e.g., here is a "dog") and figuratively ("man's best friend"). For native speakers, the meanings of words are not explicitly taught, however. When learning another language, the meanings of words are explicitly taught, but this is challenging because a word in one language does not always have a correspondence in another. Thus, direct translations are not always possible.
**metathesis.** Refers to a process of sound change in which the order of successive sounds is altered or reversed, such as the Old English *bridd* to the Modern English *bird*.
**micro-macro connection.** The connection and relationship between greater (macro) structures and processes in society with everyday encounters (micro).
**minimal pair.** A technique of doing phonemic analysis: finding a minimal pair means looking for two words that differ by only one sound, such as "bit" versus "pit."
**Mock Asian.** Fake variety of English that is characterized by fake Chinese accents, attributed to Asian Americans regardless of their ethnic origin and first language.
**Mock Spanish.** The use of Spanish-inspired phrases in English to create a fake or mock Spanish, popularized by the anthropologist Jane Hill. This type of linguistic mockery is seen as hidden racism.
**morphemes.** The smallest meaningful unit of a word, for example, *unthinkable* consists of three morphemes, *un-*, *-think-*, and *-able*.
**morphology.** The study of the formation of words and the different parts of words, such as stems and suffixes.
**morphophonemics.** The study of phonemic differences among allomorphs of the same morpheme, such as /f/ and /v/ in *knife* and *knives*, and *life* and *lives*.
**multilingual.** The ability to speak multiple languages.
**nationality.** Refers to the legal connection that an individual has to a state or country, bound by the citizenship that the individual has
**neogrammarian hypothesis.** A nineteenth-century school of linguistics claiming that sounds laws should not allow for exceptions and should be the same across languages.
**neologism.** The creation of a new lexical item or word in response to some change in the physical or social environment (e.g., the term euro for the new currency of the European Union).
**neurolinguistics.** A branch of linguistics that studies the role of the brain in speech processing.
**new ethnography.** Another name for "ethnoscience," the study of culture by using systematic linguistic-like ways of investigating it.
**nonverbal communication.** Meaningful signals and cues used in communication, either as part of speech or independently, such as gestures and facial expressions.

**norms of interpretation of communication.** What constitutes proper interaction is subject to interpretation. Interactions are interpreted differently across cultures as the norms of interpretation vary.

**overlapping distribution.** When two (or more) sounds appear in the same phonetic environment, suggesting that they are likely to be different phonemes.

**overlapping variation.** A technique of doing phonemic analysis: if sounds appear in the same phonetic environment in a set words, this implies they are likely different phonemes.

**paralanguage.** Parts of language that do not have any lexical meaning, and thus, sometimes considered optional for analysis. These include three categories: voice qualifiers (e.g., loudness and tempo), voice characterizers (e.g., giggling, crying), and vocal segregates (e.g., uh-uh, or tsk-tsk).

**participant observation.** For an extended period, fieldworkers participate in the daily activities of the people they are studying, while observing and gathering data.

**performance/performatives.** Refers to a speaker's using a language in a social context at any given time, contrasting with the speaker's actual underlying knowledge of it ("competence").

**perlocutionary effect.** In J. L. Austin's view of speech act theory, the actual effect an utterance has on a speaker, such as convincing, scaring, or insulting someone.

**phatic communication.** Speech used for social and emotive purposes and not for conveying information (e.g., formulaic greetings or small talk).

**phone.** The smallest perceptible segment of speech that, when combined with other phones, makes up an utterance. Each phone can be represented through a written symbol from a phonetic alphabet, and generally, a phone is written with brackets (e.g., [p]). For example, *apple* can be transcribed into [æpəl], in which each symbol represents each phone.

**phonemes.** The smallest meaningful unit of sound or a set of sounds in a language. These are—largely covert—idealized abstractions by native speakers who feel a group of sounds is psychologically the same, even though they can be acoustically different. For example, [p] and [b] are different phonemes in English as they contrast in forms like *pin* versus *bin*. But [p], [p$^{h}$], and [p$^{l}$] are the same phoneme because, for instance, generally native English speakers hear—and think of—the p-sounds in *spin*, *pin*, and *stop!* as being the same even though the p-sound in *pin* is "aspirated" (as a puff of air) and the p-sound in *stop!* is often "implosive" (air is not released or is sucked in). Individual phonemes are often depicted using backslashes (e.g., /p/ or /b/).

**phonemics.** The study of phonemes.

**phonetic alphabet.** A set symbols that can be consistently and unambiguously used to transcribe speech sounds, like the "letters" of a phonetic alphabet like the IPA or the American system.

**phonetic symbols.** A system of symbols used to represent speech sounds in a language.

**phonetic transcription.** The detailed representation of speech sounds using the symbols of a phonetic alphabet,.

**phonetics/phonology.** The study of sound systems, or the sound system of a particular language.

**phonology**. See **phonetics/phonology** above.

**pidgin.** A simplified language used to cross language barriers when there is a communicative need between people who speak mutually unintelligible languages.

**pitch.** Refers to the degree of highness or lowness of a tone.

**place of articulation.** Refers to the areas of the articulator where consonants are produced.

**Plato's problem.** Chomsky's name for the quandary of how speakers of a language seem to know more than what they are ever explicitly taught, evident in their ability to generate novel sentences.

**polyglots.** People with the ability to speak several languages.

**polysemy/polysemous.** Words that have multiple meanings depending on context.

**polysynthetic language.** In language typology, a language in which many affixes get attached to stems to indicate grammatical relationships; languages that can be characterized by the use of both agglutinative and inflectional elements.

**pragmatic presupposition.** What a speaker assumes upon hearing a particular sentence, as opposed to what is actually stated. For example, if a man says, "Would you like to have dinner with me tonight?" a woman might safely assume some romantic interest on his part.

**prefix.** An affix that is attached to the beginning of a word, such as *un-* in *unlikely*.

**prelanguage.** Refers to the communication system that preceded full-fledged language.

**primary sign languages.** Sign language that is used by speakers who are unable to produce verbal speech, for example, by people who are deaf, as this is their primary means of communication.

**prosodic features.** Features of speech that are important for meaning-making, such as variations in pitch, stress, and intonation. Some include things like loudness and tempo in this category, though we call such things paralanguage here. Sometimes collectively all these things are called supersegmentals.

**Proto-Indo-European.** The assumed, though largely unattested, ancestral language from which the modern-day Indo-European languages developed.

**protolanguages.** Assumed and unattested, various ancestral languages from which modern-day language families are derived (e.g., Proto-Germanic, Proto-Indo-European, etc.).

**protowords.** Refer to the reconstruction of words of a protolanguage.

**protowriting.** Refers to the very early pre-writing systems of ancient cultures, such as doodles and scratches.

**proxemic zones.** The different types of culturally appropriate distances that individuals maintain.

**proxemics.** The study of the cultural patterning of space that speakers maintain in face to-face interactions.

**race.** Contested term often used to categorize humans based on physical and biological features, and commonly equated with ethnicity; currently, race is seen as more socially constructed than physiological.

**rebus.** Traditionally referred to the use of pictures to represent words or phrases, such as a heart to represent love.

**referents/references.** Objects (concrete or abstract) in the world that are referred to by using words.

**reflexive noises.** Sounds that babies produce that have basic biological functions, such as crying and coughing.

**register.** A style of speech used in particular situations, such the "formal" speech used in a presidential address or the "preaching" in an evangelical Christian church.

**restricted code.** Relatively informal variety of speech, commonly used by members of a strong network.

**rewrite rules.** Rules used to generate sentences as part of Chomsky's generative grammar. For example, S—> NP VP, means that a sentence S is supposed to be rewritten as a noun phrase NP and a verb phrase VP; each of these phrases could be rewritten further by successive transformations.

**rules of interaction.** Communicative activity is guided by these rules, meaning that members of a speech community know what is appropriate (under normal circumstances).

**Sapir-Whorf hypothesis.** Also known as linguistic relativity, this theory is focused on the relationship between language and the mind, and specifically how a language influences the way speakers of a particular language see the world. As there are differences between languages, presumably these differences result in different worldviews.

**semantic extension.** A word to which a set of entities may be correctly applied. For example, the extension of "flower" could include rose, tulip, chrysanthemum, and so on. The term contrasts with *semantic intension*, the defining properties of a word (e.g., "flowers" are things that have petals, stems, and so on).

**semantic presupposition.** The semantic assumptions of a sentence. For example, "The King of France is in a bad mood today" implies that France indeed has a king.

**semantics.** The study of the relationship between linguistic forms and structures and their meanings.

**semiotics.** The study of signs and symbols and how they are used for meaning-making in communication.

**sentence-final particles.** Markers at the end of a sentence that indicate or express mood, intent, and identity.

**sentiment analysis.** The use of corpus linguistics, using large blocks of texts (like tweets), in an attempt to determine the public's feelings on some issue or product.

**sexual orientation.** Refers to the attraction to another individual of the same or the opposite sex.

**sign language.** Communication through the use of different hand gestures, positions, and motions to create meaningful signs.

**sign.** An entity that represents or stands for something else; this can be direct or indirect correlation, such as an icon or a symbol.

**social class.** Distinction between social groups through differences in economics, education, and familial prestige.

**social constructivism.** The idea that certain aspects of society and social phenomena are the product of cultural or other institutional forces and are not simply natural and self-evident. For example, neither gender roles nor racial categories need to be considered as preestablished, unmalleable, or sacrosanct.

**social network.** Refers to the association of individuals with whom a speaker regularly interacts.

**social power theory.** Also known as dominance theory, this theory focuses on patriarchy, male power, and unequal power relations between men and women that are manifested as language differences.

**society.** A group of people who live together in the same geographic area and typically share a common set of values.

**sociocultural.** Research conducted by looking at learned behavior (culture) and how it is linked to the values of the members of a social group (society).

**sociolinguistic change.** The understanding of linguistic change in the context or community in which the change occurs.

**Spanglish.** The blending of both English and Spanish that is spoken by speakers who know both languages to varying degrees.

**speech act.** The minimum unit of speech in the form of an utterance that is considered as an action, in which the focus is on the intention, purpose, and effect (such as an apology).

**speech act theory.** A term—associated with such linguistic philosophers as John Searle, Paul Grice, or J. L. Austin—used to describe the speaker's intentions behind the use of speech or the inferences that a listener might make from it.

**speech activity.** A collective term used to refer to various levels of speech-related activities: speech situation, speech event, and speech act.

**speech area.** A term used the ethnography of communication to refer to a geographical place where speakers of different languages share speaking rules.

**speech community.** Individuals who share the same language variety, and who have shared ways of interpreting and using that language.

**speech event.** The basic unit of verbal communication (communicative event) in which several turns of speech acts take place that are governed by social rules, like an interview or a conversation.

**speech situation.** A term used the ethnography of communication to refer to the context which speaking occurs (e.g., a family meal, school lecture, etc., which all can be distinguished from each other).

**standard speech.** Variety of a language that is more prestigious than others in a speech community. Compare to **vernacular varieties**.

**stress.** The degree of force used in producing a syllable in a word (e.g., CONtrast versus conTRAST), or the emphasis in a sentence (e.g., "Maybe WILLIAM wants to go, but KATIE certainly doesn't!").

**structuralist paradigm.** The idea that was fundamental to the field of linguistics during the first half of the twentieth century, concerned with structures and systems, until it was replaced with Noam Chomsky's generative grammar in the 1960s.

**style switch/style shift.** Refers to the shift in speech style by a speaker who moves between different communities using the same language, as opposed to shifting between different languages.

**subculture theory.** The proposal that men and women live in different linguistic worlds, as they belong to different subcultures and have their own distinct communication styles.

**suffix.** An affix attached to the end of a stem; e.g., when the suffix *-s* is attached to *car*, the plural form *cars* is created.

**syllabary/syllabaries.** Refers to symbols that represent more than one sound, as opposed to an alphabet in which ideally each symbol represents only one sound.

**symbol.** A sign that represents something else, but the meaning is arbitrary and must be learned; it is often abstract; for example, baguettes being a symbol of France.

**synchronic linguistics.** An approach in which languages are studied in a specific point in time without taking their history into account.

**synchronous/synchronic.** Communication that takes place in real time; back-and-forth communication.

**synonyms.** Refers to words with similar or the same meanings.

**syntax.** Concerns the arrangement of words within a sentence to produce a grammatically correct sentence.

**synthetic language.** In language typology, a language in which affixes are attached to other morphemes.

**transformational rules.** Statement that describes the transformation of a specific grammatical structure.

**transgender.** The situation when someone's biological sexual identity does not match that person's social gender identity. Note that this is unrelated to a person's sexual orientation.

**trilingualism.** The ability to speak three languages.

**Twitter.** A Short Messaging Service text and social networking system in which users can post and read 140-character messages called tweets.

**universal grammar.** A theory stating that the human ability to learn languages is hardwired into the brain.

**Upper Paleolithic.** The most recent period of the Old Stone Age, characterized by creativity that resulted in the production of large quantities of various objects, including weapons and art.

**vernacular.** The form of a language that is spoken in informal, everyday settings and is commonly seen as less prestigious. Compare to **standard speech**.

**vocal channel.** Modification of this area makes it possible for humans to produce sounds used for communication.

**vocal play.** Characteristic of early "baby speech," and refers to the production of a wide range of sounds that resemble consonants and vowels, typically occurring around the age of six months.

**vocal segregates.** Extralinguistic sounds, such as *uh-uh*, or *tsk-tsk*. See **paralanguage**.

**vocal tract.** The area of the human body where speech sounds are produced.

**vocal-auditory channel.** A communication method that uses spoken and audible sounds.

**voice characterizers/voice characteristics.** Refers to non-lexical parts of speech like laughing and giggling, whimpering and whining, and so on. See **paralanguage**.

**voice qualifiers.** Refers to the tone of voice and pacing of speech. This includes variation in volume, pitch, tempo, and articulation. See **paralanguage**.

**voiced sounds.** Speech sounds produced with the resonance of the vocal chords. Compare the production of *v* (voiced) with *f* (voiceless).

**voiceless sounds.** Speech sounds produced without the resonance of the vocal chords. Compare the production of *f* (voiceless) with *v* (voiced).

**vowels.** Sounds produced with an open vocal tract, meaning that your breath channel is open and not blocked. Compare to the production of consonants.

**Wernicke's area.** Area of the brain concerned with the comprehension of language. Individuals with damage in this area can produce language, but it lacks meaning.

**word order.** Refers to how words are arranged in a phrase or a sentence.

# BIBLIOGRAPHY


**ABRAHAMS, R. D.**

1972 Talking my talk: Black English social segmentation in black communities. Florida F/L Reporter 10:29–38.

**ADGER, DAVID**

2003 Core syntax: a minimalist approach. New York: Oxford University Press.

**AGAR, MICHAEL H.**

1994 Language shock. New York: HarperCollins.

**AGHA, ASIF**

2007 Language and social relations. Cambridge, UK: Cambridge University Press.

**AHEARN, LAURA**

2001a Agency. *In* Key terms in language and culture. Alessandro Duranti, ed., pp. 7–10. Malden, MA: Blackwell.

2001b Language and agency. Annual Review of Anthropology 30:109–137.

2012 Living language: an introduction to linguistic anthropology. Malden, MA: Wiley-Blackwell.

2017 Living language: an introduction to linguistic anthropology. 2d ed. Malden, MA: Wiley-Blackwell.

**AKMAJIAN, ADRIAN, RICHARD A. DEMERS, ANN K. FARMER, AND ROBERT M. HARNISH**

2010 Linguistics: an introduction to language and communication. 6th ed. Cambridge, MA: MIT Press.

**ALBERT, ROSITA DASKAL**

1986 Communication and attributional differences between Hispanics and Anglo-Americans. *In* Interethnic communication: current research, vol. 10. Young Yun Kim, ed., pp. 42–59. Newbury Park, CA: Sage.

**ALBIRINI, ABDULKAFI**

2015 Modern Arabic sociolinguistics: Diglossia, variation, codeswitching, attitudes, and identity. New York: Routledge.

**ALIM, H. SAMY**

2004 "You know my steez": an ethnographic and sociolinguistic study of styleshifting in a black American speech community. Durham, NC: Duke University Press.

**ALIM, H. SAMY, AND GENEVA SMITHERMAN**

2012 Articulate while black: Barack Obama, language, and race in the U.S. New York: Oxford University Press.

**ALIM, H. SAMY, JOHN RICKFORD, AND ARNETHA BALL**

2016 Raciolinguistics. New York: Oxford University Press.

**AMERICAN ANTHROPOLOGICAL ASSOCIATION**

1983 Professional ethics: statements and procedures of the American Anthropological Association. Washington, DC: American Anthropological Association.

**ANDRESEN, JULIE, AND PHILLIP CARTER**

2016 Languages of the world: How history, culture, and politics shape language. Malden. MA: Wiley-Blackwell.

**ANTHONY, DAVID**

2007 The horse, the wheel, and language: how Bronze-Age riders from the Eurasian steppes shaped the modern world. Princeton, NJ: Princeton University Press.

**ANTTILA, RAIMO**

1989 Historical and comparative linguistics. 2d ed. Philadelphia: Benjamins.

**ANZALDÚA, GLORIA**

1990 Introduction. *In* Making face, making soul/haciendo caras: creative and critical perspectives by feminists of color. Gloria Anzaldúa, ed. San Francisco: Aunt Lute Books.

**ASIM, JABARI**

2007 The N word: Who can say it, who shouldn't, and why. Boston: Houghton Mifflin.

**ASSOCIATED PRESS**

2013 Associated Press stylebook and briefing on media law 2013. New York: Basic Books.

**AUSTIN, J. L.**

1976 How to do things with words. 2d. ed. Oxford, UK: Oxford University Press.

**AUSTIN, PETER**

2008 One thousand languages: the worldwide history of living and lost tongues. London: Thames & Hudson.

**BAKHTIN, MIKHAIL**

1981 The dialogic imagination: four essays. Austin: University of Texas Press.

**BAQUEDANO-LÓPEZ, PATRICIA**

2006 Literacy practices across learning contexts. *In* A companion to linguistic anthropology. Alessandro Duranti, ed., pp. 245–268. Malden, MA: Wiley-Blackwell.

**BARON, DENNIS**

1986 Grammar and gender. New Haven: Yale University Press.

**BARON, NAOMI**

2000 Alphabet to email: how written English evolved and where it's heading. London: Routledge.

2008 Always on: language in an online mobile world. New York: Oxford University Press.

**BASSO, KEITH H.**

1974 The ethnography of writing. *In* Explorations in the ethnography of speaking. Richard Bauman and Joel Sherzer, eds., pp. 425–432. London: Cambridge University Press.

1990 Western Apache language and culture: essays in linguistic anthropology. Tucson: University of Arizona Press.

**BAUER, LAURIE**

2007 The linguistics student's handbook. Oxford, UK: Oxford University Press.

**BAUER, LAURIE, AND PETER TRUDGILL, EDS.**

1998 *Language Myths*. London: Penguin.

**BAUGH, JOHN**

2002 Beyond Ebonics: linguistic pride and racial prejudice. New York: Oxford University Press.

**BAUMAN, JAMES J.**

1980 A guide to issues in Indian language retention. Washington, DC: Center for Applied Linguistics.

**BAUMAN, RICHARD, AND JOEL SHERZER**

1974 (eds.) Explorations in the ethnography of speaking. London: Cambridge University Press.

1975 The ethnography of speaking. *In* Annual Review of Anthropology, vol. 4. Bernard J. Siegel et al., eds., pp. 95–119. Palo Alto, CA: Annual Reviews.

1989 (eds.) Explorations in the ethnography of speaking. 2d ed. Cambridge, UK: Cambridge University Press.

**BAZÁN-FIGUERAS, PATRICIA, AND SALVADOR FIGUERAS**

2014 The future of Spanglish: global or tribal. Perspectives on Global Development and Technology 13:261–266.

**BENEVENTO, NICOLE, AND AMELIA DIETRICH**

2015 I think, therefore, digo yo: variable position of the 1sg subject pronoun in New Mexican Spanish-English code-switching. International Journal of Bilingualism 19:407–422.

**BENOR, SARAH BUNIN**

2010 Ethnolinguistic repertoire: shifting the analytic focus in language and ethnicity. Journal of Sociolinguistics 14:159–183.

**BERGMAN, TED**

2013 Why are sign languages included in the Ethnologue? July 31, 2013. *In* ethnologue.com, SIL International Publications, http://www.ethnologue.com

/ethnoblog/ted-bergman/why-are-sign-languages-included-ethnologue #.UgW0rK44mRs.

**BERGMANN, ANOUSCHKA, KATHLEEN CURRIE HALL, AND SHARON MIRIAM ROSS, EDS.**

2007 Language files: materials for an introduction to language and linguistics. Columbus: Ohio State University Press.

**BERGVALL, VICTORIA L.**

1999 Toward a comprehensive theory of language and gender. Language in Society 28:273–293.

**BERLIN, BRENT**

1976 The concept of rank in ethnobiological classification: some evidence from Aguaruna folk botany. American Ethnologist 3:381–399.

**BERLIN, BRENT, DENNIS BREEDLOVE, AND PETER RAVEN**

1974 Principles of Tzeltal plant classification: an introduction to the botanical ethnography of a Mayan-speaking people of highland Chiapas. New York: Academic Press.

**BERLIN, BRENT, AND PAUL KAY**

1969 Basic color terms: their universality and evolution. Berkeley: University of California Press.

1991 Basic color terms: their universality and evolution. 2d ed. Berkeley: University of California Press.

**BERWICK, ROBERT, AND NOAM CHOMSKY**

2016 Why only us? language and evolution. Cambridge, MA: MIT Press.

**BESNIER, NIKO**

1995 Literacy, emotion and authority: reading and writing on a Polynesian atoll. Cambridge, UK: Cambridge University Press.

**BICKERTON, DEREK**

1981 Roots of language. Ann Arbor, MI: Karoma.

1983 Creole languages. Scientific American 249(1):116–122 (July).

1990 Language and species. Chicago: University of Chicago Press.

2009 Adam's tongue: how humans made language, and how language made humans. New York: Hill and Wang.

**BICKFORD, J. ALBERT**

1998 Morphology and syntax: tools for analyzing the world's languages. Dallas, TX: SIL International.

**BIGGAM, CAROLE P., AND CHRISTIAN KAY, EDS.**

2006 Progress in colour studies. Vol. 1: Language and culture. Amsterdam: John Benjamins.

**BIRDWHISTELL, RAY L.**

1970 Kinesics and context: essays on body motion communication. Philadelphia: University of Pennsylvania Press.

**BLACK, MAX**

1962 Models and metaphors: studies in language and philosophy. Ithaca, NY: Cornell University Press.

**BLOOMFIELD, LEONARD**

1933 Language. New York: Holt.

1946 Algonquian. *In* Linguistic structures of Native America. Cornelius Osgood, ed. Viking Fund Publications in Anthropology, no. 6, pp. 85–129. New York: Viking Fund.

**BLUM, SUSAN, ED.**

2013 Making sense of language: readings in culture and communication. New York: Oxford University Press.

**BOAS, FRANZ**

1911 (ed.) Handbook of American Indian languages, part 1. Bureau of American Ethnology, bulletin 40. Washington, DC: Government Printing Office. [Republished in 1991.]

1922 (ed.) Handbook of American Indian languages, part 2. Bureau of American Ethnology, bulletin 40. Washington, DC: Government Printing Office.

1933–38 (ed.) Handbook of American Indian languages, part 3. New York: Augustin.

1938 The mind of primitive man. Rev. ed. New York: Macmillan.

1940 Metaphorical expression in the language of the Kwakiutl Indians. *In* Race, language and culture *by* Franz Boas, pp. 232–239. New York: Macmillan.

**BOAS, NORMAN**

2004 Franz Boas, 1858–1942: an illustrated biography. Mystic, CT: Seaport Autographs Press.

**BOELLSTORF, TOM**

2004 Gay language and Indonesia: registering and belonging. Journal of Linguistic Anthropology 14:248–268.

2005 The gay archipelago: sexuality and nation in Indonesia. Princeton, NJ: Princeton University Press.

**BOKAMBA, EYAMBA**

1989 Are there syntactic constraints on code-mixing? World Englishes 8:277–292.

**BOLINGER, DWIGHT**

1975 Aspects of language. 2d ed. New York: Harcourt Brace Jovanovich.

**BOLTON, KINGSLEY, AND BRAJ B. KACHRU, EDS.**

2006 World Englishes: critical concepts in linguistics. 6 vols. London: Routledge.

**BONVILLAIN, NANCY**

2007 Language, culture, and communication: the meaning of messages. 5th ed. Upper Saddle River, NJ: Pearson Prentice-Hall.

2010 Language, culture and communication. 6th ed. Upper Saddle River, NJ: Pearson.

2013 Language, culture, and communication: the meaning of messages. 7th ed. Upper Saddle River, NJ: Pearson.

**BORODITSKY, LERA, LAUREN SCHMIDT, AND WEBB PHILLIPS**

2003 Sex, syntax, and semantics. *In* Language in mind: advances in the study of language and cognition. Dedre Gentner and Susan Goldin-Meadows, eds., pp. 61–80. Cambridge, MA: MIT Press, Bradford Book.

**BOURDIEU, PIERRE**

1987 Distinction: a social critique of the judgement of taste. Cambridge, MA: Harvard University Press.

1999 Language and symbolic power. Cambridge, MA: Harvard University Press.

**BOWEN, CLAIRE**

2008 Linguistic fieldwork: a practical guide. New York: Palgrave.

**BOWEN, CLAIRE, AND BETHWYN EVANS, EDS.**

2014 The Routledge handbook of historical linguistics. New York: Routledge.

**BRENTARI, DIANE, ED.**

2010 Sign languages. Cambridge, UK: Cambridge University Press.

**BRIGHT, MICHAEL**

1984 Animal language. Ithaca, NY: Cornell University Press.

**BRIGHT, WILLIAM**

1960 Animals of acculturation in the California Indian languages. University of California Publications in Linguistics, vol. 4, no. 4, pp. 215–246. Berkeley: University of California Press.

1992 (ed.) International encyclopedia of linguistics. 4 vols. New York: Oxford University Press.

**BROWN, CECIL H.**

1984 Language and living things: uniformities in folk classification and naming. Piscataway, NJ: Rutgers University Press.

**BROWN, GILLIAN, AND GEORGE YULE**

1983 Discourse analysis. Cambridge: Cambridge University Press.

**BROWN, PENELOPE, AND STEPHEN LEVENSON**

1987 Politeness: some universals in language usage. Cambridge: Cambridge University Press.

**BUCHOLTZ, MARY**

1999 Bad example: transgression and progress in language and gender studies. *In* Reinventing identities: the gendered self in discourse. Mary Bucholtz, A. C. Liang, and Laurel Sutton, eds., pp. 4–24. New York: Oxford University Press.

2001a Gender. *In* Key terms in language and culture. Alessandro Duranti, ed., pp. 75–78. Malden, MA: Blackwell.

2001b The whiteness of nerds: superstandard English and racial markedness. Journal of Linguistic Anthropology 11:84–100.

2004 (ed.) Language and woman's place, *by* Robin Tolmach Lakoff: text and commentaries. New York: Oxford University Press.

2011 White kids: language, race, and styles of youth identity. Cambridge, UK: Cambridge University Press.

**BUCHOLTZ, MARY, A. C. LIANG, AND LAUREL SUTTON, EDS.**

1999 Reinventing identities: the gendered self in discourse. New York: Oxford University Press.

**BUCK, CARL DARLING**

1988 A dictionary of selected synonyms in the principal Indo-European languages. Chicago: University of Chicago Press.

**BURLING, ROBBINS**

1964 Cognition and componential analysis: God's truth or hocus pocus? American Anthropologist 66:20–28.

1973 English in black and white. New York: Holt, Rinehart and Winston.

1984 (reissued with changes in 2000) Learning a field language. Prospect Heights, IL: Waveland Press.

1992 Review of Derek Bickerton: Language and species. Journal of Linguistic Anthropology 2:81–91.

2005 The talking ape: how language evolved. New York: Oxford University Press.

**BURRIDGE, KATE, AND ALEXANDER BERG**

2017 Understanding language change. New York: Routledge.

**BURTON, STRANG, ROSE-MARIE DECHAINE, AND ERIC VATIKIOTIS-BATESON**

2012 Linguistics for dummies. Missisauga, ONT: John Wiley.

**CAMERON, DEBORAH**

2005 Language, gender, and sexuality: current issues and new directions. Applied Linguistics 26:482–502.

2008 The myth of Mars and Venus: do men and women really speak different languages? New York: Oxford University Press.

n.d. Comment. *In* http://www.straightdope.com/columns/read/750/is-there-a-gender-neutral-substitute-for-his-or-her.

**CAMERON, DEBORAH, AND DON KULICK**

2006 (eds.) The language and sexuality reader. New York: Routledge.

2012 Language and sexuality. Cambridge, UK: Cambridge University Press.

**CAMERON, DEBORAH, FIONA MCALINDEN, AND KATHY O'LEARY**

1988 Lakoff in context: the social and linguistic functions of tag questions. *In* Women in their speech communities: new perspectives on language and sex. Jennifer Coates and Deborah Cameron, eds., pp. 74–93. New York: Longman.

**CAMPBELL, BERNARD G., ED.**

1979 Humankind emerging. 2d ed. Boston: Little, Brown.

**CAMPBELL, KERMIT**

2005 "Gettin' our groove on": rhetoric, language, and literacy for the hip hop generation. Detroit: Wayne State University Press.

**CAMPBELL, LYLE**

1988 Review of Joseph H. Greenberg: Language in the Americas. Language 64:591–615.

2000 American Indian languages: the historical linguistics of Native America. New York: Oxford University Press.

**CARBAUGH, DONAL, ED.**

1990 Cultural communication and intercultural contact. Hillsdale, NJ: Erlbaum.

**CARNIE, ANDREW**

2011 Modern syntax: a coursebook. Cambridge, UK: Cambridge University Press.

**CARROLL, JOHN B.**

1963 Linguistic relativity, contrastive linguistics, and language learning. International Review of Applied Linguistics in Language Teaching 1:1–20.

**CARROLL, JOHN B., AND JOSEPH B. CASAGRANDE**

1958 The function of language classifications in behavior. *In* Readings in social psychology. 3d ed. Eleanor E. Maccoby, Theodore M. Newcomb, and Eugene L. Hartley, eds., pp. 18–31. New York: Holt, Rinehart and Winston.

**CARTMILL, MATT, AND FRED H. SMITH**

2009 The human lineage. Hoboken, NJ: Wiley-Blackwell.

**CHAFE, WALLACE, AND DEBORAH TANNEN**

1987 The relation between written and spoken language. Annual Review of Anthropology 16:383–407.

**CHAIKA, ELAINE**

1982 Language, the social mirror. New York: Newbury House.

**CHAMBERLAIN, ALEXANDER F.**

1912 Women's languages. American Anthropologist 14:579–581.

**CHAMBERS, J. K., AND PETER TRUDGILL**

1998 Dialectology. 2d ed. Cambridge, UK: Cambridge University Press.

**CHESHIRE, JENNY**

2002 Sex and gender in variationist research. *In* The handbook of language variation and change. J. K. Chambers, Peter Trudgill, and Natalie Schilling-Estes, eds., pp. 423–443. Malden, MA: Blackwell.

**CHIKERSAL, PREENA, ET AL.**

2015 Modelling [sic] public sentiment in Twitter: using linguistic patterns to enhance supervised learning. In Computational linguistics and intelligent text processing: 16th International Conference, CICLing 2015, Cairo, Egypt, April 14–20, 2015, Proceedings, Part II; Alexander Gelbukh, ed., pp 49–65. Springer: Heidelberg.

**CHOMSKY, NOAM**

1957 Syntactic structures. The Hague: Mouton.

1959 Review of B. F. Skinner: Verbal behavior. Language 35:26–58.

1965 Aspects of the theory of syntax. Cambridge, MA: MIT Press.

1968 Language and the mind. Psychology Today 1(9)(1968):66.

1972 Language and mind. Enlarged ed. New York: Harcourt Brace Jovanovich.

1980 Rules and representations. New York: Columbia University Press.

1986 Knowledge of language: its nature, origin, and use. New York: Praeger.

1993 Lectures on government and binding: the Pisa Lectures. The Hague: Mouton de Gruyter.

2010 Some simple evo devo theses: how true might they be for language? *In* The evolution of human language: biolinguistic perspectives. Richard K. Larson, Vivian Déprez, and Hiroko Yamakido, eds., pp. 45–62. Cambridge, UK: Cambridge University Press.

2012 Chomsky's linguistics. Peter Graff, ed. Cambridge, MA: MIT Working Papers in Linguistics.

**CHOMSKY, NOAM, AND JAMES CHOMSKY**

2012 The science of language: interviews with James McGilvray. New York: Cambridge University Press.

**CHOMSKY, NOAM, AND MORRIS HALLE**

1968 The sound pattern of English. New York: Harper and Row.

**CHRISTIANSEN, MORTEN H., AND SIMON KIRBY, EDS.**

2003 Language evolution. New York: Oxford University Press.

**CHUN, ELAINE W.**

2009 Ideologies of legitimate mockery: Margaret Cho's revoicings of Mock Asians. *In* Beyond yellow English: toward a linguistic anthropology of Asian Pacific America. Angela Reyes and Adrienne Lo, eds., pp. 261–287. New York: Oxford University Press.

**CLAYTON, EWAN**

2015 The golden thread: a history of writing. Berkeley: Counterpoint.

**COATES, JENNIFER**

2004 Women, men, and language: a sociolinguistic account of gender differences in language. 3d ed. New York: Routledge.

**COATES, JENNIFER, AND DEBORAH CAMERON, EDS.**

1988 Women in their speech communities: new perspectives on language and sex. New York: Longman.

**COE, MICHAEL, AND MARK VAN STONE**

2005 Reading the Maya glyphs. 2d ed. London: Thames & Hudson.

**COHN, NEIL**

2010 Japanese visual language: the structure of manga. *In* Manga: an anthology of global and cultural perspectives. Toni Johnson-Woods, ed., pp. 187–203. New York: Continuum Books.

2013 The visual language of comics: introduction to the structure and cognition of sequential images. London: Bloomsbury Academic.

2015 Will emoji become a new language? *In* http://www.bbc.com/future/story/20151012-will-emoji-become-a-new-language.

n.d. Morphology of Japanese visual language. *In* http://www.visuallanguagelab.com/A/jvlmorphology.html.

COHN, NEIL, AND SEAN EHLY

2016 The vocabulary of manga: visual morphology in dialects of Japanese visual language. Journal of Pragmatics 92:17–29.

COLAPINTO, JOHN

2007 The interpreter: has a remote Amazonian tribe upended our understanding of language? New Yorker, April 16, 83:117–142.

COOK, VIVIAN, AND MARK NEWSON

2007 Chomsky's universal grammar: an introduction. 3d ed. Malden, MA: Blackwell.

COULMAS, FLORIAN

2002 Writing systems: an introduction to their linguistic analysis. Cambridge, UK: Cambridge University Press.

COWAN, WILLIAM, AND JAROMIRA RAKUŠAN

1998 Source book for linguistics. 3d ed. Amsterdam: John Benjamins.

CROWLEY, TERRY, AND CLAIRE BOWERN

2009 An introduction to historical linguistics. 4th ed. New York: Oxford University Press.

CRYSTAL, DAVID

1971 Linguistics. Harmondsworth, UK: Penguin.

1974 Paralinguistics. *In* Current trends in linguistics. Vol. 12: Linguistics and adjacent arts and sciences. Thomas A. Sebeok, ed., pp. 265–295. The Hague: Mouton.

1981 Directions in applied linguistics. New York: Academic Press.

1997 A dictionary of linguistics and phonetics. 4th ed., updated and enlarged. Oxford, UK: Blackwell.

2000 Language death. Cambridge, UK: Cambridge University Press.

2001 Language and the Internet. Cambridge, UK: Cambridge University Press.

2004 The language revolution. Cambridge, UK: Polity Press.

2007 How language works: how babies babble, words change meaning, and languages live or die. New York: Penguin.

2010 (ed.) The Cambridge encyclopedia of language. 3d ed. Cambridge, UK: Cambridge University Press.

CUMMINS, JAMES

1989 Institutionalized racism and assessment of minority children: a comparison of policies and programs in the United States and Canada. *In* Assessment and placement of minority students, *by* R. J. Samuda, S. L. Kong, J. Cummins, J. Lewis, and J. Pascal-Leone. Toronto: C. J. Hofgrefe/ISSP.

1990 Empowering minority students: a framework for intervention. *In* Facing racism in education. N. M. Hidalgo, C. L. McDowell, and E. V. Siddle, eds., pp.

50–68. Reprint Series No. 21, Harvard Educational Review. Cambridge. MA: Harvard Educational Review.

**CUTTING, JOAN**

2008 Pragmatics and discourse: a resource book for students. 2d ed. London: Routledge.

**D'ANDRADE, ROY**

1995 The development of cognitive anthropology. Cambridge, UK: Cambridge University Press.

**DANESI, MARCEL**

2016 The semiotics of emoji: the rise of visual language in the age of the Internet. London: Bloomsbury Academic.

**DANET, BRENDA, AND SUSAN HERRING, EDS.**

2007 The multilingual Internet: language, culture, and communication. New York: Oxford.

**DANIELS, PETER, AND WILLIAM BRIGHT, EDS.**

1996 The world's writing systems. New York: Oxford University Press.

**DARNELL, REGNA**

1992 Anthropological linguistics: early history in North America. *In* International encyclopedia of linguistics, vol. 1. William Bright, ed., pp. 69–71. New York: Oxford University Press.

1999 Theorizing American anthropology: continuities from the B.A.E. to the Boasians. *In* Theorizing the Americanist tradition. Lisa Philips Valentine and Regna Darnell, eds., pp. 38–51. Toronto: University of Toronto Press.

2001 Invisible genealogies: a history of Americanist anthropology. Omaha: University of Nebraska Press.

2010 Edward Sapir: linguist, anthropologist, humanist. Lincoln: University of Nebraska Press.

**DAWSON, HOPE, AND MICHAEL PHELAN, EDS.**

2016 Language files, 12th edition: materials for an introduction to language and linguistics. Columbus: Ohio State University Press.

**DE GROLIER, ERIC, ED.**

1983 Glossogenetics: the origin and evolution of language. Chur, Switzerland: Harwood Academic.

**DEFRANCIS, JOHN**

1984 The Chinese language: fact and fantasy. Honolulu: University of Hawaii Press.

1989 Visible speech: the diverse oneness of writing systems. Honolulu: University of Hawaii Press.

**DEPARTMENT OF LINGUISTICS, OHIO STATE UNIVERSITY**

2011 Language files: materials for an introduction to language and linguistics. 11th ed. Columbus: Ohio State University Press.

**DESSALLES, JEAN-LOUIS**

2007 Why we talk: the evolutionary origins of language. New York: Oxford University Press.

**DEUTSCHER, GUY**

2010 Through the language glass: why the world looks different in other languages. New York: Metropolitan Books.

**DICKINSON, PAUL**

2013 "B/w u & me": the functions of formulaic language in interactional discourse on Twitter. Linguistics Journal 7(1):7–38. *In* http://www.linguistics-journal.com/wp-content/uploads/2014/01/Volume-7-Issue-1-2013.pdf.

**DILLARD, J. L.**

1972 Black English: its history and usage in the United States. New York: Random House.

**DIMSON, THOMAS**

2015 Emojineering part 1: machine learning for emoji trends. In https://engineering.instagram.com/emojineering-part-1-machine-learning-for-emoji-trendsmachine-learning-for-emoji-trends-7f5f9cb979ad#.9hw0vo6uq.

**DIRINGER, DAVID**

1968 The alphabet: a key to the history of mankind. London: Hutchinson.

**DORIAN, NANCY C.**

1993 A response to Ladefoged's other view of endangered languages. Language 69:575–579.

**DOUGHERTY, JANET W. D., ED.**

1985 Directions in cognitive anthropology. Urbana: University of Illinois Press.

**DURANTI, ALESSANDRO**

1988 Ethnography of speaking: toward a linguistics of the praxis. *In* Linguistics: the Cambridge survey. Vol. 4: Language: the socio-cultural context. Frederick J. Newmeyer, ed., pp. 210–228. Cambridge, UK: Cambridge University Press.

1997 Linguistic anthropology. Cambridge, UK: Cambridge University Press.

2001a (ed.) Key terms in language and culture. Malden, MA: Blackwell.

2001b Linguistic anthropology. *In* International encyclopedia of the social and behavioral sciences, vol. 12. Neil J. Smelser and Paul B. Baltes, eds., pp. 8899–8906. Amsterdam: Elsevier.

2003 Language as culture in U.S. anthropology: three paradigms. Current Anthropology 44:323–347.

2006 (ed.) A companion to linguistic anthropology: Malden, MA: Wiley-Blackwell.

2009 (ed.) Linguistic anthropology: a reader. 2d ed. Malden, MA: Blackwell.

**EASTMAN, CAROL M.**

1983 Language planning: an introduction. San Francisco: Chandler and Sharp.

**ECHEVERRÍA, MAX S., AND HELES CONTRERAS**

1965 Araucanian phonemics. International Journal of American Linguistics 31:132–135.

**ECKERT, PENELOPE, AND SALLY MCCONNELL-GINET**

1992 Think practically and look locally: language and gender as community-based practice. *In* Annual Review of Anthropology, vol. 21. Bernard J. Siegel et al., eds., pp. 461–490. Palo Alto, CA: Annual Reviews.

2013 Language and gender. 2d ed. Cambridge, UK: Cambridge University Press.

**EDWARDS, JOHN, ED.**

2010 Language in Canada. Cambridge, UK: Cambridge University Press.

**EHRLICH, SUSAN, MIRIAM MEYERHOFF, AND JANET HOLMES, EDS.**

2014 The handbook of language, gender, and sexuality. 2d ed. Malden, MA: Wiley-Blackwell.

**EISENSTEIN J., B. O'CONNOR, N. A. SMITH, AND E. P. XING**

2014 Diffusion of lexical change in social media. PLoS ONE 9 (11): e113114. doi:10.1371/journal.pone.0113114.

**ENFIELD, N. J., PAUL KOCKLEMAN, AND JACK SIDNELL, EDS.**

2014 The Cambridge handbook of linguistic anthropology. Cambridge, UK: Cambridge University Press.

**EVERETT, DANIEL**

2005 Cultural constraints on grammar and cognition in Pirahã: another look at the design features of human language. Current Anthropology 46:621–646.

2008 Don't sleep, there are snakes: life and language in the Amazonian jungle. New York: Vintage.

2012 Language: the cultural tool. New York: Pantheon.

2017 How language began: the story of humanity's greatest invention. New York: Liveright.

**FARMER, ANN K., AND RICHARD A. DEMERS**

2010 A linguistics workbook: companion to linguistics. 6th ed. Cambridge, MA: MIT Press.

**FERGUSON, CHARLES**

1959 Diglossia. Word 15:325–340.

**FICKETT, JOAN G.**

1972 Tense and aspect in Black English. Journal of English Linguistics 6.17–19.

**FIELDS, CHERYL D.**

1997 Ebonics 101: what have we learned? Black Issues in Higher Education 13(24):18–21, 24–28 (January 23, 1997).

**FISCHER, JOHN L.**

1958 Social influences on the choice of a linguistic variant. Word 14:47–56.

**FISHMAN, JOSHUA A.**

1960 A systematization of the Whorfian hypothesis. Behavioral Science 5:323–339.

**FITCH, W. TECUMSEH**

2010 The evolution of language. Cambridge, UK: Cambridge University Press.

**FLANNERY, REGINA**

1946 Men's and women's speech in Gros Ventre. International Journal of American Linguistics 12:133–135.

**FORTSON, BENJAMIN**

2010 Indo-European language and culture: an introduction. 2d ed. Malden, MA: Blackwell.

**FOUGHT, CARMEN**

2006 Language and ethnicity. London: Cambridge University Press.

**FOUTS, ROGER S., AND DEBORAH H. FOUTS**

1989 Loulis in conversation with the cross-fostered chimpanzees. *In* Teaching sign language to chimpanzees. R. Allen Gardner, Beatrix T. Gardner, and Thomas E. Van Cantford, eds., pp. 293–307. New York: State University of New York Press.

**FOUTS, ROGER S., DEBORAH H. FOUTS, AND THOMAS E. VAN CANTFORD**

1989 The infant Loulis learns signs from cross-fostered chimpanzees. *In* Teaching sign language to chimpanzees. R. Allen Gardner, Beatrix T. Gardner, and Thomas E. Van Cantford, eds., pp. 280–292. New York: State University of New York Press.

**FREED, ALICE**

2003 Epilogue: reflections on language and gender research. *In* The handbook of language and gender. Malden, MA: Blackwell.

**FRISCH, KARL VON**

1967 The dance language and orientation of bees. C. E. Chadwick, trans. Cambridge, MA: Belknap.

**FROMKIN, VICTORIA, AND ROBERT RODMAN**

1988 An introduction to language. 4th ed. New York: Holt, Rinehart and Winston.

**FROMKIN, VICTORIA, ROBERT RODMAN, AND NINA HYAMS**

2010 An introduction to language. 9th ed. Belmont, CA: Wadsworth Cengage.

**GAL, SUSAN**

1979 Language shift: social determinants of linguistic change in bilingual Austria. New York: Academic Press.

**GALLOWAY, NICOLA, AND HEATH ROSE**

2015 Introducing global Englishes. New York: Routledge.

**GARBER, MEGAN**

2016 How "LOL" became a punctuation mark. March 9, 2016. In https://www.theatlantic.com/entertainment/archive/2016/03/how-lol-became-a-punctuation-mark/472824.

**GARCIA, OFELIA, AND NELSON FLORES, EDS.**

2016 The Oxford handbook of language and society. New York: Oxford University Press.

**GARDNER-CHLOROS, PENELOPE**

2009 Code-switching. Cambridge, UK: Cambridge University Press.

**GEE, JAMES PAUL**

2011 How to do discourse analysis: a toolkit. Abingdon, UK: Routledge.

**GEERAERTS, DIRK, AND HUBERT CUYCKENS, EDS.**

2007 The Oxford handbook of cognitive linguistics. New York: Oxford University Press.

**GELB, IGNACE**

1963 A study of writing. Rev. ed. Chicago: University of Chicago Press.

**GIGLIOLI, PIER PAOLO, ED.**

1972 Language and social context: selected readings. Baltimore: Penguin Books.

**GIVÓN, TALMY**

2002 Bio-linguistics: the Santa Barbara lectures. Amsterdam: John Benjamins.

**GLEASON, H. A., JR.**

1961 An introduction to descriptive linguistics. Rev. ed. New York: Holt, Rinehart and Winston.

**GLEASON, JEAN BERKO, AND NAN BERNSTEIN RATNER, EDS.**

2008 The development of language. 7th ed. Needham Heights, MA: Allyn & Bacon.

**GNANADESIKAN, AMALIA**

2008 Syllables and syllabaries: what writing systems tell us about syllable structure. *In* http://cunyphonologyforum.ws.gc.cuny.edu/files/2008/01/Gnanadesikanhandout.pdf.

2009 The writing revolution: cuneiform to the Internet. Malden, MA: Wiley-Blackwell.

**GODBY, CAROL JEAN, ET AL.**

1982 Language Files 2. Columbus: Ohio State University Press.

**GOFFMAN, ERVING**

1959 The presentation of self in everyday life. New York: Anchor/Doubleday.

1974 Frame analysis: an essay on the organization of experience. New York: Harper and Row.

**GOODALL, JANE**

1986 The chimpanzees of Gombe: patterns of behavior. Cambridge, MA: Belknap.

**GOODENOUGH, WARD H.**

1964 Cultural anthropology and linguistics. *In* Language in culture and society: a reader in linguistics and anthropology. Dell Hymes, ed., pp. 36–39. New York: Harper and Row.

**GOODY, JACK**

1987 The interface between the written and the oral. Cambridge, UK: Cambridge University Press.

**GORDON, RAYMOND**

2005 Ethnologue: languages of the world. 15th ed. Dallas, TX: SIL International.

**GOSWAMI, U.**

2006 Orthography, phonology, and reading development: a cross-linguistic perspective. *In* Handbook of orthography and literacy. R. Malatesha Joshi and P. G. Aaron, eds., pp. 463–480. Mahwah, NJ: Lawrence Erlbaum.

**GOULD, STEPHEN JAY**

2002 The structure of evolutionary theory. Cambridge: Harvard University Press.

**GOULD, STEPHEN JAY, AND RICHARD LEWONTIN**

1979 The spandrels of San Marco and the Panglossian paradigm: a critique of the adaptationist programme. Proceedings of the Royal Society of London B: Biological Sciences 205:581–598.

**GRAY, JOHN**

2012 Men are from Mars, women are from Venus: the classic guide to understanding the opposite sex. New York: Harper Paperbacks.

**GREEN, LISA**

2002 African American English: A linguistic introduction. Cambridge, UK: Cambridge University Press.

**GREENBERG, JOSEPH H.**

1987 Language in the Americas. Stanford, CA: Stanford University Press.

**GREYMORNING, STEPHEN**

2001 Reflections on the Arapaho language project, or when Bambi spoke Arapaho and other tales of Arapaho language revitalization efforts. *In* The green book of language revitalization in practice. Leanne Hinton and Ken Hale, eds., pp. 287–297. San Diego, CA: Academic Press.

**GRICE, PAUL**

1975 Logic and conversation. *In* P. Cole and J. Morgan, eds., Syntax and semantics. Vol 3: speech act, pp. 41–58. New York: Academic Press.

1991 Studies in the way of words. Cambridge, MA: Harvard University Press.

**GRODZINSKY, YOSEF, AND KATRIN AMUNTS, EDS.**

2006 Broca's region. New York: Oxford University Press.

**GUMPERZ, JOHN J.**

1958 Dialect differences and social stratification in a North Indian village. American Anthropologist 60:668–682.

1982 Fact and inference in courtroom testimony. *In* Language and social identity. John J. Gumperz, ed., pp. 163–195. Cambridge, UK: Cambridge University Press.

**GUMPERZ, JOHN J., AND DELL HYMES, EDS.**

1964 The ethnography of communication. American Anthropologist 66:6 (part 2):1–186 (special publication).

1972 Directions in sociolinguistics: the ethnography of communication. New York: Holt, Rinehart and Winston, 1972, and Blackwell, 1986 (rev. ed.).

**GUMPERZ, JOHN J., AND ROBERT WILSON**

1971 Convergence and creolization: a case from the Indo-Aryan/Dravidian border in India. *In* Pidginization and creolization of languages. Dell Hymes, ed., pp. 151–167. Cambridge, UK: Cambridge University Press.

**GUMPERZ, JOHN J., AND STEPHEN C. LEVINSON, EDS.**

1996 Rethinking linguistic relativity. Cambridge, UK: Cambridge University Press.

**HAAS, MARY R.**

1941 Tunica. *In* Handbook of American Indian languages, part 4, pp. 1–143. New York: Augustin.

1944 Men's and women's speech in Koasati. Language 20:142–149.

**HADAMITZKY, WOLFGANG, AND MARK SPAHN**

1981 Kanji and Kana: a handbook and dictionary of the Japanese writing system. Rutland, VT: Tuttle.

**HAGE, PER**

1972 Munchner beer categories. *In* Culture and cognition: rules, maps, and plans. James P. Spradley, ed., pp. 263–278. San Francisco, CA: Chandler.

**HALE, KENNETH**

1974 Some questions about anthropological linguistics: the role of native knowledge. *In* Reinventing anthropology. Dell Hymes, ed., pp. 382–397. New York: Random House.

**HALE, MARK**

2007 Historical linguistics: theory and method. Malden, MA: Blackwell.

**HALE, CONSTANCE, AND JESSE SCANLON**

1999 Wired style: principles of English usage in the digital age, rev. and updated. New York: Broadway Books.

**HALL, EDWARD T.**

1966 The hidden dimension. Garden City, NY: Doubleday.

1968 Proxemics. Current Anthropology 9:83–108.

**HALL, KIRA, AND MARY BUCHOLTZ, EDS.**

1992 Locating power. Proceedings of the Second Berkeley Women and Language Conference, vol. 2. Berkeley: Berkeley Women and Language Group, University of California.

1996 Gender articulated: language and the socially constructed self. New York: Routledge.

**HALL, ROBERT A., JR.**

1959 Pidgin languages. Scientific American 200(2):124–132, 134 (February).

**HALLOWELL, A. IRVING**

1960 The beginnings of anthropology in America. *In* Selected papers from the American Anthropologist, 1888–1920. Frederica de Laguna, ed., pp. 1–90. Evanston, IL: Row, Peterson.

**HAMMEL, E. A., ED.**

1965 Formal semantic analysis. American Anthropologist 67:5 (part 2) (special publication).

**HAMMOND, GEORGE P., AND AGAPITO REY, EDS.**

1940 Narratives of the Coronado expedition, 1540–1542. Coronado Cuarto Centennial Publications, 1540–1940, vol. 2. Albuquerque: University of New Mexico Press.

**HANKS, WILLIAM**

1995 Language and communicative practices. Boulder: Westview Press.

2010 Converting words: Maya in the age of the cross. Berkeley: University of California Press.

**HARDIN, C. L., AND LUISSA MAFFI, EDS.**

1997 Color categories in thought and language. Cambridge, UK: Cambridge University Press.

**HARNAD, STEVAN R., HORST D. STEKLIS, AND JANE LANCASTER, EDS.**

1976 Origins and evolution of language and speech. Annals of the New York Academy of Sciences, vol. 280. New York: New York Academy of Sciences.

**HARRIS, MARVIN**

1989 Our kind: who we are, where we came from, where we are going. New York: Harper and Row.

**HARRIS, ROXY, AND BEN RAMPTON, EDS.**

2003 The language, ethnicity and race reader. New York: Routledge.

**HARRIS, ROY**

1986 The origins of writing. London: Duckworth.

**HARRISON, K. DAVID**

2008 When languages die: the extinction of the world's languages and the erosion of human knowledge. New York: Oxford University Press.

**HAUGEN, EINAR**

1956 Bilingualism in the Americas: a bibliography and research guide. Tuscaloosa: American Dialect Society, University of Alabama.

**HAUGHEY, MATT**

2015 The big lebowskemoji. In https://matt.haughey.com/the-annotated-big-lebowskemoji-bb6ed62cb705#.be6hhmccu.

**HAUSER, MARK, NOAM CHOMSKY, AND W. TECUMSEH FITCH**

2010 The faculty of language: what is it, who has it, and how did it evolve? *In* The evolution of human language: biolinguistic perspectives. Richard K. Larson, Vivian Déprez, and Hiroko Yamakido, eds., pp. 14–42. Cambridge, UK: Cambridge University Press.

**HAYES, ALFRED S.**

1954 Field procedures while working with Diegueno. International Journal of American Linguistics 20:185–194.

**HAYES, BRUCE**

2008 Introductory phonology. Malden, MA: Wiley-Blackwell.

**HAYES, JOSEPH**

1981a Lesbians, gay men, and their languages. *In* Gayspeak: gay male and lesbian communication. James Chesboro, ed., pp. 28–42. New York: Pilgrim Press.

1981b Gayspeak. *In* Gayspeak: gay male and lesbian communication. James Chesboro, ed., pp. 43–57. New York: Pilgrim Press.

**HEATH, JEFFREY**

1985 Discourse in the field: clause structure in Ngandi. *In* Grammar inside and outside the clause: some approaches to theory from the field. Johanna Nichols and Anthony C. Woodbury, eds., pp. 89–110. Cambridge, UK: Cambridge University Press.

**HEATH, SHIRLEY BRICE**

1984 Linguistics and education. *In* Annual Review of Anthropology, vol. 13. Bernard J. Siegel et al., eds., pp. 251–274. Palo Alto, CA: Annual Reviews.

**HEISE, DAVID**

2010 Surveying cultures: discovering shared conceptions and sentiments. Hoboken, NJ: John Wiley.

**HELLER, MONICA**

1988 (ed.) Codeswitching: anthropological and sociolinguistic perspectives. Berlin: Mouton de Gruyter.

2011 Paths to post-nationalism: a critical ethnography of language and identity. New York: Oxford University Press.

2013 Crosswords: language, education and ethnicity in French Ontario. Berlin: De Gruyter.

**HENLEY, NANCY, AND CHERIS KRAMARAE**

1991 Gender, power, and miscommunication. *In* Miscommunication and problematic talk. Nikolas Coupland, Howard Giles, and John Wiemann, eds., pp. 18–43. Newbury Park: Sage.

**HERRING, SUSAN**

2003 Gender and power in on-line communication. *In* The handbook of language and gender. Janet Holmes and Miriam Meyerhoff, eds., pp. 202–228. Malden, MA: Blackwell.

**HICKERSON, HAROLD, GLEN D. TURNER, AND NANCY P. HICKERSON**

1952 Testing procedures for estimating transfer of information among Iroquois dialects and languages. International Journal of American Linguistics 18:1–8.

**HILL, JANE H.**

1978 Apes and language. *In* Annual Review of Anthropology, vol. 7. Bernard J. Siegel et al., eds., pp. 89–112. Palo Alto, CA: Annual Reviews.

1987 Women's speech in modern Mexicano. *In* Language, gender, and sex in comparative perspective. Susan Philips, Susan Steele, and Christine Tanz, eds., pp. 121–162. Cambridge, UK: Cambridge University Press.

2008 The everyday language of white racism. Malden, MA: Wiley-Blackwell.

**HILL, JANE, AND BRUCE MANNHEIM**

1992 Language and world view. *In* Annual Review of Anthropology, vol. 21. Bernard J. Siegel et al., eds., pp. 381–406. Palo Alto, CA: Annual Reviews.

**HILL, W. W.**

1936 Navaho warfare. Yale University Publications in Anthropology, vol. 5. New Haven: Yale University Press.

**HINNEBUSCH, THOMAS J.**

1979 Swahili. *In* Languages and their status. Timothy Shopen, ed., pp. 209–293. Cambridge, MA: Winthrop.

**HOCK, HANS HENRICH**

1991 Principles of historical linguistics. 2d ed., rev. and expanded. Berlin: Mouton de Gruyter.

**HOCKETT, CHARLES F.**

1958 A course in modern linguistics. New York: Macmillan.

1960 The origin of speech. Scientific American 203(3) (September):88–96.

1973 Man's place in nature. New York: McGraw-Hill.

1978 In search of Jove's brow. American Speech 53:243–313.

**HOCKETT, CHARLES F., AND ROBERT ASCHER**

1964 The human revolution. Current Anthropology 5:135–168 (with comments by others and the authors' reply).

**HOCKETT, CHARLES F., AND STUART A. ALTMANN**

1968 A note on design features. *In* Animal communication: techniques of study and results of research. Thomas A. Sebeok, ed., pp. 61–72. Bloomington: Indiana University Press.

**HOGAN, HELEN MARIE**

n.d. An ethnography of communication among the Ashanti. Penn-Texas Working Papers in Sociolinguistics, no. 1 (Austin).

**HOGAN, JACKIE**

2003 The social significance of English loanwords in Japan. Japanese Studies 23(1):43–59.

**HOIJER, HARRY**

1954 (ed.) Language in culture: proceedings of a conference on the interrelations of language and other aspects of culture. American Anthropological Association Memoir, no. 79. Menasha, WI: American Anthropological Association.

**HOLM, JOHN A.**

1988–89 Pidgins and creoles. 2 vols. Cambridge, UK: Cambridge University Press.

2000 An introduction to pidgins and creoles. Cambridge, UK: Cambridge University Press.

**HOLMES, JANET, AND MIRIAM MEYERHOFF, EDS.**

2003 The handbook of language and gender. Malden, MA: Blackwell.

**HOLMES, RUTH, AND BETTY SMITH**

1976 Beginning Cherokee. Norman: University of Oklahoma Press.

**HUANG, YAN**

2007 Pragmatics. New York: Oxford University Press.

**HUMBOLDT, WILHELM VON**

1907 Wilhelm von Humboldts werke, vol. 7. Albert Leitzmann, ed. Berlin: Behrs Verlag.

**HURFORD, JAMES, BRENDAN HEASLEY, AND MICHAEL SMITH**

2007 Semantics: a coursebook. Cambridge, UK: Cambridge University Press.

**HUTCHBY, IAN, AND ROBIN WOOFFITT**

2008 Conversational analysis. 2d ed. Cambridge, UK: Polity Press.

**HYMES, DELL**

2012 Linguistic anthropology. *In* Expanding American anthropology, 1945–1980. Alice Kehoe and Paul Doughty, eds., pp. 154–163. Tuscaloosa: University of Alabama Press.

**HYMES, DELL H.**

1958 Linguistic features peculiar to Chinookan myths. International Journal of American Linguistics 24:253–257.

1961 Functions of speech: an evolutionary approach. *In* Anthropology and education. Frederick C. Gruber, ed., pp. 55–83. Philadelphia: University of Pennsylvania Press.

1962 The ethnography of speaking. *In* Anthropology and human behavior. Thomas Gladwin and William C. Sturtevant, eds., pp. 13–53. Washington, DC: Anthropological Society of Washington.

1963 Notes toward a history of linguistic anthropology. Anthropological Linguistics 5:1:59–103.

1964 (ed.) Language in culture and society: a reader in linguistics and anthropology. New York: Harper and Row.

1972 Models of the interaction of language and social life. *In* Directions in sociolinguistics: the ethnography of communication. John J. Gumperz and Dell Hymes, eds., pp. 35–71. New York: Holt, Rinehart and Winston.

1974 Foundations in sociolinguistics: an ethnographic approach. Philadelphia: University of Pennsylvania Press.

1983 Essays in the history of linguistic anthropology. Amsterdam Studies in the Theory and History of Linguistic Science, vol. 25. Amsterdam and Philadelphia: Benjamins.

1989 Ways of speaking. *In* Explorations in the ethnography of speaking. 2d ed. Richard Bauman and Joel Sherzer, eds., pp. 433–445. Cambridge, UK: Cambridge University Press.

**INOUE, KYOKO**

1979 Japanese: a story of language and people. *In* Languages and their speakers. Timothy Shopen, ed., pp. 241–300. Cambridge, MA: Winthrop.

**INOUE, MIYAKO**

2006 Vicarious language: gender and linguistic modernity in Japan. Berkeley: University of California Press.

**ITOH, MASAKO, WITH NOBUKO ADACHI AND JAMES STANLAW**

2007 "I'm married to your company!" everyday voices of Japanese women. Lanham, MD: Rowman & Littlefield.

**JACKENDOFF, RAY**

1983 Semantics and cognition. Cambridge, MA: MIT Press.

2002 Foundations of language: brain, meaning, grammar, evolution. Oxford, UK: Oxford University Press.

**JACKSON, HOWARD, AND ZÉ AMVELA**

2007 Words, meaning and vocabulary: an introduction to modern English lexicology. 2d ed. London: Continuum.

**JAKOBSON, ROMAN**

1968 Child language, aphasia and phonological universals. Allan R. Keiler, trans. The Hague: Mouton.

**JANSON, TORE**

2011 The history of languages: an introduction. New York: Oxford University Press.

**JEFFERSON, THOMAS**

1944 The life and selected writings of Thomas Jefferson. Adrienne Koch and William Peden, eds. New York: Random House.

**JENKINS, JENNIFER**

2015 Global Englishes: a resource book for students. New York: Routledge.

**JESPERSEN, OTTO**

1922 Language: its nature, development, and origin. New York: Henry Holt and Company.

1955 Growth and structure of the English language. 9th ed. Garden City, NY: Doubleday.

**JETTON, JEFF**

2011 The secret of Noam: a Chomsky interview. In https://chomsky.info/20110309-2.

**JOHNSTONE, BARBARA**

2008 Discourse analysis. 2d ed. Malden, MA: Blackwell.

**JOOS, MARTIN**

1962 The five clocks. Indiana University Research Center in Anthropology, Folklore, and Linguistics Publications, no. 22. Bloomington.

**JOSEPH, JOHN**

2004 Language and identity: national, ethnic, religious. New York: Palgrave.

**JOURDAN, C.**

1991 Pidgins and creoles: the blurring of categories. *In* Annual Review of Anthropology, vol. 20. Bernard J. Siegel et al., eds., pp. 187–209. Palo Alto, CA: Annual Reviews.

**JURGENSON, NATHAN**

2011 Why Chomsky is wrong about Twitter. In www.salon.com/2011/10/23/why_chomsky_is_wrong_about_twitter.

**KACHRU, BRAJ B., ED.**

1992 The other tongue: English across cultures. 2d ed. Urbana: University of Illinois Press.

**KACHRU, BRAJ B., YAMUNA KACHRU, AND S. N. SRIDHAR, EDS.**

2008 Language in South Asia. Cambridge, UK: Cambridge University Press.

**KACHRU, YAMUNA, AND LARRY SMITH**

2008 Cultures, contexts, and world Englishes. New York: Routledge.

**KAISER, MARK, AND V. SHEVOROSHKIN**

1988 Nostratic. *In* Annual Review of Anthropology, vol. 17. Bernard J. Siegel et al., eds., pp. 309–329. Palo Alto, CA: Annual Reviews.

**KAMUSELLA, TOMASZ**

2009 The politics of language and nationalism in modern Central Europe. New York: Palgrave Macmillan.

**KANG, M. AGNES**

2009 Constructing ethnic identity through discourse: self categorization among Korean American camp counselors. *In* Beyond yellow English: toward a linguistic anthropology of Asian Pacific America. Angela Reyes and Adrienne Lo, eds., pp. 131–147. New York: Oxford University Press.

**KAPLAN-WEINGER, JUDITH, AND CHAR ULLMAN**

2015 Methods for the ethnography of communication: language in use in schools and communities. New York: Routledge.

**KATZ, JOSH**

2016 Speaking American: how y'all, youse, and you guys talk: a visual guide. Boston: Houghton Mifflin Harcourt.

**KAY, PAUL, BRENT BERLIN, AND WILLIAM MERRIFIELD**

1991 Biocultural implications of systems of color naming. Journal of Linguistic Anthropology 1:12–25.

**KAY, PAUL, BRENT BERLIN, LUISA MAFFI, WILLIAM R. MERRIFIELD, AND RICHARD COOK**

2009 World color survey. Stanford: Center for the Study of Language and Information. Chicago: University of Chicago Press.

**KEENAN, ELINOR OCHS**

1976 A sliding sense of obligatoriness: the Polynesian structure of Malagasy oratory. Language in Society 2:225–243.

**KEESING, ROGER**

1972 Paradigms lost: the new ethnography and the new linguistics. Southwestern Journal of Anthropology 28:299–332.

**KELLER, CHARLES, AND JANET DIXON KELLER**

1998 Cognition and tool use: the blacksmith at work. Cambridge, UK: Cambridge University Press.

**KELSKY, KAREN**

2001 Women on the verge: Japanese women, western dreams. Durham, NC: Duke University Press.

**KEMPTON, WILLET**

1981 The folk classification of ceramics: a study of cognitive prototypes. New York: Academic Press.

**KENDON, ADAM**

1997 Gesture. *In* Annual Review of Anthropology, vol. 26. William H. Durham et al., eds., pp. 109–128. Palo Alto, CA: Annual Reviews.

**KENNEALLY, CHRISTINE**

2007 The first word: the search for the origins of language. New York: Viking.

**KENNEDY, CHRIS, ED.**

1983 Language planning and language education. London: Allen and Unwin.

**KIMBALL, GEOFFREY**

1987 Men's and women's speech in Koasati: a reappraisal. International Journal of American Linguistics 53:30–38.

**KING, LINDA**

1994 Roots of identity: language and literacy in Mexico. Stanford: Stanford University Press.

**KLIMA, EDWARD S., AND URSULA BELLUGI**

1979 The signs of language. Cambridge, MA: Harvard University Press.

**KLUCKHOHN, CLYDE**

1949 Mirror for man: the relation of anthropology to modern life. New York: McGraw-Hill.

**KOHL-WELLS, JEANNE**

2013 The backlash over making language in Washington State laws gender neutral. Union-Bulletin.com, May 17. *In* http://www.seattletimes.com/opinion/guest-the-backlash-over-making-state-laws-gender-neutral.

**KRAMARAE, CHERIS**

1981 Women and men speaking: frameworks for analysis. Rowley, MA: Newbury House.

**KRAUSS, MICHAEL**

1992 The world's languages in crisis. Language 68:4–10.

**KRONENFELD, DAVID**

1996 Plastic glasses and church fathers. New York: Oxford University Press.

**KROSKRITY, PAUL V.**

1983 On male and female speech in the Pueblo Southwest. International Journal of American Linguistics 49:88–91.

1988 (ed.) On the ethnography of communication: the legacy of Sapir. Essays in honor of Harry Hoijer, 1984. Los Angeles: University of California Press.

1993 Language, history, and identity: ethnolinguistic studies of the Arizona Tewa. Tucson: University of Arizona Press.

2000 (ed.) Regimes of language: ideologies, polities, and identities. Santa Fe, NM: School of American Research Press.

2001 Identity. *In* Key terms in language and culture. Alessandro Duranti, ed., pp. 106–109. Malden, MA: Blackwell.

**KUBOTA, RYUKO, AND ANGEL LIN, EDS.**

2009 Race, culture, and identities in second language education: exploring critically engaged practice. New York: Routledge.

**KULICK, DON**

2000 Gay and lesbian language. Annual Review of Anthropology 29:243–285.

**LABOV, WILLIAM**

1963 The social motivation of a sound change. Word 19:273–309.

1966 The social stratification of English in New York City. Washington, DC: Center for Applied Linguistics.

1970 The logic of nonstandard English. *In* Report of the Twentieth Annual Round Table Meeting on Linguistics and Language Studies. Monograph Series on Languages and Linguistics, no. 22, pp. 1–43. Washington, DC: Georgetown University Press.

1972a Language in the inner city: studies in the Black English vernacular. Philadelphia: University of Pennsylvania Press.

1972b Sociolinguistic patterns. Philadelphia: University of Pennsylvania Press.

2005 Atlas of North American English: phonetics, phonology and sound change (with CD-ROM). The Hague: Mouton de Gruyter.

2010 Unendangered dialect, endangered people: the case of African American Vernacular English. Transforming Anthropology 18(1):15–28.

2010a Principles of linguistic change: internal factors. Malden, MA: Wiley-Blackwell.

2010b Principles of linguistic change: social factors. Malden, MA: Wiley-Blackwell.

2010c Principles of linguistic change: cognitive and cultural factors. Malden, MA: Wiley-Blackwell.

**LADEFOGED, PETER**

1992 Another view of endangered languages. Language 68:809–811.

**LADEFOGED, PETER, AND KEITH JOHNSON**

2010 A course in phonetics (with CD-ROM). 6th ed. Florence, KY: Wadsworth/Cengage.

**LAKOFF, GEORGE**

1987 Women, fire, and dangerous things. Chicago: University of Chicago Press.

**LAKOFF, ROBIN**

1975 [2004] Language and women's place. Rev. and expanded ed. New York: Oxford University Press.

**LANGACKER, RONALD W.**

1972 Fundamentals of linguistic analysis. New York: Harcourt Brace Jovanovich.

1987 Foundations of cognitive grammar. Vol. 1: Theoretical prerequisites. Stanford: Stanford University Press.

1991 Foundations of cognitive grammar. Vol. 2: Descriptive applications. Stanford: Stanford University Press.

**LARSON, RICHARD K., VIVIAN DÉPREZ, AND HIROKO YAMAKIDO, EDS.**

2010 The evolution of human language: biolinguistic perspectives. Cambridge, UK: Cambridge University Press.

**LAW, HOWARD W.**

1958 Morphological structure of Isthmus Nahuat. International Journal of American Linguistics 24:108–129.

**LE GUIN, URSULA K.**

1989 Dancing at the edge of the world: thoughts on words, women, places. New York: Grove Press.

**LEAP, WILLIAM, ED.**

1995 Beyond the lavender lexicon: authenticity, imagination and appropriation in lesbian and gay languages. Buffalo, NY: Gordon & Breach.

**LEAP, WILLIAM L.**

1981 American Indian language maintenance. *In* Annual Review of Anthropology, vol. 10. Bernard J. Siegel et al., eds., pp. 209–236. Palo Alto, CA: Annual Reviews.

**LEAVITT, JOHN**

2011 Linguistic relativities: language diversity and modern thought. Cambridge, UK: Cambridge University Press.

**LEE, PENNY**

1996 The Whorf theory complex. Amsterdam: John Benjamins.

**LEE, SAMANTHA**

2016 What communicating only in emoji taught me about language in the digital age. In https://qz.com/765945/emojis-forever-or-whatever-im-a-poet.

**LENNEBERG, ERIC H.**

1967 Biological foundations of language. New York: Wiley.

LENNEBERG, ERIC H., AND JOHN ROBERTS

1956 The language of experience: a study in methodology. International Journal of American Linguistics 22(2), supplemental memoir 13.

LEU, DONALD J., LISA ZAWILINSKI, JILL CASTEK, MANJU BANERJEE, BRIAN HOUSAND, YINJIE LIU, AND MAUREEN O'NEIL

2007 What is new about the new literacies of online reading comprehension. *In* Secondary school reading and writing: what research reveals for classroom practices. Leslie S. Rush, A. Jonathan Eakle, and Allen Berger, eds., pp. 37–69. Urbana, IL: National Council of Teachers of English.

LÉVI-STRAUSS, CLAUDE

1963 Structural anthropology. Claire Jacobson and Brooke Grundfest Schoepf, trans. New York: Basic Books.

LEVINSON, STEPHEN C.

1983 Pragmatics. Cambridge, UK: Cambridge University Press.

1996 Language and space. *In* Annual Review of Anthropology, vol. 25. William H. Durham et al., eds., pp. 353–382. Palo Alto, CA: Annual Reviews.

LEWIS, M. PAUL

2009 Ethnologue: languages of the world. 16th ed. Dallas, TX: SIL International.

LEWIS, PAUL

2009 Statistical summaries: Ethnologue: languages of the world. *In* http://www.ethnologue.com/ethno_docs/distribution.asp?by=size.

LI, WEI, ED.

2007 The bilingualism reader. 2d ed. London: Routledge.

LIPPI-GREEN, ROSINA

2012 English with an accent: language ideology, and discrimination in the United States. 2d ed. New York: Routledge.

LIVIA, ANNA

2001 Pronoun envy: the literary uses of linguistic gender. New York: Oxford University Press.

LIVIA, ANNA, AND KIRA HALL

1997a "It's a girl!": bringing performativity back to linguistics. In Queerly phrased: language, gender and sexuality. Anna Livia and Kira Hall, eds., pp. 3–18. Oxford, UK: Oxford University Press.

1997b (eds.) Queerly phrased: language, gender, and sexuality. Oxford, UK: Oxford University Press.

LJUBEŠIĆ, NIKOLA, AND DARJA FIŠER

2016 A global analysis of emoji usage. Proceedings of the 10th Web as Corpus Workshop (WAC-X):82–89. *In* https://www.researchgate.net/profile/Darja_Fiser/publications?pubType=inProceedings.

**LUCY, JOHN A.**

1992a Grammatical categories and cognition: a case study of the linguistic relativity hypothesis. Cambridge, UK: Cambridge University Press.

1992b Language diversity and thought: a reformulation of the linguistic relativity hypothesis. Cambridge, UK: Cambridge University Press.

1997 Linguistic relativity. *In* Annual Review of Anthropology, vol. 26. William H. Durham et al., eds., pp. 291–312. Palo Alto, CA: Annual Reviews.

**LYONS, JOHN**

1977 Semantics, vol. 1 and vol. 2. Cambridge, UK: Cambridge University Press.

1978 Noam Chomsky. Rev. ed. New York: Penguin Books.

**MACAULAY, RONALD**

2002 Discourse variation. *In* The handbook of language variation and change. J. K. Chambers, Peter Trudgill, and Natalie Schilling-Estes, eds., pp. 283–305. Malden, MA: Blackwell.

**MACEDO, DONALDO, ET AL.**

2003 The hegemony of English. Boulder: Paradigm Publishers.

**MACLAURY, ROBERT**

1997 Color and cognition in Mesoamerica: constructing categories as vantages. Austin: University of Texas Press.

**MACLAURY, ROBERT, GALINA PARAMEI, AND DON DEDRICK, EDS.**

2007 Anthropology of color: interdisciplinary multilevel modeling. Amsterdam: John Benjamins.

**MACNAMARA, JOHN**

1982 Names for things: a study in human learning. Cambridge: MIT Press.

**MACNEIL, ROBERT, AND WILLIAM CRAN**

2005 Do you speak American? New York: Doubleday.

**MADDIESON, IAN**

1984 Patterns of sounds. Cambridge, UK: Cambridge University Press.

**MAIR, VICTOR**

1996 Modern Chinese writing. *In* The world's writing systems. Peter Daniels and William Bright, eds., pp. 200–208. New York: Oxford University Press.

**MALINOWKSI, BRONISLAW**

1915 The natives of Mailu: preliminary results of the Robert Mond research work in British New Guinea. Transactions and Proceedings of the Royal Society of South Australia 39:494–706. Adelaide.

1922 Argonauts of the western Pacific: an account of native enterprise and adventure in the archipelagoes of Melanesian New Guinea. London: Routledge and Kegan Paul.

1923 The problem of meaning in primitive languages. *In* The meaning of meaning. C. K. Ogden and I. A. Richards, pp. 296–336. London: Routledge.

MALLORY, J. P.

1991 In search of the Indo-Europeans: language, archaeology, and myth. London: Thames & Hudson.

MANALANSAN, MARTIN

1995 Speaking of AIDS: language and the Filipino "gay" experience in America. *In* Discrepant histories: translocal essays on Filipino cultures. Vicente L. Rafael, ed., pp. 193–220. Philadelphia: Temple University Press.

MARTIN-JONES, MARILYN, AND DEIRDRE MARTIN, EDS.

2016 Researching multilingualism: critical and ethnographic perspectives. New York: Routledge.

MARTÍNEZ-FLOR, ALICIA, AND ESTHER USÓ-JUAN, EDS.

2010 Speech act performance: theoretical, empirical and methodological issues. Amsterdam: John Benjamins.

MATHUR, GAURAV, AND DONNA JO NAPOLI, EDS.

2010 Deaf around the world: the impact of language. New York: Oxford University Press.

MATTINGLY, IGNATIUS

1972 Reading, the linguistic process, and linguistic awareness. *In* Language by ear and by eye: the relationships between speech and reading. James F. Kavanagh and Ignatius G. Mattingly, eds., pp. 131–148. Cambridge, MA: MIT Press.

MAY, STEPHEN

2008 Language and minority rights: ethnicity, nationalism and the politics of language. New York: Routledge.

MCCONNELL-GINET, SALLY

1988 Language and gender. *In* Linguistics: the Cambridge survey. Vol. 4: Language: the socio-cultural context. Frederick J. Newmeyer, ed., pp. 75–99. Cambridge, UK: Cambridge University Press.

MCELHINNY, BONNIE

1995 Challenging hegemonic masculinities: female and male police officers handling domestic violence. *In* Gender articulated: language and the socially constructed self. Kira Hall and Mary Bucholtz, eds., pp. 217–243. New York: Routledge.

2003 Theorizing gender in sociolinguistics and linguistic anthropology. *In* The handbook of language and gender. Janet Holmes and Miriam Meyerhoff, eds., pp. 21–42. Malden, MA: Blackwell.

2013 Language and gender: a cross-cultural introduction. Malden, MA: Blackwell.

MCGILVRAY, JAMES

2005 The Cambridge companion to Chomsky. Cambridge, UK: Cambridge University Press.

MCGREGOR, WILLIAM B.

2010 Linguistics: an introduction. 9th ed. London: Continuum.

**MCMAHON, APRIL, AND ROBERT MCMAHON**

2012 Evolutionary linguistics. Cambridge, UK: Cambridge University Press.

**MCWHORTER, JOHN**

2003 Doing our own thing: the degradation of language and music and why we should, like, care. New York: Penguin.

2014 The language hoax: why the world looks the same in any language. New York: Oxford University Press.

2016 Words on the move: why English won't—and can't—sit still (like literally). New York: Henry Holt.

2017 Talking back and talking black. New York: Bellevue Literary Press.

**MEAD, MARGARET, AND RUDOLF MODLEY**

1968 Communication among all people everywhere. Natural History 77(7) (August):56.

**MELENDEZ, PILAR**

2015 United States has more Spanish speakers than Spain does, report says. CNN online, July 15, 2015. In http://www.cnn.com/2015/07/01/us/spanish-speakers-united-states-spain.

**MENYUK, PAULA**

1988 Language development: knowledge and use. Glenview, IL: Scott, Foresman.

**MERRIFIELD, WILLIAM, CONSTANCE M. NAISH, CALVIN R. RENSCH, AND GILLIAN STORY, EDS.**

2003 Laboratory manual for morphology and syntax. 7th ed. Dallas, TX: Summer Institute of Linguistics.

**MERRIFIELD, WILLIAM R., ET AL., EDS.**

1967 Laboratory manual for morphology and syntax. Rev. ed. Santa Ana, CA: Summer Institute of Linguistics.

**MICHAELIS, SUSANNE, ET AL., EDS.**

2013a The survey of pidgin and creole languages. Vol. 1: English-based and Dutch-based languages. New York: Oxford University Press.

2013b The survey of pidgin and creole languages. Vol. 2: Portuguese-based, Spanish-based, and French-based languages. New York: Oxford University Press.

2013c The survey of pidgin and creole languages. Vol. 3: Contact languages based on languages from Africa, Australia, and the Americas. New York: Oxford University Press.

2013d Atlas of pidgin and creole language structures. New York: Oxford University Press.

**MIHALICEK, VEDRANA, AND CHRISTIN WILSON, EDS.**

2011 Language files: materials for an introduction to language and linguistics. 12th ed. Columbus: Ohio State University Press.

**MILLAR, ROBERT MCCOLL**

2007 Trask's historical linguistics. 2d ed. New York: Oxford University Press.

**MILLER, ROY ANDREW**

1967 The Japanese language. Chicago: University of Chicago Press.

**MILLS, SARA**

1995 (ed.) Language and gender: interdisciplinary perspectives. New York: Longman.

2012 Gender matters: feminist linguistic analysis. Bristol, UK: Equinox.

**MILLS, SARA, AND LOUISE MULLANY**

2011 Language, gender and feminism: theory, methodology and practice. New York: Routledge.

**MIZUTANI, OSAMU, AND NOBUKO MIZUTANI**

1987 How to be polite in Japanese. Tokyo: Japan Times.

**MONAGHAN, LEILA, CONSTANZE SCHMALING, KAREN NAKAMURA, AND GRAHAM H. TURNER, EDS.**

2013 Many ways to be deaf: international variation in deaf communities. Washington, DC: Gallaudet University Press.

**MONTES-ALCALÁ, CECILIA**

2000 Attitudes towards oral and written codeswitching in Spanish/English bilingual youths. In Research on Spanish in the United States: linguistic issues and challenges, Ana Roca, ed., pp. 218–227. Somerville, MA: Cascadilla Press.

2009 Hispanics in the United States: more than Spanglish. Camino Real: Estudios de las Hispanidades Norteamericanas 1.0:87–115.

**MOONEY, ANNABELLE, AND BETSY EVANS**

2015 Language, society, and power: an introduction. 4th ed. New York: Routledge.

**MORGAN, MARCYLIENA**

1994 Theories and politics in African American English. *In* Annual Review of Anthropology, vol. 23. William H. Durham et al., eds., pp. 325–345. Palo Alto, CA: Annual Reviews.

1999 No woman, no cry: claiming African American women's place. *In* Reinventing identities: the gendered self in discourse. Mary Bucholtz, A. C. Liang, and Laurel Sutton, eds., pp. 27–45. New York: Oxford University Press.

**MÜHLHÄUSLER, PETER**

1986 Pidgin and creole linguistics. Oxford, UK: Blackwell.

1987 The history of research into Tok Pisin, 1900–1975. *In* Pidgin and creole languages: essays in memory of John E. Reinecke. Glenn G. Gilbert, ed., pp. 177–209. Honolulu: University of Hawaii Press.

**MULTITREE**

2009 Multitree: a digital library of language relationships. Ypsilanti, MI: Institute for Language Information and Technology (LINGUIST List), Eastern Michigan University. *In* http://multitree.org/.

**MURPHY, GEORGE**

2002 The big book of concepts. Cambridge, MA: MIT Press.

**MURPHY, JOHN**

1980 The book of pidgin English. New York: AMS Press.

**MYERS-SCOTTON, CAROL**

1993 Social motivations for code switching: evidence from Africa. Cambridge, UK: Cambridge University Press.

**NAKAMURA, KAREN**

2006 Deaf in Japan: signing and the politics of identity. Ithaca, NY: Cornell University Press.

**NETTLE, DANIEL, AND SUZANNE ROMAINE**

2000 Vanishing voices: the extinction of the world's languages. New York: Oxford University Press.

**NEWMAN, MICHAEL, AND ANGEAL WU**

2011 "Do you sound Asian when you speak English?" racial identification and voice in Chinese and Korean Americans' English. American Speech 86(2):152–178.

**NEWMEYER, FREDERICK J.**

1989 Linguistics: the Cambridge survey. Vol. 3: Language: psychological and biological aspects. Cambridge, UK: Cambridge University Press.

**NIYEKAWA, AGNES**

1991 Minimum essential politeness. Tokyo: Kodansha.

**O'BARR, WILLIAM M.**

1981 The language of the law. *In* Language in the USA. Charles A. Ferguson and Shirley Brice Heath, eds., pp. 386–406. Cambridge, UK: Cambridge University Press.

**O'BARR, WILLIAM M., AND BOWMAN K. ATKINS**

1998 "Women's language" or "powerless language"? *In* Language and gender: a reader. Jennifer Coates, ed., pp. 377–387. Oxford, UK: Blackwell.

**O'BRIEN, JODI**

1999 Writing in the body: gender (re)production in online interaction. *In* Communities in cyberspace. Marc Smith and Peter Kollock, eds., pp. 75–104. New York: Routledge.

**OCHS, ELINOR, AND BAMBI B. SCHIEFFELIN**

1982 Language acquisition and socialization: three developmental stories and their implications. Working Papers in Sociolinguistics, no. 105. Austin, TX: Southwest Educational Development Laboratory.

2006 The impact of language socialization on grammatical development. *In* Language, culture, and society. Christine Jourdan and Kevin Tuite, eds., pp. 168–189. Cambridge, UK: Cambridge University Press.

**OCHS, ELINOR, AND CAROLYN TAYLOR**

2001 The "father knows best" dynamic in dinnertime narratives. *In* Linguistic anthropology: a reader. Alessandro Duranti, ed., pp. 431–449. Malden, MA: Blackwell.

**OGDEN, C. K., AND I. A. RICHARDS**

1923 [1989] The meaning of meaning. San Diego: Harcourt Brace Jovanovich.

**O'GRADY, WILLIAM, JOHN ARCHIBALD, MARK ARONOFF, AND JANIE REES-MILLER**

2009 Contemporary linguistics. 6th ed. Boston: Bedford/St. Martin's.

**OKAMOTO, SHIGEKO, AND JANET S. SHIBAMOTO SMITH, EDS.**

2004 Japanese language, gender, and ideology: cultural models and real people. New York: Oxford University Press.

**OKRENT, ARIKA**

2009 In the land of invented languages: adventures in linguistic creativity, madness, and genius. New York: Spiegel and Grau.

**O'NEILL, P. G.**

1966 Respect language in modern Japanese. London: English Universities Press.

**ORELUS, PETER**

2011 Rethinking race, class, language, and gender: a dialogue with Noam Chomsky and other Lading scholars. Lanham, MD: Rowman & Littlefield.

**ORSI, LILIANA**

2008 Spanglish: Identifying some motivations a group of bilingual adolescents had to code-switch in informal social interactions. Master of Arts capstone paper, Department of English as a Second Language, Hamline University, Saint Paul, MN.

**OTTENHEIMER, HARRIET**

2008 The anthropology of language: an introduction to linguistic anthropology. 2d ed. Belmont, CA: Wadsworth Cengage.

2013a The anthropology of language: an introduction to linguistic anthropology. 3d ed. Belmont, CA: Wadsworth.

2013b The anthropology of language: an introduction to linguistic anthropology; workbook/reader. 3d ed. Belmont, CA: Wadsworth.

**OXFORD ENGLISH DICTIONARIES**

2015 Word of the year is. . . . In http://blog.oxforddictionaries.com/2015/11/word-of-the-year-2015-emoji.

2016 Word of the year is. . . . In https://en.oxforddictionaries.com/word-of-the-year/word-of-the-year-2016.

**PECOS, REGIS, AND REBECCA BLUM-MARTINEZ**

2001 The key to cultural survival: language planning and revitalization in the Pueblo de Cochiti. *In* The green book of language revitalization in practice. Leanne Hinton and Ken Hale, eds., pp. 75–82. San Diego, CA: Academic Press.

**PETERSON, DAVID**

2015 The art of language invention: from horse-lords to dark elves, the words behind world-building. New York: Penguin Books.

PHILIPS, SUSAN U.

1980 Sex differences and language. *In* Annual Review of Anthropology, vol. 9. Bernard J. Siegel et al., eds., pp. 523–544. Palo Alto, CA: Annual Reviews.

PHILIPS, SUSAN U., SUSAN STEELE, AND CHRISTINE TANZ, EDS.

1987 Language, gender, and sex in comparative perspective. Studies in the Social and Cultural Foundations of Language, no. 4. Cambridge, UK: Cambridge University Press.

PHILIPSEN, GERRY, AND DONAL CARBAUGH

1986 A bibliography of fieldwork in the ethnography of communication. Language in Society 15:387–397.

PHILLIPSON, ROBERT

1992 Linguistic imperialism. Oxford, UK: Oxford University Press.

PINKER, STEVEN

1992 Review of Derek Bickerton: Language and species. Language 68:375–382.

2009 How the mind works. New York: W. W. Norton.

PINKER, STEVEN, AND PAUL BLOOM

1990 Natural language and natural selection. Behavioral and Brain Sciences 13:707–784.

PI-SUNYER, ORIOL, AND ZDENEK SALZMANN

1978 Humanity and culture: an introduction to anthropology. Boston: Houghton Mifflin.

PITCHFORD, NICOLA, AND CAROLE P. BIGGAM, EDS.

2006 Progress in colour studies. Vol. 2: Psychological aspects. Amsterdam: John Benjamins.

POPLACK, SHANA

2000 Sometimes I'll start a sentence in Spanish *y termino en español. In* The bilingualism reader. Wei Li, ed., pp. 221–256. London: Routledge.

POPLACK, SHANA, AND SALI TAGLIAMONTE

2001 African American English in the diaspora. Malden, MA: Blackwell.

POSTAL, PAUL M.

1969 Mohawk vowel doubling. International Journal of American Linguistics 35:291–298.

PREMACK, ANN JAMES, AND DAVID PREMACK

1972 Teaching language to an ape. Scientific American 227(4):92–99 (October).

PREWITT-FREILINO, JENNIFER, T. ANDREW CASWELL, AND EMMI K. LAASKO

2012 The gendering of language: a comparison of gender equality in countries with gendered, natural gender, and genderless languages. Sex Roles 66:268–281.

PÜTZ, MARTIN, AND MARJOLIJN VERSPOOR

2000 Explorations in linguistic relativity. Amsterdam: John Benjamins.

QUILES, CARLOS, WITH FERNANDO LOPEZ-MENCHERO

2009 A grammar of modern Indo-European. 2d ed. Language and culture, writing system and phonology, morphology, syntax, texts and dictionary, ethnology. The European Union: Asociacion Cultural Dnghu.

RADFORD, ANDREW

1988 Transformational grammar: a first course. Cambridge, UK: Cambridge University Press.

1997 Syntax: a minimalist introduction. Cambridge, UK: Cambridge University Press.

2006 Syntax: a generative introduction. 2d ed. Malden, MA: Blackwell.

RALON, L., AND A. ELJATIB

2010 Interview with Noam Chomsky. Figure/Ground, December 17. *In* http://figureground.org/interview-with-noam-chomsky.

RAMPTON, BEN

1995 Crossing: language and ethnicity among adolescents. New York: Longman.

REETZ, HENNING, AND ALLARD JONGMAN

2009 Phonetics: transcription, production, acoustics, and perception. Malden MA: Wiley-Blackwell.

REISCHAUER, EDWIN, AND JOHN FAIRBANK

1960 East Asia: the great tradition. Boston: Houghton Mifflin.

REYES, ANGELA, AND ADRIENNE LO, EDS.

2009 Beyond yellow English: toward a linguistic anthropology of Asian Pacific America. New York: Oxford University Press.

RICKFORD, JOHN R.

1999 African American Vernacular English: features, evolution, educational implications. Oxford, UK: Blackwell.

2013 [1997] Suite for ebony and phonics. *In* Making sense of language: readings in culture and communication. Susan D. Blum, ed., pp. 372–377. New York and Oxford: Oxford University Press.

RICKFORD, JOHN R., AND RUSSELL J. RICKFORD

2000 Spoken soul: the story of Black English. New York: John Wiley & Sons.

RIEMER, NICK

2010 Introducing semantics. Cambridge, UK: Cambridge University Press.

ROBINSON, ANDREW

2007 The story of writing: alphabets, hieroglyphs and pictograms. Rev. ed. London: Thames and Hudson.

2009 Writing: a very short introduction. Oxford, UK: Oxford University Press.

ROGERS, HENRY

2005 Writing systems: a linguistic approach. Malden, MA: Blackwell.

ROITBLAT, HERBERT L., LOUIS M. HERMAN, AND PAUL E. NACHTIGALL, EDS.

1992 Language and communication: comparative perspectives. Hillsdale, NJ: Erlbaum.

**ROMAINE, SUZANNE**

1988 Pidgin and creole languages. New York: Longman.

**ROMNEY, A. KIMBALL, AND ROY GOODWIN D'ANDRADE, EDS.**

1964 Transcultural studies in cognition. American Anthropologist 66:3 (part 2) (special publication).

**ROTHMAN, JASON, AND AMY BETH RELL**

2005 A linguistic analysis of Spanglish: relating language to identity. Linguistics and the Human Sciences 1:515–536.

**ROWE, BRUCE, AND DIANE LEVINE**

2015 A concise introduction to linguistics. 4th ed. Boston: Pearson.

**SACKS, HARVEY**

1992a Lectures on conversation, vol. 1. Cambridge, MA: Blackwell.

1992b Lectures on conversation, vol. 2. Cambridge, MA: Blackwell.

**SAKEL, JEANETTE, AND DANIEL EVERETT**

2012 Linguistic fieldwork: a student's guide. Cambridge, UK: Cambridge University Press.

**SALUS, PETER H., ED.**

1969 On language: Plato to von Humboldt. New York: Holt, Rinehart and Winston.

**SALZMANN, ZDENEK**

1959 Arapaho kinship terms and two related ethnolinguistic observations. Anthropological Linguistics 1(9):6–10.

1983 Dictionary of contemporary Arapaho usage. Arapaho Language and Culture Instructional Materials Series, no. 4. Wind River Reservation, WY: Arapaho Language and Culture Commission.

**SAMARIN, WILLIAM J.**

1967 Field linguistics: a guide to linguistic field work. New York: Holt, Rinehart and Winston.

**SAMOVAR, LARRY A., AND RICHARD E. PORTER, EDS.**

1991 Intercultural communication: a reader. 6th ed. Belmont, CA: Wadsworth.

**SAPIR, EDWARD**

1916 Time perspective in aboriginal American culture: a study in method. Canada, Department of Mines, Geological Survey, memoir 90; Anthropological Series, no. 13. Ottawa: Government Printing Bureau.

1921 Language: an introduction to the study of speech. New York: Harcourt, Brace.

1922 The Takelma language of southwestern Oregon. *In* Handbook of American Indian languages, part 1. Franz Boas, ed., pp. 1–296. Washington, DC: Government Printing Office.

1949 Selected writings of Edward Sapir in language, culture, and personality. David G. Mandelbaum, ed. Berkeley: University of California Press.

**SAUSSURE, FERDINAND DE**

1913 [1983] Course in general linguistics. Roy Harris, trans. Peru, IL: Open Court.

**SAVAGE-RUMBAUGH, E. SUE**

1984 Pan paniscus and Pan troglodytes: contrasts in preverbal communicative competence. *In* The pygmy chimpanzee: evolutionary biology and behavior. Randall L. Susman, ed., pp. 395–413. New York: Plenum Press.

1986 Ape language: from conditioned response to symbol. New York: Columbia University Press.

**SAVILLE-TROIKE, MURIEL**

1982 The ethnography of communication: an introduction. Baltimore: University Park Press.

2002 The ethnography of communication: an introduction. 3d ed. Malden, MA: Blackwell.

2006 Introducing second language acquisition. Cambridge, UK: Cambridge University Press.

**SAYAHI, LOTFI**

2014 Diglossia and language contact: language variation and change in North Africa. Cambridge, UK: Cambridge University Press.

**SCANCARELLI, JANINE**

1996 Cherokee writing. *In* The world's writing systems. Peter Daniels and William Bright, eds., pp. 587–592. New York: Oxford University Press.

**SCHELE, LINDA, AND PETER MATHEWS**

1999 The code of kings: the language of seven sacred Maya temples and tombs. New York: Scribner.

**SCHENDL, HERBERT**

2001 Historical linguistics. New York: Oxford University Press.

**SCHERLING, JOHANNES**

2012 Japanizing English: Anglicisms and their impact on Japanese. Tübingen, Germany: Narr Verlag.

**SCHIEFFELIN, BAMBI B.**

1990 The give and take of everyday life: language socialization of Kaluli children. New York: Cambridge University Press.

2005 The give and take of everyday life: language socialization of Kaluli children. 2d ed. Tucson, AZ: Fenestra Books.

**SCHIEFFELIN, BAMBI B., AND ELINOR OCHS**

1986 Language socialization. *In* Annual Review of Anthropology, vol. 15. Bernard J. Siegel et al., eds., pp. 163–191. Palo Alto, CA: Annual Reviews.

**SCHIEFFELIN, BAMBI B., KATHRYN A. WOOLARD, AND PAUL V. KROSKRITY, EDS.**

1998 Language ideologies: practice and theory. New York: Oxford University Press.

**SCHNOEBELEN, TYLER**

2012 Gender and style in American English tweets. vimeo.com/46531227.

**SCHRIER, ALLAN M., AND FRED STOLLNITZ, EDS.**

1971 Behavior of nonhuman primates: modern research trends, vol. 4. New York: Academic Press.

**SCOLLON, RONALD, AND SUZANNE WONG SCOLLON**

1981 Narrative, literacy and face in interethnic communication. Norwood, NJ: Ablex Publishing.

1990 Athabaskan-English interethnic communication. *In* Cultural communication and intercultural contact. Donal Carbaugh, ed., pp. 259–286. Hillsdale, NJ: Lawrence Erlbaum.

2001 Intercultural communication: a discourse approach. 2d ed. Oxford, UK: Blackwell.

**SCRIBNER, SYLVIA, AND MICHAEL COLE**

1981 The psychology of literacy. Cambridge, MA: Harvard University Press.

**SEARLE, JOHN**

1969 Speech acts: an essay in the philosophy of language. London: Cambridge University Press.

1979 Expression and meaning: studies in the theory of speech acts. Cambridge: Cambridge University Press.

**SEBEOK, THOMAS A., ED.**

1974 Current trends in linguistics. Vol. 12: Linguistics and adjacent arts and sciences. The Hague: Mouton.

1977 How animals communicate. Bloomington: Indiana University Press.

**SHAUL, DAVID, AND LOUANNA FURBEE**

1998 Language and culture. Prospect Heights, IL: Waveland Press.

**SHELTON, TAYLOR**

2014 Hey y'all! geographies of a colloquialism. In http://www.floatingsheep.org/2014/05/hey-yall-geographies-of-colloquialism.html.

**SHERZER, JOEL**

1977 The ethnography of speaking: a critical appraisal. *In* Georgetown University Round Table on Languages and Linguistics 1977, pp. 43–57. Washington, DC: Georgetown University Press.

1987 A discourse-centered approach to language and culture. American Anthropologist 89:295–309.

**SHERZER, JOEL, AND REGNA DARNELL**

1972 Outline guide for the ethnographic study of speech use. *In* Directions in sociolinguistics: the ethnography of communication. John J. Gumperz and Dell Hymes, eds., pp. 548–554. New York: Holt, Rinehart and Winston.

**SHIBAMOTO, JANET S.**

1985 Japanese women's language. New York: Academic Press.

**SHORE, BRADD**

1996 Culture in mind: cognition, culture, and the problem of meaning. New York: Oxford University Press.

**SHUY, ROGER W.**

1984 Linguistics in other professions. *In* Annual Review of Anthropology, vol. 13. Bernard J. Siegel et al., eds., pp. 419–445. Palo Alto, CA: Annual Reviews.

**SIDNELL, JACK**

2010 Conversation analysis: an introduction. Malden. MA: Wiley-Blackwell.

**SIEBERT JR., FRANK T.**

1967 The original home of the Proto-Algonquian people. National Museum of Canada, bulletin 214; Anthropological Series, no. 78: Contributions to Anthropology: Linguistics I (Algonquian), pp. 13–47. Ottawa.

**SIEGEL, JEFF**

2008 The emergence of pidgin and creole languages. Oxford, UK: Oxford University Press.

**SILVER, SHIRLEY, AND WICK R. MILLER**

2000 American Indian languages: cultural and social contexts. Tucson: University of Arizona Press.

**SILVERSTEIN, MICHAEL**

1985 Language and the culture of gender: at the intersection of structure, usage, and ideology. *In* Semiotic mediation: sociocultural and psychological perspectives. Elizabeth Mertz and Richard J. Parmentier, eds., pp. 219–259. Orlando, FL: Academic Press.

**SIMS, CHRISTINE P., AND HILAIRE VALIQUETTE**

1990 More on male and female speech in (Acoma and Laguna) Keresan. International Journal of American Linguistics 56:162–166.

**SKINNER, B. F.**

1957 Verbal behavior. New York: Appleton-Century-Crofts.

**SMALL, LARRY**

2016 Fundamentals of phonetics: a practical guide for students. 4th ed. Boston: Pearson Educational.

**SMITH, WILLIAM**

1744 A new voyage to Guinea. . . . London: John Nourse.

**SMITHERMAN, GENEVA**

1998 Word from the hood: the lexicon of African-American Vernacular English. *In* African-American English: structure, history and use. Guy Bailey, Salikoko S. Mufwene, and John R. Rickford, eds., pp. 203–225. London: Routledge.

**SPRADLEY, JAMES**

1972 Culture and cognition: rules, maps, and plans. San Francisco: Chandler.

**STANLAW, JAMES**

1992 English in Japanese communicative strategies. *In* The other tongue: English across cultures, 2d ed. Braj Kachru, ed. Urbana: University of Illinois Press. pp. 178–208.

2002 Review of invisible genealogies: a history of Americanist anthropology. Language 78:778–780.

2004a Japanese and English: language and culture contact. Hong Kong: University of Hong Kong Press.

2004b What do cognitive scientists know, and what should linguistic anthropologists know about what they know? Teaching Anthropology SACC Notes 10(20):8–12, 33.

2005 The languages of the Internet: it's not always English anymore. Anthropology News 46(4):50–51.

2010 Wasei Eigo to Nihon-jin: gengo, bunka sesshoku no dainamizumu (Japanese-English and the Japanese people: the dynamism of language and cultural contacts). Tokyo: Shinsensha.

2014 Some trends in Japanese slang. *In* Global English slang: methodologies and perspectives. Julie Coleman, ed., pp. 160–169. New York: Routledge.

**STANLAW, JAMES, AND ALAN PESHKIN**

1991 Black visibility in a multi-ethnic high school. *In* Current perspectives on the culture of schools. Nancy Wyner, ed., pp. 67–77. Northampton, MA: Brookline Books.

**STANLAW, JAMES, AND BENCHA YODDUMNERN**

1985 Thai spirits: a problem in the study of folk classification. *In* Directions in cognitive anthropology. Janet W. D. Dougherty, ed., pp. 141–160. Urbana: University of Illinois Press.

**STANLAW, JAMES, ROBERT T. ARRIGO, AND DAVID L. ANDERSON**

2006 Colors and culture: exploring colors as an anthropologist. Module for use with "The Mind Project." *In* http://www.mind.ilstu.edu/curriculum/virtual_anthro_lab/texts/lab_manual/chap1_intro.php.

**STAVANS, ILAN**

2003 Spanglish: the making of a new American language. New York: Rayo/HarperCollins.

**STEINMETZ, KATY**

2014 TIME exclusive: here are the rules of using emoji you didn't know you were using. Time Magazine online. In http://time.com/2993508/emoji-rules-tweets.

**STELL, GERALD, AND KOFI YAKPO, EDS.**

2015 Code-switching between structural and sociolinguistic perspectives. Berlin: Walter de Gruyter.

**STOCKTON, NICK**

2015 Emoji—trendy slang or a whole new language? Wired Magazine, online. In https://www.wired.com/2015/06/emojitrendy-slang-whole-new-language.

**STOKOE, WILLIAM C., JR.**

1960 Sign language structure: an outline of the visual communication systems of the American deaf. Studies in Linguistics, Occasional Papers, no. 8. Buffalo, NY: Department of Anthropology and Linguistics, University of Buffalo.

**STROSS, BRIAN**

1976 The origin and evolution of language. Dubuque, IA: Wm. C. Brown.

**STURTEVANT, EDGAR H.**

1947 An introduction to linguistic science. New Haven: Yale University Press.

**SUNDERLAND, JANE**

2006 Language and gender: an advanced resource book. New York: Routledge.

**SUSMAN, RANDALL L., ED.**

1984 The pygmy chimpanzee: evolutionary biology and behavior. New York: Plenum Press.

**TAKAHASHI, KIMIE**

2013 Language learning, gender and desire: Japanese women on the move. Bristol, UK: Multilingual Matters.

**TAKEMARU, NAOKO**

2010 Women in the language and society of Japan: the linguistic roots of bias. Jefferson, NC: McFarland.

**TALBOT, MARY**

2010 Language and gender. 2d ed. Cambridge, UK: Polity.

**TALLERMAN, MAGGIE, AND KATHLEEN GIBSON, EDS.**

2012 The Oxford handbook of language evolution. Oxford, UK: Oxford University Press.

**TALMY, LEONARD**

2000a Toward a cognitive semantics. Vol. 1: Concept structuring systems. Cambridge, MA: MIT Press.

2000b Toward a cognitive semantics. Vol. 2: Typology and process in concept structuring. Cambridge, MA: MIT Press.

**TAMASI, SUSAN, AND LAMONT ANTIEAU**

2015 Language and linguistic diversity in the US: an introduction. New York: Routledge.

**TAMBIAH, STANLEY**

1981 A performative approach to ritual. London: The British Academy.

**TANNEN, DEBORAH**

1982 Ethnic style in male-female conversation. *In* Language and social identity. John J. Gumperz, ed., pp. 217–231. Cambridge, UK: Cambridge University Press.

1986 That's what I meant! How conversational style makes or breaks relations with others. New York: Morrow.

1994a Gender and discourse. New York: Oxford University Press.

1994b Talking from nine to five: men and women at work. New York: Quill.

1999 The display of (gendered) identities in talk at work. *In* Reinventing identities: the gendered self in discourse. Mary Bucholtz, A. C. Liang, Laurel A. Sutton, eds., pp. 221–240. New York: Oxford University Press.

2007 You just don't understand: women and men in conversation. New York: William Morrow.

TAYLOR, ALLAN R.

1994 Gros Ventre dictionary. Prefinal version. Vol. 1: A–L, Vol. 2: M–Z, and Vol. 3: Gros Ventre stem index.

TAYLOR, CHARLES

2016 The language animal: the full shape of the human linguistic capacity. Cambridge: Harvard University Press.

TAYLOR, DOUGLAS

1951 Sex gender in Central American Carib. International Journal of American Linguistics 17:102–104.

TAYLOR, INSUP, AND M. MARTIN TAYLOR

1995 Writing and literacy in Chinese, Korean and Japanese. Studies in Written Language and Literacy 3. Amsterdam: John Benjamins.

TECHNOLOGY REVIEW

2014 Computational linguistics of Twitter reveals the existence of global superdialects. In https://www.technologyreview.com/S/529836/computational-linguustics-of-twitter-reveals-existence-of-global-superdialects.

TEETER, KARL V.

1964 "Anthropological linguistics" and linguistic anthropology. American Anthropologist 66:878–879.

TERRACE, HERBERT S.

1979 Nim: a chimpanzee who learned sign language. New York: Knopf.

THIEBERGER, NICHOLAS

2014 The Oxford handbook of linguistic fieldwork. New York: Oxford University Press.

THOMASON, SARAH

2015 Endangered languages. Cambridge, UK: Cambridge University Press.

THORNE, ALAN G., AND MILFORD H. WOLPOFF

1992 The multiregional evolution of humans. Scientific American 266(4):76–79, 82–83 (April).

THORNE, BARRIE, CHERIS KRAMARAE, AND NANCY HENLEY, EDS.

1983 Language, gender and society. Rowley, MA: Newbury House.

TIME-LIFE BOOKS

1973 The first men. Emergence of Man Series. New York: Time-Life Books.

**TING-TOOMEY, STELLA**

1986 Conflict communication styles in black and white subjective cultures. *In* Interethnic communication: current research, vol. 10. Young Yun Kim, ed., pp. 75–88. Newbury Park, CA: Sage.

**TODD, LORETO**

1984 Modern Englishes: pidgins and creoles. Oxford, UK: Blackwell.

1990 Pidgins and creoles. London: Routledge.

**TOMKINS, WILLIAM**

1969 Indian sign language. New York: Dover. Originally published by the author in 1926 under the title Universal Indian sign language of the Plains Indians of North America.

**TRAGER, GEORGE L.**

1958 Paralanguage: a first approximation. Studies in Linguistics 13:1–12.

1972 Language and languages. San Francisco: Chandler.

**TRUDGILL, PETER**

1974 The social differentiation of English in Norwich. London: Cambridge University Press.

1984 (ed.) Applied sociolinguistics. Orlando, FL: Academic Press.

**TSUDA, YUKIO**

1994 The diffusion of English: its impact on culture and communication. Keio Communication Review 16:48–61.

1996 Shinryaku-suru Eigo, hangeki-suru Nihongo (Invading English, counterattacking Japanese). Tokyo: PHP.

1997 Hegemony of English versus ecology of language: building equality in international communication. *In* World Englishes 2000: selected essays. Larry Smith and Michael Forman, eds., pp. 21–31. Honolulu: University of Hawaii Press/ East-West Center.

2013 The hegemony of English and strategies for linguistic pluralism: proposing the ecology of language paradigm. *In* The global intercultural communication reader, 2d ed. Molefi Kete Asante, Yoshitaka Miike, and Jing Yin, eds., pp. 445–456. New York: Routledge.

**TWAIN, MARK**

1921 [1879] The awful German language. *In* A tramp abroad; the complete works of Mark Twain. Authorized ed., pp. 267–284. New York: Harper and Brothers.

**TYLER, STEPHEN A., ED.**

1969 Cognitive anthropology. New York: Holt, Rinehart and Winston.

**URCIUOLI, BONNIE**

1996 Exposing prejudice: Puerto Rican experiences of language, race, and class. Boulder: Westview Press.

**URLA, JACQUELINE**

2015 Reclaiming Basque: language, nation, and cultural activism. Reno: University of Nevada Press.

**VALENTINE, LISA PHILIPS, AND REGNA DARNELL, EDS.**

1999 Theorizing the Americanist tradition. Toronto: University of Toronto Press.

**VANDERWEIDE, TERESA, JANIE REES-MILLER, AND MARK ARONOFF**

2010 Study guide for contemporary linguistics. 6th ed. Boston: Bedford/St. Martin's.

**VAUX, BERT, AND SCOTT GOLDER**

2003 Harvard dialect survey. Harvard University Linguistics Department. *In* http://www4.uwm.edu/FLL/linguistics/dialect/maps.html.

**VELUPILLAI, VIVEKA**

2015 Pidgins, creoles, and mixed languages: an introduction. Amsterdam: John Benjamins.

**VOEGELIN, CHARLES F., AND FLORENCE M. VOEGELIN**

1954 Obtaining a linguistic sample. International Journal of American Linguistics 20:89–100.

1957 Hopi domains: a lexical approach to the problem of selection. Indiana University Publications in Anthropology and Linguistics, Memoir 14 of the International Journal of American Linguistics. Baltimore: Waverly Press.

1959 Guide for transcribing unwritten languages in fieldwork. Anthropological Linguistics 1(6):1–28.

1966 (comps.) Map of North American Indian languages. American Ethnological Society.

**VOEGELIN, CHARLES F., FLORENCE M. VOEGELIN, AND LAVERNE MASAYESVA JEANNE**

1979 Hopi semantics. *In* Handbook of North American Indians. Vol. 9: Southwest, pp. 581–586. Washington, DC: Smithsonian Institution.

2009 An introduction to Proto-Indo-European and the early Indo-European languages. Bloomington, IN: Slavica Publishers.

**VOEGELIN, CHARLES F., AND Z. S. HARRIS**

1952 Training in anthropological linguistics. American Anthropologist 54:322–327.

**VOYLES, JOSEPH, AND CHARLES BARRACK**

2009 An introduction to Proto-Indo-European and the early Indo-European languages. Bloomington. IN: Slavica Publishers.

**WALLESTAD, THOMAS**

2013 Developing the visual language of comics: the interactive potential of Japan's contributions. In www.lit.osaka-cu.ac.jp/cpr/arts/contents/repre/no7/003-013_wallestad.pdf.

**WALTER, HENRIETTE**

1988 Le francais dans tous les sens. Paris: R. Laffont.

**WARDHAUGH, RONALD, AND H. DOUGLAS BROWN, EDS.**

1976 A survey of applied linguistics. Ann Arbor: University of Michigan Press.

**WATANABE, SUWAKO**

1993 Cultural differences in framing: American and Japanese group discussions. *In* Framing in discourse. Deborah Tannen, ed., pp. 176–209. New York: Oxford University Press.

**WATERHOUSE, VIOLA**

1962 The grammatical structure of Oaxaca Chontal. Indiana University Research Center in Anthropology, Folklore, and Linguistics Publications, no. 19. Bloomington.

**WATSON, O. MICHAEL, AND THEODORE D. GRAVES**

1966 Quantitative research in proxemic behavior. American Anthropologist 68:971–985.

**WEINREICH, URIEL**

1980 On semantics. Philadelphia: University of Pennsylvania Press.

**WEITZ, SHIRLEY, ED.**

1974 Nonverbal communication: readings with commentary. New York: Oxford University Press.

**WESCOTT, ROGER W.**

1974 The origin of speech. *In* Language origins. Roger W. Wescott, ed., pp. 103–123. Silver Spring, MD: Linstok Press.

**WETZEL, PATRICIA J.**

2004 Keigo in modern Japan: polite language from Meiji to the present. Honolulu: University of Hawaii Press.

**WHORF, BENJAMIN LEE**

1936 The punctual and segmentative aspects of verbs in Hopi. Language 12:127–131.

1940a Science and linguistics. Technology Review 42:229–231, 247–248 (April).

1940b Linguistics as an exact science. Technology Review 43:61–63, 80–83 (December).

1941a Languages and logic. Technology Review 43:250–252, 266, 268, 272 (April).

1941b The relation of habitual thought and behavior to language. *In* Language, culture, and personality: essays in memory of Edward Sapir. Leslie Spier et al., eds., pp. 75–93. Menasha, WI: Sapir Memorial Publication Fund.

1946 The Hopi language, Toreva dialect. *In* Linguistic structures of Native America. Cornelius Osgood, ed. Viking Fund Publications in Anthropology, no. 6, pp. 158–183. New York: Viking Fund.

1950 An American Indian model of the universe. International Journal of American Linguistics 16:67–72.

2012 Language, thought, and reality: selected writings of Benjamin Lee Whorf. 2d ed. Cambridge: MIT Press.

**WILLIAMS, NORIKO KUROSAWA**

2010 The key to Kanji: a visual history of 1100 characters. Boston: Cheng & Tsui.

**WILSON, ALLAN C., AND REBECCA L. CANN**

1992 The recent African genesis of humans. Scientific American 266(4):68–73 (April).

**WILSON, DEIDRE, AND DALE SPERBER**

2012 Meaning and relevance. Cambridge: Cambridge University Press.

**WITHERSPOON, GARY**

1977 Language and art in the Navajo universe. Ann Arbor: University of Michigan Press.

**WOLFE, TOM**

2016 The kingdom of speech. New York: Little, Brown.

**WOLFRAM, WALT, AND NATALIE SCHILLING-ESTES**

2005 American English: dialects and variation. 2d ed. Malden, MA: Blackwell.

**WONDERLY, WILLIAM L.**

1951a Zoque II: phonemes and morphophonemes. International Journal of American Linguistics 17:105–123.

1951b Zoque III: morphological classes, affix list, and verbs. International Journal of American Linguistics 17:137–162.

**WOODARD, ROGER D.**

1997 Greek writing from Knossos to Homer: a linguistic interpretation of the origin of the Greek alphabet and the continuity of ancient Greek literacy. New York: Oxford University Press.

**WOOLARD, KATHRYN A.**

1989 Double talk: bilingualism and the politics of ethnicity in Catalonia. Stanford, CA: Stanford University Press.

**WOOLARD, KATHRYN A., AND BAMBI B. SCHIEFFELIN**

1994 Language ideology. *In* Annual Review of Anthropology, vol. 23. William H. Durham et al., eds., pp. 55–82. Palo Alto, CA: Annual Reviews.

**WOOLFORD, ELLEN B.**

1979 Aspects of Tok Pisin grammar. Pacific Linguistics, Series B—Monographs, no. 66. Canberra: Australian National University.

**WORTHAM, STANTON, AND ANGELA REYES**

2015 Discourse analysis beyond the speech event. New York: Routledge.

**WRIGHT, SUE, ED.**

1999 Language, democracy and devolution in Catalonia. Clevedon, UK: Multilingual Matters.

**YANO**

2013 Pink globalization: Hello Kitty's trek across the Pacific. Durham, NC: Duke University Press.

**YEGERLEHNER, JOHN**

1955 A note on eliciting techniques. International Journal of American Linguistics 21:286–288.

**YU, BEI**

2013 Language and gender in congressional speech. Literary and Linguistic Computing, January 11. *In* http://llc.oxfordjournals.org/content/early/2013/01/10/llc.fqs073.

**YULE, GEORGE**

2010 The study of language. 4th ed. Cambridge, UK: Cambridge University Press.

**ZENTELLA, ANA CELIA**

1997 Growing up bilingual. Malden, MA: Blackwell.

**ZEPEDA, OFELIA**

1983 A Papago grammar. Tucson: University of Arizona Press.

**ZHANG, HANG**

2001 Culture as apology: the Hainan Island incident. World Englishes 20:383–391.

**ZIMAN, LAL, JENNY DAVIS, AND JOSHUA RACLAW, EDS.**

2014 Queer excursions: retheorizing binaries in language, gender, and sexuality. New York: Oxford University Press.

**ZIMMER, BEN**

2011 Twitterology: a new science? In http://www.nytimes.com/2011/10/30/opinion/sunday/twitterology-a-new-science.html.

**ZSIGA, ELIZABETH**

2013 The sounds of language: an introduction to phonetics and phonology. Malden, MA: Wiley-Blackwell. 2013 Pink globalization: Hello Kitty's trek across the Pacific. Durham, NC: Duke University Press.

# INDEX